EXCHANGES
Reading and Writing About Consumer Culture

Ted Lardner
Cleveland State University

Todd Lundberg
University of Wisconsin, Milwaukee

Longman

New York Boston San Francisco
London Toronto Sydney Tokyo Singapore Madrid
Mexico City Munich Paris Cape Town Hong Kong Montreal

This book is dedicated
to Emily Decker Lardner and Evelyn Lundberg

Acquisitions Editor: Erika Berg
Developmental Editor: Leslie Taggart
Marketing Manager: Carlise Paulson
Supplement Editor: Donna Campion
Production Manager: Ellen MacElree
Project Coordination, Text Design, and Electronic Page Makeup: Electronic Publishing Services Inc., NYC
Cover Designer/Manager: Nancy Danahy
Cover Photo: "E.T.D." by Susan McMahon, woodcut, transfer drawing 24"x36". Printed by Zygote
    Press, Cleveland, Ohio, 1999.
Manufacturing Buyer: Al Dorsey
Printer and Binder: R.R. Donnelley & Sons Company
Cover Printer: Coral Graphics Services, Inc.

For permission to use copyrighted material, grateful acknowledgment is made to the copyright
holders on p. 635, which are hereby made part of this copyright page.

Library of Congress Cataloging-in-Publication Data

Lardner, Ted.
    Exchanges: reading and writing about consumer culture / Ted Lardner, Todd
Lundberg.—1st ed.
        p.   cm.
    Includes index.
    ISBN 0-321-03799-5
    1. Readers—Economics. 2. English language—Rhetoric—Problems, exercises, etc.
3. Consumption (Economics)—Problems, exercises, etc. 4. Consumer behavior—Problems,
exercises, etc. 5. Report writing—Problems, exercises, etc. 6. Readers—Consumer behavior.
7. College readers. I. Lundberg, Todd. II. Title.

PE1127.G4 L37 2001
808'.0427—dc21

                                                                    00-028737

Please visit our website at http://www.awl.com

ISBN 0-321-03799-5

1 2 3 4 5 6 7 8 9 10—DOC—03 02 01 00

Contents in Brief

Contents
in Detail

PART 2 Exchanges   46

CHAPTER 3 Consuming Choices   47

CHAPTER 8 Identity in Black and White: Negotiating Personal and Public Selves   471

CHAPTER 9 Our Places, Our Selves: Where We Come from, Who We Are   541

Preface

[A]lthough we are consumers, we are not only consumers, but parents and neighbors and citizens too. The sort of world we bring into being with our dollars does not necessarily match the world we would vote for with our hearts.

Michael Pollan in "Land of the Free Market"
(*New York Times Magazine*, July 11, 1999)

Designed for first-year writing courses, *Exchanges: Reading and Writing About Consumer Culture* gathers together a provocative set of readings to help students discover and analyze how the context of a consumer culture informs and influences the choices they make. This anthology of readings asks students to examine a variety of familiar cultural phenomena and institutions—education, entertainment, advertising, the marketplace, and others—in order to help them navigate some of the key dynamics of American life at the start of the twenty-first century.

The very ubiquity of consumerism suggests it as fertile ground for material in a writing course. It's hard to imagine a student or teacher who hasn't been to a mall, considered the impact of an advertisement, pondered the payback of a college education, or thought about the packaging of personal identity. And we have all attended to these topics in a variety of mediums, in print, on TV, through the Web. By virtue of the fact that we all bring an important measure of experience to the work, these topics facilitate sophisticated analysis and discussions.

PERSONAL GROWTH AND TECHNICAL MASTERY

Exchanges is written to help students accomplish the dual goals of personal growth and technical mastery. College students need the opportunity to use reading and writing to explore their surroundings and themselves. They need to be able to understand and evaluate the propositions and data that come at them, and they must be able to argue with analytical precision their own responses to the vast amount of information they confront in school and in everyday life. *Exchanges* helps students to gain experience in using what Lisa Delpit refers to as the "discourse of power," to broaden their horizons through self-realization, and to discover the responsibilities of citizenship. The text seeks to nurture insight, foster thoughtful interpersonal relationships, and do its part to create a literate workforce for the information age.

To accomplish these goals, we have organized our text around the idea of exchange. In the classroom, as in the larger culture, students and teachers alike get to choose roles, opinions, and goals from a dazzling array of possibilities. At the same time, they must choose from what's available in the exchange at hand. The activities of critical thinking, reading, and writing are defined by culture, but they also create room for action within the culture.

CULTURAL EXPECTATIONS AND PERSONAL CHOICES

Part One, Reading and Writing About Consumer Culture, offers a brief and practical introduction to writing as a process of exchange within a context defined by consumerism. Chapter 1, Life in a Consumer Culture, introduces some basic ideas about the relationships among cultural expectations and personal behaviors and choices. We suggest to students in Chapter 1 that learning to use language precisely will help them determine what they want, what they are willing to do to get what they want, and, even more important, what is worth wanting.

CRITICAL READING AND WRITING STRATEGIES

Specific critical reading and writing strategies are introduced in Chapter 2, Reading and Writing: Working Effectively with *Exchanges,* and are applied and extended in questions throughout the text. This chapter introduces summary, analysis, synthesis, and evaluation as processes that writers engage in, collaboratively and individually, to discover and defend positions on their place in their culture, in and out of school. Sample student papers illustrate important writing strategies, and brief activities help students explore these strategies for immediate reinforcement. Chapter 2 provides the analytic concepts and tools students can use to make sense of the challenging reading selections in Part Two.

RELEVANT, PROVOCATIVE READINGS

The readings included in Part Two of *Exchanges* touch on provocative issues and themes, all rooted in students' firsthand experience. The seven thematic chapters of Part Two encourage students to analyze and compare the perspectives of cultural critics, essayists, and journalists as well as of advertisers, CEOs, and political activists. Readings from a diverse collection of genres and sources—newspaper and magazine journalism, research articles, industry and trade journals, academic journals, memoirs, personal essays, and images—provide students with multiple points of view on some of the key exchanges of American life.

The richly diverse perspectives in Part Two invite students to engage personally and concretely in the tensions between capitalism and social welfare, individualism and community, education and achievement, market justice and other (social, ethical, legal) justices, and modernism and postmodernism.

BACKGROUND READINGS AND CASE-IN-POINT READINGS

Each thematic chapter offers two sets of readings. Background Readings provide a context in which students learn to identify the broad issues brought out in the readings, and Case-in-Point Readings ground students' thinking in familiar conditions and immediate experience. For example, in Chapter 3, Consuming Choices, the background readings examine the effects of living in a consumer society, and the case-in-point, Adventures into Shopping Malls, locates the individual and social effects of this cultural emphasis on getting and spending. In Chapter 8, Identity in Black and White, the background readings detail how our sense of who we are is defined in significant ways by our racial identity, and the case-in-point, Hip-Hop Crossover, examines how the commercial success of hip-hop's dissemination from the hood to the rural heartland stands to turn this historic, black-white binary on its head.

CAREFULLY SEQUENCED PEDAGOGY

Each thematic chapter in Part Two includes extensive pedagogy to help students understand and analyze individual texts and to position them within the broader context of consumer culture. Questions of increasing complexity are carefully crafted to help students understand their immediate personal responses and to extend their understanding to include other points of view.

Writing Activities After Each Reading . . .

Two sets of questions following each reading help students reread actively and explore their responses based on their personal observation and experience.

- **Rereading Actively** questions lead students to monitor their understanding of the text, discover rhetorical strategies, and work in groups to develop a common understanding of the reading. The aim here is to encourage students to "re-see" a text from many perspectives, to make use of individual learning styles and life experiences.

- **Exploring Your Responses** questions ask students to draw on their own experiences to find connections with the reading. Students are asked to gauge their personal reactions, to explain key terms and concepts, to analyze and take positions, and to support their gut reactions with illustrations from personal observation and experience.

Writing Activities After Each Set of Readings . . .

Writing activities after each set of Background Readings and Case-in-Point Readings offer ways for students to work through ideas collaboratively, explore Web resources, and make connections among readings and across themes.

- **Making Connections** activities ask students to write essays that explore the interplay of two or more selections. They also encourage students to explore links between different thematic units, connecting, say, advertising and entertainment or education and social class.

- **Collaborative Exchanges** allow students to work together in and out of class to consider more closely the issues raised in individual or multiple readings. Often these exchanges lead groups to engage in original field research and to report their findings to the rest of the class.
- **Net Approaches** take students to the Web, where they use search engines, link searches, and specific pages to discover a deeper context for the readings and chapter topics.

Writing Projects at the End of Each Chapter . . .

Writing Projects at the end of each chapter invite students to practice forms and genres from inside and outside the academy. These assignments often ask students to explore and employ multiple research strategies. They encourage students to approach writing as a means of investigation and problem solving, and to take a position on the pressing issues that the readings raise. Writing Projects emphasize original inquiry: the observation, analysis, synthesis, and evaluation of material growing out of independent and collaborative fieldwork.

Alternate Assignments at the End of the Book . . .

Points of Exchange, a series of sequenced assignments at the end of the book, offer alternative routes through the chapter topics and readings. Addressing topics such as gender, the wealth gap, and sustainable living, Points of Exchange draw on readings from many different chapters in an alternate set of assignments that provide maximum flexibility for using the book.

ANCILLARIES

Instructor's Manual. The Instructor's Manual provides numerous suggestions for using the text and for taking advantage of its flexible organization, along with sample syllabi for courses of different lengths and foci. ISBN: 0-321-07993-0

Companion Web site. The Companion Web site offers chapter summaries, Internet activities for research and writing, and links to resources for both students and instructors. URL: http://www.awl.com/lardner

ACKNOWLEDGMENTS

We wish to acknowledge several teachers and mentors whose vision and skill guided us to this journey: Anne Ruggles Gere, Bernie Van't Hul, Richard Meisler, Susan Wyche, Sue McLeod, Louise Schleiner, and Al Von Frank. Of our many fine colleagues with whom we have shared the work of being writing teachers, we acknowledge Arnetha Ball, Dan Melnick, Cindy Sabik, Pat Brubaker, Elaine Richardson, Harry Phillips, Tenney Hammond, David Richardson, and rock-steady Jane Dugan. Several students from ENG 506, Composition Theory, and ENG 507, Workshop in Teaching Writing, stand deserving of particular mention for the spirit in which they approached the challenge and for the inspiration they provided: Julie Candela, Stephanie Nank, Jennifer Mattingly, Mike Danko, Jim Henry, and Anna Marie Tamayo.

Of the staff at Addison Wesley Longman, we hail and salute our hero, Leslie Taggart, who knew (when we didn't) what we were trying to do. *Muchas y muchas gracias* to Anne Smith, without whom we never would have imagined ourselves authors. (We also thank Scott Hitchcock and Andrew Schwartz for their diligent care with the manuscript). And for his initial encouragement of this project we would like to thank Charles Schuster.

For the diligence and care with which they reviewed the many drafts of the manuscript, we are immensely grateful to the following writing teachers:

Richard Barney, University of Oklahoma

Jon Beasley-Murray, Duke University

Roy Bird, University of Alaska, Fairbanks

Arlene Clarke, American River College

Minerva Cruz-Solano, Tarrant County Junior College

Beth Daniell, Clemson University

Judith Doumas, Old Dominion University

Ida Egli, Santa Rosa Junior College

Julia Ferganchick-Neufang, University of Arkansas, Little Rock

Allison Fernley, Salt Lake Community College

Joan Gabriele, University of Colorado

Lisa Gerrard, University of California, Los Angeles

Alice Gillam, University of Wisconsin, Milwaukee

Helynne Hansen, Western State College of Colorado

Adam Haridopolos, Nassau Community College

Dorothy Howell, University of North Carolina, Charlotte

Christine Hubbard, Tarrant County Junior College, Southeast

Deborah Kirkman, University of Kentucky

Daniel Lowe, Community College of Allegheny County

Marjorie Lynn, University of Michigan

Laura Micciche, East Carolina University

Mary Ann Peters, University of Oregon

Leaf Seligman, University of New Hampshire

Joan Spangler, California State University, Fullerton

Lisa Tatonetti, Ohio State University

Mark Wallace, George Washington University

Mark Wiley, California State University, Long Beach

Finally, for their love, patience, and support, we thank Linda and Helen.

Ted Lardner

Todd Lundberg

PART 1

Reading and Writing about Consumer Culture

CHAPTER 1

Life in a Consumer Culture

People are social animals, and at every stage of life, we engage in making exchanges. We constantly use what we have to get what we need and desire. Even babies will use what they have—the ability to cry—to get needed food, diaper changes, and parental attention. At a very young age people start to think about what we have, what we want, and how we can get what we want with what we have. When we learn to speak, many new possibilities open up; rather than just pointing at a rattle or a cookie, we can ask for what we want, and even offer to make mutually acceptable exchanges—for example, declaring to Mom that we will be good if we can stay outside for just one more hour. In the elementary school cafeteria, we trade the dreaded tuna sandwich for the Pizza Lunchable we covet, and with friends trade baseball cards or Barbies; we have stopped merely asking for what we want or need and now start trading for it.

As we become adult members of communities, our interactions become more and more complex. Whether we are going to school, working, raising families, vacationing, retiring, or dying, we find ourselves negotiating between what we want and what is possible, or good, or even what is legal. Some would argue that many of the exchanges that we are caught up in are well outside our control. While we capitalize on the talent that we inherit, we also live in a web of relationships and perceptions determined by our circumstances. For example, one of us grew up in a small town in the Midwest. Opportunities for education, recreation, and making a living there depended largely on a farm implement manufacturing business. For generations, local families could expect to find work in the tractor factories or related businesses. All that changed in the 1970s when the factories began to shut down and the area unemployment rate crept toward double digits. Suddenly, economic survival began to require a college education and moving somewhere else for work. Dictated by these circumstances, our perception of a secure future, our expectation of raising children in familiar neighborhoods, became unrealistic. We were compelled to exchange a way of living our parents, grandparents, and great-grandparents shared for something new and uncertain.

But while circumstances like these often dictate many of our actions, people also make choices, some of them difficult, about the trades they are willing to make. We are often able to resist, for example, the ways our consumer society pressures us toward immediate gratification. We may entertain the need for present sacrifice for the sake of future rewards—i.e., what kinds of changes am I going to have to make to get the straight A's I'll need in college to give me a shot at getting into a good law school? Am I willing to do well in college, knowing that my neighborhood friends are likely to be suspicious of my success? And contrary to the prevailing messages in our culture that tell us to think of our own fortunes above all else, we may work very hard in our dealings to take, alongside our own, family and community interests into account. Should we give ourselves the luxury of dinner out once a week, or pay off those credit card bills a year earlier? Can we afford to send our children to college, and are we willing to work two jobs each for ten years to make that possible? (Can we afford *not* to send our children to college?) Our communities may also hold precedence in some important choices we make: giving up an evening at an NBA game, we might work the phones in support of a school referendum. Our concern for the working conditions in developing countries may lead us to second thoughts about the purchase of an otherwise most desirable item.

These kinds of trade-offs, where personal pleasure and fulfillment are balanced against obligations or responsibilities to a larger good, are one defining feature of a consumer culture like our own. A second feature is that exchanges that in other contexts may be more concrete—trading the potatoes you grew for the carpenter skills I have—become more abstract—trading the dollars earned on the job for the same potatoes or household improvements. Even children in our consumer culture move from concrete trades of goods and services to more and more abstract trades, negotiating away their freedom and time, bits and pieces of their future, for a wide array of goods, services, and other, ephemeral benefits: well-being, success, contentment, and pleasure. Moreover, acquisitive exchanges are pervasive. The consumption of goods and services has never so fully occupied the center of a culture as it occupies ours today. Consumer spending on things including cars, appliances, furniture, computers, and boats; on food, clothing, CDs, and cosmetics; and on entertainment, repairs, or other services adds up to two-thirds of the U.S. Gross Domestic Product.

As the activities of social interaction have become more and more involved with money and commodities, and as the number of these transactions has increased seemingly exponentially, the cultural significance of exchange has shifted in a way that, we hope you will agree, makes it an important and useful object of study. We believe that by examining some of the exchanges that define our daily lives, we can begin to discern patterns in their behavior that are related to expectations we inherit from our culture. When we recognize this relationship between cultural expectations and personal behavior, we can begin (if we wish) to exert more control over the choices we make and the contexts in which we make them.

CULTURAL EXPECTATIONS AND PERSONAL CHOICES

According to Alan Durning in *How Much Is Enough?* (1992), consumer society was born in the United States in the 1920s, when "brand names became household words, when packaged, processed foods made their widespread debut, and when the automobile assumed its place at the center of American culture" (29). Following World War II, consumer culture as we experience it took off. Durning cites a 1946 *Fortune* magazine article trumpeting "The Great American Boom," and President Eisenhower's Council of Economic Advisors proclaimed in 1953 that the "ultimate purpose" of the U.S. economy was "to produce more consumer goods." With low unemployment and expanding production, the U.S. economy grew in this period to become, according to the economist John Kenneth Galbraith in *A Journey Through Economic Time* (1994), "the pivot around which the world economy turned" (150).

By now, mass consumption as a way of life has come to seem normal to most of us. In an age of disposable income and disposable goods, we accept as part of the order of things that before their useful life is over, changing fashions and tastes will render products obsolete. We tend not to think about the ways our society molds our values and beliefs as consumers. In the ideology of consumer society, it seems natural that we want what we want, and that we seek the fulfillment of our wants in the ways that we do. Though the voluntary simplicity movement and "downshifting" stand as evidence that the tide may be turning, according to Durning, between 1967 and 1990 the percentage of American college students who "believed it essential to be 'very well off financially' rose from 44 to 74 percent" (34). For these students, the desire to acquire more and more goods and services supplanted the desire to "develop a meaningful philosophy of life" (34). On the face of it, this probably seems like a rational priority, one many of us would agree with.

Whereas some culture critics have written off consumerism, talking about "consumers" simply as people who use up the world's resources in profligate ways, others see more depth and complexity in the interactions among members of a consumer society. Through the goods and services we consume, as well as through the processes of consumption, we seek to express our identity and affiliations with others, or to exert our status in society. There is more to our behavior, these people would say, than the simple quest to get and spend. So how do we begin to analyze the exchanges through which our relationships to others are sustained, particularly when such careful thinking about the people behind the product is generally discouraged? The hum of exchange is so much a part of our life that we often don't hear the deeper resonance under its surface. Think, for example, about morning coffee. Most of us get up when our alarm clock goes off (trading sleeping in for being somewhere doing something useful.) As we get on our way to school or work, maybe we consume a cup of coffee. Whether we perk it, drip it, press it, or stir the instant powder in, whether we spend a bit of cash at a corner gas station, McDonalds, or (a bit more cash) at Starbucks, we sip and get on with our day, unfettered by responsibility for where the coffee, the coffee maker, or coffee sellers come from. Who thinks about morning coffee that way— that is, whether the means by which we satisfy our desire is a good one or not? How would we know whether it is good or not good? Often, what we focus on is the immediate exchange, the opportunity to trade what we have for what we want. The network of relationships that link us to other people in far-flung places—we rarely give ourselves reason to think about that. Life in a consumer culture is typified by this experience of exchange. Our attention is drawn to the exchange itself, dissociating the objects of exchange from the network of people who become, through the exchange, connected to one another. That cup of coffee feels warm in our hand and it tastes just right. These facts occupy us.

Likewise, we live with the awareness that what we have largely determines what we can get in our consumer culture. Some will not question spending a buck and a half on a cup of coffee. For others, the same dollar-fifty every day ($42.00 a month) would help them in the scrape to keep food on the table and a roof overhead. In our consumer culture, some people making $100,000 a year may seek to satisfy the desire for prestige by purchasing a $33,000 luxury car, a $4,000 home stereo, and a $500 electric razor, all while managing a middle five-figure mortgage on an ever-larger house. Other people, earning minimal wages, are wondering how to pay the phone and electric bills or how to cobble together complex child care arrangements with relatives they don't have to pay to make sure their kids have some adult supervision while they work the second shift. The presence or absence of money defines for most Americans the rhythms and texture of everyday life.

Many people are aware of this, at least in a general way, but few stop to think about how our consumer culture can make it seem as if having money and the things that money can buy are the be-all and end-all of our existence. "Born to Shop," a T-shirt proclaims. We get the irony of it: who is really "born to shop"? But the humor in it is rueful, coming from that little grain of truth inside the joke. It seems as if the exchange of material goods or services defines core elements of our feelings, elements we think of as having meaning and value beyond dollars and cents. A clever advertising slogan for a major credit card sums up the connection: "Some things in life are priceless. For everything else, there's Mastercard." The ad astutely acknowledges what we like to believe: there are things in life no one can put a price on. At the same time, we are encouraged by advertising and by common assumptions to behave as if such transcendent experiences are exceptional, and what really counts is the next purchase. The airwaves are filled with directions about this—messages about what to value, what to want, what kind of person to be, and how to achieve all of these things. At the same time, we are inundated by mass-produced goods, a twentieth-century marvel of dazzling proportions: sweaters, slacks, and watches; appliances and tools; cleaning products for the kitchen, bath, boat, car, garage, and basement, for odors and stains, for disinfecting, and for whiter teeth; footwear, eyewear, flatware, and software; athletic and recreational gear; home furnishings; pet supplies; collectibles; books, records, and video recordings; frozen bread, chicken nuggets, wines from major and minor continents, and seafood from the seven seas; space-age fabrics, ancient arts and crafts, and building materials. Awash in this flood of goods, it is little wonder that so many of the actions we take are directed toward choosing what products to buy.

The volume and velocity of this flood of products and this constant state of exchange can hollow out our experience and reduce us, our world, and our relationships to dollar signs. In the United States, preachers and politicians seem as interested in raising money as they are in talking about God or creating a more just and prosperous society. We, too, get caught up in the exchange: what we can buy sometimes displaces what we came looking for. When money exchanges become the fulcrum on which our daily experiences hang, our consciousness is leveraged into thoughts of making the next trade. Sorting out the relationship between money exchanges and the life experiences we value is important work, because our consumer culture does an excellent job at telling us the value of things in terms of how much they cost and how they can be purchased. Our consumer culture guides us with extraordinary skill to certain kinds of acquisitive behaviors. But is a life worth living made up of the sum total of our material exchanges? Can we buy it? Can students "buy" education? Does Disney enrich our lives? Depends on whom you ask because the ephemera of well-being—loving relationships, security, the chance to grow creatively—are so frequently closely entwined with consumerism. The economic machinery behind our consumer culture appears able to equip all of us with these intangible, valuable things. But can it? Can it equip any of us with a good life?

Probably most of us would like to have a say in shaping the social niches we occupy, to exercise our ability to resist the designs the marketers have on our desire. Most of us probably want to have a hand in defining who we will be, where we will live, how we will spend our leisure time, and who we will spend it with—choices that make up focal points for the units in this text. And indeed, the expanding economy of the United States provides an unprecedented number of residents with the means to reflect on their roots, their circumstances, and their dreams. Along with this economic prosperity, many residents of the United States have the opportunity to partake in the rich infusion of other kinds of cultural assets: unparalleled access to information, for example, and the possibility of free exchange of ideas. Participating in this expansive culture can lead to a kind of individual and social freedom and an atmosphere of excitement, change, and opportunity rarely matched in history.

Alongside this general optimism, however, we are obliged (by our duty to speak truth to power) to recognize that not every resident of the United States is able to share in this luxury of choice, nor to participate equally in the exchanges that could open parts of a shared culture. So, for example, while it is true that the stock markets have rocketed to new levels, the headline-news highs they set have created something less than genuine prosperity for the general population. According to Lester Thurow, an economist at the Massachusetts Institute of Technology, almost 90 percent of the wealth created by the increasing value of stocks has gone to the top 10 percent of American households. The bottom 60 percent of American households, owning no stock at all, is left out of the glad tidings. Further, by early in 1999, as the economy continued in the midst of the longest peacetime expansion in our history, the median family income had not risen since the early 1970s (even when adding the income of wives, who were working an average of fifteen more weeks a year). Real wages, according to Thurow, were below where they used to be for 80 percent of men in the workforce. The legal minimum wage in 1968 would be equivalent in 1999 to about $7.50 an hour, a rate that would keep a family of three just barely above the Federal government's "poverty line." It goes without saying that the actual 1999 minimum wage of $5.15 an hour would put such a family very far behind.

Therefore, one truth of our lives in consumer culture is this: In spite of the genuine prosperity, the comfortable standard of living afforded to residents of the United States by this, the most powerful economy in the history of the world, in spite of the unprecedented possibility of freedom that lies waiting here to be exercised across racial, ethnic, and religious boundaries, there remain in this society significant discrepancies between "haves" and "have-nots," between, that is, the privileged and powerful few with their luxury of choices, and the hard-working many who, wanting for the means to do so, nonetheless must answer the demand of persistent necessity. Another truth of our consumer culture is that it offers few concrete resources to help people make sense of facts like these, placing the burden of understanding on us to take up, if we care to. Unless we agree that we all really were merely "born to shop," we will begin the effort of understanding by looking anew at the familiar terrain of our consumer society. Doing so, we will endeavor to see features of our existence that it tends to smooth over or hide, to pick apart contradictions in the messages it contains, and to form new perspectives on the relationships it prescribes—relationships between ourselves and the things in life we value, including our relationships with others. The critical thinking, reading, and writing you will be asked to do in this book is the best instrument we know of to undertake this important task.

WRITING IN THE ACADEMIC COMMUNITY

We have argued that the activities of exchange are a foremost feature of consumer society. Like many other important exchanges between people, the exchanges between readers and writers that take place in college classrooms involve using language. We read texts that others have written, we write texts in response to voice our perspectives, and we talk to each other in class to explore and test our beliefs. Texts themselves are an exchange of value: a writer expresses his or her ideas on paper (or on-screen) in a way that allows readers to understand their value (at least, this is a writer's great hope!). Readers have their own, individual purposes for making this exchange—for reading this text—whether that purpose is to extract information, for example, to do well on a test; to experience pleasure, for example, in reading a novel; or to participate in a dialogue about some issue important to them as a member of society, for example, figuring out why hip-hop culture has percolated through suburban America. Thus, readers bring their own values to this exchange.

The college composition classroom offers you opportunities to learn how to make the kinds of sophisticated language exchanges that are valued in school and society. The more sophisticated your ability to use language in all variety of exchanges, the more successful you will be in articulating what you desire and fulfilling those desires intentionally. Your ability to craft or capture your precise thoughts in language, to understand the nuances of others' speech and writing, to identify in language the common interests you have with others and the way yours and others' interests mesh or compete—all these skills are going to help you get what you want. You may gain not only status, that is, recognition of your worth from others, because of course your status in this society depends in part on your ability to articulate your ideas clearly, but also a better internal sense of your own perspective. Using language more precisely will help you figure out your desires, your needs, and your responsibilities. It will help you reflect critically on how your experiences and your relationships lead you to believe what you do. In terms of writing in the classroom, it will help you decide how all these factors lead you to the points you want to make—why you think as you do, and how to explain your ideas to readers who have other desires, goals, and beliefs.

To college you bring your attitudes, beliefs, and inclinations. You also bring your ability to assemble words into sentences, and your sentences into larger statements, arguments, questions, revelations—your linguistic creativity is already hardwired in. You bring the experience and knowledge gained in your previous schooling and from your life. (Indeed, to the subject at hand—life in a consumer culture—you bring, by virtue of your ongoing participation in it, a great deal of expertise.) Together, all of these assets add up to what some people call your "cultural capital," the strength you bring to the work at hand. How can you use all this to move forward as a reader and as a writer in college?

First, you can recognize that the perspectives you have developed from past experiences probably make it easier to engage more in some kinds of verbal exchanges than in others. You may be effective in getting your friends to go to the movie you want to see, but not as effective in getting your parents to understand why you like a certain rap artist. You may be effective in making a strong argument for what you believe in the presence of someone you know shares your view, but not as effective in writing it down for your teacher. You may be able to state to yourself why you hold certain ideals or goals, but be less able to share your reasons with others. Part of your work in college will involve learning to be more flexible in explaining your point of view and thus more successful in communicating you propositions: explaining your ideas to an "authority figure," holding your argumentative ground in a class debate, letting others glimpse what you really want out of life.

If your family and your local community engaged in reading and writing in highly specific ways, if you have read a great deal and already know how to use language in the ways that are valued in school, then your work in this course will help you refine your existing skills and knowledge. If you spend more time talking, writing computer code, surfing the Web, or working with tools, your experiences in this course should help you forge connections between these valuable abilities and the verbal skills you will need for success in college. The academic world places a high value on the sophisticated use of language, and it will be part of your task to develop and refine new strategies to gain a higher level of ability in reading and writing.

One way to understand this is to consider the idea of a discourse and a discourse community. Let's say you are good at convincing your friends to go to the movies you want to see. How do you convince them? The particular answer depends on what you know about your shared experience—what words to use, what shared attitudes to touch on, what gestures or glances to make, what values you know your friends have. In short, you and they form a discourse community because you share a discourse—a set of key terms and habits, a base of knowledge, even a certain logic. Because you hold this discourse in common, you know how to approach them, to get them to act a certain way or to understand your point of view.

Now consider writing an argument to readers you don't know personally, to convince them that they should go to see a certain movie. You don't know them: you don't know what they like or dislike, what they think or don't think. You don't know what they believe or how they make decisions. You don't know whether they would agree with you about what makes a great movie, or if they do, what words would remind them of their beliefs. You don't know if they come from a farm near Des Moines, Iowa, or a barrio in L.A., and you don't know if their political beliefs are conservative or liberal, right, left, or middle of the road. In short, you don't know a thing about your readers, and what you don't know is their usual discourses. Every one of your readers will be conversant and competent with one or more discourses based on their background, education, and experiences. If some of your readers share a good deal of background and experiences, they may share a discourse. But what attitudes, beliefs, terms, and so on make up that discourse? You don't know. How can you communicate effectively with them?

That's the situation you're likely to face in college—in general, not just in writing. Each field, like English or biology, has its own discourse—a way of thinking, speaking, acting, arguing for a position, a logic for figuring things out—that is in some ways different from those in other fields. In addition, if you think of academic life in general, you will see that college overall has general expectations regarding your behavior. So, for example, college professors will often assign a paper to be written and then not mention it again until they ask you to turn it in on the due date. When you do turn it in, he or she will expect to see work that has been carried out in certain ways (ways we will explain more fully in Chapter 2). To be successful within this community, you need to figure out how to plan your work on your own, without reminders, and to do the work in the way the university expects. But to even know that this is the case, you need to understand that these habits are part of the discourse community of college.

You will also notice if you examine the different contexts of your life closely that you tend to act in different ways at home, at school, at work, with friends. At home, you may tend to be the "dutiful daughter or son," the "rebel," or the "baby of the family." In high school, you may have tended to act like a "good student," a "challenger of authority," or "a person more interested in partying than studying." With friends, perhaps you are "always loyal," a "leader," or the person "everyone turns to when they have problems." We can call these habitual ways of responding to certain social situations roles that we play; they are the public positions we take to accomplish certain purposes. In a sense, they are default identities we put on so that we will know how to act and so others will know how to act toward us. College offers you a chance to experiment with new roles. Take the example above about writing for an unknown audience. What role can you take on that would convince a bunch of people who don't know you to do as you think they should, or at least consider doing so? (Think about it. This won't be the last time you are asked this question!) In the college classroom in general, what roles can you play so that you wind up getting what you want out of the experience? Given what you know of the discourse of a particular field of study, what roles can you try on to achieve a grade of A or B? Look around at the other students in your classes. What roles can you experiment with in order to meet that interesting looking person over there?

Writing is a good way to test the effectiveness of new roles, as well as to think about what you want and whether it is worth wanting. Writing gives you time to think through the moves you can make, the words you can use, and the proposition that you might lay out for readers. In writing, you can choose very consciously and deliberately what aspects of yourself to bring to your relationship with your reader—for example, whether a humble tone or an aggressive one is likely to be more effective in a given situation. Writing can help you learn what you think and feel about an issue, help you express your thoughts and feelings so your readers will understand them (depending on the role you choose), and help you test your knowledge of the unspoken rules and habits of the disciplines you are writing in (the discourse).

Questions for Reflection

- Assess your knowledge and attitude toward American consumer culture. Ask yourself, were you "born to shop"?

- Think about the different social circles you move in, from home, to friends, to church or work. Does your way of talking change as you move from one social circle to another? Describe the different discourse communities of which you are a part.

- What are your preferred methods for dealing with the reading and writing you are assigned in school?

EXCHANGES AND YOU

We have developed *Exchanges* to offer you some starting points for paths through the exchanges at the center of American life. The first unit (Chapter 3) offers a general introduction to life in a culture of exchange, focusing on consumer culture and the shopping mall as a site of commercial exchange. The units after that span a variety of topics from social groups to advertising, entertainment to education to identity and the places we live; each offers a site where consumerism intersects with significant aspects of our lives. For each of these points of exchange, the background readings introduce general concepts to explore and to analyze and challenge. After the background readings comes a group of readings that make up a "case in point." These readings focus narrowly on a particular aspect or facet of the unit's theme. Case-in-point readings are full of observation and evidence that document American cultural exchanges, and they include a range of perspectives that writers have taken on the meanings of these exchanges. For example, in Chapter 3 on life in a culture of exchange, the case in point examines the phenomenon of the shopping mall, perhaps the single most potent symbol of the American consumer culture. Whereas some writers have lamented the destructive tendencies of our culture that shopping malls seem to represent, others examine the role of the mall as a public meeting place, where interesting kinds of exchanges can take place among a variety of people. Each unit focuses attention on one aspect of culture, but as you read, be sure you don't overlook the connections among the various paths through the exchange: the places we live have lots to do with social class; hip-hop crossover is vitally connected to advertising and fashion.

Writing and reading are all about exchanges of meaning, attitude, emotion, and information. The reading questions and writing projects in every unit, as well as the information on critical reading and writing in Chapter 2, are designed to give you opportunities to develop strategies and practice habits to become more adept at examining beliefs, trying new perspectives, and making connections that link the critical thinking, reading, and writing of college to your own experiences and perceptions, and to the world around you.

WORKS CITED

Durning, Alan Thein. *How Much is Enough? The Consumer Society and the Future of the Earth.* New York: Norton, 1992.

Galbraith, John Kenneth. *A Journey Through Economic Time: A First Hand View.* Boston: Houghton Mifflin, 1994.

CHAPTER 2

Reading and Writing: Working Effectively with *Exchanges*

The discourse of the writing classroom sets up certain expectations for the roles you will take on. As a class member, you will follow class policies in order to accomplish your goals for the course. As a reader, you may look for certain kinds of details or be alert to particular forms of bias. As a writer, you will meet your deadlines. As a reviewer of other students' work, you will comb through your colleagues' writing to find what's effective and ineffective. As a rewriter and an editor, you will examine your own writing to discover what works and what needs to be retooled. Of course, each of these roles includes other activities as well, but every role encourages certain types of mental and social moves and makes others less likely.

All of the roles that you already play call on you to work with information, to respond to circumstances, and to behave with others in a variety of ways according to your own purposes and the expectations of the people you interact with. To become a more effective learner in the university and in life, figure out how to gain the habits and strategies that go along with these new roles in a way that allows you to achieve your own goals and serve your own purposes.

How can you do that? The two major tasks of the writing classroom—learning to write and learning from writing—depend on your ability to be aware of the shifts your various roles require and to discover methods to make them happen and to control them. Every role you take on includes at least a slightly different mindset, a shift in attitude, a change of habit. The more consciously you decide to step into the roles of writer, reviewer, rewriter, editor, and so on, the more clearly you can think about whether your habits and strategies are working the way you want them to. And you'll be able to evaluate how well they are working for you based on your own sense of what you, personally, want to get out of this class.

For example, writing handbooks typically describe writing as a process involving three phases: inventing, drafting, and revising. These phases can also be thought of as three major role shifts involved in writing the kinds of papers expected in the college classroom. Writers rarely find that invention, drafting, and revising are distinct, chronological stages, but they often do know that the more completely they can step into the roles of inventor, drafter, collaborator, rewriter, and editor, the more successful their writing process will be.

In this chapter, then, we'll look at roles in two different ways. First are the roles you will play in the classroom itself—reader, inventor, writer, collaborator, rewriter, and editor. For example, to become an inventor is to leave behind for a time the analytic and critical part of your mind in favor of that part that is more open, creative, and associative. To become an editor is to step out of the writer's role as a conveyor of knowledge into a more evaluative and skeptical part of yourself. Second are the roles you can take on in the writing you do—the particular parts of yourself that you choose to reveal on paper to accomplish your purpose in writing to a certain audience of readers. As you develop a role to play in a piece of writing, you will find yourself emphasizing some attitudes and approaches over others. Sometimes, the roles you explore on paper will be in service of the point you are trying to persuade your readers to accept. Other times, your emotional stance toward a topic may make this kind of deliberate emphasis seem too cool and removed to accomplish your writing goal. Focusing on your dual roles as a student and as a writer will allow you to make deliberate choices about the exchanges you agree to make.

READING A TEXT

The readings in most college writing courses explore issues that we all live with daily. The world we live in often poses choices that are difficult to make. Even though Henry David Thoreau's *Civil Disobedience,* a text many college students have encountered, may seem to have nothing to say to contemporary life, most of us have chosen to disobey an authority—a parent, a teacher, a road sign—in order to make a point. Thoreau's ideas, and those of other authors you will read, are more relevant than they may at first seem. However, the authors you read in college may describe common experience from abstract positions

---

The Writing Process

- Inventing—discovering what you want to say and what you want your writing to do
- Drafting—writing down your ideas and accomplishing your purpose in a somewhat organized way
- Revising—viewing your writing from a new point of view and changing the writing, if necessary, to make sure it accomplishes its purpose

or describe that experience using evidence that is detailed and complex. To complicate matters further, every writer you will read has a position from which he or she writes. These writers will pose as experts, eyewitnesses, defenders of the common good, and critics of others' ideas. Not only will you have to understand what a writer is saying and doing with a text, you will also have to judge the validity of the writer's stance.

Because these texts are so often complex and dense, you need to work out an approach to them that will take you beyond the superficial. To play this role as a critical reader, you'll begin by marking important points, taking notes, and reacting to writers' propositions. You'll need to invest considerable time and energy to develop a relationship with each text, which may then cause you to embrace a new position, modify one you already hold, or resist the author's position in favor of your own—after thinking through the implications of each. As you approach the discussions of American culture in *Exchanges,* you are bound to come across ideas you don't agree with and points of view that challenge you to shift your perspective. You will encounter new information and statements of fact that you can evaluate based on your prior knowledge and experience. Despite these opportunities to develop new positions and affirm old ones, if you don't form a relationship with what you are reading, your position as a reader, writer, and human being will remain largely unchanged. You'll need to decide whether the position you already hold in relation to certain ideas will get you what you want in this course and in the rest of your education, or whether you can benefit as a student—and a citizen—by forming new approaches, habits, and values.

Reading a text closely enough to develop a relationship with it entails stepping into your role as a critical reader: doing particular kinds of work before you read, as you read, and after you read.

YOUR ROLE AS A CRITICAL READER

Think for a moment about the kinds of exchanges you make in your role as a consumer. You exchange dollars for groceries, books, clothes, movies, perhaps quarters for getting your clothes washed; you may pay rent on your room or apartment or a mortgage on your house. These exchanges are tangible and concrete: you have a purpose in mind or discover one in the process of interchange; you hand over some money, and you get back something specific in return. You need not use money as the medium of exchange in these tangible trades. You could offer to wash your friend's car if she agrees to let you use it for an evening. Whether you are consuming products like groceries or services like using a car, the exchanges are quite specific and both parties to the exchange have made an agreement to trade.

If you consider a piece of writing as a kind of a sales pitch for making a certain type of exchange, you can begin to figure out the important aspects of the role of critical reader you'll need to take on. Instead of a product like food, the writer offers you words and ideas—more intangible and abstract products, but products nonetheless. Any piece of writing is a product of language, of thought, of time, of a dynamic process of inquiry and research, and every writer, like every salesperson, has a purpose, has something to trade with others. The exchange the writer offers you, the reader, is an intellectual one, but in many ways the strategies you use to analyze and evaluate the piece of writing are similar to ones you would use in analyzing and evaluating a more familiar sales pitch.

Before Reading: Preview to Establish a Context for Reading

Before reading, your goal is to get a sense of the background of the text and an overview of its content and structure. This is like going to buy a car: Don't you want to know, before you get into all the details, what the car looks like and how much it costs? Only then can you decide how the details fit into the larger picture. You'd probably also want to know if the car dealer has a reputation, good or bad, that you should know about before committing yourself to spend money there. We call this pre-reading work previewing.

Begin previewing by thinking about why you are reading. What kind of information are you are looking for? What depth of knowledge do you need? Next, look for an abstract or an author's or editor's note that may precede the article itself and consult any background information that may be available about the author, the occasion and purpose of the writing, and its intended audience. This information will help you gain a feel for the central purpose or aim of the text. Figuring out the central purpose of the text will often help you make sense of the details.

Then, preview the text itself with the goal of forming quick impressions about its general ideas and structure. Look at the title and any subtitles; think about what these

---

The Writer's Purpose

A piece of writing often has a single central purpose: to express the writer's beliefs or feelings, to explain a topic, or to persuade a reader. Knowing the writer's primary concern will help you to predict what he or she will cover and to understand how the parts of the text fit together.

- Self-expression—The writer writes about thoughts, feelings, and memories in order to share personal experience. *Examples:* reflective journal writing, memoirs, personal narratives, essays that explore a writer's personal reaction to a topic but are unconcerned with stating a thesis.

- Exposition—The writer explains a topic that her or his reader does not understand. The writer strives to make the reader's understanding match that of the writer. *Examples:* summaries, reports, informative essays, sections in essays that present background information or facts.

- Persuasion—The writer sets out to convince a reader to believe or do something. *Examples:* argumentative essays, proposals, reviews, critiques.

In some cases, these aims overlap. In order to persuade you, a writer may decide to reveal telling personal experiences and inform you of pertinent facts along the way.

titles imply about the claims the author is making. After looking over the text as a whole, read through the introductory paragraph or section, recognizing that many authors will provide an overview of their message as well as an explicit statement of their thesis or main point in the opening portion of the text. Taking the background information, the messages conveyed by the title, note, or abstract, and the information from the opening paragraph or section into account, you should be able to form a hunch about the article's topic and the author's message. Just as you can get a general feel for a car by looking it over and sitting in the driver's seat, you can get an overview of the article's general content and structure by previewing.

Exercise 2.1 Turn to Mark Sagoff's article, "Do We Consume Too Much?" on page 48. Read the editor's note, the title and subtitles, and the first section of the article. What you do think the author's central purpose may be? What do you anticipate about the content of the article? Its structure? Share your first impressions with a group of classmates.

Reading: Finding Major Ideas and Noting Your Responses

Your initial goal as you read the text is to identify the author's most important points and to see how they fit together as a whole and how you respond to them. When a car seller starts telling you how well this car drives, how few miles it has, and details about its mechanics and special features, you're sorting through the sales pitch, listening for the points that are most important in general and important to you as an individual. When buying a car, you may be just mentally noting these important points, but when reading, you need to make written notes. As you read, make notes in the margin to identify the most important ideas, the main examples or details, and the ideas that trigger your own reactions. (If you don't want to write in the book, you can use sticky notes to record your responses.) Devise your own notation system to identify important ideas and rhetorical strategies:

Ideas: What the Text Says
- What's the author's main point?
- What claims does the author make to develop or support the main point?
- What major pieces of evidence do the main point and claims depend on?

Strategies: What the Text Does, and How
- What types of evidence—for example, statistics, stories, quotations from experts—does the author use?
- Where do major transitions between idea occur?
- What ideas, words, or phrases trigger a strong reaction in you? Why?
- What questions do you have as you read the text?

The more precise your marks are, the easier it will be to draw material from the text into your own writing. But be selective: the unfortunate tendency is to underline (or highlight) too much of a text. The shrewd reader will mark sparingly, keeping the focus on the truly important elements of a writer's ideas and strategies.

Sample Reading Annotations

The first section of Mark Sagoff's "Do We Consume Too Much?" is reprinted below, with one reader's annotations. Notice that the reader has used the left margin for notes on the content of the article ("what it says") and the right margin for notes on its structure and language ("what it does"). As you reread this section of the article and the annotations, consider whether the reader shares your ideas about what is most important. Think, too, about whether he or she has provided enough or too much annotation.

What it says

over consumption in U.S. & other industrialized nations

only so much to go around

consuming transforming nature
less nature to enjoy

I N 1994 , when delegates from around the world gathered in Cairo for the International Conferences on Population and Development, representatives from developing countries (protested) that a baby born in the United States will consume during its lifetime twenty times as much of the world's resources as an African or an Indian baby. The problem for the world's environment, they (argued) is overconsumption in the North, not overpopulation in the South.

Consumption in industrialized nations "has led to overexploitation of the resources of developing countries, a speaker from Kenya (declared.) A delegate from Antigua (reproched) the wealthiest 20 percent of the world's population for consuming 80 percent of the goods and services produced from the earth's resources.

Do we consume too much? (To some) the answer is self-evident. If there is only so much food, timber, petroleum, and other material to go around, the more we consume, the less must be available for others. The global economy cannot grow indefinately on a finite planet. As populations increase and economies expand, natural resources must be depleted: prices will rise, and humanity–especially the poor and future generations at all income levels–will suffer as a result.

Other reasons to suppose we consume too much are less often stated though also widely believed. Of these the simplest–a lesson we learn from our parents and from literature since the Old Testament–may be the best: although we must satisfy basic needs, a good life is not one devoted to amassing material possessions; what we own comes to own us, keeping us from fulfilling commitments that give meaning to life, such as those to family, friends, and faith. The appreciation of nature also deepens our lives. As we consume more, however, we are more likely to transform the natural world, so that less of it will remain for us to appreciate.

What it does

sets up a problem - gives evidence, all stated by people from developing countries -blames.

← CLAIM 1?
Not everyone?
What about Sagoff?

← CLAIM 2?

religious beliefs

well put!

protect species

God's creation

How else to express?

The reasons for protecting nature are often religious or moral. As the philosopher Ronald Dworkin points out, many Americans believe that we have an obligation to protect species which goes beyond our own well being; we "think we should admire and protect them because they are important in themselves, and not just if or because we or others want to enjoy them." In a recent survey Americans from various walks of life agreed by large majorities with the statement "Because God created the natural world, it is wrong to abuse it." The anthropologists who conducted this survey concluded that "divine creation is the closest concept American culture provides to express the sacredness of nature."

Adds moral to religious reasons— what's the difference?

philosophy

anthropology survey

Who's Muir? Temple = nature?

Nature is divine continues

During the nineteenth century preservationists forthrightly gave ethical and spiritual reasons for protecting the natural world. John Muir condemned the "temple destroyers, devotees of ravaging commercialism" who "instead of lifting their eyes to the God of the mountains, lift them to the almighty dollar." This was not a call for better cost-benefit analysis: Muir described nature not as a commodity but as a companion. Nature is sacred, Muir held, whether or not resources are scarce.

ethical/spiritual reasons

contrasts

chk

Get away from $$$ in nature

Philosophers such as Emerson and Thoreau thought of nature as full of divinity. Walt Whitman celebrated a leaf of grass as no less than the journey work of the stars: "After you have exhausted what there is in business, politics, conviviality, love, and so on," he wrote in *Specimen Days*, and "found that none of these finally satisfy, or permanently wear–what remains? Nature remains." These philosophers thought of nature as a refuge from economic activity, not as a resource for it.

philosopher & poet

running out of resources, destroying ecology

Today those who wish to protect the natural environment rarely offer ethical or spiritual reasons for the policies they favor. Instead they say we are running out of resources or causing the collapse of the ecosystems on which we depend. Predictions of resource scarcity appear objective and scientific, whereas pronouncements that nature is sacred or that greed is bad appear judgmental or even embarrassing in a secular society. Prudential and economic arguments, moreover, have succeeded better than moral or spiritual ones in swaying public policy.

*Whole new section**

CLAIM 3

But not really?

Where's Sagoff going with this?

These arguments are wrong— They are ??

These prudential and economic arguments are not likely to succeed much longer. It is simply wrong to believe that nature sets physical limits to economic growth–that is, to prosperity and the production and consumption of goods and services on which it is based. The idea that increasing consumption will inevitably lead to depletion and scarcity, as plausible as it may seem, is mistaken both in principle and in fact. It is based on four misconceptions.

chk

***MAIN POINT OF ARTICLE ***

sets up organization

Exercise 2.2 Read the rest of Sagoff's article carefully, annotating as you read. Return to your group and share your marked-up texts and marginal notes. Which of your group members' comments or annotations mirror ones that you made? Which ones do you disagree with? Which passages did other readers focus on that you did not consider? Which passages did you focus on that other readers skipped over?

After Reading: Analyzing and Evaluating

Now your goal is to review the text: to examine the content, the structure, and the language of the article in more detail, in order to refine your sense of the writer's exact purpose and to understand how and how well he or she achieved that purpose. In our car shopping analogy, the potential buyer is at the stage where he or she has decided the car seems worth examining more closely. The shopper may ask a lot of questions about the car's maintenance history, warranty, and fuel consumption—whatever seems important to that individual—and may even bring in a mechanic to give the car a careful once-over for any major systems problems. When you review a piece of writing, you will often start by examining the claims the writer lays out, the support of those claims, and the arrangement of that support. Here a well-marked text will really save you time as you sort out the structure of the text. Ask yourself:

Questions for Analysis
- Are the writer's claims clear and logical? Do they all relate directly to the main point?
- Why did the writer organize the piece in this way? What does the introduction accomplish? What functions do the individual paragraphs serve?
- What patterns of thinking does the author use to drive home the main points?
- What is the writer's tone and attitude? Is the writer being serious, humorous, angry, ironic, informative, combative? How can you tell?

Questions for Evaluation
- Are the claims, evidence, and organization effective overall in accomplishing the central purpose? What specific strengths and weaknesses do you find?
- Is the evidence relevant? Is there enough evidence to support the claims? Is the evidence verifiable? Does the evidence seem slanted or biased?
- Does the tone of the writing support or undercut the writer's position? (Consider the connotations of words and phrases the writer uses.)

Keep returning to the text to find specific examples for your analysis and evaluation. Just as in shopping for the car, at this point you're judging for yourself, in a sense, whether the initial promise of the text has been kept and how the writer's values stack up against yours. To keep track of your ideas, use your journal: identify any questions you have after this rereading, and note any insights the reading has provoked in you.

Exercise 2.3 Review Sagoff's text by answering the questions for analysis and evaluation. Be prepared to discuss your responses in class.

___

There isn't anything especially mysterious about this reading process. The main point here is that you can engage a text with more power—greater understanding and efficiency—if you preview the text, read it with a purpose and a plan, and review the text carefully after you've read it. When people try to make sense of more complex texts in the same way they would, say, a brief item in a newspaper or on a web page—starting at the first sentence and reading straight through—they tend to make more work for themselves, and they end up having to accept what they read at face value. Reading in only a linear way, you are likely to get caught up in details and lose control of the topic. Readers who quit reading because the text seems to make no sense should alter their reading strategy. Most of the students that we know don't have a lot of time to waste. Work smart. Preview, annotate, and reread.

REACTING TO THE WRITER'S IDEAS

We've talked a bit about the roles you already fill comfortably (at home, with friends, and so on) and about how each role carries with it a range of usual types of behaviors and thinking. Let's return to our car shopping analogy for a minute. What's your typical reaction to a car seller? Do you tend to get swept away in the sales rhetoric and find yourself really wanting that car, at least for as long as the salesperson is proclaiming its virtues? Or do you tend to draw back, feeling skeptical about each new part of the pitch? Most of us have a habitual response to a sales pitch, whether it's for a new car or a new idea. We're often "for" or "against," we go with the flow or we resist. Many of the early reactions you have while reading will probably fall within your usual mode of response. That's natural and feels very comfortable because it's already a habit. Writers often read at the start of a writing project with just this sort of reaction.

You can follow up on your first gut reaction to a text, or begin to move beyond it, by writing about it in your journal. For example, you can

- *React to passages*—Do you agree or disagree with the ideas raised? Why? Define and defend your position on an issue.

- *Question passages*—What is still unclear? Draft questions that you still need answered, and then try to answer them.

- *Paraphrase passages*—Rewrite a passage in your own words, and then review your paraphrase and respond to the idea(s) that you have restated.

- *Link passages to one another*—What connections between the passages triggered reactions? Label each trigger passage with a phrase, and then write explanations of how each passage connects to the next one.

- *Link your experience to passages*—What in your life experience did these passages touch? Paraphrase the passages that caught your eye, and then write about how the ideas raised there are relevant to you, developing stories, reconstructing dialogues, and describing events.

As you write in your journal, stay alert for points of connection to other pieces you have read, other ideas you've been exposed to in this class or other classes or on the job, and other ways of looking at this same topic you've wanted to explore.

Exercise 2.4 Review your annotations on the Sagoff article and then, focusing on a passage that triggered a reaction for you, try out one of the journal exercises described above. Be prepared to discuss the passage you reacted to and to share what you discovered in your journal.

WRITING SUMMARIES

Once you have expressed your early reactions to the piece, you are likely to be in a better position to step back from your personal perspective and become a more objective "observer" of a piece of writing. This role is one you play frequently as you write in school. In any academic field, being able to restate a writer's or researcher's position briefly and accurately is the beginning of responding intelligently to it. While taking class notes and writing research papers and essay exams, you will be required to write down the gist of information presented in lectures, textbooks, and other readings. When you develop your own position on complex topics, you will be expected to explain how your position relates to and is enhanced by the ideas and arguments of other writers. In such cases, you have to get the gist of what another writer says and does, and be able to report it to your readers fairly, and without bias or inaccuracy.

A summary is a brief, accurate restatement of a writer's position. A summary condenses material by using only the main ideas from the original. At times, your summaries will be single sentences in essays and papers that are otherwise full of your opinion. For example, in an essay explaining your position on school choice, you might write, "Deborah Meier argues that school choice can save public education by encouraging educators to experiment with new approaches." This single sentence catches the gist of Meier's entire essay and sets you up to agree or disagree with or to modify or expand her position as you develop your own. At other times, summary will be the purpose of your entire project. Teachers will ask you to develop paragraph and page-long summaries of difficult material, to give you a chance to understand the material better and to see how well you understand it. Whether your summary is a phrase long or a page long, you will need to play the role of a careful observer who is conveying a body of information to a reader.

To summarize a text, take brief notes to identify its purpose, thesis, audience, and main points, and then turn them into a coherent piece that others can understand. To illustrate summary writing here, we will explain the process of creating a one- or two-paragraph summary of a much longer text, a kind of writing that is also called an abstract or précis.

Taking Notes for a Summary

When you read and review in order to summarize, you need to pay close attention to what the text says and does. This will involve thinking in terms of rhetorical strategies as well as content.

- Identify briefly the author's main purpose, using your own words or a combination of your own words and a short quotation from the text. Question the text: What is the author trying to accomplish here? To reveal his or her thoughts and feelings? Inform you about an issue the writer considers important? Does the writing seek to persuade you to a particular point of view? Convince you to act in a certain way? Some combination of these? If you're not sure of the overall purpose, write down some tentative thoughts now and come back to this point later.

- Identify briefly the author's primary audience, using clues such as the place the piece was originally published, the level of difficulty of the prose, the connotations of the words the author has chosen to use, and the types of examples that may signal who the author is trying to engage. You may find it helpful to imagine a specific person who would be favorably impressed by the piece, to see if you can intuit who the author thinks the typical reader is.

- Once you have a feel for what the author is doing, look carefully at what he or she says. Find the author's thesis or main point, or if the main point is not stated in the text, write a statement describing what the piece as a whole seems to be trying to support.

- Reread the piece and mark off the main sections. Write one sentence that describes each section. To identify the sections, consider what the purpose is of each paragraph or group of related paragraphs. In longer works, headings may help you develop at least a rough sense of the major divisions, although you'll still want to pay attention to how the author uses paragraphs. You can also look for patterns of development to figure out a logical way to analyze the structure. For example, does the author compare and/or contrast items to make the main point? Use a series of examples? Suggest new or reworked definitions? Try to show what caused something else or what the effects were?

Be aware that it's not unusual for the notes you take for a summary to be longer than the actual summary that you will write.

Talking About Rhetorical Strategies

When summarizing, you should use verbs that accurately convey the writer's position and attitude. Some of the verbs listed here overlap in meaning, but they will give you a working vocabulary for talking about what writing does.

acknowledge	consider	evaluate	observe	say
add	contend	explain	offer	show
admit	craft figures	explore	persuade	solve
agree	of speech	find	point out	problems
analyze	critique	grant	pose	speculate
argue	declare	illustrate	problems	state
ask	deny	imply	propose	suggest
assert	describe	incite	action	summarize
believe	dispute	inform	reason	synthesize
claim	elaborate	insist	refute	tell stories
comment	emphasize	maintain	reject	think through
concede	endorse	narrate	report	write
conclude	establish	experience	respond	
confirm	relationships	note	reveal	

Drafting a Summary

Because your task as a summary writer is so precise, you will probably follow a fairly formal drafting process. In the very first sentence, identify the work you are summarizing by naming the title and author of the piece. Use this sentence and perhaps the next to state the author's purpose and main point in your own words.

> In "Choice Can *Save* Public Education," Deborah Meier argues that the problems of our public education system can be solved by letting parents choose where their children go to school.

> In "The Undergraduate," Erik Hedegaard describes the life of an undergraduate at one of the top "party" schools in the United States.

> In "America Has a Class System. See 'Frasier,'" Anita Gates analyzes the depiction of class conflict in this popular situation comedy.

This central assertion will be followed by the sentences you developed for each major section in the order the author used. You will probably use the author as the subject of several sentences:

> Meier then describes the successful reform of District 4 in order to demonstrate …

Stick to the really important issues, since you need to report on the whole text in only one or two paragraphs.

Once you have the material together, you'll need to go through and add transitions between your sentences so the piece reads smoothly.

Revising a Summary

Summaries must be carefully revised so that they restate the writer's main point and explain how the major pieces of the text establish the writer's point. There are several issues that you will need to attend to.

- Check to see if the verbs you have used accurately portray the writer's purpose and position (refer to Talking About Rhetorical Strategies, page 22).

- Make sure the transitions you have used to mark each major move the author makes accurately represent the text's structure (see Naming Transitional Strategies, page 24).

- Check to be sure that you have not included any personal reactions.

- Finally, as for any piece of writing you intend to share, edit and proofread your work carefully for precise grammar, accurate word choice, and clean copy (no typos, misspelled words, or the like).

Exercise 2.5 Take notes for a summary of Sagoff's essay. After you finish, meet with a group of classmates and evaluate the following draft summary of that essay. Before you read the summary itself, look over your notes on Sagoff's essay and talk about what a summary of it would have to contain. See if your group can list the major moves in the essay and craft an opening sentence for a summary of the essay. Look over the summary and evaluate how well the writer caught Sagoff's main point. Look also for transitions and biases. As a group, write an editor's note to this writer, summarizing the draft's strengths and making suggestions to shore up weaker areas.

Naming Transitional Strategies

The following categories will give you ideas for naming transitional moves.

indicate causal relationship

I shop *because* it makes me feel good. (since, therefore, thus)

indicate comparison

She was drawn to the CK brand; *similarly,* he loved the Gap. (likewise, in comparison)

indicate consequences

I am sick of buying; *therefore,* I am staying out of the mall. (hence, as a result, consequently)

indicate contrast

I am an individual; *however,* I just have to wear Nike. (but, nevertheless, on the other hand, in contrast, instead)

mark addition

The marketplace gives us freedom to choose; *in addition,* market-driven technological advances give us more time. (besides, moreover, also)

mark concession

We consume too much to be healthy *even though* we live longer than ever. (although, granted that)

mark place

The Mall of America is an amazing place. *Nearby,* the Walker Art Museum gives consumers yet another opportunity to buy. (below, above, in the vicinity)

mark restatement

Modern life is all about commodification; *that is,* we now turn every aspect of life into a good or service that can be obtained for a price. (in other words, indeed)

mark sequences

To understand consumerism, *first,* we must consider how goods and services fit into everyday life; *then* we must understand how we define consumers. (next, finally)

mark time

Historically exchanges were governed by social codes; *now* the dollar dictates. (at present, in the past, nowadays, meanwhile, in the future)

mark conclusion

In conclusion, transitions are important. (in brief, finally, in sum)

DO AMERICANS REALLY CONSUME TOO MUCH?

MICHELLE ANTONELLI

In Mark Sagoff's essay, "Do We Consume Too Much," he explores many reasons behind the differences in opinion pertaining to consumption in today's growing economy arguing that there are two different views on whether or not Americans consume too much. The one that he talks about the least is the spiritual and moral consequences of how much we consume, though he does call our attention to arguments of Muir and Thoreau who declare that nature is sacred; whether or not resources are scarce, according to these philosophers (and Sagoff by extension), they are full of divinity. He spends most of the body of his essay talking about the economic concern with supply and demand rather than moral issues. Sagoff goes on to discredit the generally held notion that the developed north inattentively uses raw materials, food and timber, and energy, and in the process exploits the south. After he talks about the economic side and tells us we aren't consuming too many of the goods, he shifts again in a short section immediately preceding his conclusion and tells us we do, in fact, consume too much, only in a different sense. Our consumption habits separate us from our friends, family, neighbors, and traditions; they deprive us of satisfaction in the spiritual terms that Muir and Thoreau talk about.

YOUR ROLE AS AN INVENTOR

Inventors invent something new, often by putting established ideas and truths together in new ways. Why do we make this obvious statement? Because it is not always clear to students that there is *no one else* who can write what you can write. No one else thinks the same way you do; no one else has the same background and interests and knowledge that you do. No one else knows everything you know.

Much of the reading you will do in college writing courses is intended to give you the raw materials to build your own ideas. Although sometimes you will be asked to leave your personal opinions and insights aside, as in a summary, mostly instructors want to read what *you* think, to see how you put together a chain of reasoning that establishes the position you've chosen to support. Unlike the book report of high school or the formal abstract of college, which are exercises in pure exposition, most of your writing tasks are going to ask you to explain and interpret a phenomenon, an event, a situation, or an issue from your own, individual point of view.

But what is your own point of view? Not many people know, or know in any thorough detail, before they start writing. The process of figuring out what you think and how best to communicate your ideas may prove frustrating or gratifying, be erratic or systematic. And the process is likely to involve somewhat different challenges for each piece you write. For many student writers, the beginning of the process is often the most intimidating, which is why the invention processes outlined next are intended to loosen up your mind and your words.

To invent a writing project, you can start with a clearly defined topic, a vague subject, or no ideas at all. If you start with a topic, you may focus on a usable idea a bit sooner; if you start with a broad subject or no ideas, you may find something really interesting to say you might not have hit on otherwise. Either way, experiment with some of these strategies to explore your stock of ideas and imagination. The role of inventor is necessarily one of risk taking. So when it's time to get started on an idea for writing, let go of your critical self, let go of your notions of what can or can't be accomplished. Stick your neck out, experiment, be daring.

Strategies for Invention

No two writers invent exactly the same way, and the same writer will use different strategies for different projects. The first strategies that we list work whether you start with no ideas or have a pretty clear sense of where you want to go.

Freewrite—Write fluidly, nonstop, off the top of your head about anything that comes to mind.
- Set a time frame, for example, six minutes, and keep writing until your time is up.
- Don't criticize, don't analyze, just keep the pen or the fingers on the keyboard moving.
- If you want, you can go back over your reading notes to refresh your memory before you begin. See what's best for you.

Loop—Do a ten-minute freewrite, then take a very short break. Read what you wrote and circle any ideas that interest you. Start with one of those ideas and freewrite about it for another ten minutes.

Brainstorm—Focus on a topic or an assignment, and list in words or brief phrases everything you think about it. Take a break; go back over your list to find surprises or related items or other interesting discoveries.

Cluster—In the center of a piece of paper draw a circle and write your topic in the circle (say, advertising). Draw short spokes out from that circle and at the end of each spoke, write a subtopic (images, language, appeals, and so on). Circle each subtopic and draw short spokes out from the subtopic circles and write sub-subtopics at the end of each spoke (for appeals, you might write humor, attention, sex, power, and peer pressure). Keep going until you work your way into concrete examples. Review your cluster and think about connections between subtopics that you discover and the reading that you have done.

If you prefer more structure or have a fair grasp of what you might be thinking, try these strategies:

Journalist's Questions—Focus on your subject and write out answers to the question words *who, what, where, when, why,* and *how.* Then look back at your answers for insights and points of departure.

Note Writing—Write a note to someone, perhaps a friend, a teacher, or an author you just read, about a topic or question.

Mini-essay—Freewrite a paragraph that raises a topic, works through some supporting examples or arguments, and comes to a conclusion.

Impromptu Essay—Write up an essay question, or focus on an actual writing assignment, and freewrite your entire answer.

Outline—List the general topics you want to cover and then put your list aside. When you come back to your list, decide how it makes sense to organize the topics and brainstorm subtopics.

Leave your invention notes aside for a time and let your ideas percolate. Go back to them and add other thoughts that surface as you read them.

Exercise 2.6 With two or three classmates, review your notes on the Sagoff essay and brainstorm ideas and passages that triggered a reaction for each of you. Focusing on one trigger issue, use an invention strategy to gather ideas for a group response to that issue.

YOUR ROLE AS A WRITER

Drafting a piece of writing requires a different mindset than inventing, although you'll likely find yourself shifting in and out of each mode of thought, each role, as we've mentioned before. The difference in role between inventor and writer is one of concentration and focus. Inventing, you let your mind soar and swoop, engaging a whole landscape of thought. Drafting, you rein it in more, stick to your central purpose, choose an idea to explore in gritty detail. Figuring out how much of the territory you have room to explore in a single piece of writing may also become part of your task in drafting.

Drafting for some people is more like inventing—open and exploratory. For others, it is more of an organizing task: How do these ideas fit together? Do they relate to larger ideas, to a more encompassing generalization? How? Which ideas are the most important, secondary in importance, and minor in importance? This second group of writers may want to develop outlines of ideas before they draft or while they are drafting. In either case, your basic tasks in drafting are to come up with an idea worth discussing, decide what you want to say about it, find examples or statistics or other kinds of data that relate to the idea, and then get it all down in some fashion on paper. That's very broad, because it must be. Every writing situation is different from the others.

Inventing, you write for yourself. Drafting, you begin to consider who else you are writing to and for. Who is your audience? In many college composition classrooms, your audience will be your fellow classmates. When you have a choice about how to say something in your draft, think about your colleagues. Which way of stating your idea would be more likely to interest them? What do they need to know before they get to your main point in order to understand it? Which of the supporting points you want to use are more and less likely to impress them?

What is your purpose? What do you want your readers to know or feel or do once they've read your piece? If you're trying to change people's minds about an issue, then you need to think about what kinds of evidence are going to be most compelling to them. If you want them to understand your analysis of an issue, then you'll need to lay out your position carefully so they can follow your logic. What exactly does your audience need to read so they can participate fully in the exchange you are offering them? Your answers may help you decide how to proceed in drafting. (If not in drafting, then certainly in revising.)

Strategies for Drafting

- **Start in the Middle**—It's sometimes easier to start drafting in the middle of the essay first, saving the introduction and conclusion for later. It's not uncommon to start out thinking one way about an issue and then move to a different point of view as you examine what you're writing. So, working through the topic first can help you better understand what you're introducing before you spend time writing an interesting opening for your piece.

- **Start from Strength**—It's sometimes easier to start with the point you feel most strongly about, because your emotion will motivate your thinking and keep your writing flowing. You can go back later and add in points that develop and balance your most immediate response to the topic.

- **Start from an Assignment**—If you have a specific writing assignment to fulfill, read the assignment very carefully before you start to draft. If the assignment has multiple parts, make sure you understand the intent of each one. In this case, drafting a thesis statement first may help keep the rest of the draft focused.

- **Write Around a Thesis**—While often you may not know what your thesis statement is until you have written a draft, sometimes you will start from the idea you want to prove or the purpose you want to achieve. This statement clarifies for you what you want to say and do, and it relates to readers both the issue you're examining and your particular point of view about the issue. Examine the following thesis statements, taken from articles in Part 2 of this book:
  - "The idea that increasing consumption will inevitably lead to depletion and scarcity, as plausible as it may seem, is mistaken both in principle and in fact." Mark Sagoff, "Do We Consume Too Much?"
  - "How you shop is who you are." Sarah Boxer, "I Shop, Ergo I Am: The Mall as Society's Mirror"
  - "Ms. Schor, an economist at Harvard University, argues that the vast majority of Americans aspire in their spending to the lifestyles of the wealthiest 20 percent." Louis Uchitelle, "Keeping Up with the Gateses?"

These three examples show different patterns for thesis statements. The first example identifies the issue (the effect of increases in the rate of consumption) and reveals the writer's point of view on it (increases need not necessarily lead to depletion). The second example names—in a very compact statement—a topic (our shopping behavior) and comments on it (it reveals our identity). The third example names a subject (research by Dr. Juliet Schor on American spending) and its most important idea (Americans pattern their lifestyles on the wealthy). Each thesis suggests a different kind of draft.

However you go about drafting, allow your thinking to develop as you go. Don't get stuck on the first thesis or outline you develop. Allow yourself to stop drafting and do more inventing when you seem to run out of things to say. And remember that drafting takes time. If you are to take advantage of what you know and how you feel about a topic, you have to discover your feelings, knowledge, and interests and then work them into a draft. This process is rarely neat, and it is almost always more time-consuming than the writer expects.

YOUR ROLE AS A COLLABORATOR

Many writing courses include collaborative exchange between readers and writers during the writing process. Whether this means talking with a small group about your ideas before drafting, receiving comments about your drafts in progress, getting editing advice, or all of these, collaborating is an opportunity to get direct feedback from an audience of readers. To make the most of the opportunity, consider the two roles in this exchange, each of which requires some care.

As a colleague commenting on another person's ideas, your role is a delicate one. You need to be honest, so the writer hears feedback useful in revising, but tactful, so the writer doesn't feel attacked or put down to the extent that he or she can no longer focus on the substance of your remarks. As a writer receiving feedback, your role is to create a bit of distance between yourself and your text, so that when you get suggestions for improvement, you can consider them critically rather than react to them defensively.

Regarding the actual task of collaborating, it helps the reader/collaborator to know what questions the writer has about the piece. Is the writer concerned about whether the thesis is clear? If the examples are given in an order that makes the piece easy to understand? If the supporting evidence seems relevant to the thesis? From the writer's point of view in this exchange, it can be helpful to receive comments in written rather than oral form. This gives the writer time to consider each remark in a methodical way that can be difficult to achieve when simply hearing the comments in the classroom.

Strategies for Working with Other Writers

Whatever the particular approach your class takes to collaboration, here are a few suggestions to help keep your role as reader of another's writing productive:

- Make a positive comment about the piece, and then move on to areas for improvement.
- State your responses using the word "I"—"I don't really understand why you …."
- Consider using an annotation system, maybe putting a straight line under strong moves and a wavy line under phrases or passages that seem less clear or less connected to the writer's purpose.
- Don't rewrite anything, but do suggest specific revisions at points of weakness and strength, for example, "I love this example! Can you use it again in the next paragraph?" or "I think that moving your third paragraph before your second would clarify their relationship to your thesis."

To take advantage of this opportunity as a writer hearing your readers' responses, consider the following points:

- Before reading your colleagues' comments, give yourself some time off after you write a draft in order to gain distance from your own perspective. This will help you to evaluate your own work more clearly.
- If you don't understand a reader's comment, ask for clarification.
- About each comment that you receive, ask yourself how revising your piece in this way will affect its ability to achieve your purpose for writing. You will probably find some comments more helpful than others, and you are the final judge of which comments to put into use.
- Do be careful if you find yourself disagreeing with all the comments you get— it's doubtful that your piece is perfect, even in the draft called "final."

THREE CRITICAL MOVES IN THE DISCOURSE OF COLLEGE

Of all the different ways people think and write, three of them—analysis, synthesis, and evaluation—form the basis for much of the work you will do in the academic community. Whether your purpose is mainly self-expression, exposition, or persuasion, you will likely draw on the strategies of analysis, synthesis, and evaluation. You already use these strategies informally in your everyday life. You may analyze a video you are thinking of renting by noticing who the actors are and whether you like each one. You may base a decision to buy a new CD on a synthesis of your friends' opinions, cuts you've heard on the radio, and a review you read in *Rolling Stone.* You may evaluate a track on that CD once you buy it to see if it matches your idea of what a good song should be, listening for its rhythm, lyrics, and melody.

Probably the main difference between using these strategies in your everyday life and using them in a college writing course is that in college, you need to state each of your ideas explicitly, so that your readers don't have to guess at the connections you are making. Just as instructors expect your thesis to be supported by ample, clearly relevant supporting evidence, they expect you to lay out the underlying ideas you use in analysis, synthesis, and evaluation so they can examine your reasoning.

Just as importantly, remember as you read the next sections that all three of these strategies are ways for you to develop and clarify your own ideas. You will use these strategies to accomplish your own purposes for writing. Don't get so caught up in figuring out the connections other writers are making that you forget to make your own. Use these strategies to deepen or extend your own thinking on an issue, taking care to emphasize your own position on the matter at hand.

Analysis

The purpose of analysis is to convey an idea you consider important to a reader by pulling apart its components, showing how they interrelate, and noting what the components, working together, show about the topic as a whole. For example, stockbrokers analyze companies to assess and predict those companies' value and health; chemists analyze compounds to determine their properties and the proportions of each component; and soybean farmers analyze soil conditions, weather patterns, and plant characteristics to schedule planting and harvesting. The word "analysis" can also describe the writing that results from such analytic activity.

In the processes of reading and writing in the composition classroom, you may take on the role of rhetorical analyst to figure out, for example, how the particular tone of voice a writer uses offers a setting for the position the writer has taken. For example:

> "My generation grew up internalizing an endless film loop of fairy-tale princesses, beach bunnies, witches, flying nuns, bionic women, and beauty queens, a series of flickering images that urged us, since childhood, to be all these things all the time."
> Susan Douglas, "Where the Girls Are"

To do such an analysis, you draw on a set of principles. In this case, you have at least a sense of a principle of writing that your instructor may call "levels of diction." That is, there are writing occasions that require more formal language and others that call for less formal language. Only by knowing this principle can you analyze the language in the example to see how it works to enhance the writer's

Questions for Analysis

As you analyze the readings in this book, ask yourself questions such as

- How does this piece of writing exemplify the theme I am studying?
- What is the writer's purpose?
- Does the writer state a thesis? Why or why not? Where?
- What key ideas or evidence does the author use to support the thesis?
- How does the tone of voice of this writing enhance the writer's position?
- How does the writer organize the text—that is, what is the progression of main ideas?
- What stance does the writer seem to take toward the subject of the article?
- What stance does the writer seem to take toward his or her readers?

position. In this example, we might say that the tone of voice draws on the informal by referring to silly images of women like "bunnies" and "flying nuns." The writer also identifies herself as a consumer of the popular culture that she describes. The content and voice is informal, but the sentence conveys a suggestive, slightly demeaning sense of the U.S. media images of women by stacking up one implausible character after another.

Try your hand at a different type of analysis: imagine what kinds of evidence the writer of the following statement should give you, the reader, in order for you to accept the statement as probably true.

> "See-want-borrow-and-buy is a comparative process; desire is structured by what we see around us."
>
> Juliet Schor, "The Overspent American"

Looking for the connections between the general statements or propositions a writer makes and the evidence used to support or verify them is a form of analysis, as we have just suggested. This analysis depends on your knowing that academic discourse demands a high standard for evidence. (In other words, you can't just throw out assertions and expect people to believe them. You need to provide the support—the evidence, definitions of key terms, logical arguments—that will establish the plausibility of your assertions.) That's the principle involved in this rhetorical analysis of the thesis by Juliet Schor. Here are some kinds of support we might expect Schor to supply to establish the believability of her thesis:

- A definition of "desire"
- Data that show how people define their positions by reference to groups or categories of other people to whom they compare themselves
- First-person accounts by consumers revealing how their desires for consumer products is triggered by what they see others buying

As you read the articles in this book, you will consistently need to ask questions about each writer's purpose and the language she or he uses to accomplish that purpose. Some of those questions will focus on the content of the piece and some on the way the writer arranges and presents the content (the rhetoric).

Exercise 2.7 With two or three classmates, brainstorm buying habits that you all share, from ordering CDs to paying tuition. Focus on one kind of purchase, and analyze the approach you—as consumers—generally take to this activity. Explain the parts of the purchasing process, the way those parts fit together, and the principles that might govern the process. Be prepared to share your analysis in a class discussion.

Synthesis

Synthesis is the opposite of analysis. Instead of dividing up a topic or idea into its parts, when you synthesize ideas, you pull them together and combine them to fashion something larger, more complex, or more important. You discover and explore the patterns among various ideas in order to create a new overall design. For example, suppose you read two articles on shopping malls. One argues that shopping malls are poor substitutes for old-fashioned marketplaces, which enhanced community. Another states that malls become what shoppers make of them, including important public meeting places for many kinds of people. From these readings, you might focus on the idea that shopping may be about something more than going into a store, finding what you want, paying for it, and returning home. Maybe shopping is one important kind of social activity that people enjoy.

Synthesis grows out of analysis. Go into a grocery store with the intention of making salsa and you will leave with tomatoes, peppers, onions, and cilantro and head for a cutting board and knife. You have used analysis to figure out what to buy and what tools to use. A recipe and a taste for salsa served as your principles. When you have chopped and mixed your ingredients, you have synthesized them—salsa is more than a tomato, more than an onion.

Before you go looking for elements (or buying ingredients), you need to have a sense for what you want to say (or cook); that is, you have to think analytically before you start a synthesis. Inexperienced writers often struggle with synthesis papers because they take the first details that they find rather than reading and thinking analytically, gaining a sense of all the pieces and the possible wholes, and only then deciding to develop a particular whole. Going into a Blockbuster video store without a clue as to what you want to see can result in discovering a great movie, but more likely, you'll wander aimlessly. There are just too many possibilities. If, on the other hand, you decide that you are looking for a comedy or a new release, you have a sense for where to look and what constitutes a potential target. Just so, it is hard to write a synthesis paper about how people use malls in different ways without first thinking about shopping as a social activity, and market places as public meeting grounds. Synthesis, then, is not a random gathering of ideas or data; it is done with purpose, in relation to principles, just as analysis is.

When you turn your hand to writing a synthesis, you have to read with the purpose of making connections. This will often mean moving through texts and looking for ideas, evidence, and passages that relate to the topic that you are pursuing. This kind of intellectual work is particularly creative and takes you well beyond reporting what one writer says. Often you will use a story from one reading, some statistical information from another, and a bit of logic from a third. These different pieces fit together because they help you build your position and they relate to the themes or principles that you are working with.

Student writers often struggle with a specific rhetorical problem that arises in writing a synthesis: How can they show their readers which ideas are their own and which come from other sources? One important point to make about this issue is that you need to keep straight which ideas and words are another writer's, and which are your own. In taking notes, you must be very careful to note what is your paraphrase or summary of a source, and what material you are quoting directly. And your own responses to each of these types of notes need to be kept clearly separate from the source material itself.

Strategies for Working with Other Writers' Material

Quotation   A direct quote duplicates the exact words of another writer, catching the tone and terminology developed by that other writer and capitalizing on his or her authority. Since you will be working to develop your own tone and authority, you will probably use direct quotes much less frequently than paraphrases and summaries.

- David Guterson, writing about his visit to the Mall of America, makes it clear that "being lost" is one of the "intentional features of the mall's psychological terrain" (93).

Paraphrase   A paraphrase is a restatement of another writer's ideas, information, or writing strategy. You will tend to paraphrase short passages that present material directly relevant to the position you are developing.

- Statistics from the United Nations Human Development Index show that since 1960, the number of people living at or below the subsistence level dropped by nearly 40 percent but over the same period, the wealthiest people increased their share of global income from 70 to 80 percent (Sagoff 59-60).
- Daniel Harris asserts that many gay magazines wrongly portray money-making as a form of social activism (139).
- Mark Sagoff dismisses as groundless the claim that excessive consumption leads to resource depletion (50).

Summary   Summaries are neutral, brief, accurate restatements of another writer's material. In synthesis writing, you will occasionally develop 100- or 200-word summaries, and frequently you will reduce whole texts to a single sentence in order to show how they generally relate to the principle or theme that you are developing.

- Lawrence Shames in "The More Factor" declares that the U.S. obsession with having more is leading to a moral crisis.

However you use other writers' materials, you need to properly identify the source of the information. This means acknowledging writers within the body of your essay and documenting source information correctly.

Questions for Synthesis

Here are some questions to get you started writing and thinking in terms of synthesis.

- What interests me about the material I am studying?
- Does there seem to be a common theme or a question running through the different sources I have consulted?
- What personal experiences come to mind as I reflect on this theme or question?
- What parts of my experiences may be relevant to the theme or question I am looking at?
- What is the context of my writing about this theme or question? (How does it relate to other work we have done in this class?)

Exercise 2.8 Brainstorm purchases that you have made in the past week and, looking at the results of your brainstorm, freewrite about the kind of consumer those purchases seem to define. Then see if you can group your purchases into categories, and explain how each category defines you as a consumer.

Evaluation

When you evaluate a subject, whether it's a piece of writing, a recipe for salsa, or a new car, you judge its worth. Evaluation is the act of valuing, of using social or personal principles to determine a thing's worth. Depending on what kind of a subject you are evaluating, you will choose different criteria to weigh the subject and find it valuable or wanting.

Some criteria are public or at least can be defended publicly. Other times, we put value on ideas or things in ways that we don't want to or couldn't defend. As a student writer, you will do public evaluations, identifying an accepted criterion and systematically applying it to the thing—texts, pieces of art, chemical compounds, geometry problems—that you are evaluating. But don't discount your personal tastes. More often than not, public evaluations begin as private inclinations. You may decide that you like Whoppers better than Big Macs, but if pressed, you could talk about their value or nutritional composition to justify your personal taste. In the same way, when you are asked to evaluate an argument, you may start from the gut feeling that the writer is just wrong and then work to prove that point publicly. As in culinary tastes, though, don't be afraid to try new things. You may start out thinking a writer is boring or wrongheaded, but give yourself a chance to change your mind (especially if you have to spend four weeks writing about the topic).

Public evaluations often proceed analytically or synthetically; that is, in order to evaluate a thing we break it down into its components or add together information or components. For instance, evaluating a Whopper could involve just biting into it and deciding whether it's good, but a hungry Burger King customer standing in line and deciding what sandwich to buy might think analytically, "Well, a Whopper is a

---

Questions for Evaluation

Here are some questions that will help you start using evaluation.

- What is the subject of my evaluation supposed to be able to do, to be, or to achieve?
- What standards or criteria would it need to meet to be considered good, effective, or worthwhile?
- Does the thing I am evaluating meet some of the criteria but not others?
- How thoroughly do I need to explain my criteria to my audience?
- How much does my audience already know about the thing I am evaluating?
- What evidence will be sufficient to demonstrate my evaluation?

---

biggish, char-broiled burger with tomato and lettuce; the parts make it worth $2." Or that customer might reflect synthetically, "The Whopper has lots of fixings but also lots of fat, and it leaves me with a peculiar aftertaste. Guess I'll go for a couple of hamburgers instead." In both cases, the evaluation is one that could be explained in a conversation.

Practically, then, your goal in writing an evaluation is to explain how well or effectively something—often a text—achieves a purpose or matches a criteria. The principle(s) and subject(s) that you decide to work with will determine whether you will address the effectiveness, credibility, evidence, or logic of your subject, whether it is an opinion, a text, a work of art, or anything else. Keep in mind that evaluations are a kind of opinionated analysis or synthesis: you decide what something should do, and then you look at it carefully (as parts or as a whole) to explain how well the thing does its thing.

Exercise 2.9 With two or three classmates, discuss the factors you took into account when selecting which college or university to attend. (Thus, you will be defining your criteria for a good college or university.) Use this list of criteria to evaluate your experience on campus so far. Be prepared to participate in a class discussion of criteria for evaluating higher education in general and your school in particular.

YOUR ROLE AS A REWRITER

Rewriting your work depends on your ability to analyze it, evaluate its strengths and weaknesses, and synthesize suggestions you may have gotten from classmates, tutors, or your teacher. The role of rewriter requires some fancy mental footwork. Revising thoroughly requires paying attention to different elements of your work, and effective revisions depend on seeing your work from the perspectives of several readers—yourself, your classmates, and your teacher(s). Each time you look at your text, keep a list of the problems you need to solve and any ideas for revising. Later, you can actually do the work of rewriting; but first, review the draft from different perspectives to get a clearer sense of what you need to accomplish in the next draft.

The first perspective is, of course, your own. What do you think of this draft, now that you have some distance from it? Where does the draft seem strong and weak? Why? Read your work aloud to yourself. Anytime you experience trouble reading it out loud, stop and mark that point in the draft for later consideration. As a reader, you are developing a system for annotating other writers' texts; as a rewriter, use the same or a similar system to work through your own text. This will mean changing your focus from "big picture" to "small piece" and back again: Do the details all help make the big picture clearer? Does the big picture seem coherent, like a table set for dinner or an alley-oop play? Or does it seem not to hang together, more like an accident or the aftermath of chaotic weather? Mark up the text and take notes as you reread.

If you received comments from your classmates, do your best to figure out why they said what they did. Check each question the draft raised for them, or jot a note in the margin to remind yourself of comments that you want to attend to in rewriting. If you didn't get feedback on the draft, think through what you know of your classmates, and imagine their responses. For example, if you've all read the same group of articles, would your classmates need to read an extended summary of an author's ideas in your piece? Also, think about discussions you may have had in class on your topic or similar ones. What objections do you think your colleagues might raise to the ideas in your paper? Consider whether you need to address these different points of view to make your piece more compelling.

You can also step into the perspective of your teacher (or tutors or other well-read adults). How would this person read your piece? What would they find interesting? What would they need to read more about to understand your thesis? To believe it? This stance will help you keep in mind the high standards for written work in the college community. You can use the questions asked in the analysis section on page 32 and the evaluation section on page 35 as a guide for the kind of critical reading your instructor would probably give your writing.

Strategies for Revision

Consider using the following strategies to revise your work thoroughly.

Outline the text to see exactly how it develops.
- Create a simple outline from your main point and claims. Leave space after each claim.
- Note for each claim what the text "says" and what that section "does" to develop the main point.

Examine transitions between ideas.
- Write on your outline brief, one- or two-sentence explanations of how each claim connects to each of the other claims.
- For claims not currently connected by transitions, write possible transition solutions on the outline.
- Describe how each part helps the text accomplish your central purpose.

Evaluate the impact of the text.

- In your journal, describe what the text seems to promise a reader. How thoroughly does it deliver on that promise?
- Review the claims. Are they clear and logically coherent? Do they all relate to the topic?
- Review the evidence. To what extent are claims backed up by evidence? How even is the distribution of the evidence? How concrete and clear is that evidence? What irrelevant material could be omitted, and what important evidence needs to be added?
- What biases do you detect? How can you correct them?

Exercise 2.10 Review the following draft—the first paragraph of which appeared above—and develop a collaborative explanation of the writer's central purpose. Then, identify passages in the draft where the writer engages in summary, analysis, synthesis, and evaluation. Be prepared to participate in a class discussion of the writer's purpose and how each critical move—summary, analysis, synthesis, and evaluation—contributes to or compromises that purpose.

DO AMERICANS REALLY CONSUME TOO MUCH?

MICHELLE ANTONELLI

In Mark Sagoff's essay, "Do We Consume Too Much," he explores many reasons behind the differences in opinion pertaining to consumption in today's growing economy arguing that there are two different views on whether or not Americans consume too much. The one that he talks about the least is the spiritual and moral consequences of how much we consume, though he does call our attention to arguments of Muir and Thoreau who declare that nature is sacred; whether or not resources are scarce. According to these philosophers (and Sagoff by extension), they are full of divinity. He spends most of the body of his essay talking about the economic concern with supply and demand rather than moral issues. Sagoff goes on to discredit the generally held notion that the developed North inattentively uses raw materials, food and timber, and energy, and in the process exploits the South. After he talks about the economic side and tells us we aren't consuming too many of the goods, he shifts again in a short section immediately preceding his conclusion and tells us we do, in fact, consume too much, only in a different sense. Our consumption habits separate us from our friends, family, neighbors, and traditions; they deprive us of satisfaction in the spiritual terms that Muir and Thoreau talk about.

Even though Sagoff's structure and points of reference at times are very confusing, as a whole the essay is very effective. He helps us think through a very important and difficult issue by explaining to us the different views about how Americans consume too much. He goes on to offer opinions from theorists about protecting nature or the natural world, but tells us that we are destroying this world because we want more material possessions. After that, he digs into a totally different issue concerning misconceptions about the way Americans consume. He points out four different times that Americans aren't consuming too much, but are given the impression they are. Then he goes on to tell us that we are not consuming too many of these goods, but finds other ways to produce other goods in place of the old ones. After he talks about the misconceptions and right before the conclusion, he adds a part in his reading relating to what the theorists talked about in the beginning of the reading. Finally in the conclusion, he sums up what he has talked about in the past three sections.

In the opening paragraphs he talks about how we should put our faith in the ideas of Thoreau, Whitman, and Muir, and other theorists. This part of the paper becomes very unclear to any reader who isn't familiar with these theorists' writing. Sagoff constantly quotes important American environmentalists, saying that Americans aren't thinking in a utopian or idealistic manner. While he fails to explain his authorities or justify his use with them, he does find in Thoreau and Muir ideas that help us. Muir states the "temple destroyers, devotees of ravaging commercialism" who "instead of lifting their eyes to the God of the mountains, lift them to the almighty dollar." Money becomes so important to us that we forget to appreciate the more important things in our lives. Sagoff continues to say "as we consume more, however, we are more likely to transform the natural world, so that less of it will remain for us to appreciate" (49). New buildings, stores, parking lots, etc., take up much of the natural world in the city. For example, people do not realize the natural world is dying from the material possessions that are desired. Thus, Sagoff uses his introduction to tell us that Americans consume too much of the material things in this world, but we don't appreciate the natural world around us.

At the end of this first section, Sagoff seems to shift emphasis, moving from moral authority to our dependence on economic authority. Sagoff mentions four misconceptions about the way we look at consumption. Initially, I was given the impression that Sagoff was saying how we consume too much was wrong. He talked endlessly about how we don't preserve our resources the way we should, and we let them go to waste. Then Sagoff mentions that the idea that increasing consumption will inevitably lead to depletion and scarcity, as plausible as it may seem, is mistaken "both in principle and in fact" (50).

In actuality, though, we aren't consuming too much and Sagoff points out great facts in each misconception, and supports them well. For example, he mentions a misconception about raw materials and quotes Paul Ehrlich, a biologist at Stanford University, who predicted that "... global shortages would soon send prices for food, fresh water, energy, metals, paper, and other materials sharply higher" (50). But the opposite of what Sagoff carefully documents happens. Raw materials are more abundant and they aren't as expensive as they were in the 1970s. Americans have found a way to make resources last, and make more of them. Resources are actually being maximized. Americans, with the help of technology, are finding way to conserve materials or come up with new and better ones.

In no way, shape, or form are these misconceptions true. The idealists seem to have it all wrong because they said that the way we were consuming was bad, and we should conserve nature. In actuality, nature is not being harmed all that much. These negative examples help us think through the issue even more. It shows that Americans are finding ways to make resources last longer so that the material possessions that need those resources last longer.

In the conclusion, Sagoff switches his argument again. He goes on to say that Americans are consuming too much, not in the sense of using materials up or wasting nature, but in the sense that our consumption is coming between our friends and family. We always want the newest product that comes out, for example, a new lawnmower or the newest model car. The attitude Americans have about always wanting more is shoving a huge wedge between what we should be concentrating on and what we are concentrating on. Traditions and family values are being depleted, not the resources or materials. I think Sagoff puts it best when he says, "We consume too much when market relationships displace the bonds of community, compassion, culture, and place" (63). He finally makes this obvious at the very end of the essay.

In the end, Mark Sagoff wrote a very effective essay, leading us through a very important issue by pointing out two important views. The first one is the spiritual and moral view which pertains to great theorists such as Muir, Thoreau, and Whitman, who point out that Americans are consuming too much of the natural world without trying to preserve the resources or appreciating or loving it the way we should. As it turns out, though, Americans are not consuming too many resources, rather they are increasing the amount of them or finding a substitute for them. Secondly, he takes a turn at the end and explains to us that now we are consuming too much, but in the sense of putting material possessions before family, friends, and traditions that we hold to be precious to us. We make material possessions more important to us than what really should be. This was a tricky essay, but I found that I liked it and that I agree with Sagoff.

Once you've enriched your view of the draft and have a set of notes and questions to work from, you can plan your revision and then actually start making changes (supposing you've actually been able to restrain yourself from starting to revise!). Working from the whole to the parts is usually an effective way to proceed. That is, look at bigger types of issues like purpose, thesis, and flow before tackling more local matters like word choice or connections between individual sentences.

No one could list every major concern that might arise in rewriting, but the basic idea is to work out the larger issues first. That gives you a context for making the next level of changes. Consider the whole text and

- Rewrite your thesis statement to make it more precise or more interesting, and make any related revisions to your supporting points.
- Rearrange sections or paragraphs to create a more logical organization.
- If needed, you might actually want to write an entirely new draft based on just a few of the better ideas in the original version.
- Replace examples that aren't as relevant as you thought.
- Add new ideas you've thought of since the last time you wrote.

Then, consider each paragraph and

- Change the order of sentences, or add transitions to sentences, to make connections between them more obvious.

- Change the order of words in a sentence to highlight its main idea, for example, putting the main idea in an independent clause.
- Choose words that say better (more precisely, or more delicately or forcefully) what you are trying to communicate.

As you analyze your writing from multiple perspectives and evaluate its strengths and weaknesses, you will generate new material that synthesizes your purpose as a writer and the needs of your readers.

Exercise 2.11 Imagine that you are collaborating in a rewrite of the following essay. Work through the text, using some of the strategies suggested above. Mark up the text and comment either on how the writer might improve the organization or increase the impact of the text on a reader.

JOHN CHENG

Mark Sagoff uses most of his *Atlantic Monthly* article "Do We Consume Too Much?" to discuss the perceived depletion of raw materials, food and lumber, energy, and the exploitation of developing nations by the industrialized nations. Besides using the article to discuss depletion, he also explains how technology and the management of resources have solved most of the world's scarcities. The point that Sagoff makes in this article doesn't focus on the world's resources but on the human need to consume. As the economy grows, so does the need to consume. Sagoff explains that in the seventies, college students were happy to be able to fit a stereo in the backseat of a bug, but as society has evolved, we have come to desire a lot more than what we can fit into a subcompact. With the ever growing need to consume, there come consequences. These consequences only serve to destroy ties within cultures, the community, family, and friends. Their moral importance in society has been shoved aside just for the satisfaction of material goods.

The intention of Sagoff's article is to persuade his readers with his view on human consumption and the rise that has occurred in our economy. Within his article, he begins with how the world has misconceived the whole idea of consumption. Sagoff looks into our assumption that resources are being depleted at alarming rates and shatters those assumptions with the fact that technology and management are finding ways to correct the abusing of resources. Through most of the article, the ideas about depleting resources are false and statistical data has proven that resources are more plentiful than first conceived.

Once he has introduced the reader to the world's scarcity problem, he makes a move towards the human side of consumption. With statistical data of growth in the economy, his idea is that we intentionally consume too much. Sagoff's evidence of our consumption leads to the idea by Benjamin Barber called the McWorld. Barber describes the McWorld as a place "… tied together by technology, ecology, communications, and commerce" (60). Sagoff brings to light that, as participants in this global network, we are unlikely to hold to local customs and traditions. These ideas bring up the point Sagoff wants to make about our own consumption. He initially wants the reader to understand that the world will take care of itself. But by raising ideas at the end of his article, he wants the reader to begin to examine their own way of life. In the end, it's not the consuming of resources but our need to consume. Do we consume too much because of our needs or wants? The moral aspect of consumption is the focus of the article. In the very end, we must examine the morals behind our consumption.

The claim behind Sagoff's article is best represented by John Muir's parody of the American ideal: "… instead of lifting their eyes to the God of the mountains, lift them to the almighty dollar" (49). This statement represents most of our economic and moral attitudes towards consumption. It represents the growth within our nation, including the world economy. As currency seems to be an ever-growing resource, there seems to be more to throw around. This idea leads to the beginning of Sagoff's article, and the fact that industrialized nations are consuming twice as much as developing nations. If we are consuming too much, then what does it have to do with natural resources? Sagoff has already told us of what is being done about the planet's resources. Economics doesn't seem to be the major problem that is plaguing the planet. With an ever-flowing economy, statistics show no evidence of decreasing resources, which brings forth the fact that the "almighty dollar" must be the reason for our overconsuming. With a healthy economy on one side, Sagoff brings up the fact that the concern should be in the way we consume. In the end, Sagoff leads his audience to the moral distinction between needs and wants.

The increasing rate of growth in the economy worldwide is suggesting that our world be like Barber's McWorld. The growth that is occurring in the world is becoming more like a fast food joint. We are able to afford the things we need and want needless of what importance they serve in our lives. To have the things we want seems to be a simple satisfaction for us instead of valuing our family and friends. The increase in the use of technology and management has made it possible to keep consumers happy. The increase in production of goods and services has slowly depleted the need for family and friends. We live in a McWorld. The integration of advanced technology and the many services all around us are making it impossible to have a coherent structure of family and friends. The conveniences we have created have only damaged much of the family structure and have created individual entities of ourselves.

Near the end of the article, he shifts the reader's view to economical authorities on consumption. In the past, economists believed that the consumer would stop consuming once they reached their goals and have satisfied all of their needs. However, as time passed and with the rise in the world's economy, our needs are even greater than before. It seems that economists have largely failed to account for the effect of technology and human desire. Sagoff repeatedly talks about technology and how it's been able to keep resources in check, but it's also one of the primary areas of what consumers desire. As the world grows and technologically becomes more advanced, the concern towards consumption increases. Everyone obviously wants the latest computer or television because the one we currently own is obsolete or doesn't satisfy us. Sagoff declares that we need to move beyond economics and consider the moral ideas that a person holds. We need to be able to sum up our ideas of consumption. We have to be able to control our motives in any of our purchases.

What is the place of nature within our economical world these days? As Sagoff ends his article, he states that people have sympathy for nature but only find economical reasons to save the natural world (61). We've seen people protest against the destruction of many species in this world. Funds have been established to help animals caught in this predicament. As the natural salmon's population shrinks, the need for them is only minor, since biotechnology has been able to create mass numbers of salmon in a laboratory (53). It seems our society has sympathy towards a species, but only if it is near the brink of extinction. Although many of us have sympathy towards many of the endangered animals and planets, the integration of technology is starting to destroy any connection to the natural world. With the advancement in cloning and other methods of recreating another species, there seems to be no way that we can get back to nature without the technology and advances in our reach.

As the world keeps on growing and the economy rises, people will want more and more as technology increasingly gets better. The world has been able to regulate the consumption of many natural resources, but its citizens, especially in the developed world, haven't been able to control their own consumption. As all our families are being raised in this society, the bond of the family may be weakened by the need for goods and services. In the end, we must decide which is important and which can be put aside. We must morally make a decision between having everything or ending up having nothing. Sagoff's intention in the article was to look at these two distinctions of the moral and human consumption. He does a great a job getting his point across and in the end allows the reader to question her or his own consumption. I know I'm thinking about mine.

Work Cited

Sagoff, Mark. "Do We Consume Too Much?" *Atlantic Monthly* June 1997: 80–96.

A final step in revising an analysis, synthesis, evaluation, or any piece of writing is assessing how well it does what it attempts to do. Of course, what constitutes good writing varies from situation to situation. In the work world, a boss or client is often the judge. In your private life, you may be. When you're writing for school, you will generally need to ask at least the following questions.

1. Did I extend my ideas beyond those I found in sources? All three modes of response require you to select and shape information from source materials to ends that you determine. To do this, you will need to draw inferences, to generalize, and to name the significance of the information you are drawing into your essay. In these ways, you are moving beyond what any one source may say about your topic; that is, you supply the connections, you forge the relationships among your sources, your ideas, and your topic.

2. Did I organize source material according to my controlling idea? These modes often result in essays that state a controlling idea clearly and use source material to support or illustrate the idea. If such an essay is your goal, you will need to check for connections between quotes, paraphrases, and summaries and your own central purpose and thesis.

3. Did I use relevant material? In each of these modes of response, it is important that you be selective in your use of source material, using only material that directly relates to your central purpose.

4. Did I use source material accurately? In all academic writing, it is important that you use source material accurately. (This is why the work of summarizing is useful and important, because it leads you to a complete and fair recognition of another writer's ideas.)

Exercise 2.12 Return to one of the student drafts included above and assess that draft in terms of two of these revision questions. Be prepared to explain your assessments and to offer evidence from the text to support them.

WRITING TO PARTICIPATE

When you respond to the American cultural exchange described in the readings and writing assignments that follow, you will likely learn a good deal about the world you live in. You will also exercise your reading and writing skills, and practice developing and formalizing a position in a fairly standard essay form. This kind of intellectual work is at the center of a college education, but it has application well beyond school. If you are to understand where you stand in the barrage of exchanges that goes on around you, if you are to make effective decisions about what to trade and, as importantly, what should and should not be traded, you will need to be able to analyze, synthesize, and evaluate. Many of the writers represented in the following chapters are not academics. They are researchers, artists, cultural critics, journalists, businesspeople, and citizens. They all manage the activities discussed in this chapter, but not because some teacher is making them. For these writers, the task, purpose, and audience have very real meanings. They write for very specific audiences with specific purposes in mind. To achieve their professional, political, and personal goals, they have all taken on specific writing roles. In doing so, they take a measure of power for themselves, becoming active members of our culture, participants in shaping the exchange.

Writing is a tool that has cultural power, because through writing you can become an active citizen rather than a passive consumer. Writing will help you to stretch and think from new positions. Suffice it to say here that taking on the role of participant (rather than bystander) is, in some important ways, the culmination of studying the American exchange. Whether you believe our consumer culture is fundamentally sound or unsound, just or unjust, liberating or stultifying, its nature is to change as a result of all of our individual decisions. We are all consumers. Being consumers may seem to trap us in a passive position, as victims of culture. But as consumers we can exercise our influence, by choosing or refusing to buy the things that are advertised, by voicing our desire for change if the system is to improve at all. Taking on the role of a writer will let you assess what you want, what you have, and how you might overcome the gap in between. As a student, a consumer, or a citizen, writing, you will discover, is one of the most powerful ways of making your way.

PART 2

Exchanges

CHAPTER 3

Consuming Choices

Consumer spending accounts for two-thirds of our national economy. Living in a consumer culture gives us access to a great availability of goods and services. As a result of our willingness to acquire more, we live in a society where many people have the chance to create pleasurable, fulfilled lives not just from food, clothing, and shelter, but also from music, travel, communication, and a staggering array of other conveniences and curiosities. Even with the stratification of wealth in our society, the least well-off among us have access to a higher standard of living, to more goods and services, than comparable groups in other societies.

While some cultural critics talk about consumers as people who use up goods and services wantonly, most of us see ourselves in our role as consumers in more ambiguous terms. On the one hand, we think of ourselves as rational individuals who are fully aware of the choices we make. We are the controlling agents in any economic exchanges, consciously responding to desires and electing behaviors that best satisfy those desires. On the other hand, we suspect this consumer life includes a measure of passivity, that we are manipulated into participation in exchanges over which we have little control. In this view, our actions are driven by desires we are hardly aware of, and we seek satisfaction in a system that depends on our never being satisfied. These aren't just two views of a situation. There is a good deal of tension here. The first view extols a consumer culture as a dynamic, prosperous space where people can choose to live however they will. The second cautions us against remaining trapped in a social structure that strips us of authentic choices, locking us into a system that benefits the few at the expense of the many, that steadily degrades the global environment, and that denies the possibility of alternative social arrangements.

The background readings in this unit present a wide range of perspectives on how people live in a consumer culture. The case in point encourages you to bring these ideas to a shopping mall near you. The most common themes center on the effect of runaway consuming. Writers wonder whether to assess a consuming culture according to fixed values (it is always wrong to spend more than you have), exchange values (it's okay to spend more than you have as long as you can find someone who will give you credit), or use values (if spending more than you have leads you to create more goods and services, then you are doing the right thing). These examinations of consuming values lead these writers to consider economic growth, the distribution of the fruits of economic growth, and the use of technology and the environment to fuel growth. To develop these themes the writers here explore issues like speculation, sustainable growth, conflicts between short-term and long-term economic and social goals, and the way consuming is represented and "sold" to the consumer.

The consumer is the center of a related set of themes. Writers try to explain how members of a consumer culture behave and desire, work and spend. They try to discover how well consumers are treated by their culture, what consumers' "quality of life" is, and whether marketers manipulate people into becoming consumers or people take up that role willingly. Implicit in all these themes is the question, "Can consumers change their culture, and should they want to?"

BACKGROUND READINGS

DO WE CONSUME TOO MUCH?
MARK SAGOFF

Mark Sagoff writes about subjects related to the future of the environment and economics, including topics like gene patenting. "Do We Consume Too Much?" (1997) appeared in Atlantic Monthly, *a magazine interested in current affairs, the arts, and the politics of contemporary culture. While his readers may be counted as members of the most robust consumer economy in the world, Sagoff explores the questions of sustainability in relation to global consumption. The issue for Sagoff is not how much we consume but the social and moral consequences of how much we consume.*

> Discussions of the future of the planet are dominated by those who believe that an expanding world economy will use up natural resources and those who see no reasons, environmental or otherwise, to limit economic growth. Neither side has it right.

In 1994, when delegates from around the world gathered in Cairo for the International Conference on Population and Development, representatives from developing countries protested that a baby born in the United States will consume during its lifetime twenty times as much of the world's resources as an African or an Indian baby. The problem for the world's environment, they argued, is overconsumption in the North, not overpopulation in the South.

Consumption in industrialized nations "has led to overexploitation of the resources of developing countries," a speaker from Kenya declared. A delegate from Antigua reproached the wealthiest 20 percent of the world's population for consuming 80 percent of the goods and services produced from the earth's resources.

Do we consume too much? To some, the answer is self-evident. If there is only so much food, timber, petroleum, and other material to go around, the more we consume, the less must be available for others. The global economy cannot grow indefinitely on a finite planet. As populations increase and economies expand, natural resources must be depleted; prices will rise, and humanity—especially the poor and future generations at all income levels—will suffer as a result.

Other reasons to suppose we consume too much are less often stated though also widely believed. Of these the simplest—a lesson we learn from our parents and from literature since the Old Testament—may be the best: although we must satisfy basic needs, a good life is not one devoted to amassing material possessions; what we own comes to own us, keeping us from fulfilling commitments that give meaning to life, such as those to family, friends, and faith. The appreciation of nature also deepens our lives. As we consume more, however, we are more likely to transform the natural world, so that less of it will remain for us to appreciate.

5 The reasons for protecting nature are often religious or moral. As the philosopher Ronald Dworkin points out, many Americans believe that we have an obligation to protect species which goes beyond our own well-being; we "think we should admire and protect them because they are important in themselves, and not just if or because we or others want or enjoy them." In a recent survey, Americans from various walks of life agreed by large majorities with the statement "Because God created the natural world, it is wrong to abuse it." The anthropologists who conducted this survey concluded that "divine creation is the closest concept American culture provides to express the sacredness of nature."

During the nineteenth century preservationists forthrightly gave ethical and spiritual reasons for protecting the natural world. John Muir condemned the "temple destroyers, devotees of ravaging commercialism" who "instead of lifting their eyes to the God of the mountains, lift them to the Almighty dollar." This was not a call for better cost-benefit analysis: Muir described nature not as a commodity but as a companion. Nature is sacred, Muir held, whether or not resources are scarce.

Philosophers such as Emerson and Thoreau thought of nature as full of divinity. Walt Whitman celebrated a leaf of grass as no less than the journeywork of the stars: "After you have exhausted what there is in business, politics, conviviality, love, and so on," he wrote in *Specimen Days,* and "found that none of these finally satisfy, or permanently wear—what remains? Nature remains." These philosophers thought of nature as a refuge from economic activity, not as a resource for it.

Today those who wish to protect the natural environment rarely offer ethical or spiritual reasons for the policies they favor. Instead they say we are running out of resources or causing the collapse of ecosystems on which we depend. Predictions of resource scarcity appear objective and scientific, whereas pronouncements that nature is sacred or that greed is bad appear judgmental or even embarrassing in a secular society. Prudential and economic arguments, moreover, have succeeded better than moral or spiritual ones in swaying public policy.

These prudential and economic arguments are not likely to succeed much longer. It is simply wrong to believe that nature sets physical limits to economic growth—that is, to prosperity and the production and consumption of goods and services on which it is based. The idea that increasing consumption will inevitably lead to depletion and scarcity, as plausible as it may seem, is mistaken both in principle and in fact. It is based on four misconceptions.

Misconception No. 1: We Are Running Out of Raw Materials

10   In the 1970s Paul Ehrlich, a biologist at Stanford University, predicted that global shortages would soon send prices for food, fresh water, energy, metals, paper, and other materials sharply higher. "It seems certain," Paul and Anne Ehrlich wrote in *The End of Affluence* (1974), "that energy shortages will be with us for the rest of the century, and that before 1985 mankind will enter a genuine age of scarcity in which many things besides energy will be in short supply." Crucial materials would near depletion during the 1980s, Ehrlich predicted, pushing prices out of reach. "Starvation among people will be accompanied by starvation of industries for the materials they require."

Things have not turned out as Ehrlich expected. In the early 1990s real prices for food overall fell. Raw materials—including energy resources—are generally more abundant and less expensive today than they were twenty years ago. When Ehrlich wrote, economically recoverable world reserves of petroleum stood at 640 billion barrels. Since that time reserves have *increased* by more than 50 percent, reaching more than 1,000 billion barrels in 1989. They have held steady in spite of rising consumption. The pre-tax real price of gasoline was lower during this decade than at any other time since 1947. The World Energy Council announced in 1992 that "fears of imminent [resource] exhaustion that were widely held 20 years ago are now considered to have been unfounded."

The World Resources Institute, in a 1994–1995 report, referred to "the frequently expressed concern that high levels of consumption will lead to resource depletion and to physical shortages that might limit growth or development opportunity." Examining the evidence, however, the institute said that "the world is not yet running out of most nonrenewable resources and is not likely to, at least in the next few decades." A 1988 report from the Office of Technology Assessment concluded, "The nation's future has probably never been less constrained by the cost of natural resources."

It is reasonable to expect that as raw materials become less expensive, they will be more rapidly depleted. This expectation is also mistaken. From 1980 to 1990, for example, while the prices of resource-based commodities declined (the price of rubber by 40 percent, cement by 40 percent, and coal by almost 50 percent), reserves of most raw materials increased. Economists offer three explanations.

First, with regard to subsoil resources, the world becomes ever more adept at discovering new reserves and exploiting old ones. Exploring for oil, for example, used to be a hit-or-miss proposition, resulting in a lot of dry holes. Today oil companies can use seismic waves to help them create precise computer images of the earth. New methods of extraction—for example, using bacteria to leach metals from low-grade ores—greatly increase resource recovery. Reserves of resources "are actually functions of technology," one analyst has written. "The more advanced the technology, the more reserves become known and recoverable."

15   Second, plentiful resources can be used in place of those that become scarce. Analysts speak of an Age of Substitutability and point, for example, to nanotubes, tiny cylinders of carbon whose molecular structure forms fibers a hundred times as strong

as steel, at one sixth the weight. As technologies that use more-abundant resources substitute for those needing less-abundant ones—for example, ceramics in place of tungsten, fiber optics in place of copper wire, aluminum cans in place of tin ones—the demand for and the price of the less-abundant resources decline.

One can easily find earlier instances of substitution. During the early nineteenth century whale oil was the preferred fuel for household illumination. A dwindling supply prompted innovations in the lighting industry, including the invention of gas and kerosene lamps and Edison's carbon-filament electric bulb. Whale oil has substitutes, such as electricity and petroleum-based lubricants. Whales are irreplaceable.

Third, the more we learn about materials, the more efficiently we use them. The progress from candles to carbon-filament to tungsten incandescent lamps, for example, decreased the energy required for and the cost of a unit of household lighting by many times. Compact fluorescent lights are four times as efficient as today's incandescent bulbs and last ten to twenty times as long. Comparable energy savings are available in other appliances: for example, refrigerators sold in 1993 were 23 percent more efficient than those sold in 1990 and 65 percent more efficient than those sold in 1980, saving consumers billions in electric bills.

Amory Lovins, the director of the Rocky Mountain Institute, has described in these pages a new generation of ultra-light automobiles that could deliver the safety and muscle of today's cars but with far better mileage—four times as much in prototypes and ten times as much in projected models (see "Reinventing the Wheels," January, 1995, *Atlantic*). Since in today's cars only 15 to 20 percent of the fuel's energy reaches the wheels (the rest is lost in the engine and the transmission), and since materials lighter and stronger than steel are available or on the way, no expert questions the feasibility of the high-mileage vehicles Lovins describes.

Computers and cameras are examples of consumer goods getting lighter and smaller as they get better. The game-maker Sega is marketing a hand-held children's game, called Saturn, that has more computing power than the 1976 Cray supercomputer, which the United States tried to keep out of the hands of the Soviets. Improvements that extend the useful life of objects also save resources. Platinum spark plugs in today's cars last for 100,000 miles, as do "fill-for-life" transmission fluids. On average, cars bought in 1993 have a useful life more than 40 percent longer than those bought in 1970.

20   As lighter materials replace heavier ones, the U.S. economy continues to shed weight. Our per capita consumption of raw materials such as forestry products and metals has, measured by weight, declined steadily over the past twenty years. A recent World Resources Institute study measured the "materials intensity" of our economy—that is, "the total material input and the hidden or indirect material flows, including deliberate landscape alterations" required for each dollar's worth of economic output. "The result shows a clearly declining pattern of materials intensity, supporting the conclusion that economic activity is growing somewhat more rapidly than natural resource use." Of course, we should do better. The Organization for Economic Cooperation and Development, an association of the world's industrialized nations, has proposed that its members strive as a long-range goal to decrease their materials intensity by a factor of ten.

Communications also illustrates the trend toward lighter, smaller, less materials-intensive technology. Just as telegraph cables replaced frigates in transmitting messages across the Atlantic and carried more information faster, glass fibers and microwaves have replaced cables—each new technology using less materials but providing greater capacity for sending and receiving information. Areas not yet wired for telephones (in the former Soviet Union, for example) are expected to leapfrog directly into cellular communications. Robert Solow, a Nobel laureate in economics, says that if the future is like the past, "there will be prolonged and substantial reductions in natural-resource requirements per unit of real output." He asks, "Why shouldn't the productivity of most natural resources rise more or less steadily through time, like the productivity of labor?"

Misconception No. 2: We Are Running Out of Food and Timber

The United Nations projects that the global population, currently 5.7 billion, will peak at about 10 billion in the next century and then stabilize or even decline. Can the earth feed that many people? Even if food crops increase sufficiently, other renewable resources, including many fisheries and forests, are already under pressure. Should we expect fish stocks to collapse or forests to disappear?

The world already produces enough cereals and oilseeds to feed 10 billion people a vegetarian diet adequate in protein and calories. If, however, the idea is to feed 10 billion people not healthful vegetarian diets but the kind of meat-laden meals that Americans eat, the production of grains and oilseeds may have to triple—primarily to feed livestock. Is anything like this kind of productivity in the cards?

Maybe. From 1961 to 1994 global production of food doubled. Global output of grain rose from about 630 million tons in 1950 to about 1.8 billion tons in 1992, largely as a result of greater yields. Developing countries from 1974 to 1994 increased wheat yields per acre by almost 100 percent, corn yields by 72 percent, and rice yields by 52 percent. "The generation of farmers on the land in 1950 was the first in history to double the production of food," the Worldwatch Institute has reported. "By 1984, they had outstripped population growth enough to raise per capita grain output an unprecedented 40 percent." From a two-year period ending in 1981 to a two-year period ending in 1990 the real prices of basic foods fell 38 percent on world markets, according to a 1992 United Nations report. Prices for food have continually decreased since the end of the eighteenth century, when Thomas Malthus argued that rapid population growth must lead to mass starvation by exceeding the carrying capacity of the earth.

25   Farmers worldwide could double the acreage in production, but this should not be necessary. Better seeds, more irrigation, multi-cropping, and additional use of fertilizer could greatly increase agricultural yields in the developing world, which are now generally only half those in the industrialized countries. It is biologically possible to raise yields of rice to about seven tons per acre—about four times the current average in the developing world. Super strains of cassava, a potato-like root crop eaten by millions of Africans, promise to increase yields tenfold. American farmers can also do better. In a good year, such as 1994, Iowa corn growers average about 3.5 tons per acre, but farmers more than double that yield in National Corn Growers Association competitions.

In drier parts of the world the scarcity of fresh water presents the greatest challenge to agriculture. But the problem is regional, not global. Fortunately, as Lester Brown, of the Worldwatch Institute, points out, "there are vast opportunities for increasing water efficiency" in arid regions, ranging from installing better water-delivery systems to planting drought-resistant crops. He adds, "Scientists can help push back the physical frontiers of cropping by developing varieties that are more drought resistant, salt tolerant, and early maturing. The payoff on the first two could be particularly high."

As if in response, Novartis Seeds has announced a program to develop water-efficient and salt-tolerant crops, including genetically engineered varieties of wheat. Researchers in Mexico have announced the development of drought-resistant corn that can boost yields by a third. Biotechnologists are converting annual crops into perennial ones, eliminating the need for yearly planting. They also hope to enable cereal crops to fix their own nitrogen, as legumes do, minimizing the need for fertilizer (genetically engineered nitrogen-fixing bacteria have already been test-marketed to farmers). Commercial varieties of crops such as corn, tomatoes, and potatoes which have been genetically engineered to be resistant to pests and diseases have been approved for field testing in the United States; several are now being sold and planted. A new breed of rice, 25 percent more productive than any currently in use, suggests that the Gene Revolution can take over where the Green Revolution left off. Biotechnology, as the historian Paul Kennedy has written, introduces "an entirely new stage in humankind's attempts to produce more crops and plants."

Biotechnology cannot, however, address the major causes of famine: poverty, trade barriers, corruption, mismanagement, ethnic antagonism, anarchy, war, and male-dominated societies that deprive women of food. Local land depletion, itself a consequence of poverty and institutional failure, is also a factor. Those who are too poor to use sound farming practices are compelled to overexploit the resources on which they depend. As the economist Partha Dasgupta has written, "Population growth, poverty and degradation of local resources often fuel one another." The amount of food in world trade is constrained less by the resource base than by the maldistribution of wealth.

Analysts who believe that the world is running out of resources often argue that famines occur not as a result of political or economic conditions but because there are "too many people." Unfortunately, as the economist Amartya Sen has pointed out, public officials who think in Malthusian terms assume that when absolute levels of food supplies are adequate, famine will not occur. This conviction diverts attention from the actual causes of famine, which has occurred in places where food output kept pace with population growth but people were too destitute to buy it.

30 We would have run out of food long ago had we tried to supply ourselves entirely by hunting and gathering. Likewise, if we depend on nature's gifts, we will exhaust many of the world's important fisheries. Fortunately, we are learning to cultivate fish as we do other crops. Genetic engineers have designed fish for better flavor and color as other traits. Two farmed species—silver carp and grass carp—already rank among the ten most-consumed fish worldwide. A specially bred tilapia, known as the "aquatic chicken," takes six months to grow to a harvestable size of about one and a half pounds.

Aquaculture produced more than 16 million tons of fish in 1993: capacity has expanded over the past decade at an annual rate of 10 percent by quantity and 14 percent by value. In 1993 fish farms produced 22 percent of all food fish consumed in the world and 90 percent of all oysters sold. The World Bank reports that aquaculture could provide 40 percent of all fish consumed and more than half the value of fish harvested within the next fifteen years.

Salmon ranching and farming provide examples of the growing efficiency of aquacultural production. Norwegian salmon farms alone produce 400 million pounds a year. A biotech firm in Waltham, Massachusetts, has applied for government approval to commercialize salmon genetically engineered to grow four to six times as fast as their naturally occurring cousins. As a 1994 article in *Sierra* magazine noted,

"There is so much salmon currently available that the supply exceeds demand, and prices to fishermen have fallen dramatically."

For those who lament the decline of natural fisheries and the human communities that grew up with them, the successes of aquaculture may offer no consolation. In the Pacific Northwest, for example, overfishing in combination with dams and habitat destruction has reduced the wild salmon population by 80 percent. Wild salmon—but not their bio-engineered aquacultural cousins—contribute to the cultural identity and sense of place of the Northwest. When wild salmon disappear, so will some of the region's history, character, and pride. What is true of wild salmon is also true of whales, dolphins, and other magnificent creatures—as they lose their economic importance, their aesthetic and moral worth becomes all the more evident. Economic considerations pull in one direction, moral considerations in the other. This conflict colors all our battles over the environment.

The transition from hunting and gathering to farming, which is changing the fishing industry, has taken place more slowly in forestry. Still there is no sign of a timber famine. In the United States forests now provide the largest harvests in history, and there is more forested U.S. area today than there was in 1920. Bill McKibben has observed in these pages that the eastern United States, which loggers and farmers in the eighteenth and nineteenth centuries nearly denuded of trees, has become reforested during this century (see "An Explosion of Green," April, 1995, *Atlantic*). One reason is that farms reverted to woods. Another is that machinery replaced animals; each draft animal required two or three cleared acres for pasture.

35   Natural reforestation is likely to continue as biotechnology makes areas used for logging more productive. According to Roger Sedjo, a respected forestry expert, advances in tree farming, if implemented widely, would permit the world to meet its entire demand for industrial wood using just 200 million acres of plantations—an area equal to only five percent of current forest land. As less land is required for commercial tree production, more natural forests may be protected—as they should be, for aesthetic, ethical, and spiritual reasons.

Often natural resources are so plentiful and therefore inexpensive that they undercut the necessary transition to technological alternatives. If the U.S. government did not protect wild forests from commercial exploitation, the timber industry would have little incentive to invest in tree plantations, where it can multiply yields by a factor of ten and take advantage of the results of genetic research. Only by investing in plantation silviculture can North American forestry fend off price competition from rapidly developing tree plantations in the Southern Hemisphere. Biotechnology-based silviculture can in the near future be expected to underprice "extractive" forestry worldwide. In this decade China will plant about 150 million acres of trees; India now plants four times the area it harvests commercially.

The expansion of fish and tree farming confirms the belief held by Peter Drucker and other management experts that our economy depends far more on the progress of technology than on the exploitation of nature. Although raw materials will always be necessary, knowledge has become the essential factor in the production of goods and services. "Where there is effective management," Drucker has written, "that is, application of knowledge to knowledge, we can always obtain the other resources." If we assume, along with Drucker and others, that resource scarcities do not exist or are easily averted, it is hard to see how economic theory, which after all concerns scarcity, provides the conceptual basis for valuing the environment. The reasons to preserve nature are ethical more often than they are economic.

Misconception No. 3: We Are Running Out of Energy

Probably the most persistent worries about resource scarcity concern energy. "The supply of fuels and other natural resources is becoming the limiting factor constraining the rate of economic growth," a group of experts proclaimed in 1986. They predicted the exhaustion of domestic oil and gas supplies by 2020 and, within a few decades, "major energy shortages as well as food shortages in the world."

Contrary to these expectations, no global shortages of hydrocarbon fuels are in sight. "One sees no immediate danger of 'running out' of energy in a global sense," writes John P. Holdren, a professor of environmental policy at Harvard University. According to Holdren, reserves of oil and natural gas will last seventy to a hundred years if exploited at 1990 rates. (This does not take into account huge deposits of oil shale, heavy oils, and gas from unconventional sources.) He concludes that "running out of energy resources in any global sense is not what the energy problem is all about."

40   The global energy problem has less to do with depleting resources than with controlling pollutants. Scientists generally agree that gases, principally carbon dioxide, emitted in the combustion of hydrocarbon fuels can build up in and warm the atmosphere by trapping sunlight. Since carbon dioxide enhances photosynthetic activity, plants to some extent absorb the carbon dioxide we produce. In 1995 researchers reported in *Science* that vegetation in the Northern Hemisphere in 1992 and 1993 converted into trees and other plant tissue 3.5 billion tons of carbon—more than half the carbon produced by the burning of hydrocarbon fuels worldwide.

However successful this and other feedback mechanisms may be in slowing the processes of global warming, a broad scientific consensus, reflected in a 1992 international treaty, has emerged for stabilizing and then decreasing emissions of carbon dioxide and other "greenhouse" gases. This goal is well within the technological reach of the United States and other industrialized countries. Amory Lovins, among others, has described commercially available technologies that can "support present or greatly expanded worldwide economic activity while stabilizing global climate—and saving money." He observes that "even very large expansions in population and industrial activity need not be energy-constrained."

Lovins and other environmentalists contend that pollution-free energy from largely untapped sources is available in amounts exceeding our needs. Geothermal energy—which makes use of heat from the earth's core—is theoretically accessible through drilling technology in the United States in amounts thousands of times as great as the amount of energy contained in domestic coal reserves. Tidal energy is also promising. Analysts who study solar power generally agree with Lester Brown, of the Worldwatch Institute, that "technologies are ready to begin building a world energy system largely powered by solar resources." In the future these and other renewable energy sources may be harnessed to the nation's system of storing and delivering electricity.

Last year Joseph Romm and Charles Curtis described in these pages advances in photovoltaic cells (which convert sunlight into electricity), fuel cells (which convert the hydrogen in fuels directly to electricity and heat, producing virtually no pollution), and wind power ("Mideast Oil Forever?" April, 1996, *Atlantic*). According to these authors, genetically engineered organisms used to ferment organic matter could, with further research and development, bring down the costs of ethanol and other environmentally friendly "biofuels" to make them competitive with gasoline.

Environmentalists who, like Amory Lovins, believe that our economy can grow and still reduce greenhouse gases emphasize not only that we should be able to move to renewable forms of energy but also that we can use fossil fuels more efficiently. Some improvements are already evident. In developed countries the energy intensity of production—the amount of fuel burned per dollar of economic output—has been decreasing by about two percent a year.

45   From 1973 to 1986, for example, energy consumption in the United States remained virtually flat while economic production grew by almost 40 percent. Compared with Germany or Japan, this is a poor showing. The Japanese, who tax fuel more heavily than we do, use only half as much energy as the United States per unit of economic output. (Japanese environmental regulations are also generally stricter than ours; if anything, this has improved the competitiveness of Japanese industry.) The United States still wastes hundreds of billions of dollars annually in energy inefficiency. By becoming as energy-efficient as Japan, the United States could expand its economy and become more competitive internationally.

If so many opportunities exist for saving energy and curtailing pollution, why have we not seized them? One reason is that low fossil-fuel prices remove incentives for fuel efficiency and for converting to other energy sources. Another reason is that government subsidies for fossil fuels and nuclear energy amounted to many billions of dollars a year during the 1980s, whereas support for renewables dwindled to $114 million in 1989, a time when it had been proposed for near elimination. "Lemon socialism," a vast array of subsidies and barriers to trade, protects politically favored technologies, however inefficient, dangerous, filthy, or obsolete. "At heart, the major obstacles standing in the way [of a renewable-energy economy] are not technical in nature," the energy consultant Michael Brower has written, "but concern the laws, regulations, incentives, public attitudes, and other factors that make up the energy market."

In response to problems of climate change, the World Bank and other international organizations have recognized the importance of transferring advanced energy technologies to the developing world. Plainly, this will take a large investment of capital, particularly in education. Yet the "alternative for developing countries," according to José Goldemberg, a former Environment Minister of Brazil, "would be to remain at a dismally low level of development which … would aggravate the problems of sustainability."

Technology transfer can hasten sound economic development worldwide. Many environmentalists, however, argue that economies cannot expand without exceeding the physical limits nature sets—for example, with respect to energy. These environmentalists, who regard increasing affluence as a principal cause of environmental degradation, call for economic retrenchment and retraction—a small economy for a small earth. With Paul Ehrlich, they reject "the hope that development can greatly increase the size of the economic pie and pull many more people out of poverty." This hope is "basically a humane idea," Ehrlich has written, "made insane by the constraints nature places on human activity."

In developing countries, however, a no-growth economy "will deprive entire populations of access to better living conditions and lead to even more deforestation and land degradation," as Goldemberg warns. Moreover, citizens of developed countries are likely to resist an energy policy that they associate with poverty, discomfort, sacrifice, and pain. Technological pessimism, then, may not be the best option for environmentalists. It is certainly not the only one.

Misconception No. 4: The North Exploits the South

50 William Reilly, when he served as administrator of the Environmental Protection Agency in the Bush Administration, encountered a persistent criticism at international meetings on the environment. "The problem for the world's environment is your consumption, not our population," delegates from the developing world told him. Some of these delegates later took Reilly aside. "The North buys too little from the South," they confided. "The real problem is too little demand for our exports."

The delegates who told Reilly that the North consumes too little of what the South produces have a point. "With a few exceptions (notably petroleum)," a report from the World Resources Institute observes, "most of the natural resources consumed in the United States are from domestic sources." Throughout the 1980s the United States and Canada were the world's leading exporters of raw materials. The United States consistently leads the world in farm exports, running huge agricultural trade surpluses. The share of raw materials used in the North that it buys from the South stands at a thirty-year low and continues to decline; industrialized nations trade largely among themselves. The World Resources Institute recently reported that "the United States is largely self-sufficient in natural resources." Again, excepting petroleum, bauxite (from which aluminum is made), "and a few other industrial minerals, its material flows are almost entirely internal."

Sugar provides an instructive example of how the North excludes—rather than exploits—the resources of the South. Since 1796 the United States has protected domestic sugar against imports. American sugar growers, in part as a reward for large contributions to political campaigns, have long enjoyed a system of quotas and prohibitive tariffs against foreign competition. American consumers paid about three times world prices for sugar in the 1980s, enriching a small cartel of U.S. growers. *Forbes* magazine has estimated that a single family, the Fanjuls, of Palm Beach, reaps more than $65 million a year as a result of quotas for sugar.

The sugar industry in Florida, which is larger than that in any other state, makes even less sense environmentally than economically. It depends on a publicly built system of canals, levees, and pumping stations. Fertilizer from the sugarcane fields chokes the Everglades. Sugar growers, under a special exemption from labor laws, import Caribbean laborers to do the grueling and poorly paid work of cutting cane.

As the United States tightened sugar quotas (imports fell from 6.2 to 1.5 million tons annually from 1977 to 1987), the Dominican Republic and other nations with climates ideal for growing cane experienced political turmoil and economic collapse. Many farmers in Latin America, however, did well by switching from sugar to coca, which is processed into cocaine—perhaps the only high-value imported crop for which the United States is not developing a domestic substitute.

55 Before the Second World War the United States bought 40 percent of its vegetable oils from developing countries. After the war the United States protected its oilseed markets—for example, by establishing price supports for soybeans. Today the United States is one of the world's leading exporters of oil and oilseeds, although it still imports palm and coconut oils to obtain laurate, an ingredient in soap, shampoo, and detergents. Even this form of "exploitation" will soon cease. In 1994 farmers in Georgia

planted the first commercial acreage of a high-laurate canola, genetically engineered by Calgene, a biotechnology firm.

About 100,000 Kenyans make a living on small plots of land growing pyrethrum flowers, the source of a comparatively environmentally safe insecticide of which the United States has been the largest importer. The U.S. Department of Commerce, however, awarded $1.2 million to a biotechnology firm to engineer pyrethrum genetically. Industrial countries will soon be able to synthesize all the pyrethrum they need and undersell Kenyan farmers.

An article in *Foreign Policy* in December of 1995 observed that the biotechnological innovations that create "substitutes for everything from vanilla to cocoa and coffee threaten to eliminate the livelihood of millions of Third World agricultural workers." Vanilla cultured in laboratories costs a fifth as much as vanilla extracted from beans, and thus jeopardizes the livelihood of tens of thousands of vanilla farmers in Madagascar. In the past, farms produced agricultural commodities and factories processed them. In the future, factories may "grow" as well as process many of the most valuable commodities— or the two functions will become one. As one plant scientist has said, "We have to stop thinking of these things as plant cells, and start thinking of them as new microorganisms, with all the potential that implies"—meaning, for instance, that the cells could be made to grow in commercially feasible quantities in laboratories, not fields.

The North not only balks at buying sugar and other crops from developing countries; it also dumps its excess agricultural commodities, especially grain, on them. After the Second World War, American farmers, using price supports left over from the New Deal, produced vast wheat surpluses, which the United States exported at concessionary prices to Europe and then the Third World. These enormous transfers of cereals to the South, institutionalized during the 1950s and 1960s by U.S. food aid, continued during the 1970s and 1980s, as the United States and the European Community vied for markets, each outdoing the other in subsidizing agricultural exports.

Grain imports from the United States "created food dependence within two decades in countries which had been mostly self-sufficient in food at the end of World War II," the sociologist Harriet Friedmann has written. Tropical countries soon matched the grain gluts of the North with their own surpluses of cocoa, coffee, tea, bananas, and other export commodities. Accordingly, prices for these commodities collapsed as early as 1970, catching developing nations in a scissors. As Friedmann describes it, "One blade was food import dependency. The other blade was declining revenues for traditional exports of tropical crops."

60   It might be better for the environment if the North exchanged the crops for which it is ecologically suited—wheat, for example—for crops easily grown in the South, such as coffee, cocoa, palm oil, and tea. Contrary to common belief, these tropical export crops—which grow on trees and bushes, providing canopy and continuous root structures to protect the soil—are less damaging to the soil than are traditional staples such as cereals and root crops. Better markets for tropical crops could help developing nations to employ their rural populations and to protect their natural resources. Allen Hammond, of the World Resources Institute, points out that "if poor nations cannot export anything else, they will export their misery—in the form of drugs, diseases, terrorism, migration, and environmental degradation."

Peasants in less-developed nations often confront intractable poverty, an entrenched land-tenure system, and a lack of infrastructure; they have little access to markets, education, or employment. Many of the rural poor, according to the environmental consultant Norman Myers, "have no option but to over-exploit environmental resource stocks in order to survive"—for example, by "increasingly encroaching onto tropical forests among other low-potential lands." These poorest of the poor "are causing as much natural-resource depletion as the other three billion developing-world people put together."

Myers observes that traditional indigenous farmers in tropical forests moved from place to place without seriously damaging the ecosystem. The principal agents of tropical deforestation are refugees from civil war and rural poverty, who are forced to eke out a living on marginal lands. Activities such as road building, logging, and commercial agriculture have barely increased in tropical forests since the early 1980s, according to Myers; slash-and-burn farming by displaced peasants accounts for far more deforestation—roughly three fifths of the total. Its impact is fast expanding. Most of the wood from trees harvested in tropical forests—that is, those not cleared for farms—is used locally for fuel. The likeliest path to protecting the rain forest is through economic development that enables peasants to farm efficiently, on land better suited to farming than to forest.

Many have argued that economic activity, affluence, and growth automatically lead to resource depletion, environmental deterioration, and ecological collapse. Yet greater productivity and prosperity—which is what economists mean by growth—have become prerequisite for controlling urban pollution and protecting sensitive ecological systems such as rain forests. Otherwise, destitute people who are unable to acquire food and fuel will create pollution and destroy forests. Without economic growth, which also correlates with lower fertility, the environmental and population problems of the South will only get worse. For impoverished countries facing environmental disaster, economic growth may be the one thing that is sustainable.

What Is Wrong with Consumption?

Many of us who attended college in the 1960s and 1970s took pride in how little we owned. We celebrated our freedom when we could fit all our possessions—mostly a stereo—into the back of a Beetle. Decades later, middle-aged and middle-class, many of us have accumulated an appalling amount of stuff. Piled high with gas grills, lawn mowers, excess furniture, bicycles, children's toys, garden implements, lumber, cinder blocks, ladders, lawn and leaf bags stuffed with memorabilia, and boxes yet to be unpacked from the last move, the two-car garages beside our suburban homes are too full to accommodate the family minivan. The quantity of resources, particularly energy, we waste and the quantity of trash we throw away (recycling somewhat eases our conscience) add to our consternation.

65   Even if predictions of resource depletion and ecological collapse are mistaken, it seems that they *should* be true, to punish us for our sins. We are distressed by the suffering of others, the erosion of the ties of community, family, and friendship, and the loss of the beauty and spontaneity of the natural world. These concerns reflect the most traditional and fundamental of American religious and cultural values.

Simple compassion instructs us to give to relieve the misery of others. There is a lot of misery worldwide to relieve. But as bad as the situation is, it is improving. In 1960 nearly 70 percent of the people in the world lived at or below the subsistence level. Today less than a third do, and the number enjoying fairly satisfactory conditions (as measured by the United Nations Human Development Index) rose from 25 percent in 1960 to 60 percent in 1992. Over the twenty-five years before 1992 average per capita consumption in developing countries increased 75 percent in real terms. The pace of improvements is also increasing. In developing countries in that period, for example, power generation and the number of telephone lines per capita doubled, while the number of households with access to clean water grew by half.

What is worsening is the discrepancy in income between the wealthy and the poor. Although world income measured in real terms has increased by 700 percent since the Second World War, the wealthiest people have absorbed most of the gains. Since 1960 the richest fifth of the world's people have seen their share of the world's income increase from 70 to 85 percent. Thus one fifth of the world's population possesses much more than four fifths of the world's wealth, while the share held by all others has correspondingly fallen; that of the world's poorest 20 percent has declined from 2.3 to 1.4 percent.

Writing in these pages, Benjamin Barber ("Jihad vs. McWorld," March, 1992, *Atlantic*) described market forces that "mesmerize the world with fast music, fast computers, and fast food—with MTV, Macintosh, and McDonald's, pressing nations into one commercially homogeneous global network: one McWorld tied together by technology, ecology, communications, and commerce." Affluent citizens of South Korea, Thailand, India, Brazil, Mexico, and many other rapidly developing nations have joined with Americans, Europeans, Japanese, and others to form an urban and cosmopolitan international society. Those who participate in this global network are less and less beholden to local customs and traditions. Meanwhile, ethnic, tribal, and other cultural groups that do not dissolve into McWorld often define themselves in opposition to it—fiercely asserting their ethnic, religious, and territorial identities.

The imposition of a market economy on traditional cultures in the name of development—for example, the insistence that everyone produce and consume more—can dissolve the ties to family, land, community, and place on which indigenous peoples traditionally rely for their security. Thus development projects intended to relieve the poverty of indigenous peoples may, by causing the loss of cultural identity, engender the very powerlessness they aim to remedy. Pope Paul VI, in the encyclical *Populorum Progressio* (1967), described the tragic dilemma confronting indigenous peoples: "either to preserve traditional beliefs and structures and reject social progress; or to embrace foreign technology and foreign culture, and reject ancestral traditions with their wealth of humanism."

70   The idea that everything is for sale and nothing is sacred—that all values are subjective—undercuts our own moral and cultural commitments, not just those of tribal and traditional communities. No one has written a better critique of the assault that commerce makes on the quality of our lives than Thoreau provides in *Walden*. The cost of a thing, according to Thoreau, is not what the market will bear but what the individual must bear because of it: it is "the amount of what I will call life which is required to be exchanged for it, immediately or in the long run."

Many observers point out that as we work harder and consume more, we seem to enjoy our lives less. We are always in a rush—a "Saint Vitus' dance," as Thoreau called it. Idleness is suspect. Americans today spend less time with their families, neighbors, and friends than they did in the 1950s. Juliet B. Schor, an economist at Harvard University, argues that "Americans are literally working themselves to death." A fancy car, video equipment, or a complex computer program can exact a painful cost in the form of maintenance, upgrading, and repair. We are possessed by our possessions; they are often harder to get rid of than to acquire.

That money does not make us happier, once our basic needs are met, is a commonplace overwhelmingly confirmed by sociological evidence. Paul Wachtel, who teaches social psychology at the City University of New York, has concluded that bigger incomes "do not yield an increase in feelings of satisfaction or well-being, at least for populations who are above a poverty or subsistence level." This cannot be explained simply by the fact that people have to work harder to earn more money: even those who hit jackpots in lotteries often report that their lives are not substantially happier as a result. Well-being depends upon health, membership in a community in which one feels secure, friends, faith, family, love, and virtues that money cannot buy. Robert Lane, a political scientist at Yale University, using the concepts of economics, has written, "If 'utility' has anything to do with happiness, above the poverty line the long-term marginal utility of money is almost zero."

Economists in earlier times predicted that wealth would not matter to people once they attained a comfortable standard of living. "In ease of body and peace of mind, all the different ranks of life are nearly upon a level," wrote Adam Smith, the eighteenth-century English advocate of the free market. In the 1930s the British economist John Maynard Keynes argued that after a period of great expansion further accumulation of wealth would no longer improve personal well-being. Subsequent economists, however, found that even after much of the industrial world had attained the levels of wealth Keynes thought were sufficient, people still wanted more. From this they inferred that wants are insatiable.

Perhaps this is true. But the insatiability of wants and desires poses a difficulty for standard economic theory, which posits that humanity's single goal is to increase or maximize wealth. If wants increase as fast as income grows, what purpose can wealth serve?

75   Critics often attack standard economic theory on the ground that economic growth is "unsustainable." We are running out of resources, they say; we court ecological disaster. Whether or not growth is sustainable, there is little reason to think that once people attain a decent standard of living, continued growth is desirable. The economist Robert H. Nelson recently wrote in the journal *Ecological Economics* that it is no longer possible for most people to believe that economic progress will "solve all the problems of mankind, spiritual as well as material." As long as the debate over sustainability is framed in terms of the physical limits to growth rather than the moral purpose of it, mainstream economic theory will have the better of the argument. If the debate were framed in moral or social terms, the result might well be otherwise.

Making a Place for Nature

According to Thoreau, "a man's relation to Nature must come very near to a personal one." For environmentalists in the tradition of Thoreau and John Muir, stewardship is a form of fellowship; although we must use nature, we do not value it primarily for the economic purposes it serves. We take our bearings from the natural world—our sense of time from its days and seasons, our sense of place from the character of a landscape and the particular plants and animals native to it. An intimacy with nature ends our isolation in the world. We know where we belong, and we can find the way home.

In defending old-growth forests, wetlands, or species we make our best arguments when we think of nature chiefly in aesthetic and moral terms. Rather than having the courage of our moral and cultural convictions, however, we too often rely on economic arguments for protecting nature, in the process attributing to natural objects more instrumental value than they have. By claiming that a threatened species may harbor lifesaving drugs, for example, we impute to that species an economic value or a price much greater than it fetches in a market. When we make the prices come out right, we rescue economic theory but not necessarily the environment.

There is no credible argument, moreover, that all or even most of the species we are concerned to protect are essential to the functioning of the ecological systems on which we depend. (If whales went extinct, for example, the seas would not fill up with krill.) David Ehrenfeld, a biologist at Rutgers University, makes this point in relation to the vast ecological changes we have already survived. "Even a mighty dominant like the American chestnut," Ehrenfeld has written, "extending over half a continent, all but disappeared without bringing the eastern deciduous forest down with it." Ehrenfeld points out that the species most likely to be endangered are those the biosphere is least likely to miss. "Many of these species were never common or ecologically influential; by no stretch of the imagination can we make them out to be vital cogs in the ecological machine."

Species may be profoundly important for cultural and spiritual reasons, however. Consider again the example of the wild salmon, whose habitat is being destroyed by hydroelectric dams along the Columbia River. Although this loss is unimportant to the economy overall (there is no shortage of salmon), it is of the greatest significance to the Amerindian tribes that have traditionally subsisted on wild salmon, and to the region as a whole. By viewing local flora and fauna as a sacred heritage—by recognizing their intrinsic value—we discover who we are rather than what we want. On moral and cultural grounds society might be justified in making great economic sacrifices—removing hydroelectric dams, for example—to protect remnant populations of the Snake River sockeye, even if, as critics complain, hundreds or thousands of dollars are spent for every fish that is saved.

80   Even those plants and animals that do not define places possess enormous intrinsic value and are worth preserving for their own sake. What gives these creatures value lies in their histories, wonderful in themselves, rather than in any use to which they can be put. The biologist E. O. Wilson elegantly takes up this theme: "Every kind of organism has reached this moment in time by threading one needle after another, throwing up brilliant artifices to survive and reproduce against nearly impossible odds." Every plant or animal evokes not just sympathy but also reverence and wonder in those who know it.

In *Earth in the Balance* (1992) Al Gore, then a senator, wrote, "We have become so successful at controlling nature that we have lost our connection to it." It is all too easy, Gore wrote, "to regard the earth as a collection of 'resources' having an intrinsic value no larger than their usefulness at the moment." The question before us is not whether we are going to run out of resources. It is whether economics is the appropriate context for thinking about environmental policy.

Even John Stuart Mill, one of the principal authors of utilitarian philosophy, recognized that the natural world has great intrinsic and not just instrumental value. More than a century ago, as England lost its last truly wild places, Mill condemned a world

> with nothing left to the spontaneous activity of nature; with every rood of land brought into cultivation, which is capable of growing food for human beings; every flowery waste or natural pasture ploughed up; all quadrupeds or birds which are not domesticated for man's use exterminated as his rivals for food, every hedgerow or superfluous tree rooted out, and scarcely a place left where a wild shrub or flower could grow without being eradicated as a weed in the name of improved agriculture.

The world has the wealth and the resources to provide everyone the opportunity to live a decent life. We consume too much when market relationships displace the bonds of community, compassion, culture, and place. We consume too much when consumption becomes an end in itself and makes us lose affection and reverence for the natural world.

Rereading Actively

1. With a partner review the first and last sections of Sagoff's essay and identify the theories of value he mentions. In your journal, make a brief list of the sources Sagoff draws on.

2. Sagoff distinguishes between economic arguments, social arguments, and moral arguments. In a small group or with a partner, write how each viewpoint addresses the problem of resource scarcity.

3. With a partner, discuss the kinds of values Sagoff argues for. Does he seem to favor one theory of values over others?

4. In each "misconception" section look at how Sagoff explains what the misconception is. In a journal entry, note the key words or phrases where Sagoff names what the truth is.

5. In each "misconception" section, evaluate the evidence Sagoff offers. Discuss with a partner whether Sagoff is clear in his presentation and whether his argument is compelling.

6. In a small group, work out a brief explanation of Sagoff's point that people's misunderstandings about consumption relate to how we view our world.

Exploring Your Responses

7. Freewrite a response to Sagoff's title: Do you consume "too much"? How much is "too much"?

8. Consider Sagoff's discussion of values. Is thinking in economic terms enough? Do you use economic considerations to make value decisions?

9. Write a brief account of an action you took that was based primarily on economic considerations.

10. Does Sagoff reach a satisfactory conclusion to the question of whether we consume too much? Why or why not?

THE SCIENCE OF SHOPPING
MALCOLM GLADWELL

"The Science of Shopping" (1996) is a narrative about marketing researcher Paco Underhill, but it is also an essay on the increasingly sophisticated world of retailing. Gladwell published this piece in the New Yorker, *an elite arts and culture magazine that appeals to an audience of educated, prosperous people. Gladwell writes like a storyteller, becoming a character who follows Paco around, stopping to reflect on what he sees Paco doing. The result is a personal and analytical consideration of the competitive strategies that drive retailing.*

Human beings walk the way they drive, which is to say that Americans tend to keep to the right when they stroll down shopping-mall concourses or city sidewalks. This is why in a well-designed airport travellers drifting toward their gate will always find the fast-food restaurants on their left and the gift shops on their right: people will readily cross a lane of pedestrian traffic to satisfy their hunger but rarely to make an impulse buy of a T-shirt or a magazine. This is also why Paco Underhill tells his retail clients to make sure that their window displays are canted, preferably to both sides but especially to the left, so that a potential shopper approaching the store on the inside of the sidewalk—the shopper, that is, with the least impeded view of the store window—can see the display from at least twenty-five feet away.

Of course, a lot depends on how fast the potential shopper is walking. Paco, in his previous life, as an urban geographer in Manhattan, spent a great deal of time thinking about walking speeds as he listened in on the great debates of the nineteen-seventies over whether the traffic lights in midtown should be timed to facilitate the movement of cars or to facilitate the movement of pedestrians and so break up the big platoons that move down Manhattan sidewalks. He knows that the faster you walk the more your peripheral vision narrows, so you become unable to pick up visual cues as quickly as someone who is just ambling along. He knows, too, that people who walk fast take a surprising amount of time to slow down—just as it takes a good stretch of road to change gears with a stick-shift automobile. On the basis of his research, Paco estimates the human downshift period to be anywhere from twelve to twenty-five feet, so if you own a store, he says, you never want to be next door to a bank: potential shoppers speed up when they walk past a bank (since there's nothing to look at), and by the time they slow down they've walked right past your business. The downshift factor also means that when potential shoppers enter a store it's going to take them from five to fifteen paces to adjust to the light and refocus and gear down from walking speed to shopping speed—particularly if they've just had to navigate a treacherous parking lot or hurry to make the light at Fifty-seventh and Fifth.

Paco calls that area inside the door the Decompression Zone, and something he tells clients over and over again is never, *ever* put anything of value in that zone—not shopping baskets or tie racks or big promotional displays—because no one is going to see it. Paco believes that, as a rule of thumb, customer interaction with any product or promotional display in the Decompression Zone will increase at least thirty per cent once it's moved to the back edge of the zone, and even more if it's placed to the right, because another of the fundamental rules of how human beings shop is that upon entering a store—whether it's Nordstrom or K Mart, Tiffany or the Gap—the shopper invariably and reflexively turns to the right. Paco believes in the existence of the Invariant Right because he has actually verified it. He has put cameras in stores trained directly on the doorway, and if you go to his office, just above Union Square, where videocassettes and boxes of Super-eight film from all his work over the years are stacked in plastic Tupperware containers practically up to the ceiling, he can show you reel upon reel of grainy entryway video—customers striding in the door, downshifting, refocussing, and then, again and again, making that little half turn.

Paco Underhill is a tall man in his mid-forties, partly bald, with a neatly trimmed beard and an engaging, almost goofy manner. He wears baggy khakis and shirts open at the collar, and generally looks like the academic he might have been if he hadn't been captivated, twenty years ago, by the ideas of the urban anthropologist William Whyte.

It was Whyte who pioneered the use of time-lapse photography as a tool of urban planning, putting cameras in parks and the plazas in front of office buildings in midtown Manhattan, in order to determine what distinguished a public space that worked from one that didn't. As a Columbia undergraduate, in 1974, Paco heard a lecture on Whyte's work and, he recalls, left the room "walking on air." He immediately read everything Whyte had written. He emptied his bank account to buy cameras and film and make his own home movie, about a pedestrian mall in Poughkeepsie. He took his "little exercise" to Whyte's advocacy group, the Project for Public Spaces, and was offered a job. Soon, however, it dawned on Paco that Whyte's ideas could be taken a step further— that the same techniques he used to establish why a plaza worked or didn't work could also be used to determine why a store worked or didn't work. Thus was born the field of retail anthropology, and, not long afterward, Paco founded Envirosell, which in just over fifteen years has counselled some of the most familiar names in American retailing, from Levi Strauss to Kinney, Starbucks, McDonald's, Blockbuster, Apple Computer, AT&T, and a number of upscale retailers that Paco would rather not name.

5   When Paco gets an assignment, he and his staff set up a series of video cameras throughout the test store and then back the cameras up with Envirosell staffers—trackers, as they're known—armed with clipboards. Where the cameras go and how many trackers Paco deploys depends on exactly what the store wants to know about its shoppers. Typically, though, he might use six cameras and two or three trackers, and let the study run for two or three days, so that at the end he would have pages and pages of carefully annotated tracking sheets and anywhere from a hundred to five hundred hours of film. These days, given the expansion of his business, he might tape fifteen thousand hours in a year, and, given that he has been in operation since the late seventies, he now has well over a hundred thousand hours of tape in his library.

Even in the best of times, this would be a valuable archive. But today, with the retail business in crisis, it is a gold mine. The time per visit that the average American spends in a shopping mall was sixty-six minutes last year—down from seventy-two minutes in 1992—and is the lowest number ever recorded. The amount of selling space per American shopper is now more than double what it was in the mid-seventies, meaning that profit margins have never been narrower, and the costs of starting a retail business— and of failing—have never been higher. In the past few years, countless dazzling new retailing temples have been built along Fifth and Madison Avenues—Barneys, Calvin Klein, Armani, Valentino, Banana Republic, Prada, Chanel, Nike Town, and on and on— but it is an explosion of growth based on no more than a hunch, a hopeful multimillion-dollar gamble that the way to break through is to provide the shopper with spectacle and more spectacle. "The arrogance is gone," Millard Drexler, the president and C.E.O. of the Gap, told me. "Arrogance makes failure. Once you think you know the answer, it's almost always over." In such a competitive environment, retailers don't just want to know how shoppers behave in their stores. They *have* to know. And who better to ask than Paco Underhill, who in the past decade and a half has analyzed tens of thousands of hours of shopping videotape and, as a result, probably knows more about the strange habits and quirks of the species *Emptor americanus* than anyone else alive?

Paco is considered the originator, for example, of what is known in the trade as the butt-brush theory—or, as Paco calls it, more delicately, *le facteur bousculade*— which holds that the likelihood of a woman's being converted from a browser to a buyer is inversely proportional to the likelihood of her being brushed on her behind while she's examining merchandise. Touch—or brush or bump or jostle—a woman on the behind when she has stopped to look at an item, and she will bolt. Actually, calling this a theory is something of a misnomer, because Paco doesn't offer any explanation for why women react that way, aside from venturing that they are "more sensitive back there." It's really an observation, based on repeated and close analysis of his videotape library, that Paco has transformed into a retailing commandment: a women's product that requires extensive examination should never be placed in a narrow aisle.

Paco approaches the problem of the Invariant Right the same way. Some retail thinkers see this as a subject crying out for interpretation and speculation. The design guru Joseph Weishar, for example, argues, in his magisterial "Design for Effective Selling Space," that the Invariant Right is a function of the fact that we "absorb and digest information in the left part of the brain" and "assimilate and logically use this information in the right half," the result being that we scan the store from left to right and then fix on an object to the right "essentially at a 45 degree angle from the point that we enter." When I asked Paco about this interpretation, he shrugged, and said he thought the reason was simply that most people are right-handed. Uncovering the fundamentals of "why" is clearly not a pursuit that engages him much. He is not a theoretician but an empiricist, and for him the important thing is that in amassing his huge library of in-store time-lapse photography he has gained enough hard evidence to know how often and under what circumstances the Invariant Right is expressed and how to take advantage of it.

What Paco likes are facts. They come tumbling out when he talks, and, because he speaks with a slight hesitation—lingering over the first syllable in, for example, "re-tail" or "de-sign"—he draws you in, and you find yourself truly hanging on his words. "We have reached a historic point in American history," he told me in our very first conversation. "Men, for the first time, have begun to buy their own underwear." He then paused to let the comment sink in, so that I could absorb its implications, before he elaborated: "Which means that we have to *totally* rethink the way we sell that product." In the parlance of Hollywood scriptwriters, the best endings must be surprising and yet inevitable; and the best of Paco's pronouncements take the same shape. It would never have occurred to me to wonder about the increasingly critical role played by touching—or, as Paco calls it, petting—clothes in the course of making the decision to buy them. But then I went to the Gap and to Banana Republic and saw people touching and fondling and, one after another, buying shirts and sweaters laid out on big wooden tables, and what Paco told me—which was no doubt based on what he had seen on his videotapes—made perfect sense: that the reason the Gap and Banana Republic have tables is not merely that sweaters and shirts look better there, or that tables fit into the warm and relaxing residential feeling that the Gap and Banana Republic are trying to create in their stores, but that tables invite—indeed, symbolize—touching. "Where do we eat?" Paco asks. "We eat, we pick up food, on tables."

10   Paco produces for his clients a series of carefully detailed studies, totalling forty to a hundred and fifty pages, filled with product-by-product breakdowns and bright-colored charts and graphs. In one recent case, he was asked by a major clothing retailer to analyze the first of a new chain of stores that the firm planned to open. One of the things the client wanted to know was how successful the store was in drawing people into its depths, since the chances that shoppers will buy something are directly related to how long they spend

shopping, and how long they spend shopping is directly related to how deep they get pulled into the store. For this reason, a supermarket will often put dairy products on one side, meat at the back, and fresh produce on the other side, so that the typical shopper can't just do a drive-by but has to make an entire circuit of the store, and be tempted by everything the supermarket has to offer. In the case of the new clothing store, Paco found that ninety-one percent of all shoppers penetrated as deep as what he called Zone 4, meaning more than three-quarters of the way in, well past the accessories and shirt racks and belts in the front, and little short of the far wall, with the changing rooms and the pants stacked on shelves. Paco regarded this as an extraordinary figure, particularly for a long, narrow store like this one, where it is not unusual for the rate of penetration past, say, Zone 3 to be under fifty percent. But that didn't mean the store was perfect—far from it. For Paco, all kinds of questions remained.

Purchasers, for example, spent an average of eleven minutes and twenty-seven seconds in the store, nonpurchasers two minutes and thirty-six seconds. It wasn't that the nonpurchasers just cruised in and out: in those two minutes and thirty-six seconds, they went deep into the store and examined an average of 3.42 items. So why didn't they buy? What, exactly, happened to cause some browsers to buy and other browsers to walk out the door?

Then, there was the issue of the number of products examined. The purchasers were looking at an average of 4.81 items but buying only 1.33 items. Paco found this statistic deeply disturbing. As the retail market grows more cutthroat, store owners have come to realize that it's all but impossible to increase the number of customers coming in, and have concentrated instead on getting the customers they do have to buy more. Paco thinks that if you can sell someone a pair of pants you must also be able to sell that person a belt, or a pair of socks, or a pair of underpants, or even do what the Gap does so well: sell a person a complete outfit. To Paco, the figure 1.33 suggested that the store was doing something very wrong, and one day when I visited him in his office he sat me down in front of one of his many VCRs to see how he looked for the 1.33 culprit.

It should be said that sitting next to Paco is a rather strange experience. "My mother says that I'm the best-paid spy in America," he told me. He laughed, but he wasn't entirely joking. As a child, Paco had a nearly debilitating stammer, and, he says, "since I was never that comfortable talking I always relied on my eyes to understand things." That much is obvious from the first moment you meet him: Paco is one of those people who look right at you, soaking up every nuance and detail. It isn't a hostile gaze, because Paco isn't hostile at all. He has a big smile, and he'll call you "chief" and use your first name a lot and generally act as if he knew you well. But that's the awkward thing: he has looked at you so closely that you're sure he does know you well, and you, meanwhile, hardly know him at all.

This kind of asymmetry is even more pronounced when you watch his shopping videos with him, because every movement or gesture means something to Paco—he has spent his adult life deconstructing the shopping experience—but nothing to the outsider, or, at least, not at first. Paco had to keep stopping the video to get me to see things through his eyes before I began to understand. In one sequence, for example, a camera mounted high on the wall outside the changing rooms documented a man and a woman shopping for a pair of pants for what appeared to be their daughter, a girl in her mid-teens. The tapes are soundless, but the basic steps of the shopping dance are so familiar to Paco that, once I'd grasped the general idea, he was able to provide a running commentary on what was being said and thought. There is the girl emerging from the changing room wearing her first pair. There she is glancing at her reflection in the mirror, then turning to see herself from the back. There is the mother looking on. There is the father—or, as fathers are known in the trade, the "wallet carrier"—stepping forward and pulling up the jeans. There's the girl trying on another pair. There's the primp again. The twirl. The mother. The wallet carrier. And then again, with another pair. The full sequence lasted twenty minutes, and at the end came the take-home lesson, for which Paco called in one of his colleagues, Tom Moseman, who had supervised the project.

15   "This is a very critical moment," Tom, a young, intense man wearing little round glasses, said, and he pulled up a chair next to mine. "She's saying, 'I don't know whether I should wear a belt.' Now here's the salesclerk. The girl says to him, 'I need a belt,' and he says, 'Take mine.' Now there he is taking her back to the full-length mirror."

A moment later, the girl returns, clearly happy with the purchase. She wants the jeans. The wallet carrier turns to her, and then gestures to the salesclerk. The wallet carrier is telling his daughter to give back the belt. The girl gives back the belt. Tom stops the tape. He's leaning forward now, a finger jabbing at the screen. Beside me, Paco is shaking his head. I don't get it—at least, not at first—and so Tom replays that last segment. The wallet carrier tells the girl to give back the belt. She gives back the belt. And then, finally, it dawns on me why this store has an average purchase number of only 1.33. "Don't you see?" Tom said. "*She wanted the belt.* A great opportunity to make an add-on sale … *lost!*"

Should we be afraid of Paco Underhill? One of the fundamental anxieties of the American consumer, after all, has always been that beneath the pleasure and the frivolity of the shopping experience runs an undercurrent of manipulation, and that anxiety has rarely seemed more justified than today. The practice of prying into the minds and habits of American consumers is now a multibillion-dollar business. Every time a product is pulled across a supermarket checkout scanner, information is recorded, assembled, and sold to a market-research firm for analysis. There are companies that put tiny cameras inside frozen-food cases in supermarket aisles; market-research firms that feed census data and behavioral statistics into algorithms and come out with complicated maps of the American consumer; anthropologists who sift through the garbage of carefully targeted households to analyze their true consumption patterns; and endless rounds of highly organized focus groups and questionnaire takers and phone surveyors. That some people are now tracking our every shopping move with video cameras seems in many respects the last straw: Paco's movies are, after all, creepy. They look like the surveillance videos taken during convenience-store holdups—hazy and soundless and slightly warped by the angle of the lens. When you watch them, you find yourself waiting for something bad to happen, for someone to shoplift or pull a gun on a cashier.

The more time you spend with Paco's videos, though, the less scary they seem. After an hour or so, it's no longer clear whether simply by watching people shop—and analyzing their every move—you can learn how to control them. The shopper that emerges from the videos is not pliable or manipulable. The screen shows people filtering in and out of stores, petting and moving on, abandoning their merchandise because checkout lines are too long, or leaving a store empty-handed because they couldn't fit their stroller into the aisle between two shirt racks. Paco's shoppers are fickle and headstrong, and are quite unwilling to buy anything unless conditions are perfect—unless the belt is presented at *exactly* the right moment. His theories of the butt-brush and petting and the Decompression Zone and the Invariant Right seek not to make shoppers conform to the desires of sellers but to make sellers conform to the desires of shoppers. What Paco is teaching his clients is a kind of slavish devotion to the shopper's every whim. He is teaching them humility.

Paco has worked with supermarket chains, and when you first see one of his videos of grocery aisles it looks as if he really had—at least in this instance—got one up on the shopper. The clip he showed me was of a father shopping with a small child, and it was an example of what is known in the trade as "advocacy," which basically means what happens when your four-year-old goes over and grabs a bag of cookies that the store has conveniently put on the bottom shelf, and demands that it be purchased. In the clip, the father takes what the child offers him. "Generally, dads are not as good as moms at saying no," Paco said as we watched the little boy approach his dad. "Men tend to be more impulse-driven than women in grocery stores. We know that they tend to shop less often with a list. We know that they tend to shop much less frequently with coupons, and we know, simply by watching them shop, that they can be marching down the aisle and something will catch their eye and they will stop and buy." This kind of weakness on the part of fathers might seem to give the supermarket an advantage in the cookie-selling wars, particularly since more and more men go grocery shopping with their children. But then Paco let drop a hint about a study he'd just done in which he discovered, to his and everyone else's amazement, that shoppers had already figured this out, that they were already one step ahead—that *families were avoiding the cookie aisle.*

20   This may seem like a small point. But it begins to explain why, even though retailers seem to know more than ever about how shoppers behave, even though their efforts at intelligence-gathering have rarely seemed more intrusive and more formidable, the retail business remains in crisis. The reason is that shoppers are a moving target. They are becoming more and more complicated, and retailers need to know more and more about them simply to keep pace.

This fall, for example, Estée Lauder is testing in a Toronto shopping mall a new concept in cosmetics retailing. Gone is the enclosed rectangular counter, with the sales staff on one side, customers on the other, and the product under glass in the middle. In its place the company has provided an assortment of product-display, consultation, and testing kiosks arranged in a broken circle, with a service desk and a cashier in the middle. One of the kiosks is a "makeup play area," which allows customers to experiment on their own with a hundred and thirty different shades of lipstick. There are four self-service displays—for perfumes, skin-care products, and makeup—which are easily accessible to customers who have already made up their minds. And, for those who haven't, there is a semiprivate booth for personal consultations with beauty advisers and makeup artists. The redesign was prompted by the realization that the modern working woman no longer had the time or the inclination to ask a salesclerk to assist her in every purchase, that choosing among shades of lipstick did not require the same level of service as, say, getting up to speed on new developments in skin care, that a shopper's needs were now too diverse to be adequately served by just one kind of counter.

"I was going from store to store, and the traffic just wasn't there," Robin Burns, the president and C.E.O. of Estée Lauder U.S.A. and Canada, told me. "We had to get rid of the glass barricade." The most interesting thing about the new venture, though, is what it says about the shifting balance of power between buyer and seller. Around the old rectangular counter, the relationship of clerk to customer was formal and subtly paternalistic. If you wanted to look at a lipstick, you had to ask for it. "Twenty years ago, the sales staff would consult with you and *tell* you what you needed, as opposed to asking and recommending," Burns said. "And in those days people believed what the salesperson told them." Today, the old hierarchy has been inverted. "Women want to draw their own conclusions," Burns said. Even the architecture of the consultation kiosk speaks to the transformation: the beauty adviser now sits beside the customer, not across from her.

This doesn't mean that marketers and retailers have stopped trying to figure out what goes on in the minds of shoppers. One of the hottest areas in market research, for example, is something called typing, which is a sophisticated attempt to predict the kinds of products that people will buy or the kind of promotional pitch they will be susceptible to on the basis of where they live or how they score on short standardized questionnaires. One market-research firm in Virginia, Claritas, has divided the entire country, neighborhood by neighborhood, into sixty-two different categories—Pools & Patios, Shotguns & Pickups, Bohemia Mix, and so on—using census data and results from behavioral surveys. On the basis of my address in Greenwich Village, Claritas classifies me as Urban Gold Coast, which means that I like Kellogg's Special K, spend more than two hundred and fifty dollars on sports coats, watch "Seinfeld," and buy metal polish. Such typing systems—and there are a number of them—can be scarily accurate. I actually do buy Kellogg's Special K, have spent more than two hundred and fifty dollars on a sports coat, and watch "Seinfeld." (I don't buy metal polish.) In fact, when I was typed by a company called Total Research, in Princeton, the results were so dead-on that I got the same kind of creepy feeling that I got when I first watched Paco's videos. On the basis of a seemingly innocuous multiple-choice test, I was scored as an eighty-nine-percent Intellect and a seven-percent Relief Seeker (which I thought was impressive until John Morton, who developed the system, told me that virtually everyone who reads *The New Yorker* is an Intellect). When I asked Morton to guess, on the basis of my score, what kind of razor I used, he riffed, brilliantly, and without a moment's hesitation. "If you used an electric razor, it would be a Braun," he began. "But, if not, you're probably shaving with Gillette, if only because there really isn't an Intellect safety-razor positioning out there. Schick and Bic are simply not logical choices for you, although I'm thinking, you're fairly young, and you've got that Relief-Seeker side. It's possible you would use Bic because you don't like that all-American, overly confident masculine statement of Gillette. It's a very, very conventional positioning that Gillette uses. But then they've got the technological angle with the Gillette Sensor…. I'm thinking Gillette. It's Gillette."

He was right. I shave with Gillette—though I didn't even know that I do. I had to go home and check. But information about my own predilections may be of limited usefulness in predicting how I shop. In the past few years, market researchers have paid growing attention to the role in the shopping experience of a type of consumer known as a Market Maven. "This is a person you would go to for advice on a car or a new fashion," said Linda Price, a marketing professor at the University of South Florida, who first came up with the Market Maven concept, in the late eighties. "This is a person who has information on a lot of different products or prices or places to shop. This is a person who likes to initiate discussions with consumers and respond to requests. Market Mavens like to be helpers in the marketplace. They take you shopping. They go shopping for you, and it turns out they are a lot more prevalent than you would expect." Mavens watch more television than almost anyone else does, and they read more magazines and open their junk mail and look closely at advertisements and have an awful lot of influence on everyone else. According to Price, sixty percent of Americans claim to know a Maven.

25   The key question, then, is not what I think but what my Mavens think. The challenge for retailers and marketers, in turn, is not so much to figure out and influence my preferences as to figure out and influence the preferences of my Mavens, and that is a much harder task. "What's really interesting is that the distribution of Mavens doesn't vary by ethnic category, by income, or by professional status," Price said. "A working woman is just as likely to be a Market Maven as a nonworking woman. You might say that Mavens are likely to be older, unemployed people, but that's wrong, too. There is simply not a clear demographic guide to how to find these people." More important, Mavens are better consumers than most of the rest of us. In another of the typing systems, developed by the California-based SRI International, Mavens are considered to be a subcategory of the consumer type known as Fulfilled, and Fulfilleds, one SRI official told me, are "the consumers from Hell—they are very feature-oriented." He explained, "They are not pushed by promotions. You can reach them, but it's an intellectual argument." As the complexity of the marketplace grows, in other words, we have responded by appointing the most skeptical and the most savvy in our midst to mediate between us and sellers. The harder stores and manufacturers work to sharpen and refine their marketing strategies, and the harder they try to read the minds of shoppers, the more we hide behind Mavens.

Imagine that you want to open a clothing store, men's and women's, in the upper-middle range—say, khakis at fifty dollars, dress shirts at forty dollars, sports coats and women's suits at two hundred dollars and up. The work of Paco Underhill would suggest that in order to succeed you need to pay complete and concentrated attention to the whims of your customers. What does that mean, in practical terms? Well, let's start with what's called the shopping gender gap. In the retail-store study that Paco showed me, for example, male buyers stayed an average of nine minutes and thirty-nine seconds in the store and female buyers stayed twelve minutes and fifty-seven seconds. This is not atypical. Women always shop longer than men, which is one of the major reasons that in the standard regional mall women account for seventy percent of the dollar value of all purchases. "Women have more patience than men," Paco says. "Men are more distractible. Their tolerance level for confusion or time spent in a store is much shorter than women's." If you wanted, then, you could build a store designed for men, to try to raise that thirty-percent sales figure to forty or forty-five percent. You could make the look more masculine—more metal, darker woods. You could turn up the music. You could simplify the store, put less product on the floor. "I'd go narrow and deep," says James Adams, the design director for NBBJ Retail Concepts, a division of one of the country's largest retail-design firms. "You wouldn't have fifty different cuts of pants. You'd have your four basics with lots of color. You know the Garanimals they used to do to help kids pick out clothes, where you match the giraffe top with the giraffe bottom? I'm sure every guy is like 'I wish I could get those, too.' You'd want to stick with the basics. Making sure most of the color story goes together. That is a big deal with guys, because they are always screwing the colors up." When I asked Carrie Gennuso, the Gap's regional vice-president for New York, what she would do in an all-male store, she laughed and said, "I might do fewer displays and more signage. Big signs. Men! Smalls! Here!"

As a rule, though, you wouldn't want to cater to male customers at the expense of female ones. It's no accident that many clothing stores have a single look in both men's and women's sections, and that the quintessential nineties look—light woods, white walls—is more feminine than masculine. Women are still the shoppers in America, and the real money is to be made by making retailing styles *more* female-friendly, not less. Recently, for example, NBBJ did a project to try to increase sales of the Armstrong flooring chain. Its researchers found that the sales staff was selling the flooring based on its functional virtues—the fact that it didn't scuff, that it was long-lasting, that it didn't stain, that it was easy to clean. It was being sold by men to men, as if it were a car or a stereo. And that was the problem. "It's a wonder product technologically," Adams says. "But the woman is the decision-maker on flooring, and that's not what's she's looking for. This product is about fashion, about color and design. You don't want to get too caught up in the man's way of thinking."

To appeal to men, then, retailers do subtler things. At the Banana Republic store on Fifth Avenue in midtown, the men's socks are displayed near the shoes and between men's pants and the cash register (or cash/wrap, as it is known in the trade), so that the man can grab them easily as he rushes to pay. Women's accessories are by the fitting rooms, because women are much more likely to try on pants first, and then choose an item like a belt or a bag. At the men's shirt table, the display shirts have matching ties on them—the tie table is next to it—in a grownup version of the Garanimals system. But Banana Republic would never match scarves with women's blouses or jackets. "You don't have to be that direct with women," Jeanne Jackson, the president of Banana Republic, told me. "In fact, the Banana woman is proud of her sense of style. She puts her own looks together." Jackson said she liked the Fifth Avenue store because it's on two floors, so she can separate men's and women's sections and give men what she calls "clarity of offer," which is the peace of mind that they won't inadvertently end up in, say, women's undergarments. In a one-floor store, most retailers would rather put the menswear up front and the women's wear at the back (that is, if they weren't going to split the sexes left and right), because women don't get spooked navigating through apparel of the opposite sex, whereas men most assuredly do. (Of course, in a store like the Gap at Thirty-ninth and Fifth, where, Carrie Gennuso says, "I don't know if I've ever seen a man," the issue is moot. There, it's safe to put the women's wear out front.)

The next thing retailers want to do is to encourage the shopper to walk deep into the store. The trick there is to put "destination items"—basics, staples, things that people know you have and buy a lot of—at the rear of the store. Gap stores, invariably, will have denim, which is a classic destination item for them, on the back wall. Many clothing stores also situate the cash/wrap and the fitting rooms in the rear of the store, to compel shoppers to walk back into Zone 3 or 4. In the store's prime real estate—which, given Paco's theory of the Decompression Zone and the Invariant Right, is to the right of the front entrance and five to fifteen paces in—you always put your hottest and newest merchandise, because that's where the maximum number of people will see it. Right now, in virtually every Gap in the country, the front of the store is devoted to the Gap fall look—casual combinations in black and gray, plaid shirts and jackets, sweaters, black wool and brushed-twill pants. At the Gap at Fifth Avenue and Seventeenth Street, for example, there is a fall ensemble of plaid jacket, plaid shirt, and black pants in the first prime spot, followed, three paces later, by an ensemble of gray sweater, plaid shirt, T-shirt, and black pants, followed, three paces after that, by an ensemble of plaid jacket, gray sweater, white T-shirt, and black pants. In all, three variations on the same theme, each placed so that the eye bounces naturally from the first to the second to the third, and then, inexorably, to a table deep inside Zone 1 where merchandise is arrayed and folded for petting. Every week or ten days, the combinations will change, the "look" highlighted at the front will be different, and the entryway will be transformed.

30   Through all of this, the store environment—the lighting, the colors, the fixtures— and the clothes have to work together. The point is not so much beauty as coherence. The clothes have to match the environment. "In the nineteen-seventies, you didn't have to have a complete wardrobe all the time," Gabriella Forte, the president and chief operating officer of Calvin Klein, says. "I think now the store has to have a complete point of view. It has to have all the options offered, so people have choices. It's the famous one-stop shopping. People want to come in, be serviced, and go out. They want to understand the clear statement the designer is making."

At the new Versace store on Fifth Avenue, in the restored neoclassical Vanderbilt mansion, Gianni Versace says that the "statement" he is making with the elaborate mosaic and parquet floors, the marble façade and the Corinthian columns is "qual- ity—my message is always a scream for quality." At her two new stores in London, Donna Karan told me, she never wants "customers to think that they are walking into a clothing store." She said, "I want them to think that they are walking into an envi- ronment, that I am transforming them out of their lives and into an experience, that it's not about clothes, it's about who they are as people." The first thing the shopper sees in her stark, all-white DKNY store is a video monitor and café: "It's about energy," Karan said, "and nourishment." In her more sophisticated, "collection" store, where the walls are black and ivory and gold, the first thing that the customer notices is the scent of a candle: "I wanted a nurturing environment where you feel that you will be taken care of." And why, at a Giorgio Armani store, is there often only a single suit in each style on display? Not because the store has only the one suit in stock but because the way the merchandise is displayed has to be consistent with the message of the designers: that Armani suits are exclusive, that the Armani customer isn't going to run into another man wearing his suit every time he goes to an art opening at Gagosian.

The best stores all have an image—or what retailers like to call a "point of view." The flagship store for Ralph Lauren's Polo collection, for example, is in the restored Rhinelander mansion, on Madison Avenue and Seventy-second Street. The Polo Man- sion, as it is known, is alive with color and artifacts that suggest a notional prewar Eng- lish gentility. There are fireplaces and comfortable leather chairs and deep-red Oriental carpets and soft, thick drapes and vintage photographs and paintings of country squires and a color palette of warm crimsons and browns and greens—to the point that after you've picked out a double-breasted blazer or a cashmere sweater set or an antique silver snuffbox you feel as though you ought to venture over to Central Park for a vigorous morning of foxhunting.

The Calvin Klein flagship store, twelve blocks down Madison Avenue, on the other hand, is a vast, achingly beautiful minimalist temple, with white walls, muted lighting, soaring ceilings, gray stone flooring, and, so it seems, less merchandise in the entire store than Lauren puts in a single room. The store's architect, John Pawson, says, "People who enter are given a sense of release. They are getting away from the hustle and bustle of the street and New York. They are in a calm space. It's a modern idea of luxury, to give people space."

The first thing you see when you enter the Polo Mansion is a display of two hundred and eight sweaters, in twenty-eight colors, stacked in a haberdasher's wooden fixture, behind an antique glass counter; the first thing you see at the Klein store is a white wall, and then, if you turn to the right, four clear-glass shelves, each adorned with three solitary-looking black handbags. The Polo Mansion is an English club. The Klein store, Pawson says, is the equivalent of an art gallery, a place where "neutral space and light make a work of art look the most potent." When I visited the Polo Mansion, the stereo was playing Bobby Short. At Klein, the stereo was playing what sounded like Brian Eno. At the Polo Mansion, I was taken around by Charles Fagan, a vice-president at Polo Ralph Lauren. He wore pale-yellow socks, black loafers, tight jeans, a pale-purple polo shirt, blue old-school tie, and a brown plaid jacket—which sounds less attractive on paper than it was in reality. He looked, in a very Ralph Lauren way, *fabulous.* He was funny and engaging and bounded through the store, keeping up a constant patter ("This room is sort of sportswear, Telluride-y, vintage"), all the while laughing and hugging people and having his freshly cut red hair tousled by the sales assistants in each section. At the Calvin Klein store, the idea that the staff—tall, austere, sombre-suited—might laugh and hug and tousle each other's hair is unthinkable. Lean over and whisper, perhaps. At the most, murmur discreetly into tiny black cellular phones. Visiting the Polo Mansion and the Calvin Klein flagship in quick succession is rather like seeing a "Howards End"–"The Seventh Seal" double feature.

35 Despite their differences, though, these stores are both about the same thing—communicating the point of view that shoppers are now thought to demand. At Polo, the "lifestyle" message is so coherent and all-encompassing that the store never has the 1.33 items-per-purchase problem that Paco saw in the retailer he studied. "We have multiple purchases in excess—it's the cap, it's the tie, it's the sweater, it's the jacket, it's the pants," Fagan told me, plucking each item from its shelf and tossing it onto a tartan-covered bench seat. "People say, 'I *have* to have the belt.' It's a lifestyle decision."

As for the Klein store, it's really concerned with setting the tone for the Calvin Klein clothes and products sold *outside* the store—including the designer's phenomenally successful underwear line, the sales of which have grown nearly fivefold in the past two and a half years, making it one of the country's dominant brands. Calvin Klein underwear is partly a design triumph: lowering the waist-band just a tad in order to elongate, and flatter, the torso. But it is also a triumph of image—transforming, as Gabriella Forte says, a "commodity good into something desirable," turning a forgotten necessity into *fashion.* In the case of women's underwear, Bob Mazzoli, president of Calvin Klein Underwear, told me that the company "obsessed about the box being a perfect square, about the symmetry of it all, how it would feel in a woman's hand." He added, "When you look at the boxes they are little works of art." And the underwear itself is without any of the usual busyness—without, in Mazzoli's words, "the excessive detail" of most women's undergarments. It's a clean look, selling primarily in white, heather gray, and black. It's a look, in other words, not unlike that of the

Calvin Klein flagship store, and it exemplifies the brilliance of the merchandising of the Calvin Klein image: preposterous as it may seem, once you've seen the store and worn the underwear, it's difficult not to make a connection between the two.

All this image making seeks to put the shopping experience in a different context, to give it a story line. "I wish that the customers who come to my stores feel the same comfort they would entering a friend's house—that is to say, that they feel at ease, without the impression of having to deal with the 'sanctum sanctorum' of a designer," Giorgio Armani told me. Armani has a house. Donna Karan has a kitchen and a womb. Ralph Lauren has a men's club. Calvin Klein has an art gallery. These are all very different points of view. What they have in common is that they have nothing to do with the actual act of shopping. (No one buys anything at a friend's house or a men's club.) Presumably, by engaging in this kind of misdirection designers aim to put us at ease, to create a kind of oasis. But perhaps they change the subject because they must, because they cannot offer an ultimate account of the shopping experience itself. After all, what do we really know, in the end, about why people buy? We know about the Invariant Right and the Decompression Zone. We know to put destination items at the back and fashion at the front, to treat male shoppers like small children, to respect the female derrière, and to put the socks between the cash/wrap and the men's pants. But this is grammar; it's not prose. It is enough. But it is not much.

One of the best ways to understand the new humility in shopping theory is to go back to the work of William Whyte. Whyte put his cameras in parks and in the plazas in front of office buildings because he believed in the then radical notion that the design of public spaces had been turned inside out—that planners were thinking of their designs first and of people second, when they should have been thinking of people first and of design second.

In his 1980 classic, "The Social Life of Small Urban Spaces," for example, Whyte trained his cameras on a dozen or so of the public spaces and small parks around Manhattan, like the plaza in front of the General Motors Building, on Fifth Avenue, and the small park at 77 Water Street, downtown, and Paley Park, on Fifty-third Street, in order to determine why some, like the tiny Water Street park, averaged well over a hundred and fifty people during a typical sunny lunch hour and others, like the much bigger plaza at 280 Park Avenue, were almost empty. He concluded that all the things used by designers to attempt to lure people into their spaces made little or no difference. It wasn't the size of the space, or its beauty, or the presence of waterfalls, or the amount of sun, or whether a park was a narrow strip along the sidewalk or a pleasing open space. What mattered, overwhelmingly, was that there were plenty of places to sit, that the space was in some way connected to the street, and—the mystical circularity—that it was already well frequented. "What attracts people most, it would appear, is other people," Whyte noted:

> If I labor the point, it is because many urban spaces still are being designed as though the opposite were true—as though what people liked best were the places they stay away from. People often do talk along such lines, and therefore their responses to questionnaires can be entirely misleading. How many people would say they like to sit in the middle of a crowd? Instead, they speak of "getting away from it all," and use words like "escape," "oasis," "retreat." What people *do,* however, reveals a different priority.

40   Whyte's conclusions demystified the question of how to make public space work. Places to sit, streets to enjoy, and people to watch turned out to be the simple and powerful rules for park designers to follow, and these rules demolished the orthodoxies and theoretical principles of conventional urban design. But in a more important sense—and it is here that Whyte's connection with Paco Underhill and retail anthropology and the stores that line Fifth and Madison is most striking— what Whyte did was to remystify the art of urban planning. He said, emphatically, that people could not be manipulated, that they would enter a public space only on their own terms, that the goal of observers like him was to find out what people wanted, not why they wanted it. Whyte, like Paco, was armed with all kinds of facts and observations about what it took to build a successful public space. He had strict views on how wide ledges had to be to lure passersby (at least thirty inches, or two backsides deep), and what the carrying capacity of prime outdoor sitting space is (total number of square feet divided by three). But, fundamentally, he was awed by the infinite complexity and the ultimate mystery of human behavior. He took people too seriously to think that he could control them. Here is Whyte, in "The Social Life of Small Urban Spaces," analyzing hours of videotape and describing what he has observed about the way men stand in public. He's talking about feet. He could just as easily be talking about shopping:

> Foot movements … seem to be a silent language. Often, in a schmoozing group, no one will be saying anything. Men stand bound in amiable silence, surveying the passing scene. Then, slowly, rhythmically, one of the men rocks up and down; first on the ball of the foot, then back on the heel. He stops. Another man starts the same movement. Sometimes there are reciprocal gestures. One man makes a half turn to the right. Then, after a rhythmic interval, another responds with a half turn to the left. Some kind of communication seems to be taking place here, but I've never broken the code.

Rereading Actively

1. Note Gladwell's section breaks, and jot in the margin a quick description of how he opens and concludes each section of his narrative. Use your journal to draw up a scratch outline from your marginal notes.

2. Work through a section at a time and note references to Paco's main characteristics (e.g., in the opening section, Gladwell tells us, among other things, that he is an "urban geographer," "engaging," and "goofy."). In your journal, write your own short description of Paco, interpreting Gladwell's description.

3. With a partner, list some of the selling strategies Gladwell reveals. In your journal, explain how these strategies attempt to control shoppers' behavior.

4. With a partner or in a small group, develop your own explanation of what Gladwell is calling "the science of shopping." Some terms from the article that may be useful to this endeavor include the "Invariant Right," "Decompression Zone," "market research," and "butt-brush."

5. Estimate Gladwell's feelings about his subject. Does he admire Paco and his company? How do you know? Review the article and note passages that hint at Gladwell's opinion of the science of shopping.

Exploring Your Responses

6. In a small group, brainstorm details from "The Science of Shopping" that stick in your mind. What examples, ideas, and assertions caught your attention?

7. Freewrite a response to this group brainstorming: Identify what you learned about the "science of shopping." Discuss how you feel about being researched.

8. Using your journal, respond to Gladwell's question: "Should we be afraid of Paco Underhill?"

9. Visualize the scenes that Gladwell describes. Have you been there? Is this scene representative of your experience as a shopper? Share your responses in a group discussion.

KEEPING UP WITH THE GATESES?
LOUIS UCHITELLE

Louis Uchitelle is a journalist who writes for the New York Times. *His subjects include business and economics, and he has written on topics ranging from productivity and the federal budget surplus to wage pressure on small retailers. In this article, published in the* Times *in 1998, Uchitelle identifies a new interpretation of consumer behavior that is motivated by "competitive consumption." Uchitelle combines summary and synthesis in this article, structuring his report around the work of two economists: Juliet Schor and Robert Frank. The work of these researchers suggests a late twentieth-century version of behavior the American sociologist, Thorstein Veblen, first described at the turn of the century, in which "conspicuous consumption" was used to claim high social status.*

Cambridge, Mass.

Her car is a second-hand 1989 Acura, a bit of resistance on the part of Juliet B. Schor to the "competitive consumption" that she describes so vividly in her new book, "The Overspent American." The television set is in the coldest, least inviting room of her house—another bit of resistance. But the well-dressed Ms. Schor gives ground on clothing, participating despite herself in the new consumerism that has been reshaping behavior since the 1980s.

Ms. Schor, an economist at Harvard University, argues that the vast majority of Americans aspire in their spending to the lifestyles of the wealthiest 20 percent. They go into debt trying to acquire the trappings of that world, or the portrayal of it offered incessantly on TV. For tens of millions of Americans, consumption has become the route to a sense of well-being and identity. But that route always seems to require more purchases, which in turn become new status markers in an endless "ratcheting up."

"The comparisons we make are no longer restricted to those in our general earnings category, or even to those one rung above us on the ladder," Ms. Schor writes. "Today, a person is more likely to be making comparisons with, or choose as a reference group, people whose incomes are three, four or five times his or her own. The result is that millions of us have become participants in a national culture of upscale spending."

In an age of income inequality, that is not easy. The incomes of the top 20 percent, which start at $75,000 a year and reside mostly above $90,000, have been growing faster than the incomes of everyone else, so keeping up means going deeper into debt. That, in fact, has been happening, particularly among households in the $25,000–to–$75,000 income range, the group that is trying hardest, in Ms. Schor's view, to rise in status. Simply having all the basics—being comfortable— now fails to be sufficient.

5   "While politicians continue to tout the middle class as the heart and soul of American society," she writes, "for far too many of us, being solidly middle class is no longer good enough."

Only determined "downshifters"—and they are growing in number, Ms. Schor reports—manage to immunize themselves, by altering their lives, working less and spending less. Ms. Schor is with them in spirit, if not always in practice. The black nylon shoulder bag that she tosses on the floor behind her as she settles into the driver's seat of her car is smart-looking and bears a designer label. Her black, knitted European suit is similarly upscale; not high couture—she got it on sale for $200, marked down from $1,200—but certainly stylish.

Two findings stood out in a lecture about the book that Ms. Schor gave last week to 50 students at Brandeis University, 20 minutes by used car from her Harvard office. Television is a big driver of consumer aspirations, she said—not just the commercials, but the stylish clothing worn by actors and the affluent settings of so many shows, particularly soap operas. Tabulating a survey of employees at a big, unnamed telecommunications company, Ms. Schor found that for every hour of television watched weekly, spending rose by $208 a year. This group watched enough TV to cost each person more than $2,200 a year.

"People from really opulent families use TV as a reality check," Ms. Schor said. "But for the vast majority of Americans, TV upscales their perceptions."

And their aspirations. Another poll asked where people wanted to end up. Eighty-five percent said they wanted to be rich or upper middle class; only 15 percent sought to "live a comfortable life"—a code phrase for middle class. The Brandeis students, in a show of hands, fit this pattern. Only one saw herself as becoming middle class, and she raised her hand meekly.

10   Ms. Schor—42, director of studies at Harvard's Women's Studies program, married to another economist, raising two children in a recently purchased three-bedroom suburban home—wrote a best-seller in 1991 entitled "The Overworked American." Instead of working fewer hours and having more leisure, which had been everyone's expectation, Americans were actually spending more time at work, she reported. It was a finding that struck a public chord and that Government data later confirmed. Among the reasons she gave for the trend: People needed the extra income to pay for their consumption.

And now, in the midst of a stock market boom and an outburst of consumption, "The Overspent American" (Basic Books) tries to explain what makes people such driven consumers. Ms. Schor, in effect, has written a modern-day version of "The Theory of the Leisure Class," in which Thorstein Veblen chronicled the "conspicuous consumption" of America's wealthy at the turn of the century, noting their spending on luxury goods (gold-handled walking sticks, for example) to call attention to their wealth and thus gain social esteem.

A half century later, after World War II, James Duesenberry, another Harvard economist, updated Veblen. Neighborhood life flourished then. Incomes were much more evenly distributed than in Veblen's day—or now—and Mr. Duesenberry popularized the phrase "keeping up with the Joneses" in his classic description of neighbors matching neighbors in the purchase of dishwashers, televisions, second cars and the like.

Another 50 years have passed and people today hardly know their neighbors. Civic activity, a potential substitute for spending, has declined. Income inequality has dissipated the egalitarian ethos. Religious and social taboos against excessive consumption have deteriorated. And the new view of life, Ms. Schor argues, is not through the kitchen window, but through the television screen or in catalogues and advertisements that endlessly promote luxury products, or in office settings where lower-level workers are often in contact with wealthier colleagues who lead fancier lives.

Ms. Schor's book describes this new milieu. The story she tells may be the most eye-catching so far, but she is not alone. Robert Frank, a Cornell University labor economist who recently co-wrote a book entitled "The Winner-Take-All Society" (Free Press), is completing a new book, "Luxury Fever," in which he shares several of Ms. Schor's views, though not her finding that most Americans are trying to mimic the lives of the upper 20 percent on the income ladder.

15   In Mr. Frank's analysis, the goal may be the top rung, but the mimicking is mainly a process of trying to keep up with those only a little higher in income. And since income inequality has created many rungs, starting at the top with Mr. Frank's big winners, it is a busy process. "If you read about someone high on the ladder buying a $50,000 wristwatch, then you don't feel like such a spendthrift if you buy a $1,000 watch," Mr. Frank said. "That is what is happening."

Both Mr. Frank and Ms. Schor would curb the spending through a consumption tax that bit hardest at the biggest spenders. A goal would be to push more spending into investment, public and private. But the solutions, particularly in Ms. Schor's case, are less interesting than the sociology and the economics.

Criticism of Ms. Schor's book is already coming from some traditional economists. The mainstream view is that consumers act rationally, buying what they need or value and can afford—if not right away, then with earnings that they expect to receive later in life. Ms. Schor accepts this thesis, but she argues—as did Veblen—that such theorizing fails to recognize that spending takes place in a social framework.

"People have choice; they can opt out of the game," she said. "What I am saying is that opting out is a socially costly thing to do. It is very difficult."

A $30,000 outlay for a Volvo or a sport utility vehicle may buy true value in the eyes of the purchaser, specifically crash protection and durability. But the payment is also made to buy status, which Ms. Schor argues is often a waste of national resources and an unnecessary invasion of savings. Her thinking helps to explain the 1989 Acura, and the decision to run her family with only one car, not two or three—another bit of American spending in which the line between utility and social pressure is often obscure.

20   The red-brick colonial home that Ms. Schor and her husband, Prasannan Parthasarathi, bought in Newton is ideal for this one-car family—within walking distance of Mr. Parthasarathi's new teaching job at Boston College, and also a short walk to the playground and the neighborhood elementary school.

The family resists, too, the home improvements so dear to Ms. Schor's new consumer. The bathrooms, never updated since the house was built in 1929, are just fine, she declares. So is the kitchen, last remodeled in the 1960's. "People say we have to change the cabinets," she said. "But we don't."

When it comes to clothing, though, sorting out value and status is not so easy.

"For most women, clothing is an area of conflict," she said. "You need an upscale wardrobe for your job. But we are also socialized in a culture that generates a lot of desire for apparel and accessories. I have that. One year, it was 1985 or 1986, I sat down and totaled up what I had spent on clothes, and I was horrified to find that I had spent $8,000 and I had only earned in the $30,000's."

The nuances of the new consumerism are noteworthy. The college-educated, Ms. Schor found in her polling, are bigger consumers than the less educated, perhaps because college raises their aspirations. Gift-giving for weddings, birthdays, bar mitzvahs and the like requires ever-more expensive presents, sucking an age-old practice "into the larger vortex of consumerism."

Less noticeable spending—expensive vacation travel abroad, say, or having children at Ivy League schools—also plays a growing role in establishing status, and people find ways to advertise these invisibles, with school decals, for example, on the family car.

25   Contrary to mainstream economic thinking, Ms. Schor found, people pass up practical purchases that add value, like aluminum siding. Siding reduces home maintenance and improves insulation, but is often rejected as déclassé. So are high-quality drugstore lipsticks, lacking only the high sticker prices of the high-fashion brands. "In fact, with lipsticks, the higher the price, the more consumers tend to purchase them," she writes, summarizing her research. "This finding flies in the face of the received wisdom that a higher price discourages buyers."

Rereading Actively

1. Uchitelle's article moves through several different topics. With a partner, look over the article, and identify the sections where each different topic is discussed. In your journal, create a brief outline of the article by listing the topic of each section you identify.

2. Much of the article discusses the work of Juliet Schor. With a partner or in a small group, identify passages in the article where Uchitelle turns from talking about Schor's scholarly work to Schor's lifestyle choices as a consumer. Review the article, looking for passages where her lifestyle and spending habits are described. Discuss what impression this information makes on you as a reader.

3. In a small group or with a partner, review Uchitelle's article and develop a list of strategies for "keeping up with the Joneses" versus "keeping up with the Gateses." Discuss whether you see evidence of either of these behaviors among people you know.

4. The article discusses the idea of consumption as a route to a sense of well-being and identity. Review passages that address the relationship between a sense of well-being or identity, and happiness. Then draft in your journal an explanation in your own words of what this relationship means.

5. Even though Louis Uchitelle refrains from stating his own opinion about the topic of his article, you might sense that the spending habits it describes call for an evaluative response. What conclusions do you draw from the work reported here? With a partner, talk about what you believe Uchitelle expects you to think about the topic of the middle class trying to emulate the upper class.

Exploring Your Responses

6. Review the article, noting the way Juliet Schor and Robert Frank discuss consumer "needs." According to these economists, what commodities are necessary? To what extent do you agree? Explain your answer in your journal.

7. In a small group, develop a definition of "necessities." Explain your definition in a journal entry, and reflect on how your group came to the definition it did.

8. Thinking personally, can you imagine a purchase you would be willing to forgo for the sake of "opting out of the game" of keeping up with the Gateses?

9. In your journal, write down in your own words an explanation of "competitive consumption." Try to think of two or three examples from behavior you have observed that illustrate this concept.

CONSUMING PASSIONS
JUDITH WILLIAMSON

Judith Williamson is an artist, journalist, and filmmaker in addition to being an observer of popular culture. She is especially interested in the how contemporary culture affects our perception of women, sex, and power. In her book Consuming Passions *(1986), she focuses on movements in British culture. The introduction to* Consuming Passions *fits nicely into an exploration of consumer culture in the United States for two reasons. First, it analyzes the psychology of consumption, looking into the desires behind buying. Second, it invites people to compare our experiences of consumption with a British woman's exploration of consumer culture.*

We are consuming passions all the time—at the shops, at the movies, in the streets, in the classroom: in the old familiar ways that no longer seem passionate because they are the shared paths of our social world, the known shapes of our waking dreams. Passions born out of imbalance, insecurity, the longing for something more, find forms in the objects and relations available; so that energies fired by what might be, become the fuel for maintaining what already is. Every desire that needs to be dulled, every sharpness at the edge of consciousness that needs to be softened, every yearning that tries to tear through some well-worn weakness in the fabric of daily life, must be woven back into that surface to strengthen it against such exposure. Consuming passions can mean many things: an all-embracing passion, a passion for consumerism; what I am concerned with is the way passions are themselves consumed, contained and channelled into the very social structures they might otherwise threaten.

The subject most avidly consumed in academic work over recent years has been 'desire', which has gained prestige in the theoretical world as a 'radical' topic. But in our society where sensuality is frozen, arrested in the streets of our cities, stretched out over every surface, public imagery has accustomed us to a sexuality that is served up in slices, and theory offers the cold slab of the dissecting table to further this operation. For academic interest in 'desire' is not unrelated to the obsession with 'revealing' sex on every hoarding. People who study things aren't fuelled by different drives from anyone else. Desire has become the subject of numerous books, conferences, articles, lunchtime lectures and so on; but the drive to read endless articles about it in theoretical journals has ultimately the same impetus as the drive to read endless articles about it in *Cosmopolitan* or *Over 21;* it is just that academic work satisfies both appetite *and* duty, and gives an important sense of control. Desire itself is channelled into this endless, obsessive theorizing about desire—harnessed in its own pursuit; and with theory, as with sex, the more elusive its object, the more interesting this pursuit is.

But passion—passion is another story. It is to be written *about,* but not *with:* for the essence of all this academic work on 'desire' is to *stay cool.* In the dominant ideology of our culture, and particularly its more 'intellectual' layers, it has never been fashionable to *over-invest* in any activity. And the bourgeois etiquette whereby any violent display of feeling is automatically taboo, any raising of the voice rude no matter what the reason, merely sets out the pattern of a much wider social phenomenon, the consensus by which any form of the 'extreme' is outlawed. Passions are fine on the cinema screen or in hi-fi advertisements—but not on the demonstration or picket line. For in the peculiar but familiar customs of consumer capitalism, our emotions are directed towards objects, rather than actions.

Marx talks of the commodity as 'congealed labour', the frozen form of a past activity; to the consumer it is also congealed longing, the final form of an active wish. And the shape in which fulfillment is offered seems to become the shape of the wish itself. The need for change, the sense that there must be something else, something different from the way things are, becomes the need for a new purchase, a new hairstyle, a new coat of paint. Consuming products does give a thrill, a sense of both belonging and being different, charging normality with the excitement of the unusual; like the Christmas trips of childhood to Oxford Street, to see the lights—and the lighted windows, passions leaping through plate-glass, filling the forms of a hundred products, tracing the shapes of a hundred hopes. The power of purchase—taking home a new thing, the anticipation of unwrapping—seems to drink up the desire for something new, the restlessness and unease that must be engendered in a society where so many have so little active power, other than to withdraw the labour which produces its prizes. These objects which become the aims of our passions are also shored up to protect us from them, the bricks of a dam held together by the very force it restrains. Passion is a longing that breaks beyond the present, a drive to the future, and yet it must be satisfied in the forms of the past.

5   For passion has no form of its own and yet, like the wind, is only revealed in forms; not a ready-made object, it is what breathes life into objects, transforming movement into shape. It is not found in things, but in ways of doing things; and the *ways* things are done are another kind of shape, less solid to our touch than products, but equally forms in which passions are consumed. These forms, not merely of objects but of our activities, provide at once our passions' boundaries and their expression: they are a shared language, for the shapes of our consciousness run right through society, we inhabit the same spaces, use the same things, speak in the same words. The same structures are found at every 'level': the property laws that underpin bourgeois capital also govern personal relationships, marriage, sex, parenthood; the deferred gratification of emotional investment mirrors the very forms and strategies of economic investment. And they are found on every 'side': the back-to-nature organic commune in Wales or California reveals many of the qualities and values of capitalist 'private enterprise' and distaste for urban politics; the need for constant change in 'radical' styles reflects a consumer system based on built-in obsolescence. The forms of oppression frequently provide the mould for its resistance; thus the Labour Party sets itself the task of producing a strong 'leader' to 'match' Mrs. Thatcher, rather than questioning the *terms* of 'leadership' in the air at the last election. And the highly visible, individual violence focused on by the media in mining communities during the miners' strike, exists in exact proportion to the less immediately visible, social violence of the plans that have caused it—plans for closures which could ravage those communities in an ultimately much more far-reaching way.

     The dominant political notion in Britain has been for decades that of a 'consensus': there are agreed limits to what is and is not acceptable, and although these are constantly shifting, they must always be seen as fixed, since they form the ground-plan of social stability. The shapes of an era are more easily found in its fashions, its furniture, its buildings—whose lines do seem to trace the 'moods' of social change—than in the equally significant outlines of its thoughts and habits, its conceptual categories, which are harder to see because they are precisely what we take for granted.

     How then *can* we 'see' them? If it is in shapes and forms that passions live—as lightning lives in a conductor—it is likely to be in images—in films, photographs, television—that such conduits are most clearly visible. Our emotions are wound into these forms, only to spring back at us with an apparent life of their own. Movies seem to *contain* feelings, two-dimensional photographs seem to *contain* truths. The world itself seems filled with obviousness, full of natural meanings which these media merely reflect. But *we* invest the world with its significance. It doesn't have to be the way it is, or to mean what it does. Who doesn't know, privately, that sense that desire lives, not in ourselves, but in the form of the person desired—in the features of their face, the very lines of their limbs? The contours of our social world are equally charged, the shapes of public life equally evocative, of passions that are in fact our own. And in the most crucial areas of meaning, public and private intersect: for example, in the way that 'Woman' carries a weight of meanings and passions hived off from the social and political world and diverted into 'sexuality', a process seen at its crudest in the way Britain's highest circulation daily paper replaces news with the page 3 pin-up. The whole drive of our society is to translate social into individual forms: movements are represented by 'leaders' ('Arthur Scargill's strike'), economic problems are pictured as personal problems ('too lazy to get a job'), public values are held to be private values ('let the family take over from the Welfare State').

This transformation of social forces into individual terms is not inevitable; but we are used to the same old furnishings of our conceptual world and frightened to grope around in the dark for different ones. It is a relief when half-formed fantasies, new outlines struggling out of old arrangements, fall back into their familiar shapes, daylight certainties stripped of danger. But even in the yearning for normality, for conformity, can be found the passion for a shared world; a sense of possibility expressed in the sensation of the obvious. There is a kind of poignancy for the way things *are,* when the familiar seems to contain more than itself: in the way that a landscape can be filled with longing, a street—as in so many songs—paved with passions. (*'I get a funny feeling inside of me, just walking up and down—Maybe it's because I'm a Londoner that I love London Town'.*) There is a passion when you glimpse what could be in what already is—in a lighted bus through a winter city, on a summer's day in a public park. In the present forms of our passions it is possible to trace, not only how they are consumed, but the very different future they might ultimately produce.

Rereading Actively

1. In a small group, list the people, places, and things that Williamson discusses. Talk about whether Williamson makes effective points in her discussion of these people, places, and things.

2. In your journal, create a paragraph-by-paragraph summary of this article by describing what each paragraph says or does.

3. Williamson continually associates passion and consumption. In your journal, explain her definitions of these words. Are passion and consumption positive or negative? How does Williamson relate them to each other?

4. Williamson draws on some very familiar issues (passion, desire, and sex) and objects (*Cosmopolitan,* malls, and cities) but also on some very abstract ideas—"bourgeois etiquette," "congealed labor," and the like. With a partner, discuss whether this essay has a thesis and conclusion: What is Williamson ultimately trying to say about these familiar issues?

5. With your partner, evaluate whether Williamson's point is persuasive or not. In your journal, note your response.

Exploring Your Responses

6. After rereading the first paragraph and the title, freewrite about the possible meanings of the phrase "consuming passions."

7. Williamson compares the "cool" view academics take of passion with the hot reality of passion. Picture one of the objects of consumption she discusses (e.g., fashion, Christmas, nature, work, entertainment) and write a cool, controlled description of your desires for this object and then write a hot, graphic narrative of how you consume the object.

8. In a small group or with a partner, reflect on your two descriptions in number 7, and discuss which description feels more natural. Which better helps you to understand consuming?

9. Williamson suggests that we can look at the "forms" of our passions in order to see how we consume them. Write a description of the form of one of your passions (how it is controlled, how it is expressed, what activities it causes you to do, how others react to it).

10. In a small group or as a class, discuss whether and how people can purchase our passions. Does buying change our passions? How?

BLUR
STAN DAVIS AND CHRISTOPHER MEYER

In 1998, business analysts Stan Davis and Christopher Meyer, working with consultants at the Young and Ernst Center for Business, published BLUR, *a book that came complete with an interactive website (www.blursight.com) and a mail-in coupon that could win readers $100. Davis—a social scientist who has taught business at Harvard, Columbia, and Boston University—has also written* Future Perfect *and* The Monster Under the Bed, *popular books that explore how business is increasingly driving culture in the United States. In* BLUR, *he and Meyer focus on how three factors—speed, connectivity, and the growth of intangible value—are structuring life. Rather than lamenting the loss of a more traditional society, Davis and Meyer identify and celebrate the opportunities and new freedoms they find in* BLUR.

Has the pace of change accelerated way beyond your comfort zone? Are the rules that guided your decisions in the past no longer reliable? If so, you are just like everyone else who's paying attention. You're not imagining things.

The elements of change that are driving these momentous shifts are based on the fundamental dimensions of the universe itself: time, space, and mass. Since the economy and your business are part of the universe, time, space, and mass are the fundamental dimensions of them as well. Until recently, this notion was too abstract to be very useful. Now, we are realizing the extraordinary power this insight has for the business world.[1]

Almost instantaneous communication and computation, for example, are shrinking time and focusing us on Speed. Connectivity is putting everybody and everything online in one way or another and has led to "the death of distance,"[2] a shrinking of space. Intangible value of all kinds, like service and information, is growing explosively, reducing the importance of tangible mass.

Connectivity, Speed, and Intangibles—the derivatives of time, space, and mass— are blurring the rules and redefining our businesses and our lives. They are destroying solutions, such as mass production, segmented pricing, and standardized jobs, that worked for the relatively slow, unconnected industrial world. The fact is, something enormous *is* happening all around you, enough to make you feel as if you're losing your balance and seeing double. So relax. You are experiencing things as they really are, a BLUR. Ignore these forces and BLUR will make you miserable and your business hopeless. Harness and leverage them, and you can enter the world of BLUR, move to its cadence and once again see the world clearly.

5 What will you see? A meltdown of all traditional boundaries. In the BLUR world, products and services are merging. Buyers sell and sellers buy. Neat value chains are messy economic webs. Homes are offices. No longer is there a clear line between structure and process, owning and using, knowing and learning, real and virtual. Less and

less separates employee and employer. In the world of capital—itself as much a liability as an asset—value moves so fast you can't tell stock from flow. On every front, opposites are blurring.

The Exchange: Every Buyer a Seller, Every Seller a Buyer

The difference between buyers and sellers blurs to the point where both are in a web of economic, information, and emotional exchange.

When Harley-Davidson customers buy their expensive, premium motorcycles, they're paying for much more than a high-flying hog. They are buying entry to a community of like-minded devotees who share a passion for all things Harley, be they branded clothing, decals, or even deodorants. The most committed bikers—whether they ride on the front of the seat or the back—further affirm their indelible loyalty to the brand with Harley-Davidson tattoos.

When Zagat's guides make money, collecting and publishing foodies' ratings of restaurants, the publisher is managing a multiple exchange: Customers get to compare notes and tell restaurant owners what they think of their offers, and they get a copy of the guide; restaurateurs get feedback on how to build business.

When Citibank provides private chat rooms on the Web for its customers, it enables them to get closer to each other—and to the bank. They can get advice on such topics as investing in real estate, or swap information with people of similar professional and financial goals. And Citicorp learns a lot about customer likes and dislikes.

Commerce used to be so simple. There were sellers and there were buyers. The seller brought a product or service to the table, and the buyer brought cash. The transaction was straightforward: The price was the price. Now, in an increasing number of business dealings, it's more difficult to determine just who is the buyer and who is the seller. A lot of the time, each is both. And even when those roles are clear, the form of payment is more convoluted. Parties are being compensated not just in money but in things like information and emotion. Thanks to the forces of BLUR—particularly the rise of Intangibles as a source of value and the spread of Connectivity—transactions are becoming anything but straightforward. The one thing you can be sure of is that the price is no longer the price.

10   A simple example is *slotting allowances,* the fees a consumer-goods manufacturer pays retailers for shelf space for a new product. For a foot of prime, eye-level position in the cookie aisle, you might pay up to $1,000 per shelf.[3] Think about this for a moment. The retailer is the customer who buys product from the manufacturer, the seller. So what's the seller doing giving money to the buyer? The manufacturer is buying marketing services from the retailer at the same time he's selling product to the retailer. They are engaging in an exchange.

At first glance, such payments seem like downright extortion. But they make good business sense when you realize that, until the product starts to sell, the retailer's real estate is more valuable than the product itself. The opportunity cost is high. The manufacturers know this, and they pony up the cash.

The distinction gets very hazy when you note that monetary payment is only a part of any given transaction. The real news in the BLUR economy is that other things—especially information and emotional engagement—make up a growing proportion of the value being exchanged in both directions. We have reached the point in our story where the Intangibles get serious.

Amazon.com, the online bookstore, is an elegant example. If the whole of that business were simply mail-order books, it would be dead in a week. Even with discounted prices to offset mailing costs, book buyers wouldn't tolerate the shipping delay. Amazon.com understands that its real edge over conventional bookstores is its capability to provide much more (and customized) information, collect and post reader recommendations, and create communities of like-minded people.

Customers pay Amazon.com not only in money but in various kinds of information that are valuable to its sales and marketing efforts. The Web site collects reader reviews and, each month, pays $1,000 in book vouchers to the amateur critic who submits the best-written item. The site also tracks virtual shopping baskets, so that it can inform someone looking at a title as to which other books were selected by fellow shoppers who bought that particular book. Meanwhile, thousands of visitors have alerted Amazon.com to their favorite authors, subjects, and book categories, and asked to be notified when new titles appear. That kind of self-selected, specialized marketing list is a direct marketer's dream.

15 Examples like this are going to become more the norm, which is why definitions of the terms "buyer" and "seller" aren't accurate anymore. The imply that the only exchange is the traditional, two-way affair where money is swapped for goods or services. The truth is, there are all kinds of value flying back and forth in a connected economy. And all these exchanges are happening so fast that there's no time—or need—to translate them into precise monetary terms. "Buyer" and "seller" just aren't descriptive enough of what's really going on. What we need to talk about instead is mutual exchange.

* * *

Buyer Redux

A common theme emerges from this discussion of exchange: The traditional buyer in the equation is gaining power and leverage relative to the seller. In the industrial model, the economic benefits of mass production created a one-way relationship, in which the manufacturer defined the product, set the price, and established the time and place of purchase. The buyer was price taker, as economists would say, and the seller a price maker. This imbalance is being redressed. After all, it wasn't always this way; the local grocer used to tell you what was good today (information) and ask about your kids (emotion). And you might point out a spot or a bruise on the melon and get a better price (economic). But now, these relationships needn't be local, or quite as simple.

In all markets, rather than simply being expected to fork over cash for an offer, the user is in a position to get economic benefits from a two-way, multifaceted exchange. Rather than just being a passive recipient of sporadic information, he is seen as a source of valuable insight and opinion. And instead of being a sap to be manipulated by emotionally charged advertising messages, he is actively engaged in an exchange of pride, satisfaction, and loyalty.

When this transformation is complete, the traditional transaction will be converted into an exchange, blurring the roles of all parties. The table below identifies some of the dimensions of this transformation.

Characteristics of the Exchange

| Characteristics | Traditional Transactions | | *BLUR* Transactions |
	Seller	Buyer	Exchange
Value Role	Create	Consume	Both Create and Consume
Value Received	Money	Product or Service Utility	Economic, Informational, and Emotional Value
Communication Role	Sender	Receiver	Interacter
Information Role	In Control	Limited Access	Shared Access and Creation
Relevant Time	Business Hours	Business Hours	Continual and Connected
Relevant Space	Point of Sale	Marketplace	Connected Anywhere

NOTES

1. This was the foundation of Stan's influential book, *Future Perfect* (Addison-Wesley, 1987, 1996).
2. Frances Cairncross, *The Death of Distance* (Boston: Harvard Business School Press, 1997).
3. The experience of RW Frookies, Inc., referenced by INC. Online, "Cookie Monsters," by Paul B. Brown, February 1989.

Rereading Actively

1. What are some of the most obvious moves that Davis and Meyer make to invite their reader into their introduction (consider direct references to the reader, examples, terms, and claims)? Who do they seem to be talking to, and what kind of reading experience is forming?

2. With a partner, brainstorm examples from your experience that illustrate the three forces of BLUR: speed, connectivity, and intangible value. Talk about whether you live in the culture that Davis and Meyer describe and whether you share the experience that they believe most of their readers share. Be prepared to share your discoveries with the class.

3. Review the examples that open the "exchange" section. In your journal, note the characteristics that these examples share and draft a paragraph that explains why Davis and Meyer might have opened this section with these examples.

4. In your journal, summarize Davis and Meyer's description of a transaction in a traditional economy and a transaction in BLUR.

Exploring Your Responses

5. Use the opening question in the excerpt—"Has the pace of change accelerated beyond your comfort zone?"—to launch a freewrite. How aware are you of changes in communications, employment, and value? Do you feel like you have a place in the BLUR world? Do you like that place?

6. In a small group, brainstorm exchanges that you make on a regular basis. Start with concrete exchanges like buying a cup of coffee, a CD, or a pair of khaki pants and then move on to more complex exchanges like eating at a restaurant, communicating online, or researching a purchase or a class project. With your group, pick one, and discuss how you go about this exchange and the values you associate with it. Be prepared to share with the class the results of your group's discussion.

BACKGROUND ASSIGNMENTS

If we were to stop and think about our behavior as shoppers, we might explain that our choice to spend money to buy things is based on *utility:* We purchase a thing because it is useful. We would perhaps also recognize that many of our choices are based on desires, that we attribute value that goes beyond utility to certain objects, brand names, or objects for which we willingly exchange our time and labor (in the form of money we have earned). How do these objects come to carry such significance for us? What compels our desire for them? How do our actions as consumers fit into a larger cultural pattern? The readings included here probe these questions, offering different perspectives on the relationships linking individual choices and life in a consumer culture.

Making Connections

1. One of us was recently blessed with the birth of a daughter. Among the surprises awaiting my wife and me as new parents was the sudden inundation of baby catalogues flooding our mailbox. Both Sagoff and Uchitelle reflect on how our culture's emphasis on consumption affects human relationships. Drawing on their claims, describe how one relationship you are familiar with—for example, child/parent, peer/peer, employer/employee—seems to be affected by consumer culture.

2. Using the claims Williamson and Gladwell make about the impact consumerism has on the desires of individuals, develop an analysis of the desire a consumer who you know has for a particular product (consider analyzing yourself). Pay attention to the way the product is represented, the way the consumer is encouraged to think about her- or himself in relationship to the product, and the ways he or she will really use the product.

3. Uchitelle and Williamson probe different assumptions about what it takes to acquire a good life and well-being in a healthy society. Write an essay that identifies the assumptions they explore and develops your own position in relationship to theirs.

4. Sagoff and Davis and Meyer see very different twenty-first centuries for the citizens of the global market. Drawing on their arguments, write an essay that explains and justifies your own sense of the future we can expect if we keep consuming as we do.

Collaborative Exchanges

1. With two or three classmates, review Gladwell's essay and visit and assess a local retail space as Gladwell might. Once you have done this work, meet as a group, compare your observations, and draft a collaborative analysis of how the store directed your attention. Be prepared to share your analysis and to talk about how well, according to the criteria Paco Underhill has developed, the store works.

2. In a small group, brainstorm types of commodities that men and women seem to consume differently, commodities like fashion, food, cars, recreation, entertainment, living spaces, and so on. Focus on a single commodity that you have all purchased or consumed, identifying similarities

and differences in how you perceive the commodity, how you consume it, and how it affects your sense of gender. Work out a general response to these questions and be prepared to share your perceptions and speculations with the class.

3. With two or three classmates, discuss your general contentment with life in a consumer world, focusing on three or four points about which you generally agree or disagree. Use arguments put forward by Sagoff or Davis and Meyer to develop those points, noting whether you come closer together or drift farther apart. Be prepared to share with the class the points you focused on and the general attitudes you have.

 Net Approaches

1. Visit the Web site of a local or regional newspaper, magazine, or other news site once a day for the next week. (You may decide to use the AJR Newslink <ajr.newslink.org> to help you find an online news site.) In a daily journal entry, keep track of the number of hits a search for "consumer culture" brings up and jot down basic descriptions of three different hits. At week's end, draft a synthesis of what you found.

2. Point your browser to HotBot.com or some other search engine and perform a search that ties together the terms "consumerism" and "culture." Sort through twenty or thirty hits, and then visit two sites that appear to take a positive view of consumerism and two sites that take a negative view. Be prepared to tell the class what sites you visited and how those sites spin consumerism.

3. Go to <www.liszt.com> and, following the internal instructions, subscribe to the digest list of the American Association of Family/Consumer Science Critical Issues (AAFCS-CI). Listen in to this listserv that "facilitates communications among AAFCS-CI subcommittee members" and after four or five days, draft a summary of the issues the AAFCS-CI members share and compare their concerns with those voiced in the readings. (If you have trouble subscribing to AAFCS-CI, subscribe to the list serve of another consumer-oriented listserv.)

CASE-IN-POINT READINGS

Adventures into Shopping Malls:
Acquiring Goods, Creating Community

The readings in this case in point examine the shopping mall as an important site of exchange in our consumer culture. The writers here approach the mall from a variety of perspectives, but underlying their different views are two general issues. The first pertains to the views that may be taken of the economic system in which consumers in the United States play a central part. Our spending as consumers, in the mechanical metaphor of much economic writing, drives the engine of production. In this view, the "getting and spending" that is made so visible in the shopping mall is a good thing, and the mall itself stands as a monument to our prosperous society. At the same time, expressions of this prosperity can be seen as wasteful, profligate—not just unnecessary but irresponsible.

The second tension pertains to individual behavior: As consumers, as participants in consumer culture, do we behave rationally and in our own best interests? When we shop, what guides our decisions? Viewed this way, the mall appears to be both inviting and deceptive—a space engineered to separate us from our money whether we mean to be or not. On the other hand, the mall also becomes a social arena defined not simply by shopping, but also by the interactions among people that it makes possible.

ENCLOSED. ENCYCLOPEDIC. ENDURED. ONE WEEK AT THE MALL OF AMERICA
DAVID R. GUTERSON

David R. Guterson is a former high school English teacher and the author of a best-selling novel, Snow Falling on Cedars *(1994), and* East of the Mountains *(1999), as well as work on education in America. Guterson's essay, "Enclosed. Encyclopedic. Endured. One Week at the Mall of America," originally appeared in* Harper's *in 1993. (*Harper's *audience tends to be well-educated liberals concerned with social justice.) Guterson relates his observations in the Mall of America (MOA) as he attempts to interpret the significance of MOA as a cultural phenomenon. In keeping with abiding themes in his work, Guterson focuses his account of MOA on the issue of community, asking what sense of community is produced by the massive, enclosed retail structures that MOA exemplifies.*

Last April, on a visit to the new Mall of America near Minneapolis, I carried with me the public-relations press kit provided for the benefit of reporters. It included an assortment of "fun facts" about the mall: 140,000 hot dogs sold each week, 10,000 permanent jobs, 44 escalators and 17 elevators, 12,750 parking places, 13,300 short tons of steel, $1 million in cash disbursed weekly from 8 automatic-teller machines. Opened in the summer of 1992, the mall was built on the 78-acre site of the former Metropolitan Stadium, a five-minute drive from the Minneapolis–St. Paul International Airport. With 4.2 million square feet of floor space—including twenty-two times the retail footage of the average American shopping center—the Mall of America was "the largest fully enclosed combination retail and family entertainment complex in the United States."

Eleven thousand articles, the press kit warned me, had already been written on the mall. Four hundred trees had been planted in its gardens, $625 million had been spent to build it, 350 stores had been leased. Three thousand bus tours were anticipated each year along with a half-million Canadian visitors and 200,000 Japanese tourists. Sales were projected at $650 million for 1993 and at $1 billion for 1996. Donny and Marie Osmond had visited the mall, as had Janet Jackson and Sally Jesse Raphael, Arnold Schwarzenegger, and the 1994 Winter Olympic Committee. The mall was five times larger than Red Square and twenty times larger than St. Peter's Basilica; it incorporated 2.3 miles of hallways and almost twice as much steel as the Eiffel Tower. It was also home to the nation's largest indoor theme park, a place called Knott's Camp Snoopy.

On the night I arrived, a Saturday, the mall was spotlit dramatically in the manner of a Las Vegas casino. It resembled, from the outside, a castle or fort, the Emerald City

Figure 3.1 The Mall of America

or Never-Never Land, impossibly large and vaguely unreal, an unbroken, windowless multi-storied edifice the size of an airport terminal. Surrounded by parking lots and new freeway ramps, monolithic and imposing in the manner of a walled city, it loomed brightly against the Minnesota night sky with the disturbing magnetism of a mirage.

I knew already that the Mall of America had been imagined by its creators not merely as a marketplace but as a national tourist attraction, an immense zone of entertainments. Such a conceit raised provocative questions, for our architecture testifies to our view of ourselves and to the condition of our souls. Large buildings stand as markers in the lives of nations and in the stream of a people's history. Thus I could only ask myself: Here was a new structure that had cost more than half a billion dollars to erect—what might it tell us about ourselves? If the Mall of America was part of America, what was that going to mean?

5   I passed through one of the mall's enormous entranceways and took myself inside. Although from a distance the Mall of America had appeared menacing—exuding the ambience of a monstrous hallucination—within it turned out to be simply a shopping mall, certainly more vast than other malls but in tone and aspect, design and feel, not readily distinguishable from them. Its nuances were instantly familiar as the generic features of the American shopping mall at the tail end of the twentieth century: polished stone, polished tile, shiny chrome and brass, terrazzo floors, gazebos. From third-floor vistas, across vaulted spaces, the Mall of America felt endlessly textured—glass-enclosed elevators, neon-tube lighting, bridges, balconies, gas lamps, vaulted skylights—and densely crowded with hordes of people circumambulating in an endless promenade. Yet despite the mall's expansiveness, it elicited claustrophobia, sensory deprivation, and an unnerving disorientation. Everywhere I went I spied other

pilgrims who had found, like me, that the straight way was lost and that the YOU ARE HERE landmarks on the map kiosks referred to nothing in particular.

Getting lost, feeling lost, being lost—these states of mind are intentional features of the mall's psychological terrain. There are, one notices, no clocks or windows, nothing to distract the shopper's psyche from the alternate reality the mall conjures. Here we are free to wander endlessly and to furtively watch our fellow wanderers, thousands upon thousands of milling strangers who have come with the intent of losing themselves in the mall's grand, stimulating design. For a few hours we share some common ground—a fantasy of infinite commodities and comforts—and then we drift apart forever. The mall exploits our acquisitive instincts without honoring our communal requirements, our eternal desire for discourse and intimacy, needs that until the twentieth century were traditionally met in our marketplaces but that are not met at all in giant shopping malls.

On this evening a few thousand young people had descended on the mall in pursuit of alcohol and entertainment. They had come to Gators, Hooters, and Knuckleheads, Puzzles, Fat Tuesday, and Ltl Ditty's. At Players, a sports bar, the woman beside me introduced herself as "the pregnant wife of an Iowa pig farmer" and explained that she had driven five hours with friends to "do the mall party scene together." She left and was replaced by Kathleen from Minnetonka, who claimed to have "a real shopping thing—I can't go a week without buying new clothes. I'm not fulfilled until I buy something."

Later a woman named Laura arrived, with whom Kathleen was acquainted. "I *am* the mall," she announced ecstatically upon discovering I was a reporter. "I'd move in here if I could bring my dog," she added. "This place is heaven, it's a *mecca*."

"We egg each other on," explained Kathleen, calmly puffing on a cigarette. "It's like, sort of, an addiction."

10   "You want the truth?" Laura asked. "I'm constantly suffering from megamall withdrawal. I come here all the time."

KATHLEEN: "It's a sickness. It's like cocaine or something; it's a drug."

LAURA: "Kathleen's got this thing about buying, but I just need to *be* here. If I buy something it's an added bonus."

KATHLEEN: "She buys stuff all the time; don't listen."

LAURA: "Seriously, I feel sorry for other malls. They're so small and *boring*."

Kathleen seemed to think about this: "Richdale Mall," she blurted finally. She rolled her eyes and gestured with her cigarette. "Oh, my God, Laura. Why did we even *go* there?"

There is, of course, nothing naturally abhorrent in the human impulse to dwell in marketplaces or the urge to buy, sell, and trade. Rural Americans traditionally looked forward to the excitement and sensuality of market day; Native Americans traveled long distances to barter and trade at sprawling, festive encampments. In Persian bazaars and in the ancient Greek agoras the very soul of the community was preserved and could be seen, felt, heard, and smelled as it might be nowhere else. All over the planet the humblest of people have always gone to market with hope in their hearts and in expectation of something beyond mere goods—seeking a place where humanity is temporarily in ascendance, a palette for the senses, one another.

But the illicit possibilities of the marketplace also have long been acknowledged. The Persian bazaar was closed at sundown; the Greek agora was off-limits to those who had been charged with certain crimes. One myth of the Old West we still carry with us is that market day presupposes danger; the faithful were advised to make purchases quickly and repair without delay to the farm, lest their attraction to the pleasures of the marketplace erode their purity of spirit.

In our collective discourse the shopping mall appears with the tract house, the freeway, and the backyard barbecue as a product of the American postwar years, a testament to contemporary necessities and desires and an invention not only peculiarly American but peculiarly of our own era too. Yet the mall's varied and far-flung predecessors—the covered bazaars of the Middle East, the stately arcades of Victorian England, Italy's vaulted and skylit gallerias, Asia's monsoon-protected urban markets—all suggest that the rituals of indoor shopping, although in their nuances not often like our own, are nevertheless broadly known. The late twentieth-century American contribution has been to transform the enclosed bazaar into an economic institution that is vastly profitable yet socially enervated, one that redefines in fundamental ways the human relationship to the marketplace. At the Mall of America—an extreme example—we discover ourselves thoroughly lost among strangers in a marketplace intentionally designed to serve no community needs.

15 In the strict sense the Mall of America is not a marketplace at all—the soul of a community expressed as a place—but rather a tourist attraction. Its promoters have peddled it to the world at large as something more profound than a local marketplace and as a destination with deep implications. "I believe we can make Mall of America stand for all of America," asserted the mall's general manager, John Wheeler, in a promotional video entitled *There's a Place for Fun in Your Life.* "I believe there's a shopper in all of us," added the director of marketing, Maureen Hooley. The mall has memorialized its opening-day proceedings by producing a celebratory videotape: Ray Charles singing "America the Beautiful," a laser show followed by fireworks, "The Star-Spangled Banner" and "The Stars and Stripes Forever," the Gatlin Brothers, and Peter Graves. "Mall of America …," its narrator intoned. "The name alone conjures up images of greatness, of a retail complex so magnificent it could only happen in America."

Indeed, on the day the mall opened, Miss America visited. The mall's logo—a red, white, and blue star bisected by a red, white, and blue ribbon—decorated everything from the mall itself to coffee mugs and the flanks of buses. The idea, director of tourism Colleen Hayes told me, was to position America's largest mall as an institution on the scale of Disneyland or the Grand Canyon, a place simultaneously iconic and totemic, a revered symbol of the United States and a mecca to which the faithful would flock in pursuit of all things purchasable.

On Sunday I wandered the hallways of the pleasure dome with the sensation that I had entered an M. C. Escher drawing—there was no such thing as up or down, and the escalators all ran backward. A 1993 Ford Probe GT was displayed as if popping out of a giant packing box; a full-size home, complete with artificial lawn, had been built in the mall's rotunda. At the Michael Ricker Pewter Gallery I came across a miniature tableau of a pewter dog peeing on a pewter man's leg; at Hologram Land I pondered 3-D hallucinations of the Medusa and Marilyn Monroe. I passed a kiosk called The Sportsman's Wife; I stood beside a life-size statue of the Hamm's Bear, carved out of pine and available for $1,395 at a store called Minnesot-ah! At Pueblo Spirit I examined a "dream catcher"—a small hoop made from deer sinew and willow twigs and designed to be hung over its owner's bed as a tactic for filtering bad dreams. For a while I sat in front of Glamour Shots and watched while women were groomed and brushed for photo sessions yielding high-fashion self-portraits at $34.95 each. There was no stopping, no slowing down. I passed Mug Me, Queen for a Day, and Barnyard Buddies, and stood in the Brookstone store examining a catalogue: a gopher "eliminator" for $40 (it's a vibrating, anodized-aluminum stake), a "no-stoop" shoehorn for $10, a nose-hair trimmer for $18. At the arcade inside Knott's Camp Snoopy I watched while teenagers played Guardians of the 'Hood, Total Carnage, Final Fight, and Varth Operation Thunderstorm; a small crowd of them had gathered around a lean, cool character who stood calmly shooting video cow-pokes in a game called Mad Dog McCree. Left thumb on his silver belt buckle, biceps pulsing, he banged away without remorse while dozens of his enemies crumpled and died in alleyways and dusty streets.

At Amazing Pictures a teenage boy had his photograph taken as a bodybuilder—his face smoothly grafted onto a rippling body—then proceeded to purchase this pleasing image on a poster, a sweatshirt, and a coffee mug. At Painted Tipi there was wild rice for sale, hand-harvested from Leech Lake, Minnesota. At Animalia I came across a polyresin figurine of a turtle retailing for $3,200. At Bloomingdale's I pondered a denim shirt with its sleeves ripped away, the sort of thing available at used-clothing stores (the "grunge look," a Bloomingdale's employee explained), on sale for $125. Finally, at a gift shop in Knott's Camp Snoopy, I came across a game called Electronic Mall Madness, put out by Milton Bradley. On the box, three twelve-year-old girls with good features happily vied to beat one another to the game-board mall's best sales.

At last I achieved an enforced self-arrest, anchoring myself against a bench while the mall tilted on its axis. Two pubescent girls in retainers and braces sat beside me sipping coffees topped with whipped cream and chocolate sprinkles, their shopping bags gathered tightly around their legs, their eyes fixed on the passing crowds. They came, they said, from Shakopee—"It's nowhere," one of them explained. The mega-mall, she added, was "a buzz at first, but now it seems pretty normal. 'Cept my parents are like Twenty Questions every time I want to come here. 'Specially since the shooting."

20   On a Sunday night, she elaborated, three people had been wounded when shots were fired in a dispute over a San Jose Sharks jacket. "In the *mall*," her friend reminded me. "Right here at megamall. A shooting."

"It's like nowhere's safe," the first added.

They sipped their coffees and explicated for me the plot of a film they saw as relevant, a horror movie called *Dawn of the Dead*, which they had each viewed a half-dozen times. In the film, they explained, apocalypse had come, and the survivors had repaired to a shopping mall as the most likely place to make their last stand in a poisoned, impossible world. And this would have been perfectly all right, they insisted, except that the place had also attracted hordes of the infamous living dead—sentient corpses who had not relinquished their attraction to indoor shopping."

I moved on and contemplated a computerized cash register in the infant's section of the Nordstrom store: "The Answer Is Yes!!!" its monitor reminded clerks. "Customer Service Is Our Number One Priority!" Then back at Bloomingdale's I contemplated a bank of televisions playing incessantly an advertisement for Egoïste, a men's cologne from Chanel. In the ad a woman on a wrought-iron balcony tossed her black

hair about and screamed long and passionately; then there were many women screaming passionately, too, and throwing balcony shutters open and closed, and this was all
followed by a bottle of the cologne displayed where I could get a good look at it. The
brief, strange drama repeated itself until I could no longer stand it.

America's first fully enclosed shopping center—Southdale Center, in Edina,
Minnesota—is a ten-minute drive from the Mall of America and thirty-six years its
senior. (It is no coincidence that the Twin Cities area is such a prominent player in
mall history: Minnesota is subject to the sort of severe weather that makes climate-
controlled shopping seductive.) Opened in 1956, Southdale spawned an era of fervid
mall construction and generated a vast new industry. Shopping centers proliferated
so rapidly that by the end of 1992, says the National Research Bureau, there were nearly
39,000 of them operating everywhere across the country. But while malls recorded a
much-ballyhooed success in the America of the 1970s and early 1980s, they gradually
became less profitable to run as the exhausted and overwhelmed American worker
inevitably lost interest in leisure shopping. Pressed for time and short on money, shoppers turned to factory outlet centers, catalogue purchasing, and "category killers" (specialty stores such as Home Depot and Price Club) at the expense of shopping malls.
The industry, unnerved, re-invented itself, relying on smaller and more convenient
local centers—especially the familiar neighborhood strip mall—and building far fewer
large regional malls in an effort to stay afloat through troubled times. With the advent
of cable television's Home Shopping Network and the proliferation of specialty catalogue retailers (whose access to computerized market research has made them, in the
Nineties, powerful competitors), the mall industry reeled yet further. According to the
International Council of Shopping Centers, new mall construction in 1992 was a third
of what it had been in 1989, and the value of mall-construction contracts dropped 60
percent in the same three-year period.

25   Anticipating a future in which millions of Americans will prefer to shop in the
security of their living rooms—conveniently accessing online retail companies as a
form of quiet evening entertainment—the mall industry, after less than forty years,
experienced a full-blown mid-life crisis. It was necessary for the industry to re-invent
itself once more, this time with greater attentiveness to the qualities that would allow
it to endure relentless change. Anxiety-ridden and sapped of vitality, mall builders fell
back on an ancient truth, one capable of sustaining them through troubled seasons:
they discovered what humanity had always understood, that shopping and frivolity go
hand in hand and are inherently symbiotic. *If you build it fun, they will come.*

The new bread-and-circuses approach to mall building was first ventured in 1985
by the four Ghermezian brothers—Raphael, Nader, Bahman, and Eskandar—builders
of Canada's $750 million West Edmonton Mall, which included a water slide, an arti-
ficial lake, a miniature-golf course, a hockey rink, and forty-seven rides in an amusement park known as Fantasyland. The complex quickly generated sales revenues at
twice the rate per square foot of retail space that could be squeezed from a conventional outlet mall, mostly by developing its own shopping synergy: people came for a
variety of reasons and to do a variety of things. West Edmonton's carnival atmosphere,
it gradually emerged, lubricated pocketbooks and inspired the sort of impulse buying
on which malls everywhere thrive. To put the matter another way, it was time for a
shopping-and-pleasure palace to be attempted in the United States.

After selling the Mall of America concept to Minnesotans in 1985, the Ghermezians joined forces with their American counterparts—Mel and Herb Simon of Indianapolis, owners of the NBA's Indiana Pacers and the nation's second-largest developers of shopping malls. The idea, in the beginning, was to outdo West Edmonton by building a mall far larger and more expensive—something visionary, a wonder of the world—and to include such attractions as fashionable hotels, an elaborate tour de force aquarium, and a monorail to the Minneapolis–St. Paul airport. Eventually the project was down-scaled substantially: a million square feet of floor space was eliminated, the construction budget was cut, and the aquarium and hotels were never built (reserved, said marketing director Maureen Hooley, for "phase two" of the mall's development). Japan's Mitsubishi Bank, Mitsui Trust, and Chuo Trust together put up a reported $400 million to finance the cost of construction, and Teachers Insurance and Annuity Association (the majority owner of the Mall of America) came through with another $225 million. At a total bill of $625 million, the mall was ultimately a less ambitious project than its forebear up north on the Canadian plains, and neither as large nor as gaudy. Reflecting the economy's downturn, the parent companies of three of the mall's anchor tenants—Sears, Macy's, and Bloomingdale's—were battling serious financial trouble and needed substantial transfusions from mall developers to have their stores ready by opening day.

The mall expects to spend millions on marketing itself during its initial year of operation and has lined up the usual corporate sponsors—Ford, Pepsi, US West—in an effort to build powerful alliances. Its public-relations representatives travel to towns such as Rapid City, South Dakota, and Sioux City, Iowa, in order to drum up interest within the Farm Belt. Northwest Airlines, another corporate sponsor, offers package deals from London and Tokyo and fare adjustments for those willing to come from Bismarck, North Dakota; Cedar Rapids, Iowa; and Kalamazoo or Grand Rapids, Michigan. Calling itself a "premier tourism destination," the mall draws from a primary tourist market that incorporates the eleven Midwest states (and two Canadian provinces) lying within a day's drive of its parking lots. It also estimates that in its first six months of operation, 5.3 million out of 16 million visitors came from beyond the Twin Cities metropolitan area.

The mall has forecast a much-doubted figure of 46 million annual visits by 1996—four times the number of annual visits to Disneyland, for example, and twelve times the visits to the Grand Canyon. The number, Maureen Hooley explained, seems far less absurd when one takes into account that mall pilgrims make far more repeat visits—as many as eighty in a single year—than visitors to theme parks such as Disneyland. Relentless advertising and shrewd promotion, abetted by the work of journalists like myself, assure the mall that visitors will come in droves—at least for the time being. The national media have comported themselves as if the new mall were a place of light and promise, full of hope and possibility. Meanwhile the Twin Cities' media have been shameless: on opening night Minneapolis's WCCO-TV aired a one-hour mall special, hosted by local news anchors Don Shelby and Colleen Needles, and the *St. Paul Pioneer Press* (which was named an "official" sponsor of the opening) dedicated both a phone line and a weekly column to answering esoteric mall questions. Not to be outdone, the *Minneapolis Star Tribune* developed a special graphic to draw readers to mall stories and printed a vast Sunday supplement before opening day under the heading A WHOLE NEW MALLGAME. By the following Wednesday all perspective was in eclipse: the local press reported that at 9:05 A.M., the mall's Victoria's Secret outlet had recorded its first sale, a pair of blue/green silk men's boxer shorts; that mall developers Mel and Herb Simon ate black-bean soup for lunch at 12:30 P.M.; that Kimberly Levis, four years old, constructed a rectangular column nineteen bricks high at the mall's Lego Imagination Center; and that mall officials had retained a plumber on standby in case difficulties arose with the mall's toilets.

30   From all of this coverage—and from the words you now read—the mall gains status as a phenomenon worthy of our time and consideration: place as celebrity. The media encourage us to visit our megamall in the obligatory fashion we flock to *Jurassic Park*—because it is there, all glitter and glow, a piece of the terrain, a season's diversion, an assumption on the cultural landscape. All of us will want to be in on the conversation and, despite ourselves, we will go.

Lost in the fun house I shopped till I dropped, but the scale of the mall eventually overwhelmed me and I was unable to make a purchase. Finally I met Chuck Brand on a bench in Knott's Camp Snoopy; he was seventy-two and, in his personal assessment of it, had lost at least 25 percent of his mind. "It's fun being a doozy," he confessed to me. "The security cops got me figured and keep their distance. I don't get hassled for hanging out, not shopping. Because the deal is, when you're seventy-two, man, you're just about all done shopping."

After forty-seven years of selling houses in Minneapolis, Chuck comes to the mall every day. He carries a business card with his picture on it, his company name and phone number deleted and replaced by his pager code. His wife drops him at the mall at 10:00 A.M. each morning and picks him up again at six; in between he sits and watches. "I can't sit home and do nothing," he insisted. When I stood to go he assured me he understood: I was young and had things I had to do. "Listen," he added, "thanks for talking to me, man. I've been sitting in this mall for four months now and nobody ever said nothing."

The next day I descended into the mall's enormous basement, where its business offices are located. "I'm sorry to have to bring this up," my prearranged mall guide, Michelle Biesiada, greeted me. "But you were seen talking to one of our housekeepers—one of the people who empty the garbage?—and really, you aren't supposed to do that."

Later we sat in the mall's security center, a subterranean computerized command post where two uniformed officers manned a bank of television screens. The Mall of America, it emerged, employed 109 surveillance cameras to monitor the various activities of its guests, and had plans to add yet more. There were cameras in the food courts and parking lots, in the hallways and in Knott's Camp Snoopy. From where we sat, it was possible to monitor thirty-six locations simultaneously; it was also possible, with the use of a zoom feature, to narrow in on an object as small as a hand, a license plate, or a wallet.

35   While we sat in the darkness of the security room, enjoying the voyeuristic pleasures it allowed (I, for one, felt a giddy sense of power), a security guard noted something of interest occurring in one of the parking lots. The guard engaged a camera's zoom feature, and soon we were given to understand that a couple of bored shoppers were enjoying themselves by fornicating in the front seat of a parked car. An officer was dispatched to knock on their door and discreetly suggest that they move themselves along; the Mall of America was no place for this. "If they want to have sex they'll have to go elsewhere," a security officer told me. "We don't have anything against sex, per se, but we don't want it happening in our parking lots."

I left soon afterward for a tour of the mall's basement, a place of perpetual concrete corridors and home to a much-touted recyclery. Declaring itself "the most environmentally conscious shopping center in the industry," the Mall of America claims to recycle up to 80 percent of its considerable refuse and points to its "state-of-the-art" recycling system as a symbol of its dedication to Mother Earth. Yet Rick Doering of Browning-Ferris Industries—the company contracted to manage the mall's 700 tons of monthly garbage—described the on-site facility as primarily a public-relations gambit that actually recycles only a third of the mall's tenant waste and little of what is discarded by its thousands of visitors; furthermore, he admitted, the venture is unprofitable to Browning-Ferris, which would find it far cheaper to recycle the mall's refuse somewhere other than in its basement.

A third-floor "RecycleNOW Center," located next to Macy's and featuring educational exhibits, is designed to enhance the mall's self-styled image as a national recycling leader. Yet while the mall's developers gave Macy's $35 million to cover most of its "build-out" expenses (the cost of transforming the mall's basic structure into finished, customer-ready floor space), Browning-Ferris got nothing in build-out costs and operates the center at a total loss, paying rent equivalent to that paid by the mall's retailers. As a result, the company has had to look for ways to keep its costs to a minimum, and the mall's garbage is now sorted by developmentally disabled adults working a conveyor belt in the basement. Doering and I stood watching them as they picked at a stream of paper and plastic bottles; when I asked about their pay, he flinched and grimaced, then deflected me toward another supervisor, who said that wages were based on daily productivity. Did this mean that they made less than minimum wage? I inquired. The answer was yes.

Upstairs once again, I hoped for relief from the basement's oppressive, concrete gloom, but the mall felt densely crowded and with panicked urgency I made an effort to leave. I ended up instead at Knott's Camp Snoopy—the seven-acre theme park at the center of the complex—a place intended to alleviate claustrophobia by "bringing the outdoors indoors." Its interior landscape, the press kit claims, "was inspired by Minnesota's natural habitat—forests, meadows, river banks, and marshes ..." And "everything you see, feel, smell and hear adds to the illusion that it's summertime, seventy degrees and you're outside enjoying the awesome splendor of the Minnesota woods."

Creators of this illusion had much to contend with, including sixteen carnival-style midway rides, such as the Pepsi Ripsaw, the Screaming Yellow Eagle, Paul Bunyan's Log Chute by Brawny, Tumbler, Truckin', and Huff 'n' Puff; fifteen places for visitors to eat, such as Funnel Cakes, Stick Dogs and Campfire Burgers, Taters, Pizza Oven, and Wilderness Barbecue; seven shops with names like Snoopy's Boutique, Joe Cool's Hot Shop, and Camp Snoopy Toys; and such assorted attractions as Pan for Gold, Hunter's Paradise Shooting Gallery, the Snoopy Fountain, and the video arcade that includes the game Mad Dog McCree.

40   As if all this were not enough to cast a serious pall over the Minnesota woods illusion, the theme park's designers had to contend with the fact that they could use few plants native to Minnesota. At a constant temperature of seventy degrees, the mall lends itself almost exclusively to tropical varieties—orange jasmine, black olive, oleander, hibiscus—and not at all to the conifers of Minnesota, which require a cold dormancy period. Deferring ineluctably to this troubling reality, Knott's Camp

Snoopy brought in 526 tons of plants—tropical rhododendrons, willow figs, bud-dhist pines, azaleas—from such places as Florida, Georgia, and Mississippi.

Anne Pryor, a Camp Snoopy marketing representative, explained to me that these plants were cared for via something called "integrated pest management," which meant the use of predators such as ladybugs instead of pesticides. Yet every member of the landscape staff I spoke to described a campaign of late-night pesticide spraying as a means of controlling the theme park's enemies—mealybugs, aphids, and spider mites. Two said they had argued for integrated pest management as a more environ-mentally sound method of controlling insects but that to date it had not been tried.

Even granting that Camp Snoopy is what it claims to be—an authentic version of Minnesota's north woods tended by environmentally correct means—the question remains whether it makes sense to place a forest in the middle of the country's largest shopping complex. Isn't it true that if people want woods, they are better off not going to a mall?

On Valentine's Day last February—cashing in on the promotional scheme of a local radio station—ninety-two couples were married en masse in a ceremony at the Mall of America. They rode the roller coaster and the Screaming Yellow Eagle and were photographed beside a frolicking Snoopy, who wore an immaculate tuxedo. "As we stand here together at the Mall of America," presiding district judge Richard Spicer declared, "we are reminded that there is a place for fun in your life and you have found it in each other." Six months earlier, the Reverend Leith Anderson of the Wooddale Church in Eden Prairie conducted services in the mall's rotunda. Six thousand peo-ple had congregated by 10:00 A.M., and Reverend Anderson delivered a sermon enti-tled "The Unknown God of the Mall." Characterizing the mall as a "direct descendant" of the ancient Greek agoras, the reverend pointed out that, like the Greeks before us, we Americans have many gods. Afterward, of course, the flock went shopping, much to the chagrin of Reverend Delton Krueger, president of the Mall Area Religious Coun-cil, who told the *Minneapolis Star Tribune* that as a site for church services, the mall may trivialize religion. "A good many people in the churches," said Krueger, "feel a lot of the trouble in the world is because of materialism."

But a good many people in the mall business today apparently think the trouble lies elsewhere. They are moving forward aggressively on the premise that the dawning era of electronic shopping does not preclude the building of shopping-and-pleasure palaces all around the globe. Japanese developers, in a joint venture with the Ghermezians known as International Malls Incorporated, are planning a $400 million Mall of Japan, with an ice rink, a water park, a fantasy-theme hotel, three breweries, waterfalls, and a sports cen-ter. We might shortly predict, too, a Mall of Europe, a Mall of New England, a Mall of California, and perhaps even a Mall of the World. The concept of shopping in a frivolous atmosphere, concocted to loosen consumers' wallets, is poised to proliferate globally. We will soon see monster malls everywhere, rooted in the soil of every nation and offering a preposterous, impossible variety of commodities and entertainments.

45   The new malls will be planets unto themselves, closed off from this world in the manner of space stations or of science fiction's underground cities. Like the Mall of America and West Edmonton Mall—prototypes for a new generation of shopping cen-ters—they will project a separate and distinct reality in which an "outdoor café" is not

outdoors, a "bubbling brook" is a concrete watercourse, and a "serpentine street" is a hallway. Safe, surreal, and outside of time and space, they will offer the mind a potent dreamscape from which there is no present waking. This carefully controlled fantasy—now operable in Minnesota—is so powerful as to inspire psychological addiction or to elicit in visitors a catatonic obsession with the mall's various hallucinations. The new malls will be theatrical, high-tech illusions capable of attracting enormous crowds from distant points and foreign ports. Their psychology has not yet been tried pervasively on the scale of the Mall of America, nor has it been perfected. But in time our market-places, all over the world, will be in essential ways interchangeable, so thoroughly divorced from the communities in which they sit that they will appear to rest like per-manently docked spaceships against the landscape, windowless and turned in upon their own affairs. The affluent will travel as tourists to each, visiting the holy sites and taking photographs in the catacombs of far-flung temples.

Just as Victorian England is acutely revealed beneath the grandiose domes of its overwrought train stations, so is contemporary America well understood from the upper vistas of its shopping malls, places without either windows or clocks where the temperature is forever seventy degrees. It is facile to believe, from this vantage point, that the endless circumambulations of tens of thousands of strangers—all loaded down with the detritus of commerce—resemble anything akin to community. The shopping mall is not, as the architecture critic Witold Rybczynski has concluded, "poised to become a real urban place" with "a variety of commercial and noncom-mercial functions." On the contrary, it is poised to multiply around the world as an institution offering only a desolate substitute for the rich, communal lifeblood of the traditional marketplace, which will not survive its onslaught.

Standing on the Mall of America's roof, where I had ventured to inspect its massive ventilation units, I finally achieved a full sense of its vastness, of how it overwhelmed the surrounding terrain—the last sheep farm in sight, the Mississippi River incidental in the distance. Then I peered through the skylights down into Camp Snoopy, where throngs of my fellow citizens caroused happily in the vast entrails of the beast.

Rereading Actively

1. Guterson approaches his task equipped with information supplied by the MOA publicity press kit, and Guterson's article may be mined for nuggets of this infor-mation. Work with a partner to list ten or twelve facts Guterson relates about MOA. Discuss what seems interesting or noteworthy about the facts you selected. Write a short entry in your journal that tells what you and your partner noticed.

2. Guterson refers to "the alternate reality the mall conjures," alluding to the design features of the mall that have a kind of disorienting, "conjuring" power. In your journal, write a brief description of how the design elements of MOA seem to disorient mall visitors.

3. Guterson is critical of several aspects of mall culture as these reflect Amer-ican consumer culture. With a partner, find passages in his article that dis-cuss these, including the emphasis on materialism above community and spiritual values, and the destructive effects materialism has on the envi-ronment. From the passages you find, explain in your own words the prob-lems Guterson sees.

4. Guterson compares and contrasts the Mall of America with other market-places throughout history. With a partner or in a small group, identify some of the ancient and contemporary marketplaces that Guterson mentions.

5. Guterson asserts that the Mall of America is different in important ways from other marketplaces. Using your own words along with short quotations from Guterson, write a brief explanation of these differences between the new kind of marketplace that MOA represents and these other marketplaces.

Exploring Your Responses

6. Guterson frames his observations in a narrative, a story with a beginning, middle, and end. "Last April," Guterson begins, "on a visit to the new Mall of America near Minneapolis …" Try your own version of Guterson's story, telling about one time when you visited a shopping mall. Focus your description on the "psychological terrain," being as detailed as you can to show how your feelings and thinking shifted or changed as you proceeded through the mall. (Take a field trip to a mall if you need to, and record your experiences there in your journal.)

7. Guterson seems to understand and to appreciate the Mall of America and those who work and shop there. On the other hand, he is critical of some aspects of the mall. With a partner, discuss Guterson's interpretation of the mall as a reflection of American consumer culture: Is Guterson persuasive? Do your views of shopping malls accord with Guterson's?

8. Guterson asks: "Here was a new structure that had cost more than half a billion dollars to erect—what might it tell us about ourselves?" Freewrite a response to Guterson's question: What does the Mall of America tell you about yourself? What does it tell you about American consumer culture?

I SHOP, ERGO I AM: THE MALL AS SOCIETY'S MIRROR
SARAH BOXER

Sarah Boxer is a veteran journalist who has written about popular culture for numerous newspapers and magazines and now is a regular contributor to the New York Times. In this article, which appeared in the Times in 1998, Boxer reports on scholarly studies that portray shopping as a form of social activity and the shopping center or marketplace as a social space. Boxer's article covers a range of history, including the (recent) emergence of cultural studies as an academic field, and the (somewhat deeper) history of shopping and the evolution of shopping spaces. Boxer identifies the emergence of the superstore as a significant turning point for these developments.

In certain academic circles, "shop till you drop" is considered a civic act. If you follow cultural studies—the academic scrutiny of ordinary activities like eating fast food, buying a house in the suburbs, watching television and taking vacations at Disneyland—you will know that shopping is not just a matter of going to a store and paying for your purchase.

How you shop is who you are. Shopping is a statement about your place in society and your part in world cultural history. There is a close relationship, even an equation, between citizenship and consumption. The store is the modern city-state, the place where people act as free citizens, making choices, rendering opinions and socializing with others.

If this sounds like a stretch, you're way behind the times. The field of cultural studies, which took off in England in the 1970's, has been popular in this country for more than a decade.

The intellectual fascination with stores goes back even further. When the philosopher Walter Benjamin died in 1940, he was working on a long study of the Paris arcades, the covered retail passageways, then almost extinct; which he called the "original temples of commodity capitalism." Six decades later, the study of shopping is well trampled. Some academics have moved on from early classical work on the birth of the department store and the shopping arcade to the shopping malls of the 1950's and even the new wide aisles of today's factory outlets and superstores—places like Best Buy, Toys "R" Us and Ikea.

Historically, the age of shopping and browsing begins at the very end of the 18th century. In a paper titled "Counter Publics: Shopping and Women's Sociability," delivered at the Modern Language Association's annual meeting, Deidre Lynch, an associate professor of English at the State University of New York in Buffalo, said the word "shopping" started to appear frequently in print around 1780. That was when stores in London started turning into public attractions.

5   By 1800, Ms. Lynch said, "a policy of obligation-free browsing seems to have been introduced into London emporia." At that point, "the usual morning employment of English ladies," the 18th-century writer Robert Southey said, was to "go a-shopping." Stores became places to socialize, to see and be seen. Browsing was born.

The pastime of browsing has been fully documented. Benjamin wrote that the Paris arcades, which went up in the early 1800's, created a new kind of person, a professional loiterer, or *flâneur*, who could easily turn into a dangerous political gadfly. The philosopher Jürgen Habermas, some of his interpreters say, has equated consumer capitalism with the feminization of culture. And now some feminists, putting a new spin on this idea, are claiming the store as the place where women first became "public women."

By imagining that they owned the wares, women were "transported into new identities," Ms. Lynch said. By meeting with their friends, they created what feminist critics like Nancy Fraser and Miriam Hansen call "counter publics," groups of disenfranchised people.

Putting Merchants in Their Place

Some feminists point out that as shoppers, women had the power to alter other people's lives. Women who spent "a summer's day cheapening a pair of gloves" without buying anything, as Southey put it, were "fortifying the boundaries of social class," Ms. Lynch said. They were "teaching haberdashers and milliners their place," taunting them with the prospect of a purchase and never delivering. It may not have been nice, but it was a sort of political power.

Women could also use their power for good. In 1815, Ms. Lynch points out, Mary Lamb wrote an essay called "On Needle-work," urging upper-class ladies who liked to do needlework as a hobby to give compensatory pay to women who did it to make a living. Lamb's biographer recently noted that this was how "bourgeois women busily distributed the fruits of their husbands' capitalist gains in the name of female solidarity."

10   The idea that shopping is a form of civil action naturally has its critics. In one of the essays in a book titled "Buy This Book," Don Slater, a sociologist at the University of London, criticized the tendency of many academics to celebrate "the productivity, creativity, autonomy, rebelliousness and even … the 'authority' of the consumer." The trouble with this kind of post-modern populism is that it mirrors "the logic of the consumer society it seeks to analyze," he said. Such theories, without distinguishing between real needs and false ones, he suggested, assume that shoppers are rational and autonomous creatures who acquire what they want and want what they acquire.

Another critic, Meaghan Morris, author of an essay called "Banality in Cultural Studies," has faulted academics for idealizing the pleasure and power of shopping and underestimating the "anger, frustration, sorrow, irritation, hatred, boredom and fatigue" that go with it.

The field of shopping studies, whatever you think of it, is now at a pivotal point. In the 19th century, emporiums in London and arcades in Paris turned shopping into social occasions; in the 20th century, academics turned shopping into civic action; and in the 21st century, it seems that megastores will bring us into a new, darker era.

Shoppers' freedoms are changing. According to Robert Bocock, writing in "Consumption," the mall walkers of today do not have the rights that the flâneurs of the 19th century had. "In the United States, 'policing' of who is allowed entry to the malls has become stricter in the last two or three decades of the 20th century."

In superstores, the role of shoppers has changed even more radically. Superstores are warehouses that stock an astounding number of goods picked out at a national corporate level, said Marianne Conroy, a scholar of comparative literature at the University of Maryland. Shoppers educate themselves about the goods and serve themselves. Thus, the superstore effectively "strips shopping of its aura of sociality," Ms. Conroy said. There is no meaningful interaction between the salespeople and the shoppers or among the shoppers. The shoppers' relationship is not with other people but with boxes and shelves.

15   Does the concept of the shopper as citizen still hold? The real test is to see how the citizen-shopper fares at the superstore. In a paper she delivered to the Modern Language Association, titled "You've Gotta Fight for Your Right to Shop: Superstores, Citizenship and the Restructuring of Consumption," Ms. Conroy analyzed one event in the history of a superstore that tested the equation between shopping and citizenship.

In 1996 Ronald Kahlow, a software engineer, decided to do some comparison shopping at a Best Buy outlet store in Reston, VA., by punching the prices and model numbers of some televisions into his laptop computer. When store employees asked him to stop, he refused and was arrested for trespassing. The next day, Mr. Kahlow returned with a pen and paper. Again, he was charged with trespassing and handcuffed.

When he stood trial in Fairfax County Court, he was found not guilty. And, as Ms. Conroy observed, the presiding judge in the case, Donald McDonough, grandly equated Mr. Kahlow's comparison shopping to civil disobedience in the 1960's. Mr.

Kahlow then recited Robert F. Kennedy's poem "A Ripple of Hope," and the judge said, "Never has the cause of comparison shopping been so eloquently advanced."

Like Canaries in the Mines

At first, Ms. Conroy suggested they both might have gone overboard in reading "public meaning into private acts," but then she reconsidered. Maybe, she said, it's just time to refine the model.

Ms. Conroy suggested that consumerism should be seen no longer as the way citizens exercise their rights and freedoms but rather as "an activity that makes the impact of economic institutions on everyday life critically intelligible." In other words, shoppers in superstores are like canaries in the mines. Their experience inside tells us something about the dangers lurking in society at large.

20   What does one man's shopping experience at Best Buy tell us about the dangers of modern life in America? The fact that Mr. Kahlow was arrested when he tried to comparison shop shows that even the minimal rights of citizen-shoppers are endangered, said Ms. Conroy. Not only have they lost a venue for socializing, but they are also beginning to lose their right to move about freely and make reasoned choices.

Without the trappings of sociability, it's easier to see what's what. Stores used to be places that made people want to come out and buy things they didn't know they wanted. And they were so seductive that by the end of the 20th century they became one of the few sites left for public life. But in the superstores, the *flâneurs* and the consumer-citizens are fish out of water. They have nowhere pleasant to wander, no glittering distractions, no socializing to look forward to and no escape from the watchful eyes of the security guards. If this is citizenship, maybe it's time to move to another country.

Rereading Actively

1. As you review the article, note in your journal dates that are linked to these three strands in Boxer's article: the emergence of cultural studies as an academic field, the history of shopping, and the evolution of shopping spaces. In your journal, create a timeline from the dates in the article, with notations indicating what the dates signify.

2. Boxer's article is divided into sections. Write down a brief summary of each section in your journal. Compare the timeline you created using the dates that Boxer mentions with the organization of her article into sections. With a partner, discuss how else the topics in this article might have been organized.

3. Boxer gives particular attention to the superstore. She uses an anecdote about Ronald Kahlow and the Best Buy outlet store in Reston, Virginia, to help make her point about this new kind of shopping space. With a partner, review the incident involving Mr. Kahlow, and discuss what effects Boxer achieves by including this incident in her article.

4. In a small group or with a partner, review Boxer's article, noting passages that characterize the role of shoppers in superstores in contrast to the role of shoppers in malls or arcades. Discuss similarities and differences in these roles, and then write a short description of these roles in your journal.

5. Boxer refers to scholarship that argues that women became "public women" when they congregated in shopping spaces. With a partner, discuss this point, and then write a short explanation of the idea in your journal.

Exploring Your Responses

6. Reflecting on your experiences and observations, respond to the idea presented in the article that the shopping space has made possible an emerging public role for women.

7. Shopping, in the view of the scholars this article focuses on, is as much or even more about creating social relationships as it is about acquiring goods that we want. Do you agree with this view, or do you tend to agree with the other work cited, that calls attention to the "anger, frustration, sorrow, irritation, hatred, boredom and fatigue" involved in shopping? Explain your view.

8. Do you prefer shopping at an outlet store or a mall? Why? What place, if any, does the social climate that each offers have in your choice of shopping spaces? What does your reflection on your preferences tell you about the contention that "how you shop is who you are" (or maybe we should say, "*where* you shop is who you are")?

9. Finally, think about your reasons for going to the mall: Is it for the ease and comfort the mall provides you? For the access it provides to major retail stores? Is it for the entertainment value that you get from visiting the mall? Which is most important to you?

CONSUMING HISTORY
DIANE BARTHEL

Diane Barthel teaches sociology at the state University of New York at Stony Brook and writes about the sociology of culture and community. Among her publications are Amana: From Pietist Sect to American Community *(1984), and* Putting on Appearances: Gender and Advertising, *(1988). In* Historic Preservation: Collective Memory and Historical Identity *(1996), from which this excerpt in drawn, Barthel looks at what cultures choose to preserve (she compares Great Britain and the United States) and how what gets saved is turned into a business. The shopping mall is no exception: apparently, we long for the intimacy and safety of the local shop but are unwilling to give up the conveniences of the shopping center.*

Historic Shopping Villages and Urban Malls

Consumer culture and postmodernism form interweaving and interpenetrating social processes. Postmodernism views consumer culture as one of the defining aspects of contemporary society. But postmodernism itself feeds back into consumerism by producing distinctive postmodern goods in literature, the arts, and the media.[1]

One of the characteristics of postmodernism is a nostalgic longing for past forms of social organization. In Britain, once but no longer a nation of shopkeepers, nostalgia is evident in historic representations that replicate Victorian shops. On the South Coast, the resort town of Eastbourne has a "How We Lived Then" Museum of Shops with over fifty thousand exhibits. Tourists are invited to relate what they see to their own nostalgic experiences: "Can you still taste Tizer or Virol and remember the 'Ovaltineys' or 'Bisto Kids?' … Remember 'Five-boys' chocolate and when sweets were weighed from jars?" Not far inland from Eastbourne, Buckleys of Battle invites visitors to "Return to the Corner Shop," be it the chemist's, the sweet shop, the pub or the pawnbroker's. Such historic representations re-create the small-scale intimacy of the village shops of days past, even as increasing numbers of out-of-town shopping centers are undermining the economic viability of actual village shops.

In the States, historic shopping experiences take different forms. Nostalgic shops rarely stand isolated on their own as historic representations: rather they are more frequently either part and parcel of Staged Symbolic Communities, or old and new are integrated in what are called "shopping villages" (since most real villages have been destroyed) and in urban malls created in the shells of historic structures.

In the post World War II years, the trend was for shopping to move away from villages and town main streets out toward new suburban shopping centers. These new shopping centers offered easy access, easy parking, wide item choice, and an environment that was clean, safe, and modern. The process spelled doom for the unfashionable main streets. What had once been centers of civic pride frequently became centers of dereliction.

5   Meanwhile, shopping centers evolved into shopping malls. They became bigger and grander, competing with each other for how many stores they could contain under a covered roof, how many major department stores anchored the projecting wings, and how many acres of parking surrounded these fortresslike constructions.

The growing need for mall security dimmed part of the original appeal, suburban safety from urban crime. Mall police and security guards became more evident, shop security systems universal, and customers began to worry about having their cars broken into or being mugged in those dark wastelands of parking lots.

Malls countered the inevitable loss of modern glamour by becoming not just bigger but more exotic. Food halls with colorful flags, banners, and mobiles offered shoppers the fast food of all nations. Atriums, with their hanging cascades of greenery and gurgling fountains, created the image of an oasis. This attracted clusters of senior citizens, who camped out on the benches without buying much. The only ones who seemed to really enter into the mall spirit were the packs of teenagers and preteenagers, who made the mall their hangout.

Unknown to the teenage hordes, some architects were trying to revive Main Street. The National Trust for Historic Preservation Main Streets Project was first launched in 1977, and in 1980 the National Main Street Center was created. Since then, it has overseen the restoration and redevelopment of Main Streets in almost eight hundred communities in thirty-four states. Through its efforts, more than $2.5 billion has been reinvested in physical improvements, more than seventeen thousand new businesses were created, and with them a net gain of more than sixty thousand new jobs.[2]

The Main Streets program had all the difficulties inherent in preservation projects: local conflicts of interest and simply different ideas as to what constituted a desirable streetscape. There were the inevitable limits of time, will, energy, and dollars. There was also no guarantee that the restoration would payoff—that suburbanites would flock back to the Main Streets once the cracked cement was dug up and replaced with bricks, and once power lines were buried and fake gas lamps installed.

10   Some developers preferred to work in less piecemeal and voluntaristic a fashion. The refusal of one recalcitrant shopkeeper could ruin the whole visual effect and also cut into profits. Developers took to the grander ideas of postmodern architects, who proposed revolutionizing consumption by returning it to its human scale. Don't revive Main Street, they advised. Make the mall over *into* Main Street.

The model for the make over was the transformation of the New Seabury Shopping Center on Cape Cod into Mashpee Commons. Developers bought the old shopping center and hired an architectural team. The architects had the asphalt torn up and divided up the larger store, creating more of a village shop effect. They added streets, sidewalks, plazas, and benches. Small storefronts now had inviting shop windows. There was a lot of postmodern architectural detail that recalled the old New England village.

To the visitor in the summer of 1991, it still looked like a shopping mall in the center of a vast parking lot. But there was a new concept behind it that was attracting developers, corporate retailers, architects, and planners from as far as Japan. As one of the developers said, "To the retail world we're a mid-size shopping center.... But we call this a downtown."[3]

The whole design was seen not simply as boosting retail sales, but as promoting a return to social connectedness and neighborliness. It would be especially valuable for the old, for whom the local housing authority had already by 1991 built twenty-four apartments close to the center. It would also be good for the young. It would keep them out of malls (even if it once had been a mall). As the developer argued, "We don't want to see (children) going to the suburban mall and living within the four walls of a car." He continued, obviously warming to the topic, "I think it's the responsibility of everyone to open the front door, get out in the yard, take a walk down the street, and get involved."[4]

Such voluntarism based on an individual sense of responsibility and civic pride would, however, be accompanied by tight planning controls and architectural guidelines. One thing that hadn't changed in the movement from modernism to postmodernism was the desire of architects to assign themselves a considerable measure of social control. However, while architecture may suggest social patterns, people do not always follow the suggestions, as the experience of Seaside, Florida, made clear. While building codes tried to enforce a small-town atmosphere, with porches for sitting and narrow streets for walking, people retreated to back porches for privacy or indoors to watch television. There's more, in short, to turning back time, to creating a supposedly organic village, than building a clock tower or a postmodern post office. Beyond providing architectural guidelines and encouraging strolling, the problem is one of reactivating the sense of social responsibility that the rise of consumer society itself has helped stifle. It is one thing to "retrofit" a market, another thing to retrofit a mentality.

15   Transforming shopping malls into historic representations of villages is a trend still new enough to carry risks for developers. And megamalls are a countertrend now in both Britain and the United States. Malls still have certain advantages. They are known commodities and are constructed to set formulas. As one developer involved said, "Because there's no formula for doing a downtown, they're much more difficult." He added, "It's easier to sign Pizza Hut to a deal than Joe's Pizza."[5]

With such social trends and fashions, that which first seems risky later becomes formulaic, even prosaic. When developer J. Rowse first proposed an urban equivalent of retro suburban shopping villages, he failed to receive financial backing. Today, his Quincy Market in Boston is an exemplar for other historical representations of urban markets in historic factories, warehouses, and civic buildings that have been adapted to the uses of consumer society.

At New York's South Street Seaport, museum and marketplace are totally confounded. Those looking for a taste of history will find it in a range of indoor galleries and outdoor maritime exhibits. The work of serious tourism is more than balanced by the play afforded by a wide range of restaurants, boutiques, and markets. On a summer's day, the Seaport area appears to be one giant playground. Japanese tourists wait patiently to have their picture taken with a young woman covered head-to-toe with green paint, in a Statue of Liberty costume. Others watch a street performer imitate a music box doll.

The South Street Seaport and similar sites combine the nostalgic leisure experience—boat or trolley rides—with myriad other forms of historic entertainments. The zone of mediation found in many Staged Symbolic Communities has been eliminated, with history and consumption totally intermingled. Such representations are better than most malls, because they are also sites. Tourists see and are seen in these new urban agoras, whose original business, be it fishmongering, canning, or producing chocolates, seems, for the most part, to have moved elsewhere.

The extent to which such historic representations, once risky business, have now become formulaic is pointed up in the comment of an NEA official monitoring the preservation and presentation of Ybor City. He feared that this distinctive site would soon join the "generic mini-malls in old structures with various chains and tourist trinket emporiums alongside living history presentations."[6]

20   In Britain, civic leaders and businesspeople want to work the same magic at historic docklands and abandoned factories in London, Gloucester, and Bristol, and also in many northern cities where the loss of industrial might has left a plethora of empty factory buildings. It has also, however, left an economically depressed population unable to shop at the trendy boutiques that often fill these representations.

Such markets are successful because they are fun. They intertwine tourism with consumerism. They satisfy the "libido for looking" and the desire to spend. Despite their atriums and fountains, malls represent by contrast the rational organization of consumption. They centralize purchases, pulling in shoppers from a wide area by means of major access roads and expressways. They standardize purchases, as shoppers are assured of finding basic goods within a predictable range.

Herbert Marcuse predicted an end to scarcity. This, he believed, would liberate people, enabling them to transcend past struggles and assume new dimensions of being. At the end of the twentieth century, this has not happened. More people are lacking the basics of life, food and shelter, and more British and Americans find themselves economically pressed, rather than economically liberated.

What *has* changed over the past century is the sheer volume and range of goods available. In today's marketplace, new goods and brands compete to find, as one student of advertising said, "a place to live in your mind." Many goods promise not just to fill a need or perform a service. They offer a form of magic, a promise, even of transcendence. While the major subject of this chapter is the historic structures that contain the goods, it is worth considering in what way historic goods—whether retro fashions and reproductions, souvenirs, or antiques and collectibles—offer this magic, promise this transcendence.

NOTES

1. Mike Featherstone, *Postmodernism and Consumer Culture* (Newbury Park, Calif.: Sage Publications, 1991). See also Edward W. Soja, *Postmodern Geographies: A Reassertion of Space in Critical Social Theory* (London: Verso, 1989); David Harvey, *The Condition of Postmodernity: An Enquiry into the Origins of Cultural Change* (London: Basil Blackwell, 1989); and Sharon Zukin, *Landscapes of Power: From Detroit to Disney World* (Berkeley: University of California Press, 1991).

2. "Facts About the National Trust's National Main Street Center" (Washington, D.C.: National Trust for Historic Preservation, 1993.)

3. Barbara Flanagan, "A Cape Cod Mail is Disappeared," *New York Times,* Thursday, 14 March 1991, p. C10.

4. Ibid.

5. Ibid.

6. Nicolas R. Spitzer, *Ybor City Folk Festival Site Visit Report, Nov. 13–15, 1987* (Washington, D.C.: National Endowment for the Arts, Folk Life Program), 5. Cited in Susan B. Greenbaum, "Marketing Ybor City: Race, Ethnicity, and Historic Preservation in the Sunbelt," *City & Society* 4, no. 1 (June 1990): 74.

Rereading Actively

1. Summarize Barthel's comments on "postmodernism." Describe one way in which you are or are not a postmodern.

2. With a partner review the article focusing on Barthel's interpretation of the history of shopping centers. Discuss the important transitional points in this history and then draft a basic timeline in your journal.

3. In her history of the mall, Barthel discusses mall architects and developers. In a journal entry, describe their role.

4. With a partner, talk about the way history is represented within shopping centers. According to Barthel, how does history sell?

5. Barthel asserts that rehabilitated markets "are successful because they are fun" (¶ 21). List the "fun" characteristics that she attributes to these markets, and explain how each one might lead to enjoyment. Then describe the extent to which these characteristics contribute to your enjoyment of the mall.

Exploring Positions

6. With two or three classmates, review the kinds of commodities that Barthel discusses, for example, food, fashion, leisure, and so on. Focus on one that you all have some experience with as buyers or at least lookers. Brainstorm a list of examples, and discuss which of those examples each of you own (or would like to own) and how you feel about them. Be prepared to tell the class the range in your perceptions of the commodity and your feelings about specific goods.

7. In a one- or two-page journal entry, reflect on whether or how an aging mall or shopping district in your local area should be dealt with. In your conclusion, note how your position compares with the history of mall redevelopment that Barthel assembles.

8. Brainstorm consumer goods that you feel a particular attachment to: your favorite jeans, your first pair of Filas, that Swiss Army watch you obsessed about. In an extended freewrite, explore what purposes that object serves for you. Barthel suggests that these objects try to find "a place to live in your mind" and "offer a form of magic, a promise, even of transcendence" (¶ 23). Review your freewrite, and reflect briefly on the extent of your awareness of how what you buy and where you buy it affects you.

Radical Shopping in Los Angeles: Race, Media and the Sphere of Consumption

John Fiske

John Fiske, a communications professor at the University of Wisconsin, is a respected culture analyst who has done groundbreaking work on the role of audiences in mass media. In this 1994 essay published in Media, Culture & Society, *a British journal for cultural studies scholars, Fiske looks at Los Angeles in the wake of riots that followed the first Rodney King verdict. Through interviews with looters and storeowners and the analysis of media representations, Fiske tries to understand the motives of rioters and the meaning of the riot. He uncovers a kind of shopping mall where consumer citizens denied economic and social access to the Mall of America on the basis of race and class go shopping in a way that allows them to define themselves as part of the consumer culture, finding satisfaction and meeting basic needs.*

In this article I wish to explore the cultural dimensions of 'looting' and its media coverage in the uprisings in South Central LA that followed the first Rodney King verdict.[1] Like the protesters, I too consider the sphere of consumption an appropriate, available and effective site for political protest. In mounting this argument, I have no desire to reopen old and unproductive debates between political economists and culturalists over the relative importance of the spheres of production and consumption. I hope that both camps recognize that social change requires struggle on every possible front—in language and on the streets, in the workplace and the market place. I hope we can accept comfortably that two decades of discussion have not brought the two camps much closer,[2] and that we can reconcile ourselves to recognizing that neither sphere can be adequately analyzed from the perspectives of the other, and that attempts to do so have often ended in reductionism or the toppling of straw figures. Each sphere requires its own methodologies and theoretical frameworks, but both camps are complementarily engaged in the common critical analysis of capitalist societies in the hope, however slender, of contributing to their change. This paper, then, gives a culturalist account of racial protests in the sphere of consumption but it is important to contextualize it with a brief sketch of the racialization of employment in the US.

Between 1982 and 1989, 131 factories closed in LA with the loss of 124,000 jobs. Driving this was the deregulation of Reaganomics which encouraged capitalists to seek higher gains and lower labor costs in the 'Third' World. The jobs that were lost were ones that disproportionately employed African Americans. And this flight of capital and employment did not occur from high or stable ground—in the four years before 1982, South Central, the traditional industrial core of LA, lost 70,000 blue-collar jobs. In Black eyes, this pattern is produced not by a raceless free market, but by racism recoded into economics: To them the 50 percent Black male unemployment in South

Central does not look like the result of neutral, let alone natural, economic laws. African Americans in South Central may be hurting badly, but they are not suffering alone: Andrew Hacker (1992) shows that, come boom or bust, between 1960 and 1980 the national unemployment rate of Blacks was always approximately double that of Whites. In the 1980s, however, the gap widened, so that by 1990 it was almost triple. Even for those with jobs, the Reaganomic years produced a national decline in wages at the lower end of the scale and a spectacular rise at the upper. Many African Americans believe that the sphere of employment is where White supremacy is most firmly secured, and that America is always as racist as it can afford to be: when it needs Black labor racism diminishes, when it does not racism increases. The recent shift to the 'Third' World of these manufacturing jobs to which the White economy has traditionally confined Black labor, together with the mechanization of agriculture, means that Black unemployment will be permanent and therefore, if this argument holds, the US of the foreseeable future will be deeply racist.

The US market place is as racialized as its workplace and consequently has a long history as a site of racial-political struggle. Before reaching the analytical substance of the article, I would like to suggest some possible reasons for this. In the sphere of consumption the immediate effects of deprivation and discrimination are more widely experienced than in that of production where they are confined to the employed (a minority of African Americans). All, however, enter the sphere of consumption; the young and old, males and females, the employed and unemployed, the married and single, the sick, the disabled and the athletes, the middle, working and under-classes, all go shopping, and they all experience, often very personally, the daily indignities of racial discrimination.

Discrimination may also bear particularly heavily in the sphere of consumption because of its presumption of equality: everyone's cash is presumed to have the same purchasing power (for both commodities and social respect) in a way that is not the case with labor and earning power in the sphere of production. Discrimination intensifies the inequalities of the workplace but does not contradict them: in a so-called 'free' market place, however, discrimination runs counter to the principles that are claimed to define and organize it. It may, therefore, get even further under one's skin.

5   The sphere of consumption may be the only place of connection with the larger social order in which the oppressed can have any presumption of equality with others. The institutions of the public sphere—education, health, welfare, the law and the police—are all too often experienced variously as discriminating, alienating, humiliating or oppressive, and employment is precarious and scarce. The consumption of commodities provides a material connection with the social order that produces them and, however unfair that social order may be, most people do not wish to feel excluded from the society into which they have been born. Discrimination and disrespect in the market place become particularly painful techniques of exclusion when the market place is the only remaining potential site of inclusion.

The places of consumption adjoin both the public and the private: people and goods move constantly between the shop, the street and the home in an intricate web of everyday, intimate connectedness between public life, private life and the sphere of consumption. This is not the case in that of production with its clear boundary and singular pathway between home and work. Public places, with their close links to the market place and to the home, are also places of visibility and are thus where the behavior of private people or consumers can be seen by TV, can be made into news and can thus gain national and international attention. Public places are readily accessible to TV and in the image-saturated world of late capitalism political protest that is not covered by TV has had most of its teeth pulled.

A position of privilege allows the powerful to speak publicly, almost at will: for the powerless, however, public space is the only position for public speech. Intentionally disruptive behavior in public is, therefore, one of the most readily available, if not the only, means of access to the media for the most deprived and repressed segments of our society. Of course, any such access will always be on the media's own terms, but even that may seem preferable to invisibility and silence. The discourse into which the media put events is inevitably one that promotes the interests of the power bloc to which they are, on most occasions, closely allied. But, despite their best efforts, discursive frames can never contain and control *all* the meanings of events, particularly ones as disruptive and polysemic as an urban uprising.

The mainstream media consistently tried to frame the events of LA in a discourse characterized by the vocabulary of 'riots', 'arson', 'murder' and 'looting'. White Republican politicians used the same discourse, and the same words peppered the speeches made by George Bush, Dan Quayle and Pat Buchanan, to mention only those who were most vigorously electioneering at the time. Very few African Americans, however, used the word 'riot'; for them the words of choice were 'insurgency' or 'rebellion', while left leaning Whites preferred 'uprising' (which is why I use it in this article). A change of word is always significant, for it indicates a change of discourse, and by discourse I refer to a socially located and politically interested way of making and circulating a particular sense of social experience.

The word 'looting' set the strugglers-over-discourse a harder task than that of 'riot'. The mainstream media and members of the power bloc used it freely, but alternative words were hard to find. Property rights appear to be as deeply ingrained in capitalism's discursive system as in its legal and economic ones, so that the only words available that refer to the transfer of property from the strong to the weak without payment are ones that put this transaction into the discourse of crime. A word such as 'confiscation' refers to the non-economic transfer of property to the strong from the weak, and not vice versa and, as another disqualification, it lacks any sense of the opportunism that characterizes the tactics of the weak. Nobody tried to coin terms like 'radical shopping', for such neologisms have no social currency and would thus be semiotically unexchangeable: a pity, for 'looting' needs the semiotic shock of a term like 'radical shopping' to deliver the discursive blow that 'rebellion' or 'insurgency' did to 'riot'.

10   'Looting' was one of the key words by which the media attempted to confine the dominant understanding of the uprising to the discourse of law and order ('arson' and 'murder' were others), and in using it, I set it within quotation marks in an attempt to disarticulate it from its normal discursive, and therefore social, relations. The power over discourse is a material power, for the power to call the activity 'looting' was also the power to put those who engaged in it into prison and to know that prison was the solution to the problem.

Of course, one sense of 'looting' must be the dominant legal one: 'looters' knowingly break the laws that underpin property rights and organize the economic relations between buyers and sellers. 'Looting' does involve grabbing goods illegally, it does involve seizing the opportunities afforded by a breakdown of law and order, and in *some* cases this may have been all that it involved—there were reports, for instance, of 'yuppies in BMWs' (Davis, 1993: 144) joining in, but limiting its meaning to its legal dimension is a strategy of the power bloc that represses others. The White media, like the White politicians, put 'looting' into the discourse of law and order in a way that colored that order indelibly White and the disorder Black or Brown. Images of Whites engaged in this 'blackened' disorder were repressed from both the airwaves and mainstream common sense. At WITI-TV, the CBS affiliate in Milwaukee, Wisconsin, for example, two reporters were compiling a round-up of the second day's events for the late night news. In an attempt to achieve a degree of balance they included footage of a White woman loading designer dresses into her Mercedes who explained her behavior with a casual 'Because everyone else is doing it.' The producer cut the footage. The producer was White, the reporters Black.[3]

To those engaged in it, 'looting' was multidimensional: it could be, for example, both a form of public speech and a statement of self-assertion. 'Looting' enabled the silenced to be heard and the overlooked to be seen. For those who are normally denied an identity and refused a social presence, 'looting' could bring self-satisfaction and could give them an opportunity to remind the nation of Frederick Douglass's words, 'We *are* here. We *are* here.' The uprisings caused Oprah Winfrey to move her show from Chicago to LA and thus to give the Black residents an opportunity for media access that is normally denied them, and one young Black woman, among many others, took it:

> The looting? OK, I'm not saying that attacking the Koreans solved the problem, but when this Rodney King verdict came down, people were angry, and I'm still angry, I get angrier daily, how are we supposed to get it? We're not allowed to rally, we were going to meet Saturday, but that was cancelled—I'm not saying attacking the Koreans was the way, but it did get national attention. We *are* here, we *are* here.[4]

Commodities are goods that speak as well as goods to use, and unequal access to commodities is part of the same system that makes access to public discourse unequal. 'Looting' can temporarily correct both inequalities in one guerrilla action. Baby Saye, a South Central resident who has spent her life on welfare, understood this clearly as she 'looted' eighteen rolls of two-ply Charmin toilet paper. 'I know what you're thinking but basically fuck you', she said, 'I've been wiping my ass and my children's asses with that scratchy shit all my life because I can't afford the good shit. Now I got Charmin, just like those white jurors. So there!' (Institute for Alternative Journalism, 1992: 36).

Calling looting 'theft' and 'senseless', as the White media so often did, involved seeing each 'looter' as an individual thief. But when 'looting' is a form of public speech, it not only makes sense, but that sense may be communal: 'looters' then become not individual criminals but popular spokespeople whose actions give voice to a communal sentiment: radical shopping is communal, not individual. One study of the 1965 Watts uprisings emphasized their popular nature by pointing out that some 50,000 to 60,000 people lined the streets cheering on the 22,000 who actually 'looted' (much, we might think, as a chorus supports a folk singer) (cited in Davis, 1993: 144). Mike Davis saw the same pattern in South Central, but estimated that the numbers were probably double though the ratio remained about the same.

15 But 'looting' was not just speech, much of it was occasioned by simple survival needs: with stores closed, power off and refrigerators not working for an unknowable period, many 'looted' as their only means of providing for their families. As a Chicana

mother said, 'No, this has nothing to do with Rodney King. This is about trying to get something to eat for the kids. Who knows where they're going to get food, now that everything has been destroyed? We have no choice' (*LA Times*, 1992: 68).

Looting makes sense only in the intertwining of class and race. Even the comparatively conservative *LA Times* (1992: 59) recognized that 'the protest over police abuse had become a poverty riot' and others referred to them as 'bread riots'. Omi and Winant (1993) consider that, for the urban poor of all races, the riots exhibited class alliances rather than racial ones, but for middle-class Blacks who identified with the rioters, the racial alliances overcame class difference. Many of this group made their way to South Central later in the uprisings, not only to check on the safety of friends and relatives, but also to express solidarity (Omi and Winant, 1993: 105–6). In general, this would seem a convincing account, but it needs complicating even more: middle-class Blacks whose businesses were attacked tended to align themselves with Koreans and Whites, and Oprah Winfrey tried (without complete success) to stop herself joining the same alliance and thus distancing herself from the economically deprived Blacks of South Central. She wobbled on a discursive tightrope as she gave 'looters' a rare chance to put their case on national television, but still equated looting with stealing and saw no sense in it. The contradictions were clear in one image on her show: a Black man passionately pointed out the differences in the African American community between the haves and have-nots, and as his words put him and Oprah into opposite economic alliances, she put her arm around his shoulder to draw them into the same racial one:

> Oprah Winfrey: Don't we all live in this world together, don't we all live in this world together?
>
> Black Youth #4: Miss Oprah, when you leave this show, you go home to a lavish place, lots of us don't go home to lavish things, we go home to empty refrigerators, you know, crying kids, no diapers, no jobs, you know what I'm saying. (*She puts her arm around him.*) Everybody ain't got it like everybody—the people who didn't want to loot didn't want to loot because you have something to live for, you had a job to go to, lots of people haven't got a job to go to, I had a job, I had a job to go to, that's why I didn't loot.[5]

In a similar attempt to negotiate the same contradiction, a Black business owner accused those who looted his store of not understanding how difficult and expensive it is for a Black business to get insurance. The power of the White economy to deny middle-class African Americans equal access to insurance, mortgages and venture capital is the same power that denies underclass African Americans equal access to jobs and commodities: the power is directed to a different class of African Americans so the place and method of its application is different. Consequently it can remain unseen and unrecognized by those who do not experience it directly. In both these cases, however, we must recognize that the divisiveness of class differences was overlooked by the successful, but loomed large in the eyes of the deprived.

For the mainstream White media, however, the complications of race and class were largely repressed. For them, 'looting' was a matter of criminality and ethics in which racial difference could be criminalized. ABC's *Nightline*, for example, in summarizing the first 24 hours of the uprisings used three main image clusters—one of attacks on White drivers (including Reginald Denny), one of burning buildings and one of looting. Against these images of disorder, it showed the order of the National Guard being mobilized. Ted Koppel's introduction conforms to the standard, if simple, journalistic definition of objectivity as giving both sides of the issue (as though an issue like this had only two!):

> It has already begun turning into another dialogue of the deaf. On the one hand those for whom the verdict in the Rodney King case confirmed yet again the insensitivity, the callousness, the downright racism of The System, capital T, and capital S. And then, on the other hand those who view the violence spreading throughout Los Angeles as an expression of sheer lawlessness, unwarranted, unjustified and unrelated to the King verdict except in so far as it is being used as an excuse. Most tragically of all, the country seems to have run out of honest brokers, anyone genuinely capable of bridging the gap between the two sides. There is a reservoir of hostility on both sides of the line.[6]

But even here the intentionality of his language (it is White journalese) betrays his professional intention: the modifier 'yet' before 'again,' and the tone of 'capital T, capital S' are discursive alienations in his account of 'their' position that have no equivalent in his description of 'ours'.

This gesture towards objectivity is as empty as it is professionally necessary; from this point on, the story is told entirely in the language of those who saw the uprisings as 'sheer lawlessness, unwarranted, unjustified and unrelated to the King verdict':

> Most of the trouble is taking place within a one hundred and five square mile area of South Central LA, but there are reports now of looting in Hollywood, Beverly Hills and several locations in the San Fernando Valley. In South Central the looting has become brazen. There seems little connection to outrage over the King verdict. Most of the looters, like these seen breaking into a Sears store, seemed to be making the most of the chaotic situation to grab some goods. In fact, one looter arrived at this location in a yellow cab.[7]

The situation may have been chaotic, but ABC's reporter on the spot was able to read the motives of the 'looters' with certainty, and could apparently differentiate looting that was merely 'grabbing some goods' from looting that expressed 'outrage over the King verdict'. Her understanding of the cab arriving at a 'looting' scene was indelibly White and middle class: she gave no pause to consider that it may have carried the driver (who was almost certainly Black or Latino) to the scene of the action, but was content with the class- and race-based assumption that cabs function only for their passengers.

CNN's Greg LaMotte walked the same path:

> The fact is there are too many looters, too many arsonists, and too few police officers to do anything about it. Police stand helplessly by as hundreds of looters bash their way into stores and take, seemingly, whatever they want. The looting is sporadic, but it is citywide, Hollywood and Beverly Hills are affected. Three major banks have been closed down out of fear of robbery, most stores have closed in the downtown area but the looters just crashed through the glass and gates with no fear of being caught. In fact, the police, when they do see it, only try to scare them away. Given the level of crime here, only a handful of people have been arrested, because police are too busy trying to contain certain areas, not make arrests. At stores that are looted, it's almost like a feeding frenzy, they pour in, grab what they want and run out. There is thick black smoke everywhere from the hundreds of fires that have been set. The National

Guard is now on the streets, but it seems as each hour passes, the strength of the masses grows—people realize that they can get away with something, so they do, and nobody seems to know when it will end.[8]

Greg LaMotte talks of a 'feeding frenzy' and of how 'senseless' it all is; he calls the people 'the masses' and so denies the uprisings any purpose because to do so would be to admit that such a purpose is directed against the white position from which LaMotte speaks. The discourse of 'masses', 'senselessness' and 'lawlessness' absolves White society from any responsibility for the uprisings. By using this as their dominant discourse, the mainstream media were able to submerge both the broader social situation in which their role is so formative and the history of dominations of which they are themselves a product. The mainstream media's refusal to see anything from a point of view other than their own represses any alternative knowledge that there was an order and a sense to the uprisings.

20   Black Liberation Radio, however, an illegal micro-radio station in Springfield, Illinois, is far from mainstream, and on it Mbanna Kantako repeatedly reminded his listeners that the burning and 'looting' was systematic, not random. Starting 4,000 fires in less than 24 hours and confining them to businesses was, for him, clear evidence of organization and purpose.[9] In South Central almost no private residences were burned or 'looted': as one gang leader put it, 'We didn't burn our community, just their stores.' A piece of graffiti made the same point: 'Day one, burn them out. Day two, we rebuild.' Sister Adwba, reporting on Black Liberation Radio by phone from LA saw order, purpose and mutual respect or politeness in the 'looting':

SISTER ADWBA (on phone from LA): … and these are the very kids that were so orchestrated and organized that nobody could stop them. And it was so organized—if you could have seen it happen, them moving around, doing businesses and stuff …

MBANNA KANTAKO: Just like we saw it, right here, last night.

SISTER ADWBA: It was something, it was really something, because with me, I had a sense of pride in me, I could see the city falling all around me, and some Black people were complaining, and they were saying 'We're destroying out community.' We have to understand the definition of a community, it's not just because you live in it, do you own it, do you control it, and do you run it? And so it wasn't our community that we destroyed, anyway.

MBANNA KANTAKO: Yes, sister, it was strategic. In fact they were more precise than those 'smart bombs' that Bush dropped on Baghdad.

SISTER ADWBA: Exactly, but then they said 'Well, our property value's going down,' and my response was, 'Good, maybe now we'll get a chance to own it.' We ought to be glad the property value's going down. So that's right, we ought to turn this around and butt out all the markets and stuff. I was very pleased, you know, I was really pleased, I was really pleased to my soul, because I told the people, I said, 'Now you'll maybe see the Black-owned grocery in our neighborhood.… It makes a Black woman like me, I was so proud, these were our children, and we had raised them correctly. The people talk about them looting and whatever, I think that 500 years of free labor is supposed to be paid for by any means necessary, and they were taking Pampers and stuff, who can blame them for looting for their babies?

MBANNA KANTAKO: Who can blame them for taking food?

SISTER ADWBA: Yes, they were so organized, brother. You've never seen so much respect and harmony and cooperation in a looting situation, half the stuff that people didn't know, they were helping each other, saying 'Excuse me'—it was beautiful, it was just beautiful.[10]

For African Americans in particular the Korean stores in South Central Los Angeles became a point where racial oppression could be physically and violently opposed. The focus of this anger was the shooting of a Black girl, Latasha Harlins, by Soon Ja Du, a Korean store owner. Three elements interweave through this incident and its aftermath: the role of the Korean store in Black neighborhoods and the Black perception of it as racialized economic exploitation: the Black perception of Koreans as White allies in their racial oppression: and the personal disrespect that African Americans perceive in their day to day relations with Korean store owners.

The shooting of Latasha Harlins was recorded on video by the store security camera, and the video of her death joined with that of Rodney King's beating as a hyper-visible sign of racial oppression in Black America. The video showed Latasha Harlins approaching the store counter. Witnesses said she had her money in her hand. Du appeared to shout at Harlins and grabbed her sweater. Harlins punched Du three times about the head. Du threw a stool at her. Harlins put the bottle on the counter, turned and began to walk away. Du pulled a gun from beneath the counter and fired. Latasha Harlins fell, with a bullet in the back of her head. The defense later argued that the gun had been modified, without Du's knowledge, to give it a hair trigger. At Du's trial, the White judge found the homicide 'justifiable', Du was released on probation, required to perform 400 hours of community service and pay a $500 fine. To African Americans this sentence made sense only in terms of a racist alliance by which Soon Ja Du was made into an honorary and temporary White.

This particular alliance of interest, embodied momentarily by Judge Karlin and Du, was understood by African Americans as an instance of a broader strategic alliance by which Korean store owners are seen to promote White interests in Black communities. From the position of the 'have-nots' the Koreans appear to have been included in the category of the 'haves', and one of the things that they 'have' that poor African Americans 'have not' is access to economic power and capital; another is a government that cares for them. As Mbanna Kantako put it on Black Liberation Radio:

> The Korean, you know what, brother, the Korean government issued a demand to the United States government, according to the crackers, of course, to protect the Korean Americans in this devil country. Who issued such a warning to this government to protect the African Americans? You'd better start thinking about this!

Korean Americans are, in the eyes of African Americans, in a close alliance with Whites who use their comparative economic success and their status as 'the model minority' to 'prove' that the cause of Black 'failure' lies in African America and not in European America: the 'model minority' strengthens White self-insulation against accepting any responsibility for the plight of other minorities, and this self-insulation affects directly the social and economic policies formulated within its enclave. The 'honorary' Whiteness of Koreans is thus a White strategy, and it remains under the control of the Whites that the Koreans are not and can never be.

Certainly, not all Koreans see themselves as honorary Whites. As a middle minority, they are vulnerable to what Sumi Cho (1993) calls 'triple scapegoating'. One level of attack upon them was physical, mainly by Blacks and Latinos, upon their stores.

Equally hostile was the refusal of White police to provide any protection, and to concentrate their resources on the defense of White, wealthier communities. Mike Davis
was also told by Koreans of their bitterness at the way the police and National Guard
protected the South Central shopping malls owned by Alexander Haagen, a generous
contributor to local political coffers, while leaving Koreans to fend for themselves. One
commented, ruefully, 'Maybe this is what we get for uncritically buying into the White
middle class's attitude towards Blacks and its faith in the police.' And when they did,
the media attacked them on the third level with a barrage of images of vigilante Koreans, armed to the teeth, firing apparently randomly into the crowd. These images, Cho
argues, resonated happily in the White conservative imagination, for they made the
Korean storekeepers into 'a surrogate army acting out the White suburban male's
American dream—bearing arms against Black men'.

25   There are clear grounds for seeing the Koreans as economic exploiters, profiteering on the poverty of African Americans. Korean stores do charge high prices, though
profiteering may not be the explanation. At one market in South Central, for instance,
a bag of diapers costs $13.99 compared to $10.99 in wealthy West LA, and 5lbs of sugar
costs $2.99 as against $1.79. Higher ticket items follow the same pattern: a refrigerator that costs $1300 in West LA costs, in South Central $2040 and, to finance the purchase, the South Central resident would pay interest rates that were higher by at least
2 percent and maybe more. The ratio of stores to residents in South Central is less than
half that in LA County, reducing both competition and choice and, as most of these
are small, for few of the high retail chains will operate there, the picture is even worse
than the statistics show.[11] Shopping is restricted by both poverty and lack of choice.
These large chain stores, whose bulk purchasing and rapid turnover enable them to
offer lower prices, prefer to do their business in wealthier white areas and to shun
South Central. Similarly there are only fourteen banks in South Central; as virtually
no bank in LA will cash checks except for their own depositors, South Central residents on welfare have to take their government checks to check-cashing stores who
charge 10 percent of the check's face value, which was meagre enough in the first place.

To those who experience this double-barrelled poverty of low income and high
prices, the Korean store is a point of economic exploitation that they cannot avoid.
There are no alternatives. A greater distance, however, allows us to see that the Korean
store has been pulled into its position by the workings of a market system that is racist
in effect if not in intention. While the system of the market may appear neutrally col-
orless, where its transactions are made between different races the exchange between
merchant and customer is inevitably racialized. And as the Korean vigilantes acted as
White surrogates as they fired upon Black bodies, so the Korean merchants are seen
as troops deployed in the White strategy of weakening the Black communal body by
ensuring that such money that it has flows into pockets other than its own. As one
South Central resident put it, 'And the money that we are giving to the stores, they're
taking it to their own community, Koreatown. If a Black man owned the store, the
money would stay among us and help build the community up.'[12]

For the Black and Latino communities, the store is an active agent in the colo-
nizing of the place where they live: it works to prevent economic as well as territorial self-determination. The absence of territorial and economic control disempowers
the dispossessed in the broader social arena. Having a place from which to speak is

vital: the more displaced a social formation is, the less the voices speaking from it will be heard. The point made by Sister Adwba when she said: 'We have to understand the definition of a community. It's not just because you live in it—do you own it, do you control it, do you run it?' was repeated unwittingly and less explicitly by CNN when it reported that, 'Unrest that at first affected a predominantly Black area in South Central Los Angeles has now spread to communities several miles away.' The code here is that 'communities' are where White people live whereas 'areas' are inhabited by Blacks.

The video of Latasha Harlins's death was so significant because, like that of Rodney King's beating, it condensed into a moment of hypervisibility long and complex histories. The transaction across Du's counter—arguments, physical blows, no money, a shot—was a material instance of larger historical and social transactions. In it we can trace multiple movements across this counter: bullets and punches; the gaze of the video camera and of the store owner; money and commodities; interpersonal and inter-racial behavior.

The bullet of Soon Ja Du carried the histories of many others. The Korean American Grocers and Retailers Organization (KAGRO) in Southern California tried to avoid exacerbating the tension between its members and African Americans but, while doing so, had to recall the forty-one Korean merchants killed by African Americans between 1975 and 1990, and the twelve African Americans killed by Koreans defending their property. From this viewpoint Du's grocery store forms the front line of a racial war, in which the transactions across its counter are skirmishes. This history of racial anxiety and antagonism is activated every day. The video-gaze that follows the Black customer with unrelenting suspicion is repeated by the store owner, and Black customers complain bitterly of the disempowerment and disrespect embedded in such surveillance.

> KOREAN MAN: It's not right to demand our respect, that we've got to give you respect …
>
> BLACK MAN #1: I do not demand respect, but I expect it. If I walk into your establishment to make a purchase and I pass by you, and I say 'Hi, how are you?' I expect the same from you. I don't want you to come out from behind your counter and follow me around the store assuming I'm going to steal from you.[13]

30 The suspicious gaze of the camera and the merchant are signs of social exclusion, of being 'othered' from one's own society. At the immediate level of personal and interpersonal experience, this excluding is experienced as 'disrespect' or 'diss'—words that in White discourse can be curiously unemphatic, if not trivial. Yet they point to the way that racial, economic, legal and social disempowerment can be condensed into a glance or a tone of voice:

> BLACK WOMAN: They [Koreans] were targeted because they are rude to us in our neighborhoods (applause), they're rude to our kids, Latasha Harlins was just an incident, I'm talking about our everyday living. I walked into the store and I spoke, 50 years old, one woman, by myself, and I spoke—one woman behind the counter, she wouldn't speak to me, in my neighborhood, you hear me![14]
>
> BLACK MAN: That shooting [Latasha Harlins's] is just proof of the problem, just another example of their disrespect for Black people. You go in their stores and they think you're going to steal something. They follow you around the store like you're a criminal. They say 'Buy something, or get out.'[15]

The store is a key site where this multiaxial disempowerment is put into practice. It is where racial power can be redirected along economic and legal axes. Du's counter, then, is encumbered with a history within which both she and Latasha are held and to which their transaction contributed. Store counters are the furniture of capitalism, the equivalent in the sphere of consumption of the workbench in that of production. The workshop and the corner shop are where the two key economic relations of capitalism are made material in interpersonal relationships between supervisor and worker, merchant and customer. And racial difference is at work in both.

For the deprived, shopping is not, as it is for the wealthy, where success in the sphere of production is materially rewarded: it is an experience of exclusion and disempowerment. Shopping is painful. The way a store owner treats a Black or Latino person entering the store is, quite literally, an embodiment and an emplacement of the way that White capitalism treats the racially unemployed or underpaid.

Under these conditions, disrespect in the stores is loaded with social and racial significance. In the interpersonal relationships of everyday life, demanding and expecting respect from other individuals, particularly those who embody signs of social privilege, is one of the few ways in which the deprived can feel that they can be accepted into the social order. If the economic, legal and racial relations of society have rejected you completely, then 'respect' in particular relationships is all you have left, and is worth fighting hard to maintain.

The cop treating Black skin as a sign of criminality, and the store owner and the surveillance camera doing the same thing, are where the White power to exclude and oppress are individually and bodily experienced. It is hardly surprising, then, that the store was a key site of struggle in the civil rights movement. The store, the restaurant, the bus and the public toilet are sites within the sphere of consumption where race relations have been experienced most acutely and contested most bitterly.

35   Lizbeth Cohen traces two crucial eras of the civil rights movement—the boycotts and sit-ins of the 1950s and early 1960s, and the ghetto riots of the late 1960s—and posits the centrality of consumerism in both (Cohen, 1992). Arguing that from the 1950s onwards, African Americans associated their sense of citizenship with free access to consumer goods and services, she emphasizes first the political motivation provided by the personal experience of indignity (or 'diss') in the sphere of consumption and, second, the political effectiveness of organized boycotts of stores, restaurants and buses in dismantling the structure of segregation.

In his study of one particular struggle in the civil rights movement, Steven Classen finds similar concerns. In organizing against the renewal of the license for WLBT, a Jackson, Mississippi, TV station, because of its racist programming, Black protesters boycotted downtown stores whose commercial interests were closely allied with WLBT's. In their letter to Jackson businessmen (sic), the protesters claimed that the boycott was aimed to end 'discrimination against Negro workers and Negro consumers', and demanded:

1. hiring of personnel on the basis of personal merit without regard to race, color or creed; and promotion of such personnel on the basis of both merit and seniority without regard to race, color or creed;
2. an end to segregated drinking fountains, an end to segregated restrooms, and an end to segregated seating;

3. service to all consumers on a first-come, first-served basis;
4. use of courtesy titles—such as 'Miss', 'Mrs' and 'Mr'—with regard to all people. (Classen, 1994: 5–6)

Three of the four demands are located in the sphere of consumption, and the last two focus specifically on racial 'disrespect'. Similar demands lay at the core of the civil rights movement. Rosa Parks's historic refusal to sit at the back of that Montgomery bus sparked one of the first uses of a consumer boycott to demand civil rights. On its first evening, a meeting organized by Martin Luther King agreed that African Americans would consider that the bus company was denying them their civil rights until (1) its drivers treated them with the courtesy they accorded whites, (2) its passengers were seated on a first-come first-served basis, and (3) it employed Black drivers (King, 1958: 47).

In LA in 1992 these rights were still being denied. One small example that in this context signifies much is provided by Judge Karlin's remarks on her sentencing of Soon Ja Du. On every one of her eighteen references to Du she gave her the courtesy title of 'Mrs'. Never did she refer to Latasha Harlins as 'Miss', and once she called her simply 'Latasha'.

There is a pattern in the media coverage of 'looting': the less mainstream the media, the more minority voices were likely to be heard. Daytime talk shows, the alternative press and illegal radio carried discursive currents that were submerged or marginalized by the nightly news and the dailies. Even on the same channel the same pattern could be observed. On CNN's *Newsnight,* for example, Greg LaMotte put the events into a discourse of which even Pat Buchanan would have approved. But on CNN's *Showbiz Tonight* Black actors such as Wesley Snipes, radical White ones such as Charlie Sheen and Latino ones such as Jimmy Smits were allowed quite lengthy expressions of sympathy with, and understanding for, the uprisers. An African American friend of mine, a member of the professional classes, told me that the best coverage of the uprisings he could find was on MTV. Mainstream television scrambled to get the pundits that Whites wanted to hear, so their analytical commentaries were provided by university professors, politicians, civil rights leaders and law enforcement officers. On MTV, however, the pundits were rap artists: they spoke from their own experiences of pauperization, of police brutality, of social exclusion and of racism, and brought to the nation's screens voices and viewpoints that its mainstream media repressed.

Rappers are the best journalists for Heather Mackey (1992: 128) also: 'When Chuck D says that rap music is like CNN for Black people, it makes complete sense to me, because I use rap as a news source. My sources of information are different from the evening news—they have to be, because I don't watch a lot of TV.' Her friends told her, time and again, how uncannily the events in South Central mirrored songs in their collections. Ice-T's 'Cop Killer' provides an example: its chorus is 'Fuck the police for Daryl Gates, Fuck the police for Rodney King.' Ice Cube's rap 'Black Korea' is about Black anger at the way Korean grocers distrust Black customers and 'watch every damn move that I make'; it ends with the threat, 'So pay respect to the Black fist, Or we'll burn your store right down to a crisp.' Ice-T and Ice Cube are both criticized by Whites for inciting violence, and 'Cop Killer' was withdrawn from sale after a campaign by the Police Federation and White supporters. But the rappers explain that they are giving information about Black experience and warnings about Black anger. Violence is incited not by rap, but by White ignorance: 'If you weren't prepared for this', Ice-T told the White liberal journalist Terry Gross on National Public Radio's *Fresh Air,* 'If you didn't think it was going to happen, or if you are at all surprised, then it's your fault.'[16] During the interview Terry Gross's questions were all posed from the unmarked space of Whiteness from which Black violence appears antisocial and Whiteness its victim. 'What have the cops done to you', she asked in pained bafflement, 'that you see them as the enemy?' Ice-T told her and her listeners in no uncertain terms:

> Put me in jail, kill a couple of my friends, beat me, harass me, look me in my eyes because I'm in my car and told me to get over, put me on the side of the road, laid me down in the street like a punk. All that has to do is to happen to you once and you'll hate them. You know, I live it. If you're not from LA you don't understand the Gestapo force of police that they have in LA. They're not humans. I just think White America, of the upper class, don't even have any way of understanding the injustices that go on in the ghetto, and until you do it's just a waste of my time explaining it to you.

This Black frustration with White refusal to listen is what Whites miss when they understand the anger in rap as merely incitement to violence. Terry Gross, for example, described the lyrics in 'Body Count' as 'inflammatory' and failed to hear the question that the album was really asking, which was, as Ice-T explained to her, 'What is a brother gotta do to get a message through?'

40 There are many voices normally excluded from the mainstream media that are allowed to speak on them in times of crisis. National Public Radio did air Terry Gross's interview with Ice-T during the uprisings, but she would have been unlikely to interview him in more normal times. And that is Ice-T's point—the uprisings were, in part, loud public speech by those whose voices are normally silenced or confined to their own media. The uprisings did force the White media make room for the occasional Black voice, and they made White American listen. 'Looting' not only threw White property rights into crisis, it also disrupted White control over whose voices should be granted public circulation.

In times of crisis the media may be forced to carry a wider range of voices than in normal times, but they do structure these voices in a hierarchy of legitimation that is a product of the dominant value system. In this hierarchy of legitimation talk shows are not only seen as lower-brow and less 'good' than the network news, but their core audience is 'lower' in the social hierarchy. Entertainment news is lower than 'real' news and MTV is 'lower' even than talk shows. Many of those who criticize the media's coverage of political issues have a structure of taste that leads them to watch the network news rather than talk shows, *Nightline* rather than *Oprah Winfrey,* and to walk the dog rather than watch MTV. The print media, from the mainstream dailies to the alternative weeklies, do cover a broader spectrum than television, but they still reproduce a similar hierarchy of legitimation. Unlike television, however, the US radical or alternative press rarely uses discourse that appeals to the structures of taste of those lower in the social hierarchy: they lack the populist tone of an Oprah Winfrey, and rarely, as do MTV and the music press, allow rappers to speak directly of their material conditions. Communal voices of the oppressed, such as those of Mbanna Kantako, are rarely quoted on their pages, whose space is more likely to be reserved for middle-class White dissidents.

The populism of tabloid TV, of MTV and the talk shows carries a wide variety of topics and points of view, only some of which would be applauded by progressive critics. But when these same critics dismiss 'low' TV or ignore it completely they are participating in the same hierarchy of legitimation as the media they criticize. Our media resources are limited, and will always be so, particularly when they are commercial or reliant on corporate sponsorship, so it is doubly important to take advantage of the range that they do offer. Even when a crisis produced from below (such as the LA uprisings) gives the oppressed opportunities for media access (such as that taken by the 'looters') we need actively to search for and listen to those rarely heard voices. Urgent speakers require engaged and motivated listeners, and the sphere of consumption is often where this communication can best occur. Late capitalist societies in particular are centered around consumption, but the commonality, the everydayness and the necessity of the market place have always made it a site of cultural as well as economic exchange. When the economically oppressed disrupt the normal economic processes of the market, the culturally silenced simultaneously disrupt its cultural processes, for the economic and the cultural are two sides of the same coin. 'Looting' gives the oppressed access to both commodities and public speech.

There can be no guarantee that bringing the dirt out from under the carpet will encourage the occupiers to clean up the room, but it is a first step. More importantly, we liberal Whites who wish to mitigate the worst effects of racial discrimination and economic deprivation cannot formulate adequate programs of action from our good intentions alone: to have any chance of success such programs must be produced by inter-racial alliances, preferably Black-led ones, and for such alliances to hold, we Whites have to listen to the voices of the racially oppressed and learn from their experiences. The mainstream media prevent this, and part of our political effort must involve searching the media margins for otherwise silenced voices. On a minor scale we can thus pick up in the sphere of media consumption some of what the 'looters' are trying to say in their disruption of the public market place.

NOTES

1. This article draws upon material that is part of a larger study of the LA uprisings in my forthcoming book *Media Matters*, University of Minnesota Press.
2. The work of Graham Murdock and of Nicholas Garnham has gone further than most in bridging the gap.
3. Personal interview with one of the reporters, Darryl Newton.
4. The *Oprah Winfrey Show*, 5 May 1992.
5. The *Oprah Winfrey Show*, 5 May 1992.
6. *Nightline*, 30 April 1992.
7. Ibid.
8. *CNN Newsnight*, 30 April 1992.
9. Black Liberation Radio, 2 May 1992.
10. Black Liberation Radio, 2 May 1992.
11. *LA Times*, 24 November 1991, p. A39.
12. *LA Times*, 13 May 1992, p. T10.
13. The *Oprah Winfrey Show*, 5 May 1992.
14. Ibid.
15. *LA Times*, 3 November 1991.
16. 1 May 1992.

REFERENCES

Cho, Sumi (1993) 'Korean Americans vs. African Americans; Conflict and Construction', in R. Gooding-Williams (ed.), *Reading Rodney King/Reading Urban Uprising*. New York: Routledge.

Classen, S. (1994) 'Standing on Unstable Grounds: A Re-examination of the WLBT-TV Case, Consumerism and Legal Standing', *Critical Studies in Mass Communication* 11.1. 5–6.

Cohen, L. (1992) 'Consumption and Civil Rights'. Paper presented at the American Studies Association Conference, Costa Mesa, CA, November 1992.

Davis, Mike (1993) 'Uprising and Repression in LA', in Robert Gooding-Williams (ed.), *Reading Rodney King/Reading Urban Uprising*. New York: Routledge.

Hacker, A. (1992) *Two Nations: Black and White, Separate, Hostile, Unequal*. New York: Ballantine Books.

Institute for Alternative Journalism (1992) *Inside the L.A. Riots*. New York: IAJ Press.

King, M.L. (1958) *Stride Towards Freedom: The Montgomery Story*. New York: Harper and Row.

LA Times (staff of) (1992) *Understanding the Riots*. Los Angeles: *LA Times*.

Mackey, Heather (1992) 'I Told You So', in Institute for Alternative Journalism, *Inside the LA Riots*, New York: IAJ Press.

Omi, Michael and Howard Winant (1993) 'The LA Race Riot and US Politics', in Robert Gooding-Williams (ed.), *Reading Rodney King/Reading Urban Uprising*. New York: Routledge.

Rereading Actively

1. Identify passages where Fiske explains the relationship between the sphere of consumption and the sphere of production and write a two- or three-sentence summary of the relationship in your journal.

2. With a partner, discuss a passage in which Fiske links consumption and race, and outline his position.

3. In a small group, identify the points that the "mainstream media" made about the riot, and then discuss Fiske's attitude toward this explanation. Summarize your group's discussion in your journal.

4. Fiske offers several interpretations of looting. List as many of these interpretations as you can, and then order them from least to most compelling.

5. Find passages where Fiske includes the exact words of looters, storeowners, and media personalities. In your journal, explain why Fiske might have used each quote.

6. With a partner, analyze the exchange between Sister Adwba and Mbanna Kantako (¶ 20). Summarize in a phrase or two the claims each speaker makes, and then draft a collaborative explanation of what the interaction adds to a reading of Fiske's article.

Exploring Your Responses

7. Freewrite your opinion about the parallel Fiske draws between rioting and shopping. Is this a valid analogy? Is it a good one? Why or why not?

8. With two or three classmates, discuss what Fiske means by the spheres of consumption and production and whether you tend to see the world from the

vantage of a consumer, producer, or a mixture of the two. Talk about how your vantage affects your view of a media event like the LA riots, a national election, a presidential scandal, or some such.

LET US ENTERTAIN YOU

MARIWYN EVANS

As the executive editor of the Journal of Property Management, *Mariwyn Evans spends considerable energy studying malls and other retail spaces. Her purpose is not so much to buy as to assess how space is designed and how effective that design is in getting shoppers to buy. In this 1999 article, she takes property developers and other business folk who are interested in the findings of the International Council of Shopping Centers and the Institute of Real Estate Management—the publisher of the* Journal of Property Management—*on a walk through the future of the shopping mall, and the future is entertaining.*

> Twenty screens, forty screens, sixty screens—Ferris wheels, petting zoos, exotic foot courts—Oh! By the way—we have stores, too.

From the frosts of Minnesota to the palm trees of Miami, the worlds of entertainment and retailing continue to merge. Symbolized by that retail/entertainment behemoth the Mall of America, shopping center owners and managers have embraced entertainment as a way to bring customers to the mall and keep them there.

As an *ICSC Research Quarterly* pointed out three years ago, entertainment has always been a component of shopping centers. Even in the 1950s, early mall developers included benches, artwork, and piped-in music to make the shopping experience more pleasurable. But today, entertainment has become "an integral part of the shopping experienced and will be a point of strategic differentiation for shopping centers of the future," according to ICSC. In a 1995 International Council of Shopping Centers survey, more than half of the retailers surveyed used the word "entertainment" to describe their businesses.

But if entertainment is a standard retailing element, opinions on its specific impact are mixed. Although several of the leading mall managers interviewed for this article are "in the process" of conducting statistical research into the effects of entertainment on mall revenues, few have much in the way of concrete data at this point. "There is not a great deal of good, solid statistical research on the impact of movies on malls, but if you visit the theaters, you do not see a lot of shopping bags," says Cindy Bohde, senior vice president and national director of marketing for Urban Retail Properties, Co., the management, leasing, and development affiliate of Urban Shopping Centers, Inc. However, notes Bohde, movie attendance does give customers "another reason and more time to explore the mall" and hopefully a reason to return.

"If a competitor has a new 20-screen cineplex with stadium seating and you don't, you have got problems," says Buddy Herring, managing director and principal of Trammel Crow Faison.

5   A 1996 survey of 11 malls sponsored by ICSC concluded movie patrons did have a positive impact on mall sales. An article in the Spring 1997 *Research Review* stated that approximately 60 percent of movie patrons shopped in a mall during a visit to the theater. Patrons that did shop spent an average of $20 on non-food items (com-

pared to $56 for the average shopper) and spent approximately 30 minutes shopping. While these sums are not large, the article does point out that much of this income is added revenue. In ICSC's Analyst Alley, William A. Speer, vice president of TrizecHahn Centers' Market Research and Financial Analysis Department, uses these 1996 finds to model the "spin-off" from sales to movie patrons. He projects that in a mall with 13 theater screens sales would increase by a weighted average of 13 percent. Food sales were the biggest gainers, with a 17-percent increase in sales.

"Large cineplexes in malls do increase property visits, but they do not benefit all retailers equally," says Michael McCarty, senior vice president and director of research for Simon Property Group. McCarty cites food courts and book and music stores as major beneficiaries of movie-generated sales. Many of these categories appeal to teenage customers, who "use the center as a club and may spend an hour or more shopping and visiting while waiting for a movie to begin." Proximity to the theaters is also a key in retailer sales success.

The layout of the box office entry points may also influence a theater's impact on sales, says Bill Maher, director of strategic research for La Salle Partners Management Services. He notes that several malls currently under construction or renovation plan to place their theaters on an upper level above the center court of the mall. "I think the-aters are confident that they can draw the crowds and are not too concerned about their location, as long as adequate parking is available," says Maher.

Food—especially a variety of fast and sit-down venues—is another key compo-nent of today's entertainment mix. "Food has a much more direct correlation than movie theaters on retail traffic. And adding destination restaurants help make shop-ping centers places where people go for a variety of things," says Bohde.

The National Restaurant Association predicts that in 1999 Americans will spend $354 billion on meals outside the home. "It is vital to have adequate food in the mall and to include a combination of restaurants that reflect different income levels and age groups," says Herring. He notes that food provides an opportunity to relax and prepare for more shopping. "If customers have to leave the center for lunch, they may just not come back," Herring says.

If It's Tuesday, This Must Be the Gap

10   The need for variety is another important component in the "entertainment" expe-rience of shopping. This is no small task when every center seems to have the same six anchors and 150 national retailers. "You often can't tell the difference between one mall and another; that is why it is so important to create a sense of architec-tural place," says McCarty. The Simon Company was a pioneer in the entertainment arena with The Mall of America and the Forum Shops at Caesar's. The Forum Shops match the high drama of Las Vegas with animated Roman statuary, a changing inte-rior skyscape, and storefronts that echo the Colosseum. But McCarty is quick to point out that what works in Las Vegas would not be appropriate in Wichita. "The sense of architecture and place has to extrapolate to each individual property; you cannot transplant the same idea or the same budget from one site to the next," he says. As an example, says McCarty, at the Lakeline Mall in Austin, a sense of place was created simply but effectively with a food-court mural depicting the historic buildings of Austin's Fourth Street. The three-dimensional installation, which is true to historic detail, creates a sense of an early shopping experience and is unique

to the site. "The mural gives people a reason to drive the extra mile to come to Lakeline," says McCarty.

Retailers are also embracing the idea of reflecting their geographic area, says Mez Birdie, senior vice president of Commercial Net Lease Realty, Inc. He notes that in Houston a Barnes and Noble has changed the store's interior with a 10-foot by 30-foot western mural. Another retailer on Florida's Intercostal Waterway has added a dock and cafe that can be reached by water taxi.

Other properties are carrying this sense of place even further by attempting to create the Main Street shopping experience under one roof. At increasing numbers of properties such as the just-opening Citrus Park Town Center in Tampa, the facades of mall shops are individually designed with street-front concepts to create a sense of a small-town shopping experience. A childrens' play area depicting a miniature small town complements the concept.

"You cannot really focus on shopping for more than one-half hour without losing concentration," says Amanda Nicholson, an assistant professor of retailing at Syracuse University. "Going in and out of stores as if you were on the High Street gives you a chance for a little fresh air."

The same sense of changing scenery can be created inside a store, says Birdie. "Take the new GNC stores as an example; each department has a different look—a spa, a sports lab—all tied into the idea of living well and healthily. The design engages the shoppers and encourages them to move on and see another motif."

15   Carts and kiosks are another way to add differentiation and excitement to a mall, says Nancy McCann, vice president of marketing for Forest City Enterprises. "Temporary tenants, kiosks, and carts can bring seasonal and regional flavor to a center. We try to find merchandise that creates a sense of a marketplace and is special to the area," she says.

Rotating mall events, long a mainstay of the entertainment mix, are also getting a new look. The ICSC research study found that events incorporating education into the mix were the most successful at attracting shoppers. McCann describes successful promotions done in conjunction with the PBS Magic School Bus and with Disney. "We have even hosted an international film festival at one of our centers that drew 30,000 guests," she notes.

Bohde is incorporating an educational/entertainment component into a renovation of Fox Valley Mall. In partnership with the DuPage County (Illinois) Children's Museum, the mall will feature a play area with periodic children's programming.

A Few Simple Things

If much of the drive toward entertainment is focused on megamultiplexes and Dinomation exhibits, mall managers have also discovered that enjoyment can come from little things. "Sometimes giving people a small, unexpected pleasure can do a lot to take the drudgery out of shopping. At certain times of the year, our greeters will hand out red lollipops or Hershey's kisses. If you make a customer smile, you create a joyful experience," says McCann.

McCann also believes that music and visual excitement play big parts in the shopping experience. "This is the MTV generation; retail today is very much show business." She uses music and highly visual displays, such as the Dragonfest, which delighted children with a 80-foot smiling dragon, and a July 4th concert that included the "1812 Overture" by the renowned Cleveland Orchestra and a laser light show, to create a sense of excitement throughout the mall.

20   At Fox Valley Center, interactive fountains and lights provide a reason to pause and feel refreshed. "It breaks up the day and gives people something to talk about," says Bohde.

Retailers are also getting into the act, says Birdie. "Now when you score a basket on the court at the Galyan's store, the lights flash and the 'crowd' cheers." Companies such as Barnes and Noble and Virgin Records create meeting places within the store and contribute to the sense of excitement.

Reality Check

As shopping centers large and small turn to entertainment as a way to draw customers in and keep them there longer, the question becomes how much entertainment is too much? Will the mall of the future—encroached on by e-commerce and catalogs— become an entertainment center that just happens to have a few shops. The answer is a rousing, "who knows?"

Still, movie theaters are not a panacea for every property cautions McCarty. "An entertainment concept can turn a good mall into a great one, but it won't make a bad mall good."

Fun Isn't Everything

"You can put in all the marble you want, what women shoppers want is a clean, convenient place to change the baby," says Amanda Nicholson, assistant professor of retail at Syracuse University. After conducting a series of focus groups in upstate New York on behalf of the Pyramid Company, Nicholson is convinced that convenience and store variety are more important to shoppers, most of whom are women, than all the bells and whistles.

25   "What we are hearing is a theme of convenience and a combination of different shopping needs," says Michael McCarty, senior vice president and director of research for Simon Property Group.

The location of necessary amenities such as bathrooms and food service have a significant impact on shopper satisfaction and length of stay. "If a shopper has to walk a half a mile to reach the food court, she will leave," says Nicholson. She emphasizes that good vertical transportation and clear signage make it easier for shoppers to negotiate the mall and cut down on frustration.

"If the kids are crying, the customer will go home," agrees Cindy Bohde, senior vice president and national director of marketing for Urban Retail Properties Co. All of Urban's new developments and renovations feature "family restrooms" that make it more convenient for fathers or mothers to accommodate small children of either sex.

Children's play areas, such as those now being built into Kroger supermarkets, are another way to make shopping less stressful—and they cut down on breakage. "Kroger has found that the play areas increase customers trips to three times a week in stores that offer the service," says Mez Birdie, CPM Registered Trademark, senior vice president of Commercial Net Lease Realty, Inc.

Incorporating more stores including Big Boxes and discounters into malls—is another new trend to accommodate time-pressed shoppers. At malls such as General Growth's Coral Ridge in Iowa City, managers are mixing power retailers with traditional stores to offer shoppers more options. "People don't just shop at one type of store anymore. You can go to a Wal-Mart parking lot and see Mercedes as well as Fords," says Birdie.

30   "People are pressed for time, so being able to combine destinations into one location is more efficient and more appealing," says McCarty.

"In Europe, you often see supermarkets in malls; there is no reason that you cannot use the same cart to buy your Nikes and your groceries," says Nicholson.

Give Me Data …

One of the major frustrations facing mall owners and managers in determining the impact of entertainment on sales is a lack of concrete data. But that may be about to change with the introduction of Maxtrak, a hand-held electronic data tool that may revolutionize the shopper survey. Unlike paper surveys, which were time consuming and expensive to tabulate, customer responses to questionnaires on preferences, product awareness, and shopping patterns now can be entered into the palm-size device and then downloaded directly into a computer, says Laura Howard, vice president of retail marketing for LaSalle Partners Management Services. Howard, who is testing the new device, notes that: "The best thing is that you get to talk to your customers directly and get immediate feedback. In that way, you can respond at once if a tenant or amenity is not meeting expectations."

Rereading Actively

1. With a partner, review the article, focusing on descriptions of specific malls and specific studies of malls. Together, develop a summary of the current uses of entertainment in malls and also a timeline of the mall developers' commitment to entertainment.

2. What is the most striking position put forward by a mall developer? In a journal entry, explain how this position affects your understanding of the way malls function.

3. Describe the different components of mall entertainment, and then illustrate each component with observations about a local mall.

4. What values do Evans and the people she interviews attribute to shoppers? In a journal entry, summarize the view of the consumer that surfaces here, and offer your initial reaction to that view.

5. What reservations does Evans seem to have about the effectiveness of entertainment as a development strategy? How does her conclusion affect your reading of the article?

Exploring Your Responses

6. According to Evans, more and more retailers believe that they sell entertainment. Revisit one of your favorite shopping haunts and recall an important purchase or a particularly meaningful trip that you made there. In a narrative reflection, reconstruct that purchase or trip, and then freewrite about what your thoughts say regarding the role entertainment plays in your shopping habits.

7. As a class, brainstorm local shopping centers, from the mall around the corner to Wal-Mart and Farm and Fleet to that renovated building with a couple of alternative shops in it. With two or three classmates, visit one of these spots and list the features that retailers have added to the basic store structure—a room, merchandise, and a cash register. Discuss the role entertainment plays in the design of this shopping space, using Evans's analysis as a guide. Then, talk about how the entertainment features—or the absence of such features— affect customers' experiences. Do you believe these features—or their absence—increase sales? Be prepared to report your findings to the class.

8. Think back to your earliest recollections of shopping. Have your shopping habits changed? Do you go to the mall in search of entertainment? In a freewrite, explore your evolution as a shopper and reflect on how shopping center design has anticipated, ignored, or missed your development.

CASE-IN-POINT ASSIGNMENTS

What we buy, why we buy, and how we feel about buying propel our consumer culture, and there are few sites where that culture is (literally) more visible than the mall. Of course, people visit malls for a variety of reasons. We eat and drink at food courts. We exercise there, walking laps around the concourses. At the GAP, we may search for freedom from the fashions of the previous generation. In specialty stores, we enter new social groups. We divert ourselves through movies and the act of purchasing. We reflect on and analyze culture as we browse in the Museum store and watch people promenade the vaulted hallways. We fall in love or flirt or fantasize. We do all of this in an environment that is carefully designed to put us in a buying mood; we may come for the community, but every detail in the place is geared to shopping. It's hard to look at the mall and not consider the "designs" that malls have on us, the implicit and explicit manipulation that is part of a space focused on purchasing. The writers here play with a few of these many variables and details and assemble a number of different positions. They wonder if consumers consume too much, but they also notice that we find power, freedom, and pleasure along the way.

Making Connections

1. Boxer, Barthel, and Evans identify trends and categories associated with shopping and shopping malls. Ranging from sociability to comparison shopping to entertainment, the kinds of use that malls provide have changed over time. Use the trends and categories these writers provide as you describe one mall in a community near you and interpret its role, showing how it is used by the people who frequent it.

2. Guterson and Fiske develop elaborate arguments about why consumers of various types shop. Drawing principles from their work, explain whether a local mall serves as a "mirror" of society (as Boxer claims) or does something quite different.

3. Drawing on the shopper characteristics developed by Guterson, Fiske, and/or Evans, explain and interpret a social interaction that takes place in

a local mall. In your conclusion, state a position on what happens to human relationships in that mall.

4. Review the essays of Barthel and Guterson and brainstorm interesting hypotheses that Barthel's interpretation raises. For example, you could ask, "Are shopping malls in my area becoming like downtowns?" Or "Do I feel nostalgic when I enter a mall?" Or "Does a mall in my area sell a retro style and am I inclined to buy that style?" With a hypothetical question in mind, take a trip to the mall to test your hypothesis (much like Guterson did). Write up a narrative of your experience that explores your question and answers it or discovers that there doesn't seem to be an answer.

5. Fiske talks about how shopping can be a means of political expression. Using his analysis and the review discourse developed by the reviewers (Bowman, Hill, and Chang) included in the Entertainment unit case in point, write a review of the Disney Store (as it exists in a local mall or on the Internet at disney.com), focusing on how the store offers children or parents a chance for political expression.

Collaborative Exchanges

1. Form a group with two or three classmates and review Guterson. Then visit a local mall, freewriting a response to what it feels like to be in that mall. After you've done this fieldwork, meet as a group to discuss your feelings about the mall, comparing them with Guterson's response to the Mall of America. Be prepared to share with the class an explanation of how your perceptions of the mall differed, along with an evaluation of Guterson's assessment of the mall as a public space.

2. In a same-sex group of three or four students, discuss what malls you go to and why you go there, noting similarities and differences in your motivations. Review Boxer's essay and drawing on her analysis and your own experiences, develop a collaborative position on how malls accommodate and define gender in order to encourage people to buy. Be prepared to argue your position in a class discussion.

Net Approaches

1. Go to <www.altavista.com> and do a link search for the Mall of America site <http://www.mallofamerica.com.> To do this, type the following string as an AltaVista search: link:http://www.mallofamerica.com. (Other search engines also enable link searches; check out search engine help pages for instructions.) Scroll through at least fifty of the several hundred linked sites, jotting down surprising ones. Then, visit the five most surprising and explain in your journal why you were surprised that each of the five sites was linked to MOA and why the site is, according to its author, linked to MOA. Finally, write a reflection on what these links tell you about the significance of MOA.

2. Visit a major Internet store like Amazon.com, Gateway.com, or Disney.com and, drawing on the points Evans makes about the role of entertainment in

mall design, explain how the Internet store improves on, differs from, or dilutes this design.

3. With a partner, review Barthel's chapter and Guterson's essay, and brainstorm commodity types—toys, entertainment, fashion, food, technology and so on—that brainstorm define shopping centers. Then, use a search engine to find a Web site that sells one of these kinds of merchandise. Together develop a collaborative description of how the item is displayed electronically.

WRITING PROJECTS

LIFE IN A CULTURE OF EXCHANGE

Project 1

Likely Readings

Background Readings
- Gladwell
- Uchitelle
- Williamson
- Evans

Case-in-Point Readings
- Barthel
- Boxer
- Guterson

Task and Purpose

Focus on a single background reading and locate an idea, principle, or theme that is interesting to you. (Maybe it's Gladwell on manipulation, Uchitelle on seeking higher status, or Williamson on consuming passions.). Decide which case-in-point reading seems to relate this idea to the shopping mall. Use this pairing to analyze shopping malls as a specific aspect of American culture. To develop your analysis, draw on descriptions of the mall in the case readings as well as your own observations and experiences.

Project 2

Likely Readings

Background Readings
- Davis and Meyer
- Gladwell
- Sagoff
- Evans

Case-in-Point Readings
- Boxer
- Fiske
- Guterson

Task and Purpose

The readings above stake out at least two different positions on the direction American consumer culture is headed. Davis and Meyer and Sagoff suggest that changes in technology and social structures have created an environment that thrives on consumption. Guterson fears that consumers are being cut off from one another and that they are being encouraged to substitute the fantasy world of the male for reality. What do you think? Pick a side, define your position (here you will need to make concrete references to the background readings), and use information (images, statistics, structures, observations) from the case in point to elaborate your position.

Project 3

Likely Readings

Background Readings
- Davis and Meyer
- Gladwell
- Sagoff
- Uchitelle

Case-in-Point Readings
- Boxer
- Guterson
- Evans

Task and Purpose

Take a walk through a mall, and write up a narrative of your experience. You will want to focus your narrative on some aspect of your response, on a theme of one sort or another, so that your audience can make sense of it. Look back at the reading we have done. Notice that especially Guterson, but also Sagoff and Gladwell, uses personal observations over time to make a point for their readers. This is more or less your task, but you will need to focus more narrowly as your narrative will run only four or five pages.

Project 4

Likely Readings

Background Readings
- Gladwell
- Williamson
- Evans

Case-in-Point Readings
- Barthel
- Guterson

Task and Purpose

As a cultural phenomenon, malls sell things in part by working to shape people's perceptions and desires. Using Williamson's or Gladwell's ideas as a backdrop and the case-in-point readings as examples, develop an analysis of a local shopping center so that your readers understand how (and how effectively) the design of that mall works.

Project 5

Likely Readings

Background Readings
- Davis and Meyer
- Sagoff
- Uchitelle

Case-in-Point Readings
- Boxer
- Fiske
- Guterson

Task and Purpose

As the readings suggest, not everyone agrees about the virtues and vices of consumer culture. Think of a theme that runs through these readings—for example greed, hype, nostalgia, shallowness, manipulation, materialism, value formation, maybe even sustainable development or the class divide. Synthesize your own position on this topic. Write a paper in which you present differing views on the topic, and explain your own view in relation to those of the writers you are considering. Do you agree or disagree with one or another of them? Why?

CHAPTER 4

Social Groups and Shared Identity

ach of us invests time and energy figuring out what we want and how we will obtain it, and we do this largely in the company of others as members of groups—for example, families and neighborhoods, a peer group at school, or social classes. We gain social recognition by our memberships in groups; through group affiliations, society organizes itself. By virtue of some social or biological "givens," we are assigned to some groups—membership is involuntary. We were born in the late twentieth century; we grew up speaking one or more languages to the exclusion of others. In other cases, we claim group membership voluntarily. We may decide to join the swimming team, listen to a particular style of music, or become a vegetarian. Finally, our membership in some groups may be partly voluntary and partly not. In the United States, a teenager may be required by the state to be a high school student, but she can decide what other students she will associate with, or how willingly she will comply with the expectations of teachers or other school officials, or the pressures put on her by her peers to act or to be a certain way. Facing these decisions as an individual, she will necessarily make her choices in relation to the range of social groups that surround her. Aware of groups she could join, she will notice as well which ones seem to exclude her.

The readings here reflect a number of important characteristics of social groups in a culture of exchange. First, we are in large measure who we are by virtue of our affiliations with various groups. Some of these groups are prominently recognized by society—race, ethnicity, gender, sexual orientation, religion. Whereas some groups

136

have high visibility because of shared attire (uniforms, colors) or coded language, other groups may be united by less tangible bonds such as those shared by a circle of friends or a poetry-writing group. Second, membership in groups is not always clear-cut, since the markers of group membership may be ambiguous, and "the group" as an abstract category will never achieve airtight descriptive precision. If we offered, for example, a group called "library users," and pointed to the twenty or thirty people we can see, here in this suburban branch library on a sweltering June afternoon, you could easily observe the numerous differences that make this group a heterogeneous one, differences in age and gender, in use of the library (it's air conditioned), and interests. Third, groups that have social visibility gain it through the labels, images, or stereotypes that are attached to them. These images and labels may come from outsiders; on the other hand, the group itself, as a way of signifying its own identity, may project them.

This unit will look at groups centered on race, ethnicity, gender, socioeconomic status, taste, and sexual preference, categories that are frequently on center stage in the United States. While the identity of social groups is a product of social practices ("race" as a concept used to categorize people is a human invention that lacks basis in genetics), we are obliged to live with these categories, though we may work to modify their boundaries or our positions within them. And while at times the discussion of social groups seems to descend into the abbreviated code of personal ads, the categories that divide our society take on important meanings as elements in a culture of exchange. (Market research firms and pollsters know a great deal about you simply by knowing your zip code.) The groups we belong to connect us to status, occupations, and privileges. Group membership can still determine how well we are treated and what we can expect to achieve. Therefore, understanding our positions in—and on—social groups requires taking a close look at how and why folks are grouped. In the case-in-point readings, we will focus these questions about the nature and function of social groups, looking specifically at the middle class.

BACKGROUND READINGS

OUT OF THE CLOSET, AND INTO NEVER-NEVER LAND
DANIEL HARRIS

Writing for publications like Harper's, Salmagundi, *and the* New York Times Magazine, *Daniel Harris is a nationally recognized voice on gay culture. His recent book,* The Rise and Fall of Gay Culture *(1997), gathers together his work in a text that tries to understand what happens to a social group when it is assimilated into the U.S. mainstream. Harris concludes that the U.S. market remains homophobic, but it is eager to include gay consumers. As he analyzes the methods through which the mainstream economy sells identity to the gay and lesbian community, he worries about whether this particular group dynamic won't ultimately undermine and even destroy the hard-won social position that gays and lesbians have fought for. This* Harper's *article published in 1995 is a part of that larger project, a set of notes on media representation of gay Americans.*

There's good news for gay Americans these days, and it comes in colorful, monthly installments. Slick, upbeat, glossy gay magazines have arrived over the last few years, pitching the "gay lifestyle." These aren't like the old gay magazines—edgy, alternative publications that focused primarily on political rights. In the new gay glossies, such concerns are lost amid fashion spreads, hair-care products, and Club Med packages. Doing their best to mimic *Details* or *Vanity Fair,* magazines such as *Out, Genre, Men's Style,* and *10 Percent* present endless images of well-adjusted gay bohemians, frolicking in a utopian never-never land where homosexuals are no longer persecuted or self-loathing. But today, as the political climate for gay rights grows colder—as state after state proposes gay-discrimination bills, reaffirms archaic antisodomy statutes, and disqualifies lesbian mothers as unfit parents—these glossies are but fantasy literature, mood enhancers for a demoralized movement.

With a circulation of 120,000, *Out* leads the pack. But it's not circulation that keeps these magazines afloat—it's ad dollars. In these pages you'll find ads for American Express, Virgin Atlantic Airways, and Apple PowerBooks, a sign that corporations are finally mustering the courage to target what the *Wall Street Journal* calls the "dream market"—upscale gay consumers, particularly the so-called DINKs (dual income, no kids). Indeed, gays and lesbians have impressive demographics: their average household income of $47,000 a year is 12 percent higher than for most Americans. *Out*'s media kit raves about the "free-spending" habits of these hungry hedonists; with no kids but a lot of hang-ups, they're "image-conscious," "style-conscious," "health-conscious," and ready to burn gay dollars. *Out* wants to get in on the deal: it's not so much a magazine as a market-penetration device.

The picture of gay life here is a sanitized one, scrubbed clean of overt sexuality and unseemly images. The only mention of sex comes in the subtitle of a less than steamy article about a homicidal lesbian. Inside, there are no nude photos or risqué personal ads. The most conspicuous omission? Images of people with AIDS. Pictures of wasted bodies would scare advertisers and destroy the giddy mood of these magazines. In an interview with the late filmmaker Derek Jarman, *Genre* took the unusual step of omitting photographs of the director altogether, tactfully describing him as "frail." Even *Poz,* the magazine devoted to those living with HIV, avoids photographs of diseased pariahs and instead showcases HIV-positive athletes with ruddy, gym-buffed physiques.

Gay culture has long doted on Hollywood icons (Bette Davis, Judy Garland), but the new glossies are positively starstruck. Celebrities are recruited for more than gossip and glamour—they're asked to show their gay credentials, to prove that they are gay-friendly. Whether it's Ricki Lake assuring *Out* readers that she's a "nice, sweet fag hag" or pop singer Nina Hagen telling *10 Percent* that she "would jump through fire" to help gay people, celebrities are constantly conferring their benedictions on the readers. This fixation on celebrities' feelings about homosexuality reflects a larger dynamic that has taken hold in gay culture: the notion that liberation lies not with politicians but with pop stars, the moral vanguard in American society. Gays are now betting that the concrete social changes they have failed to realize through conventional legal methods can be achieved by riding the coattails of mass culture; if Newt Gingrich won't help you, try Elton John.

5   The articles on film director Gus Van Sant and playwright Arthur Laurents are examples of a type of feature that figures prominently in the new gay glossies: the profile in courage—not political courage but the courage of those "making it." The editors habitually sing the praises of enterprising homosexuals who have clambered to the top of the

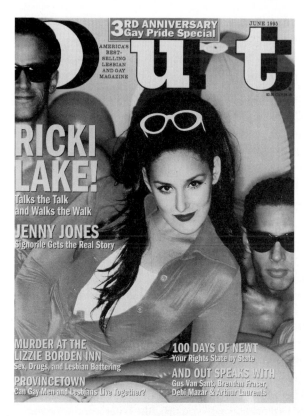

Figure 4.1 *Out* **cover**
Daniel Harris's last piece for *Harper's*, "Making Kitsch from AIDS," appeared in the July 1994 issue. He is working on a book about gay culture to be published by Hyperion.

corporate ladder and now lead prosperous lives as openly gay executives, fashion designers, investment gurus, pulp novelists, and soap-opera stars. Such rags-to-riches parables of the "velvet mafia" transform the new glossies into an oddly religious sort of inspirational literature and cunningly present money-making as a responsible form of activism, a means of seizing the reins of power. Social climbing is more than just profitable; it's a way of blazing the trail to a more equitable and homosympathetic society.

Although the words "gay" and "lesbian" appear on the cover a total of six times, it is quite possible that someone browsing through the magazines at a newsstand would mistake *Out*'s June issue for a straight publication. The crowning irony of the new glossies is that they shamelessly imitate mainstream publications while insisting on the need to cover, as *Genre* puts it, the "people and stories that the general media has long overlooked." In fact, it is the new gay magazines that are doing the overlooking—glossing over the problems of a subculture ravaged by AIDS, splintered by ideological differences, and frustrated by political stagnation. The editors of these magazines, however, are betting their readers won't notice.

Rereading Actively

1. In your journal, describe the focus of each of Harris's comments in two ways: first, notice what feature of the magazine the comment refers to, things like

features, interviews, images, and so on; second, note in a phrase the signifi-cance that Harris finds in each feature.

2. List the issues that Harris finds to be defining gay culture on this magazine cover.

3. What relationship between gay and straight culture does Harris find?

4. With a partner, review the piece and identify the characteristics that Harris attributes to old and new "gay magazines."

5. Working from your findings in the previous exercise, summarize Harris's atti-tude toward the new gay magazines. In your journal, record your response to his attitude.

Exploring Your Responses

6. In your journal, reflect on how the *Out* representation of gay lifestyle com-pares with your notion of this U.S. social group. As you conclude, consider how you feel about the mainstreaming of this often-marginalized group.

7. In a small group, discuss what the cover of a magazine that targets a specific group really says about that group, noting points of agreement and disagree-ment. Then, develop a collaborative evaluation of Harris's analysis, identify-ing and explaining the strongest and weakest points he makes. Be prepared to share your findings with the class and to participate in a debate on the mer-its of Harris's interpretation.

8. Find a magazine that targets a group to which you belong, study its cover, and then, in an extended freewrite, reflect on how many membership criteria the magazine cover offers. Explore how well you meet the criteria and what moti-vation the magazine has for developing the criteria.

DIVIDING AMERICAN SOCIETY

ANDREW J. HACKER

Andrew Hacker teaches political science at CUNY—Queens College and writes about race and social justice. In this first chapter of his book Two Nations: Black and White, Sepa-rate, Hostile, Unequal *(1992), Hacker argues that American racial dynamics are a prod-uct of cultural exchanges from the slave trade to the recent economic successes of new immigrant groups. He confronts his readers with the practices that have governed racial exchanges, choice, responsibility, opportunity, and dominance. As he traces the history of American concepts of race, Hacker seeks to understand why black Americans have not been absorbed into the white dominant culture, and whether black and white Americans can overcome the "residues" (¶ 44) of slavery.*

Race has been an American obsession since the first Europeans sighted "savages" on these shores. In time, those original inhabitants would be subdued or slaugh-tered, and finally sequestered out of view. But race in America took on a deeper and more disturbing meaning with the importation of Africans as slaves. Bondage would later be condemned as an awful injustice and the nation's shame, even as we have come to acknowledge the stamina and skill it took to survive in a system where humans could be bought and sold and punished like animals. Nor are these antecedents buried away in the past. That Americans of African origin once wore the chains of chattels remains alive in the memory of both races and continues to separate them.

Black Americans are Americans, yet they still subsist as aliens in the only land they know. Other groups may remain outside the mainstream—some religious sects, for example—but they do so voluntarily. In contrast, blacks must endure a segregation that is far from freely chosen. So America may be seen as two separate nations. Of course, there are places where the races mingle. Yet in most significant respects, the separation is pervasive and penetrating. As a social and human division, it surpasses all others—even gender—in intensity and subordination.

If white Americans regard the United States as their nation, they also see it beset with racial problems they feel are not of their making. Some contrast current conditions with earlier times, when blacks appeared more willing to accept a subordinate status. Most whites will protest that they bear neither responsibility nor blame for the conditions blacks face. Neither they nor their forebears ever owned slaves, nor can they see themselves as having held anyone back or down. Most white Americans believe that for at least the last generation blacks have been given more than a fair chance and at least equal opportunity, if not outright advantages. Moreover, few white Americans feel obliged to ponder how membership in the major race gives them powers and privileges.

America is inherently a "white" country: in character, in structure, in culture. Needless to say, black Americans create lives of their own. Yet, as a people, they face boundaries and constrictions set by the white majority. America's version of *apartheid,* while lacking overt legal sanction, comes closest to the system even now being reformed in the land of its invention.

5   That racial tensions cast a pall upon this country can hardly be denied. People now vent feelings of hostility and anger that in the past they repressed. Race has become a national staple for private conversation and public controversy. So it becomes necessary to ask what in recent decades has brought the issue and reality of race to the center of the stage.

The idea of race is primeval. Humans have given names to their varied strains since physical differences first began to appear. Nor are there signs that racial lines have grown dimmer in modern times. On the contrary, race continues to preoccupy the public mind, a reminder of a past that cannot be willed away.

Since race is part of common parlance, people have used the term in many ways. Little will be gained by asking for clear-cut definitions; or, for that matter, trying to decide exactly how many different races occupy this planet. Anthropologists have their lists, but even they disagree on criteria and classifications. Still, some major groupings recur: Negroid, Mongoloid, Australoid, Caucasoid, and Indic, with American Indians and Pacific Islanders added as two encompassing categories. But there are also finer racial divisions, such as Aryans and Semites and Dravidians. Tribes like the Watusi and Navahos have also been given racial designations. Indeed, since there is no consensus when it comes to defining "race," the term has been applied to a diversity of groups. The Irish have been called a race in their own right, as have Jews and Hindus. Many find these ambiguities unsettling, but then so is much of life. In the

United States, what people mean by "race" is usually straightforward and clear, given the principal division into black and white. Yet, as it happens, not all Americans fit into "racial" designations.

In theory, Native Americans taken together belong to what most anthropologists would call a basic race. Yet on the whole, they tend to be a loose residue of tribes, rather than a racial entity. A single primal consciousness cannot be said to bind the aspirations and interests of Chippewas and Seminoles and Aleuts. As it happens, the Native American population has undergone an unusual increase. Between 1970 and 1990, the number of persons claiming tribal antecedents rose from 827,268 to 1,516,540, which works out to more than three times the growth rate for the nation as a whole. The chief reason is that a lot of people who had concealed their native origins are now reclaiming them as their primary identity. As it happens, another group can claim an even firmer racial cohesion. It consists of descendants of Hawaii's original inhabitants, most of whom have Polynesian origins. Their growth has mirrored the Native American model, doubling from 100,179 in 1970 to 210,907 in 1990.

Until just a decade or so ago, Americans spoke of "Orientals," and the individuals so described are certainly members of what the anthropologists call the "Mongoloid" race. However, these terms—along with "yellow"—are now hardly ever heard. For one thing, many of those subsumed under the "Oriental" rubric never liked that designation. After all, it was invented and imposed by Europeans, who saw their own continent as the center of civilization, and relegated the "Orient" to Europe's eastern horizon.

10 Today, we have the generic term "Asian," which includes not only Japanese and Chinese and Koreans, but also Indonesians and Indians, along with Burmese and Thais, plus Filipinos and Pakistanis. Geographically speaking, Asia extends from the Kurile Islands to Istanbul and Israel. In fact, "Asian Americans" did not chose this title for themselves. Rather, the larger society has found it convenient to collect them into a single category that mingles racial and national origins. For this reason, obviously, "Asian" itself cannot be a race, since it embraces not only persons once described as "Mongoloid," but also Indics and Dravidians and Caucasians. Even the Koreans and Chinese and Japanese, who belong to the common "Mongoloid" race, seldom mix with one another and have few activities or interests in common. Rather than racial, their images of their identities are almost wholly national. So while in textbook terms, most Americans of Asian origin have specific racial origins, in social and political terms those identities have only a residual significance. In 1970, the census counted 1,438,544 people in what is now the Asian category. By 1990, due mainly to immigration, that group had grown fivefold to 7,273,662.

Nor can it be contended that Americans of Hispanic—or Chicano or Latino— heritage comprise a race. On the contrary, among their numbers can be found persons of almost pure European ancestry, as well as some of partial but visible African origins, along with individuals of unblemished Indian descent. But far outnumbering them are people of such varied parentages as to render any talk of race impossible. Since 1970, the Hispanic group has increased from 9,072,602 to 22,354,059, almost three times the rate for the population as a whole.

In fact, the "nonracial" character of Hispanics has been reflected in recent census reports, where individuals are allowed to describe themselves as they choose. Accordingly, in one census question, individuals may indicate that they are Latin or Hispanic. In another place, they may also fill in a race. Thus in 1990, the census located 7,687,938 residents of California who selected the Latin or Hispanic designation. Within this group, just under half—49.5 percent—chose to say that they also had a race: black or white, or, in a few cases, Asians or Native Americans. However, the other 50.5 percent told the census that in their own view, they had no "race" at all. For them, to be Hispanic was a sole and sufficient identity. (The same eschewal of "race" may be observed among Islamic immigrants from the Middle East.)

So it would seem that the country's fastest-growing groups prefer to emphasize their cultural and national identities rather than traits associated with race. However, the same cannot be said for the rest of the nation, which remains either black or white.

To give the names "black" and "white" to races might seem, on its face, quite ludicrous. Clearly, no human beings have skins of either color. Indeed, very few come even close to those tones. But then "white" and "black" stand for much more than the shades of epidermal coverings. To start, they refer to the "Caucasian" and "Negroid" races, whose facial appearances differ as prominently as their colors.

15   But more is involved than color or facial features or skeletal structure. The terms also carry cultural connotations. In its basic meaning, "white" denotes European antecedents, while "black" stands for Africa. Since the human species began in Africa, we can say that black people are those whose ancestors remained on that continent, while whites descend from those who embarked on migrations to cooler climates. This has led some to the presumption that the races are at different levels of evolutionary development. For at least half a dozen centuries, and possibly longer, "white" has implied a higher civilization based on a superior inheritance.

Europeans who colonized the western hemisphere sought to recreate it in their image, and to transform North and South America into "white" continents. With conquest comes the power to impose your ways on territories you have subdued. The treatment of the Native Americans simply ratified that view. (In some places, the native populations remained large enough to exert a reciprocal influence, as in India and most of Africa. This was not to be the case in the United States.) Still, something can be learned by looking at how "white" was originally conceived, and the changes it has undergone.

From the colonial period through the Jacksonian era, most white Americans were of English ancestry. Alexis de Tocqueville, during his visit in the 1830s, found he could characterize the country and its people as "Anglo-Americans."

Given the expansion of the population, this epithet could not last. Even so, the Anglo-American model has remained remarkably durable, with most subsequent immigrants adapting to its canons. They not only learned English, the single national language, but also adjusted their lives to the economy and technology associated with that prototype. This does not mean that the majority of white Americans regard themselves as "English" in a literal sense. They can and do identify with other origins. Even so, it could be argued that most contemporary citizens associate themselves to a greater degree with Anglo-American culture than with their actual country of origin.

To say this would seem to resurrect the conception of the melting pot, which argued that immigrants would shed their older identities and assimilate to the new culture they encountered. That view has been challenged in many quarters. Rather than as a cauldron, many commentators today prefer to see America as a mosaic or even a lumpy stew. At best, the pot still contains plenty of unmelted pieces. Hence the renewed emphasis on "ethnicity," with its focus on the country's racial and national and religious diversity.

20   Even so, assimilation has taken place and it continues apace. One of the earliest examples came with Germans, who in terms of sheer numbers made up the nation's largest immigrant group. Yet for at least a generation, it has been hard to find many people who qualify as "German-Americans" in any serious sense. Soon after their arrival, which gathered momentum following 1848, Germans quickly learned English and studied the customs of their new land. Many were merchants or farmers, familiar with the rules of a market economy. In addition, it became evident that they were not particularly committed to the country they had left behind. (In fact, there was no unified Germany at that time.) Each generation saw more intermarriage, accompanied by moves to mixed neighborhoods. Service in the Union Army during the Civil War speeded the assimilation process, which was effectively completed during the First World War. With the suburbanization of Milwaukee, only Cincinnati retains the vestiges of a German flavor.

        What also eased acceptance of German immigrants was the realization by Americans of English origin that they needed an ally. For one thing, their own stock was not being renewed by immigration. And, as often happens with groups that arrive early, the offspring they produce begin to feel they should no longer have to do society's less pleasant chores. German-Americans could see why they were being co-opted, and they welcomed the chance to show their ambitions and skills. The English had a further motive: encouraging the Germans, who were mainly Protestant, helped to hold the Catholic Irish at bay.

        It took the Irish longer to shed an alien identity. Although they arrived already knowing English, rural folkways slowed their adjustment to an urban world. Furthermore, at the time of their arrival, Catholics were not regarded as altogether "white." (Thomas Nast's political cartoons gave Irish immigrants subhuman features.) Italians may have been less fervidly Catholic than the Irish, but their acceptance was hampered by peasant habits. Many chose to return to Italy after brief sojourns here; and some of those who chose to stay took their time learning the new language.

        Jews, who arrived in large numbers at the turn of the century, were at first kept at the margin of "white" America simply because they were not Christians. Still, by a generation after their arrival, they had set themselves to mastering the tests for college admission, civil service posts, and many professions. World War II speeded the process of assimilation. At its end, people from every corner of Europe were considered fully "white." By 1990, two Americans of Irish extraction had been elected President, and being a Catholic was seldom a bar to promotion or preferment. The Chrysler Corporation has had a Lee (from Lido) Iacocca for its chairman, while an Irving Shapiro headed DuPont, and several Ivy League universities have had Jewish presidents.

        By this time, it should be clear that the question is not "Who *is* white?" It might be more appropriate to ask "Who *may* be considered white?" since this suggests that something akin to permission is needed. In a sense, those who have already received the "white" designation can be seen as belonging to a club, from whose sanctum they ponder whether they want or need new members, as well as the proper pace of new admissions.

25   Recent immigration from Asia and Latin America complicates any discussion of race. To start, we might ask if persons arriving from countries like Korea or Pakistan might somehow "become white." (Nor is this to say that they might desire the designation.) As was noted earlier, Koreans and others who were once portrayed as belonging to the "yellow" race now reject that description. Their membership in the "Asian" category conjoins them with people as far west as Istanbul. Armenians are now considered "white," as are most Lebanese and Iranians. While in theory, some Asian Indians might be thought too dark to be "white," the appellation has shown itself to possess remarkable elasticity.

In many respects, therefore, color is becoming less important. Most Asian immigrants arrive in this country ready to compete for middle-class careers. Many come with a level of educational preparation at least as good as our own. Schools in Seoul and Bombay now offer coursework as sophisticated as any in Seattle or Baltimore. As hardly needs repeating, Asia has been catapulting itself into the modern world; so if most Asians are not literally "white," they have the technical and organizational skills expected by any "Western" or European-based culture.

How Asians are currently being viewed has much in common with the ways earlier generations co-opted new talents and energies as their own were winding down. To cite a single example,... studies show that white students today spend less time on homework than their Asian classmates. At college, white undergraduates tend to select easier majors, and are opting for comfortable careers in the more sociable professions. Right now, it is in science and technology where Asian talents are being co-opted. But a glance at the list of editors of the *Harvard Law Review* suggests that they are destined for broader representation in the professions and management.

As Asians find places in the economy, they are allowed to move upward on social and occupational ladders. Middle-class whites do not object if Asian children attend their local schools or populate their neighborhoods. Even now, we are beginning to see an increasing incidence of intermarriage, although with the caveat that the first pairings will most usually involve an Asian woman and a white man. The grandchildren will undoubtedly be regarded as a new variant of white.[1]

Much the same process can be observed among Hispanics. Of course, large numbers are already quite "white." This is clearly the case with Cubans, a prominent example being Roberto Goizueta, the Yale-educated chairman of the Coca-Cola Corporation. Most Central and South Americans can claim a strong European heritage, which eases their absorption into the "white" middle class. While skin color and features still figure in social grading, they are less obstacles to mobility than was once the case. More at issue is the divide between unskilled laborers, who will continue pouring across the border for the foreseeable future, and others with the skills and schooling that allow them to enter legally.

30   With the absorption of increasing numbers of Hispanics and Asians, along with Middle Eastern immigrants, being "white" will cease to carry many of the connotations it did in the past. The future population will reflect a more varied array of national origins rather than races, since—as has been stressed—the new groups cannot be easily assigned to racial classifications.

Nor should we be too quick in proclaiming that America will become "multicultural" as well. True, one can point to exotic neighborhoods, with their parades and festivals, to foreign-language newspapers and television channels, along with calls for new kinds of courses in colleges and schools. It would be more accurate to say that the United States will continue to have a single dominant culture. It doesn't really matter whether it is called "white" or "Western" or European or Anglo-American or by another title. It would be better simply to describe it as a structure of opportunities and institutions that has been willing to use the energies and talents of people from various origins. The reception given to recent immigrants is essentially similar to that accorded to successive waves of Europeans. In neither case have the newcomers been given a very cordial welcome. Indeed, they have often met with mistrust, not to mention violence and hostility. Despite the felicitous words on the Statue of Liberty, immigrants are allowed entry on the condition that they serve as cheap labor and live unobtrusively. Many will tell you that now, as in the past, they find their religions scorned, their customs ridiculed, and their features caricatured.

Throughout this nation's history, the expectation has been that newcomers will adapt to the models they encounter on their arrival. If that means relinquishing old-country customs, there are signs that many are prepared to do just that, or at least watch as their children assimilate. Perhaps the first instance of the expanded purview of "white" was when the English founders sought the services of two talented Scots—James Madison and Alexander Hamilton—to help found this nation. The process is still going on.

As with "white," being "black" is less one's particular shade of color than physical features and continent of ancestry. Of course, very few Americans are entirely African in origin. As is well known, slave owners and other whites felt free to force themselves on black women. Still, no matter how light their skin tones, if they retained any vestige of African features, they and their descendants continue to be delineated as "black."

The United States, unlike other countries and cultures, no longer uses terms specifying finer gradations. Hence "mestizo" and "mulatto" have disappeared from our parlance, as have "creole" and "quadroon." Nor has this country retained the generic term "colored" for people whose ancestries are obviously mixed. (The last use of an intermediate term was in the 1910 census, in which interviewers identified about 20 percent of the "Negro" group as "Mulattoes.") It has been far from accidental that this country has chosen to reject the idea of a graduated spectrum, and has instead fashioned a rigid bifurcation.

35   For all practical purposes, "whites" of all classes and ethnicities now prefer to present a common front. Unlike in the past, there are no pronounced distinctions of "purer" versus "lesser" whites, or of those with older claims as against newer arrivals. While immigrants from Colombia and Cyprus may have to work their way up the social ladder, they are still allowed as valid a claim to being "white" as persons of Puritan or Pilgrim stock.

Americans of African ancestry were never given that indulgence. The reason is not that their coloration was too "dark" to allow for absorption into the "white" classification. After all, the swarthiness of some Europeans did not become a barrier to their admission. Had white America really believed in its egalitarian declarations, it would have welcomed former slaves into its midst at the close of the Civil War. Indeed, had that happened, America would not be two racial nations today. This is not to suggest how far blacks themselves would have assimilated, since a lot depends on how far members of a group want to preserve their special heritage. The point is that white

America has always had the power to expand its domain. However, in the past and even now, it has shown a particular reluctance to absorb people of African descent.

How do blacks feel about this bifurcation? Today, most express pride in their African origins, especially those who make a point of calling themselves African-Americans. While, like it or not, a lighter color remains an advantage for women, social advantage is no longer gained by alluding to white elements in one's ancestry. Black Americans are aware that much in the "black" designation represents how whites have defined the term. Still, despite attempts by whites to describe and define them, black Americans have always sought to create their own lives and sustain their sentiments and interests. It started when the first slaves created a culture of their own. Similarly, the drive to replace "colored" with "negro," followed by the move to "Negro," and then on to "black" and "African-American," have all reflected a desire to maintain an autonomous identity.

For most black Americans to be an African-American means literally that in that continent lies the primal origin of your people. The experiences of capture and transportation, of slavery and segregation, never diminished or erased the basic culture and character of tribal ancestries. Yet it is also instructive that blacks from the West Indies and other islands of the Caribbean seek to retain an independent history. Their forebears also originated in Africa and served as slaves, but blacks born in Barbados and Jamaica, or Haiti and Martinique, make clear the British or French connections that distinguish them from others of their race. This emphasis is not intended to render Haitians or Jamaicans "less black" in terms of color. Rather, they wish it known that their antecedents are not exclusively African, but also bear a European imprint.

Black Americans came from the least-known continent, the most exotic, the one remotest from American experience. Among the burdens blacks bear is the stigma of "the savage," the proximity to lesser primates. Hence the question in many minds: Can citizens of African origin find acceptance in a society that is dominantly white, Western, and European?

40   Even at a time when Americans of European backgrounds are giving less emphasis to their ancestries, it is not as easy for black men and women to assimilate into the American mainstream. Even those who aspire to careers in white institutions, and emulate white demeanor and diction, find that white America lets them only partly past the door.

Arguably, this is because the "Africa" in African-American contrasts with much of the European structure of technology and science, of administrative systems based on linear modes of reasoning. Today, Africa is the least developed and most sorrow-ridden of continents. It has more than its share of malnutrition and debilitating diseases, and at least its share of tribal rancor and bloodshed. It seems always to be petitioning the rest of the world for aid. Since the close of the colonial era, over a generation ago, there have not been many African success stories.

Yet the actual Africa of today is not really the model black Americans have in mind. Of much greater significance is how the continent is construed as a symbol: what it says about the human spirit, what it connotes as a way of life. It is more the Africa of history, before the imperial powers arrived. It is also an Africa of the imagination, of music and dance and stories. This Africa speaks for an ancestral humanity, for an awareness of the self, the bonds of tribe and family and community. If the European heritage imposes the regimens of standardized tests, the African dream inspires discursive storytelling celebrating the soul and the spirit.

But as much as anything, being "black" in America bears the mark of slavery. Even after emancipation, citizens who had been slaves still found themselves consigned to a subordinate status. Put most simply, the ideology that had provided the rationale for slavery by no means disappeared. Blacks continued to be seen as an inferior species, not only unsuited for equality but not even meriting a chance to show their worth. Immigrants only hours off the boat, while subjected to scorn, were allowed to assert their superiority to black Americans.

And in our own time, must it be admitted at the close of the twentieth century, that residues of slavery continue to exist? The answer is obviously yes. The fact that blacks are separated more severely than any other group certainly conveys that message. Indeed, the fear persists that if allowed to come closer they will somehow contaminate the rest of society.

45   What other Americans know and remember is that blacks alone were brought as chattels to be bought and sold like livestock. As has been noted, textbooks now point out that surviving slavery took a skill and stamina that no other race has been called upon to sustain. Yet this is not what others choose to recall. Rather, there remains an unarticulated suspicion: might there be something about the black race that suited them for slavery? This is not to say anyone argues that human bondage was justified. Still, the facts that slavery existed for so long and was so taken for granted cannot be erased from American minds. This is not the least reason why other Americans— again, without openly saying so—find it not improper that blacks still serve as maids and janitors, occupations seen as involving physical skills rather than mental aptitudes.

The recollections of the past that remain in people's minds continue to shape ideas about the character and capacities of black citizens. Is it possible to erase the stigmas associated with slavery? After all, a very considerable number of black Americans have achieved impressive careers, winning many of the rewards bestowed by white America. Still, there is no way that even the most talented of these men and women will be considered eligible for the honorific of "white." They are, and will remain, accomplished blacks, regarded as role models for their race. But white Americans, who both grant and impose racial memberships, show little inclination toward giving full nationality to the descendants of African slaves.

Notes

1. Nor should all Asians be categorized as immigrants. Americans of Chinese and Japanese ancestry have been in this country for many generations, particularly in California and Hawaii. Indeed, in Hawaii, these citizens hold many of its prominent positions.

Rereading Actively

1. Hacker opens this chapter with strong phrases like "savages," "slaughtered," "bondage," "shame," and "chains of chattels." How might Hacker want different readers—rich and poor, black and white—to respond to this opening paragraph?

2. What surprising details do you discover in Hacker's history of race in the United States? In your journal, list three or four details and then freewrite about what you knew about these historical references, where you obtained your knowledge, and what Hacker adds to your understanding.

3. In a small group or with a partner, discuss Hacker's analysis of the connection between economic success and racial assimilation in the United States. What does he say the nature of this connection is? How do his assertions compare with your experience and observations? In your journal, summarize your conversation about these questions.

4. In your journal, write a paragraph explaining the symbolism Hacker attributes to "black" and "Africa."

5. With a partner or in a small group, review Hacker's final references to slavery, discussing how they might affect readers' attitudes toward this chapter.

Exploring Your Responses

6. Hacker declares that Americans are "obsessed" with race. In a page or two in your journal, describe an experience you have on a regular basis that confronts you with race issues. Review your story, and freewrite an assessment of your own awareness of race.

7. Think about how race affects "assimilation" into your community, on campus or at home. Is there an "us and them" division you can detect in this local culture? Is race a factor in this division?

8. With two or three classmates, brainstorm scenes of racial separation on your campus or in your local community. Focusing on one situation, discuss the role of the "dominant culture" (¶ 31) in this scene. Consider how likely it is that the races represented your local community will ever be assimilated into a new dominant culture, one built on racial equality.

RE-THINKING THE NATURE OF WORK
BELL HOOKS

bell hooks, a professor of English at the City College of New York, is an influential feminist scholar who has written widely about race, gender, class, and American culture. Writing primarily for an academic audience, hooks's many publications include Ain't I a Woman: Black Women and Feminism *(1981),* Black Looks: Race and Representation *(1992), and* Killing Rage: Ending Racism *(1995). "Rethinking the Nature of Work" appeared in her 1984 volume,* Feminist Theory from Margin to Center. *In this essay, hooks challenges the mainstream feminist movement to engage economic oppression as a women's issue. hooks also questions received notions of the "value" of work as she seeks to re-imagine the capitalist class system—middle class (bourgeois), working class, and lower class—through which women's relationships to themselves, their relationships to men, and their relationships to each other are mediated.*

Attitudes towards work in much feminist writing reflect bourgeois class biases. Middle class women shaping feminist thought assumed that the most pressing problem for women was the need to get outside the home and work—to cease being "just" housewives. This was a central tenet of Betty Friedan's ground-breaking book, *The Feminine Mystique*. Work outside the home, feminist activists declared, was the key to liberation. Work, they argued, would allow women to break the bonds of economic dependency on men, which would in turn enable them to resist sexist domination. When these women talked about work they were equating it with high paying careers; they were not referring to low paying jobs or so called "menial" labor. They were so blinded by their own experiences that they ignored the fact that a vast majority of women were (even at the time *The Feminine Mystique* was published) already working outside the home, working in jobs that neither liberated them from dependence on men nor made them economically self-sufficient. Benjamin Barber makes this point in his critique of the women's movement, *Liberating Feminism*:

> Work clearly means something very different to women in search of an escape from leisure than it has to most of the human race for most of history. For a few lucky men, for far fewer women, work has occasionally been a source of meaning and creativity. But for most of the race it remains even now forced drudgery in front of ploughs, machines, words or numbers—pushing products, pushing switches, pushing papers to eke out the wherewithal of material existence...[1]

Critiques, like Barber's, did not lead feminist thinkers at that time to re-examine their perspectives on women and work. Even though the notion of work as liberation had little significance for exploited, underpaid working women, it provided ideological motivation for college-educated, white women to enter, or re-enter, the work force. It gave many non-college-educated white women who had been taught that a woman's place is in the home the support to tolerate low paying jobs, primarily to boost household incomes and break into personal isolation. They could see themselves as exercising new freedom. In many cases, they were struggling to maintain middle class lifestyles that could no longer be supported solely by the income of husbands. Caroline Bird explains the motivating forces behind their entry into the work force in *The Two-Paycheck Marriage*:

> Whether professional or "pink collar" work, wives didn't think of themselves in the context of economic history. They had no idea they were creating a revolution and had no intention of doing so. Most of them drifted into jobs "to help out" at home, to save for the down payment on a house, buy clothes for the children, or to meet the rising expenses of college. They eagerly sought part-time jobs, work that wouldn't "interfere" with their families. Instead of keeping women at home, children of the 1970's were the expense that drove women to earn, for wives with children at home were more apt to be earning than women in general.[2]

Although many of these women never participated in feminist movement, they did think of themselves as challenging the old-fashioned ideas about women's place.

Early feminist perpetuation of the notion "work liberates women" alienated many poor and working class women, especially non-white women, from feminist movement for a number of reasons. Campaigns like "wages for housework," whose organizers simultaneously challenged sexist definitions of work and the economic structures of capitalism, did not succeed in radicalizing the public's view of feminist definitions of work. Barber was correct when he made the point that these women often desire to quit working because the work they do is not liberating:

> Among many poorer Americans, liberation means the freedom of a mother finally to quit her job—to live the life of a capitalist stay-at-home as it were. Of course work for her has meant scrubbing floors or scouring toilets or sewing endless buttons on

discount smocks, and has more to do with self-preservation than self-realization. Even the most debasing sort of menial labor can, it is true, be perceived as an escape from the pointed dilemmas of leisure—providing it is not compulsory. To be able to work and to have to work are two very different matters.[3]

As workers, poor and working class women knew from their experiences that work was neither personally fulfilling nor liberatory—that it was for the most part exploitative and dehumanizing. They were suspicious of bourgeois women's assertion that women would be liberated via work and they were also threatened. They were threatened because they knew that new jobs would not be created for those masses of white women seeking to enter the work force and they feared that they and men of their classes would lose jobs. Benjamin Barber agreed with them:

> When large numbers of relatively well-educated women enter a rigid labor market in which large numbers of relatively unskilled workers are already unemployed, their employment will probably spell joblessness for many at the bottom. Non-white young men between sixteen and thirty, who already comprise a large proportion of the unemployed, will find it tougher than ever to get a job. At this point the need to set priorities based on some objective measure of real suffering, oppression, and injustice becomes paramount, and the real costs of feminist insistence on the term oppression become visible. Sexism exists with and not in the place of racism and economic exploitation. Liberationists cannot expect the poor to look appreciatively on what appears to be a middle class campaign to wrest still more jobs away from them.

Black women and men were among the first groups to express fears that the influx of married white women into the job market would mean fewer hirings of qualified black people, given the extent to which white supremacy has worked to prevent and exclude non-white people from certain jobs. By grouping white women of all classes with non-white people in affirmative action programs, a system was effectively institutionalized that allowed employers to continue discriminating against non-white peoples and maintain white supremacy by hiring white women. Employers could satisfy affirmative action guidelines without hiring any non-white people. While I was working towards a Ph.D. degree in English, I was continually told by my white professors and peers that I would be the first to get a job, that my blackness would make it easier for me to get a job. This always puzzled me since the majority of affirmative action positions filled during the course of my years of study went to white women. When a black person was hired (or another non-white individual) it was assumed that no other people of color would ever be considered for positions—this was not the case with white women. Unfortunately, the feminist activism that argued white women were a minority helped create a situation wherein jobs once designated primarily for qualified non-whites could be given to white women, and thus many people of color felt that the feminist movement was a threat to their liberation struggles. Had white feminist activists urged that two categories be set up in affirmative action programs—one for women distinct from oppressed ethnic groups seeking job equity—it would not have appeared that white women's liberationists were eager to advance their cause at the expense of non-white women and men.

5   The emphasis on work as the key to women's liberation led many white feminist activists to suggest women who worked were "already liberated." They were in effect saying to the majority of working women, "feminist movement is not for you." By

formulating feminist ideology in such a way as to make it appear irrelevant to working women, bourgeois white women effectively excluded them from the movement. They were then able to shape feminist movement to serve their class interests without having to confront the impact, whether positive or negative, proposed feminist reforms would have on the masses of working class women. Taking their cues from white women, many black women pointed to their having always worked outside the home as an indication that they were already liberated and not in need of feminist movement. They should have been challenging the idea that *any* work would liberate women and demanding that feminist movement address the concerns of working women.

If improving conditions in the workplace for women had been a central agenda for feminist movement in conjunction with efforts to obtain better paying jobs for women and finding jobs for unemployed women of all classes, feminism would have been seen as a movement addressing the concerns of all women. Feminist focus on careerism, getting women employed in high paying professions, not only alienated masses of women from feminist movement; it also allowed feminist activists to ignore the fact that increased entry of bourgeois women into the work force was not a sign that women as a group were gaining economic power. Had they looked at the economic situation of poor and working class women, they would have seen the growing problem of unemployment and increased entry of women from all classes into the ranks of the poor.

Now that many middle class white women divorce and find they enter the ranks of the poor and working class, feminist activists have begun to talk about the "feminization of poverty" and are calling attention to the economic plight of women in the United States. Barbara Ehrenreich and Karin Stallard's essay "The Nouveau Poor" calls attention to the increased entry of middle class white women into the ranks of the poor and emphasizes that poverty among women of all classes increased from 1967 to 1978, years many people thought were economically prosperous times for women:

> The grim economic news belies the image of the seventies as women's "decade of liberation." For some women, in some ways, it was. Women who were young, educated, and enterprising beat a path into once closed careers like medicine, law, college teaching, and middle management. In the media, the old feminine ideal of the suburban housewife with 2.3 children and a station wagon was replaced by the upwardly mobile career woman with attaché case and skirted suit. Television "anchorwomen" became as familiar as yesterday's news, chairmen became chairpersons, so that at times it seemed as if the only thing holding back any woman was a subnormal supply of "assertiveness." But, underneath the upbeat images, women as a class—young, old, black, white—were steadily losing ground, with those who were doubly disadvantaged, black and Hispanic women, taking the heaviest losses.[4]

Unfortunately, it is no accident that white women have only recently begun to focus on these losses. Classism and racism shape women's perspectives in such a way that bourgeois white women saw no need to call attention to these losses when they were not likely to be among those deprived. Concurrently, much recent attention to the issues of women and poverty (among feminists and coming from the right) implies that it is somehow more tragic, more worthy of note, more a situation in need of change because increasing numbers of white middle class women are likely to someday enter the ranks of the poor. This approach to the issue of women and poverty privileges the plight of one group of women. It encourages women to examine the impact of unemployment, divorce, etc. on bourgeois white women rather than compelling us to examine women's overall economic position. Had feminist activists been observing the entire picture all along, it would not have come as such a surprise that women as a group are losing rather than gaining ground economically and the problems could have been addressed sooner.

Approached in the right way, attacking poverty could become one of the issues that could unite women from various ethnic groups and cultural backgrounds. Ehrenreich and Stallard assert:

> The feminization of poverty—or, to put it the other way, the impoverishment of women—may be the most crucial challenge facing feminism today.

Ending economic exploitation of women could become the feminist agenda that would address the concerns of masses of women, thereby breaking down the barriers separating those small groups of women who actively participate in feminist organizations from the larger group of women in society who have not participated in organized feminist struggle. It could transform feminist movement so that it would no longer serve the class interests of a specific group. A collective attempt to address the problem of women's economic exploitation would focus on a number of issues. Some of these issues might be devising ways working conditions within the present system can be improved, though this will not radically change capitalist patriarchy. This latter point is crucial. It is a point Ehrenreich and Stallard avoid making. While they write numerous paragraphs outlining the problem, they write one paragraph suggesting a possible solution:

> We need a feminist economic program and that is no small order. An economic program that speaks to the needs of women will have to address some of the most deep-seated injustices of a business-dominated economy and a male-dominated society. Naming it will take us beyond the familiar consensus defined by the demand for equal rights—to new issues, new programs, and maybe new perspectives. Whether there are debates ahead or collective breakthroughs, they are long overdue; the feminization of poverty demands a feminist vision of a just and democratic society.[5]

Ehrenreich and Stallard suggest that women should work to envision new economic programs but they avoid explicitly criticizing capitalism in this essay. We must accept that it is a system that depends on the exploitation of underclass groups for its survival. We must accept that within that system, masses of women are and will be victims of class oppression.

Most women active in feminist movement do not have radical political perspectives and are unwilling to face these realities, especially when they, as individuals, gain economic self-sufficiency within the existing structure. They are reluctant, even unwilling, to acknowledge that supporting capitalist patriarchy or even a non-sexist capitalist system would not end the economic exploitation of underclass groups. These women fear the loss of their material privilege. As more middle class white women lose status and enter the ranks of the poor, they may find it necessary to criticize capitalism. One of the women described by Ehrenreich and Stallard acknowledges that "hard times have a remarkable way of opening your eyes."

10   As more women face the bankruptcy of the present economic system, we must strive to envision new economic programs while working to alleviate women's current economic plight through meaningful reforms. Efforts to create new jobs by shortening the work week should be supported. Women should support the efforts of couples to share one high paying position. Women should work to bring an end to the "family wage" men receive. Women should support welfare and demand welfare reform. On a very basic level, women need to learn to manage whatever money they receive more effectively. Women need help to break their addiction to compulsive consumerism. Groups of women on specific jobs need to organize collectively to demand better working conditions. Often poor working conditions make low paying jobs women hold unhealthy, unnecessarily dehumanizing, stressful, and depressing. Women who work in service jobs who do not know how to address job-related problems need somewhere they can go for guidance and advice. The list of possible reforms and progressive programs is endless. Although some of these issues are already being addressed, they could all benefit from added support. When women see that their economic concerns are a central agenda for feminist movement, they will be more inclined to examine feminist ideology.

Women are exploited economically in jobs but they are also exploited psychologically. They are taught via sexist ideology to devalue their contributions to the labor force. They are taught via consumerism to believe that they work solely out of material necessity or scarcity, not to contribute to society, to exercise creativity, or to experience the satisfaction of performing tasks that benefit oneself as well as others. Feminist focus on re-thinking the nature of work would help women workers resist psychological exploitation even though such efforts would not change the economic situation. By attributing value to all the work women do, whether paid or unpaid, feminist activists would provide alternative self-concepts and self-definitions for women. All too often, focus on professions and careers within feminist movement led participants to act as if all other jobs, especially those that are low paying, have no value. In this way, feminist attitudes towards work done by the masses of women mirrored the attitudes of men.

Many women in the job market do service work, which is either low paying or unpaid (i.e., housework). Housework and other service work is particularly devalued in capitalist patriarchy. Feminist activists who argued for wages for housework saw this as a means of giving women some economic power and attributing value to the work they do. It seems unlikely that wages for housework would have led society to attribute value to these tasks since paid service work is seen as valueless. In paid service jobs, workers are compensated economically but these compensations do not lessen the extent to which they are psychologically exploited. Their work has the same degrading stigma that is attached to housework. The anonymous authors of *Women and the New World* suggest that wages for housework is "a proposal that takes us even further down the road of capitalism since it brings us into the market-place and puts a price on activities which should fulfill human needs and not just economic independence for women." Were women to receive wages for housework, it is unlikely that it would ever cease to be designated "woman's work"; and it is unlikely that it would be regarded as valuable labor.

There have been too few works written about the value of service work and of housework in particular. (Ann Oakley's *The Sociology of Housework*, Rae Andre's *Homemakers: The Forgotten Workers*, and one anthology, *The Politics of Housework*, edited by Ellen Molos are books about housework.) Yet there are few feminist studies which examine the extent to which well done housework contributes to individual well-being, promotes the development of aesthetics, or aids in the reduction of stress. By learning housework, children and adults accept responsibility for ordering their material reality. They learn to appreciate and care for their surroundings. Since so many male children are not taught housework, they grow to maturity with no respect for their environment and often lack the know-how to take care of themselves and their households. They have been allowed to cultivate an unnecessary dependence on women in their domestic lives and as a result of this dependence are sometimes unable to develop a healthy sense of autonomy. Girl children, though usually compelled to do housework, are usually taught to see it as demeaning and degrading. These attitudes lead them to hate doing housework and deprive them of the personal satisfaction that they could feel as they accomplish these necessary tasks. They grow to maturity with the attitude that most work, not just housework, is drudgery and spend their time fantasizing about lives in which they do not work, especially service work. Had they been taught to value housework, they might approach all work differently. They might see work as an affirmation of one's identity rather than a negation. Today, many young Westerners, female and male, follow the teachings of varied Eastern religious and philosophical thought in the hopes of experiencing self-realization. During this process, they learn to re-think their attitudes towards work, especially service work. They learn that discipline begins with careful performance of all tasks, especially those deemed "menial" in this culture.

Re-thinking the nature of work is essential for feminist movement in the United States. As part of that re-thinking, women must learn to value work. Many feminist activists did not take the position that it would be a significant and meaningful gesture of power and resistance for women to learn to value the work they do, whether paid or unpaid. They acted as if work done by women could only be deemed valuable if men, especially ruling groups of men, were compelled to acknowledge its value (in the case of housework by making it wage labor). Whether men acknowledge the value of the work women do is irrelevant if women do not value that work.

15   Women, like other exploited and oppressed groups in this society, often have negative attitudes towards work in general and the work they do in particular. They tend to devalue the work they do because they have been taught to judge its significance solely in terms of exchange value. Receiving low wages or no wages is seen as synonymous with personal failure, lack of success, inferiority. Like other exploited groups, women internalize the powerful's definition of themselves and the powerful's estimation of the value of their labor. They do not develop an attitude towards work that sees it as an expression of dignity, discipline, creativity, etc. In *Revolution and Evolution in the Twentieth Century* Grace Lee Boggs and James Boggs suggest that most workers in this society, female and male, think of work as a form of slavery and need to know that they create their humanity through participation in work:

> It is inconceivable that humankind could exist without work. The new ethic of work starts out in the first place with the idea that work is a necessity for the human personality. But man/woman has struggled for so long against compulsory work that we have lost the notion that if we didn't work, we would not exist as humans. We exist at the historical conjunction of the highest point of the mass struggle against labor and the technological revolution which eliminated the old reasons to work. So we

have to reaffirm that people have to work, but they don't have to work in the old way and for the old reasons. We can't look for a new way or for new reasons unless we believe that there are human reasons for working...

We need to set up a polarization, an opposition between two attitudes towards work. Whether or not one calls these respectively the "bourgeois" and the "socialist" attitudes to work is not important as long as we recognize that at this historical juncture, this transition, there are two attitudes: one which is hatred and repudiation of work, destructive of the human personality, and the other which recognizes work as essential to the development of oneself as a human being.[6]

Traditionally, work has not been a sphere of human activity women have participated in for the purposes of developing their personalities, self-concepts, etc. This is one of the reasons why those who have achieved economic self-sufficiency are often as unable to liberate themselves from oppressive interactions with sexist individuals as those women who do no wage labor and depend on others for their economic survival. These working women often think that interpersonal relationships are the area in which they will develop personality, self-definition, etc. They may cling to the notion that they will someday be liberated from the need to work by meeting the "right" man. Such thinking leads them to support and perpetuate sexist ideology. Like working class women, they could benefit from feminist effort to re-think the nature of work. Women who cannot find work, who are unemployed and compelled to rely on welfare, are encouraged by the ruling groups to see themselves as parasites living off the labor of others. The welfare system is structured to ensure that recipients will undergo a process of demoralization in order to receive aid. This process often creates depressions that paralyze these women and make them unable to liberate themselves from the position of dependents. These women could also benefit from feminist efforts to re-think the nature of work. They could participate in feminist-promoted efforts to restructure the current welfare system to link it to a positive concept of work, to ensure that it leads to jobs.

Future feminist movement will be sustained only if the needs of masses of women are addressed. By working to rethink the nature of work, feminist activists will be shaping the direction of the movement so that it will be relevant to all women and lead them to participate.

Notes
1. Benjamin Barber, *Liberating Feminism*, p. 52.
2. Caroline Bird, *The Two-Paycheck Marriage*, p. 5.
3. Barber, p.51.
4. Barbara Ehrenreich and Karin Stallard, "The Nouveau Poor," *Ms.*, August 1982, pp. 217–224.
5. *Women and the New World*, p. 35.
6. Boggs, p. 242.

References
Barber, Benjamin. *Liberating Feminism*. New York: Dell Publishing Company, 1975.

Berg, Barbara. *The Remembered Gate: Origins of American Feminism*. New York: Oxford University Press, 1979.

Bird, Caroline. *The Two-Paycheck Marriage*. New York: Pocket Books, 1980.

Boggs, Grace Lee and Boggs, James. *Revolution and Evolution in the Twentieth Century*. New York: Monthly Review Press, 1974.

Women and the New World. Detroit: Advocators, 1976.

Rereading Actively

1. How does hooks organize the stages of the development of ideas about work?

2. Review the article with a partner or in a small group, identifying problems hooks describes and solutions she considers. Discuss whether the solutions she offers seem reasonable. That is, do they seem to be adequate solutions to the problem she analyzes? Why or why not?

3. hooks includes many references to the other feminist thinkers. How do her responses to these other writers clarify her own views of work? Analyze this article with a partner, focusing on two writers whose ideas hooks responds to. Discuss how their ideas help hooks to forward her own view of women and work.

4. Focusing on any three of the following phrases, freewrite on the position of working women as hooks presents it: bourgeois class biases, exploitative and dehumanizing work, white domination, the feminization of poverty, victims of class oppression, addiction to compulsive consumerism.

5. In your journal, write a paragraph that explains what happens to the idea of class as hooks moves to the end of her essay.

Exploring Your Responses

6. How does hooks's constant redefinition of work affect your reading of this piece? Working in a small group, find as many different descriptions of work as you can. Then, brainstorm all the kinds of work you have done, from jobs to volunteer work to chores around home. Pick five very different kinds of work and use hooks's ideas to interpret them.

7. In a page or two in your journal, reflect on the work done by one or more women you know well. Where does this work fit in relation to the double and triple standards that hooks describes? Is the woman (or women) whose work you are analyzing aware of the groups to which hooks might say she belongs?

8. Respond to the feminist approach used by hooks and the writers she quotes. Brainstorm a list of issues that hooks raises and reflect on what hooks says about these topics. What concerns did you share with her before reading the essay? Which of her concerns are new for you? Do you find these new concerns compelling? Why or why not? In a page or two in your journal, describe your thinking about hooks's approach.

9. In a page or two in your journal, explore your or your family's relationship to or experiences of work, focusing on scenes of alienation and success that you discover. Comment on this exploration, comparing your experience to the class and gender issues that hooks describes.

Children of the Future

Roberto Suro

In his 1998 book, Strangers Among Us, *Roberto Suro explores how one American group, Latino immigrants, are transforming the society at large. A journalist at the* Washington Post *and the author of several policy papers on immigration, Suro mixes anecdotes about the lives of immigrants with analysis of how those lives are shaped by and shape the economic system, the short-term gains immigration offers, and the long-term costs it inflicts. Throughout his discussion, Suro focuses on the linguistic, social, and economic exchanges that offer Latino immigrants hope, but also present this group with challenges. As Suro points out, the "migrant channels" that make Latino immigrant life possible were opened by the desire for cheap labor. At the same time, these avenues are threatened by competition between Latino immigrants and other groups for jobs, education, and economic gain. At stake in* Strangers Among Us *is the question of whether Latino immigrants as a group will be able to make a place within U.S. society or remain "a new class of outsiders."*

On Imelda's fifteenth birthday, her parents were celebrating everything they had accomplished by coming north to make a new life in the United States. Two short people in brand-new clothes, they stood in the driveway of their home in Houston and greeted relatives, friends, and neighbors, among them a few people who had come from the same village in central Mexico and who would surely carry gossip of the party back home. A disc jockey with a portable stereo presided over the backyard as if it were a cabaret instead of a patch of grass behind an overcrowded bungalow where five people shared two bedrooms. A folding table sagged with platters of tacos and fajitas. An aluminum keg of beer sat in a wheelbarrow atop a bed of half-melted ice cubes. For Imelda's parents, the festivities that night served as a triumphant display of everything they had earned by working two jobs each. Like most of the other adults at the party, they had come north to labor in restaurants, factories, warehouses, or construction sites by day and to clean offices at night. They had come to work and to raise children in the United States.

Imelda, who had been smuggled across the Rio Grande as a toddler, wore a frilly dress ordered by catalog from Guadalajara, as befits a proper Mexican celebrating her *quinceañera,* which is the traditional coming-out party for fifteen-year-old Latin girls. Her two younger sisters and a little brother, all U.S. citizens by birth, wore new white shirts from a discount store. Their hair had been combed down with sharp, straight parts and dabs of pomade.

When it came time for Imelda to dance her first dance, her father took her in his arms for one of the old-fashioned polkas that had been his favorite when a band played in the town square back home. By tradition, boys could begin courting her after that dance. Imelda's parents went to bed that night content they had raised their children according to proper Mexican custom.

The next morning at breakfast, Imelda announced that she was pregnant, that she was dropping out of school, and that she was moving in with her boyfriend, a Mexican-American who did not speak Spanish and who did not know his father. That night, she ate a meal purchased with food stamps and cooked on a hot plate by her boyfriend's mother. She remembers the dinner well. "That night, man, I felt like an American. I was free."

5   This is the promise and the peril of Latino immigration. Imelda's parents had traveled to Texas on a wave of expectations that carried them from the diminishing life of peasant farmers on a dusty *rancho* to quiet contentment as low-wage workers in an American city. These two industrious immigrants had produced a teenage welfare mother, who in turn was to have an American baby. In the United States, Imelda had learned the language and the ways. In the end, what she learned best was how to be poor in an American inner city.

Latino immigration delivers short-term gains and has long-term costs. For decades now, the United States has engaged in a form of deficit spending that can be measured in human lives. Through their hard work at low wages, Latinos have produced immediate benefits for their families, employers, and consumers, but American society has never defined a permanent place for these immigrants or their children and it has repeatedly put off considering their future. That future, however, is now arriving, and it will produce a reckoning. The United States will need new immigration policies to decide who gets into the country. More importantly, the nation will need new means of assuring political equality and freedom of economic opportunity. Soon Americans will learn once again that in an era of immigration, the newcomers not only demand change; they create change.

When I last met Imelda, she was just a few weeks short of her due date, but she didn't have anything very nice to say about her baby or her boyfriend. Growing up in Houston as the child of Mexican immigrants had filled her with resentment, especially toward her parents, and that was what she wanted to talk about.

"We'd get into a lot of yelling and stuff at home because my parents, they'd say, 'You're Mexican. Speak Spanish. Act like a Mexican girl,' and I'd say, 'I'm here now and I'm going to be like the other kids.' They didn't care."

Imelda is short and plump, with wide brown eyes and badly dyed yellow hair. She wore a denim shirt with the sleeves ripped off, and her expression was a studied pout. Getting pregnant was just one more way of expressing anger and disdain. She is a dime-store Madonna.

10   Imelda is also a child of the Latino migration. She is a product of that great movement of people from Latin America into the United States that is older than any borders but took on a startling new meaning when it gradually gained momentum after the 1960s and then turned into something huge in the 1980s. Latino immigrants were drawn north when America needed their services, and they built communities known as barrios in every major city. But then in the 1990s, as these newcomers began to define their permanent place here, the ground shifted on them. They and their children—many of them native-born Americans—found themselves struggling with an economy that offered few opportunities to people trying to get off the bottom. They also faced a populace sometimes disconcerted by the growing number of foreigners in its midst. Immigration is a transaction between the newcomers and the hosts. It will be decades before there is a final tally for this great wave of immigration, but the terms of the deal have now become apparent.

Imelda's story does not represent the best or the worst of the Latino migration, but it does suggest some of the challenges posed by the influx. Those challenges are defined first of all by demography. No other democracy has ever experienced an uninterrupted wave of migration that has lasted as long and that has involved as many people as the recent movement of Spanish-speaking people to the United States. Twelve million foreign-born Latinos live here. If immigration and birth rates remain at current levels, the total Hispanic population will grow at least three times faster than the population as a whole for several decades, and Latinos will become the nation's largest minority group, surpassing the size of the black population a few years after the turn of the century. Despite some differences among them, Latinos constitute a distinctive linguistic and cultural group, and no single group has ever dominated a prolonged wave of immigration the way Latinos have for thirty years. By contrast, Asians, the other large category of immigrants, come from nations as diverse as India and Korea, and although the Latino migration is hardly monolithic, the Asian influx represents a much greater variety of cultures, languages, and economic experiences. Moreover, not since the Irish potato famine migration of the 1840s has any single nationality accounted for such a large share of an immigrant wave as the Mexicans have in recent decades. The 6.7 million Mexican immigrants living in the United States in 1996 made up 27 percent of the entire foreign-born population, and they outnumbered the entire Asian immigrant population by more than 2 million people. Latinos are hardly the only immigrants coming to the United States in the 1990s, but they will define this era of immigration, and this country's response to them will shape its response to all immigrants.

Latinos, like most other immigrants, tend to cluster together. Their enclaves are the barrios, a Spanish word for neighborhoods that has become part of English usage because barrios have become such a common part of every American city. Most barrios, however, remain a place apart, where Latinos live separated from others by custom, language, and preference. They are surrounded by a city but are not part of it. Imelda lived in a barrio named Magnolia Park, after the trees that once grew along the banks of the bayou there. Like other barrios, Magnolia is populated primarily by poor and working-class Latinos, and many newly arrived immigrants start out there. Magnolia was first settled nearly a hundred years ago by Mexicans who fled revolution in their homeland and found jobs dredging the ship channel and port that allowed Houston to become a great city. Latinos continued to arrive off and on, especially when Houston was growing. Since the 1980s, when the great wave of new arrivals began pouring into Magnolia, it hasn't mattered whether the oil city was in boom or bust—Latinos always find jobs, even when they lack skills and education. Most of Magnolia is poor, but it is also a neighborhood where people go to work before dawn and work into the night.

Like other barrios, Magnolia serves as an efficient port of entry for Latino immigrants because it is an easy place to find cheap housing, learn about jobs, and keep connected to home. Some newcomers and their children pass through Magnolia and find a way out to more prosperous neighborhoods where they can leave the barrio life behind. But for millions like Imelda who came of age in the 1990s, the barrios have become a dead end of unfulfilled expectations.

"We could never get stuff like pizza at home," Imelda went on, "just Mexican foods. My mother would give me these silly dresses to wear to school. No jeans. No jewelry. No makeup. And they'd always say, 'Stick with the Mexican kids. Don't talk to the Anglos; they'll boss you. Don't run around with the Chicanos [Mexican-Americans]; they take drugs. And just don't go near the *morenos* [blacks] for any reason.'"

15   Imelda's parents live in a world circumscribed by the barrio. Except for the places where they work, the rest of the city, the rest of America, seems to them as remote as the downtown skyline visible off in the distance on clear days. After more than a dozen

years, they speak all the English they need, which isn't much. What they know best is how to find and keep work.

Imelda learned English from the television that was her constant childhood companion. Outside, as Magnolia became a venue for gangs and drug sales, she learned to be streetwise and sassy. Growing up fast in Magnolia, Imelda learned how to want things but not how to get them. ...

The United States sits atop the Western Hemisphere like a beacon atop a lighthouse, a sole source, powerfully distorting everything it illuminates even as it points the way. For a hundred years, it has exercised a powerful influence over Latin America, and whether the medium was the Marine Corps or the Peace Corps, the message has always been that Americans knew better, did better, lived better. Whenever the United States became scared of Nazis or Communists, it expended huge resources to portray itself as the paragon of civic virtue and a land of boundless economic opportunity. Meanwhile, the American consumer culture penetrated deep into the Latin psyche, informing every appetite and defining new desires. With TV shows, soldiers, and political ideals, the United States has reached out and touched people across an entire hemisphere. It has gotten back immigrants in return.

America beckons, but massive human flows occur only after migrant channels have evolved into highly efficient conduits for human aspirations. In Mexico's case, emigration to the United States developed out of proximity, shared history, and encouraging U.S. business practices and government policies. When the Mexican revolution displaced millions of peasants after 1910, railroad foremen greeted them at the border and recruited them into track gangs. Dispersed by the Southern Pacific and the Santa Fe railroads, they remained in hundreds of farm towns and built the first urban barrios. Aside from these permanent settlements, a kind of circular traffic developed. Many thousands of Mexicans came to the United States for sojourns of work often lasting no more than a harvesting season but sometimes stretching to years. This migration was expanded and legalized by an agricultural guest–worker program launched in 1942 to help with wartime labor shortages. American farmers liked the cheap, disposable labor so much that that program survived until 1964. By that time, 4.5 million *braceros,* as the workers were known, had learned the way north. The *bracero* program ended, but the traffic continued even as the United States started trying to control the flow. Many Mexicans had acquired some kind of legal status here, including those born in the United States to migrant-worker parents. Others came illegally and found shelter in such barrios as Magnolia and East L.A., which had become permanent Spanish-speaking enclaves. Major changes in U.S. immigration law enacted in 1965 raised the overall ceilings for legal immigration and removed biases that favored Northern and Western Europeans. The most important change in the long run, however, gave preference to immigrants who were reuniting with kin. Having a relative here became the key qualification for a visa, rather than a prospective employer or marketable skills, and immigrant flows became self-duplicating as every new legal immigrant eventually became a potential sponsor for others.

Saskia Sassen, a professor of urban planning at Columbia University, has defined two distinct stages in the history of a migration: the *beginning* of a new flow and its *continuation.* In *The Mobility of Labor and Capital,* a pioneering work on the global economy, Sassen argues that the beginning of a migration involves factors in both the sending and receiving countries that allow for "the formation of objective and subjective linkages…that make such migration feasible." Once migrant channels are established, Sassen believes, the continuation of the flow depends largely on the host country's demand for immigrant labor.

20 A long history of U.S. political and military intervention and of deep economic involvement established ties between the United States and Cuba, so that during the turmoil accompanying Fidel Castro's takeover in 1959, migration was not just feasible but natural and easy. Similar links facilitated a flow from the Dominican Republic when it underwent political upheavals in the 1960s. Although they arrived under very different circumstances, the early waves of Cubans and Dominicans prepared the ground for larger numbers of their countrymen who followed in later years.

The migrant channels from Latin America found their concrete manifestation in the barrios that began to develop in many U.S. cities in 1970s. These communities must be understood as both a cause and a result of immigration. Newcomers pour into the barrios because these communities make immigration accessible to a greater number of people by reducing the cost and difficulty of getting settled here. As the barrios grew larger and more permanent, new migrant channels evolved faster. By the 1980s, it took only a few years for robust flows to grow out of the political turmoil in Central America.

Once efficient linkages had developed, a variety of economic circumstances in the United States generated the demand for immigrant labor, which encouraged the continuation of migrant flows. Just as the rise of the industrial era created jobs for the great wave of European immigrants, the end of that era created opportunities for Latinos. Some manufacturers in old industries such as garments, furniture, and auto parts turned to low-cost immigrant labor as a way of remaining competitive with foreign producers As the U.S. population shifted south to the Sun Belt, Latinos arrived to build the new cities. Immigrants filled hundreds of new job niches as the United States developed a postindustrial service economy that saw booms in light manufacturing and all manner of consumer and financial services.

In addition to economic demand, changes in U.S. immigration law have also promoted continued movement from Latin America. The Immigration Reform and Control Act of 1986 was meant to halt illegal immigration, but it actually encouraged its growth. It created amnesties that allowed nearly 3 million former illegal aliens—nearly 90 percent of them Latinos—to acquire legal residence and eventually become eligible for citizenship. They, in turn, have become hosts to about a million relatives, who have lived in the United States illegally while applying for legal status, and to uncounted others who have no claim on residency. The 1986 reform also imposed sanctions for the first time—mostly civil fines—on employers who hire illegal aliens. No mechanism was ever created to enforce the law, and so it eventually became a meaningless prohibition. Then in 1990, Congress raised the limits on several forms of legal immigration, thus ensuring a protracted influx.

Sassen's framework—beginning and continuation—does not take into account the sudden mass movements of people that characterize the history of emigration to the United States. The Irish, for example, came across the Atlantic as early as the seventeenth century and kept coming steadily for nearly two hundred years in response to demand for low-wage workers. This well-established linkage allowed for a massive, explosive migration during the potato famine in the middle of the nineteenth century and another huge wave in the 1880s during a period of rapid industrialization. Although the U.S. government now tries to regulate immigration, Mexico resembles the Irish case. As with the Irish in the nineteenth century, the migrant channels are abundant and efficient—there are large receiving communities here and the native-born descendants of immigrants have begun to penetrate the mainstream of American society. When Mexico suffered a devastating economic crisis in the 1980s and the U.S. economy boomed, the number of Mexican immigrants living in the United States doubled in a decade. That explosion continues so forcefully that the numbers might nearly double again in the 1990s. And the explosion does not involve just Mexicans now. The flows from the Dominican Republic and El Salvador are also running at a rate headed for a doubling by the end of decade.

25   Americans are only just waking up to the size of this immigrant wave, and yet the foreign-born already account for 9 percent of the total population—the highest proportion since World War II. For fifty years after the end of the European wave in the 1920s, there was no steady immigration, and then the long lull was followed by a demographic storm. Some 7 million more immigrants, counting the estimates of the illegal flow, came to the United States between 1975 and 1995 than during the preceding half-century hiatus. Now, like Rip van Winkle aroused from his slumber, the United States is trying to understand something that is at once familiar but changed. The nation's reference points for large-scale immigration are set in an era of steamships and telegraphs, yet the United States needs to manage a massive influx at a time of jet travel and global television. Moreover, the Latino immigration is not just unexpected and unfamiliar; many Americans consider it unwanted. No national policy debate and no clear process of decision making led to formal action opening the doors to a level of immigration unfamiliar in living memory.

    When the counterreaction hit, it hit hard. In the early 1990s, an extraordinary variety of events combined to present immigration as a menacing force. It began quietly during the recession at the start of the decade and grabbed the public's attention with the nanny problems of Zoë Baird, President Clinton's first nominee for attorney general. Then came the World Trade Center bombing, perpetrated by evildoers who slipped through the immigration system. Chinese smuggling ships, Haitian boat people, Cuban rafters, and swarms of Tijuana border jumpers all fueled anxieties about a chaotic world infringing on America. Even though the United States remained more open to foreigners than any other nation, immigrants had come to represent mysterious and uncontrollable dangers.

    Fears often reflect preexisting conditions in the mind of the victim, and fear of foreigners is no different. Immigrants served as emblems for perils that had already begun to gnaw away at this country's sense of confidence. The seemingly unregulated flow of people struck many Americans as another irrational product of feckless Washington. The immigrants themselves were seen as unworthy beneficiaries of American largesse, arriving unbidden to take advantage of jobs, welfare programs, and much else. Because they are nonwhite and because Hispanic civil rights groups had pushed relentlessly for more open admissions, Latino immigrants also became associated in the minds of some whites with the era of minority-group activism and fears of "reverse discrimination." The ease with which illegal aliens flaunted border controls haunted those who believed that the United States exists in a world full of unworthy but vexing adversaries.

The most virulent expressions of the backlash emerged, not surprisingly, from Southern California, where the economic downturn of the early 1990s was most severe and where immigration was most intense. But every national poll showed that immigration caused widespread if not well-articulated anxieties. Voters indicated they wanted something done, although they were not sure what. An election-year Congress responded in 1996 with measures to keep legal immigrants off welfare and to begin a massive buildup of the Border Patrol. Then, as the economy improved and demand for labor remained high, the rhetoric cooled. The underlying causes of anti-immigrant anxieties have not changed; rather, they have been building. If the U.S. economy sours, or if a crisis in Mexico, Cuba, or Central America produces a highly visible surge of migrants, the backlash will return with even greater fury. Then, Americans are likely to demand strict limits on both legal and illegal immigration and they will hold their leaders to account for failing to develop such controls when the flow was smaller and more manageable.

Devising effective immigration control is an important challenge because without a credible immigration policy the American people are unlikely to make the kind of effort necessary to ensure the successful integration of Latino immigrants and their children. Illegal immigration and high drop-out rates in barrio schools may seem like unrelated problems, but in fact it will be difficult to muster the political will and the resources necessary to deal with the looming crisis in the barrios without first gaining control of the borders. Over the next few decades, despite efforts to close the nation's doors, immigrants will continue to come and, along with the millions already here, many will form a new class of outsiders. No one knows where these new people are supposed to fit into American society, and yet their story has become an American one.

REFERENCES

(¶ 1) *Imelda's story*: Author's account of his first encounters with Imelda appeared in the *New York Times*, January 20, 1992.

(¶ 11) *Twelve million foreign-born Latinos*: U.S. Census Bureau, *The Foreign Born Population: 1994* (Current Population Reports P20-486, 1995), Current Population Survey, March 1996, FB96CPS.

(¶ 11) *Latinos will become the nation's largest minority group*: U.S. Census Bureau, *Population Projections of the United States by Age, Sex, Race and Hispanic Origin: 1995 to 2050* (Current Population Reports P25—1130, 1996).

(¶ 11) *No single group has ever dominated a prolonged wave of immigration*: In the 1890s, for example, Italy, Russia, Austria-Hungary, and Germany had almost equal shares of the influx (around 15 percent each), with Scandinavia, Ireland, and Great Britain not far behind (around to percent each).

(¶ 11) *The 6.7 million Mexican immigrants*: U.S. Census Bureau, *The Foreign Born Population: 1994.*

(¶ 19) *Sassen's stages of immigration*: Saskia Sassen, *The Mobility of Labor and Capital: A Study in International Investment and Labor Flow* (Cambridge University Press, 1988), p. 13.

Rereading Actively

1. Why does Suro open with Imelda's story? What vision of Latino immigrants does this opening encourage? Why?

2. In your journal, list the important details that are raised in Suro's history of American immigration. Review your list and, focusing on two or three details, record your response to this version of U.S. group life.

3. Suro refers to Saskia Sassen's *The Mobility of Labor and Capital*: "The beginning of a migration involves factors in both sending and receiving countries that allow for 'the formation of objective and subjective linkages … that make such migration possible'" (¶ 19). Review this passage with a partner, and write in your journal an explanation of Sassen's theory of migration.

4. Working with the same partner, discuss how the Sassen passage (¶ 19) helps Suro develop his position on the collective experience of Latino immigrants.

5. Review your findings from the previous exercise and write a one- or two-sentence summary of the role of labor in Suro's explanation of migration.

6. What attitude does Suro seem to reveal in his final paragraphs? Does that attitude affect your reading of his text? Your understanding of the situation of Latino immigrants? In your journal, write a response to Suro's conclusion.

Exploring Your Responses

7. Suro describes a "wave" of immigrants that is "unexpected," "unfamiliar," and, for many Americans, "unwanted" (¶ 25). What is your view?

8. With a group of two or three classmates, brainstorm Latino influences and images that are visible in American culture. For example, you might think of Spanish phrases that have become part of American English, and then move to trends in popular culture and media. Reflect on your results, discussing the influences and images you identified.

9. In a journal entry, describe your group's work in the previous question, and comment on your own personal experiences with (or within) Latino culture. How do your experiences compare with the representations of Latino culture reflected in the list your group brainstormed?

BACKGROUND ASSIGNMENTS

One thing all of these writers agree on is that in our society, people's lives are defined in important ways by the groups they belong to. Indeed, the language we use when we speak of "belonging to" a group carries the implication of ownership. Standing in tension with our American sense of individualism, we find that social groups are an enduring feature of our lives. Though some of the categories discussed here predate consumerism, all of them now flow through markets and are defined in part by money and exchange. For instance, no one technically chooses her or his race or gender (though medical technology allows some to acquire alterations), yet hooks and Hacker show how maleness and femaleness, or blackness and whiteness, take on exchange values that have little to do with biology. Further, all of these writers are interested in the process by which individuals and groups try to optimize the classifications they are dealt to achieve more comfortable, more productive, or more just positions. It seems that social groupings have everything to do with fairness, opportunity, taste, and success, all crucial dynamics in our culture of exchange. As you consider these readings, you will need to sort out a disputed vocabulary and some passionately held views on the marginalization and triumphs of groups and individuals, and you will need to think through some arguments about the relationships among classifications, personal choice, manipulation, and oppression.

Making Connections

1. Both Harris and hooks suggest that consumerism may contribute to the subjugation of some groups. Compare Harris's analysis of mainstream gay/lesbian publications with hooks's critique of mainstream feminism and its definition of the value of women's work. Evaluate how effectively each author argues that consumer culture runs contrary to gay/lesbian and women's empowerment.

2. Review hooks, Suro, and Hacker, looking for passages where each talks about our identity as workers or consumers in relation to our identities based on other social groupings—ethnicity, gender, race, language, religion, and so on. Drawing on their ideas, argue whether consumer culture is incompatible with or enhances our identity as members of these other social groups.

3. Exploring the process of assimilation, Hacker and Suro probe what it takes to become recognized as a member of the mainstream or dominant culture in the U.S. Each suggests that access to membership in this group varies according to a range of factors, including economic status as well as race and ethnicity. Think about groups you are a member of, pick one, and describe the elements that might confer membership on a newcomer. Referring to Hacker and Suro, comment on the process by which individuals may (or may not) gain membership in groups they wish to join.

4. Though hooks and Suro take very different approaches to the topic, both explore the stereotypes that society has about a group and conclude that group members need to take political action to combat these stereotypes. Drawing a rationale for group action from these writers and using evidence from your experience as a group member, tell members of a group you belong to why they need to confront a stereotype.

5. Both Harris and Susan Douglas in Chapter 6 describe the methods that media use to present idealized (if not distorted) images of social groups to members of those groups. Drawing on Harris and Douglas, describe how a group you belong to is represented in the mainstream media, for example, special interest magazines, television, or films. Then evaluate the impact this representation has on your own sense of membership in the group.

Collaborative Exchanges

1. With two or three classmates, brainstorm groups to which you feel strongly attached, starting with involuntary groups based on locale, gender, ethnicity, and the like, and moving on to voluntary associations centered on fashion, hobbies, goals, social and political concerns, and so on. Pick one group to focus on and head for the Internet. Find the web site of an organization that represents your group interest; surf through the site, analyzing the group's

structure, goals, or methods of action. Prepare a summary of your findings and a general response to the organization you studied.

2. In a small group, discuss Harris's analysis of the cover of *Out* magazine, noticing what evidence he finds and how he interprets it. Then, pick a current edition of another magazine aimed at a U.S. social group (anything, for example, from *Cosmopolitan* to *Velonews*) and perform the same kind of analysis that Harris did. Write a paper summarizing your group's findings about the projection of a group image to potential group members.

Net Approaches

1. Go through the brainstorming exercise described in the first collaborative exchange above, and locate the Web site of an organization that represents a group you identify with. Then, do a link search. To do this, go to AltaVista <www.altavista.com> and enter into the search box the following string: *link: URL*. (Replace *URL* with the complete URL of your site.) After scrolling through a couple dozen hits, explore three or four connections that catch your attention—for instance, we typed in *link:http://www.now.org* and discovered a list of famous bisexual women, artists, public policy foundations, and Mensrights.com all linked to the National Organization for Women page. Be prepared to explain to the class what you stopped to look at and what the links you found indicate about the group whose web site you began with.

2. Use a search engine or <www.liszt.com> to find a chatroom or listserv that caters to a group to which you belong. (Both tools have complete instructions for joining a discussion.) Watch the discussion for a couple days, making at least one entry yourself, and then write a paper that explores how this virtual conversation affects your sense of belonging to—of being a member of—this group.

CASE-IN-POINT READINGS

THE GROUP AT THE CENTER: FINDING THE MIDDLE CLASS

The case in point focuses the themes raised in the background readings on socioeconomic class, one of the most significant groupings in a culture where exchange cuts across every boundary. Readings here look at poverty in a consumer culture, the struggle to live an "ordinary" life when that life costs too much, the responsibility that comes with wealth and privilege (inherited or earned), representations of class, and the quest for equal opportunity. These writers struggle to find a vocabulary and discourses that deal adequately with the realities of the American exchange and, not surprisingly, disagree on words and realities.

AMERICA HAS A CLASS SYSTEM. SEE "FRASIER"

ANITA GATES

In this 1998 New York Times *article, Anita Gates asserts that it is class difference that has made* Frasier *popular. (*Frasier *appeals broadly to white middle-class viewers.) She finds that a careful representation of the upper-class tastes of Frasier (Kelsey Grammer) and*

Niles (David Hyde Pierce), set in contrast to Frasier's working-class father Martin (John Mahoney), creates a vehicle for "smart," realistic drama and comedy. The dynamics she focuses on—dynamics that other class-conscious sitcoms lack—are instructive: Niles's inability to see his pretentiousness, Martin's running critique of upper-class excesses, and Frasier's consciousness of both highbrow comforts and lowbrow realities. Moreover, Gates asserts that these characters have "values"; that is, they are consistent, kind, and vulnerable despite their neuroses. Gates likes Frasier, *but the real work she accomplishes in this article is an analysis of the humor in the details of this show.*

D r. Frasier Crane's apartment says a lot about him. The tan suede sofa is a copy of one Coco Chanel had in her Paris atelier. The view is the Seattle skyline. There are Lichtensteins on the wall, a baby grand in the alcove and a finely ground Kenya blend in the coffeemaker.

All Frasier (Kelsey Grammer) really wants is to be Cary Grant, but he can never quite pull it off. Even when he, his ex-wife and his brother find themselves in bathrobes (but let's call them dressing gowns) in a great Art Deco hotel room discussing irony, superegos, eggs Florentine and—oh, by the way—a tiny sexual infidelity, as he did in a recent episode, Frasier can't help summing it all up with "Well, isn't this peachy?"

And if Frasier's own failings weren't enough to sabotage his efforts at urban sophistication, there's his father, Martin Crane (John Mahoney), retired cop, beer drinker, television watcher, plain speaker, whose sense of style is symbolized by the dreadful striped easy chair with duct-tape accents that he has plunked down in the middle of his son's elegant minimalism.

The dangers of class mobility in America have never been more eloquently addressed. And class is a subject long overdue for discussion, now that three or four people have admitted that they would have liked Paula Jones better if she'd gone to all the right schools.

5   There may be a hundred reasons that "Frasier" has been a hit sitcom since NBC introduced it in 1993 or why it has won the best-comedy Emmy Award every year it has been on the air, but for many viewers' the heart of the series is the Cranes' intrafamily culture clash, the kind that's bound to occur when blue-collar Americans send their children to Harvard.

American television has never dealt much with the class system, possibly because of the lingering belief that we don't have one. Most series have picked a socioeconomic level and stuck with it: struggling working class from "The Life of Riley" to "Roseanne," solidly, comfortably middle class from "Father Knows Best" to "Home Improvement," or filthy rich on "Dallas" and "Dynasty."

One of the few conspicuously rich households on the 1998 schedule belongs to Maxwell Sheffield on "The Nanny," a sitcom about a Broadway producer with a British accent who hires and learns to love a loud young woman with a Queens accent and very short skirts. The class gap on "The Nanny" is exaggerated for broad laughs, just as a larger gap was on "The Beverly Hillbillies" 30 years ago. Even "Fresh Prince of Bel Air," Will Smith's sitcom about an inner-city teenager relocated to his wealthy relatives' home in a posh part of Los Angeles, tended to rely on stereotypes about the stuffy rich.

The closest thing to a serious portrayal of class mobility must have been "The Millionaire," the 1950's series about a billionaire who liked to amuse himself by giving $1 million (tax free, that was the great part) to some deserving stranger. The half-hour was devoted to the story of how the lucky man or woman handled that new-found wealth—usually badly.

But on innumerable shows, especially rags-to-riches mini-series, that sort of transition is a snap. Maybe that's because television has usually treated class differences as if they were strictly about net worth. Lucy and Ricky Ricardo often had more money than Fred and Ethel Mertz, because Ricky was a successful band leader (and eventually a movie actor), but they never seemed to have different tastes in fashion, food or art. At least not to the degree found among the Cranes.

10   Viewers quickly learned who they were dealing with during the first season of "Frasier" when, over latte at Cafe Nervosa, Frasier's dapper brother, Niles, described a trick he had played on someone at his wine club: switching labels between a Château Petrus and a Foureas-Dupré. "What scamps you are!" said Frasier. "His face must have turned redder than a Pichon-Longueville." The difference between the brothers is that Frasier knows they're being pretentious; Niles honestly doesn't.

David Hyde Pierce, who plays Niles, has said that his character was originally explained to him as "what Frasier would be if he had never gone to Boston and never been exposed to the people at Cheers."

Frasier's character was created in 1984 for "Cheers," then NBC's highest-rated sitcom, as a love interest for Diane Chambers (Shelley Long). A psychiatrist with elbow patches and pear-shaped vowels, he was an educated and sophisticated contrast to the jovially working-class gang that hung out at the show's namesake Boston bar. Diane left Frasier at the altar, but he kept his seat at the bar, looking down his nose at the others' failings for eight more seasons. Luckily for Frasier, Martin never flew into town to reveal his son's humble origins. "Cheers," in the tradition of a class-free America,

Figure 4.2 Not like father
Kelsey Grammer, right; John Mahoney, center, and David Hyde Pierce of "Frasier."

acknowledged taste and economic differences, but in script after script it insisted that the postal worker and the professor might really socialize.

Back in Seattle, Frasier has given that sort of thing up, possibly because he gets enough blue-collar atmosphere at home.

Maybe, the Crane boys sometimes wonder, there was a switched-at-birth mistake at the hospital. "Frasier, is he our real father?" Niles once asked. Frasier answered tolerantly: "Now don't start that again. We've been having this discussion since we were children."

15   At times the brothers think they might be able to sophisticate Martin by exposing him to the finer things. Frasier recalls that even their own tastes were not always beyond reproach. "Remember," he tells Niles, "when you used to think the 1812 Overture was a great piece of classical music?" Niles smiles wistfully. "Was I ever that young?" he says.

But that strategy doesn't work, and neither does Frasier's attempt to buy his father an Armani suit. Martin insists on stopping at a discount store, where he finds a wrinkle-resistant sharkskin ensemble instead. Offered any restaurant in town for his birthday celebration, Dad wants to go to Hoppy's Old Heidelberg. Which may be better than the steak place he once dragged his sons to, where patrons choose their meal from "the steak trolley" and anyone wearing a necktie has it cut off—even if it's Hugo Boss.

Although Frasier earns his living in broadcasting (giving psychiatric advice on a radio call-in show), he makes fun of his father's unfortunate television habit. When he buys Martin a telescope, he says, "Just think of it as having 100 more channels to watch."

But Martin won't let his sons undermine his confidence in his common-man tastes and often gives as good as he gets. He refers to Frasier's breakfast of a bran muffin and a touch of yogurt as "girlie food" and corrects Niles when he describes the cuisine at a certain restaurant as "to die for." "Niles, your country and your family are to die for," Martin reminds him. "Food is to eat." Martin isn't oblivious to changing standards around him; he just thinks they're insane. "A dollar fifty for coffee?" he says in one show. "What kind of world are we living in?"

One of Martin's finest moments comes when Frasier, planning an old-fashioned live radio play, explains to Niles, "People of Dad's generation would sit around at night listening to the radio, absolutely mesmerized." Before Niles has a chance to say that yes, he's well aware of that, Martin gives his older son a look and says, "We were a simple people."

20   One reason "Frasier" works is that both classes are made up of good people with values, which happen to be expressed in different ways. The show gives both coastal yuppies and Middle America a good name.

Kelsey Grammer once described his character, at a Museum of Television and Radio seminar, as "flawed and silly and pompous and full of himself" but "genuinely kind" and "totally vulnerable."

And then there's Niles. Niles, who is so out of touch with the mainstream that he explains creative visualization by suggesting that a radio listener might have "a dog-eared copy of 'Middlemarch' " nearby. That he tries to order a Stoli gibson with three pearl onions at a theme restaurant. (Niles who, by the way, mentions his $400 Bruno Maglis months before O. J. Simpson mentions his.) Niles of the cute smirk and boyish blond good looks (Leonardo DiCaprio in 15 years, if he takes care of himself) and tart tongue. Lilith, Frasier's formidable ex-wife, is in town? "Ah," says Niles, "that explains why blood was pouring from all my faucets this morning."

But also Niles who, despite his elegance, can't dance ("Start with your left foot," suggests his instructor. "Which one?" Niles asks, all too honestly). And who has a painful case of unspoken, unrequited love for Daphne Moon (Jane Leeves), his father's young English (working-class) live-in physical therapist.

Which could begin a list of things the "Frasier" writers are doing right: unrequited love as an opportunity for bawdy double-entendre (Daphne to Niles: "I'm beginning to think I should spend an hour or two on the couch with you"), the lovable dog whom the lead character hates, Niles's never-seen monster of an estranged wife and occasional excursions into farce.

25   The writers throw in literary and theatrical references—without explanation, God bless them—to the likes of Dorothy Parker ("What fresh hell is this?"), "A Chorus Line" ("I'm a dancer. A dancer dances.") and "Hamlet," sort of ("We're a hit. A palpable hit.").

While most sitcoms change scenes with a shot of the exterior of a building and some perky music, "Frasier" does it with subtitles, like "A Coupla White Guys Sittin' 'Round Talkin'" and "Could Guy's Last Name Be Feydeau?"

The show is just plain smart. But America might not forgive the Crane brothers their sophistication, their culinary pretensions and their decorating budgets if they didn't have Martin around to remind them where they came from.

Rereading Actively

1. Identify passages in the article that mention the details of class differences and the comedic possibilities these differences create. Write a summary of these in your journal.

2. This piece opens with a series of references to symbols of upper-class life (e.g., Coco Chanel) and working-class life (e.g., beer). In a journal entry, describe how you respond to these symbols, the associations they bring up for you, and the effect they have on your reading of this article or viewing of *Frasier*.

3. In a small group, discuss Gates's assessment of the show overall and of each of its main characters, paying special attention to the role of class. Record your group's findings in a journal entry.

4. What does Gates seem to think a sitcom is? What are the important elements of this kind of show? What role does a sitcom like *Frasier* play in the culture, according to Gates? Freewrite a response to these questions in your journal.

5. Gates concludes that *Frasier* is "just plain smart" TV (¶ 27). Use a journal entry to explain what this assertion might mean.

Exploring Your Responses

6. Do you agree with Gates's evaluation of *Frasier* and of TV in general? Why or why not?

7. Watch an episode of *Frasier* and freewrite a response to the episode. What do you like and dislike? What was the most memorable scene? What references did you not understand? How was the class divide represented?

8. After watching an episode of *Frasier* and writing a response to it, discuss your reactions to characters, scenes, and representations of class with two or three of your classmates, noting points of agreement and disagreement. Then, brainstorm on the popularity of *Frasier* and what that popularity might say about American ideas about class. Write a brief report that explains to the class why the sitcom is popular and whether Gates's review is accurate.

MOVIES FIND A WAY TO CLOSE THE CLASS DIVIDE
WILLIAM MCDONALD

New York Times *culture critic William McDonald turns to movies and social class in this 1997 article, a review of the film* Inventing the Abbots. *The review focuses on a single scene, one in which true love conquers social class roles. The movie's "tidy solution"— lovers walking off together into a new, classless life—provokes McDonald to talk to sociologists and culture critics. He reports that they declare that this leveling of differences in education, resources, and tastes is a long-standing Hollywood myth, achieved by plot moves McDonald identifies. The people McDonald interviews admit that this myth may sell movies, but they argue that it masks the real effects of the American class system.*

"Inventing the Abbots," A new movie about an old story—the struggle of love against the barriers of social class—saves its most telling moment for last. On screen is the film's working-class hero, Doug Holt, standing alone on a sidewalk along a dark, puddled street in Chicago. He is peering through a dress shop window at his heart's desire, Pamela Abbott, a daughter of wealth. Doug, played by Joaquin Phoenix, has finally caught up with Pam after a fitful pursuit that began where they both came from, an idyllic Illinois town of the late 1950's, a place of malt shops, swinging screen doors and well-tended hedges separating the haves from the have-nots.

Pam, played by Liv Tyler, is startled to see Doug and comes out of the store to greet him. It's a tender scene: shyly, sweetly, the two profess their love. Then they go off together into the night as the camera withdraws, leaving them, presumably, to live happily ever after.

A Hollywood ending? Of course. But what's illuminating about it are the altered circumstances in which Pam and Doug find themselves by the final scene. Doug, a former soda jerk, has escaped the limited future his modest upbringing had held out; he has gone to a fancy Eastern college on a scholarship and, having just graduated, is poised to make something of himself. Pam, too, by leaving home has escaped a future that *her* social station would have demanded: that she marry a man of her own rank, someone suitably rich, and bear his children and tend to his home. Now she can marry whomever she wants and—this is the clincher—earn her place in the world. For when Doug spots her, Pam isn't buying a dress, as might be expected of a rich girl; she's working in the dress shop.

Doug, then, has come up in the world and Pam, in an act of liberation, has come slightly down. Hand in hand, they've bridged the social gap and, even more, found a happy middle ground from which they can both proceed on something close to an equal footing, a place where they won't have to think about such uncomfortable, anti-democratic notions as a class divide. They've become, in short, middle class.

5   It's a tidy solution, this social leveling, to troubling questions about class divisions in America, and it's one that Hollywood has fallen back on time and again. The formula is simple: look at class conflict through the prism of a rich-man, poor-woman romance (or, less often, the other way around) and effectively declare the issue moot. Which is to say, class differences not only don't matter, they don't exist: we're all really alike in the end, and if some people have a few more dollars than you, well, that can be remedied through good old-fashioned gumption and hard work.

"Hollywood will talk about class, if only to destroy the notion of it," says Herbert J. Gans, the Columbia University sociologist. "And of course the idea that we're class-less is nonsense." It's a view shared by the cultural critic Benjamin DeMott, whose 1990 book, "The Imperial Middle: Why Americans Can't Think Straight About Class," tried to lay bare what he calls the American "myth of classlessness."

"In love stories," Mr. DeMott says, "the point as Hollywood tells it is that nothing is an impediment. And the hard social facts of the case—the differences in education, in resources, in tastes that come as a result not of choice but of background—all those things are blown away by the power of instant affection."

One can see this happening in another movie still in theaters, "Fools Rush In," a romantic comedy starring Matthew Perry of the sitcom "Friends." He plays Alex Whitman, a junior executive who impregnates a Las Vegas casino worker, Isabel Fuentes (Salma Hayek), on a one-night stand, never guessing that she'll later reenter his life and make him see that she's the best thing that ever happened to him.

To be sure, the story as advertised is about love overcoming cultural and ethnic differences: he is white Anglo-Saxon and she is Mexican-American. But the movie is also, though less admittedly, about class: he wears a Yale T-shirt and grew up in wealthy New Canaan, Conn.; she comes from a blue-collar immigrant family and works as a casino "picture girl," one who snaps Polaroids of guests. (Alex's snobbish parents mistake her for his housekeeper.)

10   Yet the movie manages not just to bring them together but to close the social gap between them. For one thing, it ratchets Isabel up on the respectability scale by portraying her as an aspiring, and talented, photographer, the idea being that her casino job is clearly beneath her but, fear not, just temporary. To bring Alex down a little, the film has him chuck his upscale Manhattan life style in a love-is-all-that-matters epiphany and race back to Nevada without even a suitcase. And should anyone miss the point, the two seal their union (and bring their baby into the world) precisely where Arizona and Nevada meet atop the Hoover Dam. In other words, they've reached across a metaphorical canyon and found common ground smack in the middle.

Hollywood has had other ways to resolve class differences. Some take a page from "Cinderella," having a commoner hit the romantic jackpot. John Hughes's 1986 teenage romance "Pretty in Pink" comes to mind. Others wind up effectively endorsing class divisions. In "Of Human Bondage" (all three versions), the Somerset Maugham title alone is a tip-off that an affair between an ill-mannered waitress and a genteel doctor can't end well. "The Philadelphia Story" similarly allows the blue-blood Tracy Lord (Katharine Hepburn) to flirt with a reporter (James Stewart). But marry him? Not with rich, handsome C. K. Dexter Haven (Cary Grant) still available.

Figure 4.3 Rich Men, Working Women
James Spader and Susan Sarandon in the 1990 film "White Palace."

Even Spike Lee's seemingly inclusive "Jungle Fever" keeps the classes, as well as the races, separate in the end. Here a black architect patches things up with his wife, a buyer at Bloomingdale's, after his affair with a white working-class woman from Queens has run its fervid course.

"More often than not, though, class-conscious movies simply maneuver the socially mismatched up or down the social ladder toward a common rung. Among the climbers are the heroines of "Sabrina," "My Fair Lady" (by way of Broadway, by way of George Bernard Shaw) and "Pretty Woman"—servant-class women or worse who require social-rank makeovers before rich men will have them. A downwardly mobile variation is the opera-loving yuppie (James Spader) in the 1990 movie "White Palace." He ultimately throws away his lawyer's life of affluence for the love of a tough-talking fast-food waitress (Susan Sarandon).

Even those cloyingly smitten undergrads in the 1970 hit "Love Story"—a saucy baker's daughter from Rhode Island (Ali MacGraw) and a moody son of the New England aristocracy (Ryan O'Neal)—achieve a kind of parity as newlyweds, starting out in an $82-a-month walk-up after young Oliver Barrett 4th is disinherited for marrying down. Now they're actually in a position to pull themselves up by the bootstraps, all the way to a deluxe Fifth Avenue apartment, where they begin to make it on their own with the help of Harvard (his) and Radcliffe (hers) educations.

Go back to 1938 and the same sort of social equalizing occurs at the end of "The Shining Hour." Here a night-club dancer, Olivia Riley (Joan Crawford), drives off into the future with the wealthy Henry Linden (Melvyn Douglas), but only after their big house has burned down and he's virtually left with just the clothes on his back, his wealth at least figuratively left behind. It's a loud declaration, shouted during the Depression, that the rich may be different from you and me but no better.

15   Indeed, such class-blind resolutions are testimonials to the American ideal of egalitarianism.

"We strive toward a middle class melting pot, a kind of assimilation, and it's very worthy and profound," says Ken Hixon, who wrote the screenplay for "Inventing the Abbotts." He acknowledges that the movie's last scene, uniting Doug and Pam, is itself an invention. In the Sue Miller story on which the film is based, Pam and Doug don't even have a crush on each other. The Miller tale centers instead on Doug's embittered older brother, Jacey (Billy Crudup), who chafes at his lower-born status and tries to right the scales by seducing Pam as well as her two equally desirable sisters. For his sins he winds up alone, a hollow man. The brother who finds true love in the movie, Doug—and here lies the moral perhaps—is the one who seems oblivious to class distinctions. His love is pure "and obviously more sentimental," Mr. Hixon says.

"The idea was that love can transcend those mundane obstacles," he says.

But do movie audiences really believe that? If the message, that class lines are easily erasable, isn't the reality for most Americans, won't they see these movies for what they are—fantasies? "Yes, people know it's not true," Mr. Gans says. "It's one of the standard myths that make movies entertainment. People understand it's fantasy, and that's why they go to the movies."

He goes on: "The message is insidious if you take movies seriously, and I'm not sure anybody does."

20   Mr. DeMott, for one, does. He says the power and pervasiveness of movies demand that they be taken seriously. When films promote a myth of classlessness, he says, they only help keep blinders on the American public. And that, he says, has ramifications.

"Social policy is written on the basis of the argument that we are a classless society," he says. Programs like mortgage deductions, property tax exemptions and capital gains tax cuts are, in Mr. DeMott's view, a Federal donation to the middle class financed in part by the poor. "And yet," he says, "these privileges are bestowed on the ground that anybody can get into the middle class and that therefore the programs are not class-based."

To him, Americans who surmount class obstacles are the exceptions, not the rule. "Yes, people will say, since the whole thing is a fantasy, who cares? And it's true that people may walk out of the theater thinking that real life doesn't work that way. But why must we undo each movie after it's over and apply it to a reality check? Why not give us something realistic?"

A realistic story would show that class differences don't evaporate in the heat of passion, Mr. DeMott says. "I've seen marriages of people not of the same social class and the fact is, the differences don't disappear," he says. "People go on making distinctions, and these marriages have to be worked at. Some are successful, some not. In the movies, though, you get the feeling that these distinctions aren't going to come back, that it doesn't matter that you went to Utica State and your wife went to Wellesley."

Even Mr. Hixon, the screenwriter, allows that movies that contrive to place such lovers on the same side of the tracks may be missing the more interesting drama. "The contemplation of what will happen next is probably more compelling than the story you've just seen," he says.

25   But that might be more realism than the movies care to indulge in. Hollywood *is* a fantasy factory, after all. Better to avoid the domestic drama that Utica State vs. Wellesley might provide and end on a happy, if unreal, note. Or, barring that, settle the issue as "Love Story" did: have one of the lovers die.

But that would settle nothing, of course. Movies will continue to return to the subject, and therein lies a tale. For in having to assert over and over that the American dream admits to no class distinctions, Hollywood may be protesting too much, and not saying what it may actually suspect: that the dream, like a movie, is one thing and the truth, quite another.

Rereading Actively

1. McDonald's review brings the discussion of class to very familiar ground. In a small group, discuss his description of the class divide and the mythical ways in which that divide is covered up. Summarize your group's discussion of these topics in a journal entry.

2. With a partner, focus on the question raised in the previous exercise. Together, review McDonald's description of the strategies of social leveling that surface in films.

3. What is McDonald's assessment of the effect of movies on our culture? What seems to be McDonald's attitude to popular film? Where does he reveal it? Draft two- or three-sentence responses to each of these questions in a journal entry.

4. Write a paragraph summary of McDonald's position on both the role of realism in Hollywood films and the effect that realism has on depictions of class in those films.

5. In a journal entry, explain and evaluate McDonald's belief that there are some fairly direct connections between film and life.

Exploring Your Responses

6. In your experience, are people affected by what they see in movies? How does McDonald's perspective on movies compare or contrast with yours? Respond to the differences or similarities.

7. The sociologists that McDonald cites assume that American society has a fairly well-established class hierarchy but that Americans love to fantasize about a classless society. In a page or two in your journal, speculate on the ways in which your own life may be affected by class roles. What class systems do you dream about?

8. Freewrite a reaction to McDonald's description of the final scene of *Inventing the Abbotts*. Does he make you want to go and see the film? How do you respond to films that end this way? Does doing a "reality check" change your experience of a movie?

9. With two or three classmates, watch a movie, TV show, or play that depicts class difference, maybe one of the films that McDonald discusses. After viewing, discuss how believable each of you found the representation of the "myth" of class, class characteristics, and social mobility, noting differences in opinion. After your discussion, collaborate on a brief explanation of how elements of class were presented and how this representation adds to or modifies your group's sense of class in America. Be prepared to share your explanation and descriptions of one or two scenes from the film with the class. (If possible, show a couple of clips.)

AIN'T NO MIDDLE CLASS

SUSAN SHEEHAN

Susan Sheehan has been a staff writer with the New Yorker *since 1961 and has published a variety of nonfiction in article and book-length forms. While she has worked with topics that range from architecture to politics, she seems to keep coming back to American family life. On one level, this excerpt from her 1995* New Yorker *essay reads like an anthropological case study, an objective description of human behavior. (It appeared in the "Reporter at Large" section of the magazine.) Yet, while Sheehan appears to withhold judgment, the evidence and dialogue she includes give the piece a distinctive spin. A practiced nonfiction writer, Sheehan offers her interpretation through the comments of her subjects, the Mertens, and by relying on the reactions of her readers.*

At ten o'clock on a Tuesday night in September, Bonita Merten gets home from her job as a nursing-home aide on the evening shift at the Luther Park Health Center, in Des Moines, Iowa. Home is a two-story, three-bedroom house in the predominantly working-class East Side section of the city. The house, drab on the outside, was built in 1905 for factory and railroad workers. It has aluminum siding painted an off-shade of green, with white and dark-brown trim. Usually, Bonita's sons—Christopher, who is sixteen, and David, who is twenty and still in high school (a slow learner, he was found to be suffering from autism when he was eight)—are awake when she comes home, but tonight they are asleep. Bonita's husband, Kenny, who has picked her up at the nursing home—"Driving makes Mama nervous," Kenny often says—loses no time in going to bed himself. Bonita is wearing her nursing-home uniform, which consists of a short-sleeved navy-blue polyester top with "Luther Park" inscribed in white, matching navy slacks, and white shoes. She takes off her work shoes, which she describes as "any kind I can pick up for ten or twelve dollars," puts on a pair of black boots and a pair of gloves, and goes out to the garage to get a pitchfork.

In the spring, Bonita planted a garden. She and David, who loves plants and flowers, have been picking strawberries, raspberries, tomatoes, and zucchini since June. Bonita's mother, who lives in Washington, Iowa, a small town about a hundred miles from Des Moines, has always had a large garden—this summer, she gave the Mertens dozens of tomatoes from her thirty-two tomato plants—but her row of potato plants, which had been bountiful in the past, didn't yield a single potato. This is the first year that Bonita has put potato plants in her own garden. A frost has been predicted, and she is afraid her potatoes (if there are any) will die, so instead of plunking herself down in front of the television set, as she customarily does after work, she goes out to tend her small potato strip alongside the house.

The night is cool and moonless. The only light in the back yard, which is a block from the round-the-clock thrum of Interstate 235, is provided by a tall mercury-arc lamp next to the garage. Traffic is steady on the freeway, but Bonita is used to the noise of the cars and trucks and doesn't hear a thing as she digs contentedly in the yellowy darkness. Bonita takes pleasure in the little things in life, and she excavates for potatoes with cheerful curiosity—"like I was digging for gold." Her pitchfork stabs and dents a large potato. Then, as she turns over the loosened dirt, she finds a second baking-size potato, says "Uh-huh!" to herself, and comes up with three smaller ones before calling it quits for the night.

"Twenty-two years ago, when Kenny and me got married, I agreed to marry him for richer or poorer," Bonita, who is forty-nine, says. "I don't have no regrets, but I didn't have no idea for how much poorer. Nineteen-ninety-five has been a hard year in a pretty hard life. We had our water shut off in July *and* in August, and we ain't never had it turned off even once before, so I look on those five potatoes as a sign of hope. Maybe our luck will change."

5   When Bonita told Kenny she was going out to dig up her potatoes, he remembers thinking, Let her have fun. If she got the ambition, great. I'm kinda out of hope and I'm tired.

Kenny Merten is almost always tired when he gets home, after 5 P.M., from his job at Bonnie's Barricades—a small company, started ten years ago by a woman named Bonnie Ruggless, that puts up barriers, sandbags, and signs to protect construction crews at road sites. Some days, he drives a truck a hundred and fifty miles to rural counties across the state to set up roadblocks. Other days, he does a lot of heavy lifting. "The heaviest sandbags weigh between thirty-five and forty pounds dry," he says. "Wet, they weigh fifty or sixty pounds, depending on how soaked they are. Sand holds a lot of water." Hauling the sandbags is not easy for Kenny, who contracted polio when he was eighteen months old and wore a brace on his left leg until he was almost twenty. He is now fifty-one, walks with a pronounced limp, and twists his left ankle easily. "Bonnie's got a big heart and hires people who are down on their luck," he says.

Kenny went to work at Bonnie's Barricades two years ago, and after two raises he earns seven dollars and thirty cents an hour. "It's a small living—too small for me, on account of all the debts I got," he says. "I'd like to quit working when I'm sixty-five, but Bonnie doesn't offer a retirement plan, so there's no way I can quit then, with twenty-eight years left to pay on the house mortgage, plus a car loan and etceteras. So I'm looking around for something easier—maybe driving a fork-lift in a warehouse. Something with better raises and fringe benefits."

On a summer afternoon after work, Kenny sits down in a rose-colored La-Z-Boy recliner in the Mertens' living room/dining room, turns on the TV—a nineteen-inch Sylvania color set he bought secondhand nine years ago for a hundred dollars—and watches local and national news until six-thirty, occasionally dozing off. After the newscasts, he gets out of his work uniform—navy-blue pants and a short-sleeved orange shirt with the word "Ken" over one shirt pocket and "Bonnie's Barricades" over the other—and takes a bath. The house has one bathroom, with a tub but no shower. Last Christmas, Bonita's mother and her three younger brothers gave the Mertens a shower for their basement, but it has yet to be hooked up—by Kenny, who, with the help of a friend, can do the work for much less than a licensed plumber.

Kenny's philosophy is: Never do today what can be put off until tomorrow—unless he really wants to do it. Not that he is physically lazy. If the Mertens' lawn needs mowing, he'll mow it, and the lawn of their elderly nextdoor neighbor, Eunice, as well. Sometimes he gets up at 4:30 A.M.—an hour earlier than necessary—if Larry, his half uncle, needs a ride to work. Larry, who lives in a rented apartment two miles from the Mertens and drives an old clunker that breaks down regularly, has been married and divorced several times and has paid a lot of money for child support over the years. He is a security guard at a tire company and makes five dollars an hour. "If he does-n't get to work, he'll lose his job," Kenny says. In addition, Kenny helps his half brother Bob, who is also divorced and paying child support, with lifts to work and with loans.

10   Around 7:30 P.M., Kenny, who has changed into a clean T-shirt and a pair of old jeans, fixes dinner for himself and his two sons. Dinner is often macaroni and cheese, or spaghetti with store-bought sauce or stewed tomatoes from Bonita's mother's garden. He doesn't prepare salad or a separate vegetable ("Sauce or stewed tomatoes *is* the veg-etable," he says); dessert, which tends to be an Iowa brand of ice cream, Anderson Erick-son, is a rare luxury. Kenny takes the boys out for Subway sandwiches whenever he gets "a hankering" for one. Once a week—most likely on Friday, when he gets paid—he takes them out for dinner, usually to McDonald's. "It's easier than cooking," Kenny says.

Because Bonita works the evening shift, Kenny spends more time with his sons than most fathers do; because she doesn't drive, he spends more time behind the wheel. Christopher, a short, trim, cute boy with hazel eyes and brown hair, is one badge away from becoming an Eagle Scout, and Kenny drives him to many Scouting activi-ties. This summer, Kenny drove Eunice, who is eighty-five, to the hospital to visit her ninety-year-old husband, Tony, who had become seriously ill in August. After Tony's death, on September 12th, Kenny arranged for the funeral—choosing the casket and the flowers, buying a new shirt for Tony, and chauffeuring the boys to the private view-ing at the funeral home. "Everyone was real appreciative," he says.

At around eight-thirty on evenings free from special transportation duties, Kenny unwinds by watching more television, playing solitaire, dozing again, and drinking his third Pepsi of the day. (He is a self-described "Pepsiholic.") Around nine-fifty, he dri-ves two miles to the Luther Park nursing home for Bonita.

Bonita and Kenny Merten and their two sons live in a statistical land above the lowly welfare poor but far beneath the exalted rich. In 1994, they earned $31,216 between them. Kenny made $17,239 working for Bonnie's Barricades; Bonita made $13,977 at Luther Park. With an additional $1,212 income from other sources, includ-ing some money that Kenny withdrew from the retirement plan of a previous employer, the Mertens' gross income was $32,428. Last year, as in most other years of their marriage, the Mertens spent more than they earned.

The Mertens' story is distinctive, but it is also representative of what has happened to the working poor of their generation. In 1974, Kenny Merten was making roughly the same hourly wage that he is today, and was able to buy a new Chevrolet Nova for less than four thousand dollars; a similar vehicle today would cost fifteen thousand dol-lars—a sum that even Kenny, who is far more prone than Bonita to take on debt, might hesitate to finance. And though Kenny has brought on some of his own troubles by not always practicing thrift and by not always following principles of sound money management, his situation also reflects changing times.

15   In the nineteen-sixties, jobs for high-school graduates were plentiful. Young men could easily get work from one day to the next which paid a living wage, and that's what Kenny did at the time. By the mid-eighties, many of these jobs were gone. In Des Moines, the Rock Island Motor Transit Company (part of the Chicago, Rock Island & Pacific Railroad) went belly up. Borden moved out of the city, and so did a division of the Ford Motor Company. Utility companies also began downsizing, and many factory jobs were replaced by service-industry jobs, which paid less. Although there is a chronic shortage of nurse's aides at Luther Park, those who stay are not rewarded. After fifteen years of almost continuous employment, Bonita is paid seven dollars and forty cents an hour—fifty-five cents an hour more than new aides coming onto the job.

Working for one employer, as men like Kenny's father-in-law used to do, is a novelty now. Des Moines has become one of the largest insurance cities in the United States, but the Mertens don't qualify for white-collar positions. Civil-service jobs, formerly held by high-school graduates, have become harder to obtain because of competition from college graduates, who face diminishing job opportunities themselves. Bonita's thirty-seven-year-old brother, Eugene, studied mechanical engineering at the University of Iowa, but after graduation he wasn't offered a position in his field. He went to work for a box company and later took the United States Postal Service exam. He passed. When Bonita and Kenny took the exam, they scored too low to be hired by the Post Office.

Although thirty-one percent of America's four-person families earned less in 1994 than the Mertens did, Kenny and Bonita do not feel like members of the middle class, as they did years ago. "There ain't no middle class no more," Kenny says. "There's only rich and poor."

This is where the $32,428 that the Mertens grossed last year went. They paid $2,481 in federal income taxes. Their Iowa income-tax bill was $1,142, and $2,388 was withheld from their paychecks for Social Security and Medicare. These items reduced their disposable income to $26,417. In 1994, Bonita had $9.64 withheld from her biweekly paycheck for medical insurance, and $14.21 for dental insurance—a $620.10 annual cost. The insurance brought their disposable income down to $25,797.

The highest expenditures in the Mertens' budget were for food and household supplies, for which they spent approximately $110 a week at various stores and farmers' markets, for a yearly total of $5,720. They tried to economize by buying hamburger and chicken and by limiting their treats. (All four Mertens like potato chips.) Kenny spent about eight dollars per working day on breakfast (two doughnuts and a Pepsi), lunch (a double cheeseburger or a chicken sandwich), and sodas on the road—an additional two thousand dollars annually. His weekly dinner out at McDonald's with his sons cost between eleven and twelve dollars—six hundred dollars a year more. Bonita's meals or snacks at work added up to about three hundred dollars. Kenny sometimes went out to breakfast on Saturday—alone or with the boys—and the meals he and his sons ate at McDonald's or Subway and the dinners that all four Mertens ate at restaurants like Bonanza and Denny's probably came to another six hundred dollars annually. David and Christopher's school lunches cost a dollar-fifty a day; they received allowances of ten dollars a week each, and that provided them with an extra two dollars and fifty cents to spend. The money the boys paid for food outside the house came to five hundred dollars a year. The family spent a total of about $9,720 last year on dining in and out; on paper products and cleaning supplies; and on caring for their cats (they have two). This left them with $16,077.

20　　　The Mertens' next-highest expenditure in 1994 was $3,980 in property taxes and payments they made on a fixed-rate, thirty-year, thirty-two-thousand-dollar mortgage, on which they paid an interest rate of 8.75 percent. This left them with $12,097.

In April of 1994, Kenny's 1979 Oldsmobile, with two hundred and seventy-nine thousand miles on it, was no longer worth repairing, so he bought a 1988 Grand Am from Bonita's brother Eugene for three thousand dollars, on which he made four payments of two hundred dollars a month. The Grand Am was damaged in an accident in September, whereupon he traded up to an eleven-thousand-dollar 1991 Chevy Blazer, and his car-loan payments increased to $285 a month. Bonita has reproached Kenny for what she regards as a nonessential purchase. "A man's got his ego," he replies. "The Blazer is also safer—it has four-wheel drive." The insurance on Kenny's cars cost a total of $798, and he spent five hundred dollars on replacement parts. Kenny figures that he spends about twenty dollars a week on gas, or about $1,040 for the year. After car expenses of $2,338 and after payments on the car loans of $1,655, the Mertens had $8,104 left to spend. A ten-day driving vacation in August of last year, highlighted by stops at the Indianapolis Motor Speedway, Mammoth Cave, in Kentucky, and the Hard Rock Cafe in Nashville, cost fifteen hundred dollars and left them with $6,604.

The Mertens' phone bill was approximately twenty-five dollars a month: the only long-distance calls Bonita made were to her mother and to her youngest brother, Todd, a thirty-three-year-old aerospace engineer living in Seattle. She kept the calls short. "Most of our calls are incoming, and most of them are for Christopher," Bonita says. The Mertens' water-and-sewage bill was about fifty dollars a month; their gas-and-electric bill was about a hundred and fifty dollars a month. "I have a hard time paying them bills now that the gas and electric companies have consolidated," Kenny says. "Before, if the gas was seventy-five dollars and the electric was seventy-five dollars, I could afford to pay one when I got paid. My take-home pay is too low to pay the two together." After paying approximately twenty-seven hundred dollars for utilities, including late charges, the Mertens had a disposable income of $3,904.

Much of that went toward making payments to a finance company on two of Kenny's loans. To help pay for the family's 1994 vacation, Kenny borrowed eleven hundred dollars, incurring payments of about seventy-five dollars a month for two years and three months, at an interest rate of roughly twenty-five percent. Kenny was more reluctant to discuss the second loan, saying only that it consisted of previous loans he'd "consolidated" at a rate of about twenty-five percent, and that it cost him a hundred and seventy-five dollars a month in payments. Also in 1994 he borrowed "a small sum" for "Christmas and odds and ends" from the credit union at Bonnie's Barricades; twenty-five dollars a week was deducted from his paycheck for that loan. Payments on the three loans—about forty-three hundred dollars last year—left the Merten family with a budget deficit even before their numerous other expenses were taken into account.

Except in a few small instances (according to their 1994 Iowa income-tax return, Bonita and Kenny paid H & R Block a hundred and two dollars to prepare their 1993 return, and they gave a hundred and twenty-five dollars to charity), it isn't possible to determine precisely what the rest of the Mertens' expenditures were in 1994. Several years ago, Kenny bounced a lot of checks, and he has not had a checking account since. Kenny exceeded the limits on both of their MasterCards a few years ago, and the cards were cancelled. Bonita has a J. C. Penney charge card but says, "I seldom dust it off." Now and then, Bonita went to a downtown outlet store, and if a dress caught her fancy she might put it on layaway. On special occasions, she bought inexpensive outfits for herself and for Kenny. Before last year's summer holiday, she spent seven dollars on a top and a pair of shorts, and during the trip Kenny bought a seventy-five dollar denim jacket for himself and about fifty dollars' worth of T-shirts for the whole family at the Hard Rock Cafe. One consequence of Kenny's having had polio as a child is that his left foot is a size $5^1/2$ and his right foot a size 7. If he wants a comfortable pair of shoes, he has to buy two pairs or order a pair consisting of a $5^1/2$ and a 7. Often he compromises, buying sneakers in size $6^1/2$. David wears T-shirts and jeans as long as they are black, the color worn by Garth Brooks, his favorite country singer. Christopher is partial to name brands, and Bonita couldn't say no to a pair of eighty-nine-dollar Nikes he coveted last year. The Mertens spent about seven hundred dollars last year on clothing, and tried to economize on dry cleaning. "I dry-clean our winter coats and one or two dresses, but I avoid buying anything with a 'Dry-clean only' label," Bonita says.

25   The Mertens' entertainment expenses usually come to a thousand dollars a year, but that amount was exceeded in 1994 when Kenny bought a mountain bike for every member of the family. The bikes (Bonita has yet to ride hers out of the driveway) cost two hundred and fifty-nine dollars apiece, and Kenny made the final payments on them earlier this year. This July, David rode Kenny's bike to a hardware store, and it was stolen while he was inside. Kenny yelled at David; Bonita told Kenny he was being too hard on him, and Kenny calmed down.

Bonita and Kenny don't buy books or magazines, and they don't subscribe to newspapers. (They routinely borrowed Eunice and Tony's Des Moines *Register* until Tony's death, when Eunice cancelled it.) They rarely go to the movies—"Too expensive," Kenny says—but regularly rent movies and video games, usually at Blockbuster. For amusement, they often go to malls, just to browse, but when they get a serious urge to buy they go to antique stores. Kenny believes in "collectibles." His most treasured possession is an assortment of Currier & Ives dishes and glasses.

The Mertens have never paid to send a fax, or to send a package via Federal Express, and they aren't on-line: they have no computer. They even avoid spending money on postage: Kenny pays his bills in person. Bonita used to send out a lot of Christmas cards, but, she says, "I didn't get a whole lot back, so I quit that, too." They spend little on gifts, except to members of Bonita's family.

Kenny knows how much Bonita loves red roses. Twenty-two years ago, he gave her one red rose after they had been married one month, two after they had been married two months, and continued until he reached twelve red roses on their first anniversary. He also gave her a dozen red roses when she had a miscarriage, in 1973, "to make her feel better." To celebrate the birth of David and of Christopher, he gave her a dozen red roses and one yellow one for each boy. And Kenny gives Bonita a glass rose every Christmas.

On a Sunday evening this summer, the four Mertens went to Dahl's, their supermarket of choice in Des Moines. They bought four rolls of toilet paper (69 cents); a toothbrush (99 cents); a box of Rice Krispies (on sale for $1.99); eight sixteen-ounce bottles of Pepsi ($1.67); a gallon of two percent milk ($2.07); a large package of the least expensive dishwasher detergent ($2.19), the Mertens having acquired their first dishwasher in 1993, for a hundred and twenty-five dollars; two jars of Prego spaghetti sauce ($3); a box of Shake 'n Bake ($1.99); two rolls of film ($10.38), one for Kenny, who owns a Canon T50 he bought for a hundred and twenty-five dollars at a pawnshop, and one for Christopher to take to Boy Scout camp in Colorado; a battery ($2.99) for Christopher's flashlight, also for camp; a pound of carrots (65 cents); a green pepper (79 cents); some Ziploc bags ($1.89); a Stain Stick ($1.89); a box of 2000 Flushes ($2.89); a package of shredded mozzarella ($1.39) to add to some pizza the Mertens already had in the freezer; and twelve cans of cat food ($3). Bonita bought one treat for herself—a box of toaster pastries with raspberry filling ($2.05). Christopher asked for a Reese's peanut-butter cup (25 cents), a bottle of Crystal Light (75 cents), and a package of Pounce cat treats ($1.05). All three purchases were O.K.'d.

30   David, who is enchanted by electrical fixtures, was content to spend his time in the store browsing in the light-bulb section. He was born with a cataract in his left eye, and the Mertens were instructed to put drops in that eye and a patch over his "good" right eye for a few years, so that the left eye wouldn't become lazy. Sometimes when they put the drops in, they told David to look up at a light. Today, David's main obsession, which apparently dates back to the eyedrops, is light. "We'd go someplace with David, and if there was a light with a bulb out he'd say, 'Light out,'" Bonita recalls. "We'd tell him, 'Don't worry about that,' and pretty soon he was saying, 'Light out, don't worry about that.'"

At twenty, David looks fifteen. A lanky young man with copper-colored hair, hearing aids in both ears, and eyeglasses with thick lenses, he attends Ruby Van Meter, a special public high school for the city's mentally challenged. He reads at a fifth-grade level, and he doesn't read much. For years, the Mertens have been applying—without success—for Supplemental Security Income for David. In June of this year, when his application for S.S.I. was once again turned down, the Mertens hired a lawyer to appeal the decision. David has held a series of jobs set aside for slow learners (working, for instance, as a busboy in the Iowa state-house cafeteria and in the laundry room of the local Marriott hotel), but he says that his "mood was off" when he was interviewed for several possible jobs this summer, and he drifted quietly through his school vacation. He will not be permitted to remain in school past the age of twenty-one. If David could receive monthly S.S.I. checks and Medicaid, the Mertens would worry less about what will happen to him after they are gone. They have never regarded David as a burden, and although he has always been in special-education classes, they have treated him as much as possible the way they treat Christopher. Say "special ed" to Bonita, and she will say, "Both my boys are very special."

The Dahl's bill came to $44.75. When Kenny failed to take money out of his pocket at the cash register, Bonita, looking upset, pulled out her checkbook. She had expected Kenny to pay for the groceries, and she had hoped that the bill would be forty dollars or less. But Kenny was short of money. "Aargh," Bonita said, softly.

Bonita didn't want to write checks for groceries, because she has other ideas about where her biweekly paychecks—about four hundred dollars take-home—should go. Most of her first check of the month goes toward the mortgage—$331.68 when she pays it before the seventeenth of the month, $344.26 when she doesn't. Bonita likes to put aside the second check for the two most important events in her year—the family's summer vacation and Christmas. In theory, Kenny is supposed to pay most of the other family expenses and to stick to a budget—a theory to which he sometimes has difficulty subscribing. "I don't like to work off a budget," he says. "I think it restricts you. My way is to see who we have to pay this week and go from there. I rob Peter to pay Paul and try to pay Peter back." In practice, Kenny rarely pays Peter back. With his take-home pay averaging about two hundred and thirty-five dollars a week, he can't.

When a consumer counsellor, who does not know the Mertens, was questioned about the family's current financial predicament—specifically, their 1994 income and expenditures—she made numerous recommendations. Among her suggestions for major savings was that the Mertens cut their food bills dramatically, to fifty-four hundred dollars a year. She proposed stretching the Mertens' food dollars by drastically curtailing their eating out and by buying in bulk from the supermarket. She said that Kenny should get rid of his high-interest loans, and use the money he was spending on usurious interest to convert his mortgage from thirty years to fifteen. The way Kenny and Bonita were going, the counsellor pointed out, they would not finish paying off their current mortgage until they were seventy-nine and seventy-seven years old, respectively. The Mertens' principal asset is eight thousand dollars in equity they have in their house. If the Mertens wanted to retire at sixty-five, they would need more than what they could expect to receive from Social Security.

35   The counsellor had many minor suggestions for economizing at the grocery store. The Mertens should buy powdered milk and mix it with one percent milk instead of buying two percent milk. They should cut down even further on buying meat; beans and lentils, the counsellor observed, are a nutritious and less costly form of protein. She recommended buying raisins rather than potato chips, which she characterized as "high-caloric, high-fat, and high-cost."

The counsellor had one word for the amount—between fifteen hundred and twenty-five hundred dollars—that the Mertens spent on vacations: "outlandish." Their vacations, she said, should cost a maximum of five hundred dollars a year. She recommended renting a cabin with another family at a nearby state park or a lake. She urged the Mertens to visit local museums and free festivals, and go on picnics, including "no-ant picnics"—on a blanket in their living room.

Kenny and Bonita were resistant to most of the suggestions that were passed on to them from the counsellor, who is funded mainly by creditors to dispense advice to those with bill-paying problems. According to Kenny, buying a dozen doughnuts at the supermarket and then taking breakfast to work would be "boring." Bonita says she tried powdered milk in the mid-eighties, when Kenny was unemployed, and the kids wouldn't drink it. She does buy raisins, but the boys don't really like them. Bonita and Kenny both laugh at the prospect of a no-ant picnic. "Sitting on the living-room carpet don't seem like a picnic to me," Bonita says.

Bonita surmises that the counsellor hasn't experienced much of blue-collar life and therefore underestimates the necessity for vacations and other forms of having fun. "We couldn't afford vacations in the eighties, and if we don't take them now the kids will be grown," she says. Kenny reacted angrily to the idea of the boys' eating dried beans and other processed foods. "I lived on powdered milk, dried beans, surplus yellow cheese, and that kind of stuff for two years when I was a kid," he says. "I want better for my boys."

Kenny acknowledges that he tried to confine his responses to the consumer counsellor's minor suggestions, because he realizes that her major recommendations are sound. He also realizes that he isn't in a position to act on them. He dreams of being free of debt. He has tried a number of times to get a fifteen-year mortgage, and has been turned down each time. "We both work hard, we're not on welfare, and we just can't seem to do anything that will make a real difference in our lives," he says. "So I save ten dollars a bowling season by not getting a locker at the alley to store my ball and shoes, and have to carry them back and forth. So I save twenty-five dollars by changing my own oil instead of going to Jiffy Lube. So what? Going out to dinner is as necessary to me as paying water bills."

Rereading Actively

1. Most of the episodes that make up this essay open with a reference to time and place: we see Bonita arriving home at 10 P.M. and leaving for work at 1 P.M.; the Mertens go shopping "on a Saturday evening"; and a consumer counselor reviews their "1994 income and expenditures." Focus on two or three of these time references, and write about how they affect your reading of the essay.

2. What is the most surprising of the Mertens' spending habits that Sheehan reveals? Record your response to the passage in which this evidence appears.

3. With a partner or in a small group, review the article, discussing what Sheehan and her subjects think life should be like. How do they justify that view?

4. How does Sheehan's general description of Kenny and Bonita affect you? Do you end up feeling sympathy, empathy, or pity? Do you pass judgment on them? Explain how two passages shape your response.

5. Reflect on Sheehan's attitude toward the Mertens. (You may want to begin this reflection by identifying passages where she seems to reveal her attitude.) Compare her feelings about the Mertens with those of the consumer counselor and with your own.

6. At the end of this excerpt, Kenny observes, "Going out to dinner is as necessary to me as paying water bills" (¶ 39). In a freewrite, explain how this assertion affects your reading of this piece.

Exploring Your Responses

7. With two or three of your classmates, brainstorm a list of all the expenditures you have made in the past two weeks. Review your results and divide them

into three sets: essential expenditures, important ones, and frivolous ones. Note items that create disagreement among group members or are hard to categorize. Discuss and note how much time and effort you spend pursuing the items in each of the categories, again recording differences. Craft a general profile of your group's spending habits, calling attention to differences and similarities among group members, and then compare your group's general spending habits with the Mertens'. Be prepared to define the different "class" habits represented in your group and the differences and similarities between group members and the Mertens.

8. What would a consumer counselor say if she looked at your expenditures in detail? Would she find "outlandish" behavior? Write a note from a consumer counselor to yourself explaining your expectations, tastes, and spending habits and the directions these tendencies are taking you.

9. Sheehan's title, "Ain't No Middle Class," suggests that fewer and fewer Americans can achieve the American dream. Freewrite about your own prospects for achieving success, comfort, and your own home (or whatever your "dream" is). What "class" do you hope to or expect to join? Do you suspect that you will be more successful at getting into that class than the Mertens? Why or why not?

10. Compare the Mertens' situation with your own family situation. Focus on two or three points of similarity or difference, and use those points of contact to explore your own position within the social and economic hierarchy.

An Emerging Middle Class
Linda Chavez

President of the Center for Equal Opportunity, Linda Chavez is an outspoken proponent of Hispanic assimilation into mainstream American culture. A specialist in public policy, Chavez sees market competition as a boon for (legal) immigrants rather than a hostile force. In publications ranging from Time *and the* Wall Street Journal *to* Commentary, *and in this excerpt from* Out of the Barrio *(1991), she argues that Hispanic leaders have failed to see what Hispanic people everywhere know: assimilation is the ticket to a better life. Along with her opposition to bilingual education, affirmative action, and liberal immigration policies, this stance has made her a controversial figure in the Hispanic community. This discussion of the Hispanic middle class is representative of her agenda, calling attention to misreadings of the "real" situation and celebrating the values of consumer life, progress, family, work, earnings, education, and career.*

Each decade offered us hope, but our hopes evaporated into smoke. We became the poorest of the poor, the most segregated minority in schools, the lowest paid group in America and the least educated minority in this nation."[1] This view of Hispanics' progress by the president of the National Council of La Raza, one of the country's leading Hispanic civil rights groups, is the prevalent one among Hispanic leaders and is shared by many outside the Hispanic community as well. By and large, Hispanics are perceived to be a disadvantaged minority—poorly educated, concentrated in barrios, economically impoverished; with little hope of partici-pating in the American Dream. This perception has not changed substantially in twenty-five years. And it is wrong.

Hispanics have been called the invisible minority, and indeed they were for many years, largely because most Hispanics lived in the Southwest and the Northeast, away from the most blatant discrimination of the Deep South. But the most invisible His-panics today are those who have been absorbed into the mainstream. The success of middle-class Hispanics is an untold—and misunderstood—story perhaps least appre-ciated by Hispanic advocates whose interest is in promoting the view that Latinos can-not make it in this society. The Hispanic poor, who constitute only about one-fourth of the Hispanic population, are visible to all. These are the Hispanics most likely to be studied, analyzed, and reported on and certainly the ones most likely to be read about. A recent computer search of stories about Hispanics in major newspapers and maga-zines over a twelve-month period turned up more than eighteen hundred stories in which the word *Hispanic* or *Latino* occurred within a hundred words of the word *poverty*. In most people's minds, the expression *poor Hispanic* is almost redundant.

Has Hispanics' Progress Stalled?

Most Hispanics, rather than being poor, lead solidly lower-middle- or middle-class lives, but finding evidence to support this thesis is sometimes difficult. Of course, Hispanic groups vary one from another, as do individuals within any group. Most analysts acknowledge, for example, that Cubans are highly successful. Within one generation, they have virtually closed the earnings and education gap with other Americans.... Although some analysts claim that the success of Cubans is due exclusively to their higher socioeconomic status when they arrived, many Cuban refugees—especially those who came after the first wave in the 1960s—were in fact skilled or semiskilled workers with relatively little education.[2] Their accomplishments in the United States are attrib-utable in large measure to diligence and hard work. They established enclave economies, in the traditional immigrant mode, opening restaurants, stores, and other émigré-ori-ented services. Some Cubans were able to get a foothold in industries not usually avail-able to immigrants. They formed banks, specializing in international transactions attuned to Latin American as well as local customers, and made major investments in real estate development in south Florida. These ventures provided big profits for only a few Cubans but jobs for many more. By 1980 Miami boasted some two hundred Cuban millionaires and 18,000 Cuban-owned businesses, and about 70 percent of all Cubans there owned their own homes (a rate that exceeds that of whites generally).[3] But Cubans are as a rule dismissed as the exception among Hispanics. What about other Hispanic groups? Why has there been no "progress" among them?

The largest and most important group is the Mexican American population.... [I]ts leaders have driven much of the policy agenda affecting all Hispanics, but the importance of Mexican Americans also stems from their having a longer history in the United States than does any other Hispanic group. If Mexican Americans whose families have lived in the United States for generations are not yet making it in this society, they may have a legitimate claim to consider themselves a more or less per-manently disadvantaged group, like blacks. That is precisely what Mexican American leaders suggest is happening. Their proof is that statistical measures of Mexican

American achievement in education, earnings, poverty rates, and other social and economic indicators have remained largely unchanged for decades. In 1959 the median
income of Mexican-origin males in the Southwest was 57 percent that of non-Hispan-
ics.[4] In 1989 it was still 57 percent of non-Hispanic income.[5] If Mexican Americans had
made progress, it would show up in improved education attainment and earnings and
in lower poverty rates, so the argument goes. Since it doesn't, progress must be stalled.

5   In the post-civil rights era, the failure of a minority to close the social and economic gap with whites is assumed to be the result of persistent discrimination.
Progress is perceived not in absolute but in relative terms. The poor may become less
poor over time, but so long as those on the upper rungs of the economic ladder are
climbing even faster, the poor are believed to have suffered some harm, even if they
have made absolute gains and their lives are much improved. However, in order for
Hispanics (or any group on the lower rungs) to close the gap, they must progress at
an even greater rate than non-Hispanic whites; their apparent failure to do so in recent
years causes Hispanic leaders and the public to conclude that Hispanics are falling
behind. Is this a fair way to judge Hispanics' progress? In fact, it makes almost no sense
to apply this test today (if it ever did), because the Hispanic population itself is changing so rapidly. This is most true of the Mexican-origin population.

In 1959 the overwhelming majority of persons of Mexican origin living in the
United States were native-born, 85 percent. Today only about two-thirds of the people
of Mexican origin were born in the United States, and among adults barely one in two
was born here. Increasingly, the Hispanic population, including that of Mexican origin,
is made up of new immigrants, who, like immigrants of every era, start off at the bottom of the economic ladder. This infusion of new immigrants is bound to distort our
image of progress in the Hispanic population, if each time we measure the group we
include people who have just arrived and have yet to make their way in this society.

A simple analogy illustrates the point. Suppose we compared the achievement of
two classes of students in the same grade as measured by a standardized test administered at the beginning and the end of the school year, but the only information by
which we could assess progress was the mean score for the class. Let's say that the mean
score for Class A was 100 points on the initial test, a score right at the national average, and that Class B scored 75. In the test given at the end of the school year, Class A
scored 150 (again the national average) and Class B scored 110. Both classes made
progress, but Class B still had not eliminated the gap between it and Class A and
remained significantly below the national average. Having only this information, we
would be justified in believing that students in Class B were continuing to lag in educational achievement.

But suppose we discovered that Class B had grown by one-half by the time the
second test was given and that the other class had remained stable. In Class A thirty
students took the test at the beginning of the school year, and the same thirty took
it at the end. In Class B, however, fifteen new students were added to the class
between the first and the second test. We would have no way of knowing what the
average final test score meant in terms of the overall achievement of students in
Class B until we knew more about the new students. Suppose we then found out
that half of them were recent, non-English-speaking immigrants. We could reasonably assume that the addition of even five such students would skew the test
results for the entire class, presumably lowering the class mean. Unless we had more

information, though, we still wouldn't know what exact effect the scores of the new students had on the class mean or how much progress the original students had actually made over the year.

Hispanics in the United States—and the Mexican-origin population in particular—are very much like Class B. In 1980 there were about 14.6 million Hispanics living in the United States; in 1990, nearly 21 million, an increase of about 44 percent in one decade. At least one-half of this increase was the result of immigration, legal and illegal.... [T]his influx consists mostly of poorly educated persons, with minimal skills, who cannot speak English. Not surprisingly, when these Hispanics are added to the pool being measured, the achievement levels of the whole group fall. It is almost inconceivable that the addition of two or three million new immigrants to the Hispanic pool would not seriously distort evidence of Hispanics' progress during the decade. Yet no major Hispanic organization will acknowledge the validity of this reasonable assumption. Instead, Hispanic leaders complain, "Hispanics are the population that has benefitted least from the economic recovery."[6] "The Myth of Hispanic Progress" is the title of a study by a Mexican American professor, purporting to show that "it is simply wrong to assume that Hispanics are making gradual progress towards parity with Anglos."[7] "Hispanic poverty is now comparable to that of blacks and is expected to exceed it by the end of this decade," warns another group.[8]

10   Hispanics wear disadvantage almost like a badge of distinction, as if groups were competing with each other for the title "most disadvantaged." Sadly, the most frequently heard complaint among Hispanic leaders is not that the public ignores evidence of Hispanics' achievement but that it underestimates their disadvantage. "More than any group in American political history, Hispanic Americans have turned to the national statistical system as an instrument for advancing their political and economic interests, by making visible the magnitude of social and economic problems they face," says a Rockefeller Foundation official.[9] But gathering all Hispanics together under one umbrella obscures as much information as it illuminates, and may make Hispanics— especially the native-born—appear to suffer greater social and economic problems than they actually do.

In fact, a careful examination of the voluminous data on the Hispanic population gathered by the Census Bureau and other federal agencies shows that, as a group, Hispanics have made progress in this society and that most of them have moved into the social and economic mainstream. In most respects, Hispanics—particularly those born here—are very much like other Americans: they work hard, support their own families without outside assistance, have more education and higher earnings than their parents, and own their own home. In short, they are pursuing the American Dream—with increasing success.

NOTES

1. Raul Yzaguirre, speech at the Leadership Conference on Civil Rights Fortieth Anniversary Dinner, May 8, 1990.
2. See Alejandro Portes and Robert L. Bach, *Latin Journey: Cuban and Mexican Immigrants in the United States* (Berkeley: University of California Press, 1985). The earliest Cuban refugees included many businessmen, professionals, and skilled workers, but later immigrants were neither wealthy nor well educated.
3. L. H. Gann and Peter J. Duignan, *The Hispanics in the United States: A History* (Boulder, Colo.: Westview Press, 1986), 108.

4. Leo Grebler, Joan W. Moore, and Ralph C. Guzman, *The Mexican American People: The Nation's Second Largest Minority* (New York: Free Press, 1970), 187.

5. Bureau of the Census, *The Hispanic Population in the United States: March 1990*, Current Population Reports, sec. P-20, no. 449 (Washington, D.C.: GPO 1991).

6. National Council of La Raza, "The Decade of the Hispanic: An Economic Retrospective" (Washington, D.C.: National Council of La Raza, March 1990).

7. Jorge Chapa, "The Myth of Hispanic Progress: Trends in the Educational and Economic Attainment of Mexican Americans," *Harvard Journal of Hispanic Policy* 4 (1989–90): 17.

8. *Closing the Gap for U.S. Hispanic Youth: Report from the 1988 Aspen Institute Conference on Hispanic Americans and the Business Community* (Washington, D.C.: Hispanic Policy Development Project, 1988), 8.

9. Kenneth Prewitt, "Public Statistics and Democratic Politics," in William Alonso and Paul Starr, eds., *The Politics of Numbers* (New York: Russell Sage, 1987), 271.

Rereading Actively

1. In her first paragraph, Chavez summarizes the view of the Hispanic civil rights group La Raza on the place Hispanics have in the American class system and declares, "It is wrong." Why does she use this introduction strategy, and how does it affect your reading of the chapter?

2. Working in a small group or with a partner, summarize Chavez's position on progress and social mobility.

3. Chavez consistently draws distinctions between Hispanic Americans and Hispanic immigrants. In small group, review this distinction, discussing how it affects the validity of her argument and that of her opponents. Describe your group's conversation in an entry in your journal.

4. In the final sentence of this excerpt, Chavez offers an implicit definition of middle-class life and describes several paths into the middle class. Explain in your own words her definition of the middle class and then list the paths into that group.

5. How might a sympathetic reader respond to the last sentence in this excerpt? How might a member of La Raza respond? In your journal, describe the two reactions.

Exploring Your Responses

6. Chavez voices an assumption that most consumer–citizens share: Success in the "social and economic mainstream" equals "progress" (¶ 11) With a partner or in a small group, discuss whether, based on your experience and observation, this assumption is valid. Then, write your own opinion in an entry in your journal.

7. In a page or two in your journal, reflect on your own class position by drawing on Chavez's comments on the Hispanic community. How do family, work, and education seem to contribute to your own "social mobility"?

8. In a small group, develop a collaborative response to Chavez's analogy to two classes of students (¶ 7–9). Talk about what two things she is comparing and what conclusions she draws. Then, decide whether you think the analogy is

valid, noting different positions within your group. Generate a statement that integrates everyone's position. (This doesn't mean you all have to agree.) As a group, be prepared to participate in a class discussion about how immigrants fit into U.S. consumer culture.

THE YUPPIE STRATEGY

BARBARA EHRENREICH

Barbara Ehrenreich is an important feminist writer, a novelist, a columnist, and a researcher. Her work on gender, social justice, education, class, and most recently violence has appeared in Time *and* Newsweek, *specialist journals, and books. In* Fear of Falling *(1989), she turns from feminist issues to class issues, with an interest in how people who describe themselves as middle class carry on from generation to generation. In this excerpt from a chapter on yuppies, she explores a 1980s middle-class social group that defined itself and was defined by upscale consumption. Ehrenreich analyzes the sources and characteristics of this short-lived, "middle-class" rebellion and finds it to be a reflection of an American "consumer binge." She also describes a change in middle-class attitudes toward consumption and social identity. Ehrenreich employs a vocabulary of class as she delves into themes of identity, consumption, the fear of becoming poor, or looking like a mere copy of the rich. The "yuppie strategy" was, according to Ehrenreich, an attempt to found a class on the purchase of goods and services, an experiment that didn't work.*

Like every other social group to rise to fleeting prominence, the yuppies were as much invented as discovered. The term was first employed in the press for the modest purpose of explaining Gary Hart's unexpected success in the 1984 presidential primaries. Someone had voted for him, someone young, urban, and professional, and there was brief hope that this new grouping would provide the Democrats with a much-needed new constituency. But what started as a neutral demographic category evolved with alarming speed into a social slur. Four years after their "discovery," Hendrik Hertzberg wrote in Esquire:

> *Yuppie* is now understood almost universally as a term of abuse.... "You're a yuppie" is taken to mean not "you're a young urban professional" but rather "you have lousy values."

Yuppie is a hybrid category—a mixture of age, address, and class. Other social classes are, in the middle-class imagination, age groups too: the poor as children, blue-collar workers as stern though somewhat pitiable fathers. But yuppies were by definition young adults, and thus subject to the moral judgments that older and more established people routinely pass on the young. From one angle, yuppies were the good children so sorely missed by neoconservatives like Midge Decter in the sixties and early seventies. They did not waste time "finding themselves" or joining radical movements. They plunged directly into the economic mainstream, earning and spending with equal zest. To *Newsweek*, the yuppie eagerness to "go for it" was a healthy sign of the "yuppie virtues of imagination, daring and entrepreneurship."

But they were also the very worst children, the apotheosis of middle-class forebodings about the corrupting effects of affluence. No one hurled the still-potent diagnosis of permissiveness at them, perhaps because by the eighties the word referred to so much more than childraising practices. Yet here they were, displaying that dread trait customarily assigned to the poor—"inability to defer gratification"—and even the desperate "orality" Oscar Lewis had once detected in the culture of poverty. Yuppies did not devote their youth to "that patient overcoming and hard-won new attainment" that Decter had endorsed as the prerequisite to adult middle-class life. They did not study; they "networked." They did not save; they spent. And they did not spend on houses or station wagons, but on Rolex watches, Porsches, quick trips to Aruba, and, most notoriously, high-status foods. In its "Year of the Yuppie" cover story, *Newsweek* found them on "a new plane of consciousness, a state of Transcendental Acquisition."

Yuppies, of course, did not turn out to be a new constituency for liberalism. Their "virtues" of entrepreneurship and acquisition made them for the most part conservatives, though not in the fervid, ideological style of the neoconservatives or the New Right. Yuppies thought of themselves as members of an elite whose interests might naturally collide with those of the lower classes: They lived in gentrified neighborhoods from which the unsightly poor had been freshly cleared; they worked for firms intent on minimizing the "labor costs" of blue- and pink-collar workers; their lifestyle was supported by the labor of poorly paid, often immigrant, service workers—housekeepers, restaurant employees, messengers, and delivery "boys." Although they parted company with the New Right on the social issues, such as abortion and women's rights, self-interest kept them reliably Republican.

5   Yet, despite their political conservatism, everyone sensed that the yuppies were somehow connected to that last period of youthful assertiveness, the sixties. Some commentators presented them as grown-up radicals, covertly bearing the heritage of the sixties into the corporate rat race of the eighties. It was possible in fact to have been a radical in the first decade and a self-centered hustler in the second, as Jerry Rubin's transformation from rebel to networking impresario illustrates. The very word *yuppie* had originally been coined in 1983 to describe Rubin's transition from a "yippie"— the acronym for the anarcho-hippie Youth International Party organized by Rubin and Abbie Hoffman—to prototypical young urban professional. *Newsweek* saw yuppies as the "vanguard of the baby-boom generation," which had "marched through the '60s" and was now "speed[ing] toward the airport, advancing on the 1980s in the back seat of a limousine."

Actually, the stereotypical yuppie, who was about thirty in 1984, was more likely to have spent the sixties bicycling around the neighborhood than marching on Washington. With equal disregard for the normal length of generations, yuppies were sometimes presented as the rebellious children of sixties radicals, who, in a stunning reprisal, were now horrifying *their* parents with their self-centeredness and political conservatism. Actor Michael J. Fox, the only yuppie actually pictured in *Esquire*'s "Days of Wine and Sushi" cover story, can ordinarily be found in a sitcom whose single sustaining joke is the clash between Fox and his gentle, sensitive, sixties-generation parents.

What yippies and yuppies did share was their class. Despite the frequent confusion of yuppies and baby-boomers in general, yuppies—defined by lifestyle and income— made up only about 5 percent of their generation. They were exemplars not of their generation but of their class, the same professional middle class that had produced the student rebels. Like the sixties rebels, the yuppies were at the cutting edge of their class, a kind of avant-garde, charting a new direction and agenda. They were also, in their own way, rebels. Both radicals and yuppies rejected the long, traditional path to middle-class success, but the defining zeal of the yuppies was to join another class—the rich.

The actual number of demographically official yuppies—people born between 1945 and 1959, earning over $40,000 a year in a professional or managerial occupation, and living in urban areas—was only about 1.5 million, hardly enough to warrant excitement. If yuppies were further defined as greedy, shallow people prone to burble about the joys of real estate investment, like those depicted in *Newsweek's* cover story, then, as a commentator in the *New Republic* observed, there were probably no more than 113 of them nationwide. But there was certainly a yuppie style of work and consumption, as well as what could be called a yuppie strategy for success, and these embraced, to a greater or lesser extent, many thousands of middle-class people beyond the demographic category. Here I will use *yuppie* in a loose, rather than demographically precise, sense, for someone who adopted the strategy and more or less fit the style. Hardly anyone, of course, deserves to bear the full burden of the stereotype.

But even the stereotype plays an important role in our chronicle of emerging class awareness. With the image of the yuppie, the normally invisible, normally "normal" middle class finally emerged in the mass media as a distinct group with its own ambitions, habitats, and tastes in food and running gear. The class usually privileged to do the discovering and naming of classes had itself been discovered by the media and, with scant respect for its dignity, named with a diminutive that rhymes with *puppy*.

The Consumer Binge

10 The hallmark of the yuppie—male or female, married or single—was consumption. The yuppie of stereotype drove a $40,000 foreign car, vacationed vigorously in all seasons, and aspired to a condominium with an intimidating address. Even those who could not afford the big-ticket items—condos and Porsches—infused their daily lives with extravagant details: salad dressings made of raspberry vinegar and walnut oil, imported mineral water, $100 sneakers, $50 meals at the restaurant of the moment. Yuppie spending patterns represented a new, undreamed-of level of capitulation to the consumer culture: a compulsive acquisitiveness bordering on addiction, a mental state resembling the supposed "present-orientation" and "radical improvidence" of the despised underclass.

Yuppie consumerism was not simply a distortion built into the stereotype. America was on a consumer binge, or as some economists put it, in a new stage of "hyperconsumption." Someone was spending, and it was not the laid-off industrial worker or unemployed woman on a dwindling welfare allowance. In fact, even during the recession of 1982–83, even after the stock-market crash of 1987, sales of luxury goods boomed. The truly rich—roughly the 5 percent of Americans who hold over 50 percent of the nation's wealth—accounted for a disproportionate share of the boom, particularly in the markets for yachts, gems, jets, real estate, and such collectibles as classic cars. But at the low end of luxury—which includes vacation trips, restaurant meals, and sports cars—America's newly rich, double-income business professionals were holding up their share of the binge.

In defense of yuppie spending habits—and it is a tribute to the enduring anxiety of the middle class that they still needed *any* defense at the height of Reagan-era profligacy—*New Republic* editor Michael Kinsley described the yuppies as engaged in a kind of compensatory spending. The $40,000 or so that a young business person might earn did not, after all, measure up so well when compared to the purchasing power enjoyed by his or her parents a few decades ago. It would hardly be enough to cover the house, station wagon, stay-at-home spouse, and three children that the white-collar man of the fifties expected as a matter of right. So, in Kinsley's argument, the raspberry vinegar, *crème fraîche,* and so forth had to be seen as "affordable luxuries":

> They serve as consolation for the lack of unaffordable luxuries like a large house. You may not have a dining room, but you have a dining room table, and everything on it can have a complicated explanation involving many foreign words.

But the compensatory-spending argument misses the profound change in middle-class attitudes toward consumption. In a previous generation, a young couple who lacked the money for a house and other family-oriented purchases would simply have skipped the raspberry vinegar (or its fifties equivalent) and saved their pennies. Spending was the reward for saving; and "leisure products," which include all the yuppie favorites, took second place to the moral solidity represented by a house and heavy appliances. The profligacy of the yuppies, which set a standard for all the middle class as a whole, was the surrender to hedonism that middle-class intellectuals had been warning against for over thirty years.

The consumer binge of the eighties is all the more startling when contrasted to the trend that immediately preceded it—the fashionable austerity of the seventies, symbolized by Jimmy Carter's low-budget 1976 inauguration and the popularity of E. F. Schumacher's *Small Is Beautiful.* "Voluntary simplicity," as this brief interlude of abstemiousness has since been termed, gave concrete expression to the middle-class fears of affluence that had been voiced since the fifties. The counterculture and student movement of the sixties were its immediate inspiration; the oil shortage of the early seventies and the new environmentalism imbued it with a high sense of moral purpose. A 1977 Harris poll found Americans increasingly concerned with "learning to get our pleasure out of non-material experiences," rather than "satisfying our needs for more goods and services." According to a study by the Stanford Research Institute, this attitude was particularly strong among young, educated, middle-class people, who were no longer likely to be political activists but at least tended "to prefer products that are functional, healthy, nonpolluting, durable, repairable, recyclable or made from renewable raw materials, energy-cheap, authentic, aesthetically pleasing, and made through simple technology." These preferences easily accommodated the new marketing emphasis on "leisure products," such as sports equipment, cameras, and stereos. The requirements of being functional and healthy did not, however, extend to such eighties favorites as *crème fráiche* and Beluga caviar.

15   Voluntary simplicity echoed the "simplicity movement" of the emerging middle class in the Progressive Era. Both movements sought a way to express middle-class political aspirations in the form of personal behavior, or, in seventies terminology, "lifestyle." In the early twentieth century, middle-class simplicity had meant fewer and plainer items of furniture, looser clothes, and lighter meals. In the 1970s, the trend was to minimalist (or high-tech) decor, blue cotton work shirts, "health foods," and a horror of strong drink and cigarette smoke. Both movements embodied a principled rejection of the endlessly wasteful, endlessly seductive, capitalist consumer culture. And both movements ended by trivializing that rejection as a new set of consumer

options: in the 1970s, natural fiber over polyester, whole-grain bread over white, plain oak furniture over high-gloss department-store maple.

No one in the 1970s expected voluntary simplicity to fade with the mere turn of a decade. It was a "quiet revolution," according to the Harris poll summary, a "major transformation of Western values," according to the Stanford Research Institute. Moreover, voluntary simplicity seemed to have become the very hallmark of middle-class existence—not only an ethic but a set of behavioral cues that distinguished the middle class from those both above and below it. The poor and the working class smoked and ate cheeseburgers; the middle class carved out nonsmoking environments for itself and eschewed red meat, American cheese, and grease in all forms.

So entrenched were the new middle-class tastes that it began to appear as if the classes could no longer coexist in the same physical space. I recall the dilemma faced by a group of young doctors in Chicago who wanted to invite other hospital workers—aides, orderlies, technicians, nurses—to a party. The doctors, friends of mine and dedicated reformers of the medical system, hoped to celebrate in the most generous and egalitarian fashion possible. But, they agonized, would their working-class coworkers submit to the obvious (middle-class) rules: no smoking, no hard liquor, and no junk food? The doctors finally realized that they would have to make a sacrifice, at least for one evening, of their values and possibly their health.

But it was more common for middle-class practitioners of the new simplicity to simply retreat from the challenge of mixed environments. Health was usually the immediate rationale, but health had become a nebulous metaphor for other distinctions, and disguised a growing disdain for the white working class. In the early sixties, middle-class commentators had, perversely enough, seen the poor as the victims of a consumerist mentality, the slaves of sensation and impulse. As the seventies wore on, the blue-collar working class began to take the place of the poor in the moral hierarchy of the middle class. The poor themselves once again dropped from view, leaving the working class—with its tasteless home furnishings, high-fat diet, and unwholesome addictions—to serve as an object lesson in the perils of succumbing to the consumer culture.

So how was the middle class able, within a few short years, to throw itself into the consumerist binge without losing its sense of identity—its fragile autonomy from the leveling force of the consumer culture? The short answer is that it was *not* able to. The binge was experienced as a capitulation every bit as profound as the switch from relatively autonomous careers in the professions to get-rich-quick trajectories in the business world. But the short-term answer was that the middle class was able to construct a new identity around conspicuous consumption, redefining it not as surrender but as a pious form of work.

The Embrace of Affluence

20   One of the unappealing features of 1950s-style mass-marketed affluence, from a middle-class point of view, was that it allowed for only "minute distinctions" between the middle class and those immediately below, the working class. One might have more and better, but "better" was not distinctively different: thicker carpets, a car with more options, museum prints rather than dime-store reproductions on the walls. In the eighties this problem was decisively resolved. The mass market disappeared and was

replaced by two markets, which we know as "upscale" and "downscale." The change reflected the growing middle-class zeal to distinguish itself from the less fortunate, and at the same time it made such distinctions almost mandatory for anyone hoping to inhabit the social and occupational world of the successful and "upscale."

Everywhere in the retail industry there were signs of the new market polarization. Department stores, for example, faced the choice of specializing in one end of the class spectrum or the other—or else going out of business. Undifferentiated chains, like Korvette's and Gimbel's, which had aimed at both blue- and white-collar middle-income consumers, were forced to close, while Sears and J. C. Penney anxiously tried to "reposition" themselves to survive in the ever more deeply segmented market. The stores and chains that prospered were the ones that learned to specialize in one extreme of wealth or the other: Bloomingdale's and Neiman-Marcus for the upscale; K-Mart and Woolco for those constrained by poverty or thrift.

Inside the stores there was hardly any product that could not be found in up- and downscale versions, as if even lifeless commodities were being asked to take sides in an undeclared class war. Beer divided between the familiar American brands and dozens of expensive imports—Beck's, Corona, Heineken, Kirin. Food, of course, divided and subdivided frenetically, but the broad contours of change were reflected in Pillsbury's restaurant strategy: Burger King for the proletariat; Bennigan's well-appointed, trendily stocked restaurants for the yuppies. The auto industry had always had its Cadillacs and Chevys, but now there was a fresh segmentation among the imports, with Mercedes and Audis for the affluent, Toyotas for the masses. Even the most phlegmatic commodities, home appliances, began to sort themselves out as manufacturers added high-tech features to create an upscale line. According to a market analyst for the Bear Stearns brokerage firm:

> There is a consumer out there who doesn't want chain-store labels on things they buy. Kenmore [the Sears brand of appliances] is a good name but not a yuppie name. When they have friends over, these people do not want those friends to see names like Sears or Kenmore. They want people to see names like Sony or Kitchen Aid.

The split in the mass market followed the deepening fault lines within American society and was a response to those underlying shifts. Downwardly mobile people have little choice but to go for the discount goods, while the upwardly mobile are eager to transform their money into the visible marks of status. No doubt, too, the pressure to consolidate one's financial position through marriage heightened the importance of small and subtle class cues. A "nice guy" or a "good-looking gal" would no longer do, and since bank accounts and résumés are not visible attributes, a myriad of other cues were required to sort the good prospects from the losers. Upscale spending patterns created the cultural space in which the financially well matched could find each other—far from the burger-eaters and Bud-drinkers and those unfortunate enough to wear unnatural fibers. In fact, upscale department stores found a new use as cruising grounds for affluent singles. At the height of the consumer binge, a popular dating activity was a joint mission to a high-priced store like Bloomingdale's.

Whatever the reasons, the yuppie spending pattern, (whether indulged in by demographically official yuppies or not) represented a frantic positioning—an almost desperate commitment to the latest upscale fad. In the fashionable intellectual discourse of the time, possessions were important only as "signifiers," elements of an ever-shifting language that spoke of wealth and promise. The trick was to understand the language as it changed from month to month, leaving behind the ignorant and the less than affluent. As soon as an affordable fad—the example is often given of pita-bread sandwiches—sedimented down to the general public, it would be rendered useless as a mark of status and abandoned by the cognoscenti.

25   Hence that favorite magazine and newspaper filler in the mid-eighties, the list of what's in and what's out, calculated to both mock and alarm the status-conscious reader. For example, in 1985 the *Miami Herald* published a largely predictable list of what's "hot" and "not hot": Conservatives, dinner parties, and gilt were hot; liberals, cookouts, and minimalism were not. The joke was at the end of the long lists, where, under *hot,* one found *what's not hot,* and under *not hot,* of course, *what's hot.*

But there was a certain consistency to the dominant upscale tastes. Conservatism had triumphed over liberalism, gilt over minimalism, expensive over modestly priced. The obvious impetus was the sudden visibility of the truly rich, who reentered public consciousness with the triumphal display of the 1981 Reagan inauguration. The rich, of course, are always with us. But throughout most of the postwar period they had not been too eager to announce their presence, as a class, to the potentially resentful public. All this changed with the ascent to power of the New Right, whose populist language conflicted openly with its aristocratic allegiances. According to historian Deborah Silverman, the Reagan era introduced a "new cultural style" consistent with right-wing politics:

> A style aggressively dedicated to the cult of visible wealth and distinction, and to the illusion that they were well earned; a style that adopted the artifacts of Chinese emperors, French aristocrats, and English noblemen as signs of exclusivity and renunciation; a style of unabashed opulence, whose mixture of hedonism, spitefulness, and social repudiation was captured in the slogan "Living well is the best revenge."

Not to mention the even nastier and more popular slogan "He who dies with the most toys wins."

What was pathetic and ultimately embarrassing about the stereotypical yuppie was that he or she was such a poor copy of the truly rich. People who have yachts and private jets do not have to agonize over "what's hot" and "what's not." People who employ their own chefs do not have to engage in yuppie-style "competitive eating" to establish their place in the world. In moving from minimalism to gilt, from voluntary simplicity to a parodic profligacy, the upwardly mobile middle class began to lose its own fragile sense of dignity. The rich can surrender to hedonism because they have no reason to remain tense and alert. But the middle class cannot afford to let down its guard; it maintains its position only through continual exertion—through allegiance to the "traditional values" of hard work and self-denial. In the eighties, the middle class came dangerously close to adopting the presumed wantonness of the poor—that is, the actual wantonness of the very rich.

References

(¶ 1) *"Yuppie is now understood"*: Hendrik Hertzberg, "The Short Happy Life of the American Yuppie," *Esquire,* February 1988, p. 100.

(¶ 2) *The yuppie eagerness:* "The Year of the Yuppie," *Newsweek,* December 31, 1984, p. 14.

(¶ 7) *Only about 5 percent of their generation:* "The Big Chill (Revisited), or, Whatever Happened to the Baby Boom?" *American Demographics,* vol. 7, September 1985, pp. 22–25.

(¶ 8) *A commentator in the* New Republic: Alex Heard, "Yuppie Love," *New Republic,* January 28, 1985, p. 10.

(¶ 11) *Sales of luxury goods boomed:* "Despite Collapse of Stocks, Luxury Sales Bounce Back," *New York Times,* June 7, 1988.

(¶ 11) *The 5 percent of Americans:* Stephen J. Rose, *Social Stratification in the U.S.,* pp. 35–36.

(¶ 12) *Compensatory spending:* Michael Kinsley, "Arise, Ye Yuppies!" *New Republic,* July 9, 1984, p. 4.

(¶ 14) *A study by the Stanford Research Institute:* Quoted in David E. Shi, *The Simple Life: Plain Living and High Thinking in American Culture* (New York: Oxford University Press, 1985), p. 269.

(¶ 15) *Voluntary simplicity:* See T. Jackson Lears, *No Place of Grace: Antimodernism and the Transformation of American Culture, 1880–1920* (New York: Pantheon Books, 1981), chapter 2.

(¶ 16) *Quiet revolution":* Quoted in Shi, *Simple Life,* pp. 268–69.

(¶ 20) *The mass market disappeared:* Bruce Steinberg, "The Mass Market Is Splitting Apart," *Fortune,* November 28, 1983, p. 76.

(¶ 22) *"There is a consumer out there":* "Where Sears Has Stumbled," *New York Times,* June 5, 1986.

(¶ 25) *A largely predictable list:* "What's Hot, What's Not," *Miami Herald,* January 13, 1985.

(¶ 26) *"new cultural style":* Deborah Silverman, *Selling Culture* (New York: Pantheon Books, 1986), p. 11.

Rereading Actively

1. Ehrenreich opens this chapter by drawing a distinction between social "grouping" and "age, address, and class." Working with a partner, list the class characteristics that yuppies have and also the reasons that the yuppies don't seem to be a unique class. Individually summarize your findings in your journals, share your summaries, and then draft a collaborative explanation of where yuppies might fit in the American social landscape.

2. In a small group, discuss the patterns Ehrenreich finds in the tastes and political habits of the yuppies.

3. Review the article, identifying similarities and differences between the yuppies and the traditional, 1950s middle class. Describe the important characteristics of each group in an entry in your journal.

4. Ehrenreich declares that yuppies were defined by their desire to "join another class—the rich" (¶ 7). In a short journal entry, explain in your own words Ehrenreich's description of this desire, illustrating it with details she includes in her article.

5. A 1984 *Newsweek* cover story emphasized "yuppie virtues of imagination, daring, and entrepreneurship." Others, including Ehrenreich, note that the yuppie seemed to symbolize a loss of middle-class identity and a "surrender to hedonism" (¶ 13). Explain what Ehrenreich means by this, focusing on the meaning of "middle-class identity" she seems to have in mind.

Exploring Your Responses

6. In a page or two in your journal, compare your spending habits with those of the yuppies of the 1980s and the American middle class of the 1950s.

7. What spending habits have you inherited? Are your habits sustainable? Why or why not?

8. With two or three classmates, watch a recent TV program or movie that includes a view of a yuppie world. After viewing, discuss the representation of yuppie lifestyle. What characteristics did the yuppies have? What values did they seem to represent; that is, were they energetic and productive? Were they obsessed with style and display? Were they the butt of jokes or were they making jokes? After your discussion, write a joint review that focuses on the portrayal of the yuppie character, suggests how compelling the character was, and describes how that character contributes to the overall success or failure of the program or film. Be prepared to share your review and, if possible, a film clip with the class.

BOURGEOIS BLUES
DEIRDRE McCLOSKEY

Deirdre McCloskey teaches economics and history at the University of Iowa and writes both technical papers and popular articles about economic policy for magazines like American Scholar *and* Scientific American. *In addition, she is the author of numerous scholarly books of economic history. In much of her writing, McCloskey spent the 1990s praising the social virtues of the market and the bourgeoisie and so finds a friendly audience for her 1993 "Bourgeois Blues" in* Reason, *a magazine that sets itself in opposition to the "liberal media" and extols free markets and free minds. McCloskey writes an economic history of the bourgeois, arguing that the "detestation" of the bourgeois is the product of a "discourse" that writes off business folk as greedy. An important part of McCloskey's purpose here is to offer a corrective to that negative view.*

The bourgeois have won. Furthermore, they deserve to win, since they are the good guys. The 21st century will be the century of the universal middle class. It will exhibit the bourgeois virtues.

"Bourgeois virtues"? Don't make me laugh. The bourgeoisie may be useful, even necessary. But *virtuous?* Since 1848 or so the intellectuals, who at first welcomed the bourgeoisie most cordially, have been sneering this way at the very idea of "virtue" in the middle class. "Man must labor,/Man must work," says a nursery rhyme for moderns, "The executive is/A dynamic jerk."

Charles Dickens, the first and most successful of the anti-bourgeois writers, loved peasants and proletarians most warmly and had a kind word even for some of the aristocracy. But he detested the merchants and mill owners. The merchant Scrooge hurls his "Bah: humbug!" at a Christian holy day, a celebration of peasant virtues. Mr. Gradgrind, teaching little children to be wage slaves, declares, "Now, what I want is, Facts." The motto, "Facts alone are wanted in life," rejects all that is noble and aristocratic and romantic in the talk of virtue.

We talk of virtue in one of two ways only, the patrician or the plebeian, the virtues of the aristocrat or of the peasant, Achilles or Jesus. The two vocabularies are heard each in its own place, in Camp or Common. The one speaks of the pagan virtues of the soldier—courage, moderation, prudence, and justice. The other speaks of the Christian virtues of the worker—faith, hope, and charity. Achilles struts the Camp in his Hephaestian armor, exercising his noble wrath. Jesus stands barefoot on the mount, preaching to the least of the Commoners.

5   Camp and Common, the romantic hero or the working-class saint: That's been our talk of good and bad. And yet we live now in the Town, we bourgeois, or are moving to the Town and bourgeois occupations as fast as we can manage.

The prediction that the proletariat would become the universal class has proven to be mistaken. Half of employment in rich countries is white collar, a figure that's steadily rising. Jobs for peasants, proletarians, and aristocrats are disappearing. The class structure that the intellectuals analyzed so vigorously in 1848 and have since tried to keep in place is going or is gone.

The explanation is that the production of things has become and will continue to become cheaper relative to most services. In 50 years, a maker of things on an assembly line will be as rare as a farmer. The proletariat, an urban and secular version of the rural and religious peasantry, have sent their children to Notre Dame and thence to careers in plastics. Brahmins may lament, churchmen wail, bohemians jeer. Yet the universal class into which the classes are melting is the damnable bourgeoisie.

The result will be a massively bourgeois Town. It's time for the intellectuals to stop complaining about the fact and to recognize the bourgeois virtues.

To sing only of aristocratic or peasant virtues, of courage or of solidarity, is to mourn for a world well lost. We need an 18th-century equipoise, a neoclassicism of virtues suiting our condition. We are all bourgeois now. For some decades about 80 percent of Americans have identified themselves as "middle class" (such consciousness of course may be false). The ideals of nationalism or socialism have not suited our lives (refer for empirical verification to records of the Great European Civil War 1914–1990). The ideals of the townsperson, by contrast, have suited us peacefully, and no surprise.

10   Bad news? A future of selfish SOBs? The country club regnant? The death of community? No, unless you swallow the talk of Western clerks and scribblers since 1848.

The growth of the market promotes virtue, not vice. Most intellectuals since 1848 have thought the opposite: that it erodes virtue. As the legal scholar James Boyd White puts the thought in his otherwise admirable *Justice as Translation*, bourgeois growth is "the expansion of the exchange system by the conversion of what is outside it into its terms. It is a kind of steam shovel chewing away at the natural and social world."

And yet we all take happily what the market gives—polite, accommodating, energetic, enterprising, risk-taking, trustworthy people; not bad people. In the Bulgaria of old the department stores had a policeman on every floor, not to prevent theft but to stop the customers from attacking the arrogant and incompetent staff selling goods that at once fell apart. The way a salesperson in an American store greets customers makes the point: "How can I help you?" The phrase startles foreigners. It is an instance in miniature of the bourgeois virtues. As Eric Hoffer said, "It is futile to judge a kind deed by its motives.... We are made kind by being kind." Thank you very kindly.

It is usual to elevate a pagan or Christian ideal and then to sound a lament that no one achieves the ideal. The numerous bourgeois virtues have been reduced to the single vice of greed. The intellectuals thunder at the middle class but offer no advice on how to be good within it. The only way to become a good bourgeois, say Flaubert

The Classes and the Virtues

Aristocrat/Patrician	Peasant/Plebian/Proletarian	Bourgeois/Mercantile
Pagan	Christian	Secular
Achilles	St. Francis	Benjamin Franklin
Pride of Being	Pride of Service	Pride of Action
Honor	Duty	Integrity
Forthrightness	Solidarity	Trustworthiness
Courage	Fortitude	Enterprise
Wit	Jocularity	Humor
Courtesy	Reverence	Respect
Propriety	Humility	Modesty
Magnanimity	Benevolence	Consideration
Justice	Fairness	Responsibility
Foresight	Wisdom	Prudence
Moderation	Frugality	Thrift
Love	Charity	Affection
Grace	Dignity	Self-Possession
Subjective	Objective	Conjective

and Sinclair Lewis, is to stop being one. The words have consequences. The hole in our virtue-talk leaves the bourgeoisie without reasons for ethics. Since they cannot be either knights or saints they are damned, as we are all, and say: To hell with it.

Consider the virtues of the three classes, matched to their character, aristocrat, peasant, or bourgeois (the "character" of a class will sometimes be its character in the eyes of others, sometimes in its own, sometimes in fact). Thus:

15   The point is to notice the third, bourgeois column, the third estate of virtue, not to elevate it above the other two. Courage is in some personal experiences and social institutions a virtue. So is humility. But when the class left out is half the population, the old dichotomy of masters and men is not doing its ethical job.

A potent source of virtue and a check on vice is the premium that a bourgeois society puts on discourse. The aristocrat gives a speech, the peasant tells a tale. But the bourgeois must in the bulk of his transactions talk to an equal. "I will buy with you, sell with you, talk with you, walk with you, and so following…. What news on the Rialto?" It is wrong to imagine, as modern economics does, that the market is a field of silence.

Talk defines business reputation. A market economy looks forward and depends therefore on trust. The persuasive talk that establishes trust is of course necessary for doing business. This is why co-religionists or co-ethnics deal so profitably with each other, as Quakers or overseas Chinese. The economic historian Avner Greif has explored the business dealings of Mediterranean Jews in the Middle Ages, accumulating evidence for a reputational conversation: In 1055 one Abun ben Zedaka of Jerusalem, for example, "was accused (though not charged in court) of embezzling the money of a Maghribi traders, [and] merchants as far away as Sicily canceled their agency relations with him." A letter from Palermo to an Alexandrian merchant who had disappointed the writer said, "Had I listened to what people say, I never would have entered into a partnership with you." Reputational gossip, Greif notes, was cheap, "a by-product of the commercial activity [itself] and passed along with other commercial correspondence." Cheating was profitless within the community. The market does not erode communities; it makes them, and then flourishes within what it has made.

The aristocrat, by contrast, does not deign to bargain. Hector tries to, but Achilles replies: "argue me no agreements. I cannot forgive you. / As there are no trustworthy oaths between men and lions, / Nor wolves and lambs have spirit that can be brought into agreement." The Duke of Ferrara speaks of his last duchess there upon the wall looking as if she were alive, "Even had you skill / In speech—(which I have not)—make your will / Quite clear to such an one…. /—E'en then would be some stooping; and I choose / Never to stoop." The aristocrat never stoops; the peasant or proletarian stoops to harvest or to tend the machine. The bourgeois stoops daily to make his will quite clear, and to know the will and reasons of the other. The aristocrat's speech is declamation (imitated by the professoriate). The aristocrat's proofs are like commands, which is perhaps why Plato the aristocrat loved them so. They convince (*vincere,* to conquer). The bourgeois, by contrast, must persuade, sweetly (*suadeo,* from the same root as "sweet").

The bourgeoisie talks with a will. About a quarter of national income is earned from merely bourgeois and feminine persuasion: not orders or information but persuasion. One thinks immediately of advertising, but in fact advertising is a tiny part of the total. Take the detailed categories of employment and make a guess as to the percentage of the time in each category spent on persuasion. Out of the 115 million civilian employees, it seems reasonable to assign 100 percent of the time of 760,000 lawyers and judges to persuasion, and likewise all the time of public-relations specialists and actors and directors. Perhaps 75 percent of the time of 14.2 million executive, administrative, and managerial employees is spent on persuasion, and a similar share of the time of the 4.8 million teachers and the 11.2 million salespeople (excluding cashiers). Half of the effort of police, writers, and health workers, one might guess, is spent on persuasion. And so forth. The result is that 28.2 million person-years, a quarter of the labor force, persuades for a living.

20 The result can be checked with other measures. John Wallis and Douglass North measure 50 percent of national income as transaction costs, the costs of persuasion being part of these. Not all the half of American workers who are white collar talk for a living, but in an extended sense many do, as for that matter do many blue-collar workers, persuading each other to handle the cargo just so, and especially pink-collar workers, dealing all day with talking people.

And of the talkers a good percentage are persuaders. The secretary shepherding a document through the company bureaucracy is called on to exercise sweet talk and veiled threats. The bureaucrats and professionals who constitute most of the white-collar work force are not themselves merchants, but they do a merchant's business inside and outside their companies. Note the persuasion exercised the next time you buy a suit. Specialty clothing stores charge more than discount stores not staffed with rhetoricians. The differential pays for the persuasion: "It's you, my dear" or "The fish tie makes a statement."

The high share of persuasion provides a scene for bourgeois virtues. One must establish a relationship of trust with someone in order to persuade him. *Ethos,* the character that a speaker claims, is the master argument. So the world of the bourgeoisie is jammed with institutions for making relationships and declaring character, unlike that of the aristocracy or peasantry or proletariat, who get their relationships and characters ready-made by status, and who in any case need not persuade.

Hollywood producers spend hours a day "buffing," which is to say chatting with their business peers, establishing relations. On the foreign-exchange markets the opening business of the day is to trade jokes useful for making human contact with clients. *Ethos* is all, as much as with any sneering aristocrat—or maybe more, since claimed less confidently. In Thomas Mann's first novel, the story of his German merchant family, the head of the firm scolds his unbusiness-like brother, a harbinger of bohemianism in the family: "In a company consisting of business as well as professional men, you make the remark, for everyone to hear, that, when one really considers it, every businessman is a swindler—you, a businessman yourself, belonging to a firm that strains every nerve and muscle to preserve its perfect integrity and spotless reputation."

Bourgeois charity, again, if not the "charity," meaning spiritual love, of the King James translation of the Bible, runs contrary to the caricature of greed. More than the peasant or aristocrat, the bourgeois gives to the poor—as in the ghettos of Eastern Europe or in the small towns of America. Acts of charity follow the bourgeois norm of reciprocity. The American Gospel of Wealth—founding hospitals, colleges, and libraries wherever little fortunes were made—is a bourgeois notion, paying back what was taken in profit. Middle-class people in the 19th century habitually gave a biblical tenth of their incomes to charity. The intrusion of the state into charity killed the impulse, remaking charity into a *taille* imposed on grumbling peasants: I gave at the office.

25   One could go on. The bourgeois virtues are in for a long run and need exploration and praise. We already have Japanese bourgeois and now Korean and Taiwanese; later Pakistani in volume, and Mexican. The world is about to become one Rialto.

And yet the intelligentsia detests this splendid bourgeoisie. The detestation is not new. Anciently the poet Horace prefers his Sabine valley to troublesome riches or recommends stretching one's income by contracting one's desires, even while accepting large gifts in cash or land from Maecenas and Augustus. The disdain for money grubbing becomes a literary theme and merges smoothly with the Christian virtues.

But over the past two centuries the hostility to the money-grubbing class has become frantic. After a brief flirtation with pro-bourgeois writing in the 18th century (Daniel Defoe is the high point; Voltaire admired the English and bourgeois virtues; Jane Austen, late, admired at least the marriage market), literature sinks into a sustained sneer. The novel begins as the epic of the bourgeoisie but becomes with Balzac and Dickens an anti-epic, a Dunciad of the middle classes. German romantics and French statists and English evangelicals in the early 19th century were bourgeois by origin but did not like it, not one bit. Overwhelmingly the French men of letters who barked at the bourgeoisie were the sons of lawyers and businessmen. So too were German men of letters, such as Marx and Engels. The American progressives, advocating a secularized but nonetheless Christian ideal for public policy, were the sons and daughters of Protestant ministers, bourgeois all.

It's a puzzle. In his astonishing *Bohemian Versus Bourgeois: French Society and the French Man of Letters in the Nineteenth Century*, Cesar Grana asks, "What is it in the spiritual scene of modern society that may account for such intellectual touchiness, willfulness, and bitterness" among the intelligentsia against the bourgeoisie? His answer was what has since been called the "aporia of the Enlightenment project," namely, the conflict between freedom and rationalism in modern life. The bourgeoisie is seen by intellectuals such as Dickens, Weber, and Freud as the embodiment of rationalism.

Grana is probably correct. An impatience with calculation has been the mark of the romantic since Herder. Don Quixote's idiotic schemes in aid of chivalry are precisely uncalculated, irrational but noble.

30 The modern men Grana writes about, however, have been mistaken all this time. They mistook bourgeois life, the way a rebellious son mistakes the life of his father. The life of the bourgeoisie is not routine but creation, as Marx and Engels said. What has raised income per head in the rich countries by a factor of at least 12 since the 18th century is originality backed by commercial courage, not science. Dickens was mistaken to think that Facts alone are wanted in the life of manufacturing. Manufacturing depends on enterprise and single-mindedness far from cooly rational.

Weber was mistaken to think that the modern state embodies principles of rationality in bureaucracy. Anyone who thinks that a large, modern bureaucracy runs "like an army" cannot have experienced either a large, modern bureaucracy or an army. Freud was mistaken to claim that modern life forces a choice between the reality principle and eroticism. A businessperson without an erotic drive (suitably sublimated) achieves nothing.

This lack of insight by the intelligentsia into business life is odd. It reminds one, I repeat, of an adolescent boy sneering at his father: Remarkable how the old fellow matured between my 16th and 22nd birthdays. The European novel contains hardly a single rounded and accurate portrait of a businessman (Thomas Buddenbrook is an exception). The businessman is almost always a cardboard fool, unless he proves in the end to evince aristocratic or Christian virtues. Intellectuals in the West have had a tin ear for business and its values. Thus Arthur Hugh Clough in 1862, "The Latest Decalogue": "Thou shalt have one God only; who / Would be at the expense of two?" and so on in the vein of a clever adolescent down to "Thou shalt not steal; an empty feat, / When it's so lucrative to cheat. / ... Thou shalt not covet, but tradition / Approves all forms of competition."

Economics, as the science of business, has been similarly spurned since 1848, leading to more adolescent sneering at what the lad does not quite grasp. (Lad, not lass: Portraits of bourgeois women in literature are numerous and accurate from the hands of women novelists—or even from men, Defoe's Moll Flanders [ranging from whore to noblewoman, but always enterprising] or Flaubert's Madame Bovary or James's portrait of a lady, down to Brian Moore's Mary Dunne or Judith Hearne. It is bourgeois men on the job whom novelists have failed to grasp.) Early in the 19th century, writers like Macaulay or Manzoni read and understood economics and applied it intelligently. Manzoni's novel *The Betrothed* (last edition, 1840) contains an entire chapter on the unhappy effects during a famine of imposing price controls (*un prezzo giusto*).

But after 1848 the intellectuals construed economics as the faculty of Reason, arrayed against the Freedom they loved, a misunderstanding encouraged by the talk of "iron laws" among classical economists. Or else they portrayed businesspeople as mere con men (thus Twain and Howells). By the late 19th century economics had dropped out of the conversation entirely. No intellectual since 1890 has been ashamed to be ignorant about the economy or economics. It is a rare English professor—David Lodge, for example, in *Nice Work*—who can see the businessperson as anything other than The Other.

35   A change is overdue. To admire the bourgeois virtues is not to buy into Reaganism or the Me Decade. Greed is a bourgeois vice, though not unknown among other classes. But the market and capitalism produce more virtue than vice. We must encourage capitalism, it being the hope for the poor of the world and being in any case what we are, but our capitalism need not be hedonistic or monadic, and certainly not unethical. An aristocratic, country-club capitalism, well satisfied with itself, or a peasant, grasping capitalism, hating itself, are both lacking in the virtues. And neither works. They lead to monopoly and economic failure, alienation and revolution. We need a capitalism that nurtures communities of good townsfolk in South-Central L.A. as much as in Iowa City. We encourage it by talking seriously about the bourgeois virtues.

Being ashamed of being bourgeois has for two centuries amounted to being ashamed of America. The sneerers at Ben Franklin like Baudelaire and D. H. Lawrence were notorious as anti-democrats and anti-Americans. Charles Dickens hated the United States as much as he hated businessmen. But America is not the only bourgeois society: Germany is, too, though one that in its intellectual circles wishes it was not; Italians are famous townsfolk; and China, having for centuries cities larger than anywhere else, must have a bourgeois tradition counter to the peasant or aristocrat.

We live not in a global village but in a global town, and have for a long time. A myth of recency has made the virtues arising from town markets seem those of a shameful parvenu. In economic history dependent on Marx, such as Weber's *General Economic History* (1923) or Karl Polanyi's *The Great Transformation* (1944), the market is seen as a novelty. From this historical mistake arose the 19th-century fairy tales of lost paradise for aristocrats or peasants. It has taken a century of professional history to correct the mistake.

Medieval men bought and sold everything from grain to bishoprics. The Vikings were traders, too. Greece and Rome were business empires. The city of Jerico dates to 8000 B.C. The emerging truth is that we have lived in a world market for centuries, a market run by the bourgeoisie. It is time we recognized the fact and started cultivating those bourgeois virtues, of which we are to witness a new flowering.

Rereading Actively

1. McCloskey opens her essay declaring that the "bourgeois have won" because "they are the good guys," and closes it encouraging readers to "cultivate" the "bourgeois virtues" of talk, persuasion, and trust. How do her strong moral claims influence your reading? Does she make you feel at home with the topic or put you off?

2. With a partner or in a small group, summarize McCloskey's explanation of virtue in "the three classes," defining terms like bourgeois, patrician, and plebian and symbols like the "romantic hero," "working-class saint," and "intelligentsia."

3. How does McCloskey characterize her opponents (the intellectuals, aristocrats, and workers) and her friends, the bourgeois? Identify passages where McCloskey refers to these different groups of people, and with a partner, discuss the portrayal of each group.

4. Use a paragraph to explain why a member of either the aristocracy or the proletariat—the two classes McCloskey criticizes—might object to this portrayal of class.

5. McCloskey is highly critical of "sneering" intellectuals. Is her critique persuasive to you? How do you respond to her preference for "the businessperson" over "men of letters," "progressives," and "professors"? In your journal, write a paragraph explanation of your response.

6. With a partner, review the article, noting how McCloskey relates economics to her discussion of virtue. Individually or collaboratively, write a short journal entry explaining the link McCloskey makes.

Exploring Your Responses

7. In a small group, experiment with the class categories McCloskey uses, applying them to people you are familiar with. Can your group identify two members of the bourgeois, patricians, progressives, and professors?

8. Reflect on the conversation your group engaged in with the previous question: What problems did you find as you experimented with applying these categories to people you know? Are these categories sufficiently descriptive?

9. Pick an object that indicates your "class" values—maybe a favorite picture, CD, book, tool, toy, whatever. In a page or two in your journal, analyze what values the object represents. How does this kind of object circulate in society? Prepare to explain the object and its significance to the rest of your class.

CASE-IN-POINT ASSIGNMENTS

We have a contradictory relationship to class in the United States. We seem in many ways to obsess about upward mobility and striking it rich, but we are often quite reluctant to talk openly about how much or how little money we have. We perceive that opportunities flow toward the "haves" in our society, yet we profess that ours is a society where everyone, rich and poor alike, has an equal shot at success. At the center of most current discussions of class is the middle class—men, women, and children working and shopping in "middle America." When the number of middle-class households is expanding, all is well; when it declines, we question the validity of the American dream. Neither rich enough to live off inherited wealth nor so poor that they work just to stay alive, this group is the dynamo of a consumer culture. These people work, buy homes, and pour money into IRAs in hopes of being able to maintain a hedge against poverty. At the same time, they spend, sometimes far beyond reasonable means, in hopes perhaps of gaining an "upper-middle-class" existence. Indeed, the chance to be middle class keeps a capitalist society from looking like a rigged game where the rich endlessly exploit the poor. The case readings have presented you with definitions of social categories, images of life, and statistics about income brackets and group habits that are often used to divide people into classes. As you work through the assignments below, you will have a chance to come to your own conclusions about the virtues and vices of the balancing act that is middle-class life in a consumer culture.

Making Connections

1. These writers seem to assume that understanding the middle class is the key to understanding class relationships in a consumer culture. Even though artists and social critics have long considered the middle class boring and boorish, the bourgeoisie make the culture run. Write an essay that uses Chavez's definition of the middle class to analyze and explain either the problems faced by Kenny and Bonita Merten (Sheehan) or the class conflict developed by a TV program (Gates) or a film (McDonald).

2. In "The Yuppie Strategy," Ehrenreich discusses the gradual replacement, in the 1980s, of the "mass market" with two markets—"upscale" and "downscale"—a division meant to reinforce class distinctions between upper and lower ends of the middle class. Drawing on Ehrenreich's discussion, explain in what ways the TV show *Frasier* (see Gates) portrays this tension between upper and lower ends of the socioeconomic spectrum.

3. Describe and evaluate a family hero or anti-hero in light of two readings that describe that person's class. This person may have:

   - Found success (or failure) by being what tradition and class dictated.
   - Rejected the constraints of class and moved into a new neighborhood, into (or out of) money, into stability or satisfaction (or uncertainty).
   - Failed to maintain her social or economic position.

   Use the readings to explain where this person started, where she or he ended up, and how she managed the passage.

4. Think about the contemporary characteristics of a particular class, and write an analysis of how that class seems to fit within the dynamics of a consumer culture (for better or worse.) You'll need to draw on case readings that explain the virtues of the class you choose or its vices. (Gates and McCloskey talk about the elite, Ehrenreich about the middle, and Sheehan about the poor.)

5. McCloskey declares that the open market gives the most people the best chance. This same argument (open markets vs. social guarantees of equal access) is at the core of debates about what a good education should include and how it should be delivered. Drawing on McCloskey's perspective, argue whether a college education should be a tool to create equal opportunity (for example, the position of Ira Shor, page 460) or a product developed and distributed in an open market (for example, the position of the University of Phoenix as Traub explains it, page 433).

Collaborative Exchanges

1. The case writers list a number of class markers: neighborhood, parental vocation and income, family traditions, education, personal aspirations, tastes in fashion, art, and entertainment, and consumption habits, among others. With two or three classmates, brainstorm the markers of class at your campus, making special note of markers that group members believe are particularly clear or particularly ambiguous. Pick a marker from your list that is relevant

to your group's experience of class. Write individually about your perceptions of the marker, calling attention to specific examples of the marker, your personal experience with it, and your sense of how this marker affects the campus community. Compare your writing, noting points of agreement and disagreement. Be prepared to describe your marker to the class and to explain how your group perceives the marker.

2. The writers here identify several social-class problems, for example, a family that lives beyond its means, an anxious middle class that wants to be something more, an elite that fails to recognize the virtues of the bourgeoisie. With two or three classmates, pick a class problem raised by the reading. Then, search recent issues of a local or national newspaper or a news site on the Web, and find a current example of the class problem you have focused on. Do some further research by locating primary sources that offer details about the example itself and secondary sources that discuss the principles involved in the issue. Generate a joint report for the class in which you define the incident as a class problem, describe the relevant facts, and propose a solution to the problem.

3. In a small group, brainstorm images from your campus or neighborhood of stereotypical middle-class culture reflected in advertising, entertainment, fashion, food, technology, architecture, and so on. After discussing how the middle class seems to be idealized in your examples, use one or more of the readings to explain how this representation of the middle class constrains people, redefines people, or frees people to do what they will.

Net Approaches

1. Use the U.S. Bureau of Census homepage to see how issues raised in the readings look in your locale. Point your browser to <www.census.gov> and at the Census Bureau home page choose to "search" a "place" that you will identify by zip code. (A zip code map from a print version of the white pages still seems to be the best way to find zip codes.) Using the census survey tables (the Tiger map is cool but really complicated), generate a profile of a local neighborhood that reveals the size of households, ethnic and/or racial makeup, household incomes, and occupations. Then, generate the same profile for a similar or different neighborhood. Write a brief report that summarizes the profile of the first neighborhood and notes significant differences between the neighborhoods.

2. Visit the Soc Net on Class, a page maintained by the University of Chicago that serves researchers looking into class issues: <www.spc.uchicago.edu/orgs/social_class/-index.html>. This is a rich site. Choose to do one of the following:

- Explore the papers that are archived here.
- Subscribe to the moderated listserv that is supported by this site and read recent exchanges.
- Follow four links to other sites.

  Write a brief report that explains what you discovered and how this information relates to the reading you have done in this unit.

3. Go to <www.altavista.com> and do a link search for the home page identified in the preceding assignment. To do this, type the following string into an

AltaVista search box: *link:http://www.spc.uchicago.edu/orgs/social_class/ index.html*. (Other search engines also enable link searches; check out search engine help pages for instructions.) Scroll through at least two dozen links, noting sites that relate to your interest in the general topic of social class. Follow three links, and note what is stored at these sites and what additional links they include. Write a brief report in which you explain how you might use the information included in these three sites to develop a position on social class.

WRITING PROJECTS

Social Groups and Shared Identity

Project 1

Likely Readings

Background Readings
- Suro
- Harris

Case-in-Point Readings
- Ehrenreich
- Sheehan

Task and Purpose

What does it mean—what is it like—to be a member of a group? Write a paper in which you identify a group you belong to, focusing on what it's like to be a member. Start by deciding what kind of group you want to explore, perhaps one you love being a part of, one you have to be a part of, or one you are uncertain about. Look through your reading notes and find information about this group. (You may need to use the library or the Web to augment your reading.) Once you have gathered some material to work with, you can go in a couple of directions. For example, you can freewrite a typical experience you have as a member of the group and then think about what it says regarding the group, or think about why the group is significant and then brainstorm experiences that reveal that significance.

Project 2

Likely Readings

Background Readings
- Hacker
- Harris
- hooks

Case-in-Point Readings
- Ehrenreich
- Sheehan
- Chavez

Task and Purpose

Write a paper in which you study a member of a group that fascinates or confuses you, from a position outside that group. The result will be an analysis based on fieldwork similar to that which Sheehan did. Start by reviewing what you know about the group, and focus on one or two characteristics from among such elements as education, spending habits, occupation, acquisitions, and so on. Now go into the field. You might look at what the subject of your study spends money on or watches on TV, analyze his or her house or dorm room, or record what he or she eats durng a typical week. You *should* do a couple of focused interviews with your subject. Once you have done your fieldwork, use the "arc" of your study to organize your discussion, noting when different things occurred and how those occurrences informed, changed, or confirmed your point of view. You might start with your initial experiences with this group, even if those experiences took place in the past. You may move then into an interpretation of texts you read as part of your research, then of scenes you observed, then of interviews you held.

Project 3

Likely Readings

Background Readings
- Hacker
- hooks
- Suro

Case-in-Point Readings
- McCloskey
- Gates
- McDonald

Task and Purpose

How has your membership in one group or another affected your opportunities as a student? Using the reading to clarify how groups are empowered and marginalized, analyze how gender, ethnicity, class, or some other group membership may have affected your sense of your own possibilities, influenced your choice of the school you could attend, or affected the extracurricular activities you could afford. As you complete the analysis, draw some conclusions about your future goals and the effect of your group membership on achieving those goals.

Project 4

Likely Readings

Background Readings
- Hacker
- Harris
- hooks
- Suro

Case-in-Point Readings
- Ehrenreich
- Gates
- McDonald

Task and Purpose

Analyze a popular representation of a social class or group raised in one of the readings. Your options are groups based on gender, race, class (from upper to lower), sexual preference, ethnicity, and citizenship. Working with definitions and claims about group membership, analyze a text—a TV show, popular figure, movie, work of art, building, neighborhood—to explain what members appear to get from belonging to the group, how they are supposed to act, and how other groups treat them. As you move toward your conclusion, reflect on how this representation affects your view of this group.

CHAPTER 5

Advertising: The Discourse of Consumerism

In some sense, advertising is the official discourse of a consumer culture. In the flow of ads, everything—goods and services, identities, relationships, experiences, moods, places—becomes a commodity to be consumed. Through advertising, these things may also become symbols that consumers can use to create themselves, understand their desires, and communicate with others. Stop and think about ads for sport utility vehicles, for example. An SUV meets a basic human need for getting from here to there, and so at a basic level an SUV ad signals transportation. But rarely do these ads offer facts concerning transportation; instead, they call up symbols of individualism, safety, wealth, power, and environmental consciousness. Of course, as the roads fill up with high-powered, inefficient, expensive four-wheel-drive vehicles, these same symbols may also come to stand for waste, recklessness, environmental degradation, and elitism.

The flow of advertising doesn't trade in careful deliberation or rational thinking; from its suggestive murmur, we pick the meanings that appeal to us, ignoring contradictions or misinformation. We rarely trouble with the fact that advertisements call attention to price yet encourage us to disregard cost, or that many ads ignore price altogether or fill us with imagery and symbols that have nothing to with product information. Advertising mingles our concern about material needs with image, pleasure, and status (or, in more broad-minded approaches, our sense, perhaps vaguely defined, of social obligation). We come to believe we need particular images associated with certain products, and that buying is pleasurable. Ads lead us, through listening, viewing, and reading experiences, to an array of goods and services that make possible a life we would never have imagined without the cues advertising provides. Of course, we also end up with hefty credit card balances and, just maybe, an imagination and value system that is programmed by Madison Avenue.

Where supply exceeds demand, advertising comes to center stage. As a result of enormous increases in the ability to produce goods, our consumer society is awash in tidal waves of products for which demand must be artificially stimulated. Indeed, this skewed ratio between supply and demand is a precondition to a consumer-based economy. Faced with what the economist John Kenneth Galbraith in his book *The Affluent Society* (third edition, 1976) called "the urgency of numerous products of great frivolity" (118), producers turn to advertising to perform the wizardry that will "synthesize the desire for such goods" (118). Use-value and practicality have little to do with the equation that links consumer desire to products. In the global market, whether it's goods like cars, baby food, or heart medicine, or services like telecommunications, shipping, or credit, producers vie for consumers' attention and coin. Supported by this competition, the advertising industry has evolved and specialized, becoming a major cultural and economic force in its own right. The industry offers its members special achievement awards, and it continues to pursue its own forms of research and development— building on knowledge of cognition and communication to seek more and more effective ways of stimulating desire among consumers. As the speed of exchange has picked up, so has the volume and sophistication of advertising, such that we have more and more difficulty distinguishing between what we desire and what we can reasonably demand. (And if the ads are to be believed, there are no limits to what we desire.)

Whether you own a pair of athletic shoes or not, you probably know what Michael Jordan looks like. You have almost certainly seen several dozen ads today—on average, we are exposed to hundreds of ads every day. Taking a second look at the ads we see raises two questions that run through the readings: First, do ads show us options that exist in our world or do they create a world of options for us, defining a set of desires we accept as normal? For example, is there anything more than a trivial difference brands of soap? Second, is the world we see portrayed in advertising a world we should or must live in? These questions are tame as long as we're talking about selling something like soap. When we get to the case in point and the subject of illegal drugs and the ability of ads to change deeply held attitudes and public perceptions, the questions asked above become livelier.

BACKGROUND READINGS

THE SURFACE OF THE ADVERTISEMENT: COMPOSED AND CONSUMED
JIB FOWLES

In this excerpt from Advertising and Popular Culture *(1996), Jib Fowles looks at the role that advertising plays in the life of consumers. Fowles, a professor of media studies at the University of Houston—Clear Lake, analyzes the discourse of advertising and the ways advertising interacts with social values. He also describes how consumers go about decoding and ultimately using ads. Fowles has been analyzing ads for a long time; he is the author of an article called "Advertising's Fifteen Basic Appeals," which first appeared in the journal* Et Cetera *in (1982) and has since been reprinted in numerous first-year composition texts. In* Advertising and Popular Culture, *he builds on this project, responding to the work of other analysts and trends in the study of advertising.*

In directly contributing recognizable and appreciated ingredients and then in establishing a congenial setting, popular culture is providing great services to its boon companion, the domain of advertising. Important as these contributions are, however, it is only further investigation that can uncover the general thrust of advertising communication. What essentially is the content that is laid out on the surface of the advertisement? At the start of this chapter, concern is not with the totality of the compound advertisement but with the symbolic material that is left once notice of the commodity itself is subtracted from the message. That is, we are reaching for generalizations regarding the kinds of cultural symbols that advertisers strive to attach to their products, no matter what those products are.[1]

Scrutinizing the surface of the advertisement for what is presented there invariably leads to the problem of "meaning." The meaning that one person takes from an advertisement is certain to differ from what another person does.[2] How then is the content of advertising determined? The only answer is through a collection of approximations, all of them more or less imperfect but yet all of them an improvement over blanket ignorance or, worse, ascertainable untruths.

The Dominant Theme in Advertising Imagery

It is a surprisingly small palette of imagery that creative directors in advertising agencies typically turn to. The criteria for inclusion on this palette are severe, although they are not so rigid that they cannot slowly evolve in time. The imagery must be potentially meaningful to the audience, of course; the expensive display of meaningless material has no earthly purpose here. The imagery should usually be congenial, as its meanings are often intended to glide over onto the product. Unpleasant imagery is risky and hence rare (see, for example, Figure 5.1).[3] Ordinarily, the images must be pleasant to the greatest number and offensive to the fewest; the chosen pictures must, as Andrew Wernick (1992) wrote, "reach over the heads of the combatants and beyond their incompatibilities to whatever, nevertheless, can be expected to unite them all" (p. 43). Because the task of the messages is to change behavior, and the easiest, least resisted change in behaviors is in the direction of ideals, the images should usually be idealized depictions. These idealized depictions cannot be sanctimonious or insincere, or they are sure to be shunned. The number of possible themes dwindles.

Because advertisements are trying to inculcate meanings and because meanings exist only in a human context, it makes sense that the majority of advertisements contain images of people. In a study of advertising in men's and women's magazines, about 75% of all ads featured humans (Masse & Rosenblum, 1988, p. 129). The percentage is even higher in commercials—an analysis of both morning and evening network commercials determined that 87% contained human beings (Bretl & Cantor, 1988, p. 600). Because advertisements are messages designed to instigate sales, a visitor from another planet might well ask if they are selling people, since images of people typically occupy more of the purchased time and space than do images of commodities. Advertisers make this allocation because the harder job is not the display

Figure 5.1 Logitech ad
One of the rare unappealing figures in advertising, exaggerated so as to be comedic, this gentleman is not the center-piece of the Logitech campaign but a peripheral, change-of-pace character and so perhaps a relief. The computer users targeted by this ad may enjoy its collegiate whimsy but have little inclination to allow the image to color the product. Then again, isn't there a little larceny in everyone? (° 1993 Logitech Inc. Used by permission.)

of the inert product but the display of a human context that may or may not lend singular meanings to that product (a product sure to resemble all the other competing products in its class).

5   The people portrayed in American advertising are often engaged in pleasurable, leisure, off-hours activities. Swedish scholar Gunnar Andren (1978) conducted a content analysis of a carefully composed sample[4] of American print ads and found that less than 5% of the 300 ads examined showed scenes of employment (p. 130). Of the 162 ads he coded for some depicted activity, 110 (or 37%) contained leisure-time activities (p. 140). In a Canadian study, leisure was featured in just 1% of the 1930s' ads but almost 20% of the 1970s' (Leiss et al., 1990, p. 272). Using perhaps a narrower definition of leisure, Richard Pollay found leisure in evidence in 14% of his 1975 sample, still a gain from the 8% found at the start of the century (Belk & Pollay, 1987, p. 55).

The pleasures illustrated in advertising are commonly tamer and slighter than those available in popular culture; the brevity of the advertising presentation and the requirement not to violate the definitions of comportment held by potential customers dictate this. However, for one kind of pleasure—sexuality—the opinion is widespread that its depictions in advertising are on the rise. A 1986 study explored this by comparing a sample of 1964 print ads with a comparable sample of 1984 ads; the finding was that "the percentage of ads with sexual content has remained constant" (Soley & Kurzbard, 1986, p. 53). Then what can account for the general perception that the use of sex in advertising is expanding? Soley and Kurzbard (1986) provide two clues: First, although the proportion of sexual ads remained the same, the number of ads per magazine issue had climbed, which meant more sexuality in the advertising environment; and second, although the proportion of sexual ads remained constant, the sexual depictions within that percentage had become more overt, which also meant more sexuality in the advertising environment. Proportions had stayed the same, yet sexuality had increased. However, to put this into perspective, American advertising remains conspicuously prudish in contrast to its European counterpart; only 2.5% of Soley and Kurzbard's 1964 sample and 4.3% of their 1984 one were suggestive of sexual intercourse (p. 51). Fowles (1976) found strong sexual appeals in only 2% of print ads (p. 92); Pollay, studying 1975 print ads, found also that just 2% contained what he labeled "eros" (Belk & Pollay, 1987, p. 133).

Of interest is the fact that the social settings and personages characteristic of post–World War II advertising in the United States do not advance class distinctions and status markers as prominent themes. The comparative absence of class depictions has been especially clear to European observers, for in their home countries such social clues infuse advertising. "It is surprising that status does not play a major role," Andren (1978, p. 139) reported about American ads, expressing an incredulity that a native-born observer might not be susceptible to; only about 10% of the ads in his sample contained obvious status symbols. In a 1991 comparison of British and American print ads, the hypothesis that the U.S. ads would overwhelmingly depict an idealized upper-middle-class consumer and the British ads would reflect more class consciousness through a range of class portrayals was borne out in the data. Only 1% of American ads featured working-class people, whereas 24% of British ads did (Frith & Wesson, 1991, p. 222).

The relative classlessness of American advertising does not capture social reality, for every American senses that different social classes do exist, nor does it parallel popular culture offerings, where class placements and class markers are frequently conspicuous, contributing an important scale to the dramatic action in many programs and films. The muting of class information in advertising serves to eliminate an unpleasant social reminder from the message. Its removal also responds to a democratic American ideal, further confirming that advertising is the symbolic domain where ideals are advanced. The absence of class distinctions shifts the calibration from social definitions to personal definitions, from society to the individual.

Advertising imagery may be relatively free of the categorical impositions of work and of class, but just the reverse is the case with gender depictions. The liberated individuals within American advertising are sure to be highly delineated prototypes of maleness and femaleness. When Alice Courtney and Thomas Whipple (1983) complain that "women and men in society today clearly are far different from their portrayed images in advertising" (p. 24), they are unquestionably correct: Advertisers are certain that images of people as they are "in society today" will draw no more attention in advertising than do average people in the real world, whereas highly stylized paragons will attract the same fascinated gazes they would if they were spotted walking down any street in America. Thus, normal or unattractive people are rare in advertising …; only 1 of the 300 ads that Andren (1978) studied depicted a body deformed by work, sickness, or age (p. 125).

10   For females in ads, appearance was most commonly the totality of their persona, Andren determined; if any character trait shone through pictures of women, it was most likely to be "niceness" or "tenderness" (p. 128). Male appearance was most frequently and stereotypically linked to "toughness" or "expertise" (p. 128). The women in advertising conform to, as Andren says, "a very narrow ideal of female beauty" (p. 123). About half of the featured females are going to be noticeably thin (Gagnard, 1986, p. R46).[5] They are more likely than male models to be smiling (71% vs. 49%) (Choe, Wilcox, & Hardy, 1986, p. 125), a sign of amiability and acquiescence. They are also many times more likely than males to be partially or completely undressed (Andren, 1978, p. 132; Soley & Kurzbard, 1986, p. 53 …).

The presence of so many lithe and less-clothed women represents advertisers' attempt to project certain meanings onto their commodities. The objectified women are redolent in possible significations: They are vital, warm, accessible, pliable, consumable. They are the apples of many men's eyes, and some of their desirability can slide over to the inert product they are linked with. Such depictions may work with male consumers, but advertisers are convinced they work with females as well; according to Soley and Kurzbard (1986), in the 1984 ads they reviewed, the depiction of partially clad or nude models was 50% greater in women's magazines than in men's (p. 50). The implication would have to be that men are drawn to a certain portrayal of femininity and women are drawn toward occupying that portrayal; for women as well as men, a favorable disposition to the portrayal might then shift to the product.

Both males and females in advertising are certain to be youthful. This feature is so conventionalized that it may be overlooked, but it should not be, for it is suggestive of the ultimate function of advertising imagery. Busby and Leichty (1993) found that over 70% of the women in both 1959 and 1989 ads were judged to be between 18 and 34 (p. 259). There has been no discernible broadening or raising of age stereotypes over the decades for females, and the same is likely the case for males. Males' age in ads has always averaged several years older than females' (England, Kuhn, & Gardner, 1981), but there is no evidence that, as time has passed, this average has increased.

The greatest change in advertising since World War II has been the ascendant motif of the solitary figure. Andren (1978) found that illustrations of individuals occurred far more frequently than couples, families, or friends. He wrote, "When we read advertisements, we get the impression that people live completely isolated from one another in a social vacuum" (p. 142). Leiss et al. (1990) discovered that individualism rose steadily over the 20th century in their sample of Canadian print ads (p. 272). Similarly, in Fowles's (1976) study of motivational appeals in a sample of American print ads from 1950 to 1970, the sharpest climb was in the need for autonomy (p. 92). A single human figure was the most prevalent element in Masse and Rosenblum's (1988) sample of 564 print ads from 1984, prompting them to reflect about advertising that "this utopian world sustains an idealized, narcissistic self" (p. 131). A comparison of 1988 American and British print ads found that 57% of the American ads contained a single person, whereas 45% of the British advertising did (Frith & Wesson, 1991, p. 220).

A summary statement does a disservice to the outlying content in the expressive domain of advertising, but can capture the central themes. More than anything else, the imagery in advertising is that of idealized human beings. There is no requirement that this be so (advertising could feature abstract colors or pictures of ferns or no images at all), but it happens because advertisers have learned over time that this is what consumers want to look at. The people featured are largely devoid of employment and social locus and increasingly devoid of family and, in fact, others altogether (see Figure 5.2). This fascination speaks to our situation in history, to the present need to observe paragons of the self. It can be inferred that the imagery that lies on the surface of the advertisement is pertinent to the newly all-important concern for construction of the self. The imagery depicts young people because youth is the stage most given over to the formation of self-identity.[6] It shows leisure activities because those are the hours devoted to the self. It is gender-ridden because gender lies at the core of self-identity. Advertising imagery fixes on what individuals fix on, converting their needs into its forms in the hope that acceptance of these figurations will lead to acceptance of the commodities offered.

Figure 5.2 Bestform ad   What Americans primarily want to gaze at in advertising are exemplars of the individual, shorn of social trappings and pure in self-containment. They want to study the surfaces of those idealizations, first, to view acmes of attractiveness, and, second, to catch any glimpses of integrity, self-respect, and contentment. (Courtesy of Bestform Foundations, Inc.)

Social Values and Advertising

15   The imagery that lies on the surface of advertising is often subject to debate regarding whether it creates social values or simply mirrors social values already in existence. Critics of advertising usually hold the first position; defenders find solace in the second. Stuart Ewen (1988) appears to believe in the former, for he claims that advertising style is "a process of creating commodity images for people to emulate and believe in" (p. 91). Bruce Brown (1981), however, defends the latter, arguing that "advertising can be said to *reflect* middle-class cultural values" (p. 12).

Considering the fact that this debate has been raised countless times in virtually every serious treatment of advertising (including here), why is it that it has never been conclusively settled? The question is possibly a good (even if unanswerable) one, drawing out quickly and succinctly any observer's position regarding advertising. But there is also the possibility that it is a duplicitous question, appearing to address the issues but actually concealing them in such a way that they cannot be productively confronted. In truth, the relationship between advertising imagery and social values is unlikely to be a simple cause-and-effect one nor one conducted on one plane—both of these being implications in the query as originally formulated. Advertising imagery may not "cause" social values and existing social values may not "cause" advertising depictions, in any way that resembles simple causation. Nor, given the discrepancy between the heightened idealizations prominent in advertising imagery and the typically routinized lives (necessarily) of spectators, is it likely that communication would occur in a direct and level way according to the information flow presumed to exist in both arguments.

Advertising cannot create social actualities out of whole cloth, and it is folly to think it could. To believe it can impose stereotypes of its own making upon the public is to hold demeaning and, in the end, unsupportable views about the nature of the public. Consumers do not all accept the idealizations in advertising and then pattern themselves determinedly on them, or there would be much more uniformity in taste and appearance than there is. Resistance to advertising messages, or indifference to them, is revealed in the uneven marketplace successes of the commodities promoted within them. Conversely, it is clear that only a fraction of social actuality is captured in advertising; selection on some basis accounts for what is a highly circumscribed set of images. Even that selection is unlikely to mirror social realities. Attention to ads depicting what is already abundantly evident in the cultural world would be lower than the marginal attention currently paid to advertising.

Only when one reconsiders the imagery that actually lies on the surface of the advertisement can one begin to understand the relationship between advertising, consumers, and the creation or mirroring of reality. To repeat, what is seen on the surface are renderings of people in the prime of life, stripped of occupational roles, stripped of class allocations, stripped of ethnicity (an increasing number of Black and Asian models have Caucasian features), stripped of age considerations, and constituted as paragons of their genders. Missing is most of human life—work, duty, routines, small kindnesses as well as unpleasantries, not to mention the extensive variation in gender confirmation. Advertising distills from the variety of human appearances the few that will be accepted as apotheoses and returns them in perfected form to an audience desiring to see such singular renditions.

To trace this movement, the shift is from the plane of normal existence (the consumer's life, with a full cultural quotient except for nonpareils of attractiveness) to the out-of-this-world plane of idealized states (the flawless depictions conjured by advertising personnel) and back to the plane of this world (now armed with useful—perhaps even useful for purposes of rejection—epitomes of attractiveness). In circling from the quotidian to the idealized and back to the quotidian, not all of the idealized "information" will be adopted and brought back; it is the nature of ideals that they be recognized as distant and abstract, perhaps not to be incorporated but only to be acknowledged as points of cultural reference. Thus, advertisers respond to vague preferences with certain specific figurations that settle back into consciousness to both reify and vary standards of attractiveness. Advertising does not, and cannot, create these stereotypes from sources that exclude the public, nor does advertising passively mirror stereotypes; it is actively involved in the dialectical process of making and remaking them.

20 If the primary dynamic at work is not a shuttling of cause and effect in one direction or another, but rather a spiraling of need and image, that of refined preferences and further refined images, this still does not explain why the imagery consists in exactly what it does. In a national survey, 2,200 adults were asked to select their two most important personal needs from a list, and the results (in percentages) were these (Kahle, 1984, p. 78):

- Self-respect 21.1
- Security 20.6
- Warm relationships with others 16.2
- Accomplishment 11.4
- Self-fulfillment 9.6
- Being well respected 8.8
- Sense of belonging 7.9
- Fun/enjoyment/excitement 4.5

Self-respect tops the list, it can be presumed, because being at peace with oneself, feeling that the person who has been created is a person worthy of creation, remains elusive for the atomized population of Americans. In a period when the burden of identity-creation has fallen upon the individual, people are often trying to improve who they are and, accordingly, require idealizations of the self to respond to.

How Consumers Exploit Advertising

What is encoded into advertising is far from identical to what is decoded. The consumer now comes to center stage. In the face of the large literature on the subject of advertising, which Richard Pollay (1986) says is notable for "the veritable absence of perceived positive influence" (p. 19), the treatment here undertakes to valorize both advertising and consumers. The scope is thus widened to take more explicit account not only of advertising's composition but also of its reception, and the scope is further widened by reincorporating the commodity-related material into the advertising message and into consumers' consideration.

Just as a valorization of popular culture by cultural studies scholars depended on the recognition and appreciation of the powerful, interpretive role of the *user* of popular culture, so the valorization of advertising awaits acknowledgment of the truth that advertising does not exploit consumers, but, rather, that consumers exploit advertising. David Mick (1986) enjoins that "we must move beyond conceiving advertising in terms of what it does to people and view it more in terms of what people do with advertising" (p. 205). Consumers are, on the whole, adept social creatures, working to get the most from their resources in the interest of fulfilling their responsibilities and pleasures. To see consumers otherwise, as sheepish or foolish, is to do a disservice not only to them but to oneself both as a representative consumer and as a social observer. According to Mary Douglas, "Theories of consumption which assume a puppet consumer, prey to the advertiser's wiles, of consumer jealously competing with no sane motive, or lemming consumer rushing to disaster, are frivolous, even dangerous" (Douglas & Isherwood, 1979, p. 89). A position held by some feminist scholars is that a condescending view toward consumers is yet another instance of the patriarchal effort at the subordination of women, as it has long been held that production is men's work and consumption women's (Myers, 1986, p. 103). The sexist treatment of consumption would thus parallel the sexist treatment of popular culture (Huyssen, 1986).

In making selections for purchase, consumers do not rely extensively on advertising either consciously or inadvertently. Far more important are the opinions of friends and family members, the consumer's own experiences with the brand, and the price found in the store (Schudson, 1984, chap. 3). When consumers are unavoidably in the presence of advertising, as when reading a magazine or watching television, only a limited amount of the advertising is permitted to enter through the aperture of their minds. For those few advertising messages that are allowed in, many are either misunderstood or rejected outright. In one study of print advertising, 20% of the responses (from a national sample of 1,347 adults) to factual questions regarding a just-read ad evinced either miscomprehension or rejection (defined as occurring "when the receiver of the communication extracts meanings neither contained in nor logically derivable from the communication and/or rejects meanings contained in or logically derivable from the communication") (Jacoby & Hoyer, 1989, p. 437).[7] In an earlier study regarding television commercials, the average level of miscomprehension per commercial was 28% (Jacoby, Hoyer, & Sheluga, 1980, p. 73).

Decoding, the act of attaching meaning to the symbolic material of the advertising message, is clearly highly complex and interactive, with consumers bringing deeply personal readings to the process. Following the three-part scheme that Stuart Hall (1980) applied to popular culture, the meaning received could be the "preferred" one of the advertiser: for example, the consumer already thinks favorably of Candice Bergen and will consider using Sprint. Or the commercial could produce an "oppositional" meaning: the consumer finds Candice Bergen insipid, now and always, and will never use the long-distance carrier. But most likely the meaning is a "negotiated" one: perhaps the consumer has an amorous interest in Candice Bergen or has a sister who looks like Candice, perhaps the household dog is named Candy. These and a million other meanings come forward and greet the commercial.

25   For those advertising messages that the consumer does receive and supply meaning to, the content of the message will now be used for entirely personal purposes. The

appeal associated with the product first takes up its place within the sphere of stored meanings, either affirming an old one or creating a slightly altered one. The young actor who poses as a doctor or a Chinese relative in the Bud Light commercials ("Yes I am!") lends playful nuances to concepts of imposture and pretense. The image of the accompanying product may or may not be allowed to register at all ("Was that for Bud Light or Miller Lite?"). If the product is accepted, it may be mentally situated near the meaning of the appeal: The beer takes on meanings of impudence, and impudence comes to imply the beer. Or the beer may be lodged somewhere in the concentric spheres of widening meanings: defiance, self-assertion, youthfulness, fun.

For each ad that enters the mind, the consumer has chosen to reconfirm or add to the massive symbol vocabulary necessary for the conduct of a well-managed life. The appeal imagery may endorse a notion of what constitutes the good life, for example, and the product image may take on inferences of an item useful toward the realization or communication of that good life. The consumer does not in any way "believe" the ad's implied equation that the product will necessarily result in the depicted tableau of the good life. Michael Schudson (1984) calls advertising "the art form of bad faith" (p. 11) in that neither advertiser nor consumer literally "believes" the message. Yet the imagery of accepted ads has credibility because it is performing the crucial service of establishing ideals and anchoring scales of evaluation. For the consumer, the ad takes vague notions of important states and lends those a form, an image. The consumer does not want advertising to deal in realities, which already abound in the consumer's life; the consumer appreciates advertising that offers gossamer. Only a culture critic, employing inappropriate discourse standards, would rebuke advertising for being unreal.

The act of creating appropriate idealizations through the discovery of evocative imagery in advertising and may well be a pleasurable one for the consumer. There is intriguing quantitative evidence in support of this: In a carefully controlled study by Myers and Biocca (1992), college-age females who were exposed to commercial television footage edited to feature idealized female body images felt more euphoric afterward. Moreover, they judged themselves as *thinner* than they had on pretests. Trying to explain these unexpected findings, Myers and Biocca write,

> The commercials invited them to fantasize themselves in their future ideal body shape. The significant drop in depression levels suggests that subjects exposed to the body-image commercials felt better about themselves immediately after exposure to the 15 ideal-body ads. The commercials' cumulative message of "You can be thin" may have developed greater feelings of self-control in the young women.
>
> (p. 127)

By this reasoning, exposure to an ideal had invited pleasurable fantasizing of movement toward that ideal.[8] To a slight but discernible degree, the young women had permitted meanings taken from the paragon to be incorporated into the self and the self into the paragon.

As further indication of the integrity and purposefulness of consumers, it is not often that the absorption of advertising leads to actual purchases.[9] The consumer is ruthlessly selective in what will or will not be bought. Economist Stanley Lebergott (1993) has data showing that 86% of the 85,000 new products advertised in the American market over the 1980s did not survive beyond the end of 1990 (p. 18). The few advertised products that are purchased are highly likely to provide the meanings

sought. When Marxist critics Max Horkheimer and Theodor Adorno (1972) complained, "The triumph of advertising in the culture industry is that consumers feel
compelled to buy and use its products even though they see through them" (p. 167),
they were correct—but in an unintended way. Products are linked to meanings, and
if consumers see through products, it is to those meanings lying around and beyond.

The way that consumers make use of advertising—in the search for idealized
states to which a meaning connection can be made, with a passing interest in the products that may be associated with those states—has become decisive in the construction of that advertising. Advertisers and their agencies respond to the preferences of
consumers by offering up first and primarily the desired depictions and then by insin-
uating a connection between the appeal imagery and the product the advertiser is trying to sell. The appeal imagery is not what the advertiser wishes to impose on the
consumer nor what the advertiser thinks there is even a chance of imposing but, rather,
what the advertiser prays will give form to the proclivities of the consumer. Leiss et al.
(1990) confirm that "in the consumer society the consumer, not the product, is the
core of the message system about the sphere of consumption" (p. 295).

30   As it plays to the extraordinary discretion, even power, of the consumer, advertising may now be reconceptualized as almost the reverse of what the authors of the advertising critique insist upon. Advertising is not a hail of commercial barbs inflicting damage
on huddling consumers and their culture. Advertising is a buffet of symbolic imagery
that advertisers hope will prove tempting and lead to the more difficult exchange of
money for goods. Consumers pass down the table of displayed appeals, glancing here
and there, but stop only infrequently to oblige a felt inner need for a symbol and a product—and to buy. It is their favor that advertisers are assiduously courting.

NOTES

1. It can be difficult at first to separate the product from the pitch. When beer drinkers are
   asked why they choose Budweiser, they sometimes respond, "Because it's the King of
   Beers." Yet, in short order, one learns to mentally subtract all the information factually
   related to the product, leaving the nonproduct material ready for inspection. Once again,
   there need be no logical link at all between the commodity and the noncommodity material in an advertisement, and frequently there is none; mere association is sufficient for the
   transfer of meaning.
2. For a restricted yet emphatic empirical demonstration of how interpretations of advertising can differ, see Sentis and Markus (1986). In their study, they asked groups of males to
   judge depictions of aftershave lotions and found that judgments varied according to the
   respondents' self-descriptions, leading Sentis and Markus to conclude that "consumers
   take very different ideas from advertising and other brand communication depending on
   the organization and content of their self-concept" (p. 146).
3. Leiss, Kline, and Jhally (1990) indicate that fear appeals have fallen off in Canadian advertising since the 1930s (p. 268); the same is certain to be the case for advertising in the
   United States.
4. Andren (1978) and his colleagues took their sample from the 11 largest circulating magazines of 1973. The 300 ads in the sample were chosen after allowing for the various magazines' circulation sizes and annual numbers of issues. Issues were selected randomly from
   throughout the year, and within each of these issues ads were picked randomly.
5. Howard Gossage (1967) thinks he knows why models are so thin: "They are supernatural
   representations and I defy you to account for them in any other fashion" (p. 366). Their
   ethereal, unearthly quality levitates the associated products from the plane of the real to
   the plane of the magical.

6. On the prevalence of the young in advertising, and this feature's link with spectators' concerns for self-identity, Diane Barthel (1988) concurred, "It is no wonder that advertising stresses the appearance of youth and the values of youth. It is caught up with youth's crises and concerns, namely, finding identity and managing intimacy" (p. 187).

7. It is important to note that in the study by Jacoby and Hoyer (1989) respondents were handed a print ad and instructed "Please read what it says and tell me when you've finished" before being asked comprehension questions. Clearly, miscomprehension rates would have been much higher under normal reading conditions.

8. A study with contrary findings was reported by Richins (1991). Results from groups of female undergraduates suggested that "exposure to highly attractive images can negatively affect feelings about the self" (p. 81).

9. If advertising does not lead to (many) purchases, then why do advertisers advertise? There are fundamentally two reasons. The economies of mass communication mean that the cost per consumer contact is small considering the enormous number of consumers reached; if only a tiny percentage of these inexpensively contacted consumers go on to effect purchases, the effort will still be profitable. But even if the cost of advertising does not seem to be directly paying out, to pull back from this type of marketing when competitors do not is to risk extinction. Advertisers advertise to stay abreast with competitors, who are also advertising.

REFERENCES

Andren, G. (1978). *Rhetoric and ideology in advertising: A content analytical study of American advertising.* Stockholm: Liberforlag.

Barthel, D. (1988). *Putting on appearances: Gender and advertisers.* Philadelphia: Temple University Press.

Belk, R., & Pollay, R. W. (1987). The good life in twentieth century advertising. *Journal of Advertising Research, 11,* 887–897.

Bretl, D. J., & Cantor, J. (1988). The portrayal of men and women in U.S. television commercials: A recent content analysis and trends over 15 years. *Sex Roles, 18*(9/10), 595–609.

Brown, B. W. (1981). *Images of family life in magazine advertising, 1920–1978.* New York: Praeger.

Choe, J.-H., Wilcox, G. B., & Hardy, A. P. (1986). Facial expressions in magazine ads: A cross-cultural comparison. *Journalism Quarterly, 63*(1), 122–126.

Courtney, A., & Whipple, T. (1983). *Sex stereotyping in advertising.* Lexington, MA: Lexington Books.

Douglas, M., & Isherwood, B. (1979). *The world of goods: Toward an anthropology of consumption.* New York: W. W. Norton.

Ewen, S. (1988). *All consuming images: The politics of style in contemporary culture.* New York: Basic Books.

Firth, K. T., & Wesson, D. (1991). A comparison of cultural values in British and American print advertising: A study of magazines. *Journalism Quarterly, 68*(1/2), 216–223.

Fowles, J. (1976). *Mass advertising as social forecast.* Westport, CT: Greenwood.

Gagnard, A. (1986). From feast to famine: Depictions of ideal body type in magazine advertising. In E. F. Larkin (Ed.), *Proceedings of the 1986 Conference of the American Academy of Advertising* (pp. R46—R50). Norman: University of Oklahoma Press.

Gossage, H. L. (1967). The gilded bough: Magic and advertising. In F. W. Matson & A. Montague (Eds.), *The human dialogue* (pp. 363–370). New York: Free Press.

Hall, S. (1980). Encoding/decoding. In S. Hall (Ed.), *Culture, media, language* (pp. 128–138). London: Hutchinson.

Horkheimer, M., & Adorno, T. (1972). The culture industry: Enlightenment as mass deception. In M. Horkheimer & T. Adorno, *Dialectic of entertainment* (pp. 120–167). New York: Herder & Herder. (Original work published 1944)

Huyssen, A. (1986). Mass culture as woman: Modernism's other. In T. Modleski (Ed.), *Studies in entertainment: Critical approaches to mass culture* (pp. 188–207). Bloomington: Indiana University Press.

Jacoby, J., & Hoyer, W. D. (1989). The comprehension/miscomprehension of print communication: Selected findings. *Journal of Consumer Research, 15*(4), 434–443.

Jacoby, J., Hoyer, W. D., & Sheluga, D. A. (1980). *Miscomprehension of televised communications.* New York: Educational Foundation of the American Association of Advertising Agencies.

Kahle, L. R. (1984). The values of Americans: Implications for consumer adoption. In R. E. Pitts & A. G. Woodside (Eds.), *Personal values and consumer behavior* (pp. 77–86). Lexington, MA: Lexington Press.

Lebergott, S. (1993). *Pursuing happiness: American consumers in the twentieth century.* Princeton, NJ: Princeton University Press.

Leiss, W., Kline, S., & Jhally, S. (1990). *Communication in advertising: Persons, products and images of well-being* (2nd ed.). Scarborough, Ontario; Nelson Canada.

Masse, M. A., & Rosenblum, K. (1988). Male and female created they them: The depiction of gender in the advertising of traditional women's and men's magazines. *Women's Studies International Forum, 11*(2), 127–144.

Mick, D. G. (1986). Consumer research and semiotics: Exploring the morphology of signs, symbols, and significance. *Journal of Consumer Research, 13*(2), 196–213.

Myers, K. (1986). *Understains: The sense and seduction of advertising.* London: Comedia.

Myers, P. N., & Biocca, F. A. (1992). The elastic body image: The effects of television advertising and programming on body image distortions in young women. *Journal of Communications, 42*(3), 108–133.

Pollay, R. W. (1986). The distorted mirror: Reflections on the unintended consequences of advertising. *Journal of Marketing, 50*, 18–36.

Richins, M. (1991). Social comparison and the idealized images of advertising. *Journal of Consumer Research, 18*, 71–83.

Schudson, M. (1984). *Advertising, the uneasy persuasion: Its dubious impact on American society.* New York: Basic Books.

Sentis, K., & Markus, H. (1986). Brand personality and self. In J. Olson & K. Sentis (Eds.), *Advertising and consumer psychology* (Vol. 3, pp. 132–148). New York: Praeger.

Soley, L., & Kurzbard, G. (1986). Sex in advertising: A comparison of 1964 and 1984. *Journal of Advertising, 15*(3), 46–55.

Wernick, A. (1992). *Promotional culture: Advertising, ideology, and symbolic expression.* Newberry Park, CA: Sage.

Rereading Actively

1. Throughout this chapter, Fowles considers the debate over whether advertising creates or reflects social values, finally suggesting that this is the wrong question to ask. How does this maneuver affect your reading of the essay and your position on the relationship between advertising and values?

2. What does Fowles mean by "the imagery that actually lies on the surface of the advertisement" (¶ 18)? Why is staying on the "surface" so important to his analysis?

3. In a small group, review Fowles's description of the process through which ads create images and the process of "decoding" through which viewers put ads. Write a brief summary of each of these processes in your journal.

4. At the beginning of the final section, Fowles declares that he will "valorize both advertising and consumers" (¶ 21) and concludes that advertising is better described as a "buffet" than a "hail of barbs" (¶ 30). If "to valorize" means to give value to, does Fowles accomplish his intentions in the section? Why or why not?

5. Fowles contends that "consumers exploit advertising" (¶ 22). How does this happen? In your journal, explain how you have exploited a specific ad.

Exploring Your Responses

6. In a small group, brainstorm social values that advertising makes use of, values concerning sexuality, aggression, community, self-fulfillment, respect, and so on. Focusing on one of these values, discuss whether ads tend to create social values or reflect social values that people already hold. Write a description of your group's discussion in your journal.

7. With a partner, pick a currently popular ad, brainstorm target audiences for the ad, and discuss how one audience might decode the ad. Focus on (a) the relevant symbolic material, (b) the appeal associated with the product, and (c) consumers' potential evaluation of the content of the ad. Be prepared to explain to the class how a specific audience may exploit or be exploited by the ad.

8. Reflect on the ideals that advertising makes use of (starting with those Fowles lists). Focus on a single ideal that is important to you, and in a page or two in your journal, explore what advertising does with that ideal and how you respond to ads that make use of that ideal.

ADVERTISING CITIZENSHIP
IRENE COSTERA MEIJER

Irene Costera Meijer teaches communications at the University of Amsterdam and studies advertising. In this 1998 essay in the British cultural studies journal Media, Culture & Society, *she counters the academic mainstream, suggesting that advertising is, at least in part, a productive and useful public discourse, one that helps people become active citizens and not just passive consumers. To accomplish this goal, she takes on the critics of advertising on their own turf, working with the vocabulary of cultural analysis and reviewing recent positions on advertising. Once this groundwork is complete, she examines the example of an ad agency that tells "valuable stories of the good life."*

The idea that audiences actively use and interpret popular culture has become something of a truism in cultural and media studies. The parallel concept, that consumers make discerning use of commercials, advertising and other genres of consumer culture has gained less standing (Fowles, 1996). In this article I suggest ways to look at advertising's potential as a form of public communication and a setting for the actualization of notions of contemporary citizenship. The latter includes more than the Marshallian triad of civic, political and social rights and obligations. Citizenship must also be seen as a feature of culture, operative as a dimension of individual and collective identities. Thus, as various authors have argued, citizenship has also to do with belonging and inclusion (Roche, 1987; Turner, 1990). To be a citizen is to be a member of something we (metaphorically) call a community. It also has to do with participation in that community (local, historical, political or cultural). The conditions of membership and participation, the processes which determine inclusion or exclusion must be understood broadly. They refer to public life in a more general way.

To paraphrase Dahlgren (1995: 136): to be a citizen means to be included culturally, not just civically, socially and politically.

Historically, one of the main issues in critical debates on advertising, especially in relation to the representation of women, has been whether ads reflected reality more or less correctly (Friedan, 1963; Lazier-Smith, 1989; Schmerl, 1992). Another critical angle bypasses the epistemological issue of reflection and representation, and raises the question how advertising operates in the construction of identities and subjectivities (Bordo, 1992; Goldman and Papson, 1996; McCracken, 1993; Messaris, 1997; Slater, 1997). I want to widen the latter approach and explore the possibilities of advertising or promotional culture (Wernick, 1991) as a means to create positive notions of contemporary citizenship. Whereas this may seem an unexpected turn in critical approaches to consumer or promotional culture, there are enough examples to warrant an analysis of advertising's construction of so-called 'civic capital' (Charity, 1995), i.e., anything that improves the productivity of a community, its ability to meet crises, solve problems and live contentedly. Public journalists are not the only communicators who look for ways to strengthen their community's goodwill, cooperative habits, insights into where other social groups are coming from and other ground rules of democracy (Charity, 1995). Take for instance the work of an American advertising agency like Burrell Advertising. Its work is well known for its attempts to use advertising to shape people's (political) attitudes and in particular to advance racial understanding.

Burrell's ads and the other examples I will discuss more extensively can best be understood as positive forces for citizenship if we look at the performative side of advertising (Butler, 1993) rather than the epistemological one. By this I mean that we should look at advertising as the act of telling stories that enable a certain interaction with and management of 'reality' (Slater, 1997). Such a performative perspective is central to my understanding of promotional culture and involves a focus on both the production and reception of advertising: which stories are being told in promotional culture; which ones are considered worth telling; what do they animate/activate; how do they relate to other stories people tell and live in?

I will make my case for advertising using various sources and some preliminary results of my own research on outdoor advertising. First, however, I shall theorize the articulation of advertising and contemporary citizenship in more detail.

Advertising and Citizenship

5 Apart from the vocabulary, framing advertising in a context of citizenship is not a brand new idea. On the contrary, more often than not citizenship has been the governing theme in discussions about the social impact of advertising. Until recently this debate has been dominated by critics who explained how ads stifled people's aspirations for change and their abilities to think about themselves as powerful and motivating citizens. Underlying such critiques is a perceived dichotomy between the values of production and consumption that can be traced to, among other things, the classic Marxist idea that work and production constitute the proper forms of human self-fulfilment. 'The mode of consumption, on the other hand, becomes an activity of human alienation, fetishization, and reification. It is finally a mode of misrecognition' (Bermingham, 1995: 6).

That basic opposition has been reworked in various famous works on advertising. Erich Fromm, for instance, a member of the highly influential Frankfurt School, wrote in his book *Escape from Freedom* that advertising appeals were 'essentially irrational;

they have nothing to do with the quality of the merchandise, and they smother and kill the critical capacities of the customer like an opiate or outright hypnosis' (1941: 128).

According to another well known critic of Western culture Christopher Lasch (1979), advertising serves not so much to advertise products as to promote consumption as a way of life. Ads 'educate' the masses into a way of life that celebrates consumption as an end in itself. Lasch extends his critique to the consumption of new experiences as a means for more personal fulfillment. Consumption is the answer to problems like boring and meaningless jobs and empty lives. 'Consumption promises to fill the aching void; hence the attempt to surround commodities with an aura of romance; with allusions to exotic places and vivid experiences; and with images of female breasts from which all blessings flow' (Lasch, 1979: 137–8).

Lasch underscores that the 'propaganda for commodities' serves a double function. First, it upholds consumption as an alternative to protest or rebellion. Instead of changing one's life, ads are presenting goods as a cure to feelings of loneliness, sickness, weariness or lack of sexual satisfaction. Advertising proposes consumption as the cure to personal insecurity, anxiety of people about their professional and personal status or their ability as parents to nurture their children. In the second place, advertising turns alienation itself into a commodity. Ads create new forms of discontent that can only vanish or be cured by new products. Although Lasch concludes that advertising serves the status quo, he is not immune to the performing qualities of the industry.

> The apparatus of mass promotion attacks ideologies based on the postponement of gratification; it allies itself with 'sexual revolution'; it sides or seems to side with women against male oppression and with the young against the authority of elders. The logic of demand creation requires that women smoke and drink in public, move about freely, and assert their right to happiness instead of living for others.
>
> (Lasch, 1979: 139)

Lasch states that the advertising industry encourages the pseudo-emancipation of women and similarly flatters and glorifies youth in the hope of elevating young people to the status of full fledged consumers in their own right, 'each with a telephone, a television set, and a hifi in his own room' (Lasch, 1979: 140). He acknowledges that the 'education' of the masses has altered family relations, but only to subject women and children to the new laws of the advertising and fashion industry.

In a Marxist vein, Judith Williamson writes that 'advertisements obscure and avoid the real issues of society'. For her the real issues of society involve the organization of production: 'those relating to work: to jobs and wages and who works for whom' (1978: 47). In her view, advertising alters the issues concerning labour into matters of consumption. She seems to agree with Lasch as she states: 'The basic issues in the present state of society, which do concern money and how it is earned, are sublimated into "meanings", "images", "lifestyles", to be bought with products not with money' (1978: 47).

10   Thus, in many critical perspectives advertising and citizenship seem to have been solely and unambiguously defined as a contradiction in terms: advertisements choke the abilities of people to act and think as independent citizens. Advertising manipulates people into being consumers and instils false values. It extols a materialistic and consumerist ethic and it deals in emotions and irrationality because it leads people to buy unnecessary things or overvalued items. In short, advertising leads to consumerism and consumerism marks an identity and a lifestyle which are emptied of

civic virtues. The critical articulation of citizenship and consumer culture is therefore one of strong opposition.

Quite another paradigm comes from anthropology, and in particular from the work of Mary Douglas and her co-author the economist Baron Isherwood. Their joint enterprise *The World of Goods: Toward an Anthropology of Consumption* (1979) provided a different way in to consumer culture, starting from why people want to obtain goods in the first place. Douglas and Isherwood create a different link between the buying of commodities and people's sense of themselves as social beings. They argue that material possessions have carried social meanings from the beginnings of humankind and not just since the beginnings of the industrial revolution as Marxists tend to claim. Quite unlike Stuart Ewen, who warns in his book about the *Captains of Consciousness* (1976) that 'social change cannot come about in the context where objects are invested with human subjective capacities', their cultural analysis is concentrated upon the use of material goods as communicators of social meanings. People do not obtain goods to escape the real world. On the contrary, the consumption of goods lies at the core of human existence because goods make meanings manifest and provide a means for people to situate themselves within that culture (Appadurai, 1986). While the ability to ascribe meaning to otherwise inanimate objects and thus to transform commodity goods into social communicators is not solely the purview of advertising—it is in fact the necessary requisite of human culture, in which all objects, even the most mundane, must be mediated within a symbolic field in order to have any utility, value or worth at all—it is the work of advertisements to make things come alive. Douglas and Isherwood's work opens up the argumentation that ads must not be condemned beforehand as the designer tools for daily spiritual deprivation. On the contrary, they could be thought of as a rich source of information about daily life.

A question that remains, however, is why are human beings nowadays collectively involved in the enterprise of mass consumption? Recapitulating the influence of the anthropological angle, Jib Fowles (1996) underlines Douglas and Isherwood's suggestion that because people need goods to articulate meanings in their cultural world, should that cultural world for any reason enlarge, then so would the number of matters demanding new symbols and more goods. The authors turn around the critical Marxist argument of the commodification and—therefore—devaluation of values. In their interpretation, the commodification of values, the transformation of values into goods, and thus the production of new goods could be interpreted as a sign of the emergence of new values and fresh symbols for novel cultural phenomena. The enlargement of the cultural world requires an enlargement of the amount of available goods. New cultural values need new products to come alive, so to speak. Reasoning from the perspective of Douglas and Isherwood, Coca Cola is not just a very popular soft drink, not even the symbol for an ever expanding universal lifestyle for young people, but the expression of a new way of living and a new understanding of global cultural values.

This type of argument makes even more sense if we relate it to the historical emergence of the modern individual. The formation of modern human beings with their unique sense of self forms one of the main differences between earlier societies and our Western cultures. Since the 19th century, the Western concept of the individual has been in transition. The increasing prominence of the individual occurred at the expense of some of the rigour of such framing institutions as church, community, ethnicity, lineage, profession, family and gender (Fowles, 1996). Earlier, these institutions had assumed near complete responsibility for granting people firm definitions of themselves as well as social locations. Socially inscribed categories for personal defin-ition (like Catholic or Protestant, Dutch or German, Caucasian, Jewish or African-American, from Amsterdam or Veenendaal, farmer or pharmacist) now seem old fashioned and inadequate. The categories have been succeeded by the answer to ques-tions on the order of 'What is she like?' or 'What kind of person is he?' The question of individual identity becomes more prominent and is also posed introspectively: what kind of person am I (Fowles, 1996)? The project of the self has been changed from an engraving of social concepts on to the individual to practices and technologies that are used by the individual to constitute him- or herself as a subject (Foucault, 1988a).

The individuation of human life demands that not just each household but each person has to possess an adequate measure of symbolizing goods in order to manoeu-vre in the modern cultural world. The identities of the self that were once shaped by constraining and imposing social forces were now more likely to be created and nur-tured by the individual. Grant McCracken (1986: 80) notes that 'contemporary North American culture leaves a great deal of the individual undefined. One of the ways indi-viduals satisfy the freedom and fulfil responsibility of self-definition is through sys-tematic appropriation of the meaningful properties of goods'.

15   In his recent book *Consumer Culture & Modernity* Don Slater writes that con-sumerism is central to this self obsession (1997: 91). This is partly because we not only have to choose a self but, as Foucault suggests, we have to constitute ourselves as a self who chooses, as a person who consumes, a consumer. Slater claims that one implica-tion of this 'ideology of choice' is that we are deemed personally responsible for every aspect of ourselves: we could always choose to do something about our appearance, health, manners. Wearing this, eating that, looking like this are all read as reflections of the self. As a result, all aspects of our existence are monitored and scrutinized as objects of instrumental calculation in the creation of the self, and the self is itself as much a thing one must produce as the person that one is. In Slater's line of argument, consumer industries stand ready with things one can buy in order to address all these technical problems in the production of ourselves. Moreover, he underscores, adver-tising and the media routinely offer aspirational narratives of the self—images of lifestyles, goods, advice—with which the viewer can identify. Most crucially, much like Foucault's ethical technologies, they offer up the very idea of the self as a narrative form, a story to be told and retold and to be constructed through individual choice and effort.

Despite Slater's emphasis on the performative power of advertising in the con-struction of selves, he keeps on condemning the practice of advertising as the selling of false selves (disguised as authentic selves) to so-called real selves that are in fact per-manently under construction. The self constructed as a consumer does not seem to be capable of citizenship. The citizen and the consumer are still miles apart and very unlikely candidates for the same story. If Slater states that advertising offers up the very idea of the self as something you can construct through individual choice and effort, he offers a disapproving statement. Notwithstanding its postmodern views on identity, Slater's book has a firm Marxist imprint in its denunciation of advertising for instill-ing false hopes and desires. There is no such thing as a choosing self, he reminds us, choice is always and exclusively an ideological category, not an authentic possibility.

Apparently he has serious doubts about people's ability to transform themselves into the persons that they aspire to be. Furthermore, he does not believe that advertising is capable of instilling good narratives of the self, let alone good lifestyles and good advice. Indeed, consumerism may turn you into an anti-social egotistic human being. But why should it not be capable of changing you for the good?

The Commodification of Citizenship: Advertising Civic Virtues

If advertising is about setting up and instilling ideals, could not the installation of these ideals be as easily capable of transforming you into a good citizen? In order to argue that advertising has something to offer in this respect, I'll discuss two sets of advertising that offer visions of the good life and the good society: the first comes from the Burrell Agency mentioned earlier. It is the largest black-owned advertising agency in the world and is said to define the standard for quality advertising addressing black audiences. Burrell makes ads that celebrate 'black citizenship'. The second set was produced for two Dutch companies—the multinational beer brewery Heineken and a life insurance company Amev whose campaigns both incorporated enjoyable visions of cultural differences and alternative lifestyles.

The Burrell Agency

Underlying the so-called Burrell style are two key concepts: 'psychological distance' and 'positive realism' (Cassidy and Katula, 1990). The owner and founder of the agency, Thomas Burrell, describes psychological distance as a feeling of separation between the black consumer and mainstream products, like Crest toothpaste. Black people will immediately admit to the quality of these products but will not buy them because they do not envision themselves as 'belonging' to these brands. To overcome the perception that 'this product is not for me', Burrell's ads associate the product with portrayals of black people at their best—images of what Burrell calls 'positive realism': 'people working productively, people engaged in family life … people being well-rounded … and thoughtful; people with dreams and aspirations; people with ambition' (Cassidy and Katula, 1990: 94). Burrell's basic assumption is that the best way to sell products to the black consumer market is through the projection of positive images. An ad made for McDonald's may serve as the typical example: it shows a responsible, community-oriented businessman teaching a lesson in economics to school-children. In the text it says in large letters: 'John A. Dawkins has a Degree in Chemistry and Still Goes to Grade School'. In smaller letters the text continues:

> Like so many McDonald's owner-operators, John A. Dawkins believes customer service should extend far beyond the doors of his restaurants. To him, giving back means reaching out and getting involved. Because at McDonald's, community relationships start with personal relationships.

Burrell's principle of positive realism is at the heart of the McDonald's ad which clearly comes out of the concept of using the trustworthy male, the father figure, as a positive, laudatory, image of black manhood. The ad directly counters three of the current negative stereotypes of blacks: the lazy ni—er, the irresponsible father and the ghetto drug dealer. According to Burrell, the idealization of the responsible father/business figure is something that would make the female heads of households that the ad is talking to feel good about the advertisement and—by implication—the product (Cassidy and Katula, 1990). Supposedly, the black female consumer would like to have that male figure in the house, or in front of her kids' classroom. Talking from the kids' point of view, the agency used the father/business man as a key figure. The man is caring, wants to be part of the kids' life and which child would not want to have such a family man around (Cassidy and Katula, 1990).

The work of the Burrell Agency offers a new and powerful impulse to the debate around the social impact of advertising. It stimulates advertisers and marketing researchers to think about the use of positive, laudatory stereotypes that create so-called win—win situations, images which are good for the market and can change people's ideas about themselves and hopes for society.

20   There is of course another side to that approach: the positive image of the black successful business and family man is firmly based in white, middle-class values and it raises the question how much the picture shows of black culture, if anything. Such controversy over the use of positive middle-class images has also surrounded the reception of the *Bill Cosby Show,* one of the few other black mainstream media successes (Downing, 1988; Dyson, 1991; Gray, 1989; Real, 1991). Yet, it seems a bit cynical to reprehend the 'positive images' approach when the overwhelming majority of mainstream American media culture is populated by stereotypes like the lazy ni—er, the welfare mother, the irresponsible father, the ghetto drug dealer or the violent, unemployed youth. There is an additional up-side to the Burrell approach which is especially relevant in the context of the performative power of advertising. These ads not only show likeable people, they also offer new stories to live by. Carolyn Heilbrun (1989) has argued that we can only live our lives by the stories we have read or heard. The McDonald's ad makes visible and imaginable a new story of responsible black male citizenship that can be a source of inspiration and guidance for men and women, whites and blacks. The ad draws people into a valuable and a socio-cultural awareness of (good) citizenship and it calls for a new and just lifestyle.

Amstel/Heineken Beer

A Dutch counterpart of the Burrell approach can be seen in an advertising campaign for the multinational beer brewery Heineken. Its advertising agency created a story of multicultural citizenship to transform the image of one of its brands Amstel from average and middle-of-the-road to something more urban and special. Different commercials show sites of leisure like a park, grand cafe or harbour where people of different ages, colour and sex are walking different sorts of dogs, are dancing different sort of dances and are sailing different sorts of ships. The commercials share the same text: 'In the end, we all want the same thing.' Although what it is that we all want in the end remains somewhat vague, the viewer is invited to identify with a cheerful community of very diverse individuals who are relaxed in their free time, loyal and helpful towards one another, healthy looking and free-spirited. Drinking beer can elevate your spirits and is accompanied by the happy feeling of multicultural camaraderie.

The Amstel ads offer a commodified version of multicultural citizenship. The campaign explicitly and deliberately, according to Heineken's marketing director Paul Waterreus, celebrates the authenticity of every human being by stating: 'In the end we all want the same thing', which in this context refers to 'We are all different and yet all the same' (personal interview, Paul Waterreus, 18 April 1997). However, the concept of global citizenship accompanied by the message 'In the end, we all want the same thing' did not work out as expected. Marketing research suggested that Dutch consumers found the message of the campaign unsettling. Apparently, they did not want to be hailed into the utopian future of infinite friendship across ranks, classes and colours. They preferred a feeling of togetherness on a much smaller scale with family, friends and neighbours. The new Amstel campaign therefore shows a sense of brotherhood in a more literal way (friendship among young white men) and on a much smaller scale, the local pub.

Should we conclude, with the director of Heineken, that the commercial was too utopian in nature and that one must turn back to more 'realistic' and thus more intolerant portrayals of Dutch neighbourhoods or Dutch multiculturalism? I would hope not. I firmly believe that we must invent better stories. What is special about the Amstel myth is the concept that, together with the introduction of drinking beer as a crucial part of adult life, it inscribes tolerant multicultural citizenship as an essential moment of adulthood. According to marketing research (which may have its own questionable logic), something in these particular narratives provided a disturbing rather than an exhilarating experience. Maybe they were too new and too utopian. Perhaps they were loved as stories, but not as practices, as visions of 'reality'. The concept, however, is worth repeating in a different format.

Amev

Recently (autumn 1997) the Dutch life insurance company Amev made a comparable effort with their TV commercial about civic 'daring'. The famous soundtrack of Nina Simone ('Ain't got no home …') accompanies three visual messages: a young boy defies the social pressure of peer group and coach by refusing to jump off the diving board [in letters on the screen: dare to refuse]; a Turkish man, at work in a grill-room, imagines a better future, while selling a bun with *shoarma* (roasted lamb) to the chauffeur of a wealthy old man who is waiting outside in his limousine, contemplating his (probably poorer) past [text: Dare to dream!]. The last lesson is about an old and helpless looking man entering a launderette and getting help from the least expected source: an angry looking guy [text: Dare to be alone!]. A profit-making industry like a life insurance company thus produces civic capital; three televised stories of people who act and dream as citizens. Could this be a case of public advertising?

25   Like the Thomas Burrell ads, both the Amstel and the Amev commercials featuring visions of the multicultural society met with serious criticism. Critics argued that these types of commercials mythologize multiculturalism by selecting only images signifying tolerance of others and recognizing individuals' uniqueness (Goldman and Papson, 1996: 179). This goes as much for the Amstel and Amev spots as for the famous Coca Cola commercial that gathered peoples of the world on a mountain top to sing of Coca Cola as a totem of togetherness. Underlying such comments is the familiar conception of advertising as a means to transfer positive associations on to the commodity. But with the increasing 'media-savvy' of consumers, one may wonder whether this transfer does indeed take place. Nava and Nava (1992) suggest, for instance, that young people consume commercials independently of the products advertised. In the case of the public commercials, consumers would not have to transfer the positive associations of responsibility, self-confidence and friendship on to McDonald's, Amstel or Amev, but they could read such commercials as mere short stories—or fairy tales—of multicultural tolerance, human subjectivity, friendship and, in a wider sense, contemporary citizenship.

Thus, advertising may make people aware of various civic virtues and values that one would otherwise only encounter in the informative genres of the various public spheres. As more and more people turn away from those, advertising becomes one of the few mainstream and popular cultural sites where it is possible to find such narratives of utopia. An example from Mary Gillespie's (1995) research on young Punjabis living in London, further illustrates this point. Gillespie shows how they articulate their preferences, distinctions and aspirations through talk about television commercials. She describes how a classroom discussion of a group of 16- and 17-year-olds of the Levis 501 and LA Gear commercials, reveals a hierarchy of values and styles. 'Classy' types who are 'cool' are located at the top. 'Coolness' emerges as a matter of detachment from specifically local and territorially based styles. Thus being cool means being cosmopolitan which can be understood as:

> ...a willingness to engage with others, an intellectual and aesthetic stance of openness toward divergent cultural experience, a search for contrasts rather than uniformity, a matter of competence and skill in manoeuvering more or less expertly within a particular system of meaning.
>
> (Hannerz, quoted in Gillespie 1995: 183)

By contrast, at the bottom of the hierarchy of the young, are people caricatured as locked into a closed local style. Whereas the specific hierarchical order may be seen as the product of the particular and strained location of these Punjabis as intermediaries between the local cultures of India/Pakistan and England, what matters in a more general sense is the way in which commercials and consumer culture function in their construction of subjectivity and individuality. Certainly, the 'classy' authentic labels matter, yet it is not one label itself that matters, but its articulation into an overall look. Classies flee uniformity and seek to distinguish themselves as individuals. The cosmopolitan style reveals itself as a kind of civic attitude organized and produced by multinational companies and mediated by talk about their commercials.

Outdoor Advertising and Citizenship

Next to the expression and accommodation of new forms of citizenship through commercial narratives of utopia, consumer culture may produce citizenship in other, more traditional ways. As is clear from the critical reception of the commercial multicultural utopias, one (wo)man's dream is another's nightmare. My own research on outdoor advertising shows that billboards displayed in public spaces can lead to considerable debate among citizens over, for instance, the boundaries of private and public decency. Advertising thus lands in a traditional Habermasian public sphere as a legitimate object of discussion and civil consideration; some ads, like the Benetton ones, even deliberately aim to do so (Falk, 1997). Whereas one may question and distrust the sincerity of such ads, their impact nevertheless is civil agitation rather than consumerist oblivion.

In a larger, multi-method research project on consumer culture, we interviewed 54 Amsterdam inhabitants of different age, sex and ethnicity about outdoor advertising in general and shock-advertising (ranging from the so-called catastrophe adverts like Benetton's [Falk, 1997] to pictures of more or less naked men and women) in particular, because the combination of the two seems to create the most animated public discussions.[1] Many interviewees frame their opinion of outdoor advertising in terms of age. In their eyes, age is the discriminating factor between their own 'liberal' views on public respectability and the supposedly conservative opinion of (other) older people. Whereas 'feel good' advertising like the Coca Cola, the McDonald's or the Amev ads seduces people to conform to certain civic values, shock advertisements confront people with their (often subconsciously held) values and beliefs (Falk, 1997). Karel (22) calls himself a 'liberal':

> As long as outdoor ads are posted at legal places there shouldn't be any limits, as long as the images are more or less proper. As long as you do not discriminate against somebody. I think much could and should be possible.

Commenting on a shocking poster announcing a photo exhibition of Andres Serrano 'A History of Sex' (showing a beautiful young woman who urinates into an attractive young man's mouth) he volunteers:

> I thought it brave what they had done. Personally, I think that it should be allowed, but I am of a younger generation and will understand very well if other people cannot manage it.

Interestingly, older people also tried to position themselves as 'liberal' by distancing themselves from other (generally older or religious) persons. It seemed an important aspect of individual identity to be called or recognized as 'liberal', in the sense of being open-minded and tolerant to the sensitivities of others. This open-mindedness can be very well thought out and contextualized as the comments of Carmen (60) on the public display of women's bodies in advertising shows. Whereas she does not mind public nakedness as a fact in itself, she does take exception to the style of ad in which women are positioned as objects (the Pamela Anderson ads). She fears the exploitation of female bodies:

> It gives people, especially boys some ideas. I think you have to avoid being disrespectful of women. It can lead to abuse of women. I am seriously against this practice and fear its consequences.

30   Quite unexpectedly, the same woman does not mind the Serrano poster:

> Look, that's an equal situation, just like the one of van Gils [perfume ad—ICM]. You may very well use women if the situation is one of equality. That woman clearly wants this to happen and according to me, she is the one who grabs him by his hair. Yes, I consider it a very fresh photograph.

A less liberal and familiar line of argument comes from Nora (55) commenting on the thinness of the models and fearing an increase of cases of anorexia nervosa or bulimia.

> These posters of beautiful women are very dangerous, because it is not without reason that scary diseases like anorexia exist nowadays. Young girls want to look that way and they go to extremes to succeed. Horrible.

These examples show how outdoor advertising stimulates people to think about themselves in terms of liberal or conservative, masculine and feminine, even black and white. Precisely because of their public display and their resulting enforced public reception, they incite public debate much more than the private consumption of other forms of promotional culture. Outdoor advertising is experienced on the street, while walking, cycling, driving a car or waiting for traffic lights or at bus stops. While talking with others about the ads, people give meaning and substance to civic values, for those tend to be formed not in the privacy of one's own minds but by talking things through with other people (Charity, 1995).

Coming back then to the performative perspective on advertising, we can see how particular commercials tell valuable stories of the good life in postmodern, multicultural societies; stories that in their optimism and gaiety are hard to find in other forms of mainstream communication. Such stories should be seen as part of the wide array of practices and technologies with which individuals nowadays have to constitute their sense of self as—among other things—citizens of ever expanding communities. Likewise, advertising tells stories which may annoy us or which we assume will offend our fellow citizens, and as such they may inspire new civil attitudes and lifestyles. In such a light it seems impossible to maintain the modernist dichotomy between the consumer and the citizen; let's consider consumer culture instead as an as yet unmined source of civic capital.

NOTE

1. As well as 54 in-depth interviews, we carried out 200 street interviews, analysed all the billboard images shown in Europe between 1995 and 1997 and researched the decisions (between January 1995 and May 1997) of the Dutch self-regulating commission of the advertising industry, the Reclame Code Commissie, and interviewed 10 spokespersons of advertising agencies about their policies on outdoor advertising.

REFERENCES

Appadurai, Arjun (ed.) (1986) *The Social Life of Things: Commodities in Cultural Perspective.* Cambridge: Cambridge University Press.

Bermingham, A. (1995) 'The Consumption of Culture: Image, Object, Text', pp. 1–23 in A. Bermingham and J. Brewer (eds) *The Consumption of Culture, 1600–1800.* London: Routledge.

Bordo, Susan (1992) 'Reading the Slender Body', pp. 83–113 in Mary Jacobus, Evelyn Fox Keller and Sally Shuttleworth (eds) *Body/Politics: Women and the Discourses of Science.* New York/London: Routledge.

Butler, Judith (1993) *Bodies That Matter: On the Discursive Limits of 'Sex'.* New York/London: Routledge.

Cassidy, Marsha and Richard Katula (1990) 'The Black Experience in Advertising: An Interview with Thomas J. Burrell', *Journal of Communications Inquiry* 14(1): 93–104.

Charity, Arthur (1995) *Doing Public Journalism.* New York/London: The Guilford Press.

Dahlgren, Peter (1995) *Television and the Public Sphere.* London: Sage.

Douglas, Mary and Baron Isherwood (1979) *The World of Goods: Toward an Anthropology of Consumption.* New York: W.W. Norton.

Downing, J.D.H. (1988) '*The Cosby Show* and American Racial Discourse', pp. 46–74 in G. Smitherman-Donaldson and T.A. van Dijk (eds) *Discourse and Discrimination.* Detroit, MI: Wayne State University Press.

Dyson, M. (1991) 'Bill Cosby and the Politics of Race', pp. 34–40 in J. Hanson and A. Alexander (eds) *Taking Sides.* Guilford, CT: Dushkin.

Ewen, Stuart (1976) *Captains of Consciousness: Advertising and the Social Roots of the Consumer Culture.* New York: McGraw-Hill.

Falk, Pasi (1997) 'The Benetton-Toscani Effect: Taking the Limits of Conventional Advertising', pp. 64–83 in Mica Nava, Andrew Blake, Iain MacRury and Barry Richards (eds), *Buy This Book: Studies in Advertising and Consumption.* London: Routledge.

Foucault, Michel (1988a) 'Technologies of the Self', pp. 16–50 in Luther H. Martin, Huck Gutman and Patrick H. Hutton (eds) *Technologies of the Self: A Seminar with Michel Foucault.* London: Tavistock.

Foucault, Michel (1988b) 'The Political Technology of Individuals', pp. 145–63 in Luther H. Martin, Huck Gutman and Patrick H. Hutton (eds) *Technologies of the Self: A Seminar with Michel Foucault*. London: Tavistock.

Fowles, Jib (1996) *Advertising and Popular Culture*. Thousand Oaks, CA: Sage.

Friedan, Betty (1963) *The Feminine Mystique*. New York: Dell.

Fromm, Erich (1941) *Escape from Freedom*. New York: Rinehart & Winston.

Gillespie, Mary (1995) 'Cool Bodies: TV Ad Talk', pp. 175–204 in *Television, Ethnicity and Cultural Change*. London: Routledge.

Goldman, Robert and Stephen Papson (1996) *Sign Wars: The Cluttered Landscape of Advertising*. New York: The Guilford Press.

Gray, H. (1989) 'Television, Black Americans, and the American Dream', *Critical Studies in Mass Communication* 6: 376–86.

Heilbrun, Carolyn G. (1989) *Writing a Woman's Life*. London: The Women's Press.

Lasch, Christopher (1979) *The Culture of Narcissism: American Life in an Age of Diminishing Expectations*. New York: W.W. Norton.

Lazier-Smith, Linda (1989) 'A New "Genderization" of Images to Women', pp. 247–61 in Pamela J. Creedon (ed.) *Women in Mass Communication: Challenging Gender Values*. Newbury Park/London: Sage.

McCracken, Ellen (1993) *Decoding Women's Magazines: From Mademoiselle to Ms.* London: Macmillan.

McCracken, Grant (1986) 'Culture and Consumption: A Theoretical Account of the Structure and Movement of the Cultural Meaning of Consumer Goods', *Journal of Consumer Research* 13: 71–81.

Messaris, Paul (1997) *Visual Persuasion: The Role of Images in Advertising*. Thousand Oaks, CA: Sage.

Nava, M. and O. Nava (1992) 'Discriminating or Duped? Young People as Consumers of Advertising/Art', in M. Nava (ed.) *Changing Cultures: Feminism, Youth and Consumerism*. London: Sage.

Real, M.R. (1991) 'Bill Cosby and Reading Ethnicity', pp. 58–84 in L.R. Vande Berg and L.A. Wenner (eds) *Television Criticism*. London: Longman.

Roche, Maurice (1987) 'Citizenship, Social Theory, and Social Change', *Theory and Society* 16: 363–99.

Schmerl, Christiane (1992) *Frauen der Werbung: Aufklärung über Fabeltiere*. München: Frauenoffensive.

Slater, Don (1997) *Consumer Culture & Modernity*. Cambridge: Polity Press.

Turner, Bryan S. (1990) 'Outline of a Theory of Citizenship', *Sociology* 24: 189–217.

Wernick, Andrew (1991) *Promotional Culture: Advertising, Ideology and Symbolic Expression*. London: Sage.

Williamson, Judith (1978) *Decoding Advertisements: Ideology and Meaning in Advertising*. London: Marion Boyars.

Rereading Actively

1. Like others who are involved in scholarly analyses of media and culture, Meijer opens her essay with a lot of references and terms. Summarize the gist of the first three paragraphs, and then do a short freewrite on how you tend to respond to articles that begin this way.

2. What are the two basic approaches to advertising that Meijer outlines? Reflecting on your response to an ad, explain which one most closely corresponds to your experience.

3. With a partner, discuss what Meijer means when she connects advertising to "the historical emergence of the modern individual" (¶ 13). How does that connection help her to develop her argument?

4. How might some one like Don Slater, who condemns the practice of advertising, respond to Meijer's positive notions about the ability of advertising to create citizens?

5. In a small group, discuss Meijer's analysis of the Burrell Agency. Does her explanation make you inclined to accept her thesis? Why or why not?

Exploring Your Responses

6. With two or three classmates, brainstorm ad campaigns that "tell valuable stories of the good life ... stories that in their optimism and gaiety are hard to find in other forms of mainstream communication" (¶ 33). Review your findings, and then select a single ad. Using Meijer's analysis as a framework, discuss the narrative that the ad creates and the impact that narrative might have on people in a particular market segment. Record points of agreement and points of dissension. Be prepared to present your ad and its narrative to the class, and to lead a brief discussion of how and whether the ad helps consumers understand their place in contemporary society.

7. On your own, do the brainstorming sequence described in the previous exercise, directing your attention to ad campaigns that tell stories about you and your aspirations. Once you have an ad in hand, describe how this ad might have shaped or is shaping your identity.

8. In a page or two in your journal, explore the role advertising plays in the creation of values, making references to ads and/or to ideas developed by Meijer.

SHADOWS ON THE WALL
STUART AND ELIZABETH EWEN

Stuart and Elizabeth Ewen have written about the effect of mass media and advertising on American culture. This excerpt comes from Channels of Desire, *published in 1982 and updated in 1992. This text looks at how mass-produced images have largely formed the culture of exchange; this passage on advertising comes from the final chapter, "Shadows on the Wall," where the Ewens draw some conclusions through a series of pointed observations and metaphors. They are less concerned with how individual ads work than with what the continual flow of advertising does to the people and societies that participate in it. They describe the failure of boundaries between the "commercial and noncommercial," and a kind of distraction that hides reality behind a parade of increasingly meaningless choices.*

A recent TV commercial for Canon cameras shows tennis pro Andre Agassi leaping out of a sports car and onto the court. Rejecting the uniformity of "tennis whites," he is adorned in flashy, multihued spandex. The scene is defined by the screaming logo: "*REBEL!*" Heavy metal blares in the background as the tennis court dissolves to a frantic, digitized cityscape. At the moment of climax, Agassi turns away from the highly produced commotion and ejaculates: *"Image is everything!"*

Elsewhere a more sedate advertisement for Macy's men's sportswear portrays men in a medley of athletic embarrassments. One falls off a horse; another chips a golf ball into a water trap; bumbling outdoorsmen capsize their fishing dinghies and struggle under collapsing tents. Even where star performance fails, the commercial tutors, no need to worry. *"At Macy's we understand it's just as important how you look as how you play."* In the sacraments of merchandising, the athlete and the schlepp taste from the same wafer. For both, "image is everything," the over-whelming yardstick for success.

While the circulation of mass-produced, commercial images dates to the middle of the nineteenth century in the United States, the past couple of decades have witnessed a dramatic acceleration of this trend. In every imaginable venue, and employing instruments that would have staggered Walter Lippmann, visual salesmanship has become a boundless feature of life.

Just twenty years ago, if you were asked to list the commercial media, you would have responded with a discrete catalog of organs and institutions: newspapers, magazines, movies, radio, and television. A boundary between media and society still appeared to exist. Today that boundary is evaporating. Every moment of human perception is viewed, by marketers, as a potential media opportunity, a point of contact for advertising. The phone rings and a prerecorded, computer-dialed message tries to sell you a vacation home in rural Pennsylvania. Calls like this are now made two-and-a-half billion times a year. Figures on "junk mail" are incalculable. Thanks to Whittle Communications, public school "homeroom" periods are now sponsored by those advertisers who run commercials on Whittle's "Channel One," a video infotainment-news program adopted by school districts in exchange for much-needed equipment. Soon doctors' waiting rooms will be presenting "health information" videos, thinly veiled drug company ads, to captive and vulnerable audiences.

5   For people with particular preoccupations, "900" telephone numbers offer a range of services, including shopping services, confessional services, sexual services, and electronic healing. The charge per minute can be astronomical. Now, just appearing, supermarket shopping carts are being outfitted with liquid crystal display screens in the place where children used to sit. These monitors receive short-distance infrared signals from the ceiling of the store which assure that as you pass through a particular aisle, you receive a commercial for products within close reach.

The commercial and the noncommercial mingle together so seamlessly that we hardly notice the difference. Breaking down a history of "consumer resistance" that has plagued the advertising industry since the 1920s, MTV has pioneered a form of advertising—music videos—that people watch for pure "entertainment" value, often unaware that they are watching an advertisement. Paid-for "product placements" insert familiar consumer goods into the settings and story lines of Hollywood films. Testifying before a congressional committee on the Iran-Contra scandal, Oliver North affected a boyish innocence, conspicuously sipping from a red-and-white can of Coca-Cola. General Norman Schwarzkopf's press conference, announcing a cease-fire in the Persian Gulf War, was lent an air of congeniality as he hoisted a can of Diet Pepsi, repeatedly, to his lips.

On the streets of America, and around the world, people wear the exploding paraphernalia of the marketplace on their backs, their fronts, their heads. Madonna, Teenage Mutant Ninja Turtles, Air Jordan, Nike, Bud Man, Golden Arches, Fight the

Power!: all contend for the public eye, all stand for products to be purchased, all project an image of personal and group identity. Within the alluring whir of images, where the commercial media end, and life begins, is indeterminate.

At the heart of this engaging pageant of images, however, lies sweet confusion, what Walter Benjamin called a "continual state of distraction." A sense of groundedness and a connection to customary patterns of existence still have a hold on people's sense of meaning, but this is increasingly challenged by history, and by dancing shadows. To some extent the textures and tensions of this challenge can be felt in the ways that social scientists sometimes describe the dilemmas of contemporary social life. Writing in *Society* magazine in 1985, for example, David Goslin noted that "years ago options were fewer." He goes on:

> A person went to school, got a job, married for better or worse—and raised children. A woman's place was in the home, and the home, for the most part, was not far from where one was raised. Widely accepted standards of morality and conduct governed much of our behavior. During the last twenty years much of that has changed. Now we must make real choices; to marry or not to marry; to stay married or not; to remarry or not; to have children or not; to work or not; to live near our family or not.[1]

In large measure, Goslin's description is a caricature of something real. Most of the changes he enumerates are not simply *choices* that people make, but rather the ways in which history and circumstance impact upon their lives. The decision for a woman "to work," for example, is trivialized when seen merely as a *choice*. Such a description supposes that women, unlike men, are immune from necessity. Similar objections could be raised about the other *options* he describes. What is interesting, however, is the particular language by which the author *chooses* to interpret these developments, and the way that his *choices*, too, bear the footprints of history. In adopting the language of *choice*, Goslin submits the lived terms of life to the propaganda of the marketplace. In the process, the historical circumstances, the ambivalences, and the social restrictions that affect all people's biographies are neglected. Life becomes "life-style," a thing, out there on the market, to be consumed. Amid the diffusion of possible life-styles—each with its own identifiable array of purchasable images—comes the appearance of choice. This concept of electable life-styles cannot be separated from the historical swelling of a media-merchandising environment, one in which the play of images often obscures underlying realities.

10   The commercial traffic in images—each with a sale to make—has become a central force of culture, delineating ideals of behavior and social life, ideas of morality and conduct. In this play of enticing visuals, a key element of its charisma is the implicit and ritual claim that it offers an inexhaustible spectrum of choices, simply to be made. More and more, as the "free market" has been elevated to the status of a religious icon, unregulated capitalism is openly trumpeted as the fountain out of which all choice and possibility flow. The only acknowledged limit is the failure of individual backbone, an unwillingness to make (purchase) the right choice.

Built into the equation of consumption and choice, however, lies a decidedly undercratic assumption. If consumption is choice, then choice is inevitably dependent upon one's ability to consume. At a moment when, for many, basic economic survival is becoming difficult, this equation spells mass disenfranchisement. If choice is limited to the marketplace, those priced out have no voice.

Amid the celebration of unfettered options, however, there are a number of social, economic, and anthropological issues that fester beneath the spectacle of consumable freedom. Residing within this apparent panoply of alternatives is a contradiction that is marked within those institutions that serve as prime proselytizers of choice: the commercial mass media. On the surface of things—as evidenced by cable television or the array of magazines at any newsstand—it would appear that more and more media are available, simultaneously answering the purchasing needs of an increasingly inclusive audience while, at the same time, responding to its diverse and specialized tastes.

If American mass culture was once dominated by three television networks and a few general national magazines, today—according to many media business observers—there is no "mass culture" any longer, no "mass market." Instead, it is commonly argued, there are *many* markets, responding to the wills of myriad groups of people. *Consumer sovereignty reigns.*

Missing from this fairy tale, however, are a number of critical developments. First, the move toward "market segmentation" that defines media and other industries today, is not merely a response to the democratic will of the people. If anything, it is an attempt to make what was formerly a rigid conception of marketing more efficient, and more profitable. The shift began in the late sixties and early seventies, during a period of social turmoil. Marketing professionals were concerned that many sectors of the population were either not being effectively reached by or were resistant to, the appeals encoded in advertising and product design. A broad, relatively undifferentiated approach to marketing had spurred economic growth during the 1920s and then, impressively, in the 1950s. By the end of the 1960s, however, that growth had begun to stagnate. Even more alarming was the conspicuous emergence of local and subcultural forms of expression. Many of these explored the possibility of a mode of life, and of a material culture, that looked beyond the gargantuan system of production, distribution, and merchandising that had defined the American Way of Life since the 1920s.

15   Reacting to these indigenous popular trends, new-age marketers began to rely more heavily on an anthropological analysis of the heterogeneous American populace. Taking into account variations of ethnicity, gender, economic class, and sociopolitical attitude, the American population was divided into a variety of instrumentally conceived segments, each defined by its "life-style." Each "life-style" was projected according to the ways that its attitudes or circumstances suggested particular marketing techniques.[2] What—at a grass roots level—was marked by imagination, self-expression, and self-activity, was now being transformed into economically functional categories designed to influence behavior, expand markets, and maximize profits. Issues of choice were being recast as issues of *consumer choice.* Social ideas, ecological concerns, the search for meaningful identity; these became new raw materials of merchandising. This move toward consumption-defined "life-styles" is particularly evident when one analyzes the subject matter that defines much of the media diversity we find today. While it is true that there are more and more magazines on the newsstand, their orientation is becoming increasingly uniform. Whether they are addressing audiences of tennis enthusiasts, career women, new parents, audiophiles, dirt bikers, or computer users, the consumption of products provides a focal point for most of these publishing ventures. Advertising and editorial content melt together. Mean-while, general-interest journalism—defined by interests apart from consumption—is dying.

In back of the curtain of choice, it must be added, lies a planetary consolidation of economic power that puts the lie to the notion that it is individual consumers who determine the offerings of the market. This consolidation only magnifies anti-democratic trends that underlie the pretense of options. Ben Bagdikian has provided eloquent evidence of this in the realm of media ventures. In "Lords of the Global Village," he chronicles the rise of transnational information giants which, today, dominate much of what people see, read, and hear on television, in film, in newspapers and magazines, in recorded music. Behind the apparent kaleidoscope of choice, stand the boardroom decisions of a smaller and smaller number of colossal corporations. Leading the list are five powerful media oligopolies: Time Warner, Inc.; Bertelsmann AG; Rupert Murdoch's News Corporation, Ltd.; Hachette S.A.; and Capitol Cities/ABC, Inc. The next level of the pyramid is controlled by what Bagdikian terms "midsize" giants, U.S.-based media companies like Gannett, Ted Turner's Broadcasting System, General Electric. "To the eye of the consumer," Bagdikian adds,

> the global media oligopoly is not visible.... Newsstands still display rows of newspapers and magazines, in a dazzling array of colors and subjects.... Throughout the world, broadcast and cable channels continue to multiply, as do video cassettes and music recordings. But...if this bright kaleidoscope suddenly disappeared and was replaced by the corporate colophons of those who own this output, the collage would go gray with the names of the few multinationals that now command the field.[3]

The charade of choice is but a mask behind which fewer and fewer people and institutions are, in fact, making the choices that count. The inner truth of this development is ironically captured on an advertising T-shirt produced for the music publishing giant, ASCAP. It reads, simply, "There are many alternatives, but only one choice."

Beyond the contours of the market, in the confines of daily life, the proliferation of consumer "preference" coincides with a widespread breakdown of social interdependency. As marketing appeals to individual choice, the rhythms of life become increasingly fragmentary. Television watching—once termed a "family" activity—is today becoming more and more solitary. Televisions, situated throughout the household, provide electric companionship for separate individuals. When families do convene—for dinner—table discussion has given way to television spectatorship.

Not only has TV viewing become more insular, but the act of watching itself has evolved into an assembly of fragments. Increasingly, people tend to juggle several shows at once. As maestros of the remote transport themselves across the dial—from *choice* to *choice*—instantaneously, a cacophony of images becomes the norm. The environs of daily life mimic the patter of the spectacle. The sound (and visual) bite becomes not only the preferred medium of television news directors, it becomes a vernacular aesthetic. On the creative side, this montage of fragments has inspired rap music sampling. On the side of social pathology, it reinforces a culture with, as Josh Meyerowitz has described it, "no sense of place."

20   Amid the clatter of images, the cant of *choice*, the religion of the *new*, lies a general atmosphere of bewilderment, a sense of numbness. It is experienced on the level of inner life, expressed in the syndromes of estrangement and free-floating anxiety that mark the psychology of our time. "These days," notes social psychologist Robert Cialdini, "there are so many choices; so many options; so much information, so much

stimulation that we must deal with activity in a less fully considered way."⁴ Closeted within all the choice is a gnawing sense of powerlessness. To a large extent, this condition is wedded to the often-trivial nature of the choices available, and to the absence of more consequential options. While we are continually bombarded by incantations to change the things we can (hair color, style of dress, the car we drive), the notion of improving the realm of social possibility has disappeared from view.

Even pressing social issues tend to be seen as a parade of discrete products being sold. In the process they are trivialized. This can be heard in the words of Nadine Threadgill, a Silver Springs receptionist recently interviewed by the *New York Times:*

> I get home, and my mailbox is filled with little envelopes from the cancer fund, the wildlife fund, the alumni fund all asking me for money. There's the homeless problem, the drug problem, the AIDS crisis, the abortion issue. And then someone wants me to get worked up about Eastern Europe.⁵

Overwhelmed by a world depicted as a catalog of products, Ms. Threadgill eloquently demonstrates the way in which that world loses coherence, defies systematic understanding. "Infomercials" emerge as a new vehicle of public address; a sense of the distinction between reality and public relations evaporates. Products, ideas, social problems, politics come at people with the speed of light, collapsing into visual havoc, producing confusion, encouraging people to retreat into a cautious inactivity—a defensive shell of indifference.

Though much of the ennui may result from the customs and mores of contemporary culture, for the pundits of the media industries, the epidemic of disaffection is notable primarily insofar as it leads to people's tuning out of sales pitches. This can be seen in the lament of one market researcher who expressed his concern that "the American public, by nature of the assault they take from commercial ads, have become passive." Elsewhere, in business news sections and trade journals, the passivity is not complete enough; the *zapping* of television commercials assumes the urgency of a major social crisis. Marketing analyst Mona Doyan reports that many in the television audience "simply don't see [television commercials] ... anymore. They don't have to zap them out by remote. They have tuned out mentally."⁶ The *Wall Street Journal* provides a diagnostic term for alienation from endless salesmanship: "*Ad nauseum*," they call it.⁷ As democracy is diminished to the language of *consumer choice*, general feelings of disengagement are described as problems of *consumer recalcitrance*.

Within the publicized expansion of choice there resides a potentially toxic narrowing of vision. Nowhere is this contradiction more evident than in the overflowing landfills and garbage dumps that serve as the unseen graveyards of discarded choice. When Simon Patten, one hundred years ago, described the coming of a new standard of living that would be "determined, not so much by what a man has to enjoy, as by the rapidity with which he tires of the pleasure," he may have unwittingly written the eventual epitaph for our *culture of choice*. Trendy, often-transparent hype of "green marketing" notwithstanding, the identity between choice and consumption inevitably harnesses human desire to a machinery of waste. Within each new *choice* being offered is the implicit invitation to dispose of yesterday's *choices*. At the heart of this perpetual cycle is a market economy whose health depends upon the growing infirmity of the planet.

NOTES

1. David Goslin, "Decision Making and the Social Fabric," *Society,* 2 (2) (New Brunswick, 1985), p. 9.
2. The major book in the field of "life-style" market segmentation is Arnold Mitchell, *The Nine American Lifestyles* (New York. 1983). In this work he divides the population into nine American life-styles which he calls VALS (values and life-style): *Survivor, Sustainer, Belonger, Emulator, Achiever, I-Am-Me, Experiential, Societally Conscious,* and *Integrated.* Since the book's publication, there has been a reconfiguration of the system, VALS 2, which attempts to refine a more specific relationship between attitude and purchase behavior. The refined VALS 2 system segments the population into eight consumer categories: *Actualizers, Strugglers, Fulfilleds, Believers, Achievers, Strivers, Experiencers,* and *Makers.* For a description of VALS 2, see Rebecca Piirto, "VALS: The Second Time," *American Demographics,* July 1991. For a more detailed description of the development of market segmentation, see William Meyers. *The Image Makers: Power and Persuasion on Madison Avenue* (New York, 1984).
3. Ben H. Bagdikian, "The Lords of the Global Village," *The Nation,* June 12, 1989, p. 819.
4. Robert Cialdini, quoted in the *New York Times,* December 6, 1989, p. C16.
5. Lena Williams, "Free Choice: When Too Much Is Too Much," *New York Times,* February 14, 1990, p. C10.
6. Ibid.
7. Quoted by Deborah Baldwin, "The New Marketplace," *Common Cause Magazine,* May/June 1991, p. 16. This article is an excellent survey of these new marketing trends and their effects.

Rereading Actively

1. As they turn to exploring their initial examples, the Ewens talk of "the sacraments of merchandising" (¶ 2). What does this phrase mean? How does it relate to the rest of the essay? How do you respond to it?

2. The Ewens argue that the "boundary" between media and society (¶ 4), between the commercial and the noncommercial (¶ 6), has disappeared. With a partner or in a small group, review the effects they see this disappearance causing. Discuss whether your experience and observation bear out these effects.

3. With a partner, discuss the chief characteristics of a society based on "market segmentation." Does this characterization of our society seem persuasive to you?

4. In a brief journal entry, summarize the distinctions the Ewens draw between "choice" (¶ 9) and "choices that count" (¶ 17).

5. Working with one or two classmates, discuss "the machinery of waste" (¶ 23) that the Ewens describe. Share your responses to their implied connection between consumer choice and the destruction of the planet.

Exploring Your Responses

6. With a partner or in a small group, review the Ewens' sense of our attitudes toward what we do, the people with whom we interact, and where we carry out our lives. They seem to conclude that our exchange society makes a staggering array of choices available, but leaves us with an indifferent view of

those choices, almost unable to make choices that really matter. Compare their assessment of our collective state with what you see around you. Consider whether mass-produced images—especially those that circulate in ads—are truly this powerful. Write a description summarizing your conversation in your journal.

7. Pair up with a classmate of the same sex and read one another, looking for instances of what the Ewens call "the exploding paraphernalia of the market" (¶ 7). Develop a profile, first by listing brand names from clothing and accessories and then by noting the main media habits of your partner (ask questions about TV, radio, print, computer, entertainment, and so on). From this information, write a description of the market segment to which your partner belongs. Discuss your description with your partner, and note how he or she feels about belonging to this segment. Be prepared to discuss the market segments you discover and your feelings about them with the class.

Is Nothing Sacred?

Mary Kuntz

That a magazine like Business Week *could comfortably offer information about consumer groups and publications that mock advertising—the life-blood of business—is a testimony to just how central advertising is to U.S. culture. In this brief 1998 article in the marketing section, Mary Kuntz, a* Business Week *staff writer, documents a current trend in advertising, self-parody, and in the process, she shows the extent to which brands have crept into every nook and cranny of our public and private lives. Two themes are at the core of this study: many of us—advertisers included—are uncomfortable with the continuous pressure of advertising; advertising is so much a part of our market-centered society that it co-opts or squashes all criticism.*

Mad Ave Adopts Ad Haters' Most Potent Weapon—Parody

In Northern California, a band recently released *Dispepsi*, a CD pieced together from bits of music, ads, and interviews to create a scathing (and entertaining) commentary on the nation's second-largest soft-drink company. In New Jersey, a coalition of artists alters billboards in minority neighborhoods, adding touches such as a banner on a Newport cigarette ad that reads "Healthy profits don't always require living customers." And *Adbusters,* a nine-year-old Canadian quarterly devoted to the art of the "culture jam"—as such rearranged anti-advertising ads are called—reaches 30,000 subscribers, mostly in the U.S.

With sales messages assaulting us in every possible venue, it's no wonder that there's a growing cadre of activists who simply loathe ads and the industry that perpetrates them. What is more surprising is the growing sophistication of the backlash. Thanks to the advent of desktop publishing and the Internet, these grassroots critics are increasingly fighting Madison Avenue with the industry's own techniques. Just look at the fake ad on the back cover of *Stay Free!*, a tiny New York-based 'zine that critiques consumer culture. The type-face and photography look like the familiar

Dewars campaign featuring attractive, sophisticated young imbibers, but the tagline reads: "Remember how liquor used to make you vomit?"

Corporate America's reaction to these lampoons is muted. "No comment," says Jan Sharkansky, a spokesperson for Calvin Klein Cosmetics Co., when asked about an *Adbusters* "ad" that shows a musclebound young man peering intently down his fashionable underwear under the headline "Obsession." Others in the ad community say they're barely aware of culture jammers and that, in any case, there's no advantage to trying to stop such small fry.

But while advertisers may be oblivious to the politics and polemics behind culture jamming, they have been quick to intuit the value of a clever parody. Copping the same hip, ironic attitudes and playing to the same consumer cynicism, big-time marketers have begun to lampoon one another. "It punctures the pomposity because you're telling people something real," says David Suissa, chairman and executive creative director for Suissa Miller Advertising Inc., which produced a series of parody ads for Boston Chicken Inc. last year mocking Calvin Klein's anorexic models.

"Killing the Planet"

5 Adland's embrace of parody has blunted one of the culture jammers' favorite weapons, but not their ardor. Take 29-year-old Carrie Mclaren. A record promoter by day, she

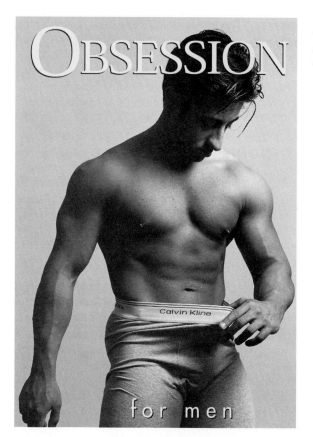

Figure 5.3 "Spoof ad"
This parody of Calvin Klein's general approach to advertising appeared on the adbusters Web page <www.ad busters.org>.

publishes *Stay Free!*—with such articles as "Singled Out: An alarmist look at ultra-targeted marketing"—largely at her own expense. Why? "It's not just advertising, it's the overall commercialization of the planet," she says. Others cite ecological concerns. "We believe that our corporate culture is unsustainable," says Kalle Lasn, *Adbusters'* editor and founder. "Economic progress is killing the planet."

Mark Hosler of Negativland, the Bay Area band that released *Dispepsi,* also believes that the sheer volume of advertising is degrading to the mental and physical environment. "It isn't that advertising per se is evil, it's the amount of it that's going on," says Hosler, whose band coined the term "culture jamming." He argues that the wealth and might of giant marketers makes it difficult for opposing viewpoints to be heard. The aim of culture jamming: to break through that clutter by playing off the powerful messages and icons already out there.

There's also a political strand. Cicada Corps of Artists, the New Jersey group, alters tobacco and liquor billboards in minority neighborhoods, which they say receive a disproportionate share of such advertising. Defacing billboards is illegal, but group member Pedro Carvajal believes their activities are justified: "Alternatives have been taken away because they [advertisers] have all the money. We had to go underground."

Advertisers say the backlash from fringe groups is simply too puny to register on their radar screens. Maybe, but some parody protest ads have begun showing up in more traditional media. During a labor dispute with a Miller Brewing Co. distributor in St. Louis three years ago, the Teamsters put up a billboard mocking a Miller ad. Instead of two bottles of beer in a snowbank with the tagline "Two Cold," the ad showed two frozen workers in a snowbank labeled "Too Cold: Miller canned 88 St. Louis workers." Ron Carver, coordinator of strategic campaigns for the Teamsters, says the union has since used similar parodies in disputes to great effect. "When you're doing this, you're threatening multimillion-dollar ad campaigns," he says.

Tobacco lampoons have also moved into the mainstream. Scott Plous, a psychology professor at Wesleyan University, is incensed at what he sees as the blatant appeal to kids by Big Tobacco. So a few years ago, he countered with his own cartoon character, Joe Chemo, who bears more than a passing resemblance to a certain familiar dromedary. With the help of various antismoking groups, Joe Chemo has moved from the pages of *Adbusters* to billboards in downtown Seattle, posters in public schools, and T-shirts given away to kids.

Lawsuits

10 Many big brands aren't as willing to shrug off the spoofs when they're done nationally by a fellow marketer. Digital Equipment Corp.'s discomfort with rival Hewlett-Packard Co.'s parody was understandable. Running just once in a few national publications, the ad replaced the "Digital" in the company's trademark red blocks with the word "worried?" in the same typeface. Appealing to customers left anxious by DEC's recent merger with Compaq Computer Corp., the ad brought in millions of dollars of business, says Nick Earle, marketing manager for HP's Enterprise Systems Group. Digital's response: a letter to HP alleging trademark infringement and demanding a halt to the ads.

Even mainstream ad parodies that aren't launched by rivals often seem to result in allegations and lawsuits. Mattel's sensitivity on the subject of Barbie is legendary. The company moved quickly to quash a recent Nissan ad that featured Barbie-and-Ken-like dolls. And Nike Inc., whose attitude-filled commercials have made it a favorite parody target, found nothing humorous about a recent campaign by Candie's Inc. for colorful new sneakers featuring actress Jenny McCarthy. The tagline: "Just Screw it." Nike fired off a cease-and-desist letter.

Heineken USA Inc. avoided litigation by taking parody a step further. A campaign for its Amstel brand involved bill-boards and TV spots denouncing it as an evil import from "free-thinking" Amsterdam. The campaign, supposedly by the fictitious Americans for Disciplined Behavior, won publicity when the prank was uncovered.

As the loop closes, it's getting harder to tell those who parody from those who are parodied, partly because it is virtually impossible to shame Madison Avenue. Two years ago Negativland's Hosler got a call from hip Portland-based ad agency Wieden & Kennedy Inc. raving about the band's work and asking if it would like to make a spot for Miller. "I think they were sort of mystified about why we turned them down," he says. And that may be the ultimate irony. Advertisers crave a hip, cutting-edge attitude—even if it comes from their most ardent detractors.

Rereading Actively

1. With a partner, talk about what "culture jamming" is, and in your journal, summarize your discussion, defining concepts like parody, backlash, 'zine, and lampoon.

2. What patterns does Kuntz find in culture jammers' opposition to advertising? How do you respond to their position?

3. Summarize the responses that advertisers have made to culture jamming.

4. Review the article and identify the parodies of ads that Kuntz mentions. Then visit the Adbusters Web site <www.adbusters.org> and look up the "spoof ads" posted there. (Figure 5.3 came from that site.) Focusing on two or three parodies from the article or from the Adbusters Web site, explain in your own words who produced each one and what they hoped their parody would achieve.

5. What is the author's attitude toward her topic? With a partner, identify two passages where she seems to reveal her attitude, and discuss what purpose she seems to accomplish with the article.

Exploring Your Responses

6. How aware of the "assault" of advertising are you? Does it bother you? Use a freewrite to explore your own response to the noise advertising creates and the culture and practices that it represents. As you get into your freewrite, focus on a single kind of advertising or a single ad and decide how you might feel about jamming that message.

7. Note in your journal the ads that you see over a twenty-four hour period along with the places that you see them. (Jot down as many as you can—shoot

for between twenty and fifty.) With a group, share your lists and pick out two ads that you reacted to strongly. Talk about your reactions—being certain to note points of dissent—and explain whether each ad message should be jammed. Then, develop a collaborative strategy for jamming one of the ads and be ready to share your strategy with the class.

BACKGROUND ASSIGNMENTS

Depending on whom you talk to, advertising is either a necessary part of doing business or a manipulative tool in the hands of corporate interests who are slowly dumbing down the culture. The writers here grapple with two related issues: an understanding of how ads work, and a sense of how advertising fits into the culture as a whole. The first issue is fairly straightforward. Advertising, as these writers describe it, may be the most powerful and carefully produced discourse in the contemporary scene. (The culture jammers that Kuntz describes fear that this discourse is slowly taking over editorial control of mainstream media.) The second issue is more complex: is advertising primarily a reflection of dynamics already present in consumer culture, or do advertisers create and direct these dynamics? As in most complex matters, attributing cause and effect is not easy, but asking the question is important. At stake is our sense of ourselves, the mythologies by which we make sense of our world and the ways we relate to our neighbors.

Making Connections

1. Use Fowles's theory of advertising to analyze the use of parody in ads as Kuntz describes it. (This will involve an explanation of how ads in general affect audiences as well as an explanation of how parody in ads works.)

2. Drawing arguments about the productive and manipulative power of advertising from Fowles and the Ewens respectively, write a pro/con essay about an ad campaign of your choice. Show how this ad campaign has the potential to help consumers develop a productive symbolic vocabulary and a sense of the good life, as well as how it may distract them from realities of life. In your conclusion, suggest which tendency you find to be dominant in the campaign.

3. Use Meijer's review of advertising theory to write an essay that explores the place advertising plays in your "choice" of lifestyle.

4. Pick an ad that is centered on a human image that is appealing to you, a perfect body, an engaging experience, complete control of a situation, the ultimate look, or whatever human form catches and holds your eye. Then, review Meijer's discussion of the way consumers use ads to form their identity (¶ 2), Fowles's analysis of the way ads idealize human appearance (¶ 15–20), and Kuntz's assessment of perceived excesses of advertising (¶ 5–9). Use these writers' ideas to write an essay that describes the human figure in the ad and evaluates the impact of that figure on the target audience of the ad.

5. Fowles and Meijer both call attention to the roles that audiences play in advertising. Narrate your experience of an ad that you find enjoyable and entertaining, and use your experience—and the ideas of Fowles and Meijer—to explain the pleasure the ad brings and the side effects the experience might have.

6. The Ewens declare that the mingling of the noncommercial and the commercial narrows our vision of life. On the other hand, Meijer contends that ads can tell us "stories of the good life" (¶ 33) that we don't see elsewhere. Does Diane Barthel's view of shoppers and shopping in Chapter 3 support one side or the other in this dispute?

Collaborative Exchanges

1. In small groups, brainstorm a list of interests you each have, like sports, fashion, computers, literature, cars, and so on. Specify your interests—you could narrow sports to fans and participants or individual sports, for example—and pick one as a group focus. Identify ads that target people with your shared interest, and then individually, using the method of decoding identified by Fowles decode an ad. Discuss your response with the members of the group, and be prepared to share with the class the differences and similarities in your reactions.

2. In a small group, brainstorm ads that are getting a lot of play on campus or in the local community and focus on one of those ads. With your group, discuss how Fowles, Meijer, and/or the Ewens would approach this the ad: what elements would they focus on, and how would they assess the ad's impact on its audience? Be prepared to present your findings about the ad to the class, along with an evaluation of the approach(es) you used.

3. With two or three classmates, review Meijer's explanation of the social role of consumption (¶ 12) and Kuntz's description of the techniques of both advertisers and culture jammers. Discuss what "values" and "cultural phenomena" (Meijer ¶ 12) the advertising industry seems to support. In response to your discussion, freewrite individually on your feelings about advertisers and power, and then share your freewrite with your group and develop a collaborative statement from your responses.

Net Approaches

1. Go to <www.altavista.com> and do a link search for the Clio Awards site www.clioawards.com. To do this, type the following string in the AltaVista search box: *link:http://www.clioawards.com.* (Other search engines also enable link searches; check out search engine help pages for instructions.) Scroll through at least twenty hits, and settle on two pages that are skeptical of the Clios and two sites that celebrate the Clios. Browse these sites and write a report that explains the range of positions on advertising awards. Be prepared to offer your own response to the celebration of ads.

2. Use Yahoo.com to find the corporate site for the producer of a major league consumer good, something in the same league as Coca-Cola, Tommy, Nike, or GM. Summarize the page and explain how it functions as an ad.

3. Go to <www.liszt.com> and find the "ad-list" listserv or a similar list oriented toward advertisers. (Search for listservs related to "advertising.") Use the internal instructions to subscribe to a listserv, and listen to the debate and gossip of advertising professionals for a week. Write a brief comparison of what you read online with what you have read in the text.

CASE-IN-POINT READINGS

Public Images of Illegal Drugs: (Un)selling Bad Habits

Have you ever seen the "fried egg ad" that combines an egg, a frying pan, and the phrase, "Any questions"? How many other anti-drug ad images and logos can you name? Since 1987, the Partnership for a Drug-Free America (PDFA)—a non-profit organization comprised of a small staff and hundreds of volunteers from the advertising/communications industries—has tried to unsell illicit drugs through one of the largest single ad campaigns in history. In 1991 PDFA ranked second to McDonald's among single brand advertisers in 1990, and 92% of U.S. teenagers recognized the fried egg ad. According to James Burke, Chairman of PDFA, and Barry McCaffrey, the Director of the Office of National Drug Control Policy since 1996, public-service advertisements and announcements (PSAs) are key methods for changing the attitudes of young people and getting accurate information to young people and their parents. Therefore, PDFA has called on some of the hottest agencies across the country, which have contributed hundreds of ads. It's hard to say how successful the Partnership's PSAs have been. Some critics wonder whether advertising, a discourse that in effect encourages consumers to obsess with commodities, can encourage consumers not to do drugs. Others question whether ads can unsell one drug, say heroin, but sell another, say alcohol. The readings here offer you a cross section of opinions and lots of data. As a writer, you can use this material to look closely at how ads work generally as instruments to shape public opinion and behavior, and at how consumers are engaged in a deeply divisive topic.

PEDDLING A SOCIAL CAUSE

ANNETTA MILLER AND ELISA WILLIAMS

This Newsweek *article appeared in 1986 just prior to the launch of the first Partnership for a Drug-Free America campaign. Annetta Miller and Elisa Williams have both written widely in the popular press about the intersection of business and culture. Here they describe what amounts to a public policy agenda for a general audience, but their interest is in how PSAs modify and make use of general advertising strategies—the article appeared in the business section. They describe advertising strategies, consider the technical and financial difficulties, and try to describe the limits of Madison Avenue's altruism.*

> It may seem grand 'cause you think you're a man
> But a bighead baby wasn't part of the plan
> This is L. L. Cool J and Cut Creator
> Telling you what happens nine months later
> —"Smart Sex Rap" by L. L. Cool J

The music may sound like just another rap tune. But tucked within the pulsating rhythms of rock star L. L. Cool J is—of all things—a public-service announcement about teen pregnancy. Smart Sex isn't the only social cause seeking an audience these days. Crusaders against drunken driving, alcoholism and smoking are increasingly turning to Madison Avenue's vice squad for help. Next month the Media-Advertising Partnership for a Drug-Free America will launch the largest public-service promotion ever. Funded in part by corporate contributions, the campaign is expected to get more than $500 million worth of advertising exposure.

Is Madison Avenue going altruistic? Well, yes and no. Advertising staffs burdened by the humdrum of peddling goods and services jump at the chance to use their ingenuity for more worthy causes. ("Public-service ads offer a fresh opportunity," says Kevin Allen, vice president of Ketchum Advertising in New York. "You can go beyond selling a box of laundry detergent.") Although ad agencies don't accept fees for creating public-service announcements (known in the trade as PSA's), they can profit in the long run. After the Minneapolis agency Clarity Coverdale Rueff offered to develop a *pro bono* ad campaign for a local YMCA, the national YMCA organization asked the agency to handle its advertising, too. Since then CCF's commercial billings have increased fivefold. The Minneapolis agency of Fallon McElligott Rice has also done well with such ads. The agency came out on top of more than 1,000 entries in a contest sponsored by the Reader's Digest to fight drunken driving. Its winning poster featured blind musician Stevie Wonder offering an unforgettable warning: "Before I'll Ride With a Drunk, I'll Drive Myself." Says one advertising executive: "They've used [a public-service announcement] to catapult themselves into prominence."

Public-service ads can also foster entrepreneurial spirits. Neal Kalisher's Public Service Radio company in Lake Worth, FL., specializes in adding public-service messages to commercials paid for by local businesses. The secret, Kalisher says, is tailoring ads to a particular client. Bars can warn motorists not to drink and drive, auto-parts stores can pitch compliance with a new seat-belt law and children's clothing stores can remind people to watch out for school buses. Kalisher, who has 300 clients for his custom-made ads, is clear about his motives. "I don't want to make us out to be crusaders," he says. "This is a for-profit business." Other enterprises work the public-service angle, too. Members Only, the New York-based sportswear chain, has announced that it will donate its entire $6 million advertising budget to an antidrug campaign featuring, among others, Yankees manager Lou Piniella and New Jersey Nets basketball star Buck Williams. The catch: Piniella and Williams appear in the advertisements wearing—what else—Members Only jackets.

Diverse Problems

Other sponsors range from the federal government and local municipalities to the American Lung Association. The social problems they combat are diverse. The Magazine Publishers' Association recently launched a $26 million campaign designed to attack adult illiteracy, while the National Council on Alcoholism is embarking on a public-service promotion to discourage drinking by children and teenagers. Other PSA's are aimed at lesser-known social problems. One city hospital produced a public-service campaign warning people to make sure their bath water wasn't too hot. A humane society sent out a message urging pet owners not to let their dogs drink antifreeze. Many, but by no means all, sponsors of public-service advertisements distribute their messages through the Advertising Council, a nonprofit organization made up of industry volunteers. The council assigns the creative work for the campaigns to agencies that volunteer their services free of charge, while the sponsor pays for production and out-of-pocket costs. Those fees can amount to $100,000 for a six-month period.

5   At its best, public-service advertising depends on the same marketing techniques used in regular product advertising. When N W Ayer embarked on its

youth-alcoholism campaign earlier this year, it relied heavily on psychographics, which measures attitudes and emotional responses to advertising. To test ideas about teenage alcoholics, executives used the most tried and true of psychographic devices: the focus group. The agency rounded up 100 suburban and inner-city children between the ages of 9 and 14 and divided them into small groups to discuss alcohol abuse among their peers and advertising approaches that would best discourage kids from getting drunk. The Ayer executives drew two major conclusions: first, the ads should use ordinary teenagers rather than models to capture the attention of teenage alcoholics; and, second, they should offer young people help in resisting the temptation of alcohol. The resulting campaign, "Say no. And say yes to life," incorporated both suggestions.

But research means nothing without well-executed ads. Benton & Bowles in New York once auditioned 100 actors before finding what it considered the perfect face for an Ad Council spot on adult illiteracy. The agency held out for an actor who could stumble realistically over his words while reading a book to his young daughter. When Ketchum Advertising chose a photographer for the print portion of its teenage-pregnancy campaign, it hired Francesco Scavullo, a leading fashion photographer with a flair for portraiture. The agency believed that Scavullo could capture the sexual intensity of teenagers and the peer pressure they face. The ads, which show attractive teenagers reciting such traditional come-ons as "Trust me, I won't get you pregnant," are accompanied by a telephone number for the city's counseling and health services.

The results of public-service campaigns are difficult to verify. But the Ad Council tracks some of its commercials each year to make sure they are effective. According to council statistics, the number of forest fires has been cut by half since Smokey Bear advertising began, and contributions to the United Negro College Fund campaign have increased from $11 million to $30 million since its ads first appeared. Campaigns in which the desired result is to change behavior as well as minds are tougher to quantify. One that did show results was a magazine ad sponsored by Utica Mutual Insurance Co. that included a "Students Against Drunken Driving Contract" for pupils and their parents. Although the advertisement could be torn out of the magazine and reproduced, Utica's home office was bombarded with requests for copies of the document.

Stiff Competition

The supply of public-service announcements far exceeds the demand. A CBS spokesman says the network received 5,500 ideas, storyboards and finished public-service announcements last year and ran nearly 17,000 spots, up from 10,700 in 1980. (Public-service announcements fulfill Federal Communications Commission regulations requiring broadcast stations to address public issues.) The number of organizations seeking to air their advertisements on the three major networks grew 40 percent between 1979 and 1985. So stiff is the competition that Kerry Crawford, associate research director at Ketchum Advertising in Pittsburgh, suggests that sponsors are beginning to recognize the need for strategic thinking and planning. In the scramble to get a good word out, nonprofit organizations may soon have to peddle themselves the way Madison Avenue peddles laundry detergent.

Rereading Actively

1. With a partner, review the article, looking for comments about the motives of advertisers. Talk about why ad agencies produce PSAs, and be prepared to participate in a class discussion of the reasons these agencies donate their creative energy.

2. In your journal, list the problems that, according to Miller and Williams, PSAs face as they attempt to change attitudes. Rank them in order of importance.

3. With a partner, identify the advertising strategies that PSA producers rely on. Discuss how these strategies relate to the strategies used to sell products. Summarize your discussion in your journal, noting which strategy was most surprising to you.

4. In your journal, draft a two- or three-sentence description of the dynamics that, according to Miller and Williams, define the world of advertising. Then, develop a paragraph explanation of how the first and last paragraphs in the article help to explain that world.

Exploring Your Responses

5. In a small group, pick one of the PSA topics that Miller and Williams mention, and discuss the strategy that advertisers have used to create awareness about the topic as well as the problems that they have had to deal with. Summarize your discussion and add to it an evaluation of the likely effectiveness of PSAs on this topic. Be prepared to share your findings with the class.

6. Think of PSAs that have targeted you and then freewrite your response to a single PSA as the primary audience of the ad. Explore how it got your attention and any impact it may have had on you. In your conclusion, reflect on just how successful the advertisers were.

7. Review Miller and Williams's conclusion (perhaps after completing exercise 4 above), and use an extended freewrite to reflect on the comparison between peddling worthy causes and peddling consumer products. What does it mean to think of teenagers as targets of messages concerning safe sex or drug-free lives? Can worthy causes be "sold" in the same way as consumer products?

THE NEXT FRONT IN THE DRUG WAR: THE MEDIA
BARRY McCAFFREY

Barry McCaffrey is a retired general, the son of a general, and the father of a major and a captain, and in 1996, President Clinton appointed McCaffrey as his drug czar, the leader in the U.S. war on drugs. Interestingly, McCaffrey has since talked about drugs in medical rather than military terms and has chosen to focus as much effort on media campaigns as on drug busts. This Christian Science Monitor *article was just one of dozens of* *press releases that paved the way for a 1998 plan to spend $1 billion on anti-drug public service ads and announcements (PSAs). Addressing the national readership for this publication, McCaffrey's purpose seems to be to lay out a rationale for the emphasis on advertising and the electronic media in combating drug use.*

Corporations spend billions of dollars on advertising because it works. The electronic media—television, radio, film, videos, Internet, CD ROM, and multimedia (including print augmented by color photography)—are the strongest educational tools of the modern world. They change attitudes and behavior among youth in the fastest, most effective way. So if Americans are serious about reducing substance abuse, an aggressive media campaign is a crucial addition to drug prevention at home, in schools, and in communities.

Congress is now considering just such a campaign—our proposal to spend $175 million to motivate young people to reject illegal drugs. Through support from the media and others in the private sector, this figure could double—allowing us to increase both paid advertisements and public service efforts.

The Need Is Clear

Such an initiative is unquestionably necessary. Even though overall drug use in our country has dropped by half in the last 15 years, teenage drug use rose precipitously. Eighth-grade use, for example, nearly tripled in the last five years. During this period, the number of antidrug public-service announcements fell by 30 percent, and many aired in time slots that attract few children.

The media initiative is only the beginning of a greater educational campaign that will use every tool available to reach US youngsters. Documentaries about the history of drug use, the impact of narco-terrorism, and the link between drugs, crime, and the justice system can be supplemented by factual, dramatic shows about the consequences of substance abuse. Young viewers would be more likely to shun addictive substances if they were better informed about the violence associated with this criminal industry, as well as the health risks posed by illegal drugs.

5   Today's kids spend more time watching television than attending classes in school. By high school graduation, the average youth has seen approximately 15,000 hours of TV, as compared to 12,000 hours in school. Whether we like it or not, electronic media have revolutionized the way people learn—much as Gutenberg's printing press and movable type changed Renaissance Europe from an oral to a written culture. In the 20th century, mass communication has brought us back to word-of-mouth, conveying information through speech and pictures that are electronically enhanced to magnify impact.

The media are more than the message; they have become our environment. The signs on buses we see when riding, the eye-catching packaging we view while eating, the music that fills our cars while we're driving, characters like Roseanne, Seinfeld, or the Bunkers who join our families at home, commentators who bring us news from around the world—all create a media envelope that shapes the way we think.

Because mass media act like a "proxy peer" to our youth, defining culture by identifying what's "cool" and what's not, a broad-based antidrug campaign can counteract pro-drug messages that youngsters receive from many sources. Ad experts suggest a minimum of four exposures a week, reaching 90 percent of the target audience (mostly children but also, parents, coaches, youth leaders, and other adults who work with young people) is necessary to change attitudes. The University of Michigan's "Monitoring the Future" study indicates that changes in behavior are preceded by changes in attitude. We believe that, over a five-year period, the right kind of media campaign—along with other prevention programs—can educate students to reject illegal drugs.

A recent study by the National Institute on Drug Abuse (NIDA) notes that media efforts work best at the community level in conjunction with other programs. To maximize impact, the new campaign will tailor ads to match the age, social, and psychological profile of target audiences. Alan Leshner, director of NIDA, points out that scientific research has established which types of ads achieve good results. For instance, messages that encourage audiences to think about issues—as opposed to celebrities delivering slogans—tend to produce enduring changes in viewers. Likewise, research-based material is more effective than scare tactics.

Creative minds in the arts and industry can help. We hope the Advertising Council, and the leadership of Jim Burke with the Partnership for a Drug-Free America, will provide experience and talent to help guide this effort.

A Powerful Counterforce

10 Education cannot be confined to classrooms any more than morality is limited to religious institutions. The electronic age has seen magazine covers, cereal boxes, food cartons, clothing, video games, and other consumer items turned into billboards. Young people are bombarded by thousands of images, many of which normalize or glamorize drug use. To counter these influences, we must use equally powerful channels of communication.

The idea is not to control young minds. Our purpose is to offer accurate data that enables maturing individuals to make rational choices. Drugs are wrong because they hurt people. We cannot stand idly by while toxic, addictive substances endanger children, family, friends, and neighborhoods.

Rereading Actively

1. In his opening paragraphs, McCaffrey announces and justifies a $175 million program. In your journal, explain the logic behind the comparison between corporate advertising and education and suggest why McCaffrey might open with this comparison.

2. Review the article with a partner, focusing on passages where McCaffrey calls attention to statistics and research. Together, draft a summary of what, according to McCaffrey, is known about anti-drug PSAs. Then, discuss the rhetorical effect that references to research have in this article.

3. McCaffrey discusses several different media in this article. Review the article, noticing the term "media," and list each kind of medium that McCaffrey mentions. Then, describe the relationship he implies between advertising and the other media.

4. What results does McCaffrey hope for? What is his most surprising hope?

5. Summarize the appeals McCaffrey makes in his final paragraph. How might these appeals affect a reader who is sympathetic to McCaffrey's program? How might a hostile reader respond to the final paragraph?

Exploring Your Responses

6. With two or three classmates, try to identify McCaffrey's assumptions about the place of the electronic media in a high school student's life, and consider whether he has an accurate perception of the role played by TV, radio, and related media in shaping teenagers' lifestyles.

7. Brainstorm a list of PSA ads that have stuck in your memory in the past couple of years. Focusing on a single ad, write a page or two in your journal describing the ad and explaining why it caught your attention.

8. With a partner or in a small group, discuss the relationship between advertising and "rational choices." Can ads enable "maturing individuals to make rational choices" (¶ 11)? Summarize your discussion in an entry in your journal.

VICTIMS OF EVERYTHING

JACOB SULLUM

Jacob Sullum is a senior editor at Reason *and an advocate of open markets and individual choice. He is in favor of discussions about the legalization of drugs, attacking the policy of former drug czar William Bennett and holding out for the possibility of the responsible use of drugs. His recent book on the antismoking crusade,* For Your Own Good *(1998), carries this same argument to the discussion of tobacco. This 1997 editorial appeared in the* New York Times *three months after fashion photographer Davide Sorrenti overdosed on heroin and a front-page* New York Times *article suggested that the fashion industry was unwilling to see connections between drug abuse and a fashion trend—"heroin chic," it has been tagged—that glorified a drugged-out look. Careful not to endorse heroin chic, Sullum evaluates the relative power of images and advertising and "human nature," and he asks to what extent can images that sell a certain look be responsible for decisions about heroin use.*

Like you, I've seen innumerable Calvin Klein ads featuring sallow, sullen, scrawny youths. Not once have I had an overwhelming urge to rush out and buy some heroin, and probably neither have you. Yet the death of Davide Sorrenti, a 20-year-old fashion photographer who overdosed on heroin in February, is now being held up as proof that such images have the power to turn people into junkies.

On Wednesday President Clinton accused the fashion industry of "increasing the allure of heroin among young people" and urged it not to "glamorize addiction" to sell clothes. "We now see on college campuses and in neighborhoods heroin becoming increasingly the drug of choice," he said. "And we know that part of this has to do with the images that are finding their way to our young people."

In reality, heroin is not "the drug of choice" by any stretch of the imagination. In the Government's 1995 National Household Survey on Drug Abuse, 0.1 percent of respondents reported that they had used the drug in the previous month. A nation-wide study done in 1994 for the Department of Health and Human Services found, about the same level of heroin use among 19- to 28-year-olds; marijuana use was 140 times as common, and alcohol was far and away the most popular intoxicant.

And there is no reason to expect that people attracted to the look promoted by Calvin Klein and other advertisers—a cynical sanitized vision of drug use that pretends to reflect a gritty reality—will also be attracted to heroin, any more than suburban teenagers who wear baggy pants and backward caps will end up shooting people from moving cars.

5   Nevertheless, the editors of the cutting-edge fashion magazines that helped popularize the heroin-chic look are professing repentance. "With Davide's death," said Long Nguyen, Detour's style director, "we realized how powerful fashion pictures are."

And how powerful is that? Leaving aside the point that Mr. Sorrenti, as a producer of these images, can hardly be seen as an unknowing victim of their influence, it is important to keep in mind what pictures can and cannot do. Clearly, they can provoke outrage. They can also pique curiosity, create awareness and elicit a range of emotional reactions. But they cannot *make* anyone buy jeans or perfume, let alone take up heroin. Nor can they make kids smoke cigars, despite the claims of critics about the power of photos showing cigar-chomping celebrities. A conscious mind must intervene, deciding how to interpret the message and whether to act on it.

Blurring the distinction between persuasion and coercion is often the first step toward censorship. In the 1950's, John Kenneth Galbraith and Vance Packard argued that corporations used advertising to manipulate consumers and create an artificial desire for their products. The Federal court that upheld the 1970 ban on broadcast advertising of cigarettes was clearly influenced by such ideas, citing "the subliminal impact of this pervasive propaganda."

We see the same line of thinking today. In calling for restrictions on Web sites promoting alcohol and tobacco, the Center for Media Education, a research group in Washington, warns that "interactivity has a hypnotic and addictive quality that some analysts believe could be stronger than television."

The aim of such arguments is to portray people not as independent moral agents but as mindless automatons. It's a view of human nature that encourages the flight from responsibility to victimhood that we see all around us: the smoker who blames a cigarette maker for his lung cancer, the heavy drinker who blames the liquor company for her baby's birth defects, the mass murderer who blames dirty magazines for inspiring his crimes.

10   So far no one has called for a ban on glassy-eyed waifs, and the critics of heroin chic have every right to decry the message they believe it sends. But they should be careful not to send a dangerous message themselves: that the dictates of fashion overwhelm our ability to choose.

Rereading Actively

1. How does Sullum use his first paragraph to draw his reader into the discussion? How do you react to the first paragraph? Share your reactions to this paragraph with a partner.

2. Summarize Sullum's explanation of what pictures can and cannot do. To what extent do you agree with him?

3. With a partner, locate Sullum's references to heroin chic and develop a collaborative explanation of his position on the look and his view of the impact of that look on viewers of fashion ads.

4. What does Sullum fear will happen as a result of Davide Sorrenti's death? What does he believe should happen? In your journal, draft a paragraph explanation of what Sullum seems to argue in his final sentence.

Exploring Your Responses

5. In a small group, brainstorm fashion looks and focus on one that you are all aware of. Discuss what—if anything—that look might encourage a vulnerable fashion consumer to do, and evaluate how compelling the encouragement of that behavior seems to be. Be prepared to report the highlights of your discussion to the class.

6. In a page or two in your journal, explore your position on advertisers' use of appeals to potentially dangerous behaviors to sell products, drawing on examples from ads you are familiar with (e.g., ads for beer, soft drinks, or sport utility vehicles that feature extreme sports).

AN OVERDOSE OF REALITY
ANN COOPER

Ann Cooper writes about culture and business for Adweek *and also publishes in the* Wall Street Journal *and other popular business journals. This 1996 essay from the "creative" section of* Adweek *takes a look at why and how ad agencies were creating anti-drug public- service announcements and ads in the mid-1990s. As a writer who knows the advertising beat and is writing for Madison Avenue, Cooper has knowledge about the personal lives of advertisers, their firsthand experience with drug abuse, and the intentions behind their* pro bono *campaigns. Cooper relates her sense of advertising strategy, and using quotations from others within the industry, she describes the status of PSAs within the advertising community.*

Heroin: Kirshenbaum Bond & Partners' Richard Yelland lost two friends to it—one overdosed, one committed suicide. Ground Zero's Kirk Souder saw two of his mates simply fade out of his life. Commercial director Philip Owen's brother died after shooting up. A speedball claimed a close buddy of Cliff Freeman's David Angelo. In the world of advertising, as in the worlds of music, film, fashion and just plain real life, heroin addiction has taken its toll. And the casualties are found not just among the dead and surviving addicts but also among those friends left behind.

The degree of concern is such that over the past two years, individually and collectively, the advertising community has been taking action. All of the creatives mentioned above (and many other volunteers, perhaps less personally affected) from agencies around the U.S. have been quietly working on a series of anti-heroin print and TV PSAs aimed at 18- to 25-year-olds. Such efforts culminated last month in Washington with the unveiling of one of the largest national anti-drug campaigns ever, through the Partnership for a Drug-Free America.

With heroin use at epidemic proportions, reasons for such a campaign abound. Today's heroin is much purer than in the past. In 1980, it was about 4 percent; now it's more like 40 percent. Such potency means neophytes can sniff or snort the stuff, thus avoiding the use of a needle and risking AIDS. (Heavy users later graduate to the hypodermic, which is the most efficient and cost-effective way to ingest the drug.) According to data from the Drug Abuse Warning Network, the number of overall heroin-related emergency-room visits increased 68 percent from 1988 to 1994. And there's a more relaxed attitude toward heroin generally. Experts estimate between 500,000 and 1 million heroin addicts in the U.S., and the Partnership's 1995 attitude-tracking study reports 50 percent of high-school seniors do not see great risk in trying heroin once or twice.

Don't forget the litany of famous heroin-related deaths, including Jerry Garcia, Nirvana's Kurt Cobain, Blind Melon's Shannon Hoon, actor River Phoenix and, most recently, Jonathan Melvoin, a keyboardist for Smashing Pumpkins. "Heroin chic" has become an accepted fashion term, and the ravaged, dark-eyed look dominates the runways. Now, the film *Trainspotting* is described by one reviewer as "the first funny, upbeat look at heroin addiction." All of this perpetuates the perception of neo-coolness for those most at risk: Generation X.

5   Two years ago, the Partnership, a nonprofit coalition of advertising pros, started researching the subject of heroin abuse. Set up 10 years ago to demystify illegal drugs through the media, it has launched more than 500 PSAs for everything from inhalants to marijuana; this is the organization's first heroin campaign.

Quality control comes via a review committee of creative directors such as Jeff Goodby, Cliff Freeman and Nina DiSesa. And creatively, while individual agency methods and executions may vary enormously, there's no mistaking the intent: to prevent rather than cure, to stop those most at risk before they start, to deglamorize the '90s drug du jour.

"It's a thin line," says Doria Steedman, the Partnership's executive vice president and director of creative development, on implementing the creative vision of the heroin ads. "How can we turn someone off without breaching our own taste levels?"

The Partnership states the ground rules up front. "Everything said or shown has to be about the actualization of addiction," Steedman says. "An actor can be used only if the portrayal's accurate." The aim: to create something hard-hitting. "There's no point in showing funerals and coffins. Young people see death as part of the allure and glamour of heroin."

One of the first to get involved in the anti-heroin fight in the spring of '94, copywriter Richard Yelland has watched a number of friends fall in with the drug. "I was seeing heroin take people out of my life," says Yelland, then at J. Walter Thompson, New York. He was also getting drawn in himself. "It was completely alluring and incredibly romantic," he says. "If I hadn't had a full-time job …" When one friend OD'd, Yelland decided to take the initiative. He and his art director, Thomas Hayo, recruited photographer Jon Gipe, known for his Richard Avedon-like shots of the homeless. Another friend, documentarist Esther Bell, was coincidentally shooting a film about a heroin addict—her former roommate and an ex-art director at a large New York agency. "[The addict] wanted to help because she'd been in advertising," says Hayo. "She trusted us and knew the process."

10   The print campaign, consisting of stark black-and-white photos, featured "Ashley" (not her real name) and several other addicts only furtively identified. One ad chronicled the story of "Tasha, ex-student"; the body copy read: "My friends. They turned me on. We'd wait in line around the block for a brand called 'Poison.' They're all dead now."

A TV campaign soon followed, based on Bell's early documentary footage. "The first time I did it, there was this warm feeling, I felt like I was floating," says the ravaged Ashley, age 28. The B&W film was juxtaposed with color photos of her at age 18 (as high-school class president) and at 23 (as art director). "We wanted it to be real-looking," Hayo explains, "but not judgmental or preachy. And I didn't want to overdesign it."

A second campaign, directed by former *Rolling Stone* photographer Frank Ockenfels 3, was based on Ashley as she is today. In "Teeth," Ashley removes first her false eyelashes, her makeup and finally her teeth. "We thought it was a startling way to deglamorize the heroin beauty myth," says Hayo.

Another spot that revolves around an addict is Cliff Freeman & Partners' "Lenny," directed by Tony Kaye and perhaps the most controversial of all the anti-heroin ads (see sidebar). One aspect of the controversy raged over the graphic nature of the documentary-style footage of "Lenny," who is shown injecting himself and whose body is covered with horrible sores. Lenny talks about heroin and his own life. The result: a fascinating, gruesome, all-too-real portrait of a junkie. In a year's time, says a delusional Lenny, "you can come back here with your cameras, and I'll be successful."

"We tried to avoid the typical pro bono approach; most consumers are pretty jaded and immune to it," says David Angelo, who worked with copywriter Glenn Porter on the spot. "We wanted to show young people what heroin can do—I mean Lenny was a lot like us—he had a certain amount of intelligence and people can relate to him. Some turn away from the spot; some stare and get involved—those are the people we want."

15   Whether to use an addict or an actor was an early issue, and it proved a difficult question for Los Angeles' Ground Zero. Research had turned up original '60s footage of a real addict going through withdrawal—but that hardly reflected today's user. "We thought, 'Do we go into someone's room and film the convulsions?" says Kirk Souder, the agency's co-founder. "It brought up moral and ethical questions—so we opted to recreate [withdrawal] with an actor."

The strategy, parodying the perceived coolness of heroin, shows someone going through withdrawal while a chirpy jingle touts heroin as the drug of choice for the "beautiful people" at "glamorous parties." In the end, copywriter Michael Burdick and art director Patrick Plutschow cast a Mormon actor who didn't do drugs. To ensure authenticity, they even had a doctor on the set. There was an added poignancy because the director, Philip Owens, of Wind-mill Lane, L.A., had just lost his brother to heroin. The final touch: the word "Heroin" designed to look like the cursive graphics of the old *Bewitched* TV series.

Hill, Holliday, Connors, Cosmopulos, Boston, opted for all actors in its print campaign shot by photographer Matt Mahurin, famous for photos with a dark, twisted vision. Fred Bertino, agency president, used copy, what he calls "lyric appreciation," to hook readers. "There once was a young man named Jack. Who decided one day to snort smack. Then during a binge, he used a syringe. Now Jack is a dope maniac" reads the limerick alongside the distorted photo of a black man. Below, the graphic of a needle and the words, "If you put heroin in your nose, you'll end up putting it in your arm."

The Politics of Pro Bono

How much does winning awards influence what gets produced in the name of pro bono work? As most creatives know, a lot. Working for a non-paying and usually receptive client provides fertile ground for ambitious creatives eager to build their book. And if a valuable community service is provided—so much the better.

Problems arise when agencies take matters into their own hands. Cliff Freeman, for example, submitted a three-minute cut of "Lenny," complete with Doris Day singing "When I Fall in Love"—without the Partnership for a Drug-Free America's permission—to the Andy Awards (where it won a Silver). No one doubts the effort that went into making the spot, but to many, it's a self-serving act that leaves a sour taste. "It's completely scandalous what they did," says copywriter Richard Yelland of Kirshenbaum Bond. "They just did it for an award—it was all about publicity for Tony Kaye and Cliff Freeman. We created our ads' own passion; they're living in a different world."

Freeman art director David Angelo refutes the accusations. "For me, it's one of the most important pieces I've ever done," he says, adding that the money won at the Andys was used to place Lenny in rehab. The Partnership's shorter versions, he says, didn't tell the whole story.

Self-aggrandizement or genuine concern for veracity? Whichever, at least attention is focused on the main issue: heroin abuse.

—A.C.

"The copy came first," says writer Baxter Taylor. "We battled it out and came up with the limerick. It had to be different, and have a different voice. We set out to talk about snorting heroin." The look, says art director Wendy Lewis, was Mahurin's. "It was his idea to use color and make it disturbing, in a current way."

Compelling, gritty, imaginative, inspiring, realistic—there's no end to the adjectives that describe these PSAs. And no one doubts the passion, the desire to make a difference, that fueled the work.

20 But their ultimate effectiveness depends on donated media exposure—so far, *Rolling Stone* has published the Hill, Holliday work. Ground Zero's spot has aired on MTV. And "Lenny" has run on CNN. Yet even if the intended audience sees them, is there any evidence they work? Doria Steedman says yes, that numerous studies all reach the same conclusion: Anti-drug advertising has a deterrent effect. "The point is, these commercials take so many different ways of attacking the problem," she says. "If one doesn't work, another might."

Rereading Actively

1. With a partner, consider the rhetorical strategy behind the first paragraph. How might this paragraph affect its primary audience, members of the advertising industry?

2. With a partner or in a small group, review the article and talk about Cooper's descriptions of the drug problem and the advertising community's response to the problem. Summarize your discussion in a journal entry.

3. List the advertising strategies mentioned by Cooper and the people that she interviews. Offer a two- or three-sentence evaluation of each strategy's effectiveness based on your own observations and experience.

4. With a partner, review Cooper's last two paragraphs. What does she conclude? To what extent has her article warranted that conclusion? Be prepared to share your conclusions with the class.

Exploring Your Responses

5. In a small group, list all the ads (with their producers) that Cooper mentions, picking one to focus on. Prepare a group evaluation of Cooper's interpretation of your chosen ad and agency.

6. Select one ad that has a strategy that seems to you to be either effective or misguided. In a page or two in your journal, explore your reaction to this ad and reflect on what your reaction says about Madison Avenue's campaign against illegal drugs.

HARD TO EARN: ON WORK AND WEALTH

DARRELL DAWSEY

In 1996 Darrell Dawsey—a former Detroit News *journalist—published* Living to Tell About It: Young Black Men in America Speak Their Piece, *a collection of interviews with men ranging from Harvard graduates to Chris Wallace, a.k.a. The Notorious B.I.G. As a strategy for exploring the issues discussed in the book, Dawsey includes his own analysis as a frame for the interviews. This approach allows Dawsey to present a firsthand look—pages are filled with the angry and blunt language of interviewees, a style that Dawsey replicates in his own analysis—at the experiences of a group of U.S. citizens who are much written about but rarely heard from in the mainstream media. In this reading, an introduction to the chapter on work, Dawsey takes the drug trade as his focus, looking at the drug economy from a perspective not represented on Madison Avenue.*

Somewhere along my road to adulthood, opium, to invert Marxist metaphor, became the religion of the people. Crack, to be precise, was the new gospel obsessing us Black boys. Selling, using, cooking it up—all exploded as the new abiding fascinations of a generation that grew so versed in the dope game that we would eventually rewrite the rule book.

I certainly wasn't above that fascination, enamored as I was with the thought that sixteen- and seventeen-year-old dropouts could earn thousands in hours without ever leaving the comfort of their own street corners. I stared enviously at the shiny Ford Broncos and Volvos that, exorbitant sound systems thundering, careened continually up and down our blocks. I marveled at how the girls flocked to the dealers when they walked into the clubs and skating rinks, at how the kleig lights glistened rainbows off their thick necklaces. I was amazed at how, seemingly overnight, niggas I'd been chucking dodgeballs at on the elementary-school playground only nine years earlier now heard their names spoken in awed whispers. Meanwhile, here I was, Mr. 3.8, without a dime to show for all those *A*'s. Damn, how I ached to be down!

I never was, though. I partied with some of the dopemen, ran the streets with a few, but I never could bring myself to join The Game.

Not that I was noble or opting instead for some moral high ground. In fact, I used to harbor a bizarre sort of shame in my refusal to sell drugs, because my reason was simple and obvious: I was afraid. Afraid of getting caught. Afraid of going to jail. And—once closer scrutiny of the rule book made us realize that murder was standard operating procedure in drug dealing—afraid of dying.

5   This isn't to say I didn't get into trouble. I did dirt, sure. I was a stickup kid off and on in high school, squandering many a late night throwing the barrel of my friend's .38 to people's heads to speed them out of their Adidas Top Tens, leather coats and Starter jackets. My sporadic little crime sprees were prompted by the usual suspects—petty greed, a desire to earn props, boredom, mischief. Yet stick-ups always seemed, to common thinking around the way, second-tier crime, at best. You robbed people on impulse, generally, just because you saw them with some fresh shit you didn't have. If they had money on them, that was a plus, but really, you were in it for the gear. Jack moves were cheaper and faster than going to the mall. Just whip out the pistol and growl: "Yo, nigga, don't turn around. Just check all that shit in. Move wrong, motherfucker, and I'm poppin' ya." As clean and quick as it was stupid, when you think about it.

But slingin' them boulders, now that was where the real fame and fortune lay. Armed robberies were juvenile by comparison. And growing up, I saw us learn early to treat drug dealing as the business adults had always known it to be. I saw teenagers cobble together cartels out of ragtag crews of childhood playmates. I saw them set up elaborate distribution networks, calculating just how many crack houses one block could support before becoming oversaturated. I learned the mechanics of Triple Beam scales in a way no science teacher had ever taught, got a firm grasp on supply-and-demand laws that had seemed like so much boring gibberish in sixth-period econ class. It was the 1980s, and greed was the greatest good.

And never had young Africans on these shores been more American. The Game for us gave truth to all those wonderful lies American schoolkids are fed about all the joyful opportunities America holds out for them. "Just go to school, get a good job and make good money" was our directive, and we were drilled on it incessantly by our parents, teachers, heroes and role models. None of us wanted to believe our squalor was of other men's making. None of us wanted to bear the weight of knowing that our station was meant to imprison us, not be a launchpad to better lives. None wanted to accept that wealth and power had been intentionally placed beyond our grasps. Nope, not while there was milk and honey to be had.

Moreover, being the hyper-Americans that Black folks can be, we took a shortcut. Education—and not just school, but the totality of learning to interpret and then control the world around us—was the middleman who got axed. After all, if the point of education was, as we'd been tricked into believing, to get money, then why waste time with Algebra 3 if flipping a few kilos would sweep you into a world of champagne wishes and caviar dreams?

The Game was about Black kids mimicking power brokers, about Black youth showing just how right-wing George Bush and Richard Darman and William Bennett and their ilk could make us. It was about rugged individualism ("I gotta get mine"), about megabucks ("Make money, money, make money, money, monaaaay"), about eschewing the welfare of the collective in favor of hoarding wealth for a few ("Don't ask me for shit!"). "It's business," Nino Brown explained, "never personal."

10   Many of us started rolling not because every dope man was a millionaire, but because, for the first time in our young lives, that kind of wealth was even possible. To be sure, most Black kids on the street didn't make the sort of money that your local Newsbeat team would have you believe. Most of the friends I saw scurrying around the neighborhood in their fancy cars were worth far less than the rides they'd leveraged themselves to the hilt to buy would tell. Most worked for what, toward the ends of the tragic arc that was many of their lives, they would come to understand was chump change. Most realized that even in The Game—or perhaps especially in The Game—the rules are stacked against them.

That is because, quite simply, white folks in America control wealth, who acquires it and how. Just like white folks in America control crime and drugs and guns and all the other growth industries they use us to front for. What we didn't know was that America, for all its pretensions about egalitarianism and equal opportunity, is an oligarchy with great PR.

Read, man, they'll tell you that themselves. They'll tell you, as the Federal Reserve did when it told you that "by 1989, the top 1 percent (834,000 households with about $5.7 trillion net worth) was worth more than the bottom 90 percent [94 million households with about $4.8 trillion net worth]." They'll tell you that that 1 percent saw a 70 percent gain in family income during the late seventies and eighties, the largest increase of all income groups. They'll tell you that the vast majority of this nation's corporations are concentrated in the clammy hands of a small number of white people. They'll tell you that the rich get richer and the poor get straight fucked.

But we don't challenge the economic disparities in our lives. We don't object to America's continued blatant mislabeling of the contents of its capitalist dogma. We don't think to ask how a people forced into slavery for two hundred years can allow anyone to suggest they're lazy. We don't think to question how we can be expected to "go out and get a job" when companies move by the hundreds not only out of our neighborhoods but the entire country. We don't talk of white politicians' "cycle of dependency" when it comes to their salaries; of the inconsistencies that come with attacking "welfare as we know it" as some sort of drain on the public coffers even as the banking system that allowed for a $500 billion S&L debacle remains intact. We don't ask ourselves why our mothers have to stand for hours on welfare lines, why being laid off is as much a part of our fathers' jobs as lunch breaks, why we cannot shape our infrastructure, economic system, form of government or much of anything else that so quietly but effectively dictates the poor quality of most Black lives.

Instead, we continue the charade that allows prominence and ostentation to pass for power and wealth. We foolishly call ourselves survivors because we'll do anything we have to to eat and stay alive, but we refuse to commit ourselves to the social struggles necessary for those lives to flourish. We watch passively as generation after generation lines itself up in front of the slot machines of American "opportunity," mindlessly plunking down our lives in hopes that something, anything, good happens.

And even when a few of us hit—a comedian here, a power-forward there—we never stop to ask who owns the casino where we're pissing away our futures.

15   I'm still afraid of The Game, less now for what it might do to me than for what it is doing to so many of the brothers I used to play dodgeball with. Add to that the unspeakable agony that crack addiction has brought to millions of individuals and families in this nation. Add to that the frustrating understanding that you can't believe much of what America promises, even when those promises are made on the hush-hush in the underground economy. Some of us see this now, too. Where we thought we were just getting paid in full, we were being bought off. And now we're paying—in the mounting body counts of Black children, in the pell-mell rush to build more prisons for a youth population that, while designated "out of control," is very much under someone's sway, in the nineties' nihilism that has arisen from the ashes of eighties' hedonism.

Crack still runs rampant, but its glamour has dulled somewhat. We know now that the streets can kill. We know, too, that wealth without the institutions of power—without judicial appointees who'll pardon us, without congressmen who'll fashion bills for us—is as fleeting as it is dangerous. Sadly, too many of us don't care. We still play The Game, as it is the only one we've ever felt we had even a modicum of control over. That money is still our faith, those successive generations of disfranchised Black children our proselytes. America's hedonism has become something of a secular faith for us. Upon crack rocks, a vital chunk of our generation—a swath of our warrior class—has built its church.

But when it's done with us, America'll be more than happy to send it all up in smoke.

Rereading Actively

1. With a partner, review the first five paragraphs and list the images of drug culture Dawsey includes, exploring how these images seem to be associated with Dawsey's own experiences growing up, and how they may relate to images of drug use that fill Partnership for a Drug-Free America ads. In a page in your journal, explain what you and your partner discussed.

2. With a partner, review the chapter, looking for references to the drug trade as a business. Develop a collaborative explanation of the business of drugs as Dawsey sees it.

3. Find passages where Dawsey relates "the Game" of selling drugs with mainstream U.S. life—careers, school, social relationships—and draft a paragraph that explains the place of the drug trade in the U.S. economy.

4. With a partner, focus on a passage that makes strong use of rhythm, slang, and figures of speech. Discuss how Dawsey's writing style affects your understanding of his topic in this passage.

5. Summarize the appeals of the drug trade, and explain its relationship to the social experience of the urban African Americans Dawsey writes about.

Exploring Your Responses

6. In a small group, review the essay, noting passages that explain the glamour of crack. Talk about why crack is glamorous in inner-city neighborhoods and

then speculate about how that glamour makes its way into mainstream ads that attempt to warn people away from drugs. Be prepared to share your findings with the class.

7. In a page or two in your journal, compare Dawsey's position on illegal drugs with yours, noting what you learn from his perspective and what he might learn from yours.

8. Dawsey declares that in the United States, images of prominence and ostentation serve to induce Black people to act as a front in the "growth industry" of the drug economy. With a partner, discuss Dawsey's point of view and respond to it. Describe your conversation in an entry in your journal.

AMERICA'S ALTERED STATES

JOSHUA WOLF SHENK

As former Washington Monthly *editor and* U.S. News and World Report *staff writer, Joshua Wolf Shenk has explored U.S. culture from advertising to foreign policy to Disney World, publishing his discoveries in magazines ranging from* Salon, *an online 'zine, to the* Economist, *that most proper of British news magazines. As he reveals in this 1999* Harper's *essay, a lifelong struggle with mental disease has consistently brought him back to write about drug policy, pharmacology, and mental illness. Here he explores the extreme and exaggerated images that his market-oriented culture has created around licit and illicit drugs. As he looks at the way we sell and unsell, buy and exalt drugs, Shenk fixes on a contradiction: altering the mind and body is good if it is done with some substances and it is bad if done with others. This essay is his attempt to explain the impact of that contradiction and to argue for a more reasonable cultural position on the topic.*

> My soul was a burden, bruised and bleeding. It was tired of the man who carried it, but I found no place to set it down to rest. Neither the charm of the countryside nor the sweet scents of a garden could soothe it. It found no peace in song or laughter, none in the company of friends at table or in the pleasures of love, none even in books or poetry.... Where could my heart find refuge from itself? Where could I go, yet leave myself behind?
>
> —St. Augustine

To suffer and long for relief is a central experience of humanity. But the absence of pain or discomfort or what Pablo Neruda called "the infinite ache" is never enough. Relief is bound up with satisfaction, pleasure, happiness—the pursuit of which is declared a right in the manifesto of our republic. I sit here with two agents of that pursuit: on my right, a bottle from Duane Reade pharmacy; on my left, a bag of plant matter, bought last night for about the same sum in an East Village bar from a group of men who would have sold me different kinds of contraband if they hadn't sniffed cop in my curiosity and eagerness. This being Rudy Giuliani's New York, I had feared *they* were undercover. But my worst-case scenario was a night or two in jail and theirs a fifteen-year minimum. As I exited the bar, I saw an empty police van idling, waiting to be filled with people like me but, mostly, people like them, who are there only because I am.

Fear and suspicion, secrecy and shame, the yearning for pleasure, and the wish to avoid men in blue uniforms. This is (in rough, incomplete terms) an emotional report from the front. The drug wars—which, having spanned more than eight decades, require the plural—are palpable in New York City. The mayor blends propaganda, brute force, and guerrilla tactics, dispatching undercover cops to call "smoke, smoke" and "bud, bud"—and to arrest those who answer. In Washington Square Park, he erected ten video cameras that sweep the environs twenty-four hours a day. Surveillance is a larger theme of these wars, as is the notion that cherished freedoms are incidental. But it is telling that such an extreme manifestation of these ideas appears in a public park, one of the very few common spaces in this city not controlled by, and an altar to, corporate commerce.

Several times a month, I walk through that park to the pharmacy, where a doctor's slip is my passport to another world. Here, altering the mind and body with powders and plants is not only legal but even patriotic. Among the souls wandering these aisles, I feel I have kin. But I am equally at home, and equally ill at ease, among the outlaws. I cross back and forth with wide eyes.

What I see is this: From 1970 to 1998, the inflation-adjusted revenue of major pharmaceutical companies more than quadrupled to $81 billion, 24 percent of that from drugs affecting the central nervous system and sense organs. Sales of herbal medicines now exceed $4 billion a year. Meanwhile, the war on Other drugs escalated dramatically. Since 1970 the federal antidrug budget has risen 3,700 percent and now exceeds $17 billion. More than one and a half million people are arrested on drug charges each year, and 400,000 are now in prison. These numbers are just a window onto an obvious truth: We take more drugs and reward those who supply them. We punish more people for taking drugs and especially punish those who supply them. On the surface, there is no conflict. One kind of drugs is *medicine,* righting wrongs, restoring the ill to a proper, natural state. These drugs have the sheen of corporate logos and men in white coats. They are kept in the room where we wash grime from our skin and do the same with our souls. Our conception of illegal drugs is a warped reflection of this picture. Offered up from the dirty underworld, they are hedonistic, not curative. They induce artificial pleasure, not health. They harm rather than help, enslave rather than liberate.

5   There is some truth in each of these extreme pictures. But with my dual citizenship, consciousness split and altered many times over, I come to say this: The drug wars and the drug boom are interrelated, of the same body. The hostility and veneration, the punishment and profits, these come from the same beliefs and the same mistakes.

I.

Before marijuana, cocaine, or "Ecstasy," before nitrous oxide or magic mushrooms, before I had tried any of these, I poked through the foil enclosing a single capsule of fluoxetine hydrochloride. My drug story begins at this point, at the end of a devastating first year of college. For years, I had wrapped myself in an illusion that my lifelong troubles—intense despair, loneliness, anxiety, a relentless inner soundtrack of self-criticism—would dissolve if I could only please the gatekeepers of the Ivy League. By the spring of freshman year, I had been skinned of this illusion and plunged into a deep darkness. From a phone booth in a library basement, I resumed contact with a psychiatrist I'd begun seeing in high school.

I told him how awful I felt, and, after a few sessions, he suggested I consider medication. By now our exchange is a familiar one. This was 1990, three years after Prozac introduced the country to a new class of antidepressants, called selective serotonin reuptake inhibitors. SSRIs were an impressive innovation chemically but a stunning innovation for the market, because, while no more effective than previous generations of antidepressants, SSRIs had fewer side effects and thus could be given to a much broader range of people. (At last count, 22 million Americans have used Prozac alone.) When my doctor suggested I take Prozac, it was with a casual tone. Although the idea of "altering my brain chemistry" unsettled me at first, I soon absorbed his attitude. When I returned home that summer, I asked him how such drugs worked. He drew a crude map of a synapse, or the junction between nerve cells. There is a neurotransmitter called serotonin, he told me, that is ordinarily released at one end of the synapse and, at the other end, absorbed by a sort of molecular pump. Prozac inhibits this pumping process and therefore increases serotonin's presence in the brain. "What we don't understand," he said, looking up from his pad, "is why increased levels of serotonin alleviate depression. But that's what seems to happen."

I didn't understand the importance of this moment until years later, after I had noticed many more sentences in which the distance between the name of a drug—Prozac, heroin, Ritalin, crack cocaine—and its effects had collapsed. For example, the phrase "Prozac eases depression," properly unpacked, actually represents this more complicated thought: "Prozac influences the serotonin patterns in the brain, which for some unknown reason is found to alleviate, more often than would a placebo, a collection of symptoms referred to as depression." What gets lost in abbreviation—Prozac cures! Heroin kills!— is that drugs work because the human body works, and they fail or hurt us because the body and spirit are vulnerable. When drugs spark miracles—prolonging the lives of those with HIV, say, or dulling the edges of a potentially deadly manic depression—we should be thankful.[1] But many of these processes are mysteries that might never yield to science. The psychiatric establishment, for example, still does not understand why serotonin affects mood. According to Michael Montagne of the Massachusetts College of Pharmacy, 42 percent of marketed drugs likewise have no proven mechanism of action. In *Listening to Prozac*, Peter Kramer quotes a pharmacologist explaining the problem this way: "If the human brain were simple enough for us to understand, we would be too simple to understand it." Yet pharmaceutical companies exude certainty. "Smooth and powerful depression relief," reads an ad for Effexor in a recent issue of *The American Journal of Psychiatry*. "Antidepressant efficacy that brings your patients back." In case this message is too subtle, the ad shows an ecstatic mother and child playing together, with a note written in crayon: "I got my mommy back."

The irony is that our *faith* in pharmaceuticals is based on a model of consciousness that science is slowly displacing. "Throughout history," chemist and religious scholar Daniel Perrine writes in *The Chemistry of Mind-Altering Drugs*, "the power that many psychoactive drugs have exerted over the behavior of human beings has been variously ascribed to gods or demons." In a sense, that continues. "We ascribe magical powers to substances," says Perrine, "as if the joy is inside the bottle. Our culture has no sacred realm, so we've assigned a sacred power to these drugs. This is what [Alfred North] Whitehead would call the 'fallacy of misplaced concreteness.' We say, 'The good is in that Prozac powder,' or 'The evil is in that cocaine powder.' But evil and good are not attributes of molecules."

10   This is a hard lesson to learn. In my gut, where it matters, I still haven't learned it. Back in 1990, I took the Prozac and, eventually, more than two dozen other medications: antidepressants, antipsychotics, antianxiety agents, and so on. The sample pills

would be elegantly wrapped. Handing them to me, the doctors would explain the desired effect: this drug might quiet the voices in my head; this one might make me less depressed and less anxious; this combination might help my concentration and ease my repetitive, obsessive thoughts. Each time I swelled with hope. I've spent many years in therapy and have looked for redemption in literature, work, love. But nothing quite matches the expectancy of putting a capsule on my tongue and waiting to be remade.

But I was not remade. None of the promised benefits of the drugs came, and I suffered still. In 1993, I went to see Donald Klein, one of the top psychopharmacologists in the country. Klein's prestige, underscored by his precipitous fees, again set me off into fantasies of health. He peppered me with questions, listened thoughtfully. After an hour, he pushed his reading glasses onto his forehead and said, "Well, this is what I think you have." He opened the standard psychiatric reference text to a chapter on "disassociative disorders" and pointed to a sublisting called depersonalization disorder, "characterized by a persistent or recurrent feeling of being detached from one's mental processes or body."

I'm still not certain that this illness best describes my experience. I can't even describe myself as "clinically ill," because clinicians don't know what the hell to do with me. But Klein gave me an entirely new way of thinking about my problems, and a grim message. "Depersonalization is very difficult to treat," he said. So I was back where I started, with one exception. During our session, Klein had asked if I used marijuana. Once, I told him, but it didn't do much. After he had given me his diagnosis, he told me the reason he had asked: "A lot of people with depersonalization say they get relief from marijuana." At that time, I happened, for the first time in my life, to be surrounded by friends who liked to smoke pot. So in addition to taking drugs alone and waiting for a miracle, I looked for solace in my own small drug culture. And for a time, I got some. The basic function of antidepressants is to help people with battered inner lives participate in the world around them. This is what pot did for me. It helped me spend time with others, something I have yearned for but also feared; it sparked an eagerness to write and conjure ideas—some of which I found the morning after to be dreamy or naive, but some of which were the germ of something valuable. While high, I could enjoy life's simple pleasures in a way that I hadn't ever been able to and still find maddeningly difficult. Some might see this (and people watching me surely did) as silly and immature. But it's also a reason to keep living.

Sad to say, I quickly found pot's limitations. When my spirits are lifted, pot can help punctuate that. If I smoke while on a downward slope or while idling, I usually experience more depression or anxiety. Salvation, for me at least, is not within that smoked plant, or the granules of a pill, or any other substance. Like I said, it's a hard lesson to learn.

To the more sober-minded among us, it is a source of much consternation that drugs, alcohol, and cigarettes are so central to our collective social lives. It is hard, in fact, to think of a single social ritual that does not revolve around some consciousness-altering substance. ("Should we get together for coffee or drinks?") But drugs are much more than a social lubricant; they are also the centerpiece of many individual lives. When it comes to alcohol, or cigarettes, or any illicit substance, this is seen as a problem. With pharmaceuticals, it is usually considered healthy. Yet the dynamic is often the same.

15   It begins with a drug that satisfies a particular need or desire—maybe known to us, maybe not. So we have drinks, or a smoke, or swallow a few pills. And we get

something from this, a whole lot or maybe just a bit. But we often don't realize that the feeling is *inside,* perhaps something that, with effort, could be experienced without the drugs or perhaps, as in the psychiatric equivalent of diabetes, something we will always need help with. Yet all too often we project upon the drug a power that resides elsewhere. Many believe this to be a failure of character. If so, it is a failure the whole culture is implicated in. A recent example came with the phrase "pure theatrical Viagra," widely used to describe a Broadway production starring Nicole Kidman. Notice what's happening: Sildenafil citrate is a substance that increases blood circulation and has the side effect of producing erections in men. As a medicine, it is intended to be used as an adjunct to sexual stimulation. As received by our culture, though, the *drug* becomes the desired effect, the "real thing" to which a naked woman onstage is compared.

Such exaltation of drugs is reinforced by the torrent of pharmaceutical ads that now stuff magazines and blanket the airwaves. Since 1994, drug-makers have increased their direct-to-consumer advertising budget sevenfold, to $1.2 billion last year. Take the ad for Meridia, a weight-loss drug. Compared with other drug ads ("We're going to change lives," says a doctor pitching acne cream. "We're going to make a lot of people happy"), it is the essence of restraint. "You do your part," it says in an allusion to exercise and diet. "We'll do ours." The specific intent here is to convince people who are overweight (or believe themselves to be) that they should ask their doctor for Meridia.[2] Like the pitch for Baby Gap that announces "INSTANT KARMA" over a child wrapped in a $44 velvet jacket, drug ads suggest—or explicitly say—that we can solve our problems through magic-bullet consumption. As the old saying goes, "Better living through chemistry."

It's the job of advertisers to try every trick to sell their products. But that's the point: drugs are a commodity designed for profit and not necessarily the best route to health and happiness. The "self help" shelves at pharmacies, the "expert only" section behind the counter, these are promised to contain remedies for all ills. But the wizards behind the curtain are fallible human beings, just like us. Professor Montagne says that despite obvious financial incentives, "there really is an overwhelming belief among pharmacists that the last thing you should do for many problems is take a drug. They'll recommend something when you ask, but there's a good chance that when you're walking out the door they'll be saying, 'Aw, that guy doesn't need a laxative every day. He just needs to eat right. They don't need Tagamet. They just need to cut back on the spicy food.'" It is hard to get worked up about these examples, but they point to the broader pattern of drug worship. With illegal drugs, we see the same pattern, again through that warped mirror.

Not long after his second inauguration, President Clinton signed a bill earmarking $195 million for an antidrug ad campaign—the first installment of a $1 billion pledge. The ads, which began running last summer, all end with the words "Partnership for a Drug Free America" and "Office of National Drug Control Policy." It is fitting that the two entities are officially joined. The Partnership emerged in 1986, the year basketball star Len Bias died with cocaine in his system and President Reagan signed a bill creating, among many other new penalties, mandatory federal prison terms for possession of an illegal substance. This was the birth of the drug wars' latest phase, in which any drug use at all—not abuse or addiction or "drug-related crime"—became the enemy.[3] Soon the words "drug-free America" began to show up regularly, in the name of a White House conference as well as in legislation that declared it the "policy of the United States Government to create a Drug-Free America by 1995."

Although the work of the Partnership is spread over hundreds of ad firms, the driving force behind the organization is a man named James Burke—and he is a peculiar spokesman for a "drug free" philosophy. Burke is the former CEO of Johnson & Johnson, the maker of Tylenol and other pain-relief products; Nicotrol, a nicotine-delivery device; Pepcid AC, an antacid; and various prescription medications. When he came to the Partnership, he brought with him a crucial grant of $3 million from the Robert Wood Johnson Foundation, a philanthropy tied to Johnson & Johnson stock. Having granted $24 million over the last ten years, RWJ is the Partnership's single largest funder, but the philanthropic arms of Merck, Bristol-Myers Squibb, and Hoffman-La Roche have also made sizable donations.

20   I resist the urge to use the word "hypocrisy," from the Greek *hypókrisis,* "acting of a part on the stage." I don't believe James Burke is acting. Rather, he embodies a contradiction so common that few people even notice it—the idea that altering the body and mind is morally wrong when done with some substances and salutary when done with others.

This contradiction, on close examination, resolves into coherence. Before the Partnership, Burke was in the business of burnishing the myth of the über-drug, doing his best—as all marketers do—to make some external object the center of existence, displacing the complications of family, community, inner lives. Now, drawing on the same admakers, he does the same in reverse. (These admakers are happy to work pro bono, having been made rich by ads for pharmaceuticals, cigarettes, and alcohol. Until a few years ago, the Partnership also took money from these latter two industries.) The Partnership formula is to present a problem—urban violence, date rape, juvenile delinquency—and lay it at the feet of drugs. "Marijuana," says a remorseful-looking kid, "cost me a lot of things. I used to be a straight-A student, you know. I was liked by all the neighbors. Never really caused any trouble. I was always a good kid growing up. Before I knew it, I was getting thrown out of my house."

This kid looks to be around seventeen. The Partnership couldn't tell me his real name or anything about him except that he was interviewed through a New York drug-treatment facility. I wanted to talk to him, because I wanted to ask: "Was it *marijuana* that cost you these things? Or was it your *behavior* while using marijuana? Was that behavior caused by, or did it merely *coincide* with, your marijuana use?"

These kinds of subtleties are crucial, but it isn't a mystery why they are usually glossed over. In Texas, federal prosecutors are seeking life sentences for dealers who supplied heroin to teenagers who subsequently died of overdose. Parents praised the authorities. "We just don't want other people to die," said one, who suggested drug tests for fourth-graders on up. Another said, "I kind of wish all this had happened a year ago so whoever was able to supply Jay that night was already in jail." The desire for justice, and to protect future generations, is certainly understandable. But it is striking to note how rarely, in a story of an overdose, the survivors ask the most important question. It is not: How do we rid illegal drugs from the earth.[4] Despite eighty years of criminal sanctions, stiffened to the point just short of summary executions, markets in this contraband flourish because supply meets demand. Had Jay's dealer been in jail that night, Jay surely would have been able to find someone else—and if not that night, then soon thereafter.

The real question—why do kids like Jay want to take heroin in the first place?—is consistently, aggressively avoided. Senator Orrin Hatch recently declared that "people who are pushing drugs on our kids … I think we ought to lock them up and throw away the keys." Implicit in this remark is the idea that kids only alter their consciousness because it is *pushed* upon them.

25   Blaming the alien invader—the dealer, the drug—provides some structure to chaos. Let's say you are a teenager and, in the course of establishing your own identity or quelling inner conflicts, you start smoking a lot of pot. You start running around with a "bad crowd." Your grades suffer. Friction with your parents crescendos, and they throw you out of the house. Later, you regret what you've done—and you're offered a magic button, a way to condense and displace all your misdeeds. So, naturally, you blame everything on the drug. Something maddeningly complicated now has a single name. Psychologist Bruce Alexander points out that the same tendency exists among the seriously addicted. "If your life is really fucked up, you can get into heroin, and that's kind of a way of coping," he says. "You'll have friends to share something with. You'll have an identity. You'll have an explanation for all your troubles."

What works for individuals works for a society. ("Good People Go Bad in Iowa," read a 1996 *New York Times* headline, "And a Drug Is Being Blamed.") Why is the wealthiest society in history also one of the most fearful and cynical? What root of unhappiness and discontent spurs thousands of college students to join cults, millions of Americans to seek therapists, gurus, and spiritual advisers? Why has the rate of suicide for people fifteen to twenty-four tripled since 1960? Why would an eleven- and a thirteen-year-old take three rifles and seven handguns to their school, trigger the fire alarm, and shower gunfire on their schoolmates and teachers? Stop searching for an answer. Drug Watch International, a drug "think tank" that regularly consults with drug czar Barry McCaffrey and testifies before Congress, answered the question in an April 1998 press release: "MARIJUANA USED BY JONESBORO KILLERS."[5]

II.

The market must be taken seriously as an explanation of drugs' status. The reason is that the explanations usually given fall so far short. Take the idea "Bad drugs induce violence." First, violence is demonstrably not a pharmacological effect of marijuana, heroin, and the psychedelics. Of cocaine, in some cases. (Of alcohol, in many.) But if it was violence we feared, then wouldn't we punish that act with the greatest severity? Drug sellers, even people marginally involved in a "conspiracy to distribute," consistently receive longer sentences than rapists and murderers.

Nor can the explanation be the danger of illegal drugs. Marijuana, though not harmless, has never been shown to have caused a single death. Heroin, in long-term "maintenance" use, is safer than habitual heavy drinking. Of course, illegal drugs can do the body great harm. All drugs have some risk, including many legal ones. Because of Viagra's novelty, the 130 deaths it has caused (as of last November) have received a fair amount of attention. But each year, anti-inflammatory agents such as Advil, Tylenol, and aspirin cause an estimated 7,000 deaths and 70,000 hospitalizations. Legal medications are the principal cause of between 45,000 and 200,000 American deaths each year, between 1 and 5.5 million hospitalizations. It is telling that we have only estimates. As Thomas J. Moore notes in *Prescription for Disaster,* the government calculates the annual deaths due to railway accidents and falls of less than one story, among hundreds of categories. But no federal agency collects information on deaths related to legal drugs. (The $30 million spent investigating the crash of TWA Flight 800, in which 230 people died, is six times larger than the FDA's budget for monitoring the safety of approved drugs.) Psychoactive drugs can be particularly toxic. In 1992, according to Moore, nearly 100,000 persons were diagnosed with "poisoning" by psychologically active drugs, 90 percent of the cases due to benzodiazepine tranquilizers and antidepressants. It is simply a myth that legal drugs have been proven "safe." According to one government estimate, 15 percent of children are on Ritalin. But the long-term effects of Ritalin—or antidepressants, which are also commonly prescribed—on young kids isn't known. "I feel in between a rock and a hard place," says NIMH director Hyman. "I know that untreated depression is bad and that we better not just let kids be depressed. But by the same token we don't know what the effects of anti-depressants are on the developing brain.... We should have humility and be a bit frightened."

These risks are striking, given that protecting children is the cornerstone of the drug wars. We forbid the use of medical marijuana, worrying that it will send a bad message. What message is sent by the long row of pills laid out by the school nurse—or by "educational" visits to high schools by drugmakers? But, you might object, these are medicines—and illegal drug use is purely hedonistic. What, then, about illegal drug use that clearly falls under the category of self-medication? One physician I know who treats women heroin users tells me that each of them suffered sexual abuse as children. According to University of Texas pharmacologist Kathryn Cunningham, 40 to 70 percent of cocaine users have preexisting depressive conditions.

30   This is not to suggest that depressed people should use cocaine. The risks of dependence and compulsive use, and the roller-coaster experience of cocaine highs and lows, make for a toxic combination with intense suffering. Given these risks, not to mention the risk of arrest, why wouldn't a depressed person opt for legal treatment? The most obvious answers are economic (many cocaine users lack access to health care) and chemical. Cocaine is a formidable mood elevator and acts immediately, as opposed to the two to four weeks of most prescription antidepressants. Perhaps the most important factor, though, is cultural. Using a "pleasure drug" like cocaine does not signal weakness or vulnerability. Self-medication can be a way of avoiding the stigma of admitting to oneself and others that there is a problem to be treated.

Calling illegal drug use a disease is popular these days, and it is done, I believe, with a compassionate purpose: pushing treatment over incarceration. It also seems clear that drug abuse can be a distinct pathology. But isn't the "disease" whatever the drug users are trying to find relief from (or flee)? According to the Pharmaceutical Research and Manufacturer's Association, nineteen medications are in development for "substance use disorders." This includes six products for "smoking cessation" that contain nicotine. Are these treatments for a disease or competitors in the market for long-term nicotine maintenance?

Perhaps the most damning charge against illegal drugs is that they're addictive. Again, the real story is considerably more complicated. Many illegal drugs, like marijuana and cocaine, do not produce physical dependence. Some, like heroin, do. In any case, the most important factor in destructive use is the craving people experience—craving that leads them to continue a behavior despite serious adverse effects.

Legal drugs preclude certain behaviors we associate with addiction—like stealing for dope money—but that doesn't mean people don't become addicted to them. By their own admissions, Betty Ford was addicted to Valium and William Rehnquist to the sleeping pill Placidyl, for nine years. Ritalin shares the addictive qualities of all the amphetamines. "For many people," says NIMH director Hyman, explaining why many psychiatrists will not prescribe one class of drugs, "stopping short-acting high-potency benzodiazepines, such as Xanax, is sheer hell. As they try to stop they develop rebound anxiety symptoms (or insomnia) that seem worse than the original symptoms they were treating." Even antidepressants, although they certainly don't produce the intense craving of classic addiction, can be habit forming. Lauren Slater was first made well by one pill per day, then required more to feel the same effect, then found that even three would not return her to the miraculous health that she had at first experienced. This is called tolerance. She has also been unable to stop taking the drug without "breaking up." This is called dependence. "'There are plenty of addicts who lead perfectly respectable lives,'" Slater's boyfriend tells her. To which she replies, "'An addict. …You think so?'"

III.

In the late 1980s, in black communities, the Partnership for a Drug Free America placed billboards showing an outstretched hand filled with vials of crack cocaine. It read: "YO, SLAVE! The dealer is selling you something you don't want… . Addiction is slavery." The ad was obviously designed to resonate in the black neighborhoods most visibly affected by the wave of crack use. But its idea has a broader significance in a country for which independence of mind and spirit is a primary value.

In *Brave New World,* Aldous Huxley created the archetype of drug-as-enemy-of-freedom: soma. "A really efficient totalitarian state," he wrote in the book's foreword, is one in which the "slaves…do not have to be coerced, because they love their servitude." Soma—"euphoric, narcotic, pleasantly hallucinant," with "all the advantages of Christianity and alcohol; none of their defects," and a way to "take a holiday from reality whenever you like, and come back without so much as a headache or a mythology"—is one of the key agents of that voluntary slavery.

35   In the spring of 1953, two decades after he published this book, Huxley offered himself as a guinea pig in the experiments of a British psychiatrist studying mescaline. What followed was a second masterpiece on drugs and man, *The Doors of Perception.* The title is from William Blake: "If the doors of perception were cleansed every thing would appear to man as it is, infinite—/For man has closed himself up, till he sees all things thro' narrow chinks of his cavern." Huxley found his mescaline experience to be "without question the most extraordinary and significant experience this side of the Beatific vision…[I]t opens up a host of philosophical problems, throws intense light and raises all manner of questions in the field of aesthetics, religion, theory of knowledge."

Taken together, these two works frame the dual, contradictory nature of mind-altering substances: they can be agents of servitude or of freedom. Though we are deathly afraid of the first possibility, we are drawn like moths to the light of the second. "The urge to transcend self-conscious selfhood is," Huxley writes, "a principal appetite of the soul. When, for whatever reason, men and women fail to transcend themselves by means of worship, good works and spiritual exercises, they are apt to resort to religion's chemical surrogates."

One might think, as mind diseases are broadened and the substances that alter consciousness take their place beside toothpaste and breakfast cereal, that users of other "surrogates" might receive more understanding and sympathy. You might think the executive taking Xanax before a speech, or the college student on BuSpar, or any of the recipients of 65 million annual antidepressant prescriptions, would have second thoughts about punishing the depressed user of cocaine, or even the person who is not seriously depressed, just, as the Prozac ad says, "feeling blue." In trying to imagine why the opposite has happened, I think of the people I know who use psychopharmaceuticals. Because I've always been up-front about my experiences, friends often approach me when they're thinking of doing so. Every year there are more of them. And yet, in their hushed tones, I hear shame mixed with fear. I think we don't know quite what to make of our own brave new world. The more fixes that become available, the more we realize we're vulnerable. We solve some problems, but add new and perplexing ones.

In the *Odyssey,* when three of his crew are lured by the lotus-eaters and "lost all desire to send a message back, much less return," Odysseus responds decisively. "I brought them back ... dragged them under the rowing benches, lashed them fast." "Already," writes David Lenson in *On Drugs,* "the high is unspeakable, and already the official response is arrest and restraint." The pattern is set: since people lose their freedom from drugs, we take their freedom to keep them from drugs.[6] Odysseus' frantic response, though, seems more than just a practical measure. Perhaps he fears his own desire to retire amidst the lotus-eaters. Perhaps he fears what underlies that desire. If we even feel the *lure* of drugs, we acknowledge that we are not satisfied by what is good and productive and healthy. And that is a frightening thought. "The War on Drugs has been with us," writes Lenson, "for as long as we have despised the part of ourselves that wants to get high."

As Lenson points out, "It is a peculiar feature of history, that peoples with strong historical, physical, and cultural affinities tend to detest each other with the most venom." In the American drug wars, too, animosity runs in both directions. Many users of illegal drugs—particularly kids—do so not just because they like the feeling but because it sets them apart from "straight" society, allows them (without any effort or thought) to join a culture of dissent. On the other side, "straight society" sees a hated version of itself in the drug users. This is not just the 11 percent of Americans using psychotropic medications, or the 6 million who admit to "nonmedical" use of legal drugs, but anyone who fears and desires pleasure, who fears and desires loss of control, who fears and desires chemically enhanced living.

40   Straight society has remarkable power: it can arrest the enemy, seize assets without judicial review, withdraw public housing or assistance. But the real power of prohibition is that it *creates* the forbidden world of danger and hedonism that the straights want to distinguish themselves from. A black market spawns violence, thievery, and illnesses—all can be blamed on the demon drugs. For a reminder, we need only go to the movies (in which drug dealers are the stock villains). Or watch *Cops,* in which, one by one, the bedraggled junkies, fearsome crack dealers, and hapless dope smokers are

led away in chains. For anyone who is secretly ashamed, or confused, about the explosion in legal drug-taking, here is reassurance: the people in handcuffs are the bad ones.
Anything the rest of us do is saintly by comparison.

We are like Robert Louis Stevenson's Dr. Jekyll, longing that we might be
divided in two, that "the unjust might go his way...and the just could walk stead-
fastly and securely on his upward path, doing the good things in which he found
his pleasure, and no longer exposed to disgrace and penitence by the hands of this
extraneous evil." In his laboratory, Jekyll creates the "foul soul" of Edward Hyde,
whose presence heightens the reputation of the esteemed doctor. But Jekyll's dream
cannot last. Just before his suicide, he confesses to having become "a creature eaten
up and emptied by fever, languidly weak both in body and mind, and solely occupied by one thought: the horror of my other self." To react to an unpleasant truth
by separating from it is a fundamental human instinct. Usually, though, what is
denied only grows in injurious power. We believe that lashing at the illegal drug
user will purify us. We try to separate the "evil" from the "good" of drugs, what we
love and what we fear about them, to enforce a drug-free America with handcuffs
and jail cells while legal drugs grow in popularity and variety. But we cannot separate the inseparable. We know the truth about ourselves. It is time to begin living
with that horror, and that blessing.

NOTES

1. Although I am critical of the exaltation of drugs, it must be noted that a crisis runs in
    the opposite direction. Only a small minority of people with schizophrenia, bipolar dis-
    order, and major depression—for which medications can be very helpful—receive treat-
    ment of any kind.
2. Fifty-five percent of American adults, or 97 million people, are overweight or obese. It is
    no surprise, then, that at least forty-five companies have weight-loss drugs in development.
    But many of these drugs are creatures more of marketing than of pharmacology. Meridia
    is an SSRI, like Prozac. Similarly, Zyban, a Glaxo Wellcome product for smoking cessation
    is chemically identical to the antidepressant Wellbutrin. Admakers exclude this informa-
    tion because they want their products to seem like targeted cures—not vaguely understood
    remedies like the "tonics" of yesteryear.
3. Declared Nancy Reagan, "If you're a casual drug user, you're an accomplice to murder."
    Los Angeles police chief Daryl Gates told the Senate that "casual drug users should be taken
    out and shot." And so on.
4. Many people believe that this is still possible, among them House Speaker Dennis
    Hastert, who last year co-authored a plan to "help create a drug-free America by the
    year 2002." In 1995, Hastert sponsored a bill allowing herbal remedies to bypass FDA
    regulations, thus helping to satisfy Americans' incessant desire for improvement and
    consciousness alteration.
5. The release describes Andrew Golden and Mitchell Johnson as "reputed marijuana
    smokers." No reference to Golden and pot could be found in the Nexis database. The
    Washington Post reports that Johnson "said he smoked marijuana. None of his class-
    mates believed him."
6. In the 1992 campaign, Bill Clinton said, "I don't think my brother would be alive today if
    it wasn't for the criminal justice system." Roger served sixteen months in Arkansas State
    Prison for conspiracy to distribute cocaine. Had he been convicted three years later, he

would have faced a five-year mandatory minimum sentence, without the possibility of parole. If he had had a prior felony or had sold the same amount of cocaine in crack form, he would have automatically received ten years.

Rereading Actively

1. With a partner, review Shenk's introduction (the headnote and first five paragraphs) and talk about the themes that he connects to the public image of drugs. Use a journal entry to summarize the themes you discover.

2. With a partner or in a small group, probe Shenk's definitions of drugs and of ways drugs are represented in the market. Summarize your findings in a journal entry.

3. Review the essay, noting section breaks. In your journal, give each section a subtitle and list under each subtitle the major kinds of evidence that are introduced. Below your outline, draft a paragraph summary of the purpose of each section.

4. Review the essay with a partner, noting the different drugs that Shenk discusses and talking about which examples are most striking. List the three drugs that are most interesting to you, and discuss how Shenk interprets each of these drugs. Be prepared to participate in a class discussion of Shenk's position on specific drugs.

5. Locate two passages where Shenk talks about his own experience. In a journal entry, explain how each of these passages might affect a reader.

6. With a partner, review the essay and identify passages that deal with advertising for and against drugs. Focusing on one discussion of drug ads and one discussion of antidrug public service announcements, talk about how Shenk uses each discussion to clarify the marketing of drugs. Summarize your discussion in a journal entry.

7. Review the final section and identify the assertions Shenk makes about (a) mind diseases, (b) mind-enhancing drugs, and (c) straight society. In a journal entry, explain how these passages bring the essay to a close and explore your personal reaction to Shenk's claims.

Exploring Your Responses

8. Review the description of buying marijuana that opens this essay. In a freewrite, explore how you respond to Shenk's openness about his own drug use. Does this story affect the persuasiveness of Shenk's claims about drug policy? Does the rest of his essay change your initial reaction?

9. With two or three classmates, brainstorm legal, over-the-counter medications and stimulants—for example, pain relievers and allergy remedies, acne medicines, diet pills. Review your list and categorize your results into groups like pain relievers, treatments for illnesses, body enhancers, image enhancers, and so on. Focusing on one category, talk about how you perceive these products

and then sketch out an anti-product PSA and a pro-product ad for this category. Be prepared to explain your ads to the class.

10. Review the essay and stop on a passage that relates a government or other mainstream antidrug position, maybe the strategy of the PDFA, President Clinton's policy proposals, or comments by Nancy Reagan, Daryl Gates, or Dennis Haster. In an extended freewrite, compare your sense of the drug issue to this official position. As you close your freewrite, consider what kind of culture this position reflects.

ADVERTISEMENTS

PARTNERSHIP FOR A DRUG-FREE AMERICA

Sometime in 1986, the CEO of the Daily Advertising Agency, Phil Joanou, began to believe that the advertising community should be mobilized to "unsell" illegal drugs. In 1987, the Partnership for a Drug-Free America (PDFA), formed with seed money from the American Association of Advertising Agencies (AAAA), began to run the first of hundreds of print, TV, radio, and billboard ads. PDFA hoped that every U.S. consumer would see at least one anti-drug message every day. In 1997, the U.S. congress approved a national anti-drug media campaign, which is coordinated by the White House Office of National Drug Control Policy. Today, PDFA images are a part of our cultural landscape. These ads represent the best appeals and artwork in the industry, and they even show how PSAs have changed with the famous "This is Your Brain on Drugs" ad of the late 1980s giving birth to a hip new version in "Frying Pan."

Rereading Actively

1. With a partner, scan the ads and for each one note how the ad catches the viewer's attention and what precisely the anti-drug message is. Review your notes and talk about which ad is most or least compelling for each of you.

2. Review either "Drain Cleaner" or "Frying Pan" and jot down the apparent anti-drug message that the ad conveys. Then, highlight words or phrases that catch your attention. In a journal entry, explain how the words and phrases you examined contribute to or seem to undercut the intended effect of the ad.

3. Review a single ad and list the three or four images that contribute most to the anti-drug message. In a journal entry, describe the themes—beauty, youth, danger, waste, criminality, responsibility, vanity, stupidity, and so on— that these images represent. Review your description and write an explanation of what the images are supposed to say to the intended audience of the ad. To what extent do the images present a convincing anti-drug message?

4. What is the attitude of PDFA toward drug use? In your journal, write a comparison of how two of these ads represent users. Review your analysis and speculate about the effects PDFA's attitude toward users might have on users of illegal drugs and on the members of "straight society."

This is your brain,

this is drugs,

this is your brain on drugs.

Partnership For A Drug-Free America

Figure 5.4 This is Your Brain on Drugs, Partnership for a Drug-Free America

Partnership for a Drug-Free America

"FRYING PAN" :30

DECC-3169

This is your brain.

This is heroin.

This is what happens to your brain...

after snorting heroin.

(SFX: PAN HITTING COUNTER)

This, is what your body goes through.

It's not over yet.

This is what your family goes through!

And your friends! And your money!

And your job!

And your self-respect!

And your future!

Any questions?

Figure 5.5 Frying Pan, Partnership for a Drug-Free America

5. With a partner, review "The Power of a Grandma" and talk about the message the ad sends to parents and grandparents. What specific appeals, and pieces of information catch your eye? Be prepared to participate in a class discussion about the effectiveness of this kind of advertising.

Exploring Your Responses

6. In an extended freewrite, reflect on your personal response to one of these ads. How does the ad affect your position on the use of illegal drugs? What

Partnership for a Drug-Free America

Figure 5.6 **Teeth, Partnership for a Drug-Free America**
Second to last screen: It's hard to face what heroin can do to you.

do you focus on in the ad? What feels unconvincing or fake? What makes you stop and think? How do you feel when you get to the end of the ad? Read over your reflection, and write a paragraph evaluation of how well this ad works on you.

7. In a same-sex group of three or four students, analyze the images of women in "Frying Pan" and "Teeth." Once you've looked carefully at these ads, look at a

Partnership for a Drug-Free America

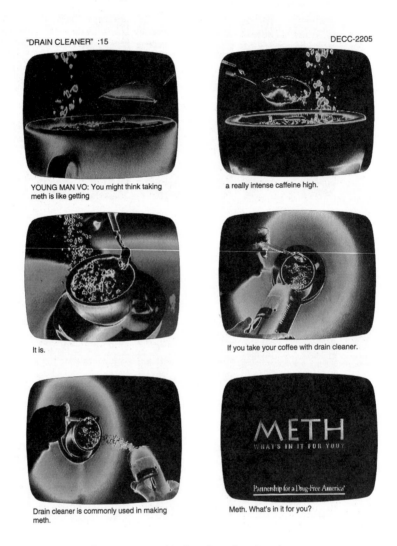

"DRAIN CLEANER" :15

DECC-2205

YOUNG MAN VO: You might think taking meth is like getting

a really intense caffeine high.

It is.

If you take your coffee with drain cleaner.

Drain cleaner is commonly used in making meth.

Meth. What's in it for you?

METH

WHAT'S IN IT FOR YOU?

Partnership for a Drug-Free America®

Figure 5.7 Drain Cleaner, Partnership for a Drug-Free America

recent issue of a fashion or lifestyle magazine that targets your gender. There are some obvious choices—women might look at *Vogue, Cosmo,* or *Self;* men, at *GQ* or *Esquire;* either group at *YM, People,* or *US.* But be creative. Once you've found a magazine, look for images of women in ads. As a group, talk about how the female characters in "Frying Pan" and "Teeth"

The power of a Grandma.

Children have a very special relationship with Grandma and Grandpa. That's why grandparents can be such powerful allies in helping keep a kid off drugs.

Grandparents are cool. Relaxed. They're not on the firing line every day. Some days a kid hates his folks. He never hates his grandparents. Grandparents ask direct, point-blank, embarrassing questions parents are too nervous to ask:

"Who's the girl?"

"How come you're doing poorly in history?"

"Why are your eyes always red?"

The same kid who cons his parents is ashamed to lie to Grandma. Without betraying their trust, a loving, understanding grandparent can discuss the danger of drugs openly with the children she adores. And should.

Use your power as an influencer to steer your grandchildren away from drugs.

If you don't have the words, we do. We'll send you more information on how to talk to kids about drugs. Just ask for your free copy of *Keeping Youth Drug-Free*. Call 1-800-729-6686.

Partnership for a Drug-Free America®

Figure 5.8 The Power of a Grandma, Partnership for a Drug-Free America

compare with the images of women in mainstream advertising. Be prepared to participate in a class discussion about whether idealized images of women can be used to unsell drugs.

8. In a freewrite, try to recall the first time you saw "This is Your Brain on Drugs." Narrate your reaction and then draft a position paper on whether the

ad would convince a curious teenager to think differently about drug use. Does "Frying Pan" successfully update its predecessor? Why or why not?

CASE-IN-POINT ASSIGNMENTS

The background readings in this unit suggest that advertisements offer consumers representations of social ideals. With every ideal comes an appeal to buy or to believe. Whether we enjoy or laugh at, embrace or dismiss these ideals, they affect us deeply. The case readings explore what happens when advertising—a discourse of ideals and appeals—becomes "public service advertising" and attempts to challenge destructive behavior like drug abuse or encourage positive behavior like staying clean and sober. All of these writers believe that anti-drug PSAs are well able to idealize clean and sober lifestyles and demonize drug culture. But, they disagree about how consumers make use of these ads, asking some difficult questions. Does a consumer culture really value being clean and sober? Is the appeal of coolness or the stigma of being a loser enough to motivate action, that is, to change behavior? How strong is an appeal to a clean and sober lifestyle? By taking a close look at these readings, you can begin to crack the code of advertising, better understanding how we respond to the continual flow of ads, and untangling the logic of consumerism. You will also have to think about whether advertising can win the war on drugs.

Making Connections

1. Fowles (from the background readings) explains how advertisers craft idealized images (¶ 18–20) and consumers use ads for personal reasons (¶ 23–29). Analyze a single PDFA ad, focusing on the ideals advertisers design in the ad and uses consumers might make of the ad. Use case readings that discuss the advertisers and consumers to develop your analysis.

2. Miller and Williams and Cooper all describe strategies used in advertisements. Shenk and Dawsey offer interpretations of the symbolism of drugs. Drawing on these writers, consider whether or to what degree PDFA ads have affected a target market of which you yourself are a part.

3. Brainstorm experiences that are mind altering, mysterious, taboo, or potentially hazardous, from getting a tattoo to bulking up on a dietary supplement to climbing buildings on campus to traveling in a chaotic country—be creative. Reflect on your attitude toward one of these experiences that you have tried or might try. Then, draw assertions about advertising and cultural taboos made by McCaffrey, Dawsey, and Cooper to analyze the direct and indirect impact that advertising might have on your attitude toward this kind of experience.

4. Are the PDFA and Office of National Drug Control Policy (ONDCP) likely to achieve success in shaping the public's perceptions of the drug culture? Drawing on information and positions from advertisers (Miller and Williams and Cooper) and critics (Shenk and Dawsey), argue for the prospects of victory in this front of the war on drugs.

5. How important is the truth in advertising aimed at public welfare? Is "full disclosure" called for or necessary? In an essay, develop a position on truth in advertising, using descriptions and criticisms of PDFA campaigns as your central examples.

6. According to most advertising theory, advertisements appeal to basic desires. In an essay, explore the desires that the anti-drug ads appeal to and speculate about how those appeals have affected the public discourse on drugs and children.

Collaborative Exchanges

1. With two or three classmates, research the PDFA's tracking studies. As a group, discuss claims of effectiveness and ineffectiveness, incorporating Shenk's explanation of anti-drug PSAs into your discussion. Draft a collaborative assessment of the situation, noting the range of opinions in your group.

2. In a small group, brainstorm public service ad strategies and campaigns similar to the PDFA's campaign. Focusing on one campaign, pick a representative ad, and draft an explanation of the basic purpose of the ad and an evaluation of the ad's success. Be prepared to present your findings to the class.

 ## Net Approaches

1. Tour the ONDCP <www.whitehousedrugpolicy.gov> and then explore links to the PDFA and Project Know <www.projectknow.com>. After acquainting yourself with each page, write a brief explanation of how the images and styles created online match up with print discussions and antidrug public service advertisements.

2. Go to <www.altavista.com> and do a link search for the PDFA site <www.drugfreeamerica.org>. To do this, type the following string into an AltaVista search: *link:http://www.drugfreeamerica.org*. (Other search engines also enable link searches; check out search engine help pages for instructions.) Find three different kinds of authors—we found cities, social service agencies, schools, TV stations, and individuals—that have created links between their personal pages and the PDFA page. Write brief profiles on the author of each page and be prepared to comment on the different interests in the PDFA that these sites represent.

3. Review the Cooper essay, focusing on the names of the ad agencies that do *pro bono* work for the PDFA. At a search engine, enter the company name (perhaps tying the company name to the term "advertising") and scroll through at least twenty hits with the goal of exploring at least three different kinds of sites. We looked for pages discussing Wieden & Kennedy and found an analysis of Wieden & Kennedy strategies, a bio of Wieden, lots of links to *AdWeek,* a couple of sample ads, and an "I hate the latest Wieden & Kennedy ads" page. After you've surfed through the sites, freewrite an explanation of what they tell you about the role of the advertising agencies in a consumer culture.

WRITING PROJECTS

Advertising

Project 1

Likely Readings

Background Readings
- Ewen and Ewen
- Fowles

Case-in-Point Readings
- Cooper
- Shenk
- McCaffrey
- Miller and Williams
- Sullum

Task and Purpose

Focusing on a single PDFA ad, describe how the PDFA can be seen to give consumers an imaginatively rich set of symbols (Fowles) but also a very narrow vision (the Ewens). Use the case readings to explore how advertisers believe PDFA ads work, and the background readings to assess the social impact of the ads.

Project 2

Likely Readings

Background Readings
- Kuntz
- Meijer

Case-in-Point Readings
- Dawsey
- Shenk
- Sullum

Task and Purpose

Take a position on the critics of the PDFA campaign. To be fair, you'll need start by sketching in the current state of affairs in advertising. Once you've established current practice, look at the complaints about PDFA and decide whether they are justified, excessive, or misdirected. Your paper will become a kind of editorial that evaluates the critics. (Look to Sullum for an example of the editorial discourse.)

Project 3

Likely Readings

Background Readings
- Fowles
- Kuntz

Case-in-Point Readings
- Cooper
- McCaffrey
- Miller and Williams

Task and Purpose

Write an explanation of the PDFA approach to unselling a specific product (marijuana, crack, heroin, or another drug) or selling a specific product or practice (information, parental involvement, or self-esteem). Make sure that you cover both the general strategies as well as a detailed description of ads for the product or practice. Your audience is a party that needs information about how antidrug PSAs work, maybe an advertising agency about to do some *pro bono* work for the PDFA or a non-profit agency that is considering funding an anti-drug media campaign.

Project 4

Likely Readings

Background Readings
- Fowles
- Kuntz

Case-in-Point Readings
- Cooper
- McCaffrey
- Miller and Williams

Task and Purpose

Working with two or three classmates, write a proposal for an anti-drug PSA. Start by doing the prewriting work for the previous project. Once you've focused on a drug or practice and a target audience, decide whether you will follow in the path of previous advertisers or move off in a new direction. Your proposal should pose a problem (explaining necessary background issues and arguing for the need for action), offer a solution (arguing a PSA will partly make the situation better), justify that solution (arguing that your proposals will work despite possible limitations), and lay out a timeline for development of the actual project. You might consider writing your proposal to the PDFA, and you'll probably want to include some graphics.

Project 5

Likely Readings

Background Readings
- Ewen and Ewen
- Kuntz

Case-in-Point Readings
- Williams and Miller
- Cooper
- Dawsey
- Shenk

Task and Purpose

In an exploratory essay, work through your response to PSAs or PSA lookalikes that use a celebrity that you find either attractive or unattractive. Start by brainstorming possible ads: Nike ads encouraging self-esteem, TV network PSAs recommending school, professional sports association PSAs, government PSAs, or PDFA PSAs. Once you've discovered an ad and a celebrity that trigger your attention, formulate a question about your personal reaction to the celebrity image: Ask why a sitcom actor talking about safe sex annoys you or why a sports celebrity's smile makes you feel good. Then, review what the readings have to say about advertising, celebrity, and celebrities in advertising. Once you've got a question and some notes together, narrate your own process of discovery. For instance, your introduction might tell the story of your brainstorming and the emotional or critical response that led you to select your topic; the first section may explain how you found an ad and how your response changed as you noticed where the ad was placed and what was really in it. Your next move might take your reader into Kuntz's article or the Ewens' chapter as you explain how thinking about current advertising practices helped you get a better sense of your response and encouraged you to find out what advertisers think they're doing, which led you to the case readings.

Project 6

Likely Readings

Background Readings
- Ewen and Ewen
- Fowles
- Meijer

Case-in-Point Readings
- Forbes
- McCaffrey
- Miller and Williams
- Sullum

Task and Purpose

Evaluate the impact of an advertising campaign—maybe but not necessarily a PSA campaign—on a target audience with which you identify strongly. Brainstorm your group memberships, tastes, aspirations, hobbies, and opinions—be specific and push toward examples about which you feel strongly. Review your work, and write next to each item a related consumer good or service. For example, you might link competitive bicycling with Pearl Izumi clothing, video gaming with Nintendo, or getting rich with a college education. Pick one group–product pairing, find some advertising that links them, and freewrite an initial response to the ad. Does the ad give you new ideas and information that help you achieve goals? Does the ad help you imagine and understand what you want? Do you suspect that the ad may manipulate your goal for the sake of a sale? Using your freewrite and the reading, assemble an analytical essay in which you explain how the ad affects someone like you, and argue whether that effect is primarily positive or negative.

CHAPTER **6**

Entertainment: The Commodification of Enjoyment

itizens around the world know something about the entertainment industry in the United State because they are exposed to it all the time. Whether it is Mickey Mouse T-shirts or Broadway shows, hip-hop or rock music, the NBA or American television, images and products circle the globe in a process that links amusement to an economic exchange. U.S. consumers alone spent over $424 billion entertaining themselves in 1996. Our consumer culture may have taken the packaging and sale of entertainment products to an extreme, but the activities that make up entertainment are as old as human communities. Through entertainment, we have always sought to forge relationships between individuals and groups; "to entertain" means "to hold mutually" or "to hold intertwined," often with strong connotations of one person or group engaging another person or group. Almost since humans have been leaving records, we've been holding rituals in hopes of entertaining or being entertained by gods and nature, potential mates or neighbors. The education of the young is in part a process of acquainting them with the entertainment media of which a local culture is particularly proud, whether it's a tribal dance, a tea ceremony, a Shakespeare play, or a poem about Winnie-the-Pooh.

Of course, entertainment isn't now—and perhaps never was—about simple engagements between people. The word carries a strong sense of amusement, of arresting another's attention and diverting it from reality. Entertainment, for better or worse, traffics in the deeply seated human urge to play. On the one hand, our willingness to play has helped us to develop technology, laugh at ourselves, and talk about important, sometimes taboo issues. On the other hand, we may reduce serious issues to fantasies and consider them, if we do at all, only when they are displayed as trivialized amusements. Moreover, some of us pay a steep price to visit a fictitious world of pleasure so that we can avoid the world we live in. Some argue, furthermore, that the packaging of entertainment for consumption has dispossessed us of the pleasure and fulfillment of participation; we are relegated to the status of audience members at a show someone else is performing. We no longer produce our own music, content to listen to someone else's song instead. Rather than make up our own stories, we watch movies. And the pervasiveness of entertainment in our lives means it is possible that being entertained may become preferable to going to work or school, even being with family and friends. So while we may have become expert at getting away and amusing ourselves, where are we going? Are we headed for a creative, fulfilling, and imaginative future? Or a tomorrow where the needs we wish to have met are also constructed by a mega-corporation?

The background readings here look at entertainment from various points along this continuum. As you read, you'll look closely at a bias that is implicit in the entertainment media. Every medium has a bias, but entertaining media seem especially to discourage us from thinking critically about what we are consuming, from noticing bias in the representations of different people, for example. The underlying message of entertainment media seems to be "don't think too hard about it, just enjoy." We are coaxed to prefer amusement over analytical or empirical responses. The readings will look at how products and services are produced for the entertainment media. Stories and images take on new and fascinating forms when they are created with a sale in mind. And all of these writers have a position on what our demand for play gives us and costs us as individual and communities and as a culture. Those positions vary from grouchiness to excitement (though no one is without at least some concerns.)

BACKGROUND READINGS

WHERE THE GIRLS ARE
SUSAN DOUGLAS

A professor of media and American studies at Hampshire College, Susan Douglas has written scholarly books as well as review articles in popular magazines like the Village Voice *and the* Nation. *In the introduction to* Where the Girls Are *(1994), she identifies herself as a white, middle-class baby boomer, an academic, and a consumer of mass media as well as "an American woman." This is the writer, then, who takes a "tour through the images" of the past four decades, confronting her reader with the patterns in which women have been "imprinted" by mainstream entertainment. Douglas points to programming and advertising that has invited and, perhaps, coerced women into buying—literally and figuratively—a contradictory identity.*

When I open *Vogue,*... I am simultaneously infuriated and seduced, grateful to escape temporarily into a narcissistic paradise where I'm the center of the universe, outraged that completely unattainable standards of wealth and beauty exclude me and most women I know from the promised land. I adore the materialism; I despise the materialism. I yearn for the self-indulgence; I think the self-indulgence is repellent. I want to look beautiful; I think wanting to look beautiful is about the most dumb-ass goal you could have. The magazine stokes my desire; the magazine triggers my bile. And this doesn't only happen when I'm reading *Vogue;* it happens all the time. The TV grilling of Anita Hill made many of us shake our fists in rage; Special K ads make most of us hide our thighs in shame. On the one hand, on the other hand— that's not just me—that's what it means to be a woman in America.[1]

To explain this schizophrenia, we must reject the notion that popular culture for girls and women didn't matter, or that it consisted only of retrograde images. American women today are a bundle of contradictions because much of the media imagery we grew up with was itself filled with mixed messages about what women should and should not do, what women could and could not be. This was true in the 1960s, and it is true today. The media, of course, urged us to be pliant, cute, sexually available, thin, blond, poreless, wrinkle-free, and deferential to men. But it is easy to forget that the media also suggested we could be rebellious, tough, enterprising, and shrewd. And much of what we watched was porous, allowing us to accept *and* rebel against what we saw and how it was presented.[2] The jig-saw pieces of our inner selves have moved around in relation to the jigsaw imagery of the media, and it is the ongoing rearrangement of these shards on the public screens of America, and the private screens of our minds, that is the forgotten story of American culture over the past thirty-five years. The mass consumption of that culture, the ways in which the shards got reassembled, actually encouraged many of us to embrace feminism in some form. For throughout this process, we have found ourselves pinioned between two voices, one insisting we were equal, the other insisting we were subordinate. After a while, the tension became unbearable, and millions of women found they were no longer willing to tolerate the gap between the promises of equality and the reality of inequality.[3]

At first blush it might seem that "He's So Fine" or *A Summer Place* had absolutely nothing to do with feminism, except that they contributed to an ideology many of us would eventually react against. Those who regard much of 1960s pop culture as sexist trash, and who remember all too well how the network news dismissively covered the women's movement in the 1970s, may be loath to regard the mass media as agents of feminism. But here's the contradiction we confront: the news media, TV shows, magazines, and films of the past four decades may have turned *feminism* into a dirty word, but they also made feminism inevitable.

To appreciate the mass media's often inadvertent role in this transformation, we must head down a memory lane that has been blockaded for far too long. We must rewatch and relisten, but with a new mission: to go where the girls are. And, as we consider the rise of feminism, we must move beyond the standard political histories of a handful of feminist leaders and explore the cultural history of the millions who became their followers. It's time to reclaim a past too frequently ignored, hooted at, and dismissed, because it is in these images of women that we find the roots of who we are now. This is a different sort of archeology of the 1950s, '60s, and '70s than we're used to, because it excavates and holds to the light remnants of a collective female past not usually thought of as making serious history.

5 What are my credentials for writing such a book? Allow me to introduce myself. I am one of those people *The Wall Street Journal,* CBS News, and *Spy* magazine love to make fun of: I am a professor of media studies. You know what that means. I probably teach entire courses on the films of Connie Francis, go to academic conferences

where the main intellectual exchange is trading comic books, never make my students read books, and insist that Gary Lewis and the Playboys were more important than Hegel, John Dos Passos, or Frances Perkins. All I do now, of course, is study Madonna. The reason I chose the media over, say, the Renaissance or quantum mechanics is that I don't like to read, don't know much about history, and needed desperately to find a way to watch television for a living.

This, anyway, is the caricature of people like me. See, if enough people think studying the media is a waste of time, then the media themselves can seem less influential than they really are. Then they get off the hook for doing what they do best: promoting a white, upper-middle-class, male view of the world that urges the rest of us to sit passively on our sofas and fantasize about consumer goods while they handle the important stuff, like the economy, the environment, or child care.[4] If it was important enough to them to spend hundreds of thousands of dollars to bring us *Mr. Ed*, Enjoli perfume ("I can bring home the bacon, fry it up in the pan, and never, ever let you forget you're a man"), and *Dallas*, then it's important enough for us to figure out why.

Now, there has been ample documentation in the past few years that the mass media are hardly a girl's best friend. It seems as if every time we turn on the TV or open a magazine advertisers try to make those of us born before 1970 feel like over-the-hill lumps of hideous cellulite in desperate need of a scalpel and a lifetime supply of Retin-A. Women like me are not too happy with the seeming insistence of those selling hair dye or skin cream that unless we all look like Christie Brinkley, act like Krystle Carrington, and shut up already about equal rights, we're worthless. Women *are* angry at the media, because a full twenty years after the women's movement, diet soda companies, women's magazines, and the *Sports Illustrated* "swimsuit issue" still bombard us with smiling, air-brushed, anorexic, and compliant women whose message seems to be "Shut up, get a face-lift, and stop eating." One of the things we are angriest about, because the strategy has been so successful, is the way we have become alienated from our own bodies. We have learned to despise the curves, bulges, stretch marks, and wrinkles that mean we've probably worked hard in and out of our homes, produced some fabulous children, enjoyed a good meal or two, tossed back a few drinks, laughed, cried, gotten sunburned more than once, endured countless indignities, and, in general, led pretty full and varied lives. The mass media often trivialize our lives and our achievements, narrowing the litmus test of female worth to one question: Does she have dimpled thighs or crow's-feet? If so, onto the trash heap of history. No wonder we want to throw our TV sets out the window whenever an ad for Oil of Olay or Ultra Slim-Fast comes on.

But our relationship to the mass media isn't quite this simple. If we are honest, we have to admit that we have loved the media as much as we have hated them—and often at exactly the same time. After all, the mass media did give us The Four Tops, Bette Midler, *The Avengers*, Aretha Franklin, *Saturday Night Live*, Johnny Carson, and *Cagney & Lacey*. And even though I spend an inordinate amount of time yelling back at my television set and muttering expletives as I survey the ads in *Glamour* or the covers of *Vanity Fair*, I don't always hate the media, or think the media are—or have been—always bad. We all have our guilty media pleasures, the ones that comfort us at the end of a rotten day or allow us to escape into a fantasy world where we really do get to soak in a bubble bath whenever we want. No, the point here is that we love *and* hate the media, at exactly the same time, in no small part because the media, simultaneously, love *and* hate women. (Here I depart from the argument in *Backlash,* Susan Faludi's important polemic on how the media have mounted a major war against women since the mid-1980s. While Faludi is extremely convincing about the breadth and depth of the backlash against feminism, she casts the media as all bad, and she suggests that this kind of backlash is relatively recent. Neither point is true. The war that has been raging in the media is not a simplistic war against women but a complex struggle between feminism and antifeminism that has reflected, reinforced, and exaggerated our culture's ambivalence about women's roles for over thirty-five years.)

Since the 1950s, women growing up in America have been indelibly imprinted by movies, television, ads, magazines, and popular music. Now it's true that, when we're born, we come with this twisted coil of DNA inside us that determines whether we'll be shy or gregarious, athletic or klutzy, cautions or daring. And we have our parents, who, for better or worse, twist that coil around in certain ways so that some kinks we can never get out, no matter how much we spend on psychotherapy or channeling—and some kinks we wouldn't want to. But we're hardly born complete, and our parents, as they will quickly attest, rarely got the last word, or even the first. Little kids have all these cracks and crevices in their puttylike psychological edifices, and one relentless dispenser of psychic Spackle is the mass media. They help fill in those holes marked "What does it mean to be a girl?" or "What is an American?" or "What is happiness?"

10   Along with our parents, the mass media raised us, socialized us, entertained us, comforted us, deceived us, disciplined us, told us what we could do and told us what we couldn't. And they played a key role in turning each of us into not one woman but many women—a pastiche of all the good women and bad women that came to us through the printing presses, projectors, and airwaves of America. This has been one of the mass media's most important legacies for female consciousness: the erosion of anything resembling a unified self. Presented with an array of media archetypes, and given morality tales in which we identify first with one type, then another, confronted by quizzes in women's magazines so we can gauge whether we're romantic, assertive, in need of changing our perfume, or ready to marry, women have grown accustomed to compartmentalizing ourselves into a whole host of personas, which we occupy simultaneously.

For kids born after World War II, the media's influence was unprecedented. The living rooms, dens, and bedrooms of America became places where people's primary activity was consuming the *mass media* in some form or other, and much of this media was geared to the fastest-growing market segment, baby boomers. Media executives knew if they were going to succeed with this group, already known for its rising rebellion against fifties conformity, they would have to produce songs or movies or TV shows that spoke to that rebellion. They would have to create products specifically for teens and definitely not for adults. And they would have to heighten the sense of distance between "cool," alienated teenagers and fuddy-duddy, stick-in-the-mud parents who yelled at us to turn the lights out when we weren't using them and often counseled fiscal restraint. Spending without guilt, and with abandon, in defiance of our parents, was "with it" and "hip." "Hey you—yeah, *you,*" yelled the advertisers, record producers, magazine publishers, and TV networks of America, "we've got something special just for you girls."

We were the first generation of preteen and teenage girls to be so relentlessly isolated as a distinct market segment.[5] Advertisers and their clients wanted to convey a sense of entitlement, and a sense of generational power, because those attitudes on our part meant profits for them. So at the same time that the makers of Pixie Bands, Maybelline eyeliner, Breck shampoo, and *Beach Blanket Bingo* reinforced our roles as cute, airheaded girls, the mass media produced a teen girl popular culture of songs, movies, TV shows, and magazines that cultivated in us a highly self-conscious sense of importance, difference, and even rebellion. Because young women became critically important economically, as a market, the suspicion began to percolate among them, over time, that they might be important culturally, and then politically, as a generation.[6] Instead of co-opting rebellion, the media actually helped promote it.

Historians will argue, and rightly so, that American women have been surrounded by contradictory expectations since at least the nineteenth century.[7] My point is that this situation intensified with the particular array of media technology and outlets that interlocked in people's homes after World War II. It wasn't simply the sheer size and ubiquity of the media, although these, of course, were important. It was also the fact that the media themselves were going through a major transformation in how they regarded and marketed to their audiences that heightened, dramatically, the contradictions in the images and messages they produced. Radio, TV, magazines, popular music, film—these were the *mass* media, predicated on the notion of a national, unified market, and their raison d'être was to reach as many people as possible. To appeal to the "lowest common denominator," TV and advertisers offered homogenized, romanticized images of America, which, especially under the influence of the cold war and McCarthyism, eschewed controversy and reinforced middle-class, sexually repressed, white-bread norms and values.

Even in the 1950s, however, there was rebellion against these sappy representations of American life, as indicated by the rising popularity of rock 'n' roll, FM radio, "beat" poetry and literature, and foreign films. These cultural insurgencies drove home the fact that the media market was not national and unified but divided—especially, but not solely, by age. Even so, media executives tried to please simultaneously the "lowest common denominator" and the more rebellious sectors of the audience, often in the same song, TV show, or film. By the 1960s, the contradictions grew wider and more obvious, and the images and messages of this period were obsessed with shifting gender codes, riven with generational antagonisms, schizophrenic about female sexuality, relentless in their assaults on the imperfections of the female face and body, and determined to straddle the widening gap between traditional womanhood and the young, hip, modern "chick."

15   These contradictions still exist, and the mass media continue to provide us with stories, images, and whopping rationalizations that shape how we make sense of the roles we assume in our families, our workplaces, our society. These stories and images don't come from Pluto: our deepest aspirations and anxieties are carefully, relentlessly researched. Then they're repackaged and sold back to us as something we can get simply by watching or buying. Despite what TV executives like to say, the mass media are not simple mirrors, reflecting "reality" to us. The news, sitcoms, or ads are not reflections of the world; they are very careful, deliberate constructions. To borrow Todd Gitlin's metaphor, they are more like fun-house mirrors that distort and warp "real-

ity" by exaggerating and magnifying some features of American life and values while collapsing, ignoring, and demonizing others.[8] Certainly there is a symbiotic relationship between the media executives, who think we're morons, and the audience, many of whom think media executives are cognitively challenged. But let's remember that they have the cameras, the production facilities, and the money, and we don't.

This doesn't mean that the media are all-powerful, or that audiences are just helpless masses of inarticulate protoplasm, lying there ready to believe whatever they see or hear. Hardly anyone with any sense believes that six rich, jowly, white guys in pinstriped suits sit together in some skyscraper and gleefully conspire to inundate all of us with the message that scrubbing the mildew off bathroom tiles is, for women, akin to a religious epiphany. Viewers *do* resist the homogenizing pull of TV, by ignoring it when it's on, yelling "Bull-shit!" at the commercials, channel clicking, or deconstructing the news.[9] We might not buy into Dan Rather's newscast, Folgers ads that pretend that having an infant is romantic, or a Rambo movie's proposals for international diplomacy. We also live real lives apart from the media, and our everyday experiences all too frequently contradict the version of reality put out by Lorimar Productions, Joan Lunden, or AT&T.

But some images and messages are harder to resist than others, like the one that insists that a forty-year-old woman should have thighs like a twelve-year-old boy's, and that no self-respecting woman should ever have wrinkles. This is because women, much more than men, have learned from ads, movies, and TV shows that they must constantly put themselves under surveillance. In standard Hollywood movies, men act—they solve crimes, engage in sword fights, right social injustice, and swing from vines—while women are on screen to be looked at. Constantly positioned on staircases, stages, rugs, beds, beaches, even tables, their bodies exposed while men are covered by sheets, robes, boxer shorts, or jungle gear, women are primarily physical specimens to be surveyed intently by the camera, the male characters in the film, and, of course, the audience.[10] Print ads in particular reinforce this, with their endless images of pouty-lipped, beautiful women looking at themselves in the mirror, being gazed at adoringly by men and by other women consumed with envy. Women learn to turn themselves into objects to be scrutinized; they learn they must continually watch themselves being watched by others, whether they're walking on the beach, drinking a beer, entering a restaurant, or rocking a baby.[11]

In part because they got us when we were so young, and in part because the mass media have been obsessed with defining—and exaggerating—codes of masculinity and femininity, they have ensnared us in an endless struggle for gender self-definition. With the recent heavy promotion of baldness remedies, bodies by Soloflex, and macho cosmetics lines, men, too, may learn the pleasures of such relentless self-consciousness. But certainly advertising, movies, and TV shows have also taught men how to look at, assess, and treat women, so this media imagery comes back at us in our own interpersonal relationships, and rarely in ways we find helpful.

Throughout our lives we have been getting profoundly contradictory messages about what it means to be an American woman. Our national mythology teaches us that Americans are supposed to be independent, rugged individuals who are achievement-oriented, competitive, active, shrewd, and assertive go-getters, like Benjamin Franklin, Thomas Edison, or Ross Perot. Women, however, are supposed to be dependent, passive, nurturing types, uninterested in competition, achievement, or success, who should conform to the wishes of the men in their lives.[12] It doesn't take a rocket scientist to see that these two lists of behavioral traits are mutually exclusive, and that women are stuck right in the middle. What a woman has to do, on her own, is cobble together some compromise between these traits that is appropriate to her class, race, and interpersonal relations with her family, friends, co-workers, and lovers.

20   Women also stand at the intersection of another major cultural contradiction: the war between what academics call the "producer" ethos and the "consumer" ethos.[13] The work ethic, with its emphasis on industriousness, thrift, deferred gratification, and self-denial, was crucial to establishing the United States as an economic giant by the late nineteenth and early twentieth centuries. But then this problem arose. Someone had to buy all the stuff the country's factories were producing. And much of what was getting produced wasn't necessities, it was conveniences and little luxuries. People who had had the virtues of the work ethic beaten into them by hickory branches and McGuffey's readers weren't going to buy all these things, especially on credit. So advertisers had to start convincing people to reverse their value systems completely, to spend, to be self-indulgent, to gratify themselves immediately, and to feel entitled to plenty of leisure time. Since this consumer ethos is extremely seductive, but the producer ethos still holds us in its unforgiving and guilt-inducing grip, we oscillate uneasily between the two. This has been especially true for women, traditionally the primary consumers in America, who were also expected to be models of productivity and efficiency, not to mention self-sacrifice, when running their households. The American woman has thus emerged as a bundle of contradictions, seeking to be simultaneously passive and active, outspoken and quiet, selfish and selfless, thrifty and profligate, daring and scared, and who had better know which persona to assume when.

My generation grew up internalizing an endless film loop of fairy-tale princesses, beach bunnies, witches, flying nuns, bionic women, and beauty queens, a series of flickering images that urged us, since childhood, to be all these things all the time. We grew up in different places, with different parents, and with wildly varying class and ethnic backgrounds. There is much that women my age don't have in common. Yet we do have a shared history of listening to the Chiffons, watching *Bewitched,* wearing miniskirts, idolizing Diana Ross, singing "I Am Woman," watching *Charlie's Angels,* being converted by Gloria Steinem, Germaine Greer, and Betty Friedan, hooting over *Dallas* and *Dynasty* (but not missing a single week), and, as a result, becoming women with a profound love-hate relationship with the mass media, and with the cultural values the mass media convey.

Like all histories, my account of our relationship with this popular culture is neither objective nor exhaustive; rather, it is idiosyncratic, and replete with the sorts of biases that come from my having been raised in a particular place and time. I am a white, middle-class woman—now a wife and mother—who grew up in a place that was something between a small town and a suburb, who went to college and then to graduate school, who has always lived in the Northeast, and who has a proven track record of consuming vast amounts of media imagery. I write this book not from the perspective of someone who was ever a feminist leader or a political activist but rather from the perspective of someone who, like most women, watched from the sidelines, yet who found being a spectator an increasingly political and politicizing act.

Because of who I am, this history cannot speak for everyone. Every woman has her own story. Some of us were smiling baton twirlers, or domesticated members of the Junior Homemakers of America, or gum-popping, leather-clad hair hoppers who hung out at the Laundromat. Some of us were quiet and shy, members of none of these stereotypically female groups. But because we were all culturally united, in an often sick and twisted way, by Walt Disney, the nightly news, Mark Eden Bust Developers, *The Mary Tyler Moore Show,* Cyndi Lauper, and ads for skin creams with "advanced delivery systems," we recognize this history as a shared history. Although I can hardly speak for women of color, working-class women, or lesbians, we often experienced the same very narrow, parochial kind of imagery that made white, upper-middle-class lives the norm and everything else deviant.

In my tour through the images of the past four decades, my goal is to expose, review, and, at times, make fun of the media-induced schizophrenia so many of us feel, while showing how it has produced tension, anger, and uncertainty in everyday women. Most women take for granted their own conflicted relationships to the mass media. They assume they are the only ones who love and hate *Vogue* at the same time, the only ones riddled with internal contradictions about whether to be assertive or diplomatic, gentle or tough. And too many assume that such contradictory feelings are unusual, abnormal. They aren't. Most women feel this because they've been socialized by the mass media, and women should know that feeling these contradictions on a daily basis is what it means to be an American woman. And, contrary to media stereotypes, such contradictions and ambivalence are also at the heart of what it means to be a feminist.

25   Our pop culture past isn't *all* embarrassing, and it's not irrelevant to how we feel or what we face today. Some of it was pretty goofy—I mean, identical cousins, get real—but much of it requires a second look. History, including this history, matters. It may help to explain why American women are both mad as hell and yet resigned, at times even happy, to leave things the way they are. This history also helps to explain why so many women are ambivalent about feminism, shunning the label but embracing so many of the precepts. And in the end it reveals why the mass media are both our best allies and our most lethal enemies.

Notes

1. Various feminist scholars have studied and documented women's contradictory responses to the mass media. See Janice Radway, *Reading the Romance* (Chapel Hill: University of North Carolina Press, 1984); Linda Williams, "'Something Else Besides a Mother': *Stella Dallas* and the Maternal Melodrama," in Christine Gledhill, ed., *Home Is Where the Heart Is* (London: British Film Institute, 1987); Judith Mayne, "The Woman at the Keyhole: Women's Cinema and Feminist Film Criticism," in Mary Ann Doane et al., eds., *Re-Vision: Essays in Feminist Film Criticism* (Frederick, MD: University Publications of America, 1984); Susan McClary, *Feminine Endings: Music, Gender and Sexuality* (Minneapolis: University of Minnesota Press, 1991). Feminist video artists also were some of the first to explore these contradictory relationships to the media. See Joan Braderman, *Natalie Didn't Drown,* © 1983, distributed by Video Data Bank, Chicago.
2. For a summary of the media's power, and of viewers' resistance to that power, see Justin Lewis, *The Ideological Octopus* (New York: Routledge, 1991).
3. Chantal Mouffe, "Hegemony and New Political Subjects: Toward a New Concept of Democracy," in Cary Nelson and Lawrence Grossberg, eds., *Marxism and the Interpretation of Culture* (Urbana: University of Illinois Press, 1988), pp. 94–95.

4. For scholarly analysis and documentation of the biases and impact of the news media, see Herbert Gans, *Deciding What's News* (New York: Vintage, 1980); Todd Gitlin, *The Whole World Is Watching* (Berkeley: University of California Press, 1980); Michael Parenti, *Inventing Reality* (New York: St. Martin's Press, 1986); and Noam Chomsky and Edward Hermann, *Manufacturing Consent: The Political Economy of the Mass Media* (New York: Pantheon, 1988).

5. Landon Jones, *Great Expectations: America and the Baby Boom Generation* (New York: Coward, McCann & Geoghegan, 1980), p. 73.

6. This point has been emphasized by Barbara Ehrenreich, Elizabeth Hess, and Gloria Jacobs in *Re-Making Love: The Feminization of Sex* (Garden City, NY: Anchor Press, Doubleday, 1986), p. 29.

7. Carroll Smith Rosenberg, *Disorderly Conduct: Visions of Gender in Victorian America* (New York: Alfred A. Knopf, 1985). See Wini Breines's discussion of the contradictions surrounding girls in the 1950s in *Young, White and Miserable*.

8. Gitlin, *The Whole World Is Watching*, p. 29.

9. John Fiske has been one of the most important advocates of viewer resistance to mass media images. See "Television: Polysemy and Popularity," in *Critical Studies in Mass Communication,* vol. 3, December 1986, pp. 391–408; *Television Culture* (London: Methuen, 1987); and "British Cultural Studies," in Robert Allen, ed., *Channels of Discourse* (Chapel Hill: University of North Carolina Press, 1987).

10. Laura Mulvey, "Visual Pleasure and Narrative Cinema," *Screen,* Autumn 1975, pp. 6–18.

11. John Berger, *Ways of Seeing* (New York: Penguin, 1977), pp. 46–47.

12. Mirra Komarovsky, "Cultural Contradictions and Sex Roles," *American Journal of Sociology,* vol. 52, 1946, pp. 184–189; Maren Lockwood Carden, *The New Feminist Movement* (New York: Russell Sage Foundation, 1974), p. 23.

13. Much of this work on cultural contradictions within the media was inspired by Jürgen Habermas, *Legitimation Crisis* (Boston: Beacon Press, 1975). For an impressive application of these ideas to popular culture see George Lipsitz, "The Meaning of Memory: Family, Class and Ethnicity in Early Network Television," in Lipsitz, *Time Passages* (Minneapolis: University of Minnesota Press, 1990); and T. J. Jackson Lears, "From Salvation to Realization: Advertising and the Therapeutic Roots of the Consumer Culture, 1880–1930," in Richard Wightman Fox and T. J. Jackson Lears, eds., *The Culture of Consumption* (New York: Pantheon, 1983).

Rereading Actively

1. Douglas grounds her introduction with a series of contradictions, including the idea that women hate and love the entertainment media that empowers and objectifies them. With a partner or in a small group, discuss why Douglas raises these contradictions. What rhetorical purpose is served by beginning this way?

2. Review the article and identify passages that explain the contradictory identity of women as it is portrayed in entertainment media. What is this contradictory identity, according to Douglas?

3. In a small group, review the article, focusing on passages that elaborate Douglas's theory of media. Discuss these passages, and then write a brief summary of Douglas's theory in your journal.

4. What purposes seem to be served by Douglas's frequent references to "her" experiences and those of "her generation"?

5. Explain Douglas's reference to feminism in the final paragraph. Why does she distinguish between the "label" and the "precepts" of feminism? How might this move affect a reader's response to her introduction?

Exploring Your Responses

6. Drawing on your own experience with entertainment media, freewrite a dialogue with Douglas about her media history. Tell her which parts of her history are compelling and which parts seem unpersuasive.

7. In a small group, brainstorm contradictory images of men and women in the entertainment media. Discuss the different meanings these images have for men and women, in terms of how they may empower individuals or force them to accept stereotypes.

8. Freewrite a reflection on how your gender is represented in a mass-media entertainment you like to consume.

9. Review Douglas's conclusion and then write a reflection on how you feel about the "label" feminism and the principles of gender equality.

THE ENTERTAINMENT ECONOMY

MICHAEL MANDEL, MARK LANDLER ET AL.

This collaborative effort by Business Week *staff writers in New York, Los Angeles, Miami, Philadelphia, and San Francisco first appeared in 1994 as a* Business Week *cover story. The purpose of the article is to offer information about the emergence of entertainment as a major sector of the U.S. and global economy. Writing in a magazine targeted at people interested in changing business opportunities, the authors treat the entertainment industry with a distinctly pro-market spin—even gambling may have some productive possibilities. But the authors also ask some economic and moral questions about the social impact of the new "entertainment industrial complex."*

Lee A. Iacocca knows a good opportunity when he sees one. Three weeks after he retired from Chrysler Corp. in late 1992, Iacocca and his wife visited Branson, MO, a small town nestled in the Ozarks that has become a mecca for country music. Strolling along Branson's rialto, a garish strip called Route 76, Iacocca was stunned to see crowds pouring out of theaters and dozens of construction cranes looming overhead. "I was never at Sutter's Creek during the Gold Rush," he says. "But that's what I imagine this was like."

Iacocca immediately wanted to get in on the action. And today, he is a partner in a production company that is bringing Broadway's *The Will Rogers Follies* to Branson. Separately, Iacocca is starting a merchant bank to finance new ventures in video games and entertainment. Why is he betting on fun and frolic? "I asked myself, 'What is the growing business in America that's exciting?'" he explains.

When one of the leading industrialists of the 1980s says that entertainment is the growth industry of the 1990s, it's a sure sign the U.S. economy is changing in dramatic ways. Indeed, Iacocca's instincts are confirmed by some startling numbers. Using data from the Bureau of Labor Statistics, *Business Week* calculates that the entertainment and recreation industries added 200,000 workers in 1993—a stunning 12% of all net new employment. That's more workers than were hired last year by the health-care industry, the preeminent job creator of the 1980s (chart, see below).

Or just look at the $340 billion that Americans spent last year on old-fashioned and newfangled ways to amuse themselves, from video rentals to theme parks to casinos. Europe and Japan used to mock America by calling it a "Mickey Mouse" economy. Well, they're right. By any yardstick, Mickey and his friends have become a major engine for U.S. economic growth. Since the economy turned up in 1991, entertainment and recreation—not health care or autos—have provided the biggest boost to consumer spending (chart, see below).

5   The entertainment economy has not revved up without some noisy backfires. The loudest by far came on Feb. 22, when Bell Atlantic Corp. called off its megamerger with Tele-Communications Inc. Four months earlier, Wall Street had hailed the deal as a sign that telephone and cable companies were ready to throw a ribbon of electronic highway across the country, bringing TV viewers a rich menu of entertainment and information. But after the FCC cut cable rates, the Bell Atlantic-TCI deal turned out to be built on speculative sand.

Still, the sinking of one merger should not obscure the already huge momentum of the entertainment economy. Interactive technology isn't likely to produce much revenue until the late 1990s. But whatever their interest in the prospect of 500 TV channels tomorrow, it's clear that Americans already have an almost insatiable thirst for the forms of entertainment that are here today.

Staggering Array

Consider that over the last 10 years, entertainment and recreation have claimed a steadily increasing share of consumer spending (chart, see below). Or that since 1991, consumers have boosted their outlays on entertainment and recreation by some 13%, adjusted for inflation—more than twice the growth rate of overall consumer spending. Small wonder, then, that the day after he scuttled his merger, TCI President John C. Malone was already plotting his next sally—by some accounts an investment in a Hollywood studio or in home-video giant Blockbuster Entertainment Corp.

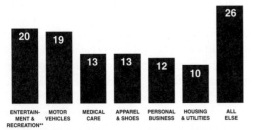

FUN POWERS SPENDING...

INCREASE IN CONSUMER SPENDING, 1991-93*
BILLIONS OF 1987 DOLLARS

ENTERTAIN-MENT & RECREATION**	MOTOR VEHICLES	MEDICAL CARE	APPAREL & SHOES	PERSONAL BUSINESS	HOUSING & UTILITIES	ALL ELSE
20	19	13	13	12	10	26

*GROWTH IN REAL SPENDING ABOVE THAT ACCOUNTED FOR BY POPULATION GROWTH
**EXCEPT HOME COMPUTERS

DATA: COMMERCE DEPT., *BUSINESS WEEK*

...AND EMPLOYMENT GROWTH

	EMPLOYMENT GROWTH, 1992-93 THOUSANDS OF WORKERS	1993 EMPLOYMENT THOUSANDS OF WORKERS
ENTERTAINMENT AND RECREATION All producers and distributors of entertainment and recreation products and services	204	4,482
HEALTHCARE Makers of pharmaceuticals and medical equipment; drugstores; hospitals; doctors' offices; and related industries	187	11,793
AUTO INDUSTRY Makers of motor vehicles and parts; auto dealers; gas stations and auto repair shops; and related industries	33	4,272

DATA: BUREAU OF LABOR STATISTICS

Americans stand to gain much from this frenetic activity. Like the defense and financial-services industries in the 1980s, the entertainment economy is creating tremendous prosperity. From Branson to Las Vegas to Orlando, companies such as Walt Disney, Blockbuster, and Matsushita's MCA are breaking ground for a staggering array of theme parks, theaters, casinos, and ballparks. More than $13 billion in big entertainment projects are in the pipeline, with many more to come....

Dino Designs

Beneath the ground, TCI, Time Warner, and other cable-TV and telephone companies are snaking fiberoptic wires that will bring interactive services, such as movies and games at the touch of a button, into America's living rooms. Silicon Valley is riding the wave as well by designing the software and networking systems to turn the TV set into a multimedia machine.

10   "The entertainment industry is now the driving force for new technology, as defense used to be," says Edward R. McCracken, CEO of Silicon Graphics Inc., one of a growing number of companies that supply technology and software to the entertainment industry. "Making a dinosaur for *Jurassic Park* is exactly the same as designing a car."

It may also be more—well—fun. Iacocca notes that the auto industry "is tough and cyclical as hell." By contrast, entertainment and recreation saw consumer spending increase right through the recession. And entertainment is profiting from the exploding global appetite for American movies, TV programs, and other entertainment products. Indeed, Hollywood earned foreign revenues of some $8 billion in 1993, which took a big bite out of the $63 billion foreign trade gap.

At home, the entertainment boom is receiving added lift from potent economic forces. With the economy recovering sharply and productivity on the rise, personal incomes are starting to climb again. In 1993, real wages and salaries for U. S. workers went up significantly for the first time since 1986. At the same time, one of their key expenses—medical bills—is rising more slowly than the breakneck pace of the late 1980s. The result: Consumers have more discretionary money to spend on fun.

Demographics play a key role as well: The number of households headed by 34- to 54-year-olds is growing, and they spend far more on entertainment and recreation than anybody else. "Baby boomers are moving into middle age," says Gerald M. Levin, chairman of Time Warner Inc. "And they seem to have brought their movie-loving habits with them." Not just movies, either: Time Warner is luring record numbers of boomers and their children to its Six Flags amusement parks.

Not everyone views the entertainment economy with unalloyed enthusiasm. For one thing, the fastest-growing part of the industry is gambling, which until recent years had an unseemly taint and was restricted to casinos in Vegas and Atlantic City. Now, starved for revenue, states and cities are allowing casinos to sprout from Indian reservations to riverfronts. Televised gambling is still illegal. But Raymond W. Smith, chairman of Bell Atlantic, points out that if it were legalized, interactive technology could turn gambling on TV into a vast new business.

15   In the face of staggering social problems such as homelessness and a troubled public education system, there's some reason to wonder whether spending billions on gambling is a wise idea. Even more innocent forms of entertainment—consumed in great quantities—may deprive us of the chance to enrich ourselves through

reading, conversation, or real experiences that haven't been filtered and packaged as entertainment commodities....

Uncertain Appetite

Even some media moguls, most of whom also publish books, profess to be uneasy. "I'm quite worried about reading," says Levin. "But I worry more about the quality of our education system than about whether entertainment is a big negative factor in our country's reading habits."

Social worries aside, the surge in entertainment investment could lead to overcapacity problems down the road if it outruns consumer demand. Companies are planning to spend tens of billions on the Information Highway over the next 5 to 10 years even though the savviest executives admit they can't predict the consumer appetite for interactive-TV services. And the flurry of building could eventually end in a glut not unlike the one that provoked the real estate crash of the early 1990s.

The result could be lost jobs, economic disappointment for regions that rely too heavily on the industry, and the ignominy of bankruptcy for some entertainment companies. "The question is: Will the market grow quickly enough to accommodate all the new players at the table?" asks Frank J. Biondi Jr., chief executive of Viacom Inc. "I think probably not."

Biondi is careful to distinguish between the growing home-entertainment market and what he thinks are more risky out-of-home ventures. After all, Viacom intends to merge with Blockbuster. The company arranged the deal to help it prevail in a takeover battle for Paramount Communications Inc., an entertainment company with a film studio. Still, Paramount also owns theme parks and sports teams. So by spending almost $10 billion for the company, Biondi and his boss, Sumner M. Redstone, are making a breathtaking bet on the vibrance of the entertainment economy—indoor and outdoor.

20   For now, the statistics seem to vindicate that gamble. Take the film industry: Wilkofsky Gruen Associates Inc., an economic consulting firm, estimates that domestic spending on filmed entertainment—box-office admissions, home video, and television—will total some $30 billion in 1994, up 7.4% from the previous year. To satisfy such demand, the major Hollywood studios will produce 198 films this year, up 10% from 1993.

Luddites

Americans are also buying more electronic gizmos on which to watch all those flicks. Sales of TVs and VCRs are up some 23% over the last two years, according to the Electronic Industries Assn. Meanwhile, over the same period, video-game sales, which were turbo-charged by hot games, such as Sonic the Hedgehog, rose by 18%, to $4 billion. Sales of electronics may grow even faster at the end of 1994, says Michael P. Schulhof, president of Sony Corp. of America. That's because Sony and other manufacturers are rolling out new products, such as multimedia video games.

Luddites among us still seem to be flocking to low-tech attractions, such as pro sports. Major League Baseball and the National Football League each added two new teams last year. And the National Hockey League added five franchises in the last three seasons, attracting new owners such as Blockbuster Chairman H. Wayne Huizenga and Walt Disney Co. Anaheim's Mighty Ducks may be fourth in their division, but Disney has sold 12,500 season tickets at up to $6,800 apiece. Huizenga, meanwhile, plans to build an arena for his Florida Panthers near a stadium for his newly acquired football team, the Miami Dolphins. The NHL is trying to grow by luring more families to its games. To do that, NHL Commissioner Gary B. Bettman is installing interactive games and other attractions in the unused portions of some of his arenas.

Family is the watchword for other entertainment categories as well. Both Blockbuster and Viacom's Nickelodeon unit are among those planning to build regional amusement centers that cater to boomers and their kids. Overall attendance at theme parks reached record levels in 1993, helped by attractions such as a stunt show based on the film *Batman* at Six Flags' Magic Mountain park in Valencia, CA.

Even live theater—which a few years ago seemed to be on the wane—is now booming. Consumer spending on country music, rock concerts, and other live attractions has soared over the last two years, to $6 billion, according to the Commerce Dept. Productions of *Phantom of the Opera* and *Cats* have raked in $2.5 billion worldwide. And so far this season, box-office receipts for stage shows in North America are 15% ahead of last year's record pace and may hit $1.1 billion.

Riverboat Bets

25 Such results have enticed Disney to produce its first Broadway show, based on the film *Beauty and the Beast.* Eventually, says Walt Disney Studios Chairman Jeffrey Katzenberg, dozens of Disney stage shows could be playing around the country. Disney also recently pledged $8 million to renovate the dilapidated New Amsterdam theater off New York City's Times Square. If it revitalizes the area, Disney would add a new chapter to the uneven history of entertainment companies and urban redevelopment....

Of all the entertainment engines, right now gambling is humming the fastest. Casinos took in about $13 billion in 1993, a figure gambling experts say will double by the year 2000. Throw in state lotteries, offtrack betting, and other forms of gambling, and Americans spent $27 billion on legal gambling last year, according to the Commerce Dept. That's as much as they spend on airline tickets. "People just love the excitement of betting," says Fort Worth investor Richard E. Rainwater, who holds options to buy 14% of slot-machine operator United Gaming Inc.

Casino operators are laying huge bets of their own with a bevy of new palaces in Las Vegas. At $1.1 billion, Kirk Kerkorian's MGM Grand is the most opulent. But Mirage Resorts isn't far behind with its $475 million Treasure Island. Both casinos are playing the family card by including theme parks and stunt shows in their vast complexes. But you don't have to travel to gamble anymore: Colorado, Mississippi, and Connecticut are among the states that allow riverboat or casino gaming, in an effort to generate needed revenue.

The states are also lured by gambling's promise of new jobs. The MGM Grand alone employs 8,000 people, from croupiers to cocktail waitresses. By comparison, BMW's new assembly plant in Spartanburg, S. C., will employ 2,000 workers. In New Orleans, which will soon have a $600 million Harrah's casino, gambling could create 15,000 jobs. And in Chicago, where gaming may soon be legalized, the number could be closer to 18,000. Depending on how many states legalize it, gaming could generate 500,000 new jobs nationwide in the next decade, says President Philip G. Satre, of casino operator Promus Cos.

Jobs Bonanza

True, casino jobs are generally unskilled and low-paying. But proponents of gambling argue that casinos offer an option for workers who might otherwise be left out of today's high-tech economy. Says J. Thomas Johnson, chairman of the Illinois Gaming Board: "They are the kinds of jobs needed for the workforce that's available."

30   The same argument is true of theme parks. Disney, for example, plans to spend $700 million on Disney's America, a theme park outside Washington that could generate thousands of jobs in the region. And Matsushita's MCA will create thousands more in Orlando, where it plans to build a second theme park and entertainment complex to complement its Universal Studios. Theme parks, and attractions already employ more than 40,000 workers in the Orlando area.

But the entertainment economy isn't only for ticket-takers and cocktail waitresses. As Hollywood ramps up, it will add more directors, producers, and key grips. Even below Arnold Schwarzenegger's level, movie employees are well paid. Average annual earnings for Hollywood are about $38,000, 50% above the average for manufacturing workers—and the gap is widening.

From the perspective of wages, the most promising segment of entertainment is the evolving business of multimedia technology. Companies are luring educated and creative people with well-paying jobs. Crystal Dynamics Inc., for example, now employs 60 staffers, up from 3 just 15 months ago, to design computer games for PCs and the new 3DO player. Salaries for new hires at the Palo Alto-based company range from $30,000 to $100,000.

Of course, job security in such a nascent industry is unpredictable. So, too, are jobs at casinos such as the MGM Grand. With so many vying for customers—even an expending pool—some will inevitably fail. For that matter, the entire entertainment economy may experience a wrenching shakeout if it ends up overbuilding or if consumers fail to embrace new interactive-TV services.

Slots in the Skills

Some experts also question whether the industry will be at war with itself, since it is pouring money into both home entertainment and out-of-home diversions. If consumers truly use their TV sets for a panoply of new activities, will they have time to visit Disneyland? "People need to get out of their homes," says Disney Chairman Michael D. Eisner. "Kids need to get away from their parents, the parents away from the kids." Eisner, whose company gets 40% of its revenue from theme parks, fervently hopes this economy is not only for the sedentary.

35   Of all the segments of the entertainment economy, the Information Highway generates the most angst among executives. They know it will be powered by entertainment. But the capital investments are gigantic: Time Warner and its telephone partner, US West Inc., have committed $5 billion to upgrade their networks for multimedia services. Next to these players, even MGM Grand's free-spending owner, Kirk Kerkorian, seems a piker.

The sums would be less daunting if executives knew that consumers really want to do more than vegetate in front of their TV sets. "We don't have the slightest idea of what people are going to buy," says Rupert Murdoch, who owns the 20th Century Fox studio.

Levin and other champions of the highway argue that it's not such a leap into the unknown. Despite technological snags, Time Warner still plans to offer interactive services to 4,000 cable subscribers in Orlando this year…. But the company is adding services only piecemeal. That way, it can determine what consumers want.

Skeptics argue that the new services will cannibalize existing businesses, such as home video. That's true, to a degree. But new delivery systems also enlarge the overall market. While some people will watch *The Fugitive* on video, rather than see it in a theater, more will see it—one way or the other. And some will see it both ways. Companies can recycle their products in other ways. Disney is using its Anaheim hockey team as an excuse to release a sequel to its 1992 film, *The Mighty Ducks.*

Finally, the industry is betting that technology will make entertainment more convenient for consumers, allowing them to pack fun into every nook and cranny of the day. Virgin Atlantic Airways Ltd., for example, is testing a machine that allows travelers to gamble while on international flights: Insert your credit card to play the slots or poker at 30,000 feet.

40   With an economy more and more dependent on amusement, though, Americans must ask themselves a serious question: Can we play hard enough to justify all the work and money now being spent? More than a good time hangs in the balance.

Rereading Actively

1. Mandel et al. open this article with an anecdote about Lee Iacocca. What does this reference seem to say about their assumed audience?

2. Review the article, identifying passages that explain the phrase "'Mickey Mouse' economy" (¶ 4). Write a short explanation of the multiple meanings of this phrase in your journal.

3. With a partner or in a small group, list and discuss the core dynamics of the entertainment economy. What makes it grow and contract, and how does it affect people?

4. Identify three passages where Mandel et al. discuss the downside of the entertainment economy. Explain their view of this downside in a brief journal entry.

Exploring Your Responses

5. Respond to the authors' view of the downside of the entertainment economy: Do their concerns seem valid to you? Why or why not?

6. In a small group, discuss one of the dynamics that were listed in question 3 as you see it in terms of a specific entertainment product that is available on campus or in the local community (e.g., Web surfing, a TV program, a movie, a sporting event). Develop a collaborative statement describing the convenience of the product as well as its impact on local consumers.

7. What are your entertainment consumption habits? In an extended freewrite, list the three forms of entertainment that you consume most and reflect on how healthy your habits are.

THE BLOCKBUSTER SCRIPT FACTORY
JAIME WOLF

A contributor to the New York Times Sunday Magazine *(from which this piece was excerpted) as well as other publications including the* Los Angeles Times, Mirabella, *and the* New Yorker, *Jaime Wolf reports on the film industry in addition to writing screenplays. So when he took this look behind the scenes in Hollywood in 1998, he had a clear view of the process of making entertainment for a mass market. To illustrate his thesis, he fabricates the production history of a fictitious movie. While he is poking fun at the recent crop of blockbusters, Wolf also offers a detailed description of how those movies are put together, implying there are reasons that blockbusters often seem to lack a "good script."*

In the course of what hollywood types refer to as "development," a screenplay's journey from first draft to production will frequently take it through the hands of several writers. Not long ago, I told my lawyer that the latest draft of an action-comedy a friend and I are writing for Columbia Pictures was nearly finished, and he replied, "Good, you'll hand it in just in time to be replaced." He was joking, but he also was not—"Small Soldiers," for instance, originally written by Gavin Scott, was purchased by Steven Spielberg in 1992, and successively revised by Anne Spielberg, Danny Rubin, Frank Deese and Lewis Colick, before a version by Adam Rifkin, incorporating Spielberg's suggestion that the titular soldiers be divided into two warring factions, was green-lighted for production last year. But in a world (to borrow the phrase favored by stentorian coming-attractions narrators) dominated by giant summer action movies, the development process hardly stops once a movie is deemed actually ready to shoot. These days, that's often when it picks up speed.

More and more commonly, screenwriters who labor to get a movie green-lighted merely stand at the head of a conveyor belt designed by producers and studios to precision-tool hits, sending their scripts along for subsequent handling by a small army of additional writers, each one specifically directed to beef up action scenes, to polish dialogue, to throw in some romance or ladle zingers over the proceedings. Within the industry, it's an open secret that the authors of elevated fare like "Chinatown," "Schindler's List," "Silence of the Lambs" and "Apollo 13" are regularly called in to make anonymous contributions to popcorn movies like "Con Air," "Twister," "Eraser" and "Mission: Impossible." As Robin Swicord, who is known for her adaptations of literary material like "Little Women," puts it: "What's the old saying? 'A camel is an animal built by committee.' Well, these movies are like camels."

As a way of illustrating the process a little more completely, meet Tim D.[1], one of those hot young screenwriters you hear about every so often who has yet to see any of his scripts produced. While working on an effects-driven fantasy called "Francis Ford Coppola's Sigmund Freud's The Interpretation of Dreams," which Dreamworks is developing for the famous director, Tim comes up with a new idea: what if, in a preapocalyptic near-future with the country riven by internal conflict, armed terrorists, in an attempt to chip away at national morale, started hijacking entire baseball teams, holding them hostage and forcing them to miss their games?

Suppose on July 4 weekend, they kidnapped the New York Yankees, threatening their traditional Independence Day contest against the Red Sox? What if the Pentagon recruited an elite squad of smooth-fielding, power-hitting anti-terrorists whose job it was to play in the absent team's stead while also hunting down the bad guys and rescuing the hostage ballplayers? Baseball Commandos! Imagine the opening scene, when after the Red Sox players are introduced and run onto the field, a jet plane streaks overhead, and 15 men parachute down into the stadium, the announcer's voice introducing them, one by one. America's team: the Baseball Commandos!

Tim runs the idea by his agent, summarizing it as "'The Dirty Dozen' on a ball field." His agent responds enthusiastically to the pitch, sure that he can sell it, though he points out that baseball teams really only have nine players. "O.K.," Tim says, "it's 'Die Hard' in New York City." The agent reminds him that "Die Hard With a Vengeance" had already been "Die Hard" in New York City. "Your players, the Commandos," he says, "they should be underdogs, right? Sure, they can defuse a bomb, but can they hit the sinking curve? It's 'The Mighty Ducks' with guns."

5   This potent catch phrase, "'The Mighty Ducks' with guns," along with a panoramic description of the team's entrance, puts "Baseball Commandos" over. It is a clear-cut summer movie, a slam-bang actionfest, with roles for several stars. Every studio in town bids on the project, and when the dust settles, Tim is hired to turn his idea into a screenplay.

While Tim is off writing his first draft, the studio sends a story outline of "Baseball Commandos" to several major stars. Bruce Willis commits to the role of Boog Parker, the Commandos' first baseman, hostage negotiator and team leader. Will Smith agrees to play Freedom "da Bomb" Washington, a hotshot outfielder and demolitions expert. Kurt Russell, who played minor-league ball in real life, also expresses interest in being on the team. In short, decisions that will affect the film's final shape start being made before anybody has even seen a script.

Tim's first draft is full of potential, but incomplete. It is too schematic, simply alternating from the drama of the baseball game between the Commandos and the Red Sox to the battle between the evil terrorists and the Commandos. There is something flat and video-game-ish about it. This is always the crucial point, where the studio considers pulling the plug, but there are other considerations, including the actors' commitments—how can you *not* make a movie with Willis and Smith?—and deals for promotional tie-ins. Ultimately, the decision is made to crash the project through.

The studio calls in Jonathan Hensleigh[2] to address the overall structure of the script. Beefing up the suspense and dramatic logic of the story, Hensleigh disguises the Commandos as the Yankees' Newark farm club, flown in to substitute. To make Spartan Sizemore, the terrorist leader, a more compelling villain, Hensleigh has the group now not only hold the Yankees hostage, but also wire the stadium to blow. Overall, he punctuates the film with a steady rhythm of escalating action sequences.

When he is finished, casting continues: to appeal to women, Lucy Lawless, Linda Hamilton and Roseanne are cast as Commandos, a move that will necessitate the rewriting of their parts. Callie Khouri[3] is brought in for the job, contributing, among other things, a memorable line spoken by Roseanne's character, catcher Ruth "Babe" Orsini: "You gotta wonder about ballplayers who run around calling themselves Pee Wee." Separately, Michael Tolkin[4] and Steven Zaillian[5] are hired to work on the human element, deepening the story lines of several of the fans in attendance at the game: a pair of Boston teenagers who ride the bus to New York City for the first time; a Puerto Rican from East Harlem and his girlfriend, and a Bronx homegirl who takes her brother's ticket after he is shot by a man who turns out to be one of the terrorists and who ultimately helps Will Smith find the detonator beneath the stadium. Ron Shelton[6], who doesn't usually do rewrite work, is prevailed upon to take over the baseball scenes, adding the part of an autistic relief pitcher—Pearl Jam's lead singer, Eddie Vedder, in his first major film role. (He also agrees to write and perform for the soundtrack.) For a motivational speech that Bruce Willis delivers during the seventh-inning stretch, Shelton cribs from the writings of A. Bartlett Giamatti, comparing baseball to Renaissance poetry. However, his metaphorical master stroke is a gambit that Willis's character will deploy, called "throwing the screwball," in which, by means of calculated double talk and nonsense, he consistently confuses and disarms the terrorists. ("Throwing the screwball" is also used by the Commandos as a euphemism for "doing the nasty.")

10   When the Japanese superstar "Beat" Takeshi Kitano is cast—ratcheting up both the hipness quotient and the appeal to Asian audiences—Quentin Tarantino[7] is hired to write his character. It is his idea that first Will Smith, and then ultimately the whole team, refer to Kitano as Astro Boy, in homage to the famous Japanese TV cartoon. He also throws in a riff in which Smith points to Kitano's cell phone, asking if he knows that the Swedish word for such things is *yuppie-nalle,* or "yuppie teddy bear." Perhaps more important, Tarantino models Kitano's character on the fabled Tokyo Giants home-run king, Sadaharu Oh, who refined his batting technique by studying traditional Aikido and swordfighting skills, which come in handy during a skirmish with Sizemore's terrorists on the D train between the third and fourth innings.

As shooting is about to start, Zak Penn[8] and Carrie Fisher[9] are brought in to address the humor of the story, a job made easier by the casting of Steve Buscemi as the Commandos' smart-aleck batboy, Bill Murray as an addled play-by-play announcer and Garry Shandling as the vain, craven Yankees owner. Finally, Sean Connery, who has agreed to play the terrorist Sizemore, requests a writer to polish his dialogue. Frank Darabont[10] is brought in for the job.

Unhappy at being shunted aside so quickly, Tim leaves "Baseball Commandos" to write a new script, a clever twist on an old idea called "Viet Kong," concerning a giant ape discovered in the jungles of Southeast Asia and trained by the N.V.A. to fight U.S. and South Vietnamese troops. Warner Brothers buys it for Oliver Stone to direct, and Tim's off on the rewrite treadmill once again.

Producers and studio executives tend to justify this approach in terms of insurance: they're spending $100 million, and want to know that every moment, every gesture, every line is as good as it can be. A script is never perfect. It's never right enough, it's never funny enough, there's not enough suspense. So producers want to be able to call on writers who can do those things. Says Glickman: "Everyone wants a guy who's done it before. You have to understand, it extends beyond writers—you want a director who's already made a big movie, a cinematographer, an editor. The stakes are so high."

Members of the elite and publicly invisible class of writers created by the system can earn as much as $200,000 a week for their contributions. In their own way, they are not unlike the Baseball Commandos, each with his own special skills, dropping down from above to save the day. "Part of the allure," says Paul Attanasio, "is precisely the anonymity of it. You can come in and help out and it's exciting, like being a relief pitcher and coming in and facing three batters without registering a win or a loss."

15   The downside, of course, is that a piecemeal method can lead to the dissolution of a film's organic unity, leaving viewers with the feeling, as Janet Maslin wrote in her *New York Times* review of "Armageddon," that it is "constructed as if it were shish kebab." And many writers, despite the lucrative inducements to rewrite others, are increasingly unhappy with the seeming disposability of their own work and have begun more vocally to decry the practice.

But to the blockbuster way of thinking, a script is far less a literary or an imaginative undertaking than it is a business plan for a start-up company that requires some $70 million to $100 million in initial capitalization. In essence, studios are investment banks that specialize in financing this kind of venture; their executives are experts in evaluating such plans in terms of particular elements that are thought to guarantee a good return. When these elements are deemed to be in place, then the business is financed and the movie is made. A cynical person might conclude that the scripts for movies like "Baseball Commandos" are fairly irrelevant—a point of view supported by Steven Spielberg's court testimony regarding the genesis of "Twister," in which he stated that its screenplay was responsible for only about 5 percent of the film's success relative to special effects, star power, advertising and marketing.

But no one who is about to spend the equivalent of the G.N.P. of Tonga ever sets out to make a bad movie. Even under ideal circumstances, as David Koepp, whose blockbuster experience includes both "Jurassic Park" movies and "Mission: Impossible" as well as this summer's "Snake Eyes," has pointed out, the more fantastic the premise of a film, and the more effects technology it necessitates, "it's difficult to have any kind of human drama that doesn't seem incompatible." Says Daniel Waters, whose quirky sensibility has informed movies like "Hudson Hawk" and "Demolition Man": "People who've written a big-budget screenplay never blame the script. People who haven't always do. I remember coming out of the first 'Batman' movie and saying: 'Oh, my God, they had such amazing visuals! If only there had been a decent script!' Then, three years later, after I'd done heartbreaking work writing 'Batman Returns,' I was walking out of the premiere, when I overheard someone saying: 'Man, what a great-looking movie. If only they had a good script....'"

THE PRODUCTION LINE

1. **Tim D.** *does not exist.*
2. **Jonathan Hensleigh** *A protégé of George Lucas's who got his start writing "The Young Indiana Jones Chronicles," Hensleigh is widely regarded as one of the premier architects of large-scale action-adventure movies. The instigator and primary writer of "Armageddon," he also restructured and rewrote significant portions of "Con Air," "The Rock" and next winter's "Virus." He says, "I am either made aware of or offered every action-adventure script in Hollywood."*

3. **Callie Khouri** *The Oscar-winning screenwriter of "Thelma and Louise" specializes in strong women. She was recently hired to work on a forthcoming remake of "Mighty Joe Young," starring Charlize Theron.*

4. **Michael Tolkin** *The writer-director of the thoughtful, edgy independently produced films "The Rapture" and "The New Age" focuses on layering dramatic story lines, as in "Deep Impact." He is also one of the many writers to take a crack at the "Mission: Impossible" sequel. The author of the novel and screenplay for "The Player," Tolkin is a seasoned observer of Hollywood mores and practices and says, "I've learned never to believe it when a studio movie has a sole writing credit."*

5. **Steven Zaillian** *A serious writer known for "Schindler's List," "Searching for Bobby Fischer" and the forthcoming "A Civil Action," he has also lent his trademark moral intensity to "Twister," "Mission: Impossible" and "Clear and Present Danger."*

6. **Ron Shelton** *The writer-director of "Bull Durham," "Cobb," "White Men Can't Jump" and "Tin Cup" specializes in sports films.*

7. **Quentin Tarantino** *Hired on "Crimson Tide" to sprinkle pop-culture references throughout, he also trades in glib, obsessive dialogue.*

8. **Zak Penn** *A joke specialist, Penn co-wrote the original script for "The Last Action Hero" and did uncredited work on "Men in Black" and "The Mask of Zorro." Comedy writers are often called on at the last minute. Channing Gibson, for example, was never supplemented by other writers on "Lethal Weapon 4," but Michael Curtis and Greg Malins ("Friends") wrote pages of joke ideas, several of which Gibson used. Similarly, Michael Leeson, who has written for Garry Shandling, did punch-up work on "The Truman Show."*

9. **Carrie Fisher** *The actress, novelist and wit jacks up the humor. She has written for Rene Russo in "Lethal Weapon 3," for "Outbreak" and for romantic comedies like "The Wedding Singer."*

10. **Frank Darabont** *The writer-director of "The Shawshank Redemption" and the forthcoming "The Green Mile," Darabont, an all-around utility man, did uncredited script work on "The Fan," "Eraser" and "Saving Private Ryan."*

Rereading Actively

1. As Wolf introduces his readers to his topic, he talks of scriptwriters like himself being "replaced" (¶ 1) or standing "at the head of a conveyor belt" (¶ 2). What do phrases like this reveal about his position on the topic? How do these phrases affect a reader's entry into the article?

2. In your journal, outline the stages *Baseball Commandos* goes through. Which one is most surprising? What's Wolf's implicit evaluation of each stage? What's your evaluation?

3. Works of art are often analyzed in terms of producer, product, performance, and audience. Find references to each of these terms, and explain Wolf's assessment of two of them in regard to blockbusters.

4. What might Wolf mean by the phrase "the dissolution of a film's organic unity" (¶ 15)? In your journal, define this phrase.

5. In his conclusion, Wolf notes the tension between fantastic premises and good scripts, pointing to recent Batman films as a case in point. In your own words, explain this tension.

6. Summarize Wolf's feelings about the marketing of movies in no more than three sentences. How sympathetic are you to his view? Why?

Exploring Your Responses

7. Wolf refers to a categorization of films that ranges from "elevated fare" to "popcorn movies" (¶ 2). Categorize a movie that you either love or hate, and then, drawing on Wolf's explanation of the production process, reflect on what your response says about you as a movie consumer. Are you drawn to popcorn flicks with good jokes, car chases, emotional moments, and super-stars even though they have a "video-game-ish" (¶ 7) feel? Do you look for films that tell a consistent story with lots of texture? What are you willing to pay $9 for and what does that say about you?

8. In a small group, brainstorm movies that you've seen recently, and then pick one to focus on. (Choose a movie you like or dislike.) Talk about the catch-phrases the writers and their agents might have used to sell the film to a producer; then, talk about why the film's stars were cast in those roles. Finally, produce a collaborative evaluation of the effect of the production process on the quality of the film. Be ready to argue your position in a class discussion.

9. Recall your response to the last several big-budget movies that you have seen, and freewrite about how you feel as you walk out of a blockbuster. (This could become a narrative description of your thoughts as you stand up and walk out of the theater or get up and turn off the VCR.) In your conclusion, consider how your reaction compares with Wolf's.

LIFE THE MOVIE
NEAL GABLER

Winner of the Los Angeles Times *Book Prize for* An Empire of Their Own: How the Jews Invented Hollywood *(1988) and the* Time *Nonfiction Book of the Year for* Winchell: Gossip, Power and the Culture of Celebrity *(1994), Neil Gabler has gained wide recognition for his careful look at entertainment. While his formal training is in the analysis of film, he turns in* Life the Movie *(1998)—the source of this excerpt—to look more at the lives of consumers of entertainment than at the entertainments they consume. His hypothesis is that life has begun to be a medium all its own and that the lives of Americans are increasingly structured by the entertainment media to look like a movie. Analyzing why "entertainment became the primary value of American life" and what the implications are, he seems to be a bit pessimistic about the choices consumers make.*

Though he couldn't possibly have known it at the time, in 1960 the novelist Philip Roth posed what would become one of the central questions of our age: How could fiction possibly compete with the stories authored by real life? As anyone could see from browsing the daily newspapers, life had become so strange, its convolutions so mind-boggling that, Roth lamented, the "American writer in the middle of the twentieth century has his hands full in trying to understand, and then describe, and then make credible much of American reality. It stupefies, it sickens, it infuriates, and finally it is even a kind of embarrassment to one's own meager imagination. The actuality is continually outdoing our talents, and the culture tosses up figures almost daily that are the envy of every novelist."[1]

At virtually the same time Roth was describing the challenge of reality to fiction, historian Daniel Boorstin, in his pathbreaking study *The Image: A Guide to Pseudo-Events in America,* was describing how everywhere the fabricated, the inauthentic and the theatrical were driving out the natural, the genuine and the spontaneous from life until reality itself had been converted into stagecraft. As Boorstin saw it, Americans increasingly lived in a "world where fantasy is more real than reality,"[2] and he warned, "We risk being the first people in history to have been able to make their illusions so vivid, so persuasive, so 'realistic' that they can live in them."[3]

Roth was talking about real-life melodrama in America, and Boorstin about the deliberate manipulation of reality in America, but both were addressing what, in hindsight, was the same root phenomenon, one that may very well qualify as the single most important cultural transformation in this country in the twentieth century. What they recognized was that life itself was gradually becoming a medium all its own, like television, radio, print and film, and that all of us were becoming at once performance artists in and audiences for a grand, ongoing show—a show that was, as Roth noted, often far richer, more complex and more compelling than anything conceived for the more conventional media. In short, life was becoming a movie.

To compare life to a movie is not to say, as the cliché has it, that life imitates art, though surely there is truth to that. Nor is it to say that life has devised its own artistic methods and thus reversed the process—art imitates life—though that also is true, as one can see from the number of novels, movies and television programs that have been inspired by real-life events. Rather it is to say that after decades of public-relations contrivances and media hype, and after decades more of steady pounding by an array of social forces that have alerted each of us personally to the power of performance, life has *become* art, so that the two are now indistinguishable from each other. Or, to rework an aphorism of the poet Stéphane Mallarmé, the world doesn't exist to end in a book; when life is a medium, books and every other imaginative form exist to end in a world.[4]

5 One need look no further than the daily news to realize how true this is now. It does not minimize the media excesses of the penny press, the yellow press and the original tabloids, to recognize that in the nearly forty years since Roth's essay the news has become a continuous stream of what one might call "lifies"—movies written in the medium of life, projected on the screen of life and exhibited in the multiplexes of the traditional media which are increasingly dependent upon the life medium. The murder trial of former football star O. J. Simpson, the life and death of Diana, Princess of Wales, the ongoing soap-operatic sagas of Elizabeth Taylor or television talk show hostess Oprah Winfrey, the shooting of Long Island housewife Mary Jo Buttafuoco by her husband's seventeen-year-old paramour, the bombing of the federal office building in Oklahoma City by right-wing dissidents, the repeated allegations of extramarital dalliances by President Bill Clinton, to name only a handful of literally thousands of episodes life generates—these are the new blockbusters that preoccupy the traditional media and dominate the national conversation for weeks, sometimes months or even years at a time, while ordinary entertainments quickly evanesce.

But however much we may be preoccupied with them, it is not just these "lifies" that make life a movie. As Boorstin observed, the deliberate application of the techniques of theater to politics, religion, education, literature, commerce, warfare, crime, *everything*, has converted them into branches of show business, where the overriding objective is getting and satisfying an audience. Acting like a cultural Ebola virus, entertainment has even invaded organisms no one would ever have imagined could provide amusement. Dr. Timothy Leary, onetime proponent of hallucinogens, turned his death into entertainment by using his computer Web page to chronicle his deterioration from prostate cancer, a show which ended with a video of him drinking a toxic cocktail in what he called a "visible, interactive suicide."[5] A group of teenage thugs in Washington, D.C., videotaped their depredations, even posing for the camera after beating a victim while an "audience" of by-standers cheered.[6] And one enterprising entrepreneur converted a former Nazi command post on the eastern front in Poland into a theme resort, while another planned an amusement park outside Berlin with the motif of East Germany under communism.[7]

What traditional entertainment always promised was to transport us from our daily problems, to enable us to escape from the travails of life. Analyzing the mechanism through which this was achieved, literary scholar Michael Wood in his book *America in the Movies* described our films as a "rearrangement of our problems into shapes which tame them, which disperse them to the margins of our attention,"[8] where we can forget about them. This is what we really mean when we call entertainment "escapist": We escape from life by escaping into the neat narrative formulas in which most entertainments are packaged. Still, with movies there was always the assumption that the escape was temporary. At the end of the film one had to leave the theater and reenter the maelstrom of real life.

When life itself is an entertainment medium, however, this process is obviously altered. Lewis Carroll, commenting on a vogue among nineteenth-century cartographers for ever larger and more detailed maps, once cautioned that the maps might get so large they would interfere with agriculture, and waggishly suggested that the earth be used as a map of itself instead.[9] Carroll's is an apt analogy for the new relationship between entertainment and life. By conflating the two and converting everything from the kidnapping of the Lindbergh baby to the marital misadventures of Elizabeth Taylor into entertainments that transport us from our problems, we need never leave the theater's comfort. We can remain constantly distracted. Or, put another way, we have finally learned how to escape from life into life.

While there are certainly those who will disapprove, one is almost compelled to admit that turning life into escapist entertainment is a perversely ingenious adaptation to the turbulence and tumult of modern existence. Why worry about the seemingly intractable problems of society when you can simply declare "It's morning in America," as President Reagan did in his 1984 reelection campaign, and have yourself a long-running Frank Capra movie right down to the aw-shucks hero? Why fret over the lack of national purpose during the doldrums of the post–Cold War era when you can convert a shooting war into a real-life war movie that reaffirms your destiny, as America did in 1991 with the Gulf War? Movies have always been a form of wish fulfillment. Why not life?

10   The conversion of life into an entertainment medium could never have succeeded, however, if those who attend the life movie hadn't discovered what the early movie producers had discovered years before: that audiences need some point of identification if the show is really to engross them. For the movies the solution was stars. For the life movie it is celebrity. Though stardom in any form automatically confers celebrity, it is just as likely now to be granted to diet gurus, fashion designers and their so-called supermodels, lawyers, political pundits, hairdressers, intellectuals, businessmen, journalists, criminals—anyone who happens to appear, however fleetingly, on the radar of the traditional media and is thus sprung from the anonymous mass. The only prerequisite is publicity.

Celebrity is by now old news, but it says a great deal about modern America that no society has ever had as many celebrities as ours or has revered them as intensely. Not only are celebrities the protagonists of our news, the subjects of our daily discourse and the repositories of our values, but they have also embedded themselves so deeply in our consciousness that many individuals profess feeling closer to, and more passionate about, them than about their own primary relationships: Witness the torrents of grief unleashed by the sudden death of Princess Diana in 1997, or the mourners who told television interviewers that her funeral was the saddest day of their lives. As Diana confirmed, celebrity is the modern state of grace—the condition in the life movie to which nearly everyone aspires. Once we sat in movie theaters dreaming of stardom. Now we live in a movie dreaming of celebrity.

Yet this is not nearly as passive as it may sound. While the general public is an audience for the life movie, it is also an active participant in it. An ever-growing segment of the American economy is now devoted to designing, building and then dressing the sets in which we live, work, shop and play; to creating our costumes; to making our hair shine and our faces glow; to slenderizing our bodies; to supplying our props—all so that we can appropriate the trappings of celebrity, if not the actuality of it, for the life movie. We even have celebrities—for example, lifestyle adviser Martha Stewart—who are essentially drama coaches in the life movie, instructing us in how to make our own lives more closely approximate the movie in our mind's eye.

Of course, not everyone is mesmerized. Many have deplored the effects of entertainment and celebrity on America, and there is certainly much to deplore. While an entertainment-driven, celebrity-oriented society is not necessarily one that destroys all moral value, as some would have it, it *is* one in which the standard of value is whether or not something can grab and then hold the public's attention. It is a society in which those things that do not conform—for example, serious literature, serious political debate, serious ideas, serious anything—are more likely to be compromised or marginalized than ever before. It is a society in which celebrities become paragons because they are the ones who have learned how to steal the spotlight, no matter what they have done to steal it. And at the most personal level, it is a society in which individuals have learned to prize social skills that permit them, like actors, to assume whatever role the occasion demands and to "perform" their lives rather than just live them. The result is that *Homo sapiens* is rapidly becoming *Homo scaenicus*—man the entertainer.

As the culture submits to the tyranny of entertainment, as life becomes a movie, critics complain that America has devolved into a "carnival culture" or "trash culture," where everything is coarsened, vulgarized and trivialized, where the meretricious is more likely to be rewarded than the truly deserving and where bonds of community that were once forged by shared moral values and traditions are now forged by tabloid headlines, gossip and media. "We had fed the heart on fantasies," wrote William Butler Yeats. "The heart's grown brutal from the fare."[10]

15   No doubt Americans who hold this view of modern culture will want a program of action that will help us "disenchant" ourselves and restore our reality and our values. One can certainly sympathize with them. But to pretend that one can provide a remedy would be not only naive but duplicitous, since it would necessarily indulge the same sort of fantasy that got us here in the first place: that problems, like crises in movies, are susceptible to simple narrative solutions. You simply present a monster in the first reel and then have the hero vanquish it in the last.

Anyone looking for heroes, solutions or even high dudgeon will not find them here. While this book is not without an attitude, particularly toward some of the absurdities to which entertainment has driven us, readers are here forewarned that it is diagnostic rather than prescriptive, an investigation rather than a screed. Its object is to provide a new context for something so gargantuan that it has slid beyond the borders of context and frequently beyond our powers of analysis. That context is entertainment.

There is obviously no such thing as a unified field theory of American culture, but if there were, one could do worse than to lay much of what has happened in late-twentieth-century America to the corrosive effects of entertainment rather than to the effects of politics or economics, the usual suspects. Indeed, Karl Marx and Joseph Schumpeter both seem to have been wrong. It is not any ism but entertainment that is arguably the most pervasive, powerful and ineluctable force of our time—a force so overwhelming that it has finally metastasized into life.

As a tool of analysis, entertainment may just be what undergirds and unites ideas as disparate as Boorstin's theory of manufactured reality, Marshall McLuhan's doctrine of media determinism, the deconstructionist notion that culture is actually a collectively scripted text, and so much of the general perspective we call postmodernism. If so, understanding how and why entertainment permeates life as it does may enable us to comprehend the brave and strange new world in which we live—the world of postreality.

What Daniel Boorstin said of *The Image* may also be true of this volume: "This is a large subject for a small book. Yet it is too large for a big book."[11] It is a vast territory we tread, nothing less than life itself, and no one could possibly chart it all. Every day the life medium generates new episodes. Every day someone finds more inventive applications for its use. The profusion is so bewildering that the Italian semiotician Umberto Eco, acknowledging the voraciousness of the mass media to devour everything, believed we could ease our minds around the issue only by taking a whole new cognitive approach to our reality. "We have to start again from the beginning," Eco wrote, "asking one another what's going on."[12]

20   This book is an attempt to start again and ask what's going on: to understand why entertainment became the primary value of American life, to examine what the implications have been for our public culture and to analyze how it has changed and continues to change our lives.

Notes

1. the "American writer in the middle of the 20th century ..." "Writing American Fiction," in Philip Roth, *Reading Myself and Others* (New York: Farrar, Straus & Giroux, 1975), p. 120.
2. a "world where fantasy ..." Daniel J. Boorstin, *The Image. A Guide to Pseudo-Events in America* (New York: Atheneum, 1987 [1961]), p. 37.
3. "We risk being ..." Ibid., p. 240.
4. Stéphane Mallarmé's aphorism. Marshall McLuhan, *Understanding Media: The Extensions of Man,* 2nd ed. (New York: McGraw-Hill, 1964), p. 66.
5. "visible, interactive suicide." Edward Rothstein, "Technology," *New York Times,* April 29, 1996, p. D23.
6. D.C. teenagers. Tracy Thompson, "Tolerance or Survival? Video Case Reveals Street Reality," *Washington Post,* June 16, 1991, pp. C1, C9. The purpose of the video, apparently, was to show New York City gangs how tough District of Columbia gangs could be.
7. Nazi-themed resort and Communist theme park. Gary Krist, "Tragedyland," *New York Times,* November 27, 1993, p. A17.
8. "rearrangement of our problems ..." Michael Wood, *America in the Movies: or "Santa Maria, It Had Slipped My Mind!"* (New York. Delta: 1976), p. 18.
9. Lewis Carroll's cartographers. McLuhan, p. 60. A similar parable was told by Jorge Luis Borges. For an elaboration, see Jean Baudrillard, *Selected Writings,* ed. Mark Poster (Stanford, CA.: Stanford University Press, 1988), p. 166.
10. "We had fed the heart on fantasies." W[illiam] B[utler] Yeats, *The Collected Poems of W.B. Yeats* (New York: Macmillan Company, 1933), p. 202.
11. "This is a large subject ..." Boorstin, p. ix.
12. "We have to start again ..." Umberto Eco, *Travels in Hyperreality,* tr. William Weaver (New York: Harcourt Brace Jovanovich, 1987), p. 150.

Rereading Actively

1. Why does Gabler open this piece with references to novelist Philip Roth and historian Daniel Boorstin?
2. With a partner, talk about what Gabler means when he says, "life is a medium" (¶ 3–8). Work together to define this sense of the word "medium" to explain what life is like when it "is" a medium, and to evaluate Gabler's assertion based on your own experience and observation.
3. In your own words, explain what Gabler means by the "techniques of theater" (¶ 6). To what extent is your life theatrical in Gabler's sense of the word?
4. What are the basic purposes and components of entertainment, according to Gabler? How does the purpose and makeup of entertainment change as life becomes a movie?
5. Gabler is himself an entertainment critic. With a partner, note the places where he discusses the role of critics and record your findings in a journal entry.

6. In his final paragraphs, Gabler explains his purpose in writing. How does his explanation affect your reading of this book introduction? Does it make you want to keep reading? Why or why not?

Exploring Your Responses

7. If life is a movie, then Martha Stewart is the ultimate agent and acting coach. Watch an episode of Martha Stewart's television program, read a copy of her magazine, or make a visit to her Web site: <www.marthastewart.com>. With notes in hand, get together with two or three classmates and draw up a collaborative description of the central purpose and activities of the life that Stewart recommends. Then, drawing on Gabler's analysis, draft a paragraph explanation of how Stewart fits into or contradicts Gabler's "world of postreality" (¶ 18).

8. Brainstorm the activities that you like most and least. Focusing on a couple of activities, reflect on how movie-like, in Gabler's terms, your pursuit of those activities is—that is, the extent to which you find yourself performing for an imaginary audience when you do these things.

9. Record your entertainment consumption for forty-eight hours, from TV to movies to going to the gym (depending, of course, on your purpose at the gym). Look over your field notes and draft a reflective essay that explores the extent to which you live in a movie.

SILENCE, PLEASE
SALLIE TISDALE

*A prolific nonfiction writer who has published in a range of magazines—*Vogue, *the* New York Times Sunday Magazine, *and* Audubon—*Sallie Tisdale takes us in this* Harper's *essay (1997) to a place most of us have been, the public library. Her analysis of the past, present, and future of the library affords a look at how entertainment value has altered this institution she argues was once "a commonly held trust" at the core of American democracy. Tisdale explores what happens to knowledge when it becomes a commodity. She argues about what a library should be, in contrast to what it has become, and she identifies who she believes is responsible for the change.*

When I entered the library as a child, I walked up several imposing steps to a door of respectful size, through a small foyer—and through the looking glass. The librarian's large desk stood guard over the small building, braced by books on three sides. The rooms were close, filled with big, heavy tables that had dictionaries open on reading stands; tall, sweet-smelling, precarious shelves; leather armchairs; rubber-coated wheeled stepstools; and other readers, silent and absorbed. They formed an open maze through which I threaded myself, hour after hour.

This was a place set outside the ordinary day. Its silence—outrageous, magic, unlike any other sound in my life—was a counterpoint to the interior noise in my crowded mind. It was the only sacred space I knew, intimate and formal at once, hushed, potent.

I didn't need to be told this—I felt it. In the library I could hunker down in an aisle, seeing only the words in my lap, and a stranger would simply step over me and bend down for his own book with what I now think of as a rare and touching courtesy. That place was then, and remains, the Library; what Jorge Luis Borges knew all along was more than that: it was "the Universe (which others call the Library)." Only outside the door, on the steps, did one take a deep breath, blink at the sudden light, pause to shift the weight of new books in one's arms, and go out again into the world.

I am disabled by this memory. I still show up at ten in the morning at the central branch of the Multnomah County Library, in Portland, Oregon, where I now live, impatient for the doors to open. I always find people ahead of me, waiting on the wide stone steps, and I wait with them, knowing better. The library I knew, the one I remember, is almost extinct.

In the last few years I have gone to the library to study or browse or look something up, and instead have found myself listening to radios, crying babies, a cappella love songs, puppet shows, juggling demonstrations, CD-ROM games, and cellular telephone calls. ("It's okay, I'm just at the library," I heard a man say recently.) Children run through the few stacks still open to patrons, spinning carts and pulling books off shelves, ignored by parents deep in conversation with one another. A teenager Rollerblades through, playing crack-the-whip by swinging himself around the ends of the shelves. I browse (with considerably less frequency than a few years ago) to the sound of librarians on the telephone, arguing, calling to one another across the room. Patrons hum along with their earphones, stand in line for the Internet screens, clackety-clack on keyboards. Silence, even a mild sense of repose, is long gone. Today's library is trendy, up-to-date, plugged in, and most definitely not set outside the ordinary day. It's a hip, fun place, the library. You can get movies there and Nintendo games, drink cappuccino and surf cyberspace, go to a gift shop or a cafeteria, rent a sewing machine or a camera. There is a library in a Wichita supermarket and a Cleveland shopping mall. But the way things are going, in a few years it's going to be hard to tell the difference between the library and anything, everything, else.

5   Again and again, for more than 150 years, the public library has endured a cycle of crisis and change, a continual confusion over purpose. Every few decades the cry has gone up: too few people use libraries, too many people are reluctant to read, intimidated by books, ignorant of all that the library offers. And then a new campaign begins to draw more people into the library, to do more things for larger numbers—to be, in many of these campaigns, all things to all. We're in the midst of one of these campaigns today. The public library of the last decade has been pushed and pulled by professional librarians and by policy makers responsive to the trend of the times. Changing and oftentimes shrinking tax bases, growing populations of immigrants as well as rootless Americans, the Internet and rapidly evolving CD-ROM technology all have had their effects on the public library. Bonds pass; new buildings are built, and old ones are renovated; computer systems are bought and upgraded; collections are sorted, discarded, and replaced; directors are fired and hired—all out of sight of the patrons hurrying in on their lunch hour.

There are almost 9,000 public libraries in the United States, used each year by about two-thirds of the adult population. Both as a physical place in a community and as a symbol of the American cultural aspiration, the library is familiar, mundane, taken largely for granted, perhaps because it is, as government institutions go, remarkably efficient. Public libraries cost about $19.16 per person annually, and although this expense has increased by more than 90 percent since 1982, it nonetheless accounts for less than one percent of all tax monies. Library money is in a volatile state, up in one region and down in another, new buildings going up and old buildings being remodeled even as branches are being closed, staff reduced, and hours curtailed. Major libraries are being built or remodeled in Cincinnati; Cleveland; Portland, Oregon; Chicago; San Francisco; Los Angeles; Little Rock; Rochester, New York; Charleston, South Carolina; and Oklahoma City. New York City just opened a new Science, Industry, and Business Library. The famously popular Baltimore libraries have had big budget cuts. Last year, the Los Angeles City library system had a policy that would have allowed, with some restrictions, anyone donating a million dollars to have a library named after him or her. There were no takers. The central branch here in Multnomah County is being remodeled at a cost of about $25 million. Meanwhile, half of the branches are going to be closed for lack of funds.

The argument about what a library is for—what a library is—began its lengthy cultural play with Ben Franklin, more than 200 years ago. When Franklin donated a collection of 116 books to the eponymous town of Franklin, Massachusetts, in 1790, thereby founding the first public library of any sort in the United States, he said that his purpose was to serve "a Society of intelligent respectable Farmers, such as our Country People generally consist of." The moneyed class, after all, already had private subscription libraries. Franklin's notion of moderately equal opportunity offended some of the townspeople, and it was more than two acrimonious years before the town meeting voted to accept the proposition. It was another forty-three years before the first tax-supported library was founded in New Hampshire, and not until the Boston Public Library opened in 1852 did the library as we know it today begin. Public libraries didn't really multiply until the early twentieth century, when Andrew Carnegie donated $56 million for the construction of 2,509 library buildings throughout the country.

Franklin hoped reading would improve people's "conversation." Carnegie saw libraries partly as a means of social improvement for "the best and most aspiring poor." Chicago librarian William F. Poole, in a massive government report issued in 1876, saw libraries as "the adjunct and supplement of the common school system" and a source of "moral and intellectual improvement" for adults. Michael Harris, then a professor of library science at the University of Kentucky, claimed in 1973 that libraries were consciously intended by the upper classes as tools for the assimilation and Americanization of immigrants, for "disciplining the masses," who often seemed intent on recreation rather than social uplift. At various times libraries have been said to exist for the active reader, the amateur scholar, the educated citizen, the uneducated citizen, the illiterate poor, the elderly, the schoolchild, and the dime-store-novel lover—all alike, and sometimes all at once.

The current trend in libraries is to do away with all that refinement in favor of a more familiar atmosphere. Libraries, I was told recently, used to be "discouraging—discouraging places to work, and discouraging to learn in." (The woman who said this has retired from library service to act as a technology consultant.) That I never felt this way—that I am deeply discouraged by the library today—is simply proof, I suppose, that I am out of touch. She meant that libraries were discouraging because they were quiet, because you were expected to behave respectfully toward other readers, because they were, as she put it, "about books."

10   I have written to my library administration with various suggestions and complaints over the years. Last year I complained about the CD-ROM dinosaur game in my small branch. Two children argued over the game while it played at full volume; my browsing that afternoon was done to the shrieks of both *T. rex* and the siblings. The deputy director responded to my letter by saying that CD-ROM games are "attractive to children that [*sic*] are reluctant readers, reluctant library users, and reluctant students.... We are pleased that they are enjoying this new way of presenting information." This is a surprisingly quaint emphasis, often tried, often abandoned. Campaigns to increase the number of patrons by offering recreation have failed as surely as attempts to direct them away from popular fiction and toward the classics. "The progressive library is a fisher of men," wrote a librarian in 1909. "And it will catch them whether it baits its hook with books, music, pictures or lectures." Or, later in the century, with social work, concerts, handicraft classes, dances, parties, and athletic meets. Or, as is being tried now, with dinosaur games and the Internet.

Perhaps the Internet is the big secret, the one seduction librarians have sought for centuries. Certainly it's the one form of recreation that seems to draw nonreaders to the library again and again. Wherever Internet connections are offered—and almost half of American public libraries provide them now—they are enormously popular.[1] In a sense the library is made more popular by the addition of Internet stations and CD-ROM games. A free showing of *Independence Day* would bring a big surge in attendance, too. But it wouldn't mean that a whole bunch of people had suddenly become library patrons, unless (and this is what I fear) the word "library" has ceased to mean much at all. The Internet/CD-ROM trend becomes essential to libraries only when we want libraries to be changed in an essential way.

In 1978 a committee of the American Library Association released a stirring statement about what the library owed the nation: "*All information* must be available to *all people* in *all formats* purveyed through *all communication channels* and delivered at *all levels of comprehension*....All information means *all* information." This amazing concept didn't simply disappear in a rush of laughter, as one might expect. Its progeny are everywhere: disappearing shelf space replaced by computer terminals, entire book collections thrown out for being archaic, an embrace of every myth about the Internet ever told. A recent story in *Time* describing Microsoft's $3 million grant to the Brooklyn Public Library for Internet connections makes the insupportable claim that "more knowledge comes down a wire than anyone could ever acquire from books." More data, perhaps, but knowledge? That a journalist could mistake one for the other is telling.

I find today's library literature strangely infatuated, unquestioning, reflecting a kind of data panic, and filled with dire fantasies of patrons left behind—woebegone hitchhikers on the information superhighway. A press release from the U.S. National Commission on Libraries and Information Science says that communities without library Internet connections will become "information have-nots." The emblematic image, continually evoked as reason enough, is the "schoolchild doing research," who shouldn't be stuck with stodgy print encyclopedias or forced to browse through the stacks and read books—not when screens and CD-ROMs abound, not when search engines and keywords can do the browsing for her. Says an ALA press release touting the virtues of the electronic resource, "Instead of tracking down volumes on the shelves, students can press a computer key and read the information they need on the screen, in some cases, complete with sound and moving images." Much of the praise for the library as an electronic-information center presumes that we are headed toward an accelerated, saturated vanishing point—and that it is the library's duty to make this as fun as possible, and to make sure everyone is on board. To criticize such an outlook is to be labeled a Luddite, a spoilsport, a stick-in-the-mud.

The reality of the electronic library is painfully obvious to anyone who has noted the national destruction of card catalogs.[2] Almost 90 percent of urban libraries now use electronic catalogs, and many have destroyed their cards, which represent decades of human labor and ingenuity. My library system switched to an electronic catalog in the late 1980s; even now it's not complete. Almost all the cards are gone, and I now have to pay ten cents a page for a computer printout.

15   A few months ago I went to the library to help my daughter get a book about cheetahs. The computers were down. I wasn't surprised—annoyed, but not surprised. Repeated "upgradings" have locked patrons out of the catalog for as long as a week, and slowdowns and freezes are common. This time, I asked a librarian to point me toward the section for animals.

"Don't know," he said, and turned to go.

"Can you tell me the classification number for animals?" I asked.

"Don't know," he said, more stonily this time.

"Do you have a list of Dewey decimal numbers I can look at?" There were none posted that I could see.

20   "I'll ring for the reference librarian," he said, and walked away.

I attended all five days of the most recent biannual Public Library Association convention, held in March of 1996 in Portland, Oregon, along with almost 6,000 other people. The PLA is part of the American Library Association, which claims 57,000 members and an annual budget of about $30 million. This larger body wanted Bill Gates to deliver the keynote address at its own convention this year, but it ended up with Harvard law professor Charles Ogletree. The PLA keynote was given by Jack Valenti, president of the Motion Picture Association of America. The theme was "Access for All."

Wandering through the echoing exhibit hall and dozens of panel discussions and lectures broken up by private parties and confabs, I was struck first of all by the amount of time and space devoted to the Internet and its various permutations. There were panels on "Community Information on the Internet," "CD-ROM to Go," "Virtual Communities," "Electronic Document Delivery," "Taking Control of the Internet," and "Internet Job Search," to name but a few.[3] The central theme of the exhibit hall was "The Future," and that future is not only electronic but expensive. There were larger booths— and many of them—for Internet-server systems costing several thousand dollars each, CD-ROM games and reference sources, a program called Dewey for Windows, periodical-access systems, electronic research programs, and cataloging systems. Just about everyone at every booth handed out business cards listing his or her Web site.

Even in the few discussions focused on books and reading, the interest was largely on genre fiction, and "read-alikes." A "read-alike" is a book "like" another—for the patron who says, "I love Judith Krantz and want to read something like that." In 1922, a few large libraries started readers' adviser services, in which patrons would check in with the adviser for direction and follow prescribed reading lists. It wasn't a very popular program. Today's readers' advisers are staffers familiar with the work of certain popular authors and ready to recommend read-alikes. At one convention booth, I played with a computer program called NoveList, which contains 11,000 plot summaries and "subject access" to 36,000 novels divided by title, genre, and plot. Type in *Carrie* by Stephen King, and NoveList tells you which books have matching "elements"—horror, female adolescents, high school proms, telekinetic murder. Choose a subject—say, "horror, high school seniors"—and a list of titles appears. Describe a plot—"high school senior murders entire class at prom"—and the program tells you if any such book has been written.

Duncan Smith, NoveList's creator and salesman, watched me play. Smith is himself a librarian, soft-spoken and, like almost every salesman at the PLA, carefully and conservatively dressed. "NoveList assumes that frequently people can tell you they've read a book and liked it, but they can't tell you why," he told me. "We don't want the reader to have to do the hard work of figuring that out."

25   The many disadvantages of electronic reading and learning have been dealt with in detail elsewhere; so have the myriad pragmatic and financial problems of a wholesale shift to electronic documentation. One of the most interesting aspects of today's library is how completely those disadvantages are being ignored. Shiny exhibits and chirping screens feed the erroneous belief that electronic delivery is the best form for both information and ideas, and further seduce people into believing that the technology needed to build a truly electronic library is even available now—let alone reliable, affordable, and tested.

Books are expensive objects, but their cost is small when compared with the real costs of electronic "delivery" of the same kind of material. Beyond the original costs of hardware, software, installation, and training—and the ongoing costs of replacing all this equipment, given the rapid obsolescence of electronic technology—there are the much higher losses possible with vandalism and theft and the costs of significant staffing changes to be considered. And no one seems to mention the enormous expense—in money, technical service, and natural resources—of printing out the information people want to take home. There are other hidden costs as well, such as the need to train staff to teach patrons how to use these tools, even while staff budgets are being trimmed to pay for the tools in the first place. Even something that seems at first glance to be cost-effective, such as a CD-ROM encyclopedia, has hidden costs. Only one person can use such a source at a time, because all the "volumes" are bound together, and an entire computer station must therefore be dedicated to that one person's research.

Once you buy the premise that information—and *entertaining* information—is the point, you have to buy the equipment, even if it is a Faustian deal. The ALA has accepted another offer from Microsoft: $10.5 million to forty-one library systems for Internet access and "multimedia personal computers." An executive with the ALA, in praise of Bill Gates's altruism, says, "Today, access to electronic information is not a luxury—it's a necessity." I have seen my own future as a library patron: the expensive new central branch being built here will have hundreds of Internet stations, partly thanks to Microsoft, but it won't have a single quiet reading room.

In their book *Future Libraries: Dreams, Madness & Reality,* Walt Crawford and Michael Gorman call the American library the "museum of failed technology." A recent survey showed that patron use of online services was dropping, even as more and more libraries added stations. The result of change for change's sake is obvious in every dusty microfiche reader and discarded box of eight-track tape.

There are, of course, voices of moderation, among them Arthur Curley, director emeritus of the Boston Public Library. He sees a lot of potential in electronic media but remains cautious. "The more limited your budget, the more important it is to acquire materials of lasting value," he told me recently. "I don't think we should be pioneers." Curley thinks the library building itself is an important symbol of the intellectual life. "I know it's a corny term, but it really is a beacon of hope. We want it to be beautiful and inviting; we want it to be a refuge."

30   The new library is not only electronic; a number of people hope it will be virtual, a "no walls" library, accessible by (and limited to) individual computers scattered throughout a community. We've seen this begin to happen, in workplaces and in a few schools, with entertainment: an isolating intrusion of false connectivity. But it is most alarming in the library, which I have always found one of the most tangible sanctuaries in society. Now it seems more and more something to be used from a distance, a place you don't have to go to—physical contact being, in the words of Kenneth Dowlin, the director of the San Francisco Public Library, a notion "less viable in a networked instant access world." Like a lot of librarians, Dowlin is playing both sides of the issue; he's a leading proponent of the virtual library, but he's also ensconced in a brand-new $140 million building.

Designed by James Ingo Freed and Cathy Simon, the new San Francisco Public Library building, with its soaring empty spaces, limited book shelving, and computer terminals to spare, has been cited by *Newsweek* and other publications as state-of-the-art, the library of the future. I've only seen photographs, but a friend who visited recently said, in a stunned monotone, "That building was designed by someone who hates books. Who *hates* books."

Perhaps books are an archaic concept in mainstream American culture. Certainly a lower percentage of library budgets is spent on materials now than in 1950, and 40 percent of that is spent on technology, not books. One of the first budget items cut when money gets tight in a library is new acquisitions, and the first books done without are those labeled "assumed or potential use"—books by unknown authors, archaic popular novels and reference materials, obscure historical works, and so on. Dollars are finite, and every library must make choices. Certain libraries, such as the New York and Boston public libraries, because they are relatively well funded, have always been "libraries of last resort," source libraries with the broadest and deepest possible collections. By contrast, a small branch outside Iowa City may largely provide interlibrary loans, community information, and introductory materials. But in both cases, the question of *what a library is for* must be asked. Should libraries be market-driven? Or do they have an intrinsic value that can be held up to the community at large, regardless of profitability and popularity? When such values prevail, books rarely read are seen as books without value.

Then libraries must be above all good businesses, anticipating the trends and dumping last year's fashions. Critical acclaim, esoteric detail, revisionism, experimental styles, controversial and unconventional points of view, and, in the end, literary depth itself are regarded as matters of no importance. Library development is meant to happen "just in time, not just in case"—that is, materials are bought "on demand." The quality of market demand, of course, adheres largely to mainstream tastes, and what the mainstream demands these days is the World Wide Web and Michael Crichton.

Midway through the PLA convention, I had lunch with Charles Robinson, director emeritus of the Baltimore County system, past president of the Public Library Association, and now editor of the *Library Administrator's Digest.* We ate and talked in a noisy, crowded downtown Portland hotel lounge. Robinson is amusing in a self-consciously acerbic way, and he is well rehearsed; he has said the things he said to me many times before.

"My vision of a public library and what it should be doing is based on what the taxpayers want," he said when I asked him what a library is for. "You have to be careful watching what people use libraries for—which can be very different from what people *say* they use libraries for. The value of a library doesn't depend on how many books it has. It depends on how many books it has that people actually want to use." Robinson castigates librarians who want libraries to be educational. "Most of our use is people getting entertained. While they're being entertained, they are also getting educated. Against their will, maybe."

35   I told Robinson that I was in the midst of reading through old cook-books for a project I was working on and that I was having trouble finding the ones I wanted. If he were my librarian, would he have such things around?

"I'm not interested in serving you," he said. "I don't give a damn. Go someplace else. We'll help you find it on interlibrary loan, if we can. But what I want to do is serve 90 percent of the people 90 percent of the time. If I want to serve 95 percent of the people, it'll double my budget."

My own local librarians have told me to seek elsewhere for quiet reading rooms, archaic material, specialized journals, even old cookbooks. In Umberto Eco's essay "How to Organize a Public Library," his Rule Number 8 is that "The librarian must consider the reader an enemy, a waster of time (otherwise he or she would be at work)." I feel, if not like the enemy, then more and more like an unwelcome foreigner.

One of the several ways I seem to be out of touch with the new library is that I consider "potential use" to be one of the most important aspects of any library—because the things subsumed under that term are often found nowhere else. When I am searching for the odd fact, the little-known detail, the forgotten idea, I am a pilgrim, searching alone. When I am looking without knowing what I am looking for, I am a voyager across my own extraordinary landscape. This is what the library does best: it provides a place where the culture is kept, without judgment or censor, a record of life as it was, is, and may be. And the most important part of that record is what cannot be found anywhere else and will be lost forever if the library doesn't keep it. I see cultural exchanges becoming ever more transitional, frail, unenduring. The public library could, in the face of such change, claim its place as the community's holder of what stays, as an exacting delineation of a thinker's world. Instead, it is close to becoming as frail as what it sells. The widely read novel, the mainstream idea, the ephemeral data of the day are available in lots of places; that's what makes them mainstream. There will be no shortage of Judith Krantz and John Grisham novels in the world, no shortage of screens inviting distraction in a worldwide web of impulsively offered words. But there is, more and more, a threat to unique, anomalous, unconventional knowledge.

I've been reading *Library Journal* and *Public Libraries* and *American Libraries* and other such literature, and talking to librarians off and on for months now, and no one mentions something else I miss very much: *silence.* That is, no one mentions it in a positive way; public-relations stories these days often cite the lack of silence as a *good* thing. Some librarians now post NO SILENCE PLEASE signs as part of their marketing campaigns. Number 11 on the ALA list of "12 Ways Libraries Are Good for the Country" is that they "Offer Sanctuary"—"a physical reaction, a feeling of peace, respect, humility, and honor." This, of course, is something no virtual, modem-connected information system can possibly do. Cyberspace hopping may be a solitary activity, but it's a crowded isolation—noisy separation rather than communal quiet.

40   Toward the end of the PLA convention, I spoke with Jo Ann Pinder, a suburban librarian from Gwinnett County, outside Atlanta. "We don't have a community," she said. "We don't have sidewalks, we have subdivisions. Instead of front porches, we have decks in the backyard. All that brings us together is our churches, our schools, our libraries. What happens when we provide remote access to the library?"

The silence I remember from my childhood library, and still find on occasion in a few big-city reading rooms, is the thick, busy silence one sometimes finds in an operating room. It is profoundly pleasing, profoundly full. There used to be such silences in many places, in open desert and in forests, in meadows and on riverbanks, and something of this kind of silence was common, a century or so ago, even in small towns, broken only by the unhurried sounds of unhurried people. There is no such silence in the world now; in every corner we live smothered by the shrill, growling, strident, piercing racket of crowded, hurried lives. The street is noisy, stores and banks and malls are noisy, classrooms are noisy, virtually every workplace is noisy. National parks and ocean shores and snowy mountains are noisy. And now the library is noisy, which is supposed to be a good thing. It is less "intimidating."

The boundaries that have kept the library a refuge from the street and the marketplace are being deliberately torn down in the name of access and popularity. No one seems to believe that there is a public need for refuge; no one seems to understand that people who can't afford computers and video games can hardly afford silence. In a world of noise and disordered information, a place of measured thought is the province once again of the wealthy, because it is invaluable.

Call me a curmudgeon. Or a romantic. Certainly my discomfort with the new library resides in that messy, hard-to-measure world of the aesthetic, the subtle, and the private. These are internal passions, as a reader's passions often are. I like a roomful of books, with its promise, its slow breath of mystery, the physical presence of history large and small. I have great faith in reading and in the immense possibilities of stories. And I believe that there is something vital about a community institution devoted to the pursuit of these things. Books and stories connect readers; their use by readers is kinetic and tactile, and readers leave evidence of their passing. But in the electronic world of marching data bits, the trail is purely local, and one's passing leaves no trace. As we slide from one transitory Web site to another, wondering what to believe—or believing everything, not knowing any better—no one bends near, in quiet courtesy.

The public library represents—at least in theory—a truly radical vision of democracy. At its best, it is an amalgam of anarchy and meritocracy. Franklin knew this, 200 years ago. It is, or could be, a huge, commonly held trust, not only of ideas but in one another—a kind of demand we've made on ourselves, a challenge, an expectation that the privilege of ideas, and the silence in which to consider them, will be cared for and exercised, and that its exercise will make us strong.

45   A few weeks ago I found myself in a large, carpeted, book-filled room. People of various colors and ages sat in armchairs, reading; soft classical music played over hidden loudspeakers; a dozen people browsed the nearby shelves. A few children read on the floor. No one spoke; each was lost in a world of carefully chosen words. It was a marvelous place, this Universe, this Library. But I was at a Barnes & Noble.

Notes

1. The Internet throws all librarians and patrons back to the arguments made in Franklin, Massachusetts. What does equal access mean on the Internet? Librarians have always exerted control over which books to buy, where to shelve them, how to catalog them, what to keep off open stacks. Should librarians exert any control over which sites are reached on the Internet, and by whom, and for how long? Will libraries "buy" every Internet address when they've never bought every book?

2. Nicholson Baker, whose persuasive article in the October 14, 1996, issue of *The New Yorker* delineated his deep-seated dislike of the new San Francisco Public Library building, its administrators, and all it and they represent, is now suing the SFPL for access to records documenting the destruction of more than 200,000 books. The library administration claims to have discarded half that number of books, all for legitimate reasons. They also took 50,000 catalog cards with notes written by patrons and made them wall decorations. Ian Shoales wrote last spring that the advent of electronic catalogs seems "as though some overenthusiastic bunch of bureaucratic technophiles came striding purposefully out of a focus group, and decided to dump baby, bathwater, towels, and soap out the window. What did they replace them with? Icons of baby, bath-water, towels, and soap." (A good line, though he doesn't mention the fact that he wrote this for *Salon*, an online magazine.)

3. I was especially curious about the big splashy exhibit put on by IAC, the Information Access Company. IAC sells Info Trac and SearchBank, systems that allow patrons to print out full-text magazine articles. IAC sells a fair portion of my own work without my permission—in fact, in spite of my "cease-and-desist" letters. My own local library offers patrons copies of dozens of different stories I've written, at ten cents per page; it bought the rights to sell my work from IAC, not from me. When I asked a salesman at the IAC booth about copyrights, he leaned over conspiratorially and said, "Don't worry, we take care of all that." Later, when I attended several panel discussions on electronic document delivery, problems with copyright and piracy went unmentioned.

Rereading Actively

1. Summarize the difference between library users like Tisdale and the new library user she describes.

2. With a partner or in a small group, discuss Tisdale's explanation of market issues like "library money" (¶ 6), "big surge[s] in attendance" (¶ 11), and "costs" (¶ 26). What are Tisdale's views of these issues?

3. Identify passages where Tisdale talks about goals libraries should embrace and write a brief explanation of these goals in your journal.

4. In a small group or with a partner, review the article, discussing the groups of library users that Tisdale identifies.

5. What effect does Tisdale gain by concluding her article with a reference to Barnes & Noble?

Exploring Your Responses

6. How do you respond to the comparison Tisdale makes between a national bookstore chain and the library? In your view, is there really a difference between browsing at a bookstore as opposed to at a library?

7. Describe your last trip to a library. What brought you there, and what did you do? Would Tisdale's ideas about "social uplift," "refinement," "knowledge," and "education" (¶ 7–9) apply?

8. With a partner or in a small group, take a trip to your local public library and observe the people who are using it. Compare your observations with what Tisdale describes.

9. Freewrite about the function that libraries fulfill, of making information available to the public.

BACKGROUND ASSIGNMENTS

The production and consumption of entertainment involves people in myriad exchanges. As these different writers assess the role of entertainment in American society, they try to work out what happens to people when entertainment becomes a property marketed to us by corporations. These writers are equally interested in what happens to a society when those entertainments become so sophisticated and pervasive that they begin to transform the very imaginations and tastes of the viewers. The approaches they take to the topic lead them to a variety of conclusions. All of these writers struggle with who is responsible for the effect of entertainment: some point to producers, some to audiences, some to the process through which the products are distributed. They draw distinctions between art and popular culture, worry about whether the commercialization degrades the efforts of artists and the experiences of audiences, explain how the marketplace can match artists to audiences with greater efficiency, and offer vocabularies, methods, and contexts for analyzing entertainment.

Making Connections

1. Brainstorm the kinds of entertainment that you pursue regularly. Focusing on one type, analyze your perception of the entertainment product, the process through which it is produced or performed, and your characteristics as a member of an audience that consumes it. Compare your consumption habits with those described by Gabler and Mandel et al.

2. Does our culture's appetite for entertainment affect other areas of our lives, for example, education, art, recreation, personal relationships? Drawing on Mandel et al.'s discussion of the potential energy of the entertainment economy, and following Tisdale's example of the conversion of libraries into a kind of entertainment center, show how our entertainment habits influence other areas of our lives.

3. Using Wolf and Mandel et al.'s discussions of the business of entertainment, analyze how business structures an entertainment that you like, and evaluate the effect the "business side" has on the end product.

4. Douglas declares that the entertainment media "continue to provide us with stories, images, and whopping rationalizations that shape how we make sense of the roles we assume in our families, our workplaces, our society" (¶ 15). In an essay, narrate your experience with a kind of entertainment that has been formative for you. Consider Tisdale as you evaluate the impact of this entertainment on your life.

5. Review Douglas's and Gabler's ideas about the purpose of entertainment critics, and write an essay that evaluates the role of a critic. Focus on the role, for example, that a sports page columnist, a movie, TV, or music reviewer, or one of the entertainment critics included in this text—does play in contrast to the role that such a critic ought to play.

6. In writing about advertising, Jib Fowles and Mary Kuntz (Chapter 5) note the vital connection between ads and entertainment. Choose an advertisement that you find entertaining. Use the description of the process of entertainment media offered by Douglas to explain how it entertains and affects an audience.

Collaborative Exchanges

1. In a small group, brainstorm mainstream entertainments and agree to focus on one. Then, talk about what separates art and popular entertainment, using Wolf's explanation of movie scripts as a guide. Develop a collaborative position on whether the entertainment you are focusing on qualifies as an art form or whether it just seeks the largest possible paying audience. Talk as well about whether you feel the distinction between entertainment and art is a good one. Be prepared to explain your analysis, the criteria you used, and your conclusion to the class.

2. In a small group, brainstorm entertainments that seem to be typed by gender—that is, that are "guy things," or for women. Focusing on one, use Douglas's ideas about how entertainment media "provide" consumers with images of gender and "shape" their understanding of gender roles. Discuss what kind of effect this shaping of roles has on gender relationships.

3. With two or three classmates, walk around your campus and visit your campus Web site, noting every kind of entertainment that you find. (Gabler, Tisdale, and Mandel et al. offer lists of different types.) Review your notes, and discuss the economic and social impact of entertainment in your campus environment. Be prepared to present your findings to the class. (You may find the essay by Mark Edmundson in the education unit to be helpful.)

Net Approaches

1. Explore the Web site for *Entertainment Tonight* <www.etonline.com>—a leader in entertainment reporting—and follow at least three embedded links. Freewrite on what these links tell you about the state of U.S. entertainment.

2. Point your browser to <www.liszt.com> and find a newsgroup focused on "entertainment." Scroll through the archived postings, and draft an analysis of the approach the group takes to entertaining itself. Be prepared to share your findings with the class.

3. Point your browser to <www.yahoo.com> and search for the home page of a major entertainment producer—a professional sports team, a motion picture producer, a TV network, a major dance company, opera, or symphony, or the like. Use Yahoo because it identifies "official" sites easily. Do a link search on your producer's site. To do this, go to AltaVista <www.altavista.com> and enter into the search box the string: *link:URL*. (Replace *URL* with the address of the official homepage of the producer; of course, other search engines also enable link searches and offer instructions for doing this on their help pages.) Scroll past thirty or forty hits to get a sense of the connections, and then look for vendors who use the entertainment producer as free advertising. Keep a list of what gets sold in the wake of this producer, and freewrite a reaction to what you find.

CASE-IN-POINT READINGS

WOMEN OF WALT DISNEY: SELLING FEMININITY FROM CINDERELLA TO MULAN

Since *Snow White* (1937), the Walt Disney Company has entertained children and adults alike with animated images of girls growing into womanhood. But the Disney heroine has also played an important role in building a business empire—in 1997 Disney generated over $22 billion in revenues—and shaping several generations' perceptions of femininity. Disney insiders defend the art and the brand; outsiders are fascinated with the products but anxious about their production and consumption, and as they dissect Disney, they reveal assumptions about what entertainment is and what it should be.

DISSECTING DISNEY
SCOTT HELLER

Scott Heller is a staff writer with the Chronicle of Higher Education, *the self-proclaimed "#1 news source for college and university faculty and administrators." This biweekly newspaper covers the higher education beat from jobs and funding to educational policy to trends in academics, students, faculty, technology, and curriculum. "Dissecting Disney" (1994) appeared in the "scholarship" section, a regular discussion of hot topics for scholars across the curriculum. In this piece of reporting, Heller weaves together the comments of several Disney critics along with reviews of recent scholarly studies of the Magic Kingdom, touching on the role Disney has come to play in popular culture. He also hints at Disney's attempt to control its public image and looks into a general academic uneasiness about a culture that is increasingly "disneyfied."*

Never one for highfalutin criticism, Walt Disney sniffed at the idea that his movies had deep meaning. "We just try to make a good picture," he told *Time* magazine in 1937. "Then the professors come along and tell us what we do."

Nearly 30 years after his death, when the entertainment empire he founded is more successful than ever, the professors have arrived to evaluate Disney's place in American cultural history. In cartoons, films, television shows, theme parks, design concepts, and merchandising strategies, they find ideal raw material to dissect and explain mass culture and consumer society in the 20th century.

Scholars are at once awed by Disney's reach, suspicious of his impact, and fearful of the company's legal wrath. "Disney has had its corporate finger in more sociocultural pies than perhaps any other twentieth century producer of mass entertainment," writes Eric Smoodin in *Disney Discourse: Producing the Magic Kingdom,* a collection of essays he is editing for Routledge.

Making Sense of an Enterprise

Art historians and film scholars were the first to take up Disney, focusing on the man and his ground-breaking animated films. Now historians, anthropologists, and cultural critics try to make sense of the entire corporate enterprise and its impact on American—and world—culture.

5   Telling the Disney story is part of a larger effort to explain American cultural history. "Popular culture is a mainstream field in American history now," says David Thelen, editor of *The Journal of American History.* "It's at the center of a lot of interpretive issues in the humanities."

Besides the Routledge collection, due out in May, Basic Books and Duke University Press each have scholarly projects on Disney in the works. Next month the Johns Hopkins University Press will publish *Walt in Wonderland: The Silent Films of Walt Disney,* by Russell Merritt and J. B. Kaufman.

Prince Charming kisses Cinderella and the Big Bad Wolf blows a couple of houses down, but in the new scholarly writing, another moment in the company's history is just as memorable: the bitter 1941 animators' strike, when Disney himself said Communist agitators were taking over the union. "The labor strike is a good way at getting at the tensions in a product that at first glance seems tensionless," says Mr. Smoodin, an associate professor of English at American University.

A Familiar Face

In Burbank, CA, on Mickey Avenue near Dopey Drive, sits the studio's corporate archive. Steven Watts, an associate professor of history at the University of Missouri at Columbia, has become a familiar face there as he gathers material for *The Magic Kingdom: Walt Disney and Modern American Culture,* expected out from BasicBooks next year. Among other things, Mr. Watts says he will trace how the Depression and the cold war were crucial to Disney's politics and the studio's works. The book will include interviews with Disney's wife, Lilly, and animators from the early days.

Academics have struggled to write about Disney. In 1942, an art historian at Harvard University wrote a book that hailed Disney as a great American artist. The historian lost his job—in part, Mr. Smoodin says, because he gave so much attention to a popular-culture figure.

10   Times have changed, if slowly. For nearly 10 years, Karal Ann Marling of the University of Minnesota has taught a popular class on Disney's art. In a forthcoming book, *As Seen on TV: The Visual Culture of Everyday Life in the 1950's* (Harvard University Press), she discusses how the Disney theme parks have influenced American architecture. But she is skeptical about the new round of Disney scholarship, because she says academic writing about the studio has been poorly researched and snobbish. "There's a lot of unconsidered slamming that still goes on," says Ms. Marling, a professor of art history and American studies.

Late last year the Walt Disney Company announced plans to build a theme park in Virginia that would depict key episodes in American history. Debate has already begun about whether the park will sugarcoat events in its displays on slavery and the Civil War.

"Instinctive Populism"

Scholars argue that Disney and his empire have been writing a version of American history all along.

In an essay being reviewed for publication in *The Journal of American History,* Mr. Watts argues that Disney's artistic creations were a bridge between Victorian values and a rapidly modernizing nation. "He makes people more comfortable with the new by casting it in familiar ways," says Mr. Watts. Ultimately, he adds. Disney's "instinctive populism" gave way to a reactionary streak, and the studio's animation became less experimental and more realistic.

Disney Discourse features articles on the company's international impact, including an analysis of Tokyo Disneyland and pieces on the studio's representations of Latin America in *The Three Caballeros* and *Saludos Amigos.* Those films, made as part of a cultural-goodwill effort in the 1940's, also helped open the Latin American market to the studio's productions.

15   In the book, Richard deCordova, an associate professor of communication at DePaul University, explains how Disney solidified a children's consumer market through the merchandising of its movies and spin-off products. He focuses on Mickey Mouse Clubs—not the television show of the 1950's but Saturday film clubs of the 1930's. To join, children would sign up in the toy department of a department store, as they wound through the collections of Mickey Mouse paraphernalia.

Today complaints about Saturday-morning television and pushy marketing to children are legion. Ironically, the response was very different in the early days of the Mickey Mouse Club, Mr. deCordova says. He maintains that the clubs drew on the language used by educational reformers, who said that children's play was healthy. By cross marketing toys and movies, he says, Disney was able to convince critics that movies were not harmful to children, while persuading children to gain satisfaction through shopping.

Obscure Cartoons

Besides editing *Disney Discourse,* Mr. Smoodin is the author of *Animating Culture: Hollywood Cartoons From the Sound Era* (Rutgers University Press, 1993). In it, he focuses on often-obscure cartoons, some of which were produced for political purposes. "Even cartoons," he writes, "those childish and unimportant cultural artifacts, are intertwined with behavior, with social control, and even with transnational relations."

That was especially true during World War II, Mr. Smoodin says, when the studio worked almost exclusively for the federal government, producing propagandistic short subjects and cartoons. Now scholars are taking a new look at those works, most of which are not included on the company's now-ubiquitous videotape compilations, according to Mr. Smoodin. "Disney has tried to eliminate anything the corporation considers timely," he says.

Mr. Smoodin highlights aspects of the uneasy relationship between the studio and the government in *Animating Culture*. For while Disney produced work for the government and came to testify against supposed Communists in the film industry, he was held in suspicion by J. Edgar Hoover, director of the Federal Bureau of Investigation. FBI records examined by Mr. Smoodin show that the agency monitored how its agents were to be portrayed in various Disney projects.

20   In 1942 the studio and the Treasury Department fought over who would pay for *The New Spirit,* an eight-minute cartoon that used Donald Duck to explain to American audiences the new income-tax system. Like a spoonful of sugar from Mary Poppins, the film was meant to make tax-paying go down easier, especially among the working class. In the cartoon, a resistant Donald Duck is persuaded that paying is patriotic, in part by a radio voice that relates the threat from Germany and Japan.

Big Reaction to Cartoon

In reviewing letters and reports to the Treasury Department, Mr. Smoodin found audiences mixed about the message. Lower-middle-class viewers were suspicious, but the use of a "star" like Donald Duck helped. Upper-class viewers, on the other hand, wrote to complain that they resented being treated like children. Others noted that the cartoon trivialized patriotic sentiments. Still others complained that the cartoon drummed up patriotic fervor through racist depictions of the Japanese and Germans.

All this over a cartoon? Mr. Smoodin argues that audience reaction to *The New Spirit* hints at the ways in which efforts to generate war-time consensus were limited. He and other cultural-studies scholars are less interested in what a text says and more in how audiences make sense of it and what that says about particular historical moments. "All of this is about showing that the intersections of culture and polities are very complex," Mr. Smoodin says.

One article not included in *Disney Discourse* is by David Kunzle, a professor of art history at the University of California at Los Angeles. Mr. Kunzle's piece dealt with imperialist messages in Disney's comic books. The article was dropped from the collection, he says, because editors couldn't guarantee that the company would give copyright clearance for illustrations. "This is the way Disney intimidates critics," Mr. Kunzle says.

Ultimately, Routledge decided not to include any illustrations in the book. "They're going the cowardly route," says Mr. Kunzle, who has dropped plans to do further scholarship on Disney because publishers don't want to battle a company known for taking copyright matters to court. (One article in the book describes several notable cases in which the company threatened legal action over use of its copyrighted characters.)

25   Edward Branigan, a film professor who brought the Disney collection to Routledge, says the matter came down to money. The press could neither pay for so many images nor claim fair use of comic-book reproductions, he says.

In 1992, at the last minute, Westview Press dropped the planned cover for *Vinyl Leaves: Walt Disney World and America,* by Stephen M. Fjellman, a professor of anthropology at Florida International University. Promotional materials for the book showed a color photograph of Cinderella Castle. Under pressure from the company, the press substituted a sketchy drawing of a castle, says Gordon Massman, senior editor at Westview.

Case-by-Case Basis

Ken Green, a Walt Disney Company spokesman, says the company handles all permission matters including scholarly requests on a case-by-case basis. "Any company whose products are creative will be careful of what they allow to be copied," Mr. Green says.

Mr. Watts of Missouri says the company has been very cooperative with his requests for access. But other scholars say they worry that Disney will be difficult about copyright, access to its archive, or other matters. Richard E. Foglesong, a professor of politics at Rollins College, plans to write a book that measures Walt Disney World's impact on the economy of Orlando, Fla., against the company's promises. So far, though, publishers have been wary of the project.

"I am not trying to write a hit-job book," Mr. Foglesong says. "Publishers, I have found, are gun-shy about getting involved in a book that might be critical about Disney." On the other hand, local groups opposed to the Virginia theme park want to hear more about his Florida research.

30   The Duke press plans to issue next year *Inside the Mouse: Work and Play at Disney World,* which grew out of an issue of *South Atlantic Quarterly.* Photographs taken of visitors at Disney World accompanied the journal. But the book's authors wonder whether they can include such illustrations—which feature people wearing Mickey Mouse T-shirts and riding Dumbo—in the book. "Everything within the boundaries of this private playland includes reference to copyrighted material," says Susan Willis, an associate professor of English at Duke. She is writing the book with Shelton Waldrep and Jane Kuenz, Duke graduate students, and Karen Klugman, a photographer and essayist.

Emphasis on Consumption

Inside the Mouse will try to understand the ways in which visitors accept or resist Disney World and its messages, especially the emphasis on consumption, Ms. Willis says. The book will also include interviews with park workers who have a love-hate relationship with their jobs.

Ms. Willis says the authors will have to grapple with a fact both simple and complex: Disney products, including Disney World itself, are fun. The goal, she says, "is not to be celebratory, but to give recognition to the types of pleasure that are possible in a consumerist culture."

Rereading Actively

1. Heller opens this article with a reference to Walt Disney and to the "entertainment empire" (¶ 2) he founded. Review the first three paragraphs, and then use a journal entry to describe their purpose and the attitude toward Disney and Disney critics that Heller seems to set up.

2. Review the article with a partner and list every kind of Disney product that Heller mentions, from animated features to afternoon cartoons to cartoon characters to theme parks and beyond. Review your list, and talk about which items play the biggest role for the scholars Heller profiles and which ones are most memorable for you yourselves. Summarize your discussion in a journal entry. Be prepared to compare the professors' view of Disney with that of the consumers of Disney products.

3. With the same partner from the previous exercise, review the article, focusing this time on Disney strategies like labor practices, representing history, marketing tie-ins, and protecting the brand. Link each strategy with a passage or two, and then in a collaborative journal entry explain Disney's likely purpose for pursuing each strategy as well as the critics' likely interest in the strategy. Review your list, write separate evaluations of the critics' understanding of Disney strategies, and share your evaluations.

4. Summarize the cultural role of Disney, as Heller presents it. How does his view compare with your sense of the company?

5. How do the final topics that Heller covers—Disney's protection of its intellectual property and the book *Inside the Mouse*—affect your sense of Disney and its critics? In a journal entry, analyze Heller's possible purposes for ending this article this way.

Exploring Your Responses

6. Freewrite about your favorite, least favorite, most confusing, or most memorable Disney moment, reflecting on the role Disney has played in your life. Review your freewrite, and then freewrite about whether or how a moment like this one should be the subject of a professor's analysis.

7. As a class, list all the studies that Heller mentions, and then break the class into groups of three or four students, assigning each group one of the studies. Working with your group, find the study in question or find reviews of that study or other work by that study's author. Summarize the material that you find—if your group is working with a book, summarize the introduction and the table of contents—and evaluate the contribution this material makes to an understanding of U.S. popular culture. Be prepared to present your findings to the class, perhaps turning your summary into a handout.

8. Reflect on Disney's attempt to control the Disney brand and to restrict academic use of Disney images. Draft a position paper on the cultural role of Disney, siding with either Michael Eisner—the Disney CEO—or a professor trying to study Disney.

CONSTRUCTION OF THE FEMALE SELF: FEMINIST READINGS OF THE DISNEY HEROINE
JILL BIRNIE HENKE, DIANE ZIMMERMAN UMBLE, AND NANCY J. SMITH

Jill Birnie Henke and Diane Zimmerman Umble study and teach communications and theater; Nancy Smith teaches education and directs a women's studies program. These three professors from different disciplines got together to write an article for a 1996 spe-cial issue of Women's Studies in Communications. *They come to Disney to analyze the role Disney has played in the way young women are understood and understand them-selves. To achieve this goal, they apply feminist frames of analysis, but they also draw on their own experience as "media consumers, teachers, scholars, and mothers of daughters." While the focus here is on the girls, the analysis of the roles boys and men play in the Dis-ney ideal of femininity are also important.*

This essay examines the way in which the female self is constructed in five Disney films: *Cinderella, Sleeping Beauty, The Little Mermaid, Beauty and the Beast,* and *Pocahontas.* Standpoint feminist theory and feminist scholarship on the psychologi-cal development of the perfect girl are used to form questions about selfhood, rela-tionships, power, and voice. Although heroines have expressed voice and selfhood in some of the later films, Disney's interpretations of children's literature and history remain those of a white, middle-class, patriarchal society.

Americans swim in a sea of Disney images and merchandise. Children can watch Disney videos before they brush their teeth with Disney character toothbrushes, go to sleep in *Beauty and the Beast* pajamas, rest their heads on *The Little Mermaid* pillow cases, check the time on *Pocahontas* watches, and drift off to sleep listening to Cin-derella sing, "No matter how your heart is grieving, if you keep on believing, the dream that you wish will come true" on their tape recorders. American children and their families watch Disney stories over and over again courtesy of their home video recorders. The Disney corporation produces myriad texts that form part of the cul-tural experience of American children and adults. Not only does Disney create a "won-derful world" of images, but the corporation also makes money in the process.

Disney re-releases its animated features to theaters on a seven-year rotation as a marketing strategy to attract a following in each new generation (Landis, "Hiberna-tion," p. 5D). Following theatrical showings, video cassettes are sold for a limited time. *Aladdin* earned $200 million in theaters in 1993, while its predecessor *Beauty and the Beast* grossed $20 million from the sale of videotapes alone (Landis, "Princely," p. 1D). This home video library provides families with opportunities for repeated viewing of such Disney films as *The Little Mermaid, Sleeping Beauty, Cinderella,* and *Pocahontas.*

This essay focuses on five animated features that span over fifty years of Disney storytelling and that portray a heroine as central to the story line: *Cinderella* (1950), *Sleeping Beauty* (1959), *The Little Mermaid* (1989), *Beauty and the Beast* (1991), and *Pocahontas* (1995.)[1] In light of the ubiquity of Disney's images, sounds, and stories, we examine the kind of world the Disney corporation constructs through its animated feature films, specifically what it means to be young and female.

This project grew out of our own experiences as media consumers, teachers, schol-ars, and mothers of daughters. We began with the assumption that mass media artic-ulates cultural values about gender by portraying women, men, and their relationships in particular ways. In addition, Julia Wood (1994) argues that the media also repro-duces cultural definitions of gender by defining what is to be taken for granted. Disney stories, then, have become part of a cultural repertoire of ongoing performances and reproductions of gender roles by children and adults; moreover, these stories present powerful and sustained messages about gender and social relations. Because our analy-sis is shaped by conversations with our daughters and our students as they began to adopt a critical stance toward Disney texts, the analytical framework we apply to these films is based on a synthesis of two streams of feminist thought: the psychological development of females, and standpoint feminist theory. Together, the perspectives illuminate the meaning and implications of Disney's filmic portrayal of girls.

The Oxymoron of Power and the Perfect Girl

5   Research by Carol Gilligan and her colleagues chronicles the psychological development of women's conceptualizations of the self. Gilligan (1982) argues that women learn to value connections with others and at least in part define themselves through their relationships with others. Orenstein (1994), who examines the related concern of how gender is constructed in the classroom, describes the hidden curriculum that teaches girls to view silence and compliance as virtues. Those values present a dilemma for bright girls who must simultaneously be "selfless and selfish, silent and outspoken, cooperative and competitive" (pp. 36–37). After studying white middle-class girls at all-girls schools, Brown and Gilligan (1992) suggest that the solution to this dilemma rests with females' invention of a self: the "perfect girl." The perfect girl, in white middle-class America, is "the girl who has no bad thoughts or feelings, the kind of person everyone wants to be with, the girl who, in her perfection, is worthy of praise and attention, worthy of inclusion and love.... [She is the] girl who speaks quietly, calmly, who is always nice and kind, never mean or bossy" (p. 59). Yet, these same girls know from their own experiences that people do get angry, wish to speak, and want to be heard. The consequence of these contradictory gender/social messages is that a girl is "caught between speaking what she knows from experience about relationships and increased pressure to negate this knowledge for an idealized and fraudulent view of herself and her relationships" (p. 61). Hence, Brown and Gilligan (1992) conclude that on the way to womanhood a girl experiences a loss of voice and loss of a sense of self as she silences herself.

During the process of this intellectual and emotional silencing, girls also are developing physically in new ways. According to Brown and Gilligan (1992), changes in girls' bodies "visually disconnect them from the world of childhood and identify them in the eyes of others with women" (p. 164). Girls conflate standards of beauty and standards of goodness by learning to pay attention to their "looks" and by listening to what others say about them. They learn to see themselves through the gaze of others, hear about themselves in ways that suggest they can be perfect, and believe that relationships can be free of conflict. These girls "struggle between knowing what they know through experience and what others want them to know, to feel and think" (p. 64). As a result, girls learn that speaking up can be disruptive and dangerous because it might put relationships at risk. The cruel irony is that by withholding their voices, girls also risk losing relationships that are genuine and authentic. In effect, girls struggle daily with the "seduction of the unattainable, to be all things to all people, to be perfect girls and model women" (p. 180).

Julia Wood's (1992) critique of Gilligan's line of research expands our application of Gilligan's work on the construction of the female self to Disney films. Wood explores the tension between Gilligan's apparently essentializing stance and a poststructural stance which emphasizes the structural effects of cultural life on individuals. The result is what Wood calls "standpoint epistemology."

"Standpoint theory prompts study of conditions that shape lives and the ways individuals construct those conditions and their experiences within them" (Wood, 1992, p. 15). For women, this theory helps explain how a female's position within a culture shapes her experiences. Because cultures define people by gender, race, and class, they often impose limits on women's experiences and women's ability to appreciate the experiences of others. Standpoint feminism argues that women have been and still are treated as "others" and "outsiders" in patriarchal societies. Although women's experiences are diverse to be sure, Wood (1992) argues that scholars should look for conditions among women that unify them. Oppression, for example, is one condition that seems universal among women: "Survival for those with subordinate status often depends quite literally on being able to read others, respond in ways that please others, and assume responsibility for others' comfort" (p. 16).

Yet, differences among women, as individuals and as members of identifiable categories within broadly shared social conditions, should not be overlooked. Our analysis of Disney characters responds to this call by articulating their similarities and their differences. Indeed, our analysis suggests that one value of standpoint feminist epistemology lies in unveiling which differences are conspicuously absent. For example, the heterosexist assumption underlying all five Disney films is not only the dominant social construct influencing relationships, it is the only social construct. None of the female figures questions that assumption. Standpoint theory, then, provides the means to understand how women's voices are muted and how women can regain their voices and become empowered (Wood, 1991).

10   Mary Parker Follett, an American intellectual whose ideas were touted by the business community in the 1940s, wrote about the construction and use of power in society in *Creative Experience* (1924). "Coercive power," Parker Follett wrote, "is the curse of the universe; coactive power, the enrichment of every human soul" (p. xii). In later works she defined two types of power—"power-over" and "power-with": "It seems to me that whereas power usually means power-over, the power of some person or group over some other person or group, it is possible to develop the conception of power-with, a jointly developed power, a co-active, not a coercive power" (1944, p. 101). While Parker Follett did not explicitly use the expression "power from within," this understanding is embedded in her discussion of the need for social constructs which preserve the integrity of the individual. She argues that a society can only progress if individuals' internal needs are met in the processes adopted by the group.

Parker Follett's conceptualization of power, in conjunction with the principles contained in standpoint feminist theory and Gilligan's perspective on the psychological development of girls, forms the foundation for a series of questions that the following analysis of Disney's animated films hopes to answer: How do the worlds of Disney films construct the heroine's sense of self? To what degree is her self-knowledge related to or in response to her relationships with others? Do Disney heroines model the "perfect girl"? On the way to womanhood, what does the Disney heroine give up? What are the ways in which the female characters experience their lives as "others" and themselves as strangers in their relationship to self and others? And what are the power dynamics of those relationships?

Until the recent publication of *From Mouse to Mermaid: The Politics of Film, Gender, and Culture* (Bell, Haas, & Sells, 1995), few scholarly analyses addressed the foregoing questions about gender constructions in the worlds of Disney animated films.[2] However, with the Bell, Haas, and Sells' edition, critical analyses of Disney discourses entered a new phase. This edited collection maps "the ideological contours of economics, politics, and pedagogy by drawing Disney films as vehicles of cultural production" (p. 7). Within this ideological map, the cultural reproduction of gender is examined by several authors.

For example, Jack Zipes (1995) argues that characterizations of Disney heroines remain one-dimensional and stereotypical, "arranged according to a credo of domestication of the imagination" (p. 40). The values imparted in Disney fairy tales are not those of original folk tellers, nor of the original writers such as Perrault or Andersen; instead, they are the values of Disney's male writers. Thus, even when the fairy tale is supposed to focus on the heroine (Snow White, Cinderella, Sleeping Beauty, Beauty, or the Little Mermaid), "these figures are pale and pathetic compared to the more active and demonic characters in the film" (p. 37). These alleged heroines are "helpless ornaments in need of protection, and when it comes to the action of the film, they are omitted" (p. 37). In contrast, while Laura Sells' (1995) Marxist feminist analysis of *The Little Mermaid* sees the story's resolution as a "dangerous message about appropriation" (p. 185), Sells remains hopeful nevertheless because "Ariel enters the white male system with her voice—a stolen, flying voice that erupted amidst patriarchal language, a voice no longer innocent because it resided for a time in the dark continent that is the Medusa's home" (p. 185).

Our analysis elaborates upon the two themes that Zipes and Sells introduce: the relative power or powerlessness of the Disney heroine, and the discovery or loss of that heroine's voice. Thus, our exploration of the construction of the female self and the interaction of that self with other film characters corroborates and extends the work of Bell, Haas, and Sells. We utilize standpoint feminist theory, Follett's theories of power, and Gilligan and Brown's theories of female psychological development to chronicle the nature and evolution of Disney's construction of the female self.

Construction of the Female Self

15   Disney's early heroines, Cinderella and Aurora, are portrayed as helpless, passive victims who need protection. Indeed, Cinderella is the quintessential "perfect girl," always gentle, kind, and lovely. Their weaknesses are contrasted with the awesome and awful power of the evil women with whom they struggle. However, later Disney films shift from simple stories of passive, young virgins in conflict with evil, mature women to more complex narratives about rebellion, exploration, and danger. Heroines Ariel, Belle, and Pocahontas display an increasingly stronger sense of self, of choice, and of voice.

This growing empowerment of Disney heroines is reflected in shifting depictions of their intimate relationships. While early heroines fall in love at first sight and easily marry to live happily ever after, love relationships for the later heroines come at a cost. Ariel temporarily gives up her voice and ultimately relinquishes her cultural identity. Belle discovers love only through trials, sacrifice, and learning to look beneath the surface. Ultimately, though, her love releases the Beast from the bonds of his own selfishness so they, too, are "empowered" to live happily ever after together.

Of all of Disney's characters, Pocahontas seems to break new ground. The narrative begins with her as a young woman in possession of a strong, well-developed sense of self, and a conviction that her destiny only remains to be discovered. Unlike other Disney heroines, she resists losing her identity to another for the sake of a marriage relationship. Her position and value in her community, her relationships with other females, and her understanding of her interdependence with the earth provide the most holistic picture yet of a co-actively empowered character in Disney animated films.

In her classic essay, "The Solitude of Self," Elizabeth Cady Stanton (1892) advanced a feminist vision in which women experience the sovereignty of the self, and women and girls are empowered from within. Stanton indicted patriarchy for systematically denying women the skills and rights to exist as sovereign selves. Over a century later, feminists still envision a diversity of female figures acting on the world from knowledge of their own worth and dreams. Are traces of these visions contained in Disney's filmic heroines?

The five films we examine situate the central female character—who is portrayed as gentle, kind, beautiful, and virginal—in an oppressive social milieu where mothers or other sources of female guidance and wisdom are largely absent. Until *Pocahontas,* in fact, these young heroines faced the challenges of their lives without the benefit of other women's support, nurturance, or guidance.

20   Cinderella, Aurora, Ariel, Belle, and Pocahontas also share another quality: they all have dreams. Each differs, however, in her power to make that dream come true. The conventional Disney tale introduces the heroine near the film's beginning through a song in which she expresses these dreams. For example, viewers first meet Cinderella when she awakens from a dream and sings, "No matter how your heart is grieving, if you keep on believing, the dream that you wish will come true." Minutes later, viewers discover that her daily reality is anything but dreamy. Supported by an army of mice and barnyard animals who come to her aid, Cinderella is continuously reminded by humans in the household that she is unworthy of their "refined" company. Cinderella's stepmother and stepsisters control Cinderella, keeping her locked away from both society and opportunity. Cinderella is portrayed as powerless to act on her own behalf. Hence, she can only dream.

Perhaps Cinderella best illustrates the Disney pattern of subjugating and stifling heroines' voices and selfhood. Her gentleness and goodness are defined by her lack of resistance to abuse by her stepfamily in the film's world. She never disobeys an order, never defends her rights, and never challenges their authority over her. She rarely eats, seldom sleeps, and receives not even the simplest of courtesies, except from her animal friends. Her father's fortune is squandered for the benefit of her stepsisters. She is powerless to control her own fate in her own home. Unable to control her own time, she also is unable to control her own destiny. Cinderella does not act, she only reacts to those around her, a sure sign of both external and internalized oppression. In the face of all this abuse, she somehow remains gentle, kind and beautiful—the perfect girl.

Similarly, *Sleeping Beauty*'s Aurora is a playful teenager whose friends are forest animals, and whose dream is expressed in the song "Some day my prince will come." Aurora is on the verge of celebrating her sixteenth birthday—the day her identity will be revealed to her. At this point she has no knowledge that she really is a princess who was betrothed at birth. Her parents' choices for her define Aurora's destiny and she has no voice in shaping that destiny.

Like Cinderella, Aurora is obedient, beautiful, acquiescent to authority, and essentially powerless in matters regarding her own fate. Furthermore, there is no one Aurora can trust. Although the fairies "protect" her from the truth about her identity and the curse on her future "for her own good," Aurora can take no action on her own behalf. Passively, she is brought back to the castle where she falls under the spell of Maleficent, touches the spinning wheel, and sleeps through most of the film while others battle to decide her future. When she awakens, she finds her "dream come true," a tall, handsome prince who rescues her from an evil female's curse.

Beginning with *The Little Mermaid,* however, the female protagonist shows signs of selfhood. Near the beginning of the film, Ariel sings of her dream to explore and her feelings of being misunderstood. She also expresses frustration and resistance: "Betcha on land they understand. Bet they don't reprimand their daughters. Bright young women, sick of swimmin', ready to stand." She asks, "When's it my turn?"

25   In contrast to the two previous demure female protagonists, Ariel is characterized as willful and disobedient. She follows her dreams even though she knows her actions run counter to the wishes of her father, King Triton. As a result, Triton charges the crab, Sebastian, with chaperoning his daughter "to protect her from herself." One might also read his actions as patriarchy's efforts to prevent her from achieving an independent identity. However, despite Triton's efforts to control Ariel, she explores, she asks questions, she makes choices, and she acts. For example, she rescues the human, Prince Eric, from the sea. She strikes a bargain with the sea witch, Ursula, to trade her voice for legs. Additionally, she prevents Eric's marriage to Ursula and protects him from Ursula's attack in the film's final battle. Nevertheless, it is Eric who finally kills the sea witch and it is Triton whose power enables Ariel to return to the human world by transforming her permanently into a human. Thus, while Ariel chooses to leave her own people for a life with Eric, it is still not her power but her father's power which enables her dreams to come to fruition.

Articulating one's own dreams and wishes—possessing an autonomous voice—is a strong indicator of the development of selfhood. Little wonder, then, that alarms sound for feminists concerned with the psychological development of girls and women's sense of self when Ariel literally sacrifices her voice and mermaid body to win Eric's love. What is gained by females who silence themselves in a masculinist society? What are the costs to their psychic selves for not doing so? Scholars in feminist psychological development describe the seductiveness of external rewards by denying one's selfhood (Brown & Gilligan, 1992). Having a voice, a sense of selfhood, is risky because it is inconsistent with images of the "perfect girl" or the true woman. When one's loyalty is not to the "masculinist system," one can end up on the margins at best and at worst socially "dead." Ultimately, Ariel's voice is silenced and she sacrifices her curiosity to gain the love of a man.

Reality for Belle in *Beauty and the Beast* means being female and wanting to experience adventure in the "great wide somewhere." Like the earlier Disney heroines, Belle dreams of having "so much more than they've got planned." Belle is the first of the Disney heroines to read, but her reading also alienates her from others in the community. She experiences herself as an "other." Townspeople call her peculiar and say that "she doesn't quite fit in." While Belle is aware of their opinions of her, and understands that she is supposed to marry a villager, raise a family, and conform, she also knows that she *is* different and *wants* something different—something "grand." Although Belle is unsure about how to attain her dreams, she does refuse to marry Gaston, the community "hunk" and its most eligible bachelor. She reads rather than socialize with the villagers, and she accepts that she can be nothing other than different from them. Belle likes herself and trusts her own judgment. Nevertheless, Belle is marginalized by the community for her uniqueness, for her sense of self.

Unlike her counterparts in *Cinderella* and *Sleeping Beauty*, Belle is no damsel in distress. Neither is she a helpless witness to the film's action nor removed from it. Belle occupies double the screen time of any other character in the film (Thomas, 1991), and Belle acts for herself. She dreams of more than a "provincial life"; she wants adventure and, as she sings, "for once it might be grand, to have someone understand, I want so much more than they've got planned." The line might have continued, "for a girl!"

Gaston, the village brute, is attracted to Belle because of her appearance not her brain. He sings that she's "the most beautiful, so that makes her the best." He offers her a place in the community with his marriage proposal. While other women swoon for his attention, Belle rejects him: "His little wife. No, sir. Not me!" Belle's sense of self is strong enough that she refuses to settle for less than a relationship which acknowledges and values her mind, in essence, her self. However, when her father is captured by the Beast, Belle comes to his rescue and offers herself in his place. By trading her life for her father's, she seems to have relinquished her selfhood. Once a prisoner in the Beast's castle, she laments to Mrs. Potts, a kind teapot, that she has lost her father, her dreams, "everything." However, this lament suggests that she still has dreams of her own and a sense of identity apart from that of a dutiful daughter.

30   Belle's dilemma occurs in part because she has a caring, co-active power relationship with her father (Parker Follett, 1944). Decision making undertaken by women who attempt to maintain selfhood but also exist in a power-with relation to others becomes much more complex, as Gilligan (1977) notes. This complexity is further illustrated by the choices that Belle subsequently makes in her relationship with the Beast. Belle negotiates the conflict she feels between freedom from the Beast and her growing affection for him. She decides not to leave him in the woods after he rescues her from wolves. Although she could escape, she chooses to help him instead. Later in the film, she again chooses to return to the Beast's castle to warn him of the impending mob, even though the Beast has released her from her promise to stay in his castle.

Like Ariel, Belle has freedom to make choices and to act on her own behalf as well as on the behalf of others; and she exercises that freedom. However, whereas Ariel at least initially seems to act out of a sense of rebellion, Belle's motivation appears to come from a craving for intellectual engagement. A simple masculinist interpretation might be that Belle acts out of a sense of personal honor or duty (to sacrifice her freedom first to help her father and later to keep the Beast). A more feminist interpretation based on Gilligan's psychoanalytic developmental work and standpoint theory might be that Belle acts as a result of the tension from seeking selfhood and relationships with others simultaneously. Thus, Belle's actions can be read as a series of complex decisions about when to act, and when to care for someone, how to administer comfort, when to take matters into her own hands, when to risk her personal safety. She is concerned not only with others but with herself as well, and her actions speak to both needs.

No victim, Belle sets the terms for the bargains she makes. In this sense, she exercises more power on her own behalf than previous Disney heroines. For Cinderella, Aurora, and Ariel, someone in power established the conditions within which their dreams could be realized. For example, Cinderella's fairy godmother gave her only until midnight to make her dream come true. At Aurora's christening, the good fairy Merryweather saved Aurora from Maleficent's death curse by decreeing that Aurora would sleep until awakened by a prince's kiss. And when Ariel gave her voice to Ursula in return for the sea witch's magical ability to transform Ariel into a human, Ursula placed a three day time limit on Ariel's pursuit to win Eric's love. Unlike Belle, these females have limited and tenuous opportunities to achieve their dreams. In contrast, Belle exercises substantial control over setting the terms of her own fate. She preserves her own options—by refusing Gaston's overtures and brushing off the villagers' criticisms, and she gives others options—by freeing her father from the Beast's prison, becoming a prisoner herself, and saving the Beast from the wolves. *She* holds *their* futures in her hands. Yet, ironically, one reading of the narrative conclusion is that Belle's liberation of the Beast from his spell ends with her becoming yet another "perfect girl" who marries the prince and lives happily ever after.

Another theme introduced in *Beauty and the Beast*—heroine as teacher—is expanded in *Pocahontas*. Just as Belle teaches the Beast how to be civil, gentle, and caring, Pocahontas teaches John Smith, her tribe, and the Englishmen about nature, power, and peace. Like Belle, Pocahontas exercises power over her future. Viewers first are introduced to Pocahontas going where the wind (the spirit of her mother) leads her; as the chief's daughter, however, she knows that she must take "her place" among her people. Her father tells her, "Even the wild mountain stream must someday join the big river." She sings, "We must all pay a price. To be safe, we lose our chance of ever knowing what's around the river bend.... Why do all my dreams stand just around the river bend.... Is all my dreaming at an end?"

Like Ariel, Pocahontas defies her father in exploring her world. Like Belle, she is an active doer, not a passive victim. She also has a savage to tame in the form of an Englishman. Pocahontas introduces John Smith to the colors of the wind and to the mysteries of the world of nature. She takes political stances such as advocating alternatives to violence, and she makes choices about her life. For example, Pocahontas' decision to reject both her father's wish that she marry Kocoum, the Powhatan warrior, and John Smith's plea to go with him back to England signify that the power to control her actions are in her hands. Pocahontas' choices reflect a sense of selfhood that is a bold stroke for a Disney heroine. A feminist psychological reading might see in her decision to embrace her cultural roots an alternative to Disney's typical heterosexual narratives in which the "perfect girl's" destiny is a monogamous relationship with a (white) man. Indeed, far more than Belle, Pocahontas finds power within to express a self which is separate from that defined through relationships to a father or love interest.

35   Our reading of Pocahontas implies that she is clearly the most elaborate and complex character in this group of heroines. Her dreams direct her choices. She weighs the risks of choosing a smooth course versus seeking the unknown course to see what awaits her just around the river bend. With counsel from female mentors, Grandmother Willow and the spirit of the wind that symbolizes her mother, Pocahontas finds the strength to listen to her own inner voice, and to choose the less safe, uncharted course of autonomous womanhood. When confronted with the option of leaving her community in order to accompany her love interest, John Smith, she rejects his offer and instead takes her place as an unattached female leader of her people.

Pocahontas brings to the forefront the absence of diversity among Disney's previous female characters. From Cinderella through Belle, Disney's female protagonists easily could be the same characters with only slight variations in hair color. Pocahontas, too, varies only slightly in skin color, but she is the first non-Anglo heroine who is the subject of a Disney animated film. Furthermore, although some of the women may not have difficult family circumstances, (e.g., Cinderella), as Caucasians, they all belong to the privileged class in their societies, as daughters of kings, Indian chiefs, and educated inventors.

As this examination of Cinderella, Aurora, Ariel, Belle, and Pocahontas demonstrates, over time Disney's female protagonists have begun to look beyond home, to practice resistance to coercion, and to find their own unique female voices. Indeed, in Pocahontas Disney offers an adventurous female who develops a sense of self in a culture other than the dominant Anglo culture, and who chooses a destiny other than that of heterosexual romantic fulfillment.

Construction of Self in Relation to Others

Evolving constructions of the female self affect the heroine's relationship to other humans in the world of Disney, and the power dynamics of those relationships. In *Cinderella* and *Sleeping Beauty,* males and evil older females hold "power over" other marginalized groups, including the young, naive, inquisitive heroines. However, in later Disney films, especially *Pocahontas,* these female characters enact "power-with" other humans. For example, by fostering cooperation between the English and the Native Americans near the end of the film, Pocahontas exercises "power-with" relationships rather than the traditional patriarchal "power-over" relationships that can result in conflict or violence. Pocahontas' actions invite viewers to interrogate assumptions about the nature and sources of power because her power orientation goes against the grain of conventional patriarchal patterns of power, and is effective in resolving conflict. Her "power-with" pattern may well be motivated by her desire to preserve relationships—a quality often associated with women, or may be a Disney anomaly since Pocahontas is a doubly marginalized other—i.e. Native American and female; regardless, the film makes the enactment of "power with" visible and potent.

Similarly, the dynamics of power in heterosexual romantic relationships evidence change over time. In the early Disney animated classics, love was sparked instantly. Cinderella and Aurora fall in love with a prince at "first sight." In both cases, a man (prince) in love rescues Cinderella and Aurora from the clutches of jealous, malicious, older women who hold "power over" them. However, while their marriages to these princes liberate them from desperate circumstances, neither Cinderella nor Aurora exercises much personal choice in the unions. In *Cinderella,* the king decrees that the prince will marry the girl whose foot fits the glass slipper; in *Sleeping Beauty,* the king betroths Aurora at birth to Prince Philip. Cinderella and Aurora merely move from one relationship to another in which others have "power-over" them. What they gain is material and marital security.

40   In contrast, Ariel and Belle exercise considerably more personal choice in their unions. Ariel falls in love with Eric the moment she sees him, and she sets out to win his love at great personal risk and physical pain. After she saves Eric's life, she then sets out on a quest to secure his love with only her good looks but not her voice. Her success leads her powerful father, Triton, to relent and permit her to leave the sea to live on the land. However, Ariel has had to sacrifice her voice and intellectual curiosity for a man's love and move from Triton's "power-over" her to a world in which her power is dependent on her affiliation with Eric.

Unlike Ariel, Belle is not the pursuer but the pursued. However, the drama in *Beauty and the Beast* also centers on a female's quest for "freedom to." In this story, the heroine (not an evil stepmother, witch, or controlling father) sets the terms for her relationships. When Belle demands more than Gaston's good looks and physical prowess, and Gaston subsequently refuses to accept her on those terms, she rejects his courtship. Further, it is Belle who controls the Beast's destiny, for he must follow her lead if he is to be freed from his curse. Only when Belle and the Beast begin the hard work of learning to love do both find love and liberation (Rich, 1986). Their relationship represents a "power with" approach in its expression of mutuality, compromise, and shared sacrifice. Nevertheless, their marriage still follows the old Disney power script—the *king*dom is restored.

Aside from obvious historical inaccuracies, Disney's *Pocahontas* subsumes its love theme within the larger theme of personal destiny. Love takes second seat to a larger story about a young woman in pursuit of a dream. The love of a man is neither necessary nor sufficient for the accomplishment of her goal. Pocahontas' happiness, then, is not determined by whom she marries, but by her own discovery of selfhood. This is shown initially when she resists her father's edict to marry Kocoum and therefore find stability and security. Her father tells her that Kocoum would make a fine husband: "He is a handsome, sturdy warrior who builds handsome sturdy walls." At the end of the story, and in an unusual shift for Disney, Pocahontas appears to reject marriage altogether. Her acceptance of herself and her leadership role within her community are the keys to her happiness.

We suspect it is not accidental that the heroine with whom Disney makes this latest shift from "power with" to "power to" is not from the dominant white culture. From a standpoint feminist perspective, one critical concern should be that the only Disney female figure who maintains selfhood independent of a heterosexual love relationship comes from a culture which has been marginalized (Collins, 1986; Harding, 1991). From another perspective, this Disney portrayal sustains a denial of the genocide of Native Americans, thereby lessening the impact and threat of a female embodying selfhood.

In the world of these Disney animated films, the young heroines hold relationships with other women as well as with men. In contrast to the limited power of the heroines, many of the supporting female characters display various kinds of power in their relationships. However, those depicted as evil clearly are characters who have more "power over" and "power to." For example, the Fairy Godmother in *Cinderella* has the power to grant Cinderella's wish to attend the Prince's ball. She can transform pumpkins into a coach and mice into horses. She creates an elegant gown with the wave of her wand. However, her "power over" is limited for it is effective only until midnight when everything becomes as it was. The Fairy Godmother apparently also lacks the power to intervene in Cinderella's conflict with the stepmother who abuses her and squanders her inheritance. Thus, the "good" Fairy Godmother has limited "power over" the world of dreams, but no "power over" Cinderella's physical realities which go unchallenged. The "power over" Cinderella's everyday life lies in the hands of a stepmother who is cold, cruel, and bitterly jealous. She makes Cinderella a slave in her own house and controls what Cinderella is and does. Cinderella herself is powerless to change her situation. It is the mice who enable her to escape the locked room and to try on the glass slipper.

45   Similarly, in *Sleeping Beauty,* the chubby, bumbling kindhearted fairies have the power to amend Aurora's death curse into one hundred years of sleep, but Maleficent's evil power cannot be overcome entirely by their good powers. Nevertheless, the good fairies contribute to the resolution of the conflict by equipping Prince Philip with weapons which bring Maleficent down and determine Aurora's fate.

In *The Little Mermaid,* fairies and godmothers give way to male protectors. Sebastian (a crab), Scuttle (a sea gull), and Flounder (a fish) prove to be no match for Ursula, the powerful sea witch. Ursula is both seductive and repulsive. She skillfully wields power over the Merpeople who want to become more physically attractive to the opposite sex, and turns hapless Merpeople into groaning, clutching, mournful seaweed who line the walls of her cave. She manipulates Ariel into complicity with her plan to overthrow King Triton by sending her eels to convince Ariel that Ursula can help her. In exchange for giving Ariel human form, Ursula takes her voice, believing that Ariel is the key to Triton's undoing. In the end, a helpless Ariel is rescued by her father who then must relinquish his power to Ursula in exchange for Ariel's life. These dynamics can be characterized as a struggle between Ursula and Triton to exert "power over" Ariel in an effort to gain control.

While Fairies and Godmothers are females who use their powers for good, they also are limited in strength, bumbling, inept, and absentminded. Disney's evil females are magnificent in their strength, presence, and rage. Visually, they loom large and dark on the screen as they trick, manipulate, and threaten. They control others' options and access to money, shelter, and relationships with men. These evil females—Cinderella's stepmother, Maleficent, and Ursula—often are alienated from their communities. In Disney tales, evil women are driven by the desire to have what isn't theirs—purity, beauty, acceptance, love. For example, in *Cinderella,* no matter how hard the stepmother tries to turn her ugly daughters into beauties, the stepsisters never acquire what comes naturally to Cinderella—beauty, kindness, and a lovely voice. In *Sleeping Beauty,* Maleficent rails at the king and queen for omitting her from the guest list for Aurora's christening. For this social slight, Maleficent curses the baby to die on or before her sixteenth birthday. And in *The Little Mermaid,* when Ursula's ambitions lead to her banishment from the sea kingdom by Triton, she vows revenge by using Ariel, his favorite, beautiful, and youngest daughter. In each case, however, the use of power by these strong, evil females results in each's literal or social death. Cinderella's stepmother and stepsisters experience social ostracism; Maleficent dies at the hands of Prince Philip; and Ursula is destroyed after being pierced by the mast of a ship captained by Prince Eric. Ironically, these villainesses' drives for power are thwarted, in part, by forces marshalled in defense of the innocence and beauty of the ones they hope to destroy.

In Disney's versions of these tales, women are more often pitted against one another than supportive of one another. For instance, in the original *Cinderella* fairy tale, Cinderella ultimately invites her stepmother to live in the castle, and her stepsisters are married to dukes, thus improving everyone's station in life. In the classic *Sleeping Beauty,* there are seven good fairies to the one old, evil one. The fairies all have equal power, and the prince does not kill the evil fairy—she dies of old age. There is no competition or power inequities between good and bad fairies in the tale. In Andersen's version of *The Little Mermaid,* a wise grandmother counsels the little mermaid in the ways of the sea world where she is surrounded by a community of loving sisters; such sources of female wisdom and companionship disappear in Disney's version.

In *Beauty and the Beast* and *Pocahontas,* female villains disappear. Belle's social landscape features few females. While Mrs. Potts (the teapot) offers comfort, she can do little to change Belle's circumstances. Other females either play only minor, comic parts—like the buxom feather duster and the picky wardrobe, or are shown in stark contrast to Belle—i.e., the village maidens who swoon over Gaston. Belle is the only female in the film empowered to take action on her own.

50   Pocahontas, however, lives in a supportive community of female mentors and friends. She seeks guidance from mother wind, from Grandmother Willow, and from her friend, Nacoma. Each female character has Pocahontas' best interests at heart. Rather than competing with her, these women cooperate to help Pocahontas find her sense of self, her voice, and her destiny. For example, when she comes to Grandmother Willow for counsel, the tree tells her that the truth she is seeking lies within;

Pocahontas must listen to herself. The depiction of female relationships in *Pocahontas* compared to *Cinderella, Sleeping Beauty,* and *The Little Mermaid* dramatically symbolizes the differences between "power-with" and "power-over."

Conclusion

As our analysis of these five films illustrates, the portrayal of female heroines in Disney animated features has changed with time. Increasingly, Disney heroines have acquired the ability to articulate their dreams and to enact changes in their lives as they pursue those dreams. Yet, we suggest that this evolution may well function hegemonically to maintain the patriarchal status quo while tacitly acknowledging the changing roles of women in contemporary society. This leads us to conclude that Disney films provide at best ambiguous and at worst troubling postfeminist messages for young viewers. Clearly, more recent Disney heroines acquire a greater sense of selfhood; however, Cinderella, Aurora, Ariel, and even Belle still end up reinforcing the image of the "perfect girl." Four of the five heroines are destined to live "happily ever after" with their white, male princes; forgotten are their explorations and dreams of something "grand." Perhaps the idea of "grand" or of "something more than they've got planned" is indeed a marriage to a prince in a castle. Four of the five heroines settle for class privilege, and marital and material security.

Consistent with Wood's (1992) discussion of standpoint epistemology as a guide for assessing the impact of social constructs on individuals, we conclude that patriarchal constructs control the development of women's construction of self in four of the five Disney films we examined. Disney heroines can change the circumstances of their oppression, but only from wicked stepmothers, protective fathers, uncivilized, boorish beasts, and simple villagers. And, these heroines all opt for royal lives replete with privilege provided by a prince. Ariel goes even further, sacrificing her own culture and identity as a mermaid.

Disney films also evidence change in the nature of power in the relationships affecting the heroines' lives. In the earlier films, these relationships consist predominantly of "power-over" relationships with the heroines. More contemporary heroines like Belle and Pocahontas demand and achieve "power-with" relationships, although we wonder whether Belle's relationship with the Beast, now a prince, will sustain any "power-with" qualities as they begin their conventional marital lives.

Only in *Pocahontas* does the heroine maintain her selfhood throughout the film; consequently, only in Pocahontas is the heroine likely to maintain "power with" and "power to" relationships. Pocahontas chases her destiny; and she flies in the face of both males and females who attempt to oppress her. She continues to strive for a better world regardless of the difficulty of her path. She rejects marriage as the goal within her own culture (Kocoum) or another culture (John Smith). People *listen* to her, take her seriously, and trust her. At no time is Pocahontas like Ariel, chaperoned in order to save her from herself; nor is she trivialized by members of her own community, as is the case with Belle. Pocahontas is clearly not a "perfect girl" for she speaks and acts as she believes she should, not as others would like her to be. Because her sense of power comes from within, she enables herself to act on her world and in her own behalf.

55   Yet, at this point, Pocahontas is an anomaly among Disney heroines. In a world in which women still struggle to be heard, the preferred reading of Disney's image of

women is one which affirms heroines like Ariel who give up their voices in order to use their looks to pursue the love of a man. Equally unfortunate, in a world in which women struggle to expand their social and intellectual horizons, Disney films reify the image of the "perfect girl," while punishing inquisitive girls by labeling them disobedient and peculiar. Several of the heroines in these films suffer for challenging conventional expectations, and eventually all but one abandons her dreams for a definition of happiness within marriage. We also find it disquieting to witness adventurous and interesting role models like Ariel and Belle inevitably succumbing to the dominant heterosexual, patriarchal notion that, in the final analysis, satisfaction is defined not by self-knowledge, being, or accomplishments, but by a role prescribed through marriage.

Although there are bright spots among the more recent heroines, the overall image of Disney heroines is problematic. One lesson we draw from this analysis is that Disney heroines are largely essentialized within patriarchy. The pervasiveness of this image echoes a dominant concern of standpoint feminist epistemology; that women as sovereign selves are both victims of imposed social conditions and actors in the unfolding of their constructions of self. Even Belle and Pocahontas confront social constraints in their constructions of self. However, like them, we also can and do make choices, including the choice to "read" Disney heroines' narratives, and to read them in particular ways.

Notes

1. When we first began our study of the Disney animated heroines, *Snow White* had not been released on video nor re-released in the theaters, so it was not included among the films we analyzed. However, the themes introduced in the two earliest films, *Cinderella* and *Sleeping Beauty*, were also present in *Snow White*. We did not include *Aladdin* because the story really centers around the boy, Aladdin, whereas Princess Jasmine is cast in a secondary role and commands little screen time. Princess Jasmine is important, however, in that she is Disney's first non-Caucasian princess.
2. Brody (1976) describes the success of Disney fairy tales from a psychoanalytic perspective. Trites (1991) contrasts Disney's version of *The Little Mermaid* with the original Hans Christian Andersen tale from a Freudian perspective. Other analysis (May, 1981; Stone, 1975) critique the way in which Disney selectively appropriates classics of children's literature. Sex role stereotyping is the focus of work by Levinson (1975) and Holmlund (1979). They extend concerns about stereotyping using a Marxist feminist, approach to the sexual politics of Disney films. Some work has celebrated the Disney tradition for its connections with the oral tradition (Allan, 1988) and its artistic accomplishments (Morrow, 1978).

References

Allen, R. (1988). Fifty years of Snow White. *Journal of Popular Film and Television, 15,* 156–163.

Bell, E., Haas, L., & Sells, L. (Eds.). (1995). *From mouse to mermaid: The politics of film, gender, and culture.* Bloomington, IN: Indiana University Press.

Brody, M. (1976). The wonderful world of Disney—Its psychological appeal. *American Image, 33,* 350–360.

Brown, L., & Gilligan, C. (1992). *Meeting at the crossroads: Women's psychology and girl's development.* Cambridge, MA: Harvard University Press.

Collins, P. (1986). Learning from the outsider within. *Social Problems, 33,* 514–532.

Follett, M. (1924). *Creative experience.* New York: Longmans, Green.

Follett, M., Metcalf, H., & Urwick, L. (Eds.). (1944). *Dynamic administration: The collected papers of Mary Parker Follett.* New York: Harper.

Gilligan, C. (1982). *In a different voice: Psychological theory and women's development.* Cambridge, MA: Harvard University Press.

Gilligan, C. (1977). In a different voice: Women's conceptions of self and of morality. *Harvard Educational Review, 47,* 481–517.

Harding, S. (1991). *Whose science? Whose knowledge? Thinking from women's lives.* Ithaca, NY: Cornell University Press.

Holmlund, C. (Summer, 1979). Tots to tanks: Walt Disney presents feminism for the family. *Social Text,* 122–132.

Landis, D. (9 February 1993). Disney classics go into hibernation. *USA Today,* p. 5D.

Landis, D. (28 September 1993). Princely predictions for 'Aladdin' video." *USA Today,* p. 1D.

Levinson, R. (1975). From Olive Oyl to Sweet Polly Purebread: Sex role stereotypes and televised cartoons. *Journal of Popular Culture, 9,* 561–572.

May, J. (1981). Walt Disney's interpretation of children's literature. *Language Arts, 4,* 463–472.

Morrow, J. (1978). In defense of Disney. *Media and Methods, 14,* 28–34.

Murphy, P. (1995). The whole wide world was scrubbed clean: The androcentric animation of denatured Disney. In E. Bell, L. Haas, & L. Sells (Eds.), *From mouse to mermaid: The politics of film, gender, and culture* (pp. 125–136). Indianapolis, IN: Indiana University Press.

Orenstein, P. (1994). *School girls.* New York: Anchor Books, Doubleday.

Rich, A. (1986). *Of woman born: Motherhood as experience and institution.* New York: W.W. Norton & Co.

Sells, L. (1995). Where do the mermaids stand?: Voice and body in "The Little Mermaid." In E. Bell, L. Haas, & L. Sells (Eds.). *From mouse to mermaid: The politics of film, gender, and culture* (pp. 175–192). Indianapolis. IN: Indiana University Press.

Stanton, E. (1892). Solitude of self. Convention of National American Suffrage Association. Washington, D.C.

Stone, K. (1975). Things Walt Disney never told us. *Journal of American Folklore, 88,* 42–50.

Thomas, B. (1991). *Art of animation: From Mickey Mouse to Beauty and the Beast.* New York: Hyperion.

Trites, R. (1991). Disney's sub/version of Andersen's "The Little Mermaid," *Journal of Popular Film and Television, 18,* 145–152.

Wood, J. (1992). Gender and moral voice: Moving from women's nature to standpoint epistemology. *Women's Studies in Communication, 16,* 1–24.

Wood, J. (1994). *Gendered lives: Communication, gender, and culture.* Belmont, CA: Wadsworth.

Zipes, J. (1995). Breaking the Disney spell. In E. Bell, L. Haas, & L. Sells (Eds.). *From mouse to mermaid: The politics of film, gender, and culture* (pp. 21–42). Indianapolis, IN: Indiana University Press.

Rereading Actively

1. The first two paragraphs call readers' attention to Disney's ability to fabricate a virtual world and to make money from that virtual world. Write a brief summary of these points in your journal.

2. What rhetorical purpose is served by opening the article with a focus on money and the "virtual world" of Disney products?

3. In a small group or with a partner, review the article, focusing on passages that talk about the "construction of the female self." Explain the authors' understanding of the phrase, "the female self" and the process through which the female self is constructed.

4. With a partner or in a small group, discuss the pattern the authors find in the historical cross section of Disney heroines. In your journal, describe this pattern in your own words.

5. Review the article with a partner or in a small group, discussing the role of men in Disney's "construction of the female self." Write an explanation of this role in your journal.

6. What conclusions do the authors draw from their analysis of Disney? How might Michael Eisner, the CEO at Disney, respond to Henke et al.'s conclusions?

Exploring Your Responses

7. In an extended freewrite, compare your reaction to one of these heroines with that of Henke et al., noticing points of agreement and disagreement. Be sure to address the formative role this heroine may have played for you or your peers.

8. With two or three classmates, find an ad for one of the films discussed in the article. (Check out the Disney homepage <www.disney.com>, find a newspaper from the year and month the film was released, or look at a video jacket.) Discuss the characteristics of the ad that seem designed to appeal to its audience, especially to young girls. Analyze how what you observe compares with what Henke et al. discovered.

9. Write a comparison of your favorite and least favorite of the characters the authors mention, going into what you like and don't like in Disney's portrayal of women. Review your writing, and explore what your response says about Disney's construction of female characters.

WHERE DO THE MERMAIDS STAND?

LAURA SELLS

Laura Sells has taught communications and women's studies at the University of South Florida and edited Hypatia: A Journal of Feminist Philosophy. *Though some may argue that as a scholar, Sells is not the intended audience of* The Little Mermaid, *she explains that she has in fact been engaged and even entertained by the animated movie. "This essay was published in* From Mouse to Mermaid: The Politics of Film, Gender, and Culture *(1995), a collection of essays about the Magic Kingdom. In the essay, Sells analyzes Ariel (the little mermaid herself) as an idealized image of a young girl. She contrasts Disney's version of this story with the original fairy tale by Hans Christian Andersen, and she locates her analysis in the context of the "identity politics" surrounding women's roles in the family and in society.*

Where to stand? Who to be?

—Cixous (1975) [1986], 75)

A young pastor, finding himself in charge of some very energetic children, hit upon a game called "Giants, Wizards and Dwarfs." "You have to decide now," the pastor instructed the children, "Which you are…a giant, a wizard or a dwarf?" At that, a small girl tugging on his pants leg asked, "But where do the mermaids stand?" The pastor told her there are *no* mermaids. "Oh yes there are," she said. "I am a mermaid."

—Barbara Bush (1990)

In spring 1990 Barbara Bush addressed the graduating class of Wellesley College, facing a hostile crowd of young feminist women who challenged her ability to represent the woman they all hoped to become as they entered the "real world." Arguing that Bush was selected as the wife of an important figure rather than as someone with accomplishments of her own, students first circulated a petition that one-fourth of the class signed, and later wore to the graduation ceremony purple armbands, which signified their protest, their graduating class color, and their first-ranked choice of commencement speaker, Alice Walker. The controversy received national media coverage, which, incidentally, characterized the protesting students as hysterics.[1]

In response to her audience's rejection, Bush gracefully defended her lifestyle, spoke about the need for women to have multiple choices, and implicitly criticized the limits placed on women by American feminism. After indirectly exalting women's role as wife and mother in the heterosexual family, she invoked the image of a mermaid as the master trope of her speech: "For over 50 years, it was said that the winner of Wellesley's annual hoop race would be the first to get married. Now they say the winner will be the first to become C.E.O. Both of those stereotypes show too little tolerance for those who want to know where the mermaids stand." The mermaid thus became Bush's attempt to broaden the spectrum of representations of women while simultaneously invoking a cartoon-like, stay-at-home Mom as a viable option. Framed by this oxymoron, the mermaid is an ironic figure that critiques the narrowness of identity politics in contemporary feminism; yet it simultaneously valorizes an equally narrow and conservative image of acceptable positions for women in American culture. This speech marks an interesting moment in the struggle to invent appropriate and liberatory images for American women, a moment in which "woman" slides between the complicated terms of mother, citizen, and subject.

Earlier that school year, in November, the Walt Disney Corporation conjured another cartoon image of woman as mermaid in their animated feature *The Little Mermaid* (1989).[2] A hallmark Disney film, *The Little Mermaid* is their first commercially successful animated feature since Walt's death in 1966, and the first in a spate of new animated features that reaffirm Disney's position as one of the largest producers of "acceptable" role models for young girls. The film portrays the story of the teenage mermaid, Ariel, who first desires independence and entry into the human world, and who eventually desires the handsome Prince Eric. She trades her voice to the Sea Witch Ursula for a human body and for access to the Prince and his world. The narrative recounts the ritual slaughtering of the archetypal evil feminine character and the marital union of the girl and her prince. Embedded within this classic narrative about an adolescent girl's coming of age is a very contemporary story about the costs, pleasures, and dangers of women's access to the "human world."

Undoubtedly, feminists have criticized *The Little Mermaid*'s Ariel because she seems to have little ambition beyond getting her prince (Trites 1990). I find this criticism somewhat reductionist. The message of *The Little Mermaid* is more insidious and also more liberatory. On the one hand, with the traditional fairy-tale trappings of finding true princely love, the Disney rendition can be seen as more insidious because it sanitizes the costs of women's access to the "male sphere" by vilifying women's strength and by erasing the pain that so often accompanies "passing." On the other, I see *The Little Mermaid* as also more liberatory because it contains the means of its own undoing in the camp character of Ursula the Sea Witch, and in Disney's compulsory happy ending, which bestows the mermaid with both access *and* voice.

5   Clearly, both Bush's and Disney's versions of the mermaid can be read as conservative images. Yet both versions of the mermaid critique the narrow range of options that constrain women's lives, and both emphasize issues of choice and agency. This essay situates *The Little Mermaid* within the context of contemporary American feminism and the struggle over the cultural definitions of "woman." By reading against the backdrop of Bush's speech, and the media's representation of the Wellesley students, I find that *The Little Mermaid* reflects some of the tensions in American feminism between reformist demands for access, which leave in place the fixed and complementary definitions of masculine and feminine gender identities, and radical refigurings of gender that assert symbolic change as preliminary to social change. In this context, then, the mermaid figure becomes both an icon of bourgeois feminism and a sign of the stakes in reinventing the category of "woman," or reimagining women as speaking subjects.

Upward Mobility

"Bright young women, sick of swimmin', ready to stand...."

—Ariel's song

In 1837, Hans Christian Andersen wrote the original literary fairy tale of "The Little Mermaid." Like most of Andersen's work, the tale is considered autobiographical, an expression of his lack of social acceptance in the aristocratic circles that offered him patronage, a personal narrative of the pleasures and dangers of "passing." Ever the outsider, Andersen "projects his nagging sense of deprivation" in his writings (Spink n.d.; Bredsdorff 1975; Zipes 1983).[3] If a fairy tale is chameleon-like, as Joseph Campbell suggests, putting on "the colors of its background," living and shaping itself to "the requirements of the moment" (1972, 850), then Disney's contemporary version has shifted colors from class to gender privilege. Given the autobiographical theme of "passing" in Andersen's literary version, the Disney version, along with its ritual affirmation of women's coming of age, invites a reading of this film as a parable of bourgeois feminism. Ariel's ascent to the "real world" easily becomes metonymic of women's access to the white male system.

The Little Mermaid establishes the world on land and the world under the sea as two contrasting spaces, one factual and one fictive, one real and the other imaginary. In this dualistic and hierarchical construction, the human world can be aligned with the white male system and the water world situated outside that system. In *Women's Reality* (1981), Ann Wilson Schaef uses the term "white male system" to characterize the dominant culture of American patriarchy. According to Schaef, the white male system operates on several contradictory myths, at least two of which are relevant to the complementary worlds of this film. First, nothing exists outside the white male system; and second, the white male system knows and understands everything (¶ 8–9). Those who are privileged by the white male system are oblivious to anything outside the system, while those outside the system know about the dominant culture as well as their own marginalized culture. These two contradictory myths speak to the relationship between the land and sea worlds: the sea world is rendered either invisible or mythic while the land world is endowed with cultural validity. As contradictory and complementary, the two-world motif creates permeable yet dangerous borders, furthers the plot, and establishes a hierarchy of desires.

As Pat Murphy convincingly argues in his ecofeminist critique of *The Little Mermaid,* the film firmly establishes a colonialist, first-world/third-world relationship between the human and sea worlds. The world under the sea, despite its aristocratic decor, is the colonized space of marginalized or muted cultures, often invisible to the inhabitants of the white male system. Sebastian, and many of the other sea creatures, have the facial features of people of color. When in their own world, the sea creatures spend their days singing and dancing to calypso music. When they venture across the boundary into the "real world," they risk being reduced to human food....

This human oblivion to other worlds becomes a major plot device in the film. In a characteristic Disney moment of ironic self-referentiality, Eric and his companions dismiss the undersea world and its inhabitants as mere "fairy tales." With the blinders of his world, Prince Eric believes that he is saved from drowning not by a mermaid but by a human girl, thus complicating Ariel's efforts to win his affection. Like real animals, Eric's dog cannot speak, and cannot tell Eric the truth about Ariel.

10   The repeated depictions of land and sea as complementary also create a hierarchical relationship in which Eric's human world on land is privileged as the real world. This is most frequently reinforced through the language and imagery of "up there" and "down here." One notable instance is during Ariel's song, "Part of Your World," in which she yearns to be "up there." Indeed, this Ashman-Menken musical formula is described in Disney production circles as the "I Want" number (Avins 1992, 70). During this "I Want" scene, the spatial imagery supports the hierarchy of dominant and muted cultures: the cartoon's simulation of camera shots either positions the audience as omniscient viewers looking downward on Ariel, or we see upward through Ariel's eyes. All of this is embedded in sweeping seascapes which resemble Georgia O'Keeffe paintings, rich with the female imagery of sea shells and cave openings.

In these contrasting worlds of dominant and muted cultures, Ariel's song "Part of Your World" becomes more than an adolescent yearning for adulthood. As Ariel sings of access, autonomy and mobility, she yearns for subjecthood and for the ability to participate in public (human) life. She is figuratively and literally an upwardly mobile mermaid.[4] As the film opens, her adolescent curiosity and rebelliousness are both immediately apparent. She is late for her singing debut, a coming-of-age ritual ordained by her father, because she is out and about salvaging forbidden human objects from sunken ships.[5] Her curiosity about the human world, and her rebelliousness toward her father and his prohibitions against human contact, are particularly evident in her song. The song intones her desire to run, walk, and dance, all synonyms for mobility. While singing, she caresses a book that she cannot read, expressing her longing for knowledge. Her desire for access is characterized by her hunger and fascination with a different world in which she believes she can have autonomy and independence.

Autonomy and independence, as many feminists have recognized, is never easy; the cost for participating in the white male system can be quite dear. About to enter the real world, Ariel faces the pain of conforming to impossible ideals as she physically mutilates her own body by exchanging her fins for the mobility of human legs. Even more disheartening, she purchases this physical transformation with her voice. Like so many women who enter "the workforce" or any other "male sphere," Ariel wrestles with the double-binding cultural expectations of choosing between either voice or access, but never both. Our culture's continued difficulty with sexual difference is evident in the public persona of figures such as Geraldine Ferraro and Hillary Clinton. Ferraro failed in her 1984 vice-presidential bid in part because voters considered her too aggressive after hearing her forceful "masculine" speaking style (Jamieson 1988). Similarly, Hillary Clinton has been called the "Lady Macbeth of Little Rock," the "Evita Peron of America," and Bill's co-president. The Bush presidential campaign sought to discredit Hillary Clinton by suggesting she was "not a real woman" (qtd. in Wood 1994, 299–300). Women so often find themselves in a position much like Andersen's, a position in which access is really just a form of passing that compromises personal integrity and immolates voice.

Disney, however, obscures these costs through several related sanitizing maneuvers that contrive to create a bizarre erasure of "the feminine." Irigaray writes that Western patriarchy is constructed on a history of matricide, and on the expropriation of women from the mother's genealogy to the father's. As the film concludes with Ursula being impaled on a phallic mast from a ship and with Ariel being passed from her father to her prince, *The Little Mermaid* enacts this expropriation and makes Ariel's choices appear to be cost-free.

First, Ariel's fascination with the human world becomes transformed into love for Prince Eric. Through this sanitizing maneuver Disney obscures Ariel's interest in the human world as metonym for access to power. Once she meets the prince, her curiosity is minimized and her drive becomes externally motivated rather than self-directed. As Ariel passes from her father's hands to her husband's hands, the autonomy and willfulness that she enacted early in the film becomes subsumed by her father's "permission" to marry Eric. In other words, the marriage plot (Radner 1993) prevails as her interest in the role of citizen becomes supplanted by her interest in the role of wife.

15   Many feminists found objectionable this transformation from the Andersen version. In Andersen's tale the mermaid dies because she fails to earn the prince's love. Upon her death, the daughters of the air grant her the ability to earn an immortal soul through three hundred years of service. Trites argues that the Disney version subverts the mermaid's self-actualization process, and that Andersen wanted the mermaid to earn a soul on her own, not as an attachment of someone else: "Andersen offers women several paths toward self-realization, so the message to children is much more farsighted than Disney's limited message that only through marriage can a woman be complete" (1990/91, 150). Andersen's version, however, is not quite that liberatory. As Zipes suggests, Andersen's reward was never power over one's own life, but security in adherence to power—in the little mermaid's case, the power of servitude to god (1983, 84).

Second, Disney erases the pain of access by sanitizing the physical, bodily pain of Ariel's self-mutilation when she trades her fins for feet. Within the context of the first sanitization, and of Ursula's song about beauty and looks ("poor unfortunate souls … this one longing to be thinner …"), the legs indicate Ariel's compliance with the beauty culture, rather than her desire for access, mobility, and independence. Ariel becomes "woman as man wants her to be" rather than "woman for herself." In Andersen's version, the mermaid feels incredible pain, as if a sword goes through her body and knives pierce her feet with each step; the pain is so deep that her feet bleed. For Andersen, the pain reflected his discomfort and the price of his own integrity as a peasant whose literary talents earned him entry into aristocratic circles (Zipes 1983). His story expressed his own discomfort and loss of voice as he attempted to "pass" in high society. Disney masks the pain of self-mutilation that often accompanies this access by excising the pain from Andersen's story. By eliminating this pain, however, Disney only enhances Andersen's original version. As Zipes puts it, "Ideologically speaking, Andersen furthered bourgeois notions of the self-made man or the Horatio Alger myth, which was becoming so popular in America and elsewhere, while reinforcing a belief in the existing power structure that meant domination and exploitation of the lower classes" (1983, 81). The Disney version thus becomes a bourgeois feminist success story in which access is achieved with minimal cost.[6]

Third, Ariel sacrifices her connection to the feminine in the matricide of Ursula, the only other strong female character in the film. Eventually, Ariel achieves access by participating with Eric in the slaughtering of Ursula, relegating her and that which she signifies to silence and absence. Ursula is reassigned to the position of the repressed that keeps the system functioning. Embedded in gynophobic imagery, Ursula is a revolting, grotesque image of the smothering maternal figure (Trites 1990/91). Of course, within Disney's patriarchal ideology, any woman with power has to be represented as a castrating bitch. Ariel's entry into the white male system is at the expense of her connection with the mother. The gynophobic imagery sanitizes this cost, making it more palatable. By vilifying feminine power in the figure of Ursula, Disney simplifies Ariel's choice: in the white male system it is much easier to be silent than to be seen as monstrous.

Admittedly, the film is a problematic text for a feminist resistant reading, because it teaches us that we can achieve access and mobility in the white male system if we remain silent, and if we sacrifice our connection to "the feminine." We all know the storyline about Ariel sacrificing her voice. Indeed, Ursula tells an ancient story when she convinces Ariel that her voice will be useless in the human world. Although Ariel severs her connection with the one strong female character of the film, Ursula, she ultimately retrieves her voice. This final sanitization is clearly the product of Disney's compulsion for rainbows, violins, and happy endings. If voice is a symbol of identity, then Ariel retains a measure of autonomy and subjecthood. Philosopher Margaret Whitford argues that women cannot be social subjects until they are subjects of language (1991, 43). In this final sanitization lies the film's undoing.

In the House of Divine

> "This little girl knew what she was and she was not about to give up on either her identity or the game."
>
> —Barbara Bush (1990)

If the Little Mermaid is, indeed, a budding young woman severing her connection to the feminine symbolic, what possible sites of resistance and pleasure are available? Where do I find hope for Ariel as she enters the white male system, passed from the hands of her father to the hands of her husband? How can Ariel's compliance with the laws of the Father be recuperated? Much like Ariel, I find myself turning to Ursula for answers to these questions. Trites tells us that the wealth of gynophobic imagery precludes us from reading Ursula's wry comments ironically: "Although some viewers might perceive those of Ursula's statements that capitalize on Ariel's inexperience as ironic and as an intended tribute to feminism, these comments are voiced in the midst of too much gynophobic imagery to honestly promote feminism" (1990/91, 152, n7). But beyond the gynophobic imagery, the character of Ursula, who is unlike any other Disney villain, teaches a different lesson about access, mobility, and voice. Ursula can retrieve Ariel from her destined alliance with patriarchy. Not only does she give Ariel legs, she schools her in disruptive reconstructions of gender and harbors her voice in the feminine home of jouissance. Ursula teaches Ariel that performance and voice are manifestations and liberations of gender.

20   The lessons that Ursula gives Ariel about womanhood offer an important position from which to resist narrowly drawn patriarchal images of women, a position absent in Disney's previous fairy tales. During her song about body language, Ursula stages a camp drag show about being a woman in the white male system, beginning "backstage" with hair mousse and lipstick. She shimmies and wiggles in an exaggerated style while her eels swirl around her, forming a feather boa. This performance is a masquerade, a drag show starring Ursula as an ironic figure. According to the directing animator, Ruben Acquine, Ursula was modeled on the drag queen Divine, while the voice and ethos behind Ursula belong to Pat Carroll. Both of these character actors are known for their cross-dressing roles. Ursula's theatricality is undeniable; to prepare her voice for her role, Carroll envisioned Ursula as an aging Shakespearean actress because, as she says in *People* (11 December 1989), "only someone who has done the classics has that kind of arrogance." A composite of so many drag queens and camp icons—Joan Collins, Tallulah Bankhead, Norma Desmond, Divine—Ursula is a multiple cross-dresser; she destabilizes gender.

Reading Ursula as a drag queen is not implausible considering two important elements that contribute to shaping the Disney narrative. Smuggled into the Disney version are the multileveled tensions of Andersen's original tale. Given his sexual ambiguity (one historian suggests that his pining away for a number of lost loves was a performance to disguise his homosexuality—see Bredsdorff 1975), his own uncomfortable and self-policed passing in aristocratic circles, and the double-consciousness motif that informs the "original" tale, *The Little Mermaid* is storied as layers of conflicting desires and codes of performance. Additionally, the influence of songwriters Howard Ashman and Alan Menken, the creators of the camp *Little Shop of Horrors,* guided musical characterizations. Ashman and Menken were brought in as cocreators of the project, and the score was written before any animation began. Consequently, the plot and characters are substantially developed through the film's music (Grant 1993, 333–42). The influence of Ashman and Menken undermines Disney's sanitizations.

In Ursula's drag scene, Ariel learns that gender is performance; Ursula doesn't simply symbolize woman, she *performs* woman. Ursula uses a camp drag queen performance to teach Ariel to use makeup, to "never underestimate the importance of body language," to use the artifices and trappings of gendered behavior. Ariel learns gender, not as a natural category, but as a performed construct. As Ariel stumbles away from the shore into Eric's arms, she winks to her undersea companions, indicating that she is *playing*: "The game is dangerous, and has a compulsive quality, but it *is* play. We may hope that when this game isn't fun any more Ariel may use her stubbornness, if not her beauty, to play another, more interesting one" (White 1993, 191).

Drag performances such as Ursula's and Ariel's are spectacles that can teach us something important about gender. Gender is composed of repeated, publicly performed, regulated acts that are "dramatic" and therefore "contingent" embodiments of meaning. Drag denaturalizes gender by showing us its imitative structure; it operates on the contradiction between anatomical sex and gender identity, a contradiction that is interrupted by the performance itself. Defining gender as a performative production dismantles the illusion of a natural category (Butler 1990; Butler 1991; Capo and Hantzis 1991; Garber 1992). Mary Russo puts it more simply: "To put on femininity with a vengeance suggests the power of taking it off" (1986, 224). Butler, however, refutes this equation of gender with style, as something to be put on or taken off as a conscious choice: "Performativity has to do with repetition, very often with the repetition of oppressive and painful gender norms to force them to resignify. This is not freedom, but a question of how to work the trap that one is inevitably in" (1992, 84).

Andersen, who inhabited a position that was radically other than himself, struggled with working this trap. "Throughout his life Andersen was obliged to act as a dominated subject within the dominant culture despite his fame and recognition as a writer," as Zipes reminds us (1983, 77). Indeed a recurrent theme in many of Andersen's fairy tales is to dismantle what Butler calls "zones of legitimacy": *pace* "The Emperor's New Clothes." Andersen's writing is often simply about passing, but passing in itself is not subversive. For drag to be subversive, it must go beyond exposing an ideal as uninhabitable. Drag becomes subversive when it "dissolves and rearticulates" ideals (Butler 1992, 89). The ideal woman represented by the mermaid image is immobile, her only power in her sexuality. As one journalist describes Bush's mermaid: "Those free-floating mermaids she mentioned are sheathed in glittering, confining, fantasy fins that really get the sailor going but leave the woman foundering if she tries to walk" (Johnson 1990). Ariel is a dissolution and rearticulation of this gender ideal: she is a mermaid passing as a human with both legs and voice, or mobility and subjecthood.

25   Just as Ursula's drag performance destabilizes and deconstructs gender, her excessive figure provides the site upon which we can reconstruct the image of the mermaid. It is no accident that Ursula is an octopus, an inverted Medusa figure. Very early in the film we learn that she is exiled by King Triton from the world of the merpeople. She represents that which is outside even the patriarchally domesticated outside, and hence, outside patriarchal language. Ariel's outside, the undersea world, is a colonized outside ruled by the patriarchal father, King Triton, who has the power to name his daughters. Ursula, who is banished from Triton's realm, is outside the outside. Ursula is a double-voiced, multiple character. The sprawling seascapes of Ursula's home are what Cixous calls "the dark continent" of the feminine body. To visit Ursula, Ariel must enter through the toothy jaws of a gigantic mouth, and swim through womb-like caves. Ursula is the female symbolic encoded in patriarchal language as grotesque and monstrous; she represents the monstrosity of feminine power. This is why Ariel trades her voice to the Sea Witch in the first place.

Feminist theories of women's *jouissance* help us to understand the metaphors of voice, body, and language as they create a force that displaces the dualistic order of the white male system. The multiplicity of women's *jouissance*, or women's bodily, sexual plea-sure, cannot be represented dualistically. Although it means woman's pleasure, *jouissance* cannot simply be translated into bodily pleasure. It connotes sensual enjoyment, the enjoyment of rights, and the enjoyment of language. *Jouissance* implies "total access, total participation, as well as total ecstasy." The multiplicity of woman's sexuality indicates "she has the potential to attain something more than total, something extra—abundance and waste, Real and unrepresentable" (Wing 1986, 165–66). The language of women's bod-ies jams the machinery of phallocentric discourse that generates a dualistic world view, disrupting the symbolic system that demands the complementarity of gender and the dual world construction of land and sea. A voice that has spent time with Ursula, that has spoken in the language of *jouissance*, could never return to innocence.

The configuration of voice, bodily excess, rupture and the feminine is established by the visual alignment of images in the climax of the film. In the first wedding scene, Ursula wears Ariel's voice in a shell around her neck in her disguise as Vanessa, Ariel's evil double. The bird Scuttle swoops down and shatters the shell, freeing Ariel's voice. The metaphor of flying/stealing (*voler*) is central to Cixous's notion of *l'écriture fem-inine*, because "to fly/steal is a woman's gesture, to steal into language to make it fly ... for all the centuries we have only had access to having by flying/stealing" (1986, 96). Ariel's voice literally becomes "the spoken word, exploded, blown to bits by suffering and anger, demolishing discourse. Broken from her body where it was shut up and forbidden" (94). The freeing of Ariel's voice literally interrupts the wedding, or the rit-ual enactment of patriarchal symbolic order.

This release of Ariel's voice also releases Ursula, who then seizes King Triton's crown and the phallic scepter. Just as Disney transforms Ariel's desire for autonomy and access into desire for a husband, Disney also warps Ursula's desire into a form of penis envy, or in this case, scepter envy. With the scepter in hand, Ursula swells into an enormous monster, exploding, diffusing, overflowing. Her growth is more rupturing than an erec-tion. Eventually, Ursula dies as Eric pierces her with the phallic mast of a ship. This undeniable event makes a recuperation of *The Little Mermaid* rather questionable. As the film concludes with Ariel in Prince Eric's arms, the dangerous message about appro-priation and the sanitized cost of access cannot be ignored. Yet, even though Ariel has been complicit in the death of Ursula, and the destined alliance with patriarchy is ful-filled, I remain hopeful. After all, Ariel enters the white male system with her voice—a stolen, flying voice that erupted amidst patriarchal language, a voice no longer inno-cent because it resided for a time in the dark continent that is the Medusa's home.

Notes

The author would like the thank the women of the Pagoda at St. Augustine, Florida, for providing the space to draft this essay.

1. See, for instance, Mike Barnicle's *Boston Globe* column in which he describes Wellesley students as "a pack of whining, unshaved feminists" who cause the Boston College students to "appre-ciate the virtue of celibacy" (*Boston Globe,* 26 April 1990). The controversy provoked the pro-duction of T-shirts sporting the slogan: "Just a bunch of whiny unshaven radical spinster tartlets" ("The Wellesley Protest, Beyond Barbara Bush," *The Washington Post,* 29 May 1990).

2. *The Little Mermaid* is the first animated fairy tale released by Disney in thirty years. It broke national box office and video store records for "first release" animations, making it Dis-ney's most successful feature-length animation (surpassed by *Beauty and the Beast* in 1991) (Thomas 1991). As Susan White points out in "Split Skins," mermaids have become a

pervasive cinematic symbol of the girl's difficult rite of passage to womanhood (1993, 186): *Splash* (1984), a Disney/Touchstone film directed by Ron Howard; Richard Benjamin's *Mermaids* (1990); and of course, Madonna's music video "Cherish" (1991). Likewise, Tori Amos's song, "Silent All These Years" (1991), evokes the configuration of the mermaid and voice.

3. See Zipes for a brief discussion of the literary and folk origins of the tale and for an insightful class analysis of Andersen's version (Zipes 1983, chapter 4).

4. Ann Wilson Schaef's (1981) terminology is particularly useful to discuss Ariel's desire to participate in the human world. Like many people who theorize about dominant and marginal cultures, Schaef agrees that marginalized people often experience a double consciousness, or an awareness both of dominant culture and of their own marginalized cultural systems (see also, for instance, Sandra Harding 1991). Unlike cultural critics who see this double consciousness as a product of political struggle, Schaef recognizes this double vision as simply the (frequently inchoate) recognition of being disenfranchised and disconfirmed as a member of a muted group. While Ariel certainly doesn't have a politicized consciousness, she is indeed aware of her own relative lack of power.

5. Ariel's desire to acquire human objects is interesting within the context of Hilary Radner's (1993) discussion of consumption as a way for women to negotiate the constraints placed on a sexual identity within the public sphere. *The Little Mermaid* can be seen as a variation on that theme. Indeed, a frenzy of consumption has sprung up around the mermaid motif as young girls buy everything from Mermaid toothbrushes to Mermaid video games (White 1993). In addition, the obvious analogy between Ariel and Barbie suggests that Ariel teaches girls that adult female sexuality is inextricably linked to consumption (see Motz 1983).

6. By shifting the focus from class to gender, Disney creates what one reviewer calls "the fall of a fishy, feminist Horatio Alger" (Roberts 1992).

References

Amos, Tori. 1991. "Silent All These Years." *Little Earthquakes.* Atlantic Recording Corporation.

Andersen, Hans Christian. (1837) 1974. "The Little Mermaid." *The Complete Fairy Tales and Stories.* Trans. Erik Christian Haugaard. Garden City, NY: Doubleday.

Avins, Mimi. 1992. "Aladdin." *Premiere,* December: 67–69, 111.

Bredsdorff, Elias. 1975. *Andersen, What Was He Like.* London: Phaidon.

Bush, Barbara. 1990. Remarks of Mrs. Bush at Wellesley College Commencement. Wellesley, MA: Wellesley College Office of Public Affairs.

Butler, Judith. 1990. *Gender Trouble.* New York: Routledge.

———. 1991. "Gender Trouble, Feminist Theory, and Psychoanalytic Discourse." In *Feminism/Postmodernism,* ed. Linda J. Nicholson. New York: Routledge.

———. 1992. "The Body You Want: Liz Kotz Interviews Judith Butler." *Artforum,* November: 82–89.

Campbell, Joseph. 1972. "Folkloristic Commentary." In *The Complete Grimm's Fairy Tales.* New York: Pantheon, Random House.

Capo, Kay Ellen, and Darlene M. Hantzis. 1991. "(En)Gendered (and Endangered) Subjects: Writing, Reading, Performing and Theorizing Feminist Criticism." *Text and Performance Quarterly* 11: 249–66.

Cixous, Hélène. (1975) 1986. "Sorties." In *The Newly Born Woman.* Trans. Betsy Wing. Minneapolis: University of Minnesota Press.

Garber, Marjorie. 1992. *Vested Interests: Cross-Dressing and Cultural Anxiety.* New York: Harper Perennial, Harper Collins.

Grant, John. 1993. *Encyclopedia of Walt Disney's Animated Characters.* New York: Hyperion.

Harding, Sandra. 1991. *Whose Science, Whose Knowledge?* Ithaca: Cornell University Press.

Jamieson, Kathleen Hall. 1988. *Eloquence in an Electronic Age: The Transformation of Political Speechmaking.* New York: Oxford University Press.

Johnson, Rheta Grimsley. 1990. "What Mrs. Bush Didn't Say." *Dallas Morning News,* 10 June.

Motz, Marilyn Ferris. 1983. "I Want to Be a Barbie Doll When I Grow Up: The Cultural Significance of the Barbie Doll." In *The Popular Culture Reader,* ed. Christopher D. Geist and Jack Nachbar. Bowling Green: Bowling Green University Popular Press.

Murphy, Patrick. 1995. " 'The Whole Wide World Was Scrubbed Clean': The Androcentric Animation of Denatured Disney." In *From Mouse to Mermaid,* ed. Elizabeth Bell, Lynda Haas, and Laura Sells. Bloomington: Indiana University Press.

Radner, Hilary. 1993. "Pretty Is as Pretty Does." In *Film Theory Goes to the Movies,* ed. Jim Collins, Hilary Radner, and Ava Preacher Collins. New York: Routledge.

Roberts, Susan C. 1992. "Fractured Fairy Tales." *Common Boundary,* September/October: 17–21.

Russo, Mary. 1986. "Female Grotesques: Carnival and Theory." In *Feminist Studies/Critical Studies,* ed. Teresa de Lauretis. Bloomington: Indiana University Press.

Schaef, Anne Wilson. 1981. *Women's Reality.* San Francisco: Harper and Row.

Spink, Reginald. n.d. "Hans Christian Andersen: Fairy Tales in a Hundred Languages." *Fact Sheet/Denmark.* Copenhagen: Press and Cultural Relations Department of the Ministry of Foreign Affairs of Denmark.

Thomas, Bob. 1991. *Disney's Art of Animation: From Mickey Mouse to Beauty and the Beast.* New York: Hyperion.

Trites, Roberta. 1990/1991. "Disney's Sub/Version of *The Little Mermaid.*" *Journal of Popular Television and Film* 18: 145–59.

White, Susan. 1993. "Split Skins." In *Film Theory Goes to the Movies,* ed. Jim Collins, Hilary Radner, and Ava Preacher Collins. New York: Routledge.

Whitford, Margaret. 1991. *Philosophy in the Feminine.* New York: Routledge.

Wing, Betsy. 1986. "Translator's Glossary." In *The Newly Born Woman,* by Hélène Cixous and Catherine Clément. Trans. Betsy Wing. Minneapolis: University of Minnesota Press.

Wood, Julia T. 1994. *Gendered Lives.* Belmont, CA: Wadsworth.

Zipes, Jack. 1983. *Fairy Tales and the Art of Subversion: The Classical Genre for Children and the Process of Civilization.* New York: Wildman Press.

Rereading Actively

1. Sells finds *The Little Mermaid* both "insidious" and "liberatory" (¶ 4). Review the article, and explain what Sells means by this paradoxical assertion.

2. Sells relates Ariel, an animated mermaid, to, among other figures, Barbara Bush, American feminism, Hans Christian Andersen, and Hillary Clinton. In a small group or with a partner, review these associations, and discuss how they create a context for Ariel as an idealized image.

3. In a brief journal entry, summarize Sells's interpretation of the Ursula character. Why might Sells's reading of Ursula surprise readers? How did you respond?

4. In a small group, review a scene from *The Little Mermaid.* Discuss how the scene develops the plot, and how Sells's analysis might be applied to it.

5. Explain the role Sells sees for "*jouissance,* or women's bodily, sexual pleasure" (¶ 26), in the film. How does this concept fit with Sells's questions about Ariel as an idealized image?

6. Why does *The Little Mermaid* leave Sells feeling hopeful?

Exploring Your Positions

7. Has reading Sells changed your response to *The Little Mermaid*? How? With a partner, discuss your responses to the film before and after reading Sells.

8. In a small group or with a partner, discuss Sells's analysis of *The Little Mermaid* in terms of how persuasive it is to you. What elements of her discussion make sense to you? What parts seem less persuasive? Reflect on your discussion in a journal entry.

9. Reflect on Sells's interest in and concern for idealized images of girls. Do you detect common ground between yourself and Sells?

MOVIE REVIEWS

- James Bowman, "Everything Old Is New Again." *The American Spectator* (1992)
- Richard W. Hill, Sr., "The Pocahontas Phenomenon." *Native Americas* (1995)
- Elizabeth Chang, "Noted with Resignation." *The Washington Post* (1998)

These three review articles find that Disney's heroines from Cinderella to Mulan are surprisingly more than thin-waisted princesses waiting for princes. While each expresses reservations about elements of the film being reviewed (e.g., violence, sentimentalization, merchandising), all three critics find the Disney girls to be appealing, maybe too appealing. The reviewers disagree about whether the movies are worth seeing. Written for popular audiences, these reviews study how Disney's construction of women makes good and entertaining film and how people actually consume them. As film critics, these authors hold assumptions about what children's movies should and should not achieve. All three reviews are shaped by an awareness of the way Disney films portray women. (Differences in audience are worth noting here: Bowman is writing to political conservatives about several 1992 entertainment offerings, Hill addresses people interested in the status of Indians in mainstream culture, and Chang seems to speak to parents of young girls.)

"EVERYTHING OLD IS NEW AGAIN"
JAMES BOWMAN

This Christmas, according to the *New York Times*, nostalgia was in. Erector sets and Lincoln Logs, reproduction Western Flyer bicycles and Fleet Arrow sleds. Flintstones Cookie Jars and the Cleaver family refrigerator magnet all comforted those old enough to remember such things with the thought that neither they nor Santa Claus nor the solid world of the 1950s nor their childhoods had quite vanished from the face of the earth.

Naturally enough, the movies got into the act. *Star Trek* and *The Addams Family*, *Beauty and the Beast* and *Peter Pan*, *Father of the Bride* and *Cape Fear* all came back from the past in new and updated versions to make us feel similarly refreshed by the familiar. The question that the discriminating movie-goer wants answered, however, is whether these pictures have anything going for them except nostalgia.

It is the same kind of sanitizing and banalizing of potentially dangerous reality that I object to in the Walt Disney instant classic, *Beauty and the Beast*. Even if you discount the fact that I consider any feature-length animation project as being at best an accomplishment on the order of that of the Indian gentleman who has, I believe, transcribed the entire New Testament onto a grain of rice, this film is tripe. I know that it is supposed to be for the kiddies, but I cannot forbear to protest against it on behalf of mature taste—partly because it is selling an adult product.

Fairy tales are meant to be scary in the way that life is scary to children. Dark forests, grotesque ugliness, arbitrary rules with terrible punishments for breaking them, weak parents who can't protect you anymore—these are the essential ingredients of others besides *Beauty and the Beast.* It would take a child already on the verge of a nervous breakdown to be afraid of anything in this movie. Adults have sanitized it.

5   The cuddly beast looks like an American bison except that he defies evolutionary logic by having the teeth of a carnivore rather than a ruminant. In character, however, he is mostly bovine, and his rages are probably less terrifying than those of most kids' daddies. Certainly, Belle (as Beauty is called in this Frenchified version) shows no fear of him at all, presumably because it would compromise her as the true feminist heroine that adult sensibilities have made her. In fact, there is a whole invented subplot, too ridiculous for words, involving a male chauvinist hunter called Gaston, which is designed precisely to establish her feminist credentials.

It is true that she still marries the beast in the end and that he still turns into a handsome prince, but the thing is done in such a way as to make all but invisible the most terrifying thing about the story, which is the need to love blindly, to love before we can know that it is safe to love. In fact, one scene in which Belle goes poking around the beast's castle has no point unless it is to suggest that a glimpse of recognition of the beast's eyes in a torn portrait of a man (could it be a prince?) has tipped her off that this isn't really a beast after all.

Outrageous! What's the use of him if he isn't a real beast, if he hasn't scared the woman out of her wits before she learns to love him? The real beast in this film is Gaston, the hairy-chested hunter fawned over by bosomy village cuties who contrast strikingly with the rather androgynous Belle. He spends his time slaughtering cuddly animals, expresses a low opinion of women's intellects, thinks education is wasted on them, is vain and arrogant and expects Belle to jump at the chance to marry him, and turns out, of course, to be a bully and a coward.

Only this beast is not one that anyone has to love; instead, we are meant to cheer when the only human male of marriageable age in the film gets offed by a manic-depressive in a buffalo suit. Meanwhile, a clock, a candlestick, and a teapot are singing and dancing away to beat the band. You've got to wonder what kind of values kids are going to take away from a picture like this. I guess the little girls, at least, will get something out of it if they learn to stick with the guy who owns the castle instead of the handsome ne'er-do-well who spends all his time in the woods, hunting.

"THE POCAHONTAS PHENOMENON"
RICHARD W. HILL, SR

The world's largest film premiere took place in New York City's Central Park in June. On four of the largest screens ever assembled, an animated Pocahontas came alive for a new generation, but does it signal a new trend in images of Indians, or is it another attempt to cash in with Indian clichés? The answer is never simple, but in this case it appears to be a conflicting combination of new sensibilities and old stereotypes. Certainly the new Disney Indians are better than the old Disney Indians. Remember the Big Chief of the Red Men in the 1953 animated version of Peter Pan? He was an ugly buffoon who explained that Indians are red because once an Indian prince kissed a maiden and started to blush and "we've been blushing ever since." The new Pocahontas does more than kiss.

With this new film, Disney embarks on a major course of events to bring a new version of Indians to the big screen. Pocahontas is just part of that plan. It is their first animation to feature actual historical characters. However, their plan started with the proposed theme park, Disney America, that was supposed to be built in Virginia until the locals protested against it. The plan was to feature a 17th century Powhatan village, the home place of Pocahontas. Visitors, inspired by the movies and the commercial hype, would walk back in time to see how Pocahontas used to live. Their plan also included the movie Squanto, a film that had new insights about Indians, but never caught on to those who seek some kind of reconciliation with Indians through movies. Their plan also includes the media campaign to bring the spirit of Pocahontas to Burger King, Wal-Mart, Payless shoes, and countless other commercial spin-offs. Pocahontas is going to become the most famous Indian ever. Children around the world will be playing Indian once again.

But what of the images it projects? The Chief wears a warbonnet, reminiscent of the Plains Indians. He has a big hooked nose, just like all the other cartoon Indians from the last fifty decades. In contrast, Pocahontas has been drawn with practically no nose at all. She is a dark version of a runway model. She wears a deerhide minidress, with one shoulder strap to make her look sexier. In fact, the press has already made the point that Pocahontas is the sexiest woman Disney animators have produced. The film also presents the sexiest tension between the two more explicitly than any other children's movie. What does this film tell children about Indian women?

Unfortunately, she is the same old white man's fantasy of an Indian princess. She comes off as a woodland pleasure seeker, an untapped sex object just waiting for a white man to set her passions free. She is also a super Indian woman. She can sing, paddle a canoe, talk with the animals, and save a white man in under two hours. Disney tries to balance all of this with a healthy does of Native spiritual philosophy to show that not only can an Indian woman be amorous, but she can teach you about the birds and bees in a new way.

"Noted with Resignation"
Elizabeth Chang

You must understand, I am not a huge Disney fan. I never wanted my daughters to be of the someday-my-prince-will-come, I'll-wear-a-bikini-top-while-I-wait mentality. But one thing you learn as a parent of a small child is that you'll have about as much luck escaping Disney as you will ear infections. You might not buy your children Disney videos, books or toys, not to mention T-shirts, lunch boxes, shoes or underwear, but, rest assured, your friends and relatives will.

Thus, despite scant encouragement from her father and myself (we are guilty of purchasing a couple of "classic" Disney music CDs, exactly two videotapes and one Pooh T-shirt), our preschool daughter, Rachel, has become devoted to Disney. Disney is more than a source of entertainment for her, it's a source of reference, a canon as familiar and enduring as Mother Goose. She pretends to be Disney characters, assigns us Disney roles ("You're the evil stepmother"), even dissects plots and motivations. We recently had a discussion about running away, based on a Disney character's actions. "Why didn't you tell her it's just a movie?" my mother-in-law asked. It never occurred to me. To Rachel, Disney is as real and relevant as the evening news is to adults.

To her parents, however, Disney, even in its newer releases, is almost medieval in its depiction of female characters, with their limited ambitions and male-centered happily-ever-afters. We blanched at the passive Sleeping Beauty, the simpering Wendy, the Little Mermaid who was willing to give up her voice to catch a prince. But, realizing that it was impossible to entirely shield Rachel from Disney, and fearing that an outright ban would simply drive her into the enemy's big, brawny arms, we decided to engage in selective defense, formulating video viewing policy with the earnest deliberativeness of The Hague.

After careful consideration, for example, we allowed Rachel to watch "Cinderella" and "The Little Mermaid" to a looping soundtrack of parental commentary that emphasized Cinderella and Ariel's positive qualities, and de-emphasized the soft-focus on the princes. We were so relieved to find several redeeming features in Belle of "Beauty and the Beast—she liked to read!—that we even let Rachel see the production on ice. But we banished the historically inaccurate "Pocahontas" with her ridiculous Barbie doll figure and plunging-neckline get-up.

5 Despite our best efforts, though, we eventually had a princess- and mermaid-obsessed child who was running around the house trailing blankets on the floor like "marrying dresses" and belting out Ariel's signature song, "Part of Your World." A child whose efforts to put life in order included such comments as, "Mom, there are three bells: Belle, Tinkerbell and Taco Bell." A child who would come only when called, variously, Cinderella, Belle or Ariel.

More seriously, our then-3-year-old began to create imaginary scenarios in which princes were going to save her, and started to fret about whom she was going to marry. And our beautiful, brown-skinned, big-eyed, shiny-haired Asian-Caucasian child said she wanted red hair like Ariel's, or blond hair like Cinderella's.

It was at that low point that Disney itself handed us the most powerful weapon in our war against its insidiously stereotypical images. It was, paradoxically, another Disney movie—a movie that finally treats girls like boys, by putting adventure and heroics first and making romance a vague afterthought. "Mulan," the Disney release based on an ancient Chinese legend of a girl who takes her disabled father's place in the emperor's army and saves all of China, has finally provided an antidote to Ariel and her ilk.

Surprisingly for Disney, "Mulan" features a strong, ordinarily proportioned, modestly dressed female character. Not as surprisingly, it, too, enchanted Rachel. She went around the house swinging the vacuum cleaner extension wand as a sword (which her father cautioned her to always use for good, and never for evil). She requested a Mulan party for her fourth birthday, and picked out party favor swords for herself and her friends. She asked for a Mulan dress, but also asked for Mulan armor. (Disney; of course, doesn't make Mulan armor. Dresses, shoes, pajamas, combs and jewelry, yes, but no armor.) Instead of waiting to be saved by a prince, she announced she was going off to save China.

Sure, there are things wrong with "Mulan" (for example, all those swords, if you're a nonviolent type). But I'm willing to forgive Disney those shortcomings because it has created a character who breaks the princess mold not only in attitude, but in appearance. And Rachel has noticed both.

10 "Mom," she said to me one day, "I look like Mulan!"

"Really?" I asked. "How do you look like Mulan?"

"Here," she said, pointing to her face.

Now I, who once downplayed Disney and refused to buy Ariel pajamas, am happy to have my daughter identify with a Disney movie character—one who is brave, clever, capable, kind and respectful. A character who has a realistic figure and an Asian face, and wears clothing that manages to cover all sensitive body parts. A character more interested in fulfilling her own interests and abilities than in finding a man.

Perhaps "Mulan" is simply a cynical attempt on Disney's part to capture another, more feminist segment of the market. If so, it has succeeded: I have given in, become yet another consumer of "Mulan" and its myriad product spinoffs. Part of me is rueful but a bigger part can't help but wonder: How much could Disney do for girls if it used its awesome power for good?

Rereading Actively

1. Each of these reviews appeared at the opening of a film. What expectations are reviewers supposed to meet in writing this kind of piece?

2. With a partner or in a small group, identify passages that talk about Disney's construction of women. Discuss what each reviewer says about reasons for not liking Disney's portrayal of women.

3. With a partner, describe the context that each writer creates for her or his discussion of the film. In your journal, explain how each context affects each writer's position on the heroine.

4. Examine the reviews, underlining passages that reflect a sense of the social purpose each reviewer ascribes to the movie being written about. In a brief journal entry, describe your sense of this social purpose in each film.

5. Each reviewer evaluates the movie. Find passages where reviewers turn their thumbs up or down. What qualifications do they offer?

6. With a partner, develop a brief summary of each review that includes the strengths and the faults that each reviewer mentions.

Exploring Your Responses

7. In a page or two in your journal, explore your response to a Disney heroine, discussing how your response is similar to or different from the view expressed by any of the reviewers.

8. In a small group, discuss ways that Disney's images of the feminine relate to your own sense of how a girl or young woman should really be. Write a description of this conversation in your journal.

9. With two or three of your classmates, find five more reviews of one of these three films and draft a report that notes the range of responses and the characteristics that reviewers seem to focus on.

THE DISNEY DOCTRINE
STEVEN WATTS

In 1997, Steven Watts, a history professor at the University of Missouri, published a "part biography and part cultural analysis" of Walt Disney titled The Magic Kingdom. *This is a detailed volume, of some 453 pages, including 57 pages of notes. Watts considers a man who to some symbolizes the American dream of entrepreneurial success and who to others stands for the hucksterism that is at the core of a consumer society. In an attempt to get beyond the legends, Watts reads Walt Disney the man against the entertainment products the Walt Disney Company created. In this excerpt, Watts focuses on the post-World War II era, and links Disney's own preoccupation with family to the animated features and live-action films the Disney Studio produced in the 1950s. Watts argues that society's concern at the time for order and security in the domestic sphere was echoed in Disney's idealized depictions of gender roles, marriage and family.*

In 1953, Walt Disney contributed an interesting essay to American Magazine. Entitled "What I've Learned from the Animals," it presented his thoughts on the True-Life Adventure series, dwelling on animals' incredible sense of "family devotion and parental care," especially among females:

> Take the care and raising of young birds, for example. Nowhere else do we find more hard-working and sympathetic mothers during the egg-hatching and forced-feeding period, nor more stern and unyielding ones when the time for independence has arrived ... In spite of what I've said about the devotion of female birds to their young, I think that bears are the best mothers. Photographing in the wilds of Montana and Wyoming, we spied on Mrs. Black Bear, handsome in her fine fur coat, for the better part of two seasons. We saw her come out of her winter cave with two fat little cubs and begin their education. Father Bear had nothing to do with the rearing of his youngsters. But Mrs. Bear stayed with her kids two years, taught them where to find food, hugged them with affection, cuffed them when they were unruly, and brought them up a credit to her name and to bear society.[1]

These musings suggest that like many Americans in the postwar era, Disney had become preoccupied by family issues in thinking about social cohesion. As a special 1954 issue of *McCall's* informed its readers, domestic togetherness was crucial to the new age of abundance. The most impressive feature of American consumption, education, and travel was that "men, women and children are achieving it *together*. They are creating this new and warmer way of life not as women *alone,* or men *alone,* isolated from one another, but as a *family* sharing a common experience." Behind this idealization of the family lay several concrete social influences—a drop in the average age at marriage, a decline in the divorce rate, and a rise in the birthrate, to its highest point in the twentieth century. The government had created unprecedented support for the family with the G.I. Bill of 1944, which made low-interest mortgage loans available to young families, and the Housing Act of 1949, which provided financial incentives to contractors to build single-family houses. Even more important was a powerful cultural movement to link domestic life to a set of compelling images—the suburban home as an emblem of abundance and locus of consumption, private life as the training ground for virtuous citizenship, the family as the mold for the individual's vibrant personality and self-fulfillment.[2]

Against this backdrop, Disney's persistent engagement with an array of domestic issues produced a powerful social resonance. It resulted in what might be called the Disney Doctrine: a notion that the nuclear family, with its attendant rituals of marriage, parenthood, emotional and spiritual instruction, and consumption, was the centerpiece of the American way of life. Illustrated through a long string of productions, this idea became a bulwark in America's defense against enemies, both foreign and domestic.

Interestingly, Disney's earlier, animated films had betrayed a pointed ambivalence about domestic security. Almost invariably, family units had been splintered, and those that appeared intact seldom existed in a state of tranquillity. For both Mickey and Minnie Mouse and Donald and Daisy Duck, for instance, an awkwardly defined relationship suggested cohabitation but explicitly rejected marriage, and children who appeared in these cartoons were orphans or distant relatives rather than real offspring. Moreover, the protagonists of feature films such as *Pinocchio, Dumbo,* and *Bambi* were typically orphans or children otherwise isolated from their families, desperately insecure and frantically searching for stability. But in the atmosphere of Cold War America, Disney modified his emphasis. His films continued to portray threats to family integrity, but the dangers were increasingly blunted or trivialized, and they appeared mainly as a pretext for the triumph of domestic stability at story's end.

5   Disney also began to develop a new, highly self-conscious emphasis on the *concept* of family entertainment. A special 1954 issue of the *Motion Picture Herald,* for example, informed readers that "Walt Disney believes the motion picture's first obligation to itself and its public is to be true to the American family without deviation." In public statements, Disney sprinkled his comments with allusions to the family focus of his entertainment vision. He described the evolution of movies in the twentieth century as a process wherein "mass entertainment began to take hold of American families" and announced that this genre, when developed by the right hands, "need never stale for the family taste." He asserted his dedication to enhancing "the sanctity of the home ... [and] all that is good for the family and for our country." While other Hollywood studios aimed at more sophisticated or prurient tastes, Disney's famous sentiment that he never made a movie that he didn't want his family to see gradually became an article of faith among the American public.[3]

The studio's animated shorts, for instance, began to depict familiar Disney characters in new ways. These heretofore rural or urban sprites, often forced to scratch out a living, now were magically transformed into prosperous suburbanites with humorous stories rooted in domestic situations. Whereas movies such as *Window Cleaners* (1940), *The Riveter* (1940), and *Bellboy Donald* (1942) had portrayed Donald Duck as an urban worker, the 1950s saw the emergence of a domesticated, middle-class, fatherly fowl. The duck's short films increasingly revolved around his comic misadventures with his nephews Huey, Louie, and Dewey, as in *Spare the Rod* (1954), where Donald gets a lesson in child psychology. *Donald's Diary* (1954) displays a suburbanized Donald wrestling with the question of marriage to his sweetheart, Daisy Duck. Such short films as *Inferior Decorator* (1948), *The Greener Yard* (1949), and *The New Neighbor* (1953) took their humor from his encounters with the vexations of modern suburban life—home furnishing, lawn care, and neighborly relations.

Goofy became a suburban family man even more dramatically. His 1950s cartoon shorts presented him as a well-meaning but not too bright father confronting a series of family difficulties: in *Get Rich Quick* (1951), a scolding wife who confiscates all of his winnings from a poker game; in *Fathers Are People* (1951), a mischievous offspring who puts him through the wringer of parenthood; in *Two Weeks Vacation* (1952), the unexpected difficulties of finding genuine relaxation; and in *Father's Weekend* (1953), the pitfalls of spending a "restful" Sunday afternoon with the family. Fleeing the big city or streaming in from the countryside like thousands of their flesh-and-blood fellow Americans, Disney's animated characters settled into subdivisions to enjoy the fruits of American abundance. As suburban knights, Goofy and Donald ventured forth from their split-level castles to do battle with an array of new enemies—lawn pests and annoying neighbors, vacation vexations and family psychodramas, recalcitrant wall paper and a rambling golf swing.

Disney's feature-length animated films in this period relied less on gags and suburban settings and offered a more complex picture of subversive forces facing the family. They focused on the fierce struggle often required to preserve its integrity and stability. In *Cinderella,* a cruel stepmother and scheming stepsisters torment the young heroine with degrading labor and emotional abuse, creating a hellish domestic scene which brightens only when a fairy godmother and a host of animal friends maneuver her toward marriage and family bliss. In like fashion, *Sleeping Beauty's* trio of good fairies try to give Princess Aurora a semblance of normal family life while protecting her against the machinations of an evil fairy, and after many crises they eventually succeed in moving the young woman into a love match with her betrothed.

Another pair of Disney animated features from the 1950s were less mythic in form. Utilizing a format that substituted dogs for humans, these whimsical stories explored many of the disruptions of modern domestic life. *Lady and the Tramp* (1955) followed an upper-class female canine and her adventurous romance with a roguish male dog from the wrong side of town. Lady is evicted from the warmth of her family home when a mean aunt takes a dislike to her during her owners' absence, and the rakish Tramp valiantly saves her from a series of dangerous scrapes. The plot resolves itself when the two marry, settle down, and produce a quartet of puppies. *One Hundred and One Dalmatians* (1961) offered a defense of family virtue under threat from an evil, greedy villainess. Pongo and Perdita, two love-struck dalmatians, maneuver their single owners into a romance, and when the two humans marry, the dogs follow suit. A litter of puppies arrives in a short time, but this domestic felicity is destroyed when a scheming family friend, Cruella de Vil, kidnaps the puppies to make a spectacular fur coat. When the police are unable to help, the dogs take things into their own paws, and a canine network eventually locates the puppies in an abandoned country estate. After a hair-raising escape, the human and dog families are reunited.

10 The studio's live-action films from this period, contrary to the sugary Disney stereotype, also stressed the precarious nature of domestic well-being. These movies frequently pictured families as incomplete, harsh, occasionally abusive, and usually struggling to survive in one form or another. *So Dear to My Heart* (1948), for instance, concerned a young orphan who lived alone with his grandmother as they toiled on a small homestead. *The Littlest Outlaw* (1957) based its story on a

ten-year-old who runs away from his cruel stepfather, while *Westward Ho the Wagons* (1956) showcased a wagon train of families who faced the onslaught of hostile Indians as they journeyed across the frontier. The protagonist of *The Light in the Forest* (1958), Johnny Butler, was a white youth who grew up among the Delaware Indians and found returning to his real parents an excruciating experience. In *Toby Tyler* (1959), yet another orphaned boy ran away to join the circus after being harshly treated by an abusive uncle. These tales of families under duress, however, always ended in reconciliation and healing as the characters found some semblance of domestic stability. And therein lay the great strength of Disney's domestic ideology in the 1950s: it resulted not so much from saccharine platitudes about togetherness as from a recurring dynamic of hard-fought achievement, where the family prospered only after struggling to overcome the most daunting challenges. Disney's Cold War audience seemed to be seeking, and finding, the gratifying message that while obstacles to family solidarity certainly loomed, they could be overcome by sustained, virtuous effort.

Disney's family ideology also gained considerable power from its gender formulations. In many of his 1950s films, the male characters carved out a domain within a consensus that was protective of family and hearth but clearly positioned outside it. The idealized female characters, however, were self-sacrificing moral instructors, skilled domestic managers, and compassionate caregivers. Yet, contrary to the stereotype, Disney did not offer a simple, saccharine female model characterized only by subordination, primness, and domestic imprisonment. His heroines, clearly dealing from a position of moral strength in the domestic realm, were not only physically attractive and even sexy in a subtle and wholesome way, but also frequently assertive and individualist as they defended and promoted their own interests. In Disney's films, women certainly presided over the family sphere, but they were not afraid to venture into the public realm when duty called.[4]

Idealized images of women as wives, mothers, and active moral agents were strewn throughout Disney's animated films in this era. In *Lady and the Tramp,* for example, a movie filled with appropriately stereotypical names, a demure wife named Darling cooks and cleans, sews, looks after her businessman husband, and generally appears "the epitome of the ideal American housewife of the 1950s," even though the story is set in 1910. She also dotes on her dog, Lady, who quickly becomes the canine guardian of the family's infant. After a series of harrowing adventures, Lady not only tames her rascally male suitor but becomes the proud mother of her own brood. Similarly, *One Hundred and One Dalmatians* presented the pretty and personable Anita as the owner of a female dog, Perdita, both of whom marry and settle into domestic harmony. While Perdita becomes a proud mother, she also proves unafraid to help with the heroic, dangerous rescue of her puppies after their kidnapping.[5]

In contrast with the girlish appearance and prepubescent sensibility of earlier protagonists such as Snow White, Disney's animated females in the 1950s also began to display a noticeable, if wholesome, sex appeal. *Peter Pan's* Tinker Bell, for example, not only "throws off star dust in the proper tradition, but she is also a particularly endearing little vixen compounded of blond hair, feminine curves, and a pout," noted a *Newsweek* reporter, "and just a little too bosomy to squeeze through an oversized keyhole." Disney claimed in a newspaper article that Tinker Bell's full figure had been inspired by the popularity of the sexpot actress Marilyn Monroe.[6]

Perhaps the clearest animated image of the Disney female came early in the decade with *Cinderella,* the 1950 film that helped reestablish the studio's reputation. Its heroine was, quite simply, the ideal American woman of the period. Many articles described her as a young woman with a keen awareness that "matrimony was the object" of female endeavor. After observing how she appeared to be pursued by while actually pursuing Prince Charming, one writer suggested that "if Cinderella is honest—and she has all the noble virtues—she will, like all honest girls should, admit that at least she 'inspired' the proposal." As another piece observed, such feminine wiles were attractively packaged in an "athletic type" who was pretty without being a dazzling beauty. In interviews, Disney Studio artists admitted that certain characteristics had been drawn into this figure: "We didn't want to make her a 'sweater girl,' but her curves are obvious and correctly placed … We want her to appeal to all women. Thus she can be neither too beautiful nor too homely. We want her to be a universal type, so any woman looking in a mirror will see something of Cinderella in herself…We gave her spunk. In the books, her fairy godmothers made things too easy for her. We made her problems tougher and gave her the guts to go after what she wanted." Cinderella, one critic concluded bluntly, was "the ideal American girl." The Disney Studio not only knew this but exploited it handsomely. The movie character inspired a whole line of clothing for young women: "With laced-up basque tops, puffed peplums that look like quaint overskirts, with ruffles and full skirts, this line of dresses hits a little girl just where her fairy tale heart is." Moreover, in early 1950, Disney officially sanctioned a series of contests in cities around the United States to find local Cinderellas. Publicity for the one held in Chicago stressed that the winning candidate "must have character, personality, charm. It is not just beauty. It can be a cheerful disposition, a friendly helpful nature or a particular talent for making others happy."[7]

15 Throughout the 1950s, the studio populated its movies with vivid countertypes to illustrate persistent threats to the feminine ideal. The animated features presented a gallery of villainous women whose baleful behavior explicitly violated every postwar standard of proper womanly conduct. They rejected domestic duty, and their public actions were selfish and corrupt. In *Cinderella,* for example, the haughty, cunning stepmother treats the young heroine as a slave, while the stepsisters are spoiled, selfish, shrill, and mean. Maleficent, from *Sleeping Beauty,* had a more striking impact. This tall, thin, black-clad evil fairy hates everything virtuous, commands a squadron of goons to do her dirty work, and literally transforms into a dragon to fight Prince Phillip. Cruella de Vil, with her wild shock of black-and-white hair and twirling cigarette holder, is a wealthy, sleazy sophisticate who kidnaps children, commits robbery, disrupts family peace, and generally destroys anything smacking of secure domestic life. These animated antiheroines not only frightened and disgusted but reinforced the idealized standard of female virtue. Once again, rather than simply displaying an ideal, Disney's films stressed that it must be the result of hard-fought achievement.

Notes

1. WD, "What I've Learned from the Animals," 23, 106–8.

2. "Live the Life of McCall's," "A Man's Place Is in the Home," "Ed and His Family Live Together and Love It," and "The Importance of Being Father," *McCall's*, May 1954, 27–35, 61. See also Lynn Spigel, *Make Room for TV: Television and the Family Ideal in Postwar America* (Chicago, 1992), 33–34, 37; May, *Homeward Bound*, 11, 16–36, 162–82.

3. William R. Weaver, "Walt Disney, Artist and Storyteller," *Motion Picture Herald*, Nov. 20, 1954, 42; WD, "Film Entertainment and Community Life," *Journal of the American Medical Association*, July 12, 1958, 1344; WD, "The Future of Fantasy," *Catholic Preview of Entertainment*, April 1959, 36.

4. In a certain sense, Disney's domestic ideology revived traditional Victorian categories of female and male "separate spheres." But as Joanne Meyerowitz has noted, in mainstream 1950s ideology, "domestic ideals coexisted in ongoing tension with an ethos of individual achievement that celebrated nondomestic activity, individual striving, public service, and public success." See "Beyond the Feminine Mystique: A Reassessment of Postwar Mass Culture, 1946–1958," in Meyerowitz, *Not June Cleaver: Women and Gender in Postwar America, 1945–1960* (Philadelphia, 1994), 23.

5. John Grant, *Walt Disney's Animated Characters: From Mickey Mouse to Aladdin* (New York, 1993), 248.

6. "Peter Pan: Real Disney Magic," *Newsweek*, Feb. 16, 1953; Maltin, *The Disney Films*, 109.

7. See "Disney's 'Cinderella': Of Mice and Girls," *Newsweek*, Feb. 13. 1950, 84–88; " 'Cinderella' Poses Moot Question about Courting," Columbus, Ohio, *State Journal*, Feb. 22, 1950; Jack Quigg, "Cinderella, Tough Girl to Cast, Emerges as Athletic, Curvy Type by Disney," Washington, D.C., *Star*, Sept. 4, 1949; Cynthia Cabot, "Fairyland Glamour," *Philadelphia Inquirer Magazine*, Jan. 29, 1950, 24–25; "A Thrilling Search for the Girl Who Is Chicago Area's Modern Cinderella," Chicago *Herald-American*, Jan. 29, 1950.

Rereading Actively

1. Watts's discussion opens with a lengthy quotation in which Walt Disney comments on the virtues of a mother bear. Considering the focus on Disney's heroines in the second half of this reading, what rhetorical effect does Watts achieve by including this quotation?

2. With a partner or in a small group, identify passages where Watts refers to the historical context of American society in the 1950s. Discuss the features of this society that were a major concern to Walt Disney. How were these elements of society reflected in the animated features and films produced by Disney Studios in this era?

3. In an entry in your journal, restate the "Disney Doctrine" (¶ 3) in your own words.

4. Disney seems to have insisted that the happy endings in his films were to be the result of "hard-fought achievement" (¶ 10). According to Watts, what was Disney's rhetorical purpose in writing his films this way? What message was Disney apparently trying to convey?

5. Disney's "family ideology" (¶ 11) included idealized portrayals of women. With a partner or in a small group, review Watts's discussion of Disney's hero-

ines, then in a page or so in your journal, write a description of the "ideal" woman as depicted by Disney.

Exploring Your Responses

6. With a partner or in a small group, reflect on the roles of women as these are discussed in the article, focusing on the relevance of Disney's portrayals (created in the 1950s) to women today. In a journal entry, describe your conversation about this subject.

7. Watts alludes to Disney's creation of female characters such as Tinker Bell and Cinderella who are said to possess a "wholesome sex appeal" (¶ 13). Focusing on either of these characters or another of your choosing, write a journal entry describing what attracts or repels you about the image of feminine beauty they portray.

8. Among the virtues said to be possessed by Disney heroines, Watts mentions both physical attractiveness and moral strength (¶ 11). In a journal entry, consider whether this is this still true today, either for Disney heroines or for women in our society. Then consider: Do moral strength and physical attractiveness have anything essential to do with one another?

9. Watts's discussion seems to establish a close connection between Walt Disney's own preoccupations with family and the portrayal of idealized family relationships in Disney films and cartoons. But what is the nature of this connection? In a journal entry, consider whether Disney's products reflect a reality already there in society, or whether they create an idealization, a myth we are meant to try to live up to every day.

A WORK IN PROGRESS

MICHAEL EISNER

In late 1984, Michael Eisner resigned the presidency of Paramount Pictures and weeks later accepted the position of CEO at Walt Disney Company. Since Eisner has held the "keys to the kingdom," Walt Disney Co. has grown from a company that had never made more than $100 million in annual profit to a corporate giant that had $22.5 billion in revenue in 1997. Disney now has a hand in nearly every form of entertainment, from Internet search engine Infoseek to ABC to the Disney Cruise Line to Bill Nye the Science Guy. In 1993, Eisner and his partner Frank Wells decided to write a book that would explain to Disney employees and others what the Disney brand could stand for. Five years later—four years after Wells died in a skiing accident—Eisner published A Work in Progress, *a memoir that explains Eisner's management of the biggest entertainment complex in the world. This excerpt focuses on how animated movies and TV shows fit into Disney's game plan.*

The enormous video market for our animated films prompted [an] epiphany, namely, the huge potential upside to be realized in stepping up production of new animated films. When we arrived at Disney, one new animated movie was being released approximately every four years. In the aftermath of Oliver and Roger Rabbit, we set a goal of producing one every twelve to eighteen months. In Jeffrey [Katzenberg's] short-hand, the chant became "Bigger, better, faster, cheaper." The tension level at animation rose perceptibly. Artists trooped into Roy [Disney's] office, complaining that Jeffrey was a "slavedriver." Roy came to me directly and expressed his concern that greater volume would occur at an expense to excellence. Increasing our output, I felt, had the potential to improve not just our profits but even the quality of our films. Endless time isn't necessarily a good thing. Deadlines, pressure, and exhaustion often lead to breakthroughs as artists are forced to exceed what they believe is possible. Increasing our production also forced us to seek out new talent.

In December 1989, Peter Schneider wrote a long memo summarizing the state of animation. It was possible, he argued, to be bigger, better, and faster with our animated movies—to break ground with each one, and to produce more of them—but it wasn't possible to do so more inexpensively. "If cheaper means not squandering money," he wrote, "we are making strides to improve the efficiency and better manage the process. If cheaper means smaller budgets for our movies, then this is in conflict with 'Bigger, Better.' With Jeffrey and Roy's desire to make truly top production value movies, it will cost more money. In my opinion, the reason that Disney animated movies were and can again be great is the ability to throw out and redo and make it better. The money spent during the making of *Mermaid* made a good movie into a great movie."

As *The Little Mermaid* prompted our feature-animation business to explode, we enjoyed a parallel success reviving television animation. For the first time, Disney emerged as a major player in Saturday morning children's television—and without relying on the mindless violence that characterized the low-cost, low-quality shows from nearly all our competitors. We were even more ambitious about producing animated shows for weekday afternoons. By the fall of 1990, we'd created four half-hour shows that we began selling as a group called the *Disney Afternoon*. It quickly became the most profitable part of our television division, consistently earning more than $40 million a year. As with most programming success, however, it was not destined to last forever.

The competitor primarily responsible for the eventual decline of the *Disney Afternoon*—Barry Diller and his Fox Television Network—had initially been its strongest supporter. Within six months after Barry took over as chairman of Twentieth Century Fox, Rupert Murdoch purchased the studio from Marvin Davis. With Rupert's backing, Barry was finally able to realize the dream we had first conceived together back at Paramount: launching a fourth television network. Fox began running its first shows in 1986. When we decided to launch the *Disney Afternoon*, Barry committed on the spot to run it on all his Fox-owned stations. Fox-affiliated stations eventually comprised more than 80 percent of the stations that carried the *Disney Afternoon*.

5   Still, my relationship with Barry wasn't free of conflict for long. Virtually from the moment that he took over Fox and I moved to Disney in 1984, we had a series of disagreements over various business deals. None was quite so dramatic as the one that emerged over the *Disney Afternoon*. It began in early 1990, when we purchased KHJ, an independent television station in Los Angeles, renamed it KCAL, and began looking for ways to improve the station's performance. One obvious move was to take the *Disney Afternoon* away from Fox's station and put it on KCAL.

This decision infuriated Barry. Having supported *Disney Afternoon* from the start, he believed that he was entitled to continue running it on his flagship Los Angeles station. "I helped bring you to where you are," he told Rich Frank and Jeffrey, "and you can't just take the shows away from us." I certainly understood his feelings, but there was no way for us to justify depriving our new station of highly desirable Disney programming.

Barry responded by immediately canceling the *Disney Afternoon* on his other six stations. Then he made a decision that would ultimately prove even more devastating to us: producing his own children's television programs. Much later, I would learn that this idea was conceived by several Fox affiliates. In any case, before very long we began to hear from our salespeople in the field that Fox was putting intense pressure on its affiliated stations all across the country to carry the network's new programming. If they didn't agree to replace the *Disney Afternoon* with Fox's new children's programs, they were told, then they risked being dropped as affiliates.

In February 1990, we filed a lawsuit against the Fox Broadcasting Company, charging it with contract interference and an unlawful attempt to monopolize children's TV. One of our most valuable assets was now in jeopardy. If you don't respond aggressively when that occurs, your competitors soon learn that they can run over you, and ultimately your shareholders are hurt. Because of my long relationship with Barry, the battle immediately took on an added personal dimension. He felt betrayed that we hadn't left the *Disney Afternoon* at KTTV. I was angry that he seemed to be urging the Fox affiliates to dump our programming in favor of his.

In the meantime, Barry moved ahead to produce his own slate of children's programs. They became his best revenge. The *Power Rangers* series emerged as the hottest children's show on television, and Fox began to dominate afternoon children's programming as we lost outlets. In the wake of our lawsuit, Fox probably proceeded more cautiously with affiliates than it might have otherwise. As a result, the *Disney Afternoon* stayed on the air in enough markets to remain highly profitable for another two years. Finally, in early 1992, we dropped the suit, in part because the dispute made it difficult for us to do any other kind of business with Fox and its parent, News Corp., around the world. Barry and I have long since reconciled, making new deals and fighting over others.

10   Even at its height, the profit from television animation paled against what we were earning in filmed animation. Over time, this business occupied more and more of Jeffrey's attention, not just because it was such a huge profit center but because it proved so well suited to his temperament. In live action, authority had to be shared with—and sometimes ceded to—strong producers, powerful directors, and big-name actors. This wasn't true in animation. Peter Schneider ran the operation day to day, keeping a huge and still-expanding group of artists working effectively together. Roy talked regularly to Peter, maintaining contact with key artists, and also screening and providing notes on the rough cuts of each of the new films. But it was Jeffrey who served as conductor of the animation orchestra and commanded center stage.

An animated movie took four years to produce, and Jeffrey drove his team relentlessly. He didn't always have a solution to a problem, but he was very good at spotting them. "If you showed Jeffrey a piece of material," Alan Menken later told me, "he always had an immediate gut reaction. You might agree with him or disagree, but he always provoked you." Jeffrey worried over the details on a daily basis. I came in at longer intervals and tried to focus on the big picture. Was a certain character's action credible? Did a particular scene evoke the intended emotion? Did the third act really work? Jeffrey sought and received more independence and authority, but I still believed I added an important perspective. In animation, we released only one movie a year, and each one took on enormous importance.

After each rough-cut screening, we all gathered together—producers, writers, and directors—to discuss our movies. I also continued to speak intermittently to Peter, Tom, and other creative executives beneath Jeffrey, much as I did to people at various levels in Disney's other divisions. It was a way to stay truly connected to the process.

The only significant artistic misstep we made during the first several years in animation was *The Rescuers Down Under.* Released in the fall of 1990, it was the first movie to make significant use of CAPS, and the quality of the animation took a quantum leap—especially in the scene of the soaring flight by the eagle Marahute, drawn by Glen Keane and conceived by Chris Sanders. In retrospect, however, the movie lacked at least three of the ingredients that audiences responded to most strongly in *The Little Mermaid:* great music, a central theme, and a strong, emotional story. It was also a sequel to the original *Rescuers,* released in 1977. However much audiences valued the Disney signature on animated movies, they also came to each one looking for something wholly new and original.

Beauty and the Beast put us back on track, but not before overcoming its own rocky start. The project began as a purely dramatic version of the classic fairy tale. A year of intensive work went into the script. After looking at the first twenty minutes in storyboards, it was clear to all of us that it didn't work. The movie was too dark, depressing, and overbearing. Finally, in the fall of 1989, Jeffrey brought in Howard Ashman and Alan Menken, fresh from their success with *The Little Mermaid.* They reconceived *Beauty* as a musical and began writing songs. The biggest problem was Ashman's health. Though he had suffered from various ailments for some time, he assured his colleagues that they were all stress-related. In mid-1990, soon after Ashman and Menken won the Academy Award for *The Little Mermaid,* Ashman acknowledged to Menken and a few close friends that he'd developed AIDS. When travel became difficult for him, Peter Schneider arranged to move the development of *Beauty* from Glendale to the Residence Inn, in Fishkill, New York, near Ashman's home.

15   A makeshift workplace was set up in one of the conference rooms, using giant foam boards on which storyboard sketches could be pinned. A Yamaha piano was rented for Menken. Despite his deteriorating health, Ashman once again became the guiding voice. Referring to himself as "the simplicity police," he argued that each scene in a powerful drama had to be both accessible and emotionally strong at its core. He fought to retain the archetypal appeal of *Beauty and the Beast*—a love story built on the premise that a tender heart lies beneath even the toughest exterior—even as he helped to create its distinctive narrative and musical identity.

It was Ashman who first recognized that the story ought to be told not from Belle's point of view but from the Beast's. He also thought of transforming Gaston from a blandly foppish suitor into a wonderfully boorish chauvinist pig. And it was Ashman who had the whimsical but touching idea of giving human voices to the servants who have been reduced by the Beast to inanimate objects, such as a mantel clock (Cogsworth) and a candlestick (Lumiere). Together, Ashman and Menken created the film's extraordinary songs. The first time that they played their opening number for us—"Belle"—we were warned that it ran seven minutes. "You're going to find it too long, too theatrical, and too unconventional," Howard said. In fact, "Belle" was a classic show stopper, which set up the whole movie and worked brilliantly in spite of its length.

Although Ashman's health continued to deteriorate, he insisted on staying at his work, even when he began to lose his eyesight and his voice. He died on March 14, 1991, at the age of forty-one—just six months before *Beauty and the Beast* opened. It was a tragic loss on both a personal and an artistic level. Beloved by those who collaborated with him, he had managed to work at the height of his creative powers until the very end of his life. In the fall of 1991, *Beauty and the Beast* became the first animated movie ever to be screened at the opening night of the New York Film Festival. When *Beauty* opened in theaters two months later, it earned by far the best reviews yet for our animated movies. It also quickly surpassed the previous leader, *The Little Mermaid,* at the box office. *Beauty* ultimately earned more than $145 million domestically. On video, it eventually sold nearly 22 million copies, compared to 9 million for *The Little Mermaid* a year earlier. Most notably of all, *Beauty and the Beast* became the first animated film ever to win an Academy Award nomination for Best Picture.

As Ashman and Menken were finishing their work on *Beauty and the Beast* during 1990, they returned to the songs for another movie that they had temporarily put aside, *Aladdin.* I had always been slightly uneasy about a film set in the Middle East, a part of the world that I didn't know and didn't feel comfortable trying to portray. Nor was I convinced that the story held together until John Musker and Ron Clements, the directors of *The Little Mermaid,* came aboard to produce and direct. In the wake of Ashman's death, Peter managed to broker a new partnership between Alan Menken and the lyricist Tim Rice, who had long been Andrew Lloyd Webber's collaborator. Together, Menken and Rice finished the song score. What made *Aladdin* most distinctive, however, was Robin Williams's brilliant, hilarious, often extemporaneous performance as the voice of the Genie. For all that, *Beauty* seemed like a tough act to follow, and most of us were surprised when *Aladdin* became an even bigger hit during the summer of 1992. In hindsight, the reasons seem clear. *Aladdin* was exotic yet accessible, engaging but also exceptionally funny, a movie that adults could enjoy every bit as much as their kids. It also benefited from the momentum created by *The Little Mermaid* and *Beauty and the Beast.*

Rereading Actively

1. This excerpt opens with Eisner's epiphany about the massive market awaiting more Disney animation. How does his pragmatic view of entertainment products affect you? In your journal, note your reaction to Eisner's matter-of-fact business perspective on entertainment.

2. With a partner, identify passages in the article that discuss or reveal Eisner's attitude toward Disney's audience, paying particular attention to the role audience appeal plays in product development. Summarize Eisner's view of Disney's audience and product appeal in a short entry in your journal.

3. Eisner's expertise is in creative management and product development. Locate passages where Eisner talks about the creative process and passages where he

describes his work with artists, project managers, and other entertainment executives. In your journal, discuss a passage in which he takes a management approach to a Disney character or product.

4. How does the control of product distribution relate to Eisner's agenda? Review the excerpt, looking for references to distribution, and in your journal respond to Eisner's attempt to control the Disney brand.

5. In a small group, review the excerpt and locate concrete and specific references to a character, song, and scene. Discuss how Eisner's interpretation of these familiar artifacts affects your understanding of the Disney brand. Summarize the different views of your group in a journal entry.

6. Review the excerpt, noting passages where Eisner emphasizes previous decisions he had made or talks about how his connections, experience, or management style enabled him to solve problems. In your journal, make a short list of the kind of statements that you found, and follow that list with a paragraph in which you define and react to the Eisner character that surfaces here. (You may want to do this exercise in connection with the first exercise in this set.)

Exploring Your Responses

7. In a page or two in your journal, reflect on your feelings about the entertainment business behind Ariel, the Little Mermaid, Belle, the princess from *Aladdin,* or a female character from the Disney afternoon lineup (pick one). Explore how knowing the business of creating character affects your consumption of the product and your relationship to this character.

8. In a small group, identify Disney films centered on heroines that your group has seen. Pick a film. With your group, find a review—a film review, a video review, or a scholarly critique—of the movie and compare this view of Disney with Eisner's. Prepare an explanation of the similarities and differences between Eisner's perspective and that of the reviewer.

9. Reflect on your access to a Disney character. Where do you see it? What do you have to do in order to see it? Could you avoid it if you wanted to? In a freewrite, consider how your access to the character is restricted and what other products and experiences come along with this character.

CASE-IN-POINT ASSIGNMENTS

The case readings suggest that Disney is more than many of us imagine. With access to billions of dollars in revenues and facilities that produce entertainment in every major media, the company is an omnipresent entertainment provider. The writers here point out the dominant position Disney has in children's entertainment, but children aren't the only citizens in the magic kingdom: Disney exerts remarkable control over representations of childhood and family, the production of American myths, and even the nightly news. If we are as addicted to entertainment as many writers seem to say we are, Disney is the biggest supplier on the block. The question the case writers struggle with is what Disney says about the feminine and how this message affects viewers' sense of what it means to be a girl or a woman.

Making Connections

1. Michael Eisner and Laura Sells have different views of Disney's mission. Compare their views, explaining how their understanding of Disney's purpose affects their interpretations of *The Little Mermaid*. Conclude by suggesting how your position on Disney and *The Little Mermaid* compares with theirs. (This will involve watching at least part of the film.)

2. Some would argue that in our world, Disney has become an influential babysitter, since Disney's products occupy so much of the time of children and young people. Drawing on Watts, Chang, and Henke et al., develop a position on the role Disney should and should not play in the lives of children and their parents.

3. Using your own experience with a Disney heroine as the basis for your argument, answer two of the writers among the case-in-point readings, exploring the validity of their analyses of Disney's images of girls.

4. Dolls, underwear, neckties...Drawing on comments about Disney tie-ins made by Henke et al. and Chang as well as, perhaps, a visit to a Disney Store or a conversation with a child, write an essay that explains the marketing potential represented by Disney's animated heroines. Focus on how these characters are designed so that they appear as idealized images, and how that idealization is used to sell other products.

5. In Chapter 8, Mark Spiegler and Eric L. Smith describe the marketing and demographics behind the phenomenon of hip-hop crossover. Using these sources of information as well as readings you have done about Disney, compare the marketing success of hip-hop style with the marketing of Disney. Reflecting on both, do you see these as serving a larger social good? Why or why not?

Collaborative Exchanges

1. In a small group, discuss your reaction to Henke et al.'s interpretation of two heroines and Watts's description of Walt Disney's personal attitude toward women, on screen and off. Develop a collaborative comparison of the view of Disney heroines from inside and outside the company. Be prepared to tell the class which view your group found to be more accurate.

2. Heller explains several critical approaches to Disney, suggesting why Disney is culturally significant and important to think about. In a small group, view and take notes on a thirty-minute Disney cartoon and the commercials that accompany it, and discuss the images of girls and women that you saw. Decide which of the critical positions described by Heller best help you to explain those images. Be prepared to explain your interpretation of the cartoon to the class.

3. With two or three classmates, find five reviews of one of the heroine-centered, animated Disney films that Eisner discusses. Develop a report that summarizes the reviewers' opinions, relates them to Eisner's description of how the films were brought to market, and takes a position on how well Eisner understands how Disney's images of girls really function in our society.

Net Approaches

1. First, visit <www.disney.com>, surf around, and be amazed. Try to story-board—keep track of the structure of links and embedded pages—what you see, and write about the apparent logic behind the structure of the page.

2. Go to the "movies" link on the Disney page and search for the title of a hero-ine-centered film. Review the hits that the title brings up, noting the different kinds of merchandise Disney links to its female characters. Once you have written down a dozen different tie-ins, go back over the list, jotting down the target consumer for each item and then sketching a profile of whom Disney believes this character appeals to.

3. Take the same movie title you used in the previous exercise to <www.hotbot.com> and connect it to "disney" but exclude the words "sale" and "sales." One way to script this search is the following: *((little mermaid) and disney) not sale**. Scroll thirty or forty hits in and look for nonvendor pages. We found a *Girl's Life Magazine* contest that asked girls to "write about how you are like your favorite Disney Princess" and a number of personal pages belonging to folks who just like Disney images. Keep track of interesting hits and be prepared to participate in a class discussion of how Disney exists in the noncommercial Web.

WRITING PROJECTS

ENTERTAINMENT

Project 1

Likely Readings

Background Readings
• Douglas
• Tisdale

Case-in-Point Readings
• Eisner
• Sells

Task and Purpose

Tell a story about your experience with a specific kind of entertainment, preferably one produced by the folks at Disney. First, think about a movie, program, sport, or book that has had a substantial effect on you; then, decide what that effect is. Skim over your reading notes, and decide how that kind of entertainment is produced and how audiences respond to it. As soon as you have focused on a kind of entertainment and an effect that it has had on you, freewrite your interaction with it. Think about how you played the role of audience member and how your experience crossed over into less "entertaining" parts of your life. From this freewrite, construct a narrative that shows your audience how entertainment has made you who you are.

Project 2

Likely Readings

Background Readings
- Douglas
- Gabler
- Tisdale
- Wolf

Case-in-Point Readings
- Bowman
- Chang
- Hill
- Sells

Task and Purpose

Analyze the impact of a specific entertainment product—maybe a Disney product—on a local culture that you know well. You will need to start from a theory of the effect of entertainment or by asking people, including yourself, some direct questions about how this entertainment makes them feel and what it makes them think about. You will also need some indirect questions about, say, what toys they buy for young girls or boys or what they think about marriage, love, gender, sex, or whatever other themes the entertainment touches on. You may also want to get first-person reactions to characters, actors, sets, music, and other details of the performance and its distribution. Once you have a sense for how your subject relates to a group of people, tear the entertainment apart, looking for connections between what goes on "on stage" and how people respond. Try not to draw conclusions until you have done the analysis, and after it's done, make sure your conclusions are based on what you have examined.

Project 3

Likely Readings

Background Readings
- Douglas
- Mandel et al.
- Tisdale
- Wolf

Case-in-Point Readings
- Heller
- Hill
- Eisner

Task and Purpose

Write a report on some aspect of the entertainment industry (perhaps on some aspect of the Walt Disney Co.) that synthesizes information from the reading to show a reader how the business works now and how it is likely to expand or contract. You will need to offer clear, neutral evidence as well as logical, well-supported recommendations. Start by picking a narrow topic within the broad subject areas of "the entertainment industry" or "Disney"; you might focus on a professional sports team or a film director, an individual Disney product or production area (e.g., TV programming or animated feature films). Once you have a topic (likely one the reading has mentioned), think about who would want to know about this topic. (You may want to start the whole process by thinking first of an audience.) With topic and audience in mind, outline the information the audience needs to know about the topic and the speculations that are likely to be helpful. Pull together a set of subtitles that subdivide the topic, and get to writing.

Project 4

Likely Readings

Background Readings
- Douglas
- Tisdale
- Wolf

Case-in-Point Readings
- Bowman
- Chang
- Heller
- Henke et al.
- Hill
- Sells
- Watts

Task and Purpose

Review Disney's *Little Mermaid* on video. Your purpose here is halfway between a standard newspaper review and an essay like Laura Sells's. You will need to call your readers' attention to the content of the film with the understanding that all or almost all of them have either seen or heard about the movie. Imagine writing for a publication that speaks primarily to parents or to nonparents: the audience you choose will determine what you emphasize, what tone you take, and whether your thumb goes up or down. As you get into this project, recall that a review is an evaluation that does a certain amount of analysis but also a good deal of synthesis. Reviews break films down into their elements but they also call attention to what other reviewers have said and how the culture in general is responding to the product in question.

Project 5

Likely Readings

Background Readings
- Douglas
- Wolf

Case-in-Point Readings
- Bowman
- Chang
- Eisner
- Henke et al.
- Hill
- Sells

Task and Purpose

Research the development of an entertainment character—perhaps a Disney heroine—and write a researched report that explains the key idea behind your character, its problems in development, and its creators' assessment of their success.

CHAPTER 7

Education: Investing in the Future

I n the 1600s, the English verb "to educate" meant little more than "to rear or bring up children." Since the eighteenth century, the word has come to refer to organized teaching. In the United States and most other market-oriented, democratic cultures, the word "education" has been connected to the universal instruction of informed voters and citizens, workers and consumers. At the same time, market competition has created a system of accessible public and elite private schools. For us, then, education encompasses the process of socializing children into a culture and also enabling citizens to participate actively in that culture. It also sorts us into groups based on both merit and the ability to pay tuition. In prosperity, more folks gain access to education and the chance for more training and stable lives and success; in lean times, education can serve to restrict access to upward mobility by controlling access to the credentials that education can provide.

In a democracy, though, education isn't only about training and credentials. Education leads to new ideas and information that need have nothing to do with the marketplace. In the United States, education is supposed by many to level the playing field and to craft the public future: educational institutions offer critiques of the very societies of which they are a part. As children and young adults, we go to school to discover ourselves, enjoy culture, and deepen our view of history and our place in it. Along the way, we sometimes confront culturally or historically embarrassing facts. And sometimes we begin to formulate new social arrangements.

This tension between the conservative and radical purposes of education raises the thorny questions that the background readings explore. Should students share a common experience in a neighborhood school, or should they choose where and what to study? Should faculty give students what they need in a core curriculum, or should students pick what they want from a smorgasbord of electives? Who should pay, and how much? Should students regard their own educations as investments in a future, the return for which they will realize in economic terms? How can the product they consume be tested or assessed? These questions anticipate a case in point focused on higher education. As consumers of higher education, what are students' rights and what can they demand? Clearly, education that is responsive to student and employer markets can be innovative and self-reforming. But when education becomes a product and students become consumers with rights and expectations, the chance to deliberate human development, truth, and access may be replaced by an educational stock market of sorts. Each of the writers in this unit has a position on the costs and benefits of a market-based approach to bringing up and training students.

BACKGROUND READINGS

KIDS AS EDUCATION CUSTOMERS
REBECCA JONES

Rebecca Jones is a senior editor at the Executive Educator, *a publication aimed at school board members and administrators. This essay appeared in the* Executive Educator *in 1996 and was reprinted in* Education Digest *the following year. As a representative of the American Association of School Boards, Jones takes a tentative trip into hotly contested territory and puts a primarily positive spin on educational consumerism. Drawing on examples from across the country, Jones identifies the pressures that are opening public schools to the marketplace and notes responses that teachers and administrators have made.*

"Service with a smile" won't prepare them for a competitive, less caring world. Maybe your mother was right. Maybe you can't please everyone. But if you're working in public schools today, you're probably trying. You're smiling, listening, nodding, sympathizing, and always, always, accommodating. You're certainly not alone in offering students and parents service with a smile, but is education really a consumer item?

Seattle (Washington) Superintendent John Stanford thinks so. He's been pushing for better customer service since he came to the district in September of 1995. He tells school employees he expects phones to be picked up by the first three rings and letters answered within 48 hours. "Everyone we deal with is a customer," he says. "We are a business here which produces a product—achievers. Poor customer service must be a firing offense."

Principal Ann Blakeney Clark also thinks good service is at the heart of a good education. Once or twice a week, she gets a call at home from a kid who's left something in a desk or locker at Alexander Graham Middle School, in Charlotte, North Carolina. Clark responds by going to the school and unlocking the building so the student can fetch the forgotten item. "I'd rather be seen as too accommodating than as not accommodating enough," she explains.

New Richmond, Ohio, Principal David Riel shares Clark's philosophy. He tells parents, "If you need a ride to your parent conference, we'll get you." And before school opens every year, the New Richmond Elementary School sponsors Readyfest, where all kids, regardless of family income, can get free tennis shoes, T-shirts, toothbrushes, crayons, pencils, lunchboxes, and dozens of other items and services. Riel compares the freebies, donated at no cost to the school, to "loss leaders" at a store. "We have a product that we're trying to sell," he says, "and that product is knowledge."

5   What's going on here? The concept of selling education isn't new, of course. Isn't that how Socrates built his reputation? But today, educators seem to be feeling more pressure to accommodate students, parents, taxpayers, even each other. Folks in the customer-service crowd are a pretty agreeable lot; the closest they come to an argument is when they try to identify which customer has top priority.

Driven by the same missionary zeal that drew them to the profession in the first place, many educators are waging all-out campaigns to win over their communities. Some say their people-pleasing efforts have gone too far, but others keep looking for new ways to satisfy their clientele.

At L'Ouverture Computer Technology Magnet Elementary School, in Wichita, Kansas, for example, Principal Howard Pitler says he's constantly seeking "customer intimacy"; he wants to know the kids and their families so well that the school can satisfy their needs before they even know they have them.

Worry

It hasn't always been this way, of course. Marc Salzman, assistant director of the public Academy of Environmental Science, in New York City, remembers what he calls "a real us-against-them attitude in New York City schools" when he began teaching there in 1968. Now, despite a waiting list of students eager to enroll, the academy staff worries when it finds out, usually from the district office, that a kid wants to transfer out.

"We call the parents and ask them to come in to talk," Salzman says. "Once we identify the problem, we can do something about it." Sometimes this means arranging for a bus pass or settling a teacher conflict by arranging a four-way conference with the teacher, the student, the parent, and an administrator. Salzman says his 86-year-old mother is appalled at the accommodations the school is willing to make. "When we went to school, the teacher was always right," she tells him.

People-Pleasers

10   Why the change? Why have schools switched from being rule-makers to people-pleasers? Educators tick off the reasons: defensiveness created by years of publicity about poor test scores and unresponsive bureaucracies; worsening difficulties in getting bond issues passed; the competition created by vouchers and schools of choice; the willingness which has been demonstrated by middle-class parents to decamp to private schools.

Some educators reach deeper into the nation's psyche, back to a generation jarred by an unpopular war and a governor barring a schoolhouse door to black students. Today, no one wants to be seen as enforcing stupid or unfair policies. And everyone, as Robert J. Samuelson writes in *The American Dream in the Age of Entitlement* (1945–1995), seems to think the government and its agencies have the obligation to guarantee a good life for all.

"People are demanding their rights," Salzman says. And many educators are handing them over cheerfully—or, at least, with smiles on their faces. They routinely cede to parents' wishes, host retreats, query focus groups, conduct surveys, and share decision making with anyone willing to attend the meetings."

Community surveys almost always show taxpayers are looking for bargains. Some districts try to woo senior citizens—often the most vociferous of taxpayers—with special services for retired people. Wareham, Massachusetts, for instance, began offering classes for senior citizens in the schools' technology labs after 3 p.m. "They really want to know what this new technology is all about," says Superintendent Jim Nolan, who now heads schools in nearby Norwood.

David and Susan Carroll, authors of *How Smart Schools Get* and *Keep Community Support*, say schools will have to pay even more attention to senior citizens in the future as baby boomers enter their retirement years. David Carroll, himself a boomer, predicts how his peers will react to school bond issues once their own children are out of school: "We have other problems now. We have college, we have retirement, we haven't saved sufficiently."

15   As parents, though, boomers have presented schools with wish lists of add-ons. Harry Hufty, principal of Blackburn Elementary School, in Prince George, British Columbia, quotes a mentor: "Everybody is reasonable, except when it comes to their kids."

Many schools routinely conduct surveys that measure parents' satisfaction and needs. Of course, schools don't hear from everyone—Salzman says many questionnaires "die in the kids' bookbags"—but the surveys that do make it home and back again speak with force.

Parent surveys at L'Ouverture, for instance, led to Saturday morning computer classes for parents and a latchkey program that keeps the school open from 7 a.m. to 7 p.m. year-round. "We've also made a very conscious effort to make sure parents feel welcome in our building," Pitler says. "We don't require appointments, we have sign-up sheets (for volunteers) in every classroom, and we all wear name tags here."

Other schools put name tags on their staff members, too, in an apparent effort to make visitors feel as comfortable at school as they do at the (also cheerfully name-tagged) local McDonald's.

The pay-off comes in volunteer support and, Pitler says, in "something we don't talk about enough—trust." When the L'Ouverture staff wanted to do away with letter grades, a parents' group resisted at first, then approved the plan, Pitier says, "because they said 'we trust you.'" The school spent a year trying out different reporting methods, always asking for parent input along the way.

20   The method they chose ran smoothly, Pitler says, until another survey—this one of former L'Ouverture students now in middle school—showed the kids were doing well but weren't ready for the shock of letter grades in middle school." The school responded quickly, and this year's fifth-graders will get a one-semester taste of letter grades before they head off to middle school.

Noting Preferences

Pitler is so eager to please parents he even invites them to express their preferences in teachers for the following year. (He says he can afford to do that because he has a school full of "great teachers.") Other administrators at other schools, perhaps in less rosy situations, broach this subject with far more trepidation.

Hufty, who says Blackburn Elementary is a Total Quality Management school, carefully builds classes for a good social and academic mix and tries to talk parents out of any objections to their child's placement. "But that's not one of the things I'm willing to go to the wall on," he says. If the parents insist, he places their child with another teacher. "It's not something I'm proud of" he says, "but it's something we do."

The customer-service approach has trickled down to—or maybe up from—teachers. "The teacher's job is to deliver the goods," Hufty says, and the good ones design their lessons and activities to catch a kid's fancy. Many also routinely give out their home phone numbers, buy presents for students, and host parties—even sleep-overs—in their own homes.

Fifth-grade teacher Janice Novello often takes kids, on her own time, to a museum, a play, or even a barbershop for a haircut. "We all do it," she says of her colleagues at Neil Armstrong Elementary School, in Bettendorf, Iowa. "We do it for the neediest of the neediest." And they don't limit their efforts to impoverished children: Novello recalls how terrible teachers felt when two kids transferred to a private school last year. "We felt like we had failed them," she says. "We all wrote them letters, telling them how much we missed them."

25   Not even the most customer-oriented schools can satisfy everyone every time, and perhaps they shouldn't try. "There are times when we get into conflict with our customers, honestly," Pitler says. "There are times we draw lines, too, and say, 'Past this point I cannot work with you.'" Pitier draws his line against parents who want the school to teach religion or who want to change their child's grade placement against the staff's recommendation. When school officials decided to move one child from the second to the fourth grade last year, six other parents piped up with similar requests for their children, but Pitier says he "counseled them out of it."

Hufty says he puts his foot down over baseball caps and what he deems "offensive T-shirts"; neither is allowed in the building. "We say, as we click our heels together and salute with our right hands, that hats are symbols and will not be tolerated," Hufty says. When he makes kids turn offensive T-shirts inside out, he says, "Parents ask what business is it of mine, and I say, 'It's my business because we have standards.'"

But when it comes to academics, standards and customer satisfaction don't necessarily go hand in hand. Albert Shanker, president of the American Federation of Teachers, bristles at the idea of treating students—or their parents—as customers who need pleasing. Quoting Socrates—"The student is the worker, not the consumer"—he says that "Attracting students is different from educating students. I've never met a kid yet who opens a Shakespearean tragedy and says, 'Ah, I can't wait to get into this.'"

Customer-service advocates insist their schools maintain rigorous academic standards, but critics say efforts to please kids and their parents can go too far and undercut standards. As Jerry Taylor, technology coordinator at Arcadia Middle School, in Greece, New York, observes: "If a kid gets an A in my class, then the parent is satisfied. Well, shoot, you know as well as I do that I can make a kid get an A, and I can make a kid get an F. I can make tests easy, and I can make tests hard."

That attitude might explain why efforts to please parents and kids have had an "absolutely deleterious effect on public education over the past 30 years," says Joan Carris, author of *S.A.T. Success* and other books that help students prepare for the Scholastic Assessment Test. "We started giving kids a lot of freedom in the '60s and '70s, including the freedom not to learn. And kids have grabbed that one with both hands."

30   It's hard to fault educators for reaching out to help kids who are out of control and who refuse to learn—that's what the idea of teaching the "whole child" is all about. But sometimes the central purpose of education can get lost in the customer-service shuffle.

"It seems like every time a problem comes up," Taylor says, "our first reaction is always [to ask], 'What can we do to change so we can meet the needs of this kid?'" By being so accommodating, he says, schools have taught kids there's no penalty for failing a test or ignoring a rule they don't like: "They don't need to worry about it, because the system will very quickly change to suit them."

The surprise comes, Shanker and others agree, when the kids leave school and find a competitive world that's not so accommodating.

Rereading Actively

1. Jones is writing to education professionals. How might they respond to her first paragraph? How do you respond?

2. What patterns do you notice in the anecdotes of people-pleasing that make up the second section of this article (¶ 11–21)? In your journal, list the programs mentioned and then describe how each one relates to providing an education.

3. Review the article with a partner and look for instances where Jones recognizes the constraints of resources, safety, and performance. Discuss how these constraints challenge the notion of student as consumer, and in your journal, evaluate Jones's interpretation of these constraints.

4. Jones is an educational administrator. How does she view academics? Look for references to course content, grades, and learning, and then draft a summary of her position on the relationship between student growth and student consumerism.

5. In her introduction and conclusion, Jones mentions a "competitive" world. How does this theme frame her discussion? Is her use of this theme effective? Why or why not?

6. What role do ideas such as improved attitude, performance, and participation play in the overarching idea of students as customers?

Exploring Your Responses

7. In a small group, talk about the service you received in high school, and then develop a position on whether teachers should perceive students as customers. You'll need to defend your position with arguments about improved attitude, performance, participation, and so on.

8. In a page or two in your journal, respond to the question Jones poses at the end of her second paragraph: "[I]s education really a consumer item?"

9. Speculate about how your high school experience would have been different if you and/or your parents had been consistently invited to talk about your satisfaction with school. What might you have said? How might your high school have accommodated your needs?

On the Uses of a Liberal Education
Mark Edmundson

Mark Edmundson is a University of Virginia English professor and a contributing editor for Harper's, *where this essay first appeared. A look at his publications reveals Edmundson's interest in literature, culture, and the liberal arts. This article presents a critique of what Edmundson calls "watered down" college offerings that seem to be taking the place of the core liberal arts curriculum. An important part of Edmundson's purpose here is to justify a return to a liberal arts foundation. Edmundson tries to establish the negative influence of a pervasive consumer worldview on the curriculum, and to argue that such an outlook is incompatible with liberal education.*

I. As Lite Entertainment for Bored College Students

Today is evaluation day in my Freud class, and everything has changed. The class meets twice a week, late in the afternoon, and the clientele, about fifty undergraduates, tends to drag in and slump, looking disconsolate and a little lost, waiting for a jump start. To get the discussion moving, they usually require a joke, an anecdote, an off-the-wall question—When you were a kid, were your Halloween getups ego costumes, id costumes, or superego costumes? That sort of thing. But today, as soon as I flourish the forms, a buzz rises in the room. Today they write their assessments of the course, their assessments of *me,* and they are without a doubt wide-awake. "What is your evaluation of the instructor?" asks question number eight, entreating them to circle a number between five (excellent) and one (poor, poor). Whatever interpretive subtlety they've acquired during the term is now out the window. Edmundson: one to five, stand and shoot.

And they do. As I retreat through the door—I never stay around for this phase of the ritual—I look over my shoulder and see them toiling away like the devil's auditors. They're pitched into high writing gear, even the ones who struggle to squeeze out their journal entries word by word, stoked on a procedure they have by now supremely mastered. They're playing the informed consumer, letting the provider know where he's come through and where he's not quite up to snuff.

But why am I so distressed, bolting like a refugee out of my own classroom, where I usually hold easy sway? Chances are the evaluations will be much like what they've been in the past—they'll be just fine. It's likely that I'll be commended for being "interesting" (and I am commended, many times over), that I'll be cited for my relaxed and tolerant ways (that happens, too), that my sense of humor and capacity to connect the arcana of the subject matter with current culture will come in for some praise (yup). I've been hassled this term, finishing a manuscript, and so haven't given their journals the attention I should have, and for that I'm called—quite civilly, though—to account. Overall, I get off pretty well.

Yet I have to admit that I do not much like the image of myself that emerges from these forms, the image of knowledgeable, humorous detachment and bland tolerance.

I do not like the forms themselves, with their number ratings, reminiscent of the sheets circulated after the TV pilot has just played to its sample audience in Burbank. Most of all I dislike the attitude of calm consumer expertise that pervades the responses. I'm disturbed by the serene belief that my function—and, more important, Freud's, or Shakespeare's, or Blake's—is to divert, entertain, and interest. Observes one respondent, not at all unrepresentative: "Edmundson has done a fantastic job of presenting this difficult, important & controversial material in an enjoyable and approachable way."

5   Thanks but no thanks. I don't teach to amuse, to divert, or even, for that matter, to be merely interesting. When someone says she "enjoyed" the course—and that word crops up again and again in my evaluations—somewhere at the edge of my immediate complacency I feel encroaching self-dislike. That is not at all what I had in mind. The off-the-wall questions and the sidebar jokes are meant as lead-ins to stronger stuff—in the case of the Freud course, to a complexly tragic view of life. But the affability and the one-liners often seem to be all that land with the students; their journals and evaluations leave me little doubt.

I want some of them to say that they've been changed by the course. I want them to measure themselves against what they've read. It's said that some time ago a Columbia University instructor used to issue a harsh two-part question. One: What book did you most dislike in the course? Two: What intellectual or characterological flaws in you does that dislike point to? The hand that framed that question was surely heavy. But at least it compels one to see intellectual work as a confrontation between two people, student and author, where the stakes matter. Those Columbia students were being asked to relate the quality of an *encounter*, not rate the action as though it had unfolded on the big screen.

Why are my students describing the Oedipus complex and the death drive as being interesting and enjoyable to contemplate? And why am I coming across as an urbane, mildly ironic, endlessly affable guide to this intellectual territory, operating without intensity, generous, funny, and loose?

Because that's what works. On evaluation day, I reap the rewards of my partial compliance with the culture of my students and, too, with the culture of the university as it now operates. It's a culture that's gotten little exploration. Current critics tend to think that liberal-arts education is in crisis because universities have been invaded by professors with peculiar ideas: deconstruction, Lacanianism, feminism, queer theory. They believe that genius and tradition are out and that P.C., multiculturalism, and identity politics are in because of an invasion by tribes of tenured radicals, the late millennial equivalents of the Visigoth hordes that cracked Rome's walls.

But mulling over my evaluations and then trying to take a hard, extended look at campus life both here at the University of Virginia and around the country eventually led me to some different conclusions. To me, liberal-arts education is as ineffective as it is now not chiefly because there are a lot of strange theories in the air. (Used well, those theories *can* be illuminating.) Rather, it's that university culture, like American culture writ large, is, to put it crudely, ever more devoted to consumption and entertainment, to the using and using up of goods and images. For someone growing up in America now, there are few available alternatives to the cool consumer worldview. My students didn't ask for that view, much less create it, but they bring a consumer weltanschauung to school, where it exerts a powerful, and largely unacknowledged, influence. If we want to understand current universities, with their multiple woes, we might try leaving the realms of expert debate and fine ideas and turning to the class-rooms and campuses, where a new kind of weather is gathering.

10   From time to time I bump into a colleague in the corridor and we have what I've come to think of as a Joon Lee fest. Joon Lee is one of the best students I've taught. He's endlessly curious, has read a small library's worth, seen every movie, and knows all about showbiz and entertainment. For a class of mine he wrote an essay using Nietzsche's Apollo and Dionysus to analyze the pop group The Supremes. A trite, cultural-stud-ies bonbon? Not at all. He said striking things about conceptions of race in America and about how they shape our ideas of beauty. When I talk with one of his other teach-ers, we run on about the general splendors of his work and presence. But what inevitably follows a JL fest is a mournful reprise about the divide that separates him and a few other remarkable students from their contemporaries. It's not that some aren't nearly as bright—in terms of intellectual ability, my students are all that I could ask for. Instead, it's that Joon Lee has decided to follow his interests and let them make him into a singular and rather eccentric man; in his charming way, he doesn't mind being at odds with most anyone.

It's his capacity for enthusiasm that sets Joon apart from what I've come to think of as the reigning generational style. Whether the students are sorority/fraternity types, grunge aficionados, piercer/tattooers, black or white, rich or middle class (alas, I teach almost no students from truly poor backgrounds), they are, nearly across the board, very, very self-contained. On good days they display a light, appealing glow; on bad days, shuffling disgruntlement. But there's little fire, little passion to be found.

This point came home to me a few weeks ago when I was wandering across the university grounds. There, beneath a classically cast portico, were two students, male and female, having a rip-roaring argument. They were incensed, bellowing at each other, headstrong, confident, and wild. It struck me how rarely I see this kind of full-out feeling in students anymore. Strong emotional display is forbidden. When con-flicts arise, it's generally understood that one of the parties will say something sarcastically propitiating ("whatever" often does it) and slouch away.

How did my students reach this peculiar state in which all passion seems to be spent? I think that many of them have imbibed their sense of self from consumer cul-ture in general and from the tube in particular. They're the progeny of 100 cable, chan-nels and omnipresent Blockbuster outlets. TV, Marshall McLuhan famously said, is a cool medium. Those who play best on it are low-key and nonassertive; they blend in. Enthusiasm, à la Joon Lee, quickly looks absurd. The form of character that's most appealing on TV is calmly self-interested though never greedy, attuned to the conven-tions, and ironic. Judicious timing is preferred to sudden self-assertion. The TV medium is inhospitable to inspiration, improvisation, failures, slipups. All must run perfectly.

Naturally, a cool youth culture is a marketing bonanza for producers of the right products, who do all they can to enlarge that culture and keep it grinding. The Inter-net, TV, and magazines now teem with what I call persona ads, ads for Nikes and Reeboks and Jeeps and Blazers that don't so much endorse the capacities of the prod-uct per se as show you what sort of person you will be once you've acquired it. The Jeep ad that features hip, outdoorsy kids whipping a Frisbee from mountaintop to mountaintop isn't so much about what Jeeps can do as it is about the kind of people who own them. Buy a Jeep and be one with them. The ad is of little consequence in itself, but expand its message exponentially and you have the central thrust of current consumer culture—buy in order to be.

15   Most of my students seem desperate to blend in, to look right, not to make a spectacle of themselves. (Do I have to tell you that those two students having the argument under the portico turned out to be acting in a role-playing game?) The specter of the uncool creates a subtle tyranny. It's apparently an easy standard to subscribe to, this Letterman-like, Tarantino-like cool, but once committed to it, you discover that matters are rather different. You're inhibited, except on ordained occasions, from showing emotion, stifled from trying to achieve anything original. You're made to feel that even the slightest departure from the reigning code will get you genially ostracized. This is a culture tensely committed to a laid-back norm.

Am I coming off like something of a crank here? Maybe. Oscar Wilde, who is almost never wrong, suggested that it is perilous to promiscuously contradict people who are much younger than yourself. Point taken. But one of the lessons that consumer hype tries to insinuate is that we must never rebel against the new, never even question it. If it's new—a new need, a new product, a new show, a new style, a new generation—it must be good. So maybe, even at the risk of winning the withered, brown laurels of crankdom, it pays to resist newness-worship and cast a colder eye.

Praise for my students? I have some of that too. What my students are, at their best, is decent. They are potent believers in equality. They help out at the soup kitchen and volunteer to tutor poor kids to get a stripe on their résumés, sure. But they also want other people to have a fair shot. And in their commitment to fairness they are discerning; there you see them at their intellectual best. If I were on trial and innocent, I'd want them on the jury.

What they will not generally do, though, is indict the current system. They won't talk about how the exigencies of capitalism lead to a reserve army of the unemployed and nearly inevitable misery. That would be getting too loud, too brash. For the pervading view is the cool consumer perspective, where passion and strong admiration are forbidden. "To stand in awe of nothing, Numicus, is perhaps the one and only thing that can make a man happy and keep him so," says Horace in the *Epistles,* and I fear that his lines ought to hang as a motto over the university in this era of high consumer capitalism.

It's easy to mount one's high horse and blame the students for this state of affairs. But they didn't create the present culture of consumption. (It was largely my own generation, that of the Sixties, that let the counterculture search for pleasure devolve into a quest for commodities.) And they weren't the ones responsible, when they were six and seven and eight years old, for unplugging the TV set from time to time or for hauling off and kicking a hole through it. It's my generation of parents who sheltered these students, kept them away from the hard knocks of everyday life, making them cautious and overfragile, who demanded that their teachers, from grade school on, flatter them endlessly so that the kids are shocked if their college profs don't reflexively suck up to them.

20   Of course, the current generational style isn't simply derived from culture and environment. It's also about dollars. Students worry that taking too many chances with their educations will sabotage their future prospects. They're aware of the fact that a drop that looks more and more like one wall of the Grand Canyon separates the top economic tenth from the rest of the population. There's a sentiment currently abroad that if you step aside for a moment, to write, to travel, to fall too hard in love, you

might lose position permanently. We may be on a conveyor belt, but it's worse down there on the filth-strewn floor. So don't sound off, don't blow your chance.

But wait. I teach at the famously conservative University of Virginia. Can I extend my view from Charlottesville to encompass the whole country, a whole generation of college students? I can only say that I hear comparable stories about classroom life from colleagues everywhere in America. When I visit other schools to lecture, I see a similar scene unfolding. There are, of course, terrific students everywhere. And they're all the better for the way they've had to strive against the existing conformity. At some of the small liberal-arts colleges, the tradition of strong engagement persists. But overall, the students strike me as being sweet and sad, hovering in a nearly suspended animation.

Too often now the pedagogical challenge is to make a lot from a little. Teaching Wordsworth's "Tintern Abbey," you ask for comments. No one responds. So you call on Stephen. Stephen: "The sound, this poem really flows." You: "Stephen seems interested in the music of the poem. We might extend his comment to ask if the poem's music coheres with its argument. Are they consistent? Or is there an emotional pain submerged here that's contrary to the poem's appealing melody?" All right, it's not usually that bad. But close. One friend describes it as rebound teaching: they proffer a weightless comment, you hit it back for all you're worth, then it comes dribbling out again. Occasionally a professor will try to explain away this intellectual timidity by describing the students as perpetrators of postmodern irony, a highly sophisticated mode. Everything's a slick counterfeit, a simulacrum, so by no means should any phenomenon be taken seriously. But the students don't have the urbane, Oscar Wilde—type demeanor that should go with this view. Oscar was cheerful, funny, confident, strange. (Wilde, mortally ill, living in a Paris flophouse: "My wallpaper and I are fighting a duel to the death. One or the other of us has to go.") This generation's style is considerate, easy to please, and a touch depressed.

Granted, you might say, the kids come to school immersed in a consumer mentality—they're good Americans, after all—but then the university and the professors do everything in their power to fight that dreary mind-set in the interest of higher ideals, right? So it should be. But let us look at what is actually coming to pass.

Over the past few years, the physical layout of my university has been changing. To put it a little indecorously, the place is looking more and more like a retirement spread for the young. Our funds go to construction, into new dorms, into renovating the student union. We have a new aquatics center and ever-improving gyms, stocked with StairMasters and Nautilus machines. Engraved on the wall in the gleaming aquatics building is a line by our founder, Thomas Jefferson, declaring that everyone ought to get about two hours' exercise a day. Clearly even the author of the Declaration of Independence endorses the turning of his university into a sports-and-fitness emporium.

25   But such improvements shouldn't be surprising. Universities need to attract the best (that is, the smartest *and* the richest) students in order to survive in an ever more competitive market. Schools want kids whose parents can pay the full freight, not the ones who need scholarships or want to bargain down the tuition costs. If the marketing surveys say that the kids require sports centers, then, trustees willing, they shall have them. In fact, as I began looking around, I came to see that more and more of what's going on in the university is customer driven. The consumer pressures that beset me on evaluation day are only a part of an overall trend.

From the start, the contemporary university's relationship with students has a solicitous, nearly servile tone. As soon as someone enters his junior year in high school, and especially if he's living in a prosperous zip code, the informational material—the advertising—comes flooding in. Pictures, testimonials, videocassettes, and CD ROMs (some bidden, some not) arrive at the door from colleges across the country, all trying to capture the student and his tuition cash. The freshman-to-be sees photos of well-appointed dorm rooms; of elaborate phys-ed facilities; of fine dining rooms; of expertly kept sports fields; of orchestras and drama troupes; of students working alone (no overbearing grown-ups in range), peering with high seriousness into computers and microscopes; or of students arrayed outdoors in attractive conversational garlands.

Occasionally—but only occasionally, for we usually photograph rather badly; in appearance we tend at best to be styleless—there's a professor teaching a class. (The college catalogues I received, by my request only, in the late Sixties were austere affairs full of professors' credentials and course descriptions; it was clear on whose terms the enterprise was going to unfold.) A college financial officer recently put matters to me in concise, if slightly melodramatic, terms: "Colleges don't have admissions offices anymore, they have marketing departments." Is it surprising that someone who has been approached with photos and tapes, bells and whistles, might come in thinking that the Freud and Shakespeare she had signed up to study were also going to be agreeable treats?

How did we reach this point? In part the answer is a matter of demographics and (surprise) of money. Aided by the G.I. bill, the college-going population in America dramatically increased after the Second World War. Then came the baby boomers, and to accommodate them, schools continued to grow. Universities expand easily enough, but with tenure locking faculty in for lifetime jobs, and with the general reluctance of administrators to eliminate their own slots, it's not easy for a university to contract. So after the baby boomers had passed through—like a fat meal digested by a boa constrictor—the colleges turned to energetic promotional strategies to fill the empty chairs. And suddenly college became a buyer's market. What students and their parents wanted had to be taken more and more into account. That usually meant creating more comfortable, less challenging environments, places where almost no one failed, everything was enjoyable, and everyone was nice.

Just as universities must compete with one another for students, so must the individual departments. At a time of rank economic anxiety, the English and history majors have to contend for students against the more success-insuring branches, such as the sciences and the commerce school. In 1968, more than 21 percent of all the bachelor's degrees conferred in America were in the humanities; by 1993, that number had fallen to about 13 percent. The humanities now must struggle to attract students, many of whose parents devoutly wish they would study something else.

30   One of the ways we've tried to stay attractive is by loosening up. We grade much more softly than our colleagues in science. In English, we don't give many Ds, or Cs for that matter. (The rigors of Chem. 101 create almost as many English majors per year as do the splendors of Shakespeare.) A professor at Stanford recently explained grade inflation in the humanities by observing that the undergraduates were getting smarter every year; the higher grades simply recorded how much better they were than their predecessors. Sure.

Along with softening the grades, many humanities departments have relaxed major requirements. There are some good reasons for introducing more choice into curricula and requiring fewer standard courses. But the move, like many others in the university now, jibes with a tendency to serve—and not challenge—the students. Students can also float in and out of classes during the first two weeks of each term without making any commitment. The common name for this time span—shopping period—speaks volumes about the consumer mentality that's now in play. Usually, too, the kids can drop courses up until the last month with only an innocuous "W" on their transcripts. Does a course look too challenging? No problem. Take it pass-fail. A happy consumer is, by definition, one with multiple options, one who can always have what he wants. And since a course is something the students and their parents have bought and paid for, why can't they do with it pretty much as they please?

A sure result of the university's widening elective leeway is to give students more power over their teachers. Those who don't like you can simply avoid you. If the clientele dislikes you en masse, you can be left without students, period. My first term teaching I walked into my introduction to poetry course and found it inhabited by one student, the gloriously named Bambi Lynn Dean. Bambi and I chatted amiably awhile, but for all that she and the pleasure of her name could offer, I was fast on the way to meltdown. It was all a mistake, luckily, a problem with the scheduling book. Everyone was waiting for me next door. But in a dozen years of teaching I haven't forgotten that feeling of being ignominiously marooned. For it happens to others, and not always because of scheduling glitches. I've seen older colleagues go through hot embarrassment at not having enough students sign up for their courses: they graded too hard, demanded too much, had beliefs too far out of keeping with the existing disposition. It takes only a few such instances to draw other members of the professoriat further into line.

And if what's called tenure reform—which generally just means the abolition of tenure—is broadly enacted, professors will be yet more vulnerable to the whims of their customer-students. Teach what pulls the kids in, or walk. What about entire departments that don't deliver? If the kids say no to Latin and Greek, is it time to dissolve classics? Such questions are being entertained more and more seriously by university administrators.

How does one prosper with the present clientele? Many of the most successful professors now are the ones who have "decentered" their classrooms. There's a new emphasis on group projects and on computer-generated exchanges among the students. What they seem to want most is to talk to one another. A classroom now is frequently an "environment," a place highly conducive to the exchange of existing ideas, the students' ideas. Listening to one another, students sometimes change their opinions. But what they generally can't do is acquire a new vocabulary, a new perspective, that will cast issues in a fresh light.

35   The Socratic method—the animated, sometimes impolite give-and-take between student and teacher—seems too jagged for current sensibilities. Students frequently come to my office to tell me how intimidated they feel in class; the thought of being embarrassed in front of the group fills them with dread. I remember a student telling me how humiliating it was to be corrected by the teacher, by me. So I asked the logical question: "Should I let a major factual error go by so as to save discomfort?" The student—a good student, smart and earnest—said that was a tough question. He'd need to think about it.

Disturbing? Sure. But I wonder, are we really getting students ready for Socratic exchange with professors when we push them off into vast lecture rooms, two and three hundred to a class, sometimes face them with only grad students until their third year, and signal in our myriad professorial ways that we often have much better things to do than sit in our offices and talk with them? How bad will the student-faculty ratios have to become, how teeming the lecture courses, before we hear students righteously complaining, as they did thirty years ago, about the impersonality of their schools, about their decline into knowledge factories? "This is a firm," said Mario Savio at Berkeley during the Free Speech protests of the Sixties, "and if the Board of Regents are the board of directors,…then…the faculty are a bunch of employees and we're the raw material. But we're a bunch of raw material that don't mean…to be made into any product."

Teachers who really do confront students, who provide significant challenges to what they believe, *can* be very successful, granted. But sometimes such professors generate more than a little trouble for themselves. A controversial teacher can send students hurrying to the deans and the counselors, claiming to have been offended. ("Offensive" is the preferred term of repugnance today, just as "enjoyable" is the summit of praise.) Colleges have brought in hordes of counselors and deans to make sure that everything is smooth, serene, unflustered, that everyone has a good time. To the counselor, to the dean, and to the university legal squad, that which is normal, healthy, and prudent is best.

An air of caution and deference is everywhere. When my students come to talk with me in my office, they often exhibit a Franciscan humility. "Do you have a moment?" "I know you're busy. I won't take up much of your time." Their presences tend to be very light; they almost never change the temperature of the room. The dress is nondescript: clothes are in earth tones; shoes are practical—cross-trainers, hiking boots, work shoes, Dr. Martens, with now and then a stylish pair of raised-sole boots on one of the young women. Many, male and female both, peep from beneath the bills of monogrammed baseball caps. Quite a few wear sports, or even corporate, logos, sometimes on one piece of clothing but occasionally (and disconcertingly) on more. The walk is slow; speech is careful, sweet, a bit weary, and without strong inflection. (After the first lively week of the term, most seem far in debt to sleep.) They are almost unfailingly polite. They don't want to offend me; I could hurt them, savage their grades.

Naturally, there are exceptions, kids I chat animatedly with, who offer a joke, or go on about this or that new CD (almost never a book, no). But most of the traffic is genially sleepwalking. I have to admit that I'm a touch wary, too. I tend to hold back. An unguarded remark, a joke that's taken to be off-color, or simply an uncomprehended comment can lead to difficulties. I keep it literal. They scare me a little, these kind and melancholy students, who themselves seem rather frightened of their own lives.

40   Before they arrive, we ply the students with luscious ads, guaranteeing them a cross between summer camp and lotusland. When they get here, flattery and nonstop entertainment are available, if that's what they want. And when they leave? How do we send our students out into the world? More and more, our administrators call the booking agents and line up one or another celebrity to usher the graduates into the millennium. This past spring, Kermit the Frog won himself an honorary degree at Southampton College on Long Island; Bruce Willis and Yogi Berra took credentials away at Montclair State; Arnold Schwarzenegger scored at the University of Wisconsin–Superior. At

Wellesley, Oprah Winfrey gave the commencement address. (*Wellesley*—one of the most rigorous academic colleges in the nation.) At the University of Vermont, Whoopi Goldberg laid down the word. But why should a worthy administrator contract the likes of Susan Sontag, Christopher Hitchens, or Robert Hughes—someone who might actually say something, something disturbing, something "offensive"—when he can get what the parents and kids apparently want and what the newspapers will softly commend—more lite entertainment, more TV?

Is it a surprise, then, that this generation of students—steeped in consumer culture before going off to school, treated as potent customers by the university well before their date of arrival, then pandered to from day one until the morning of the final kiss-off from Kermit or one of his kin—are inclined to see the books they read as a string of entertainments to be placidly enjoyed or languidly cast down? Given the way universities are now administered (which is more and more to say, given the way that they are currently marketed), is it a shock that the kids don't come to school hot to learn, unable to bear their own ignorance? For some measure of self-dislike, or self-discontent—which is much different than simple depression—seems to me to be a prerequisite for getting an education that matters. My students, alas, usually lack the confidence to acknowledge what would be their most precious asset for learning: their ignorance.

Not long ago, I asked my Freud class a question that, however hoary, never fails to solicit intriguing responses: Who are your heroes? Whom do you admire? After one remarkable answer, featuring T. S. Eliot as hero, a series of generic replies rolled in, one gray wave after the next: my father, my best friend, a doctor who lives in our town, my high school history teacher. Virtually all the heroes were people my students had known personally, people who had done something local, specific, and practical, and had done it for them. They were good people, unselfish people, these heroes, but most of all they were people who had delivered the goods.

My students' answers didn't exhibit any philosophical resistance to the idea of greatness. It's not that they had been primed by their professors with complex arguments to combat genius. For the truth is that these students don't need debunking theories. Long before college, skepticism became their habitual mode. They are the progeny of Bart Simpson and David Letterman, and the hyper-cool ethos of the box. It's inane to say that theorizing professors have created them, as many conservative critics like to do. Rather, they have substantially created a university environment in which facile skepticism can thrive without being substantially contested.

Skeptical approaches have *potential* value. If you have no all-encompassing religious faith, no faith in historical destiny, the future of the West, or anything comparably grand, you need to acquire your vision of the world somewhere. If it's from literature, then the various visions literature offers have to be inquired into skeptically. Surely it matters that women are denigrated in Milton and in Pope, that some novelistic voices assume an overbearing godlike authority, that the poor are, in this or that writer, inevitably cast as clowns. You can't buy all of literature wholesale if it's going to help draw your patterns of belief.

45   But demystifying theories are now overused, applied mechanically. It's all logocentrism, patriarchy, ideology. And in this the student environment—laid-back, skeptical, knowing—is, I believe, central. Full-out debunking is what plays with this

clientele. Some have been doing it nearly as long as, if more crudely than, their deconstructionist teachers. In the context of the contemporary university, and cool consumer culture, a useful intellectual skepticism has become exaggerated into a fundamentalist caricature of itself. The teachers have buckled to their students' views.

At its best, multiculturalism can be attractive as well-deployed theory. What could be more valuable than encountering the best work of far-flung cultures and becoming a citizen of the world? But in the current consumer environment, where flattery plays so well, the urge to encounter the other can devolve into the urge to find others who embody and celebrate the right ethnic origins. So we put aside the African novelist Chinua Achebe's abrasive, troubling *Things Fall Apart* and gravitate toward hymns on Africa, cradle of all civilizations.

What about the phenomenon called political correctness? Raising the standard of civility and tolerance in the university has been—who can deny it?—a very good thing. Yet this admirable impulse has expanded to the point where one is enjoined to speak well—and only well—of women, blacks, gays, the disabled, in fact of virtually everyone. And we can owe this expansion in many ways to the student culture. Students now do not wish to be criticized, not in any form. (The culture of consumption never criticizes them, at least not *overtly.*) In the current university, the movement for urbane tolerance has devolved into an imperative against critical reaction, turning much of the intellectual life into a dreary Sargasso Sea. At a certain point, professors stopped being usefully sensitive and became more like careful retailers who have it as a cardinal point of doctrine never to piss the customers off.

To some professors, the solution lies in the movement called cultural studies. What students need, they believe, is to form a critical perspective on pop culture. It's a fine idea, no doubt. Students should be able to run a critical commentary against the stream of consumer stimulations in which they're immersed. But cultural-studies programs rarely work, because no matter what you propose by way of analysis, things tend to bolt downhill toward an uncritical discussion of students' tastes, into what they like and don't like. If you want to do a Frankfurt School–style analysis of *Braveheart,* you can be pretty sure that by mid-class Adomo and Horkheimer will be consigned to the junk heap of history and you'll be collectively weighing the charms of Mel Gibson. One sometimes wonders if cultural studies hasn't prospered because, under the guise of serious intellectual analysis, it gives the customers what they most want—easy pleasure, more TV. Cultural studies becomes nothing better than what its detractors claim it is—Madonna studies—when students kick loose from the critical perspective and groove to the product, and that, in my experience teaching film and pop culture, happens plenty.

On the issue of genius, as on multiculturalism and political correctness, we professors of the humanities have, I think, also failed to press back against our students' consumer tastes. Here we tend to nurse a pair of—to put it charitably—disparate views. In one mode, we're inclined to a programmatic debunking criticism. We call the concept of genius into question. But in our professional lives per se, we aren't usually disposed against the idea of distinguished achievement. We argue animatedly about the caliber of potential colleagues. We support a star system, in which some professors are far better paid, teach less, and under better conditions than the rest. In our own profession, we are creating a system that is the mirror image of the one we're dismantling in the curriculum. Ask a professor what she thinks of the work of Stephen Greenblatt, a leading critic of Shakespeare, and you'll hear it for an hour. Ask her what her views are on Shakespeare's genius and she's likely to begin questioning the term along with the whole "discourse of evaluation." This dual sensibility may be intellectually incoherent. But in its awareness of what plays with students, it's conducive to good classroom evaluations and, in its awareness of where and how the professional bread is buttered, to self-advancement as well.

50   My overall point is this: It's not that a left-wing professorial coup has taken over the university. It's that at American universities, left-liberal politics have collided with the ethos of consumerism. The consumer ethos is winning.

Then how do those who at least occasionally promote genius and high literary ideals look to current students? How do we appear, those of us who take teaching to be something of a performance art and who imagine that if you give yourself over completely to your subject you'll be rewarded with insight beyond what you individually command?

I'm reminded of an old piece of newsreel footage I saw once. The speaker (perhaps it was Lenin, maybe Trotsky) was haranguing a large crowd. He was expostulating, arm waving, carrying on. Whether it was flawed technology or the man himself, I'm not sure, but the orator looked like an intricate mechanical device that had sprung into fast-forward. To my students, who mistrust enthusiasm in every form, that's me when I start riffing about Freud or Blake. But more and more, as my evaluations showed, I've been replacing enthusiasm and intellectual animation with stand-up routines, keeping it all at arm's length, praising under the cover of irony.

It's too bad that the idea of genius has been denigrated so far, because it actually offers a live alternative to the demoralizing culture of hip in which most of my students are mired. By embracing the works and lives of extraordinary people, you can adapt new ideals to revise those that came courtesy of your parents, your neighborhood, your clan—or the tube. The aim of a good liberal-arts education was once, to adapt an observation by the scholar Walter Jackson Bate, to see that "we need not be the passive victims of what we deterministically call 'circumstances' (social, cultural, or reductively psychological-personal), but that by linking ourselves through what Keats calls an 'immortal free-masonry' with the great we can become freer—freer to be ourselves, to be what we most want and value."

But genius isn't just a personal standard; genius can also have political effect. To me, one of the best things about democratic thinking is the conviction that genius can spring up anywhere. Walt Whitman is born into the working class and thirty-six years later we have a poetic image of America that gives a passionate dimension to the legalistic brilliance of the Constitution. A democracy needs to constantly develop, and to do so it requires the most powerful visionary minds to interpret the present and to propose possible shapes for the future. By continuing to notice and praise genius, we create a culture in which the kind of poetic gamble that Whitman made— a gamble in which failure would have entailed rank humiliation, depression, maybe suicide—still takes place. By rebelling against established ways of seeing and saying things, genius helps us to apprehend how malleable the present is and how promising and fraught with danger is the future. If we teachers do not endorse genius and self-overcoming, can we be surprised when our students find their ideal images in TV's latest persona ads?

55   A world uninterested in genius is a despondent place, whose sad denizens drift from coffee bar to Prozac dispensary, unfired by ideals, by the glowing image of the self that one might become. As Northrop Frye says in a beautiful and now dramatically unfashionable sentence, "The artist who uses the same energy and genius that Homer and Isaiah had will find that he not only lives in the same palace of art as Homer and Isaiah, but lives in it at the same time." We ought not to deny the existence of such a place simply because we, or those we care for, find the demands it makes intimidating, the rent too high.

What happens if we keep trudging along this bleak course? What happens if our most intelligent students never learn to strive to overcome what they are? What if genius, and the imitation of genius, become silly, outmoded ideas? What you're likely to get are more and more one-dimensional men and women. These will be people who live for easy pleasures, for comfort and prosperity, who think of money first, then second, and third, who hug the status quo; people who believe in God as a sort of insurance policy (cover your bets); people who are never surprised. They will be people so pleased with themselves (when they're not in despair at the general pointlessness of their lives) that they cannot imagine humanity could do better. They'll think it their highest duty to clone themselves as frequently as possible. They'll claim to be happy, and they'll live a long time.

It is probably time now to offer a spate of inspiring solutions. Here ought to come a list of reforms, with due notations about a core curriculum and various requirements. What the traditionalists who offer such solutions miss is that no matter what our current students are given to read, many of them will simply translate it into melodrama, with flat characters and predictable morals. (The unabated capitalist culture that conservative critics so often endorse has put students in a position to do little else.) One can't simply wave a curricular wand and reverse acculturation.

Perhaps it would be a good idea to try firing the counselors and sending half the deans back into their classrooms, dismantling the football team and making the stadium into a playground for local kids, emptying the fraternities, and boarding up the student-activities office. Such measures would convey the message that American colleges are not northern outposts of Club Med. A willingness on the part of the faculty to defy student conviction and affront them occasionally—to be usefully offensive—also might not be a bad thing. We professors talk a lot about subversion, which generally means subverting the views of people who never hear us talk or read our work. But to subvert the views of our students, our customers, that would be something else again.

Ultimately, though, it is up to individuals—and individual students in particular—to make their own way against the current sludgy tide. There's still the library, still the museum, there's still the occasional teacher who lives to find things greater than herself to admire. There are still fellow students who have not been cowed. Universities are inefficient, cluttered, archaic places, with many unguarded corners where one can open a book or gaze out onto the larger world and construe it freely. Those who do as much, trusting themselves against the weight of current opinion, will have contributed something to bringing this sad dispensation to an end. As for myself, I'm canning my low-key one-liners; when the kids' TV-based tastes come to the fore, I'll aim and shoot. And when it's time to praise genius, I'll try to do it in the right style, full-out, with faith that finer artistic spirits (maybe not Homer and Isaiah quite, but close, close), still alive somewhere in the ether, will help me out when my invention flags, the students doze, or the dean mutters into the phone. I'm getting back to a more exuberant style; I'll be expostulating and arm waving straight into the millennium, yes I will.

Rereading Actively

1. Why does Edmundson open this essay with an anecdote about student evaluations? How does this story set up his initial thesis?

2. With a partner or in a small group, discuss Edmundson's attitude toward students. Focus on how he reveals that attitude in two examples of student behavior, and then reflect on how you respond to each example. How does the attitude he conveys contribute to his argument?

3. In a small group, identify the most striking claims Edmundson makes about students and about faculty, and discuss why these assertions seem striking to you.

4. What is "genius," according to Edmundson, and what's the status of genius in a consumer culture?

5. Read through the essay looking for what Edmundson finds lacking in current university education and, by implication, what he feels a proper university education involves. What generalizations about higher education does he make, and what kind of evidence does he use to establish them? In a journal entry, summarize Edmundson's general critique.

6. Summarize Edmundson's conclusion—he signals it three paragraphs from the end of the essay—and explain how his "solutions" and the tone in which they are presented affect your reading of his essay.

Exploring Your Responses

7. How do you respond to Edmundson's introductory description of student evaluation day? How accurate is the scene? How does it make you feel about Edmundson and his topic?

8. In a small group, discuss whether this essay represents the complaint of a grouchy professor with an ax to grind, a valid critique of the current state of higher education, or a bit of each. In your journal, write your own response to this question, reflecting on comments your group members made.

9. In a page or two in your journal, compare your approach to being a student with that of Joon Lee.

10. In a small group, brainstorm the elements of student life that Edmundson mentions, from student evaluations and student consumerism to apathy and grades—nothing is too trivial. Review your findings and sort them into categories—for example, student behavior, cultural trends, faculty behavior, the business of education, genius, curriculum issues, and so on. With your group,

talk about your collective experience with these issues, Edmundson's interpretation, and alternative interpretations. Be prepared to tell the class how well Edmundson explains these issues.

THE CLOISTER AND THE HEART

JANE TOMPKINS

This is the final chapter from A Life in School, *Jane Tompkins's recent reflection on her experience as a student and teacher. After taking a B.A. from the small, elite college Bryn Mawr, Tompkins went on to receive a Ph.D. from Yale University, and she then taught at Temple, Columbia, and Duke. She has had a distinguished career and is well known in English studies as an important theorist. In this conclusion to her 1996 memoir, she works toward a holistic view of higher education, one that values not only the mind but also the spirit. Hence the central metaphors: the cloister and the heart.*

I've been struggling with the concept of college as cloister. I know not every university enjoys this privileged seclusion. I went to a college that did—Bryn Mawr—and taught for many years at one that didn't—Temple University. What I have to say applies more to the first kind of school than to the second, but it's relevant to most institutions of higher learning because most of them emulate what the cloister stands for: a place hallowed and set apart. It was the experimental courses I taught at Duke, courses in which I got to know the students much better than I did when I taught in the normal way, that led me to question the usefulness of college as a cloister and also to see the cloister as a missed opportunity. It was those courses that let me see how cut off from life the students were, how cut off from the world they were about to enter, and at the same time, how cut off from themselves. It was also those courses that recalled to me the tremendous passion that the quest for knowledge had aroused in me when I was an undergraduate.

When I was in college, I didn't worry much about what would happen afterward; and as far as I know, neither did my friends. Either you got married, or you got a job, or you went to graduate school, in which case you had a scholarship or your parents paid. The issue seemed straightforward and not a problem. Besides, what happened after college had very little reality while I was still in school.

The opposite is true for undergraduates today. They seem tasked and shadowed by the future. My student, Shannon, who confessed that she hated to read, but had come to Duke because if she hadn't, she thought she'd end up at McDonald's, is not the exception but the norm. Students who go to schools like Duke are afraid that if they don't get an expensive, high-status liberal arts degree, they'll end up in a low-level job, usually conceived as working for a fast-food chain. And even if they complete the four years successfully, they're afraid of not finding a job when they leave. The other day, crossing the quad, I heard one female undergraduate say to another, in a wail: "I'll be unemployed, have no place to live, and be a hundred thousand dollars in debt!"

Many students, driven by the fear of not getting a good enough job after they graduate, make choices that go against the grain of their personalities. One student I had who was an actor and loved the theater was majoring in economics. When I questioned him about it briefly, he seemed not to have considered a career that would make use of his talents. It was as if his love of the theater and his career plans were on two separate tracks. Over and over I've been surprised to learn that a student in one of my classes was planning to attend law school or medical school—vocations that seemed to bear no relation to his or her aptitudes or interests.

5   Over time I've come to think about my undergraduate students, whom I treasure and admire and have tremendous affection for, under the metaphor of a train journey. Someone, a parent or other influential adult in their lives, has given them a ticket. On it is stamped medical school, or law school, or business school, or in rarer cases, graduate school. They're on the train and holding this ticket, the countryside is going by very fast, and they're not getting to see much of it. All they know is that when the train arrives at their stop, they'll be getting off.

My experimental courses were about helping students to discover who was holding the ticket so that they could make up their own minds about whether the destination was right for them. More than once, a student would explain why it wasn't right and then turn around and hotly defend the choice anyway. What my experiments revealed was how pressured the students felt to perform in a way that would get them approval from their parents and their peers. They seemed to have little knowledge of themselves, little knowledge of what possibilities the world had to offer, and little sense that they really could choose on their own behalf.

This last point, the students' sense of not being agents on their own behalf, troubles me the most. I think it's the result of an educational process that infantilizes students, takes away their initiative, and teaches them to be sophisticated rule followers. Of course, as professors, we don't see the ways in which what we do as teachers narrows and limits our students: for we ourselves have been narrowed and limited by the same process.

From the teacher's point of view, the classroom is a place of opportunity. Here students can enrich themselves, are inspired, motivated, made curious, enlightened by the professor. Here students participate in producing knowledge themselves, since most professors nowadays would agree that students need to be active learners. The great example of student participation in the learning process is class discussion. From the teacher's perspective, class discussion constitutes freedom. It gives students a chance to express themselves. Instead of the teacher talking, the students talk. They air their opinions, exchange ideas; they disagree with one another, and sometimes they even disagree with the instructor. They raise their hands, they speak, their voices are heard.

But one day my cousin, Jane Dibbell, and I were talking about teaching—she is both a lifelong teacher and an actress, whose view of the classroom is sensitive to its theatricality. She started to mimic what happens when students talk in class, and a new vision of classroom dynamics opened up for me. She raised her hand and began to wave it, her voice filled with anxiety: "Am I smart?" she said. "Am I really smart? Am I the smartest?"

10   In class discussion, students compete with one another for the teacher's approval. They seek reassurance, and they want to be rewarded with praise. It's a performance they're engaged in, not a spontaneous utterance, and a performance on which a lot depends: their own self-esteem, the regard of their fellow students, the good opinion of the teacher, and ultimately their grade and their grade point average. There are many ways to fail.

You can go wrong by parroting what the teacher has already said, or by *not* repeating what she's said. You can use the wrong vocabulary or misunderstand the question.

You can appear so knowledgeable that the teacher becomes uncomfortable and the other students jealous. You can find out to your surprise that nobody agrees with you. You can say something inadvertently funny, and everyone will laugh. You can come across as naive and dorky, a nerd....

Practically everything about you is open to inspection and speculation when you talk in class, since, in speaking, your accent, your vocabulary, the intonations of your voice, your display of feeling or lack of it, the knowledge you can call on, or not, all contain clues about who you are—your social class, ethnic background, sense of yourself as a gendered being, degree of self-knowledge, the way you relate to other people. You can seem aggressive, defensive, shy, manipulative, exhibitionistic.

My cousin was right in intuiting the theatrical nature of the college classroom. People who take the classroom seriously have invested themselves in perfecting a certain kind of performance. Knowing just how to answer the question, performing exactly right for the teacher, learning how not to offend the other students become the guidelines for success in life. Slowly, with practice, the classroom self becomes the only self. At preprofessional colleges where students (largely as a result of parental influence) are headed for law school, medical school, business school, graduate school, the performance mentality intensifies; people are so grade conscious and worried about doing well on their LSATs, MCATs, or GREs, that how they do on tests and papers becomes the measure of their worth as human beings.

My point is that classroom learning can constrict a person's horizons even as it broadens them. Learning too well the lessons of the classroom exacts a price. Its exclusive emphasis on the purely intellectual and informational aspects of learning, on learning as individualistic and competitive, can create a lopsided person: a person who can process information efficiently, summarize accurately, articulate ideas, and make telling points; a person who is hardworking, knows how to please those in authority, and who values high performance on the job above all things.

15 Everything I have learned in the last ten years has shown me that this is not the sort of person to become. But the educational deck is stacked against becoming anything different. Keith Johnstone, the British playwright, director, and teacher of actors writes of the destructive effects of schooling:

> I tried to resist my schooling, but I accepted the idea that my intelligence was the most important part of me. I tried to be *clever* in everything I did. The damage was greatest in areas where my interests and the school's seemed to coincide: in writing, for example (I wrote and rewrote, and lost all fluency). I forgot that inspiration isn't intellectual, that you don't have to be perfect. In the end I was reluctant to attempt anything for fear of failure, and my first thoughts never seemed good enough. Everything had to be corrected and brought into line.

It's the people who are most susceptible to authority who suffer the most from their schooling, and who must liberate themselves later on from its effects. Many of those who do not wake up to their condition remain in school as teachers, pleased with the rewards of having performed well, so the codes of the classroom are passed on.

The *format* of higher education, its mode of delivery, contains within itself the most powerful teachings students receive during their college years. But most college professors, being products of the system, have given little thought to the ways in which the conventions of classroom teaching stunt and warp students as well as enabling them to expand their horizons. Johnstone writes.

One day, when I was eighteen, I was reading a book and I began to weep. I was astounded. I'd had no idea that literature could affect me in such a way. If I'd have wept over a poem in class the teacher would have been appalled. I realised that my school had been teaching me *not* to respond.

When I look back at my schooling today, I see what Johnstone sees—a person who was taught not to feel. The long process of coming back into possession of my feelings, learning to recognize their presence, then learning to express them in safe situations, allowing them to be there instead of pushing them down as I had always done—*this* education has dominated the last several years of my life. When I look at my undergraduate students, I see how their schooling is forcing them into the same patterns I have struggled to overcome: a divided state of consciousness, a hypertrophy of the intellect and will, an undernourished heart. I see how compartmentalized the university is, with the philosophy department at one end of the campus, the gymnasium at the other. I see how conditioned the students are—though not terminally so— to keeping their own experience out of the learning process. And I am filled with an inchoate yearning for integration.

But I hear the voices of my friends and colleagues saying, *Aren't you forgetting how much you wanted to become an intellectual? Aren't you forgetting your old love of knowledge? of books and ideas? Aren't you turning your back on something precious? And aren't you forgetting how hard it was to enter the gates of academe, to become an initiate, to learn the trade so that you could take part in the central activities of your profession?*

20   *What about all the people who are eager to have even a glimpse of the life you seem so willfully to throw away?*

Isn't your discontent the result of too much privilege?

I listen to these voices and I want to say, Of course, of course; each person's situation is different. Many people did not suffer what I suffered, or enjoy the advantages I enjoyed. My critique of school comes from my experience of it, which is limited, as all experience is. Yet I believe that the lesson I learned holds good for many people other than myself. Human beings, no matter what their background, need to feel that they are safe in order to open themselves to transformation. They need to feel a connection between a given subject matter and who they are in order for knowledge to take root. That security and that connectedness are seldom present in a classroom that recognizes the students' cognitive capacities alone. People often assume that attention to the emotional lives of students, to their spiritual yearnings and their imaginative energies, will somehow inhibit the intellect's free play, drown it in a wash of sentiment, or deflect it into the realms of fantasy and escape, that the critical and analytical faculties will be muffled, reined in, or blunted as a result. I believe the reverse is true. The initiative, creativity, energy, and dedication that are released when students know they can express themselves freely shows, by contrast, how accustomed they are to holding back, playing it safe, avoiding real engagement, or just going through the motions. Besides, it's not a question of repressing or cutting back on intellectual inquiry in school, but rather of acknowledging and cultivating wholeness. As Maria Montessori wrote in *The Absorbent Mind,* education is not just "of the mind," nor should it be thought of as "the mere transmission of knowledge…. For what is the use of transmitting knowledge if the individual's total development lags behind?"

The real objection to a more holistic approach to education lies in a fear of emotion, of the imagination, of dreams and intuitions and spiritual experience that funds commonly received conceptions of reality in this culture. And no wonder, for it is school, in part, that controls reality's shape. The fear of these faculties, at base a fear of chaos and loss of control, is abetted by ignorance. For how can we be on friendly terms with those parts of ourselves to which we have never received a formal introduction, and for which we have no maps or guides? The strength of the taboo can be gauged by the academician's inevitable recourse to name-calling when emotion, spirituality, and imagination are brought into the curricular conversation: "touchy-feely," "soft," "unrigorous," "mystical," "therapeutic," and "Mickey Mouse" are the all-time favorites, with "psychobabble" and "bullshit" not far behind. The implication is always that something mindless, dirty, and infantile is being recommended, which in a certain sense is true, since the faculties in question have not been allowed to mature and remain in an unregulated state. The concern that things will fall apart and no one will learn anything if these unruly elements are allowed into the picture stems precisely from their historic exclusion from our system of education. The less we know about these unpredictable domains, the less we want to know.

Throughout this discussion of the compartmentalization of learning, two themes have been running parallel to each other. One concerns the intense focus on performance, geared to the perceived necessity of gaining a foothold in a fiercely competitive marketplace; the other concerns higher education's exclusive emphasis on intellectual development. As things stand now, these two emphases reinforce one another; there are very few ways to excel academically, and thus to become marketable, that include attention to creativity, self-knowledge, and compassion for oneself and others.

25   I became so interested in this problem, which I called the problem of preprofessionalism, that I came back from leave and created a temporary job in order to study it and report on it to the deans of liberal arts at my university. The process of gathering information was revealing in itself. Like an animal loose in the forest for the first time, I roved at will and discovered how little I had learned, in the course of my academic life, about what goes on in a university. I talked to people who, as a full-time professor, I'd never gotten to know before: the dean and assistant dean of academic advising, the head of the Career Development Center, the head of Counselling and Psychological Services, the vice provost for student affairs, the deans of residential life, the university chaplain, the resident advisors in the dorms. I found that these people did essential, life-sustaining work, that they gave of themselves generously, that they had been thinking for some time about issues that were new to me, and that they were generally under-recognized and underpaid.

Professors, I realized, are the Chinese emperors of the institution—with students as the crown princes. Without knowing it, I had occupied an isolated, privileged space, unaware of what kept the institution running day to day, ignorant of the lives my students led outside the classroom, of the people who helped them when they needed help. I had been generally uninterested in these matters, which, I tacitly assumed, were being taken care of by people with intellects and qualifications vaguely inferior to my own—for if not, wouldn't they have Ph.D.s and tenure-track positions?

This hierarchical structure, which places people who take care of students' emotional, physical, and spiritual lives lower on the ladder than people who deal only with their minds, kept troubling me as I went about my business. I didn't know what it had to do with the problem of preprofessionalism, but it wouldn't go away. Finally, some months later, it dawned on me that the hierarchy reflected exactly what I felt was wrong with undergraduate education. It depreciates those aspects of being human that are missing from the curriculum and from our pedagogy. The way we perceive the process of schooling—the mastering of skills and the ingesting of information by disembodied minds—is reflected in the way we organize the institution.

This is not lost on the students themselves.

Not surprisingly, the students I talked to in my researches had by far the most trenchant critiques of the university, since they are less invested in it than faculty and staff, whose income and sense of identity largely depend on the institution. I met with various student groups and talked with individual students and soon formed a picture of the problem as they see it. The students complained of the tremendous pressure they were under to get good grades in order to be competitive in the rush to professional school and on the job market. They were headed in this direction so that they could find work, work that would pay back their loans or satisfy their parents, who wanted to see some financial return on their $100,000 investment. So much in the students' experience seemed constrained by this motive: they chose majors that would satisfy the requirements of professional school and took electives that would not spoil their grade point averages.

30   At the same time, students wanted to explore; they wanted to study marine botany, take a course in twentieth-century religious cults, learn Russian, and write short stories. Their advisors told them: "Take what you love." Meanwhile, their parents pressured them to major in economics. One student summed it up dramatically by saying that he felt caught in a kind of schizophrenia. "Duke wants to produce competitive students, and it wants to encourage self-exploration. Sure, students want to 'take what they love,' but people don't want to be beachcombers."

The most ringing critique I heard came from two students I'd taught two years before. I'd called up the students I'd had in Reading for Yourself, who were about to graduate. I wanted to find out what the Duke experience had been like for them, and to see them one more time before they left, for I loved them. I asked: What did you like best about your education, and what would you change if you could?

One of the students had been premed and had gotten into a prestigious medical school; he was planning to go the following fall. His was a success story, but not to hear him tell it. I took notes on our conversation because I was stunned by the harshness of his views.

He began by citing statistics: the university had a 90 percent rate of acceptance to medical school, a 95 percent rate of acceptance to law school, and was, in his words, "a preprofessional warehouse, an expensive stepping-stone." "I used Duke," he said, "and Duke used me…. It's like Monopoly, a money mill…. Learning is second. Achievement is first."

The bitterness in his tone struck me. "What would help?" I asked. "Someone like me saying the things I'm saying to you," he replied.

35   At freshman orientation for premed and pre-law students, he said that he had been told what grades he needed to make. The message freshmen ought to get, he said, was "Learn for learning's sake, not just to get a grade."

The other student whose reactions impressed me, an English major, who in the flush of graduation week said that everything about her Duke experience had been perfect, later wrote a long reflective letter in a darkened tone. She, too, began by citing statistics. "Of the 1,400 people in my class, 600 are going to law school in the fall, and 300 are going to medical school." Of the remainder, she said, some would go to graduate school. "I guess most everybody got what they came for—a ticket to some other place."

She continued: "Why aren't we ever encouraged to believe that a liberal arts education is enough?... Does my Duke degree lose its lustre if it's not joined by another? The practices of medicine and law and the academy do not need 1,000 Duke students, but the world does." Like the medical student, she felt keenly that her education had had too little application to the world.

The end product of an educational system that fails to help its students find out who they are and where in the world their talents might best be employed is not difficult to foresee. One day I was telling a friend who is a senior partner at a premier Washington law firm about how career driven my students were. He said he couldn't count the number of younger colleagues who ended up in his office saying that they were miserable but didn't know what to do. They'd gone to the best colleges, had gotten the highest grades, gone to the best law schools, made law review, been hired by a top firm and then—it turned out they hated the work. *Hated* it. But they'd never made any independent decisions, had never stepped off the track; they didn't dare leave for fear of being seen as failures. They felt trapped.

I understand the argument that the university can't do everything. Academic courses, it goes, *are* for the mind. Let the home and the church and the psychotherapist and the athletic program attend to the spirit and the body and the rest. We professors have our hands full already trying to get across the riches of our subject matter in fourteen weeks. We can't be therapists and doctors and spiritual directors, too.

40   What I am asking for is a more holistic approach to learning, a disciplinary training for people who teach in college that takes into account the fact that we are educators of whole human beings, a form of higher education that would take responsibility for the emergence of an integrated person.

I'll never forget an incident told to me by a professor of Portuguese language and literature from UMass Amherst, a dedicated teacher who had been teaching for a long time. One day, she said, she was walking down the street in Amherst when she saw this striking woman crossing the street—the woman seemed powerful and fearless as well as beautiful. Then the professor did a double take. This was the same undergraduate who had huddled in a seat at the back of her language class all semester, never opening her mouth. My friend said she never forgot that moment—how strong and free, full of life and energy the student seemed, compared to the weak, mousy person the professor had imagined her to be, because she wasn't very good at Portuguese.

One way of making education more holistic is to get outside the classroom and off the campus. It interrupts the programming twelve years of classroom conditioning automatically call up; the change in environment changes everything. The class becomes a social unit; students become more fully rounded human beings—not just people who either know the answer or don't know it. Inside the classroom, it's one kind of student that dominates; outside, it's another. Qualities besides critical thinking can come to light: generosity, steadfastness, determination, practical competence, humor, ingenuity, imagination. Tying course content to the world outside offers a real-world site for asking theoretical questions; it answers students' need to feel that their education is good for something other than a grade point average. And it begins to address the problem of the student who has no conception of what is possible after graduation.

The head of Duke's Career Development Center told me: There are two things students trust, their parents and their own experience. If their parents are pressuring them to attend professional school, then the only thing they have to place in the balance against that is some firsthand experience of the world. Staying inside the classroom won't provide them with that. As Montessori wrote in *The Absorbent Mind* in 1915: "The world of education is like an island where people, cut off from the world, are prepared for life by exclusion from it."

All the same, while speaking about the advantages of moving the classroom off-campus, I'm troubled by the memory of my own college days. I loved college, and the main reason I loved it had to do with being in a cloistered atmosphere. Without knowing it, I chose a small liberal arts college for women located in an affluent suburb because it did not ask me to cope with too many new things at once.

45   It was intellectual achievement above everything at Bryn Mawr, and I identified with that. It was bliss to be in a place where if you scored 100 on your tests, it didn't mean people wouldn't like you. It was bracing to be indoctrinated in Bryn Mawr's ethos: that women not only could but should be intellectuals, could and should compete successfully with men in the world of mind, where, presumably there was no marrying or giving in marriage. So saturated was I in the values emanating from Bryn Mawr's unofficial motto—Only our failures marry (though I didn't take it literally; I knew you could get married and not be a failure as long as you also got your Ph.D.)— that I went to the best graduate school in my field and became a professor.

I realize as I write that one can never second-guess reality, that it's folly to look back and say, I should have done this or not done that. Bryn Mawr's seclusion was probably right for me at the time, all I could have understood and coped with, given who I was. Though who knows? Perhaps if the college had offered a carefully crafted apprenticeship program or the chance to sample a variety of work situations, I might have sprung for the experience and ended up as a social worker or an editor or a journalist. Whatever the case may be, it was a different kind of omission that my education really suffered from, a more intrinsic lack. I wish that the college I bound my identity over to had introduced me to my heart. I wish it had set mercy and compassion before me as idols, instead of Athena's cold brow. I wish I had been encouraged to look inward, been guided on a quest for understanding my own turmoil, self-doubts, fears. How much pain it might have saved me later on.

This was a use for the cloister: to screen out the world and enable the gaze to turn inward in contemplation. For the growth of human beings an environment set apart and protected from the world is essential. But the cloister needs to be used for the purposes for which it was originally intended: quiet reflection, self-observation, meditative awareness. These are the gifts of the cloister that allow the heart to open without fear.

Most institutions of higher learning in our country do not address the inner lives of their students, except as a therapeutic stopgap. To get help with your self you have to go to a clinic and be assigned a psychiatric counsellor to help you with your problem, or, if you are a member of a mainstream religious denomination, you can go to its representative in the campus ministries. As far as the university is concerned, the core of the human being, his or her emotional and spiritual life, is dealt with as a necessary evil, on the sidelines, and the less heard about it the better. We don't want people to think of our students as having problems. But having a problem with your self is the existential dilemma, the human condition. Learning to deal with our own suffering is the beginning of wisdom. I didn't learn this—that is, that I had to start with myself—until I was in my late forties. I could have begun sooner.

The curriculum of American education, kindergarten through graduate school, is externally oriented. Even psychology and religion are externalized bodies of knowledge, with terminologies and methodologies and histories to be mastered like anything else. Every freshman can tell you that Socrates said, "Know thyself," but is she or he then given any way to carry out the charge? Undergraduates, you may say, are preoccupied with nothing but themselves. They are self-absorbed to a fault. Perhaps, but their self-preoccupation is a function of the stage of life they're at; they want to ask the big existential questions, and they want to know themselves in the Socratic sense. But instead of giving them the means, or the incentive, our present system sidelines this hugely important phase of human development and relegates it to the dormitory. Whoever wants to know herself is strictly on her own.

50   Occasionally in a literature class, or a women's studies class, undergraduates will be asked to write or speak from their own experience. Often they do so passionately, eloquently. But this is a kind of exception practiced in the corners of humanities departments and is widely regarded as "soft," unrigorous, not a substitute for history, methodology, theory, terminology, information. And of course it's not a substitute; it's simply knowledge of a different kind, but of a kind that, although essential to the conduct of every single human life, has practically no standing in our curricula.

I am not advocating a curriculum devoted exclusively to the pursuit of self-knowledge. I too well remember the rapture of my undergraduate days in the east wing of the Bryn Mawr library reading the thirteenth-century Italian poets. I loved the voyage out. It was full of wonder and excitement. But in order to have a balanced, nonobsessive relation to the world outside yourself, some inner balance and self-understanding are needed. Otherwise, your engagement with the world sooner or later becomes captive to the claims of obscure actors to whom you are paying hush money behind your own back. The old unmet demons—anger, fear, self-hatred, envy, you name it—end up running the show, under the guise of doing sociolinguistics, or molecular biology, or tax litigation, or child advocacy, or ikebana, or whatever it happens to be.

Inside and outside, the cloister and the world. We need both. But somehow higher learning has evolved to a point where it offers neither. Neither contact with the world nor contact with ourselves. This has come about because the university has relinquished responsibility for envisioning life as a whole. Instead, it has become an umbrella organization under which a variety of activities go on, but one that has no center and no soul. Correspondingly, the university doesn't see the student as a whole person but only as a kind of cutout part of a person, the intellect—a segment that it services diligently.

I don't know how to bring into being the world I'm trying to imagine here. I can't imagine it, really. All I can imagine are the kinds of adjustments I suggested in my report to the deans, such as: educating parents about the purpose of a liberal arts education, expanding and deepening the role of advisors, introducing more experience-based courses into the curriculum, finding ways to de-emphasize grades. In fact, I'm *afraid* to envision the kind of world my experience has taught me to reach for because I fear it would seem too outlandish, too impossible. I don't think most of us ever try to imagine our ideal world as educators. We're not encouraged to, certainly. I have taught in colleges and universities for thirty years, but no one has ever said to me: "Tompkins, have your vision of an ideal university on my desk by tomorrow morning." When did anybody ever say that?

The university has come to resemble an assembly line, a mode of production that it professes to disdain. Each professor gets to turn one little screw—his specialty—and the student comes to him to get that little screw turned. Then on to the next. The integrating function is left entirely to the student. The advising system, which could be of great help, seems to exist primarily to make sure people don't bollix up their graduation requirements.

55   Higher education, in order to produce the knowledge and skills students need to enter certain lucrative professions, cuts students off from both their inner selves and the world around them. By not offering them a chance to know themselves and come into contact with the actual social environment, it prepares them to enter professional school but not to develop as whole human beings. Although parents might object— what, all that tuition and no ticket to financial security and social success?—it would be more helpful to students if, as a starting point, universities conceived education less as training for a career than as the introduction to a life.

Rereading Actively

1. Tompkins opens this chapter by reflecting on her personal struggle to understand students' experience in higher education. Does this perspective successfully shed light on her topic? Does it seem like an effective way to begin?

2. What's Tompkins's attitude toward college faculty? Does her attitude surprise you? Why or why not?

3. Which student story is most striking? Explain how that story helps to develop Tompkins's reflection.

4. Tompkins concludes with the final opposition of "training for a career" versus "introduction to life" (¶ 55). With a partner or in a small group, analyze the distinctions Tompkins draws between these orientations.

5. Tompkins says of students, "They're on [a] train and holding [a] ticket [purchased by someone else], the countryside is going by very fast, and they're not getting to see much of it. All they know is that when the train arrives at their stop, they'll be getting off" (¶ 5). With a partner or in a small group, discuss the metaphor of college education as a ride on a fast train. What experiences does this metaphor suggest to you?

6. Identify several other metaphors Tompkins uses to understand the process of education, starting with "the cloister" and "the heart." In your journal, explain two or three of these figurative comparisons and suggest how they add to or take away from Tompkins's point.

Exploring Your Responses

7. With two or three of your classmates, surf through the Duke home page <www.duke.edu>, trying to get a feel for the mission and mode of instruction that are idealized there as well as the student experience. As a group, compare what you find on the Duke page to the ideals published by your school in a home page or catalogue. Focus on four similarities and differences, and develop a collaborative report that explains what kind of life the two campuses introduce students to.

8. In a freewrite, explore the "train ride" college is or will be for you. In your conclusion, reflect on how you feel about the trip.

9. With a small group, brainstorm experiences you have each had with an adviser or faculty person. Discuss these experiences, comparing them with the ones Tompkins describes. Reflect on your group's discussion and Tompkins's account in an entry in your journal.

FADING DREAMS, ENDURING HOPE
CHRIS LISKA CARGER

While teaching and tutoring in inner city Chicago, Chris Liska Carger met Alejandro, a Mexican-American boy, and his family. In her book, Of Borders and Dreams *(1996), she traces Alejandro's progress through middle school. (The publisher of this book, Teachers College Press, is a leading source of scholarship by and for progressive-minded educators.) The chapter included here reflects on Alejandro's graduation from middle school and on the meaning of his struggle to become educated in English—for both Alejandro and his family, especially his mother, Alma. Through her observations and interpretations of Alejandro's experience, Carger explores how, more than reading, writing, and arithmetic, education is a social process that opens paths to some futures and blocks others.*

> Multiple interpretations constitute multiple realities; the "common" itself becomes multiplex and endlessly challenging, as each person reaches out from his/her own ground toward what might be, should be, is not yet.
>
> —*The Dialectic of Freedom*, M. Greene

A s Alejandro reached out from his own ground, what was it that he tried to grasp? As a Mexican-American minority of limited English proficiency, will he be confronted with "the wall" that Langston Hughes (1968) described in the following poem?

> It was a long time ago.
> I have almost forgotten my dream.
> But it was there then,
> In front of me,
> Bright as a sun—
> My dream.
> And then the wall rose,
> Rose slowly,
> Slowly,
> Between me and my dream.
> Rose slowly, slowly

Dimming,
Hiding,
The light of my dream
Rose until it touched the sky.

Maxine Greene, who cited Langston Hughes's poem, wrote of her conviction that we who are in education cannot know, cannot truly know how it was, how it is, "… we cannot truly understand the walls immigrants and minorities face. But we can attend to some of the voices, some of the stories" (1988, pp. 88–89).

In attending to Alejandro's story, a young man emerges who wishes for economic success, and blue eyes.

"I wish I had blue eyes," he said one summer day as we walked along Lake Michigan. "Blue eyes are the best."

5   "Yeah," laughed his oldest sister. "He really wants blue eyes."

"I wanna get a nice, you know, a good job," he says, "to work downtown or maybe as a carpenter. I'll probably go to college, like just for 2 years, they're too expensive. I wanna get married but like when I'm 21 to 23…. Yeah, I wanna be a dad some day."

The dreams are vague but they are his, rooted in the ground that a strong family of inimitable faith has tilled and turned. Implicit to their realization is the need for English literacy. When he was younger, his mother recalled, Alejandro talked about wanting to be a doctor or a lawyer. She was clearly proud of those aspirations. As time went on, Alma began to question the schooling demands of such professions, began to suspect that perhaps it was already too late to hope that her son could realistically pursue those vocations. During his eighth-grade year, Alejandro himself began to pare down his career goals, and I found it difficult to discourage the direction he was taking. As realities of academic challenges settle in, he has already scaled down his dreams of employment to that of an office worker.

Alma, too, was vague about her hopes for Alejandro's future. "We've been so fortunate, people have helped us out so much. I'd like to see Alejandro do something where he could help people. I don't know what, but I think it would be nice for him to help other people." She recognized with disappointment that, due to his academic challenges and their monetary reality, this helping profession she envisioned will not likely be medicine or law. However, as is typical of Alma, she switched gears and focused on realistic alternatives. "I want him to continue going to school, I know," she gazed wistfully out her living room windows as we talked. "My husband and I tell him all the time to take advantage of the opportunity of going to school. We didn't have a chance to and it holds us back."

What Alma and her husband were very clear on is what they do not hope for their son. "We don't want him to end up in jobs like we have, bad factory jobs. We're held back because we can't fill out forms, we can't get promoted like other people we see, we don't know enough English. We work and work and never earn much."

10   Their aspirations for their son in terms of employment and education get translated into constant social restraints for Alejandro. Alma related their warnings to Alejandro not to think about marriage until his mid-twenties, when school is done and he has a good job.

"Some day he's going to realize that I was only 16 when I got married and here I'm telling him he can't even date till he's 18 or think of getting married till he's 24 or 25. I've always lied to the kids about the date of our marriage but now they're starting to realize how old I am and how old they are. They're figuring it out," Alma grins. But she is adamant that her son will not marry at an early age like she did.

"You know, Christina, Alejandro is very innocent," she told me one morning as we drove together to the social security office to investigate special educational allotments for her oldest daughter's vision and learning problems. "Last week my sister and I were talking and cooking in the kitchen and Alejandro asked why he felt sweaty and funny when a girl in his class touched his ears and neck. He was very serious, Christina, poor thing. My sister and I tried to keep a straight face. He went on to describe how odd he felt, how he had butterflies in his stomach, you know. He's very naive, very innocent about things between girls and boys."

"I think you and your husband need to talk to him about those things, don't you?" I asked.

"Oh, yes, yes. I told my husband that he had to sit down and have a 'facts of life' talk with him. And he did. He told Alejandro that's how it starts. You start touching a girl's face and one thing leads to another and you have babies. He told him he shouldn't date until he's older, at least 18."

15　　"But I don't think he really understands how everything happens. Alma, I think he needs to know. He's almost 14, right?"

Alma agreed but it was clear that neither she nor her husband would frankly explain sexual intercourse to their son. It was out of the question. He would receive a healthy dose of Catholic taboos surrounding "it" and admonitions to avoid "it," but to discuss "it" openly or scientifically was asking them to do something culturally inappropriate. Their focus would be a moral one.

"I tease Alejandro because he's told me he doesn't like dark hair, you know, like mine. I say, 'So you're not going to look for a girl like your Mom to marry?' But he has always liked blond hair. I told him, 'Then that means you're not going to marry a Mexican?'" she laughs. Despite the good-natured teasing about his preference in looks and his emerging ability to dance at family parties and events like *quinceaños* [15-year-olds' coming-out parties], he is closely monitored to keep things on a friendly, casual basis with girls.

"There are two güeras [Anglo girls] in the neighborhood who have noticed Alejandro. When he and his father are cutting the grass they walk by the house again and again. My husband tells Alejandro he should be friendly and chat with them. He tells him he should chat with your daughter, too. It would help his English," she smiles. "He's just too shy, he's embarrassed about his English."

A 14-year-old Mexican-American boy, who finds that girls like his looks yet who doesn't quite understand what to do about it, emerged from the 10-year-old I once tutored. He still struggled to read and write in English, preferred blond hair and blue eyes (obviously picking up society's biased preferences through the T.V. shows and movies he so loves), and was kept bonded closely to his family in order to resist peer influences upon him. He did not particularly like Mexico, felt more comfortable in his old "hood" than his new, prettier, cleaner, safer (at least for Caucasians) neighborhood of Brighton Park, and was frightened at the prospect of attending a large urban high school.

20　　"I miss Sorrowful Mother," he told me that summer, "but not the teachers; not Mrs. Wright. I have friends at school *only*, you know. We did lots of things together. I mean now we're gonna start all over. I mean none of my friends are gonna come (to Crown High School). I'm gonna feel like, how you say, embarrassed?"

"Why will you feel embarrassed?" I asked Alejandro.

"Well, cause I don't even know the people that go there." I remembered the relief I saw in Alejandro's face almost a year ago when Shepherd Elementary School could not take him into their overcrowded eighth grade and he had the chance to go back into the arms of Sorrowful Mother. He most likely will be reprieved as well from attending the high school he fears, for at least a while. Sara called to tell me that with fiscal problems being what they are at the Chicago Board of Education, she strongly doubts that Crown will open on time in September. She suggested enrolling Alejandro in the college's tutoring program in the fall for double sessions so that he could keep up on some type of work with his reading and writing. This tutoring was already promised in the petitioning process for Alejandro's acceptance into Crown, in addition to an updated educational evaluation during the summer.

The summer provided a more relaxed context for me to share time with Alejandro. I learned a lot observing him out of his classroom. The burden of terrifically difficult homework was lifted from our relationship, at least temporarily. The Juarez children, my daughters, and I wandered through zoos, museums, and parks together. Alejandro teased me about my "field trips," as he called them, and is finally comfortable enough with me to express his own opinions, though still cautiously.

"I don't like museums so much," he grinned. "Why don't we go to the movies instead? I like going to the movies."

25 "Well, I promised my younger daughter we'd go to the aquarium and the Field Museum today, but next week we'll go to a movie, okay?" I suggested.

"Oh, yeah! I wanna see *My Boyfriend's Back*," he said.

"*My Boyfriend's Back?* Isn't that the one where someone returns from the dead?" I asked.

"Oh, yeah, Chris. It looks good. Don't worry!" he laughed.

As we drove to and from his weekly diagnostic evaluations this summer and on our "field trips" Alejandro brought along tapes he had recorded from the radio. He told me the categories of music each group plays. "This is techno, Chris, and this one, this is plain rap." Some have a Latin beat but all have lyrics in English. He subvocalized all the words from the songs and could decipher hard-to-understand lines for me. This from a student who could not remember how to spell three-letter, primary-level words in school.

30 "He listens to his music all day," said Alicia, his oldest sister. "That's all he does any more."

"Yeah," he laughed. "I don't even watch no T.V. much any more," Alejandro added. "I haven't been out all week since the detectives," he referred to the incident when his cousin unknowingly wore a cap backwards as they played basketball in their alley and was accosted by two Chicago detectives.

Is it the repetition, I wondered? Is it the rhythm that could be helping him to memorize, to comprehend line after line of songs packed with English words? Or is it the meaning these tapes hold for him? They are esteemed by his peers with whom he talks on the phone, tape player at one ear, phone receiver at the other.

I also have watched Alejandro carefully during my field trips that summer and although he often began disinterestedly, he readily joined in activities that are hands-on.

At both the zoo and the Field Museum he perked up when exhibits had buttons to push, flaps to open, sounds to hear. He approached them with the same enthusiasm as his younger brother, Ricardo, who is a bright, animated, adventurous learner. But Alejandro did not attempt to use reading to gain information about what he was experiencing, not even single-word labels.

"What's this?" he would ask, completely ignoring the sign next to the button he had just pushed at the zoo's African exhibit. There he had to analyze simple clues to figure out situations in the wild. Integrating the clues seemed beyond him as the younger children excitedly explained answers to him. At the museum I pointed out that the word next to a button he quickly pressed named the animal in the scene in front of him that made the sound he heard. I pointed to the label next to the button "grouse" and the matching label near the stuffed grouse in the scene. Alejandro had a "light bulb over the head" reaction. His face lit up as he suddenly grasped a totally new concept. His reading teacher spoke of the same type of reaction she would notice when, clearly, meaning broke through for him as they discussed a reading topic he had initially decoded successfully but with no comprehension.

35   "I know he can learn," said Ms. Gonzales. "I've seen his expression change and his whole face light up and I know, he's got it now. He understands. But he has to be pushed to do it. If I had him more for reading that's what I would do with him. Really go through the material…make connections and make him think about it."

I saw the need for that "push" this summer too. Alejandro preferred the safe, the comfortable, like his world of tapes. Although he never refused to come on our "field trips" and has even declined my offer to bring along a friend of his, he would rather do something more familiar to him. He spoke of being bored by things he used to like to do with his family and often faced his days with lassitude, not expressing interest in the world around him. Yet, he seemed to value the time we spend together.

"I don't want to ask a friend to come," he told me clearly one day. "I'm goin' out to be with you, not with a friend." When we talked on the phone to make arrangements for our outings, he enjoyed long conversations, relating his family's activities, his plans, even asking me to listen to a song he's taped that he thinks I'll like. Although I had to coax him to read the books I found for him that summer, he offered to chat, to clean, to cut grass, to do other things he feels more competent in.

"But I want you to read, Alejandro, not to cut my grass," I told him.

"I'm gonna do it, really, Chris. I like the book. I've kind of, ya know, gotten into it. It's a good story, like a mystery." I was encouraged as he related details of a new book I bought him, written by a local author who set out to compose an interesting book series for middle-grade to junior high students with reading difficulties.

40   "I've been busy 'cause I cleaned my father's car, all day. I really did. Then he took me to Dunkin' Donuts. And tomorrow we have to go to my cousin's wedding," he explained. I saw more clearly as well that summer how narrow his world of experience is. Alejandro would not go swimming with me and my family this summer. Neither would Alicia, Almita, or Ricardo. Only his younger sister Lupita would venture into the 3-foot children's pool. Alicia, Almita, and Ricardo said they were afraid. Alejandro said he just didn't like swimming. They all still cringed at my pet cat if they even caught a glimpse of him in another room. Alejandro's parents have managed to negotiate at Dunkin' Donuts, which is a treat for their children. Lack of English and low textual literacy have restricted the family's willingness to try new stores, restaurants,

or amusements. His parents hear about things within their social network but are very cautious to attempt things that move them outside of their family and Spanish-speaking friends, and with good reason. For it is not only linguistic fears that limit them; neighborhood gang activity is always a concern.

Not long after graduation, Alma related a terrifying incident to me revolving around a family outing not far from their home. After shopping, she and her sister's family stopped at a nearby McDonald's to eat. Apparently a gang that dominated the restaurant came and encircled the entire Juarez table, staring at them, arms folded over chests. Alma and her sister quickly grabbed their food and ushered their families back into their cars. "Alicia was so upset she couldn't stop crying," Alma recounted. "None of us wanted to eat after that. It was very scary. We were afraid they were going to follow us out to our cars or start something with Alejandro."

Alma switched to a day shift as of that summer, and Alejandro, Sr. quit his second job. To their credit, I felt, they did this to spend more time with their children.

"My husband says that finally we can all eat supper together. He said he used to feel like *un perro abandonado* [a stray dog] because I always left food for him while I was away at work. Alejandro, Jr. ate more than I've seen him eat in a long time last night. I said to him, 'You must have been really hungry.' He said no; it was just that it felt so good to have his mother home cooking for him and serving the dinner that he didn't want it to end," Alma laughed. "I don't feel right. I think it's because I worked nights for so many years and my system isn't used to this change. But I know I did what was right for my family. My friends at work say they miss me. My two sisters I work with cried. They say it's not as good without me there. I always talked a lot and kind of fooled around, you know. It made the time go faster. They're begging me to come back. But I won't. I'm sorry, but my family needs me. I have to think of them first."

A lot happened for Alejandro that year, his last at an elementary school where he felt safe. He was "discovered" by girls and enjoyed that attention. He faced the reality of a public high school education and lowered his goals in terms of his choices of professions. He found that in the old "hood" and the new one, his color, Latino features, and accent are liabilities in the eyes of the "law." And for the first time in several years his family spent evenings together, in large part due to their concern for him.

45   Lately, Alejandro was more successful at "breaking the code" and orally reads noticeably better, yet he still battles with severe comprehension difficulties. He learned how to retreat into a world of popular music, phone calls from friends, and the household cleaning duties he has always excelled at. His borders as an adolescent Mexican-American became more dangerous as he faced the very real menaces of gangs, neighborhood violence, and blatant discrimination. The wall of his academic and economic difficulties impinged upon his hopes and dreams. He didn't quite know what he wanted to do, so frequently he did nothing. Yet, most of the time, he was a pleasure to be with—a sincere, kind young man.

He has come to trust a friend outside the family, who pushes him to read, to write, to think, to express his feelings. Someone who has no right to have examined his world but someone he and his family have graciously permitted to do so. Someone who has tried to tell his story. Although the notes, recordings, and interviews will now end, the friendship and concern will not. I have found, in particular, a strong, sweet friend in Alma.

Paths have crossed; connections were forged. I have told only part of the borders and dreams of a strong young man; and I have learned much more than I could ever return. And Alma, so central to this narrative, Alma has asked me to teach her, to work with her "the way you do for my son."

"I've thought of asking you for a while now. Maybe I could learn some English and to read a little. Maybe then I could help the kids more. I might not be able to do it but I just wonder, Christina." I wonder too.

References

Greene, M. (1988). *The dialectic of freedom*. New York: Teachers College Press.

Hughes, L. (1968). As I grew older. In A. Chapman (Ed.), *Black voices* (p. 426). New York: New American Library.

Rereading Actively

1. Review the chapter with a partner, noticing who expects what from school. List the stakeholders and the expectations that you identify.

2. Look also for the threads of the market—entertainment and advertising, but also fluid identities and group memberships—that are woven into Alejandro's experience, and identify some of these elements in a journal entry.

3. How does Carger distinguish between "dreams" and "hope"? Explain one example of each and then suggest what the title of the chapter implies.

4. We discover that Alejandro has a growing interest in girls and a wish for blue eyes. Find passages where Carger calls attention to Alejandro's desires, and explain the purpose of these passages in the story that she tells.

5. How do Carger's references to limited opportunities, dead-end jobs, and gang violence affect your understanding of Alejandro's education?

6. Why does this chapter conclude with Alma, Alejandro's mother and her desire for education? In your journal, explain your reaction to the final paragraphs.

Exploring Your Responses

7. In a freewrite, explore how in middle school or high school you "reached out from [your] own ground" (¶ 1), from the economic, social, and personal "realities" that defined you then.

8. In a same-sex group of three or four people, discuss how your family's "dreams" about cultural values, career goals, relationships with the opposite sex, personal identity, safety, and so on affected your schooling. Freewrite individually about how your family communicated expectations to you in high school. Then, as a group, organize your experiences along a continuum from "traditional borders" to "blurred borders" and talk about how each situation could strengthen or compromise a student's performance.

9. Reflect on a connection you formed as a high school student with an adult outside your family, and explore how this connection helped or now helps you see the cultural and social borders that you had to cross.

CHOICE CAN SAVE PUBLIC EDUCATION
DEBORAH MEIER

Deborah Meier has spent the past twenty years doing school reform in east Harlem, pioneering small schools that graduate over 80 percent of their students. She now works with Brown University to spread the approach to education that she articulated in her book The Power of Their Ideas *(1995). These ideas—student and parent involvement, small class size, student-centered curriculum, and faculty autonomy—have become topics of discussion for teachers and administrators from kindergarten to professional school. In this article, Meier Walnates school choice as a vehicle for reform. The* Nation, *where this article appeared in 1991, is a progressive American weekly magazine often critical of conservative, establishment politics; it takes a special interest in issues of social justice. For the* Nation *to publish an article that argues in favor of school choice, a cause usually associated with conservative education reformers, is therefore somewhat surprising.*

Before deciding to go down in history as a war President, George Bush called himself our "education President," announcing ambitious goals to make American schoolchildren first in the world by the year 2000. These goals were applauded by politicians, educators and corporate leaders across the political spectrum. America's future itself, they all declared, is at stake, but, unlike the gulf war, they believe this future can be bought cheaply.

The conservatives have the answer: choice. It's a solution, they note, that doesn't require throwing money at schools. And furthermore it's politically correct. The marketplace, they remind us gloatingly, will cure what a socialistic system of schooling has produced: the miseducation of our young. The most articulate and contentious proponents of marketplace choices in education are John Chubb and Terry Moe, whose articles, speeches and book, *Politics, Markets, and America's Schools,* have sparked widespread debate. But this is not merely a battle of words. A number of localities and several states have initiated systems of choice, often using Chubb and Moe's data to support their programs. While Chubb and Moe contend that they favor public education, what they mean is public funding for education. Public institutions are their enemy. They make no bones about it: Private is good, public is bad. Private equals enterprising, public equals stifling bureaucracy and destructive political influence.

The original right-wing challenge to public education, vouchers for private schools, went down to a resounding defeat. The newest star on the right, choice, is both a more powerful challenger and a more interesting one. Because progressives are on the defensive, their concern with equity leads them to attack choice reflexively as inherently elitist (naturally, it has few friends among educational bureaucrats either). This is, I believe, a grave mistake. The argument over choice, unlike the one about vouchers, offers progressives an opportunity. After all, it wasn't so long ago that progressive educators were enthusiastically supporting schools of choice, usually called "alternative schools." However, those alternatives were always on the fringe, as though the vast majority were doing just fine, thanks. We now have a chance to make such alternatives the mainstream, not just for avant-garde "misfits" and "nerds" or those most "at risk."

Americans have long supported a dual school system. Whether schools are public or private, the social class of the students was and continues to be the single most significant factor in determining a school's intellectual values and how it works. The higher the student body's socioeconomic status, the meatier the curriculum, the more open-ended the discussion, the less rote and rigid the pedagogy, the more respectful the tone, the more rigorous the expectations, the greater the staff autonomy. Numerous studies have confirmed a simple fact: The primary factor in determining the quality of schools (as well as programs within schools) is not whether they are public or private but who attends them. Changing this is what education reform is all about. What we need is strategies for giving to everyone what the rich have always valued. After all, the rich have had good public schools as well as good private schools. If we use choice to undermine public education, we will increase the duality of our educational system. If we want to use it to undermine the historic duality of our schools, the kind of plan we adopt is more important than choice advocates like Moe and Chubb acknowledge.

5   When I first entered teaching, and when my own children began their long trek through urban public schools, I too was an unreconstructed advocate of the strictly zoned neighborhood school. I knew all about choice, a favorite tactic of racists escaping desegregation. There were even moments when I wished we could legally outlaw any selective public or private institutions, although I could readily see the risks—not to mention the political impossibility—of doing so. That's no longer the case. My change of heart has personal overtones: I've spent the past sixteen years in a public school district in East Harlem that has pioneered choice, and I have founded a network of small schools of choice in that community: the Central Park East schools. All of District 4's schools are small, largely self-governing and pedagogically innovative. They are schools with a focus, with staffs brought together around common ideas, free to shape a whole set of school parameters in accord with those ideas.

It would have been impossible to carry out this ambitious agenda without choice. Choice was the prerequisite. It was an enabling strategy for a District Superintendent, Anthony Alvarado, who wanted to get rid of the tradition of zoned, factory-style, bureaucratically controlled schools that has long been synonymous with urban public schooling and replace it with a different image of what "public" could mean. The District 4 way was deceptively simple; it required no vast blueprint, just a new mindset. Within ten years, starting in 1974, District 4 totally changed the way 15,000 mostly poor Latino and African-American youngsters got educated without ever pulling the rug out from under either parents or professionals. The words "restructuring" and "reform" were never used—this was, after all, the late 1970s and early 1980s. The Superintendent sidestepped resistance by building a parallel system of choice, until even its opponents found themselves benefiting from it.

To begin with, Alvarado initiated a few model schools open to parental choice, locating them within existing buildings where space was available. He sought schools that would look excitingly different, that would have a loyal, if small, following among families and would have strong professional leadership. Alvarado and his Alternate Schools director, Sy Fliegel, gave such schools extraordinary support in the form of greater flexibility with regard to staffing, use of resources, organization of time, forms of assessment and on-site advice and counseling. Wherever possible, they also ran interference with Central Board of Education bureaucracy. When people in the "regular" schools complained of favoritism, Alvarado and Fliegel assured them that they'd be favorites too if they had some new ideas they wanted to try. Some even accepted the challenge. Each year, more schools were added. They generally started with a few classes and the largest grew to no more than 300 students. Some stayed as small as fifty. Within half a dozen years most of the students in the middle and junior-high grades were attending alternative schools, and each district building housed several autonomous schools.

Schools were no longer equated with buildings. Where there had been twenty-two schools in twenty-two buildings, in less than ten years fifty-one schools occupied twenty buildings (along with two housed in a nearby high school). Only then did the Superintendent announce Stage Two: Henceforth no junior high would serve a specific geographic area. All families of incoming seventh graders would have to choose. The district provided sixth-grade parents and teachers with lots of information to assist them in their choice, although probably word-of-mouth was the decisive factor (as it is in private schools). Sixteen neighborhood elementary schools remain intact, with space reserved first for those living within the designated zone, but Alvarado promised that parents were free to shop around if space existed. In addition, the district supported the creation of twenty alternative elementary schools, eight of them bilingual. As a result, the neighborhood elementary schools became both smaller and, in effect, also schools of choice. Alvarado even enticed a former independent elementary school to enter the public sector, leaving intact its parental governing board.

A majority of the new schools were fairly traditional, although more focused in terms of their themes (such as music, science or journalism) and more intimate and family-oriented due to their small size. Size also meant that regardless of the formal structure, all the participants were generally informally involved in decisions about school life. Most of the schools were designed by small groups of teachers tired of compromising what they thought were their most promising ideas. As a result there was a level of energy and esprit, a sense of co-ownership that made these schools stand out. They developed, over time, differences in pedagogy, style of leadership, forms of governance, tone and climate. A few schools (such as the three Central Park East schools) used this opening to try radically different forms of teaching and learning, testing and assessment, school/family collaboration and staff self-government. In this one small district, noted only a decade earlier as one of the worst in the city, there were by 1984 dozens of schools with considerable citywide reputations and stature, alongside dozens of others that were decidedly more humane, where kids found it hard to fall through the cracks and teachers were enthusiastic about teaching. A few were mediocre or worse; one or two had serious problems. The consensus from the streams of observers who came to see, and those who studied the data, was that the change was real and lasting. What was even more important, however, was that the stage was set for trying out more innovative educational ideas as professionals had the opportunity to be more directly involved in decision making. It was not a cost-free idea, but the added expense was small compared with many other heralded reform efforts; it was less than the cost of one additional teacher for every newly created school.

10   If this were the best of all possible worlds, the next ten years would have been used to launch Stage Three. The district would have studied what was and was not happening within these fifty-three small schools, examined more closely issues of equity, tracked their graduates over time, studied the families' reasons for making choices and looked for strategies to prod schools into taking on tougher challenges. The Central Board would have worked out ways to legitimize these "wildcat" schools while also encouraging other districts to follow a similar path. Under the leadership of Alvarado's

successor, Carlos Medina, District 4 launched Stage Three. But it was not the best of all worlds, and the district found itself on the defensive for reasons that had nothing to do with education in the fifty-three schools. As a result, Medina's efforts to move ahead were thwarted, and new leadership hostile to choice was installed. Today, in 1991, District 4 stands once again at a crossroads, with new sympathetic leadership both within the district and at the Central Board, although badly hobbled by the threat of draconian budget cuts. That the fifty-three schools have survived the past few years in a system that not only never officially acknowledged their existence but often worked to thwart them is a tribute to the loyalty and ingenuity that choice and co-ownership together engender.

While the District 4 story suggests that choice is fully compatible with public education and an efficient vehicle for setting in motion school reform, it is foolhardy not to acknowledge that in the political climate of the 1990s choice runs the risk of leading to privatization.

However, it's not enough these days to cry out in alarm at the possible demise of public education. If public schools are seen as incapable of responding to the demand for wholesale reform, why should we expect the public to resist privatization? Maybe private schools aren't much better, but if public education has proved so inept at meeting the challenge, if it has had such a poor history of serving equity or excellence, it's easy to see the lure of privatization. Given this history, why not just let the chips fall where they may?

The question is a good one. If we want to preserve public education as the norm for most citizens then we'd better have important and positive reasons for doing so, reasons that are compelling to parents, teachers and the broader voting public. To do so we must make the case that the rationale for improving education goes far beyond the problem employers face in recruiting sufficient numbers of competent and reliable workers or our chagrin at finding the United States at the bottom in test scores for math and science. At least as important is the role education plays as a tool in reviving and maintaining the fabric of our democratic institutions. While public education may be useful as an industrial policy, it is *essential* to healthy public life in a democracy. The two go together, and never has this been clearer than it is today. If we cannot make a convincing case for this, we will see our public schools dismantled in one way or another, either by a misused choice or by erosion and neglect as funds dry up for public education and private schooling becomes the norm for those who can afford to opt out. The status quo plus cosmetic changes won't save public education, at least not in our major urban areas.

The alternative to privatization is good public education, and choice is an essential tool in the effort to create such education. It is the necessary catalyst for the kind of dramatic restructuring that most agree is needed to produce a far better educated citizenry. Virtually all the major educational task forces, for example, agree that dramatic changes will require removing the stifling regulations that presently keep schools tied to outmoded practices, to doing things in lockstep. They agree that if we want change, we'll have to put up with nonconformity and some messiness. We'll have to allow those most involved (teachers, administrators, parents) to exercise greater on-site power to put their collective wisdom into practice. Once we do all this, however, school X and school Y are going to start doing things differently. How then can we ignore personal "tastes"? Besides, it's a lot easier to undertake difficult innovations successfully if teachers, parents and students are in agreement.

15   We can't expect the marketplace, public or private, to stimulate this kind of reform magically. Private schools as an example of the market at work aren't very inspiring when it comes to innovation. They may encourage livelier educational practice, but in general they are as convention-bound as public schools. They mostly differ in an invidious way, much like their public school sisters. There's a hierarchy among them, based mostly on how choosy the school can be about whom it accepts. The fact that the choosiest schools attract higher-status families and select only the most promising students insures their success; replication, by definition, is impossible. Their value lies in their scarcity. This kind of marketplace has led not to innovation but to imitation on a steadily watered-down basis, appealing not so much to different "tastes" but to different means and expectations. The dual system has remained alive and well in the private sector. But if the marketplace is not a magical answer, neither, experience suggests, can we expect that forced change from the top down will work. What results from such bureaucratically mandated change is anger and sabotage on the part of unwilling, unready parents and professionals as well as the manipulation of data by ambitious bureaucrats and timid administrators. The end result: a gradual return to the status quo.

To improve education for all children will require more than one simple cure-all. It requires a set of strategies. For starters, federal, state and local initiatives can stimulate districts to adopt one or another variation of the District 4 story: providing incentives to districts to break up their oversized buildings and redesign them into many small schools, easily accessible for families to choose from. Once we think small, we can even imagine locating new schools in other available public and private spaces, near workplaces as well as residences, in places where young people can interact with adults going about their daily business. While no system of rules and regulations can insure equity, public policy can assure that resources are fairly allocated. It can go further by establishing guidelines that promote appropriate social, ethnic, racial and academic diversity.

We'll also need a better quality of information if we want to promote long-range school change. We'll need a public that is not confused by misleading data or quickly discouraged by the absence of dramatically improved statistics. Who knows today what the definition of a high school dropout is or what "reading on grade level" means? We'll need to place less reliance on standardized high-stakes testing systems. Good lay information will encourage the kind of lively, even contentious, dialogue about the nature and purpose of education that is so badly needed. Choice offers no guaranteed solution to these concerns, but the existence of clear and coherent alternatives encourages such debate.

Similarly, greater school-based autonomy goes well with choice. School-based management itself does not trigger innovation, but it offers a much better audience for such innovation. Empowered faculties and families are better able to hear new ideas and less likely to sabotage them. Innovation no longer appears threatening. School-based management combined with the idea of small schools of choice allows both parents and teachers to embrace new ideas even if they cannot convince all their colleagues or all the school's parents. Furthermore, once we set loose those who are

already eager to "restructure," it will be easier to encourage successive waves of inno-
vators and risk takers. While R&D in education can't take place in labs separate from
real life, as it can in most industries, no one wants to be a guinea pig. Creating a school
different from what any of those who work in the system are familiar with, one that
runs counter to the experiences of most families, is possible only if teachers, parents
and students have time to agree on changes and a choice on whether or not they want
to go along with them.

Since school officials, like parents, are naturally conservative and reluctant to
change their habits, we don't need to sign them all up at once. What's needed first is
a range of models, examples for teachers and the public to scrutinize and learn from.
Credibility will require a critical mass of such schools; at this stage it is hard to know
how many. But we can go only as fast and as far as those who bear the burden of change
can tolerate. Putting more money into schools does not guarantee success but it can
accelerate the pace of change. Of course, taking money out slows down the possibilities for change too.

20   In short, choice is necessary but not sufficient. There's something galling about
the idea that you're stuck in a particular school that's not working for you unless
you are rich enough to buy yourself out of it. Still, if it worked for most students,
we'd put up with it, but it doesn't. What's not necessary is to buy into the rhetoric
that too often surrounds choice: about the rigors of the marketplace, the virtues of
private schooling and the inherent mediocrity of public places and public spaces.
By using choice judiciously, we can have the virtues of the marketplace without
some of its vices, and we can have the virtues of the best private schools without
undermining public education.

Rereading Actively

1. Meier opens this essay on education with references to war, politics, the marketplace, and public institutions. How do each of these issues relate to education for Meier?

2. With a partner, review the article and summarize Meier's use of the word
   "choice."

3. With a partner, identify and discuss the patterns Meier finds in Anthony
   Alvarado's reform of District 4. Summarize your discussion in a short entry
   in your journal.

4. Summing up the inability of public schools to offer equity and excellence,
   Meier states that "it's easy to see the lure of privatization" (¶ 12). What arguments does she offer against privatization as the solution to our nation's educational shortcomings?

5. With a partner or in a small group, discuss Meier's alternative to privatization. Does it seem practical? Desirable? Summarize your conversation in an
   entry in your journal.

6. How does Meier relate the marketplace and schooling in her conclusion? To
   what extent has she proved her point?

Exploring Your Responses

7. How does the story of District 4 compare with your experience in school?

8. In a page or two in your journal, explore the role "choice" played in your school experience. Identify some choices that were important to your education. How aware were you of the choices your parents and teachers made? How did these choices affect your development as a person and student?

9. In a small group, discuss the school experiences you each had, focusing on what you would choose to maintain and what you would change in the curriculum, teacher expectations, and the character of the student body. As you talk, listen carefully for differences in experience. Be prepared to explain to the class what is good, bad, and controversial about your schooling.

BACKGROUND ASSIGNMENTS

The readings here have questioned whether consumer-driven educational institutions can (and should) liberate the soul and serve the underprivileged, and whether education should serve to reproduce tradition or to challenge it. As you consider these general questions in light of the assignments below, you can take advantage of your immediate experience and, probably, strong feelings about education. You will also need to keep in mind your audiences—classmates, teachers, and others who have been reading about education but who perhaps have begun with very different experiences from yours. Your job as a writer is to bring this audience to the position you craft from the evidence offered by other writers and from the details of your life as a student.

Making Connections

1. What is the proper role of customer service in a college? Use Jones's ideas about customer service at school to explain the problems Edmundson sees in the university, explaining whether those problems are the result of consumer students or Edmundson's failure to understand the educational process. Conclude with your own position on whether you would prefer to study with Jones or Edmundson.

2. Use Meier to compare your experiences with those of Alejandro, the subject of Carger's ethnographic study. Focus your comparison on the choices you made, or that were made for you by parents, teachers, and school officials, in the search for the best possible education. In your conclusion, reflect on the extent to which you, as a middle and high school student, had to concentrate on crossing social and economic borders the way that Alejandro did.

3. Though they share a commitment to the cultivation of genius, Tompkins and Edmundson take seemingly opposed positions on the purpose and method of higher education. In an essay, compare their ideas about the purpose of college and the roles of students and faculty with your own experience. Use your conclusion to explore the strengths and weaknesses of your college experience so far.

4. Use the images of personal growth sketched by Carger and Tompkins and your own development as a student to write an essay that explains how you have grown up in school.

5. Drawing on the ideas presented by Meier and Jones and on your own experience, explore the pros and cons of choosing a consumer-oriented school or a traditional one.

6. In a consumer culture, colleges advertise—a lot. Find a set of promotional materials for your school, and use Jib Fowles's and Irene Costera Meijer's thoughts about advertising (Chapter 5) to analyze the way your campus promotes itself. Use your findings to argue whether the campus is helping students see their future or, as Edmundson believes, building a consumer vision that doesn't contribute to real education.

Collaborative Exchanges

1. Divide the class into groups of three or four people with related majors—arts and sciences, business, education, undecided, and so on. With your group, discuss how people in your major are affected by considering themselves consumers who are buying a product. Be prepared to share an outline of your discussion with the class.

2. With two or three classmates, review what Jones and Meier have to say about choice in education. Discuss the important educational choices you each have made (or had made for you) and how these choices have prepared you for college. Develop a collaborative statement on how much freedom of choice a high school student needs.

3. Edmundson talks about the University of Virginia. Tompkins talks about Duke University. In small groups, review Edmundson's essay and visit the University of Virginia home page; review Tompkins's essay and visit the Duke home page. Talk about the kind of educational environment that seems to emerge from these texts, and be prepared to explain why you would or would not want to attend school in that kind of environment.

 ## Net Approaches

1. College Web sites function partly as promotional material and partly as a source for information. Explore your campus's web site, looking for invitations made to prospective students, information about faculty and departments, and career services information. (Alternatively, you can look at the site for a campus you intend to attend or dream of attending.) Freewrite about how the site defines students, faculty, and curriculum and what you find attractive and troubling there.

2. Point your browser to <www.liszt.com> and search for listservs that deal with education—when this text went to press, there were more than forty options. Select a list that deals with a topic of interest to you—distance education, middle school, home schooling, school administration—and follow the Liszt.com

instructions for subscribing to the listserv. Notice there are also instructions for canceling a subscription; you'll probably want to unsubscribe when the project is done. Listen in for a week, participating if it makes sense. (Most of the participants will be teachers, so listening quietly may be as productive as submitting.) Generate a report that explains the interests participants have and the connections between their postings and the reading you have done in this unit.

3. Visit a local or regional newspaper, magazine, or other searchable online news site. (You may decide to use the AJR Newslink <ajr.newslink.org> to help you find an online news site.) Limiting your query to the last six or eight months, search for the following string: *education and consumerism and level.* (Replace *level* with middle school, high school, college, or adult.) Scroll through the headlines, abstracts, or articles—we got 23 searching the *Chicago Tribune* but could only look at headlines and opening paragraphs. Make note of references to school choice, competition, career-oriented students, disinterest in learning, and other themes mentioned in the reading for this unit. In your journal, sketch in some generalizations about the local feel for the topic.

CASE-IN-POINT READINGS

Higher Education: Looking for the College Premium

The case-in-point readings use the vocabulary and core issues defined by the background writers to explore a topic near to your experience: the purchase of a college degree. These analyses and evaluations work with many of the terms developed in the background readings, but they focus on the costs and benefits of delivering higher education as a consumer good. Here you will find a number of similar accounts of the recent history of higher education in the United States. Campuses grew in response to the needs of the consumer culture that sprouted after World War II, but when the baby boomers left campus, colleges and universities raised tuition and went in search of new markets in order to keep faculty, staff, and facilities busy. Now campuses struggle to retain "nontraditional" students (and their tuition dollars) while services are cut along with government funding.

While all these writers agree that a college education has been and continues to be a good buy, they raise important questions about how education should be financed, what and how students should study, and what students will ultimately do with their degrees. Depending on who you ask, you'll discover that the advent of student consumerism has dumbed down higher education or made it more fun, made it even more of a necessity or made a trip to the university irrelevant. As you read, consider the behaviors of students and parents, faculty and administrators, and the writers who describe these behaviors. While they are concerned with the process of getting an education, their positions are not always argued in the same terms, with the same assumptions, or with similar kinds of logic and evidence.

THE UNDERGRADUATE

ERIK HEDEGAARD

For decades, pop culture magazines including Playboy *and* Rolling Stone *have created rankings of the top party schools among U.S. colleges. Erik Hedegaard is a regular contributor to* Rolling Stone *who writes about education, pop culture figures such as Jerry Springer and Chris Farley, and other topical issues. In this 1997 article, Hedegaard presents a profile of one student at Florida State University (FSU): Bert is presented as the #1 party guy at the #1 party school, and Hedegaard's purpose is to show* Rolling Stone *readers (an enormous percentage of whom are themselves college students) what that distinction entails. The lush descriptions and vividly detailed accounts of binge drinking and weeklong partying are presented in contrast to our traditional sense of the purpose of college as Hedegaard explores issues including career preparation, instruction and discipline, and growing up.*

The other day, on a Tuesday, shortly before the noon hour, Bert Kreischer splashed a bit of Peachtree schnapps into a glass of orange juice, topped it off with some vodka and thought he'd probably skip class. He was a student at Florida State University, in Tallahassee. Florida State had recently been named the No. 1 party school in the nation by an organization called the Princeton Review. This fact had been trumpeted all over the nation, in radio reports and on television. College-bound kids everywhere pricked up their ears. All of a sudden, they thought maybe they should go to Florida State and enjoy the kind of life that one might enjoy at the No. 1 party school in the nation. The kind of glorious life, in fact, that Bert Kreischer, age 24, an English major, had already been leading for many years now.

Bert yawned and scratched at some of the stubble on his chin. He stuck a finger into his drink, tinkling the ice cubes floating around there. He thought about the day. If he didn't go to class, he'd play Frisbee instead. In the early evening, he'd hoist a few beers here at home, then hit the bars until some o'clock in the morning. Tomorrow, maybe he would go to class. But without doubt, he'd be drinking again by around sundown. Hopefully he wouldn't black out. Odds were against his blacking out, because he hadn't in a while. Then, looking forward in time, Bert saw Thursday evening—a great big bash on his back deck, with a live band and lots of beer. And Friday evening—getting soused wherever. And, finally, Saturday—he'd be superloaded before, during and after the football game. Beyond that, into the further reaches of adulthood, he could not see. Why should he? He was deeply into the moment of now. He'd structured his entire existence—in which he always seemed to be vying for the honor of being the top partyer at the nation's top party school—around this moment of now.

Hutch strolled in. Hutch was one of Bert's three roommates. He was a tall, tangy, happy-go-lucky marketing major. Hutch said, "Oh, man, what a day! This is the most beautiful day I've ever seen!"

He plopped down on the couch, laughing. "Hey, Bert, I made it to class today!" he shouted. "That's the first time it's happened in like a month and a half. When I walked in, I was like, 'What the hell?!' I couldn't recognize half my classmates!"

5   Bert snorted, rubbed his forehead and said, "God, it was one of those nights last night." He picked up the phone. It dangled in his hand while he stared off into space. He was wearing Birkenstocks, tan shorts and a white shirt. He looked a bit like the

actor Jon Cryer, only with a good number of extra pounds tacked on. He had a man's hairy chest and belly, and a happy, round face that sometimes flushed to a bright pink when he was especially excited. He loved to laugh and crack jokes. In fact, he was the most comical guy lots of people at Florida State had ever known. He could also be highly, raucously obscene. He'd twice run for office at his fraternity, Alpha Tau Omega. The first time, he made his big campaign speech in the nude and lost. The second time, he dropped the idea of a speech; instead, he appeared before his brothers in the nude and took a crap on a pizza box. General bedlam ensued. He won by a landslide. These days, however, that triumph was not one he so willingly recalled. He'd grown some since then. He was in his sixth year at Florida State. Sometime soon he just might grad-uate. He didn't want to, necessarily. But it was a possibility.

"Who am I trying to call?" Bert asked. It could have been his lovely girlfriend, Kristen; his concerned dad, Al; his easygoing mom, Gege; or any one of his pals. He couldn't remember. A warm fuzziness spread across his forebrain. He shrugged and put the phone down.

It had, indeed, been one of those nights. Then again, when was it not one of those nights?

Thirty thousand students attend Florida State University. According to the sta-tisticians, these students, most of them native Floridians, enter the school with an aver-age verbal SAT score of 580 and an average math SAT score of 590. This suggests that they aren't the best and the brightest in the land, but neither are they the thickest. Mostly they're the kind of students who attend good public universities everywhere. In the end, great numbers of them choose to major in criminology, communications and psychology, and not many fewer lean toward business, engineering, nursing and hotel management—which at Florida State is known as hospitality, as in, "Hi, I'm a hospitality major!" Basically they're good kids with stable political outlooks. Accord-ing to university officials, most of them are also quite serious about getting a good education and do attend class regularly. That being the case, these officials were cha-grined to learn that their institution had been named the nation's top party school, an award based on the results of a survey that asked students about drug and alcohol use, hours of study each day and the popularity of the fraternity system. Certainly the school had its partyers, even its problem partyers, but that's true of all schools. Plus, there's so much more to Florida State than parties. There's the Seminoles football team, which last year ranked No. 3; there's the marching band, the Marching Chiefs, which is the country's largest; etc.

Yet, for reasons still largely unknown to the people who run the school, Florida State does seem to have this reputation as one fine place at which to get blotto. Take a stroll across campus and the faintest breeze seems to carry along with it the vegetable scent of hops flowing freely from any number of just-tapped kegs. It mixes well with the natural Florida heat. The two together summon forth images of fermentation, of ripening processes. It makes people happy. In fact, you've never seen a happier student body. Everyone seems happy to be there. And once they've graduated, they're only too happy to return any time they can, arriving by the carload on football weekends, setting up tail-gate parties near the grand, mortared expanse of Doak Campbell Stadium—"By God, it's got the biggest brick foundation in the entire fucking United States!" many an alum has said—to get positively hammered just like they used to, so many years ago, when they were still students at their beloved Florida State and still had a chance of becoming legendary party guys at a soon-to-be-legendary party school.

10   One time we were driving home from Mardi Gras, a car pulls up next to us, and suddenly we see a naked guy hanging out the window, feet and all. It's Bert!"

"One time I went to the gym to work out, and there's a guy on the treadmill with his pants jacked up his ass, with an apple jammed in there. It's Bert!"

"I haven't met Bert yet, but he's well-known at the Tri Delt sorority. 'If you ever meet a guy named Bert, run like hell.' That's what they said. 'Run. Like. Hell.'"

"A wonderful person. The funnest guy ever."

"He's just hilarious, but he has a soft side, too."

15   "Could be a great salesman."

"A great person to talk to."

"I find him offensive."

"He's out of control."

"Bert can get away with anything!"

20   About Bert, everyone on campus seemed to have an opinion or at least a representative and highly emblematic Bert story, perhaps apocryphal, probably not. In many ways, over the years he had become larger than life—a figure of vaguely totemic proportions who could often be seen dancing joyously into the cross-town traffic on Tennessee Street, on his way to one of the many bars doing bang-up business there; or playing a mad-dash round of Frisbee golf down the broad tongue of Landis Green, bouncing the Frisbee off the steps of Strozier Library, just grazing the startled bookworms; or wheeling his black Jeep Cherokee around the fountained circle at the Wescott Building, headed for Ivy Way, where he would turn up 2Pac on his stereo so loud that all the fricking-cool black chicks would swivel their heads his way—he loved that so much. At various times, he also could be seen cruising along Stadium Drive by hallowed Doak Campbell Stadium.

Bert loved Doak. He loved the Seminoles. And he loved what was inside the stadium, on the 50-yard line, smack in the middle of the field: a Seminole Indian head painted on the hard ground, in blacks and whites, garnets and golds. It was where, one day, luck and girlfriend permitting, he hoped to enjoy some sweet, midnight-hour nooky. It was one of his most fervent college-years ambitions.

At the moment, he lived with a ton of other Florida State students in a leafy-green townhouse complex called Indian Village. Besides Hutch, who had a grade point average of 3.1, Bert had two other roommates: Blair, a 3.2-GPA marketing-major senior, the son of a heart surgeon; and Jimmy, a junior, baseball-playing communications major with a GPA of 3.0, a straight arrow until moving in here. Bert himself had a GPA of 2.27, just above failing. He grew up in Tampa, FL, attended a private Jesuit high school; his dad was a real-estate attorney; his mom worked in early childhood development. Outside Bert's Tallahassee apartment, a thousand cigarette butts covered the ground. His Jeep Cherokee, a gift from his parents on his 22nd birthday, was nuzzled deep into the carport, facing the blue waters of the complex's suburban-dream swimming pool. Upstairs, Bert was just lounging around, goofing off, not worrying about any schoolwork that might be due that day, as he explained just how sweet life can be at Florida State.

"OK, like, here's the deal," he said with a laugh. "There are way more girls than guys at Florida State. So guys here will break up with a hot girl simply because they think they can get something better. In the real world, you get a hot girl, and you're like, 'Whew—my buddies like her; I like her; she wants me; I'm staying with her.' Well, here, you'll have a hot girl, and you'll be like, 'Screw it, I can do better.' Because you really can."

He spread his arms and gestured toward his own slightly flabby, slightly thin-of-hair self. "I mean, look at me," he said. "I'm not a great-looking guy, I'm 20 pounds overweight, but I can show you pictures of girls I've hooked up with, and you'd be like, '*Whooosh!*' I'm telling you, it's just so easy to hook up here."

25 He went to the front door and opened it, flooding the apartment with the sunlight of yet another gorgeous Florida day. The sunlight covered the surfboards stashed away under the steps leading to the second floor, the mountain bikes, the Frisbees, the golf clubs. It caught a thousand bits of dust rising from the living-room carpet. It glanced off a couple of stray CD covers, shot back into the recesses of the kitchen, collided with a huge box of Frosted Mini-Wheats and a half-full bottle of ibuprofen tablets, then splintered off to illuminate the labels of the myriad empty liquor bottles on top of the kitchen cabinets: labels for vodkas, rums and gins; the main whiskeys (bourbon, Scotch); bad wines; syrupy concoctions such as used to make Janis Joplin bend and weep; all sorts of casked distillates that draw their potency from the fermenting of innocents—herbs, grasses, leaves, seeds, corn, barley, juniper berries, sugar cane, the cactuslike plant known as *Agave tequilana weberi.*

In the midmorning heat, Bert perspired lightly. Jimmy and Blair walked in and flopped down. They held forth on various sporting events, hotly. The phone rang. Bert answered it with a mock thug accent: "No, this isn't Bert. No, Bert's out partying, taking bong hits, smoking beer. Who is this?"

Afterward, he talked for a long time about his friends. "I think I've got the coolest friends in the entire world, I really do," he said. Besides Hutch, Blair and Jimmy, there were OB, Clint, Philly, Mason, Pat, Dudash, Big Country (a huge, hulking figure who actually got lots of play), Seth, Hemstreet, McBay, Trip and Grimes. Bert laughed loudly, shook his head in disbelief and slapped his knee as he told stories about each of them and their lives together, their special moments in time.

Bert grunted happily at the memories, then jumped up a flight of stairs to the bathroom to douse his scalp with Rogaine. "This is such a boom-boom school, it really is," he continued brightly. "No one goes to classes. No one's taking fucking notes in class. I think I've only been to my Introduction to Public Relations class twice—and that was for the two tests. My Shakespeare class, I have a pretty poor attendance record in, too. But I did write a paper, a critical analysis of *The Taming of the Shrew.* My theory was, Kate's not a bad girl, because her first words in the whole play are nice words. That means to me we're getting a good girl. It's just the circumstances. Everyone acted like an asshole to her, so she acted like a bitch back to them. She had to. Her father is a cocksucker. Her sister's a cunt. Even Petruchio was kind of an asshole." Bert paused. "I don't know if the teacher feels the same way I do, but I sure hope so."

Purposefully, Bert took no classes that started before 12:30 in the afternoon. With equal purpose, he'd seen to it that none of his classes fell on a Monday or a Friday, thus extending his pure party time. Later, he recalled a class he once took called Alcohol

Use and Abuse. In it, he'd filled out a survey to see if he qualified as an alcoholic. "According to that thing, I was a raving alcoholic," Bert said with a kind of distant chuckle. "I mean, one of the questions was, 'Do you blow off prior engagements to go drink?' Well, yes. But I think we're in such a different little microcosm here. There's always something going on that includes drinking."

30   If it wasn't at some shindig put on by a friend, fraternity or sorority, it was at the bars. Tallahassee was loaded with them. There was A.J.'s, Po' Boys, Potbelly's, Club Park Ave., Fusions, Yiannis, Ken's, Bullwinkle's and Floyd's—with its Sunday Old Wave Night, featuring the retro sounds of the good old '70s and '80s.

As it happened, Bert viewed this multitude of options as a good thing, and sometimes his head swam with how great it all was at Florida State—the bars, the classes, the girls, the weather, the friends, the memories, everything.

"There are days where I'm like, 'Oh, my God, I'm so happy I'm living the life I'm living,'" he said. "I mean, I'm having such a great time that somebody's got to be having a shitty time...."

His teachers thought about him often.

"He's kind of unique, isn't he?" Pat MacEnulty, his creative-writing teacher, said. The words hung there pregnantly.

35   "He's one of the brighter students I've taught and one of the most entertaining people I've ever met," said Donofrio, his public-speaking teacher. "He did a speech on Rogaine. It was gutsy. He completely captivated the audience. Students came up to me afterward and said, 'Why can't I be like Bert?'"

The way people sometimes talked about Bert, it was almost like he was a rare commodity or like maybe he was someone the MacArthur grant people should consider for a genius grant, as if those such as him should be allowed to create their own place and station in life so they wouldn't get lost or have their essential Bert-like qualities extinguished by having to take jobs selling carpets or home alarm systems in South Florida.

His parents, of course, fretted about him constantly. His mom, Gege, would bravely say, "I don't know whether the world is ready for Bert or not!" She talked about how he started walking at two months and was "a party in progress" starting from the age of 2. "The drinking? Does it bother me? I have eight brothers; four of them are [recovering] alcoholics, and two of those have said that Bert has the same pattern. The only thing I can do is talk openly with him." She didn't know what he would do after college, either, but it wouldn't bother her if he went after any of his more far-fetched dreams, like being a stand-up comic. "The average American has such limits on themselves and the way they think," she said. "Bert can't fit into that mode." Bert's father, though, really wished he would. Six years earlier, Al had wanted Bert to go to Duke University, because Duke wanted him to play on its baseball team. "Bert was an excellent ballplayer," Al used to say. "I was dying for him to play." Now he hoped his son would just find what he wanted out of life, but mostly he hoped Bert would find a job. He thought Bert was a creative kid, a sensitive kid, a good kid. "Also," he would say, "he's an unusual kid."

At a bash at his place, with a live band thrashing on the back deck, eight kegs flowing on the lawn, a good 200 kids getting sloshed and the Tallahassee police keeping a watchful eye from a distance, Bert wore a pair of overalls, a brown ski hat, a thumb ring, a toe ring, a few earrings and some dark makeup around his eyes. "Guys don't understand it, but girls like it," he said to explain the makeup. His father, of course, would not only not understand it, he would have hated it, just as he hated Bert's goatee. He once offered Bert $500 to get rid of it. The only reason Bert had grown it was to cover his double chin. But for the bucks, he shaved it off. Seeing it gone, the first thing his father had said was, "Fat Boy!" He hadn't meant to be cruel, but Bert was hurt. Before long, the goatee was back.

Bert worked his way into the crowd. He came up to a guy who was quite clearly trying to hook up with a girl. The guy was leaning forward, the girl was leaning back. Bert appraised the situation. Though he didn't know either of them, he spoke right up, calling the guy Joe. "Joe!" he said, incredulously. "Joe—you're going to be sleeping with her tonight? OK! Yeah! And what's your name? Sarah? Gonna give him a blow job probably?"

40   Sarah looked shocked. "Hey … hey," she said.

Bert started to move away. "All right, I'll go over here, if you don't mind."

When Bert had left, Sarah looked at Joe, shrugged, smiled and leaned his way just a little. She seemed to sparkle. It was like Bert had sprinkled her with some kind of sparkle dust.

When it was time to go to Tennessee Street, Kristen hopped into the driver's seat, Bert into the passenger seat and their friend OB, a rather contemplative English major, into the back seat. Every time Kristen ran over a beer bottle, it exploded. Pow! Pow! Pow! "It's a Jeep," Bert yelled. "It's a Jeep!" The three of them howled. When they arrived at Yiannis, with its long line of people waiting to get in, Bert stuck his head out the window and shouted, "OB wants pussy!" On the way inside, Bert ran into Hutch and Blair. Jimmy was there, too. By Bert's side were Kristen and OB. He was surrounded by all his friends. He had the best of all possible worlds. He was potted. His forebrain was clouded over. This was it.

That Saturday, at Bert's place, OB passed around a poem he loved. It was by e.e. cummings. OB had typed it out on a sheet of white paper.

```
l(a

le

af

fa

ll

s)

one

l

iness
```

45   "It's a great image," OB said.

"A leaf falls on loneliness," Bert said. "That's a shitty poem. It doesn't even rhyme. Now, Snoop's poetry sings to me a little harder."

OB said, "Think about it, Bert."

Bert said, "Think about it?"

He didn't want to think about it. It was Game Day. He had a plastic bag full of vodka stuffed into his pants, ready to be smuggled into the stadium. He hopped up.

Everyone hopped up. They joined the masses of people headed to see the Seminoles in action. Bert saw a group of pretty sorority girls. "Hey, ladies!" he shouted.

50   "Hey, Bert!" the girls shouted back.

Some cops looked over. "You guys got the drugs?" Bert hollered. Mirthfully he clapped his hand to his mouth. "Cops! Oh, shit!" he yelped. "I'm just joking—no drugs here! Only kiddie porn—right in their satchels! You can smuggle porn into the stadium but no alcohol, right?"

Up in the stands, Bert turned to the people sitting in the bleachers behind him—a staggering number of people, hundreds of them, in row after row, mostly adults, mostly strangers.

"You guys want to dance?" he asked them all. "Maybe?"

No one looked at him. They avoided him. He took a sip of his drink. "Jesus Christ, that's a strong drink."

55   Suddenly, Bert grabbed a camera and turned again to the people behind him.

"Everybody!" he shouted. "I'm taking a picture. If you could crowd around real quick, I want my parents to think I have a lot of friends. Oh, by the way, I'm Bert. Now, everybody say, 'Hi, Mom!'"

"Hi, Mom!" lots of people shouted.

Bert clicked the picture. "*Whoo, whoo!* I made friends! I made friends! OK, now let me tell you my problems."

Everyone laughed and began talking to Bert. A few of the people said his name out loud. They said it not as if they were asking a question or wanted his attention, but just as if they were testing it out, the sound of it as it left their mouths and joined all the other sounds in the stadium. "Bert," they said.

60   Bert focused his attention on the field. Right in the middle, on the 50-yard line, was the Seminole head, plastered there in field paint. It was the nooky spot, representing the crowning ambition of his college years. It existed today, in the moment of now. Bert squinted at it.

"I know I can do it tonight," he said happily. "I just know I can!"

Rereading Actively

1. Why does Hedegaard introduce readers to college life by talking about partying and skipping class? How do you react to the opening scene?

2. Hedegaard says that FSU students are "[b]asically...good kids with stable political outlooks" (¶ 8). Explain what he seems to mean by "good" and why, based on what he shows you in the article, you are inclined to agree or disagree with this assertion.

3. In a small group, discuss which characteristics of FSU student life seem most striking. Do you find the students here appealing or repellent? Why?

4. What appears to be Hedegaard's attitude toward FSU students? Write a summary of his descriptions of campus life, and then write a two- or three-sentence description of his evaluation of the students he followed.

5. Explain how two passages help determine your final position on Bert. The question you'll need to begin to answer is, "What kind of education are Bert

and his friends getting?" Write a page or two in your journal showing how your two passages help you get at this question.

Exploring Your Responses

6. With two or three classmates of the same sex, discuss your experience of campus life, evaluating the importance of friendships, socializing, and partying. Once you've listened to one another, freewrite individually on how friendships, socializing, and partying contribute—positively or negatively—to your education.

7. In a page or two in your journal, speculate about how being at a school like FSU might change your college experience. If you are already at a school like FSU, reflect on how the side of college that Hedegaard explores is affecting you.

DRIVE-THRU U
JAMES TRAUB

In this 1997 New Yorker *essay, James Traub analyzes the University of Phoenix, a division of a publicly traded corporation, the Apollo Group. Traub is a Harvard-educated writer who gained attention most recently for his book* City on a Hill *(1995), in which he describes his experiences sitting in on classes during a year and a half at City College, one of the campuses in the City University of New York system. While* City on a Hill *captures the decline of historically important university, "Drive-Thru U" describes the rise of a new form of university. Traub describes University of Phoenix's claim to be the "second largest private university in the United States" and its pride in selling what "education provides for [students]" rather than "education" itself. Traub notes that, at a time when traditional universities are in decline, this "para-university" has grown by serving a market segment—adults looking for functional and quick diplomas—with efficiency.*

Higher education for people who mean business.

AT the University of Phoenix, which describes itself as the second-largest private university in the United States, terms that normally have a clear and literal meaning are used in an oddly evanescent way; this seems especially true of the language that evokes our most romantic feelings about higher education. The university has, for example, a "bookstore" on the ground floor of its central administration building. The store is a boutique offering backpacks, T-shirts, coffee mugs, beer glasses, and ties, all bearing the school logo; the only books are textbooks, which you have to order from someone standing behind a counter. The U. of P.'s "library" can be found, as Kurt Slobodzian, the librarian, likes to say, "wherever there's a computer"; students can access thousands of journals via the Online Collection. And the word "campus" is understood, at the University of Phoenix, to mean "site," or even "outlet." The university is a franchise operation, with forty-seven sites all over the West and in Michigan, Florida, and Louisiana; most of them consist of an office building, or merely a few floors of a building, just off a highway exit ramp. When I was talking to the director of the university's "distance learning" program, I noticed that he was using the word "campus" to apply to himself and three other people, who ran the program from a suite of offices. The University of Phoenix is, in fact, a para-university. It has the operational core of higher education—students, teachers, classrooms, exams, degree-granting programs—without a campus life, or even an intellectual life. There are no tenured professors, and the most recent issue of the university's only academic journal contained but a single academic article, about copyright law.

You cannot get a rise out of the university's top officials by pointing any of this out. William Gibbs, a former Price Waterhouse manager, who is the president of the U. of P., said to me, "The people who are our students don't really want the education. They want what the education provides for them—better jobs, moving up in their career, the ability to speak up in meetings, that kind of stuff. They want it to *do* something for them."s

Apparently, it does. Enrollment may be flat at élite institutions, but the U. of P. has grown from three thousand students to forty thousand over the last decade. It offers accredited bachelor's-degree programs in business, nursing, and education, and an M.B.A. as well. The university is also the principal subsidiary of a profit-making company called the Apollo Group. Since late 1994, when the company first offered shares on the NASDAQ exchange, Apollo stock has increased in value from two dollars to thirty-five dollars, on a split-adjusted basis. One broker I spoke to said that most of his customers were professors at Arizona State, who had concluded that the U. of P. delivered pretty much the same product they did, only more efficiently. The University of Phoenix is competing not with the Ivy League but with the big state schools and the small, unheralded private colleges; where most students enroll. It's a Darwinian world out there: some two hundred colleges have closed during the last ten years.

College, for most of us, means greenswards, dreamy spires, professors with elbow patches, old volumes in the stacks; but no more than several dozen colleges answer to this description. Higher education in America is now a vast industry that accommodates two-thirds of America's high-school graduates, or more than fourteen million people. Most of the nation's thirty-seven hundred colleges see themselves as market-driven institutions trying to satisfy customer demand. As I drove around Phoenix, I kept hearing ads on the radio for Ottawa University, a Kansas institution that has three campuses in Arizona and others in Singapore, Malaysia, and Hong Kong. "Ottawa," the announcer said, "majors in *you.*"

5   Almost half of America's freshmen attend community colleges, institutions with no residential facilities and, often, no campus. According to a study conducted by Arthur Levine, the president of Teachers College, at Columbia University, only a sixth of America's college students fit the stereotype: full-time students, living on campus. Levine says that a survey of the five-sixths who do not has found that "they wanted the kind of relationship with a college that they had with their bank, their supermarket, and their gas company. They say, 'I want terrific service, I want convenience, I want quality control. Give me classes twenty-four hours a day, and give me in-class parking, if possible.' These are students who want stripped-down classes. They don't want to buy anything they're not using." Such students understand clearly that higher education has become an indispensable passport to a better life.

In a 1994 book entitled "Dogmatic Wisdom," a history professor named Russell Jacoby faults critics on both the left and the right for focussing on the intellectual melodramas that agitate a tiny number of institutions—"canon wars" and battles over "speech codes"—while ignoring the "narrow practicality" that dominates educational practice at almost all the others. Jacoby quotes a Department of Education study showing that of a million bachelor's degrees awarded in 1991 seven thousand three hundred were in philosophy and religion, twelve thousand in foreign languages, and about two hundred and fifty thousand in business. The institution that sees itself as the steward of intellectual culture is becoming increasingly marginal; the others are racing to accommodate the new student. And the University of Phoenix, according to Arthur Levine, "is the first of the new breed."

John Sperling, the founder of the University of Phoenix and the chairman of the Apollo Group, is a blunt, ornery seventy-six-year-old from the Ozarks. In the company's bland and studiously polite environment, he stands out for his willingness to call an idiot an idiot. Sperling is an economic historian by profession, and, like many economists, he considers himself one of the few rational people on earth. Among the people he counts as idiots are those who believe that market forces can be ignored; during one of several conversations, he observed that the principal effect of the war on drugs was that it forced users to commit crimes. Along with George Soros and Peter Lewis, Sperling helped finance the Arizona referendum to permit the medical use of marijuana.

Sperling himself had a classical education—a B.A. in history at Reed, a master's in history at Berkeley, and a D. Phil. in economic history at Cambridge. He recalls his time at Berkeley as among the happiest years of his life. He was, however, far too restless to stick with the academic routine. In the early seventies, while teaching courses in the humanities at San Jose State, Sperling won a government contract to offer a variety of classes to teachers and police officers, and that was the beginning of what he considers his real education. "They were the best students I ever had," he told me. "They really fell in love with education. It wasn't long before they said, 'We'd like to get a degree.' So I went to the administration, and they said, 'No way.' I said, 'I'm bringing you students.' And they said, 'We don't need no stinking students.'"

Sperling developed a program with twenty-five hundred teachers and police at the University of San Francisco and two other colleges in California, but he claims that the regional accrediting body said, "Either get rid of these programs or we'll pull your accreditation for the whole university." Sperling came to see higher education as a closed system whose gates were manned by the accrediting agencies—a racket designed to squelch the forces of individual choice.

10   Sperling reached the Wild West of the free-market system in 1976, when he went to Phoenix, visited a local law firm, and drew up a charter for a new university and, just like that, the University of Phoenix opened for business. He targeted the niche market that he had already begun serving—the adult learner. The University of Phoenix would accept anybody who was twenty-three or older and was working. Students had to have sixty college credits when they arrived, so the need for general education, liberal arts, and all the other stuff that takes up so much time and money at

college could be dispensed with. Sperling wanted to provide a useful and profitable service, not replicate higher education. What interested him was not so much what to teach this population as *how* to deliver it. "Higher education is one of the most inefficient mechanisms for the transfer of knowledge that have ever been invented," Sperling said. "I decided to go back to my economics and conceive of education as a production function, in which you specify the learning outcomes that you want—they're your product—and then do a regression and figure out the most efficient way of producing them."

Just as the Ivy League model was developed two centuries ago to accommodate aspiring clerics, so the University of Phoenix is shaped by the needs of working adults in the corporate economy. And because it was created all at once it's a highly rational institution. Classes are held at night, from six to ten. Courses consist of five or six weekly sessions, taken one at a time and one right after another. Each degree program is identical from one campus to the next. Laura Palmer Noone, whose title is vice-president for academic affairs—elsewhere she would be called "provost"—says, "What we have found is that adults don't want all that much flexibility, they want it to be simple."

One of Sperling's early insights was that adults also put very little stock in academic opinion. He concluded, "You were going to have to draw your faculty from the world they were familiar with—the world of work. If you had a Ph.D. that didn't mean shit." Marketing would be taught by a marketing executive, and accounting by an accountant. In a vocational setting, these teachers had the credentials that mattered. The "practitioner" system also, and not incidentally, allowed the university to deliver coursework far more cheaply than its competitors, since it paid its instructors an average of about a thousand dollars for each five-week course. Many of the teachers, and especially the businessmen, say they do their nighttime job for the sheer satisfaction of it. Hugh McBride, the executive director and chair of the graduate business programs, told me, "It's really a joy to have someone say, 'You know, Hugh, I used that last week in the company.'"

Faculty members are required to have a master's degree, but few, if any, of them have academic credentials that remotely rival Sperling's. Hugh McBride, for example, spent twenty years in the Army doing systems work, earned his M.B.A., and went to work for Citicorp and the Metro-North rail service. Larry Gudis, the director of the Phoenix campus, is a former high-school teacher and assistant principal who spent three years working as a training manager at Intel. When he walked out of his office for a minute, I glanced at the three books he had on his shelf. Their titles were "Training and Performance," "The Miracle of Personal Leadership," and "Team and Organizational Development."

The traditional American university occupies a space that is both bounded and pastoral—a space that speaks of monastic origins and a commitment to unworldliness. The headquarters of the University of Phoenix, by contrast, consists of two buildings of banded glass and brick with a fig leaf of grass in between and a parking lot all around them. The central campus happens to be situated in the middle of an industrial park near Sky Harbor Airport. As with the forty-six other facilities, the area was chosen with an eye to convenience in an automotive culture. The university leases multiple sites in many of the cities where it operates, choosing them so that no student has to drive more than twenty minutes to get to class. (In Phoenix, there are four sites, with two more scheduled to open soon.) And as the culture shifts from an automotive to an electronic one the U. of P. is moving to abridge space altogether. The on-line program offers classes to two thousand five hundred students who work out of their homes, including military personnel stationed all over the world. A separate service, the Center for Distance Education, provides one-on-one study for two thousand more students. Hundreds of colleges now offer some form of distance learning, but the U. of P. is one of the few where you can earn a degree without ever mingling with other students or even meeting a professor.

10   One evening, I attended a meeting of Business Communication Skills, a course known as COMM 202. The class met on the fourth floor of the taller of the two buildings at the central campus. The view outside the plate-glass windows was mesmerizing: waving palms; sawtooth mountains; airplanes sailing through a deepening blue sky. The teacher, Katherine Barnett, who was the assistant department chair for General Studies at the university, was a blond woman in her late forties with an ingratiating smile and a brittle manner. During the day, she taught reading and English at a public high school. She taught twenty-five or thirty classes a year at the U. of P., and did some curriculum consulting as well. It sounded like a staggering burden, but she had kids to put through college.

There were about fifteen students. Most had been in a prior course together, and they had already found a comfort zone consisting of friendly chatter. Since this was COMM 202's first session, Barnett asked the students to talk briefly about themselves. They volunteered in order of courage. Maria Surrell was a long-distance operator for Sprint, Tammy Walter was a full-time mother; Ben Burns ran the laundry at a V.A. pharmacy center; Jody Gagnon was the contract administrator for a construction firm. The youngest student in the group, Jared Annes, was twenty-four; he had spent four years in the Army after high school and now worked for a computer firm that designed telephone voice systems. "I want to be more than just Joe Programmer; that's why I chose the Business and Information Systems degree," he had told me before the class. To the others he now said, with a laugh, "When I grow up, I want to be rich." One of the oldest students, Dean Williams, slight and earnest, said that he was in "food management." He had got a job at an Albertson's supermarket when he was a teen-ager; the money was good, and at the time he couldn't see any reason to stay in school. Now it was twenty years later, and he was managing the produce department in one store. He wanted to move up, but, he said, "it seemed like I got to a stopping point because I didn't have that degree."

Barnett agreed. "The days are gone when you could make your way to the top of the ladder by sheer guts," she told the class. "Now you have to have that piece of paper." The class was designed to teach the kind of oral-presentation skills that are required in business. Group work—a simulacrum of the team-oriented business environment—is an integral part of U. of P. pedagogy: for COMM 202, the final project would consist of a group presentation of a business meeting. Students would also make individual speeches. Barnett told the class that she would be giving hints on how to reduce the stress of making public presentations. She sounded forgiving. "If you make a mess of it but you try anyway, you're going to get the grade," she said.

COMM 202 was for students who had arrived at the University of Phoenix with fewer than twenty-four credits; in effect, it was for freshmen. Later that evening, I attended a session of Advanced Marketing Management, for students working on their

M.B.A. They were required to turn in papers each week, and to do considerable reading, the final group project would be to devise a marketing strategy to capture one per cent of the beverage market. The teacher, George Francisco, had been a brand manager for Philadelphia Cream Cheese and other products at Kraft. He talked about the idea of a mature market. The soda business had stopped growing, he explained, so the big players were branching out into flavored teas and bottled waters. One student said, "We had a caffeinated water we tried to market—Aqua Java." It hadn't worked. They talked about high-stakes presentations. "Let me tell you what happened at Kraft," Francisco said. "If you went over an hour and a half, they walked out of the room." There was a little collective gasp.

The University of Phoenix has been denigrated as a "diploma mill," but in this class and the others I attended the students were engaged and the discussion was spirited. What was a little hard to get used to, though, was the lack of intellectual, as opposed to professional, curiosity. Ideas had value only insofar as they could be put to use—if they could *do* something for you, as Bill Gibbs had said. Here was a university formed around the idea that practiced experience is superior to abstract understanding—a proposition that almost seemed self-negating. Indeed, the U. of P.'s greatest contribution to curriculum design may be its Assessment of Prior Learning, a system that allows students to earn credit for courses by proving that they have had equivalent personal experience. You can even take a course in the subject, which allows you to get credit for mastering the "theory" behind the system and also gives you the tools to successfully "challenge" other courses. Norma Turner, who often teaches this course, told me about a student who earned nineteen credits—plus three more for the class itself—by writing essays demonstrating his mastery in such subjects as Parenting, Family Life, and Loss and Bereavement.

20   The University of Phoenix is not cheap compared with many of its competitors. At two hundred and sixteen dollars a credit, a bachelor's degree could come to more than twenty thousand dollars. But I didn't meet a single student who questioned the value of the investment. Many of them had chosen the University of Phoenix after a good deal of comparison shopping. They had tried Arizona State University but had found that they had difficulty scheduling all their classes at night. They had enrolled in community college but had been unable to tolerate the juvenile atmosphere. They had tried to register elsewhere but had grown tired of waiting in line for courses that turned out to be closed. In a consumer-driven market, the U. of P. had adapted itself to their needs more effectively than the competition had; it was doing unambiguously what the others were doing haltingly. Scott Safranski, a professor of management at St. Louis University, who headed a visiting accreditation-review team that looked at Phoenix last year, notes that detractors have called the school the McDonald's of higher education but says, "I'm not sure that's entirely derogatory. They've provided a uniform product in a consistent way which is convenient to the consumer at an affordable price." He adds, "I certainly hope they don't take my market away too quickly."

THE University of Phoenix is still one of the few for-profit academic institutions established to date; but the distinction between profit-making companies and educational institutions is becoming increasingly moot. Several education experts I spoke to volunteered the idea that a new kind of institution would come into being as the result of an alliance between a state-university system, a "content provider," like Disney, and a technology firm, like Motorola. The fastest-growing sector of higher education is, in fact, the "corporate university," which typically provides training for middle and upper management. A 1994 book by Stan Davis and Jim Botkin entitled "The Monster Under the Bed" observes that the increase in "classroom contact hours" for corporate employees in one year, 1992, exceeded the enrollment growth at all the colleges built between 1960 and 1990. The authors foresee the business model, with its focus on "competition, service, and standards," supplanting the current educational model.

This may be a bit premature, but the line between corporate training and academic education has clearly blurred. One day, I drove into Tempe, a suburb just beyond Phoenix (itself a sprawling suburb), to visit Motorola University, a gleaming facility on landscaped grounds that looks more like a university than the University of Phoenix does. Motorolans, as they are known, were taking courses in Behavioral Interviewing and Developing Your Human Potential, along with some in recondite aspects of computer-chip design. The curriculum sounded a lot like the one at the University of Phoenix, and, in fact, the U. of P. offers several of its courses on the campus. Motorola does not provide an academic degree, as some corporate universities do, but Arizona State offers a master's in Management of Technology on the Motorola campus, using teachers from both institutions. In Phoenix, if not yet in Boston or New York, the corporate university is part of a web, not of a pecking order—one of several kinds of "providers" filling in different aspects of a "learner"'s needs. Arthur Levine, of Teachers College, predicts that several generations from now "we'll still have some number of residential colleges and some number of research universities, but most of the rest will disappear." Corporations may simply make postsecondary education an in-house function. Non-élite institutions, Levine suggests, will be reduced largely to examining and certifying students for workplace readiness.

Like any successful business, the University of Phoenix is oriented toward growth, and in recent years it has begun to expand into the realm of the conventional university. The number of credits required for admission has dropped from sixty to zero. The U. of P. has created a General Studies department, which offers courses not only in Oral Communications but in Philosophy and Religion. (Bill Gibbs, though, says that he would like to see the Religion course focus on such practical advice as how to do business among different bodies of believers.) In effect, it is now taking responsibility for the entire undergraduate education of many of its students. The administration hired William Pepicello, who has a Ph.D. in linguistics from Brown and a manner that is identifiably academic, to establish a Gen. Ed. curriculum and embody the school's new identity. Last year, the U. of P. sought permission from accreditors to offer undergraduate degrees in whatever subjects it wished, and to establish a doctoral program. Both of these proposals were rejected—a decision that infuriated many at the school. The general view in Phoenix is that the forces of convention which have been trying to throttle John Sperling for a quarter of a century still have the upper hand in academe. An alternative point of view is that there are still standards for an academic education, and the university may have been threatening to transgress them. Stephen Spangehl, an official of the North Central Association, which is the regional accrediting body, declines to give specific reasons for the decision but says that the group was concerned about, among other things, the university's lack of rigorous academic assessment. "They seem more concerned about customer satisfaction," Spangehl says. "Our focus has always been on learning."

It's that sort of curt dismissal that makes John Sperling furious. "Jesus, they're disgusting," he said when I asked him about the decision. But he was moving ahead, looking for new markets. He had recently returned from a trip to the Far East. There were, he said, a million potential customers for information-systems training in Malaysia alone, and the China market was incalculable. The Apollo Group was making a big push into distance learning, and that may well be the growth market for postsecondary education. Moreover, the whole public-school market was opening up. Jorge Klor de Alva, a former anthropology professor at Berkeley, who is now the chair of the U. of P.'s academic cabinet, told me that the advent of school vouchers "will create huge opportunities for private, for-profit schools." Apollo could own a chain of schools, provide management services, and market curricular material. Once you conceive of education as a product, and regress from the needs of the consumer, a whole world of possibilities presents itself.

25   Sperling himself seems unable to decide whether he has created a superior model for higher education or a viable alternative to the existing one. As we were having dinner one evening, he started going on about the uselessness of classical education. "One of my favorite books is 'Tom Jones,'" he said. "I read 'Tom Jones' for the sheer pleasure, but I didn't go out and rut with some maid in the canebrakes. It's all part of what happens up here." He pointed to his head, but he sounded so thoroughly exasperated that he might as well have been talking about his appendix. "The University of Phoenix causes you to *apply* what you've learned *the next day at work*." Then, lest I get the wrong idea, he reminded me of how deeply he had loved Berkeley.

"Why don't you want all your students to have the experience you had?" I asked.

"Because they can't afford to."

"Wouldn't it be good if they could?"

Sperling gave me a weary look, and said, "I'm not involved in social reform." He had once tried to build a chain of technical schools for inner-city youth, he told me, and when that failed he had vowed never again to create something there wasn't a demand for. "Microsoft is a much more powerful force shaping the world than Harvard or Yale or Princeton," he said. "So if you can't beat 'em, join 'em."

Rereading Actively

1. Explain the opposition Traub develops in the first paragraph between the University of Phoenix and more "romantic" universities, and then describe how that first paragraph might affect readers.

2. In a small group, discuss three passages in which Traub develops an image of University of Phoenix officials. What is the overall image of the University of Phoenix that Traub conveys? What's your response to this image of the administration and faculty?

3. Summarize the traditional college experience—the current educational model to which Traub and others refer—that is alluded to in the essay. What roles does money play in student access to the traditional college experience? Does

Traub do an adequate job of factoring the role of money into his analysis of higher education? Why or why not?

4. Why might traditional college administrators and faculty believe that there is a contradiction between "customer satisfaction" and a focus on "learning"? In a journal entry, speculate about why Stephen Spangehl, an official with a university accrediting body, feels that there is a contradiction between the two emphases, and then explain the relationship that you see between customer satisfaction and learning.

5. With a partner, look for points where Traub seems to reveal his own position on the University of Phoenix. Based on these observations of his text, what would you say Traub's view is?

6. Why does Traub conclude the essay with the University of Phoenix's John Sperling explaining his sense of his company and its students? How does this conclusion affect your understanding of the University of Phoenix and of Traub's purpose in writing this essay?

Exploring Your Responses

7. With two or three classmates, make a virtual trip to the University of Phoenix <www.uophx.edu>. After surfing through the page, focus on a single node and develop a collaborative summary and evaluation of that part of the University of Phoenix program. Be prepared to report your findings to the class.

8. In a freewrite, compare your college experience with that of a University of Phoenix student. First, describe one of the following: your interaction with a professor, a walk across your campus, or the apparent purpose of one of your courses. Then, go back to Traub's essay and review passages that focus on the topic you freewrote about. Finally, speculate about how life would be different if you were at the University of Phoenix.

9. Reflect on Traub's conclusion and the comments of John Sperling that are recorded there. What is your response to Sperling—a man with a master's from UC Berkeley and a doctorate from Cambridge—and his belief that his students "can't afford" (¶ 27) the educational experience that he had?

THE LAST SHOT
DARCY FREY

Darcy Frey is a contributing editor to Harper's *and the* New York Times Magazine. *In addition, his articles have appeared in* Sports Illustrated *and other magazines. In this* Harper's *article (1993), later collected in a book titled* The Last Shot: City Streets, Basketball Dreams *(1994), Frey chronicles the year he spent following four talented basketball players from Coney Island's Abraham Lincoln High School as they seek to gain athletic scholarships to Division I colleges. Through the narrative he constructs, Frey explores a different perspective on the "worth" of a college education, presenting his readers with the complicated reality of big-time college ball and its promise of a ticket out of poverty and the old neighborhood.*

Russell Thomas places his right sneaker one inch behind the three-point line, considers the basket with a level gaze, cocks his wrist to shoot, then suddenly looks around. Has he spotted me, watching from the corner of the playground? No, something else is up: he is lifting his nose to the wind like a spaniel, he is gauging air currents. He waits until the wind settles, bits of trash feathering lightly to the ground. Then he sends a twenty-five-foot jump shot arcing through the soft summer twilight. It drops without a sound through the dead center of the bare iron rim. So does the next one. So does the one after that. Alone in the gathering dusk, Russell works the perimeter against imaginary defenders, unspooling jump shots from all points. Few sights on Brooklyn playgrounds stir the hearts and minds of the coaches and scouts who recruit young men for college basketball teams quite like Russell's jumper; they have followed its graceful trajectory ever since he made varsity at Abraham Lincoln High School, in Coney Island, two years ago. But the shot is merely the final gesture, the public flourish of a private regimen that brings Russell to this court day and night. Avoiding pickup games, he gets down to work: an hour of three-point shooting, then wind sprints up the fourteen flights in his project stairwell, then back to the court, where (much to his friends' amusement) he shoots one-handers ten feet from the basket while sitting in a chair.

At this hour Russell usually has the court to himself; most of the other players won't come out until after dark, when the thick humid air begins to stir with night breezes and the court lights come on. But this evening is turning out to be a fine one—cool and foggy. The low, slanting sun sheds a feeble pink light over the silvery Atlantic a block away, and milky sheets of fog roll off the ocean and drift in tatters along the project walkways. The air smells of sewage and saltwater. At the far end of the court, where someone has torn a hole in the chicken-wire fence, other players climb through and begin warming up.

Like most of New York's impoverished and predominantly black neighborhoods, Coney Island does not exactly shower its youth with opportunity. In the early 1960s, urban renewal came to Coney Island in the form of a vast tract of housing projects, packed so densely along a twenty-block stretch that a new skyline rose suddenly behind the boardwalk and amusement park. The experiment of public housing, which has isolated the nation's urban poor from the hearts of their cities, may have failed here in even more spectacular fashion because of Coney Island's utter remoteness. In this neighborhood, on a peninsula at the southern tip of Brooklyn, there are almost no stores, no trees, no police; just block after block of gray cement projects—hulking, prison-like, and jutting straight into the sea.

Most summer nights an amorphous unease settles over Coney Island as apartments become too stifling to bear and the streets fall prey to the gangs and drug dealers. Options are limited: to the south is the stiff gray meringue of the Atlantic; to the north, more than ten miles away, are the Statue of Liberty and the glass-and-steel spires of Manhattan's financial district. Officially, Coney Island is considered a part of the endless phantasmagoria that is New York City. But on nights like these, as the dealers set up their drug marts in the streets and alleyways, and the sounds of sirens and gunfire keep pace with the darkening sky, it feels like the end of the world.

5   Yet even in Coney Island there are some uses to which a young man's talent, ambition, and desire to stay out of harm's way may be put: there is basketball. Hidden behind the projects are dozens of courts, and every night they fill with restless teenagers, there to remain for hours until exhaustion or the hoodlums take over. The high-school dropouts and the aging players who never made it to college usually show up for a physical game at a barren strip of courts by the water known as Chop Chop Land, where bruises and minutes played are accrued at a one-to-one ratio. The younger kids congregate for rowdy games at Run-and-Gun Land. The court there is short and the rims are low, so everyone can dunk, and the only pass ever made is the one inbounding the ball. At Run-and-Gun, players stay on the move for another reason: the court sits just below one of the most dreaded projects, where Coney Island's worst hoodlums sometimes pass a summer evening "getting hectic," as they say—tossing batteries and beer bottles onto the court from apartment windows fifteen stories above.

The neighborhood's best players—the ones, like Russell, with aspirations—practice a disciplined, team-driven style of basketball at this court by the O'Dwyer projects, which has been dubbed the Garden after the New York Knicks' arena. In a neighborhood ravaged by the commerce of drugs, the Garden offers a tenuous sanctuary. A few years ago, community activists petitioned the housing authority to install night lights. And the players themselves resurfaced the court and put up regulation-height rims that snap back after a player dunks. Russell may be the only kid at the Garden who practices his defensive footwork while holding a ten-pound brick in each hand, but no one here treats the game as child's play. Even the hoodlums decline to vandalize the Garden, because in Coney Island the possibility of transcendence through basketball is an article of faith.

Most evenings this summer I have come to the Garden to watch Russell and his friends play ball. The notion that basketball can liberate dedicated players like these from the grinding daily privations of the ghetto has become a cherished parable, advanced by television sportscasters, college basketball publicists, and sneaker companies proselytizing the work ethic and $120 high-tops. And that parable is conveyed directly to the players at the Garden by the dozens of college coaches who arrive in Coney Island each year with assurances that even if a National Basketball Association contract isn't in the cards, a player's talent and tenacity will at least reward him with a free college education, a decent job, and a one-way ticket out of the neighborhood. But how does this process actually unfold? And what forces stand in its way? How often is basketball's promise of a better life redeemed? It was questions like these that drew me to this court, between Mermaid and Surf avenues.

"Just do it, right?" I glance to my left and there is Corey Johnson, smiling mischievously, eyes alight. He nods toward the court—players stretching out, taking lay-ups—and it does, in fact, resemble a sneaker commercial. "Work hard, play hard, buy yourself a pair of Nikes, young man," Corey intones. Corey is a deft mimic and he does a superb white TV announcer. "They get you where you want to go, which is out of the ghet-to!" He laughs, we shake hands, and he takes up an observation post by my side.

Corey is Russell's best friend and one of Lincoln High's other star seniors. He, too, expects to play college ball. But he specializes in ironic detachment and normally shows up courtside with his Walkman merely to watch for girls beneath his handsome, hooded eyes. Tonight he is wearing a fresh white T-shirt, expertly ripped along the back and sleeves to reveal glimpses of his sculpted physique; denim shorts that reach to his knees; and a pair of orange sneakers that go splendidly with his lid—a tan baseball cap with orange piping, which he wears with the bill pointing skyward. From his headphones come the sounds of Color Me Badd, and Corey sings along: *I—wanna—sex—you—up*…He loops his fingers around the chicken-wire fence and says, "I tell you, Coney Island is like a disease. Of the mind. It makes you lazy. You relax too much. 'Cause all you ever see is other guys relaxing."

10   Although a pickup game has begun at the basket nearest us, Russell still commands the other. As the last light drains from the sky, he finishes with three-pointers and moves on to baby hooks: fifteen with the left hand, fifteen with the right; miss one and start all over again. Corey smiles at his friend's hair-shirt discipline. Russell, it is hoped, will play next year in the Big East, one of the nation's top college conferences, in which Seton Hall, St. John's, Georgetown, Syracuse, and others compete. Russell is six feet three, 180 pounds, with a shaved head and a small goatee that seems to mean business. Last spring the Lincoln team, with Russell leading the way, won the New York City public-school championship in a rout at Madison Square Garden that was broadcast citywide on cable TV. But one can never predict what may happen to Russell, because, as Corey observes, "Russell is Russell." I can guess what this means: Russell lives in one of the neighborhood's toughest projects, and misfortune often seems to shadow him. Last year a fight between Russell and his girlfriend turned violent. Terrified that his college scholarship had just been replaced by a stiff prison term, Russell climbed to the top of one of Coney Island's highest buildings. It took almost half an hour of reasoned talk by his high-school coach and members of the Sixtieth Precinct to bring him back from the edge.[1]

Russell may be tightly wound, but no Coney Island player can avoid for long the agonizing pressures that might bring a teenager with his whole life ahead of him to the edge of a roof. Basketball newsletters and scouting reports are constantly scrutinizing the players, and practically every day some coach shows up—appraising, coaxing, negotiating, and, as often as not, making promises he never keeps. Getting that scholarship offer is every player's dream—in anticipation, no one steps outside in Coney Island without a Syracuse cap or a St. John's sweat-shirt. But in reality only a handful of the neighborhood's players have ever made it to such top four-year programs; most have been turned back by one obstacle or another in high school. Others who have enrolled in college never saw their dream to completion. The list is grim: there was Eric "Spoon" Marbury, who played for the University of Georgia but never graduated, and ended up back in Coney Island working construction; his younger brother Norman "Jou-Jou" Marbury, who lost his scholarship to highly ranked Tennessee because of academic problems in high school; and now David "Chocolate" Harris, a talented player who never even graduated from high school. He dropped out of Lincoln after his freshman year and became a small-time drug dealer. Earlier this summer police found him in an abandoned lot, his hood pulled over his head and a bullet through his skull. He was seventeen. Some of the players warming up at the Garden have written on the tongues of their sneakers, CHOCOLATE: R.I.P.

The orange court lights have come on now, displacing the encroaching darkness. Two players on either end of the court climb the fence and sit atop the backboards, hanging nets—a sign that a serious game is about to begin. Suddenly a ferocious grind-

ing noise fills the air. It gets louder and louder, and then a teenage kid riding a Big
Wheel careers onto the court. He darts through the playground crowd, leaving a wake
of pissed-off players, then hops off his ride and watches it slam into the fence. "Ah,
yes, Stephon Marbury," Corey says dryly, "future of the neighborhood."

Stephon—Eric and Norman Marbury's kid brother—is barely fourteen, has yet
to begin high school, but already his recruiting has begun. At least one college coach
is known to have sent him fawning letters in violation of National Collegiate Athletic Association rules; street agents, paid under the table by colleges to bring top
players to their programs, have begun cultivating Stephon; and practically every
high-school coach in the city is heaping him with free gear—sneakers, caps, bags—
in an attempt to lure him to his school. At first glance, Stephon doesn't look like the
future of anything: he's diminutive, barely five feet nine, with the rounded forehead
and delicate features of an infant. He sports a stylish razor cut and a pierced ear,
and the huge gold stud seems to tilt his tiny bald head off its axis. Caught somewhere between puberty and superstardom, he walks around with his sneakers
untied, the ends of his belt drooping suggestively from his pants, and half a Snickers bar extruding from his mouth.

With Stephon here, Corey wanders onto the court. Russell, too, is persuaded to
give up his solo regimen. Basketball, it is commonly said, is a game of pure instinct,
but the five-on-five contest that begins here is something else. Corey and Stephon are
cousins, and Russell is as good as family—the three of them have played together since
they were in grade school. They seem to move as if the spontaneous, magical geometry of the game had all been rehearsed in advance. Stephon, the smallest by far, is doing
tricks with the ball as though it were dangling from his hand by a string, then gun-
ning it to his older teammates with a series of virtuoso no-look passes: behind-the-
back passes, sidearm passes, shovel passes. Corey is lulling defenders with his sleepy
eyes, then exploding to the basket, where he casually tosses the ball through the hoop.
Russell is sinking twenty-footers as if they were six-inch putts.

15   The game has just begun when a crowd starts to form: sidelined players, three
deep, waiting their turn. A prostitute trolling for clients. A drunk yelling maniacally,
"I played with Jordan, I played with Jabbar. They ain't shit. And neither are *you!*" A
buffed-out guy in a silk suit and alligator shoes arrives, swigging from a bottle of Courvoisier. An agent? A scout? The crowd gives him elbow room. A couple of teenage
mothers with strollers come by; they get less elbow room.

Basketball is so inextricably woven into the fabric of Coney Island life that almost
everyone here can recite a complete oral history of the neighborhood's players. People remember the exact scores of summer tournament games played at this court ten
years ago, or describe in rapturous detail the perfect arc that Carlton "Silk" Owens put
on his jumper before he was shot in the elbow in 1982. Dog-eared copies of a ten-year-
old University of Georgia catalogue with a picture of Spoon Marbury playing with
future NBA great Dominique Wilkins get passed around like samizdat.

Russell, Corey, and Stephon are the natural heirs to this vaunted tradition. But
this is a complicated business: given the failures that have preceded them, the new crew
is watched by the neighborhood with a certain skittishness, a growing reluctance to
care too deeply. Yet Coney Island offers its residents little else on which to hang their
pride. So the proceedings here take on a desperate, exalted quality, and by unspoken
agreement the misfortunes of bygone players are chalked up to either a lack of will or

plain bad luck—both of which make possible the continuance of hope. Silk didn't go pro, it is said, "because that was the year they cut the college draft from three rounds to two." Another player, the explanation goes, had that pro game, went to the hoop both ways, "but he was done in by a shyster agent."

Still, the suspicion lingers that something larger and less comprehensible may be at work. Ten years ago, the Long Island City projects in Queens produced New York's best players, but the drug industry and the collapse of that neighborhood into violence, broken families, and ever-greater poverty put an end to its dynasty. In recent years the torch has passed to Coney Island, which struggles to avoid a similar fate.

It's past midnight now, and the ambient glow of Manhattan's remote sky-scrapers has turned the sky a metallic blue. Standing courtside, we can see only the darkened outlines of the projects, looming in every direction, and the shirtless players streaking back and forth, drenched in a pool of orange light. For Russell, Corey, and Stephon, the hard labor of winning their scholarships lies ahead; for now this game is enough. Corey, sprinting downcourt, calls out, "Homeboy! Homeboy!" Standing under his own basket, Stephon lets fly with a long, improbable pass that Corey somehow manages to catch and dunk in one balletic leap. The game is stopped on account of pandemonium: players and spectators are screaming and staggering around the court—knees buckling, heads held in astonishment. Even Mr. Courvoisier loses his cool. Stephon laughs and points to the rim, still shuddering fearfully from its run-in with Corey's fists. "Yo, cuz," he yells. "Make it bleed!" Then he raises his arms jubilantly and dances a little jig, rendered momentarily insane by the sheer giddy pleasure of playing this game to perfection....

SEPTEMBER

20   Most of the coaches are leery of Corey right now; he spends too much time with girls and, despite his intelligence, his grades are among the worst on the team. Stephon is, as far as the NCAA rules are concerned, off-limits for the next three years. So they come to see Russell. In the first week of school, Wichita State, St. Bonaventure, and the University of Delaware have paid him visits. After school today he sits down with Rod Baker, the head coach at the University of California at Irvine.

"My apologies for not coming to see you before, but the fact is one of our players just dropped out and suddenly we need another guard." Coach Baker is a trim, handsome black man wearing a natty blue suit, tasseled loafers, and a gleaming gold NCAA ring. "And the first person we thought of was Russell Thomas. I'm not bull-shitting you. Frankly, I think you're an impact player, a franchise player. Five years from now, I wouldn't be surprised if people were saying, 'Remember when Russell Thomas came in and changed the fortunes of Cal-Irvine?'" Baker runs a finger down each side of his well-groomed mustache. Russell smiles uncertainly.

"Now let me tell you about California. Ever been there?" Russell shakes his head. "Well, you're gonna think you died and went to heaven. I'm serious. What is it today— seventy degrees? Nice and sunny? In California this is a shitty day in December. That's the God's truth. And the other thing about going to school on the West Coast ..." Baker looks down, allows himself a moment to collect his thoughts, then looks up at Russell. "Everybody's got certain things they want to get away from in their past." How on earth does Baker know about Russell's incident on the roof? "In California, Russell, you can get away from that, from all the stuff that brings you down in Coney Island. At Cal-Irvine you can be whoever you really want to be."

After Coach Baker leaves, Russell and I walk out to the football field behind the school, a lovely, tree-lined expanse of green in an otherwise barren urban setting. It's one of those crystalline September afternoons, with fall in the air but the sun pulsing down on the aluminum bleachers where we sit with the last warmth of summer. (Weather like this may ruin a Californian's day, but in Brooklyn this is as good as it gets.) "I was impressed with Coach Baker. I felt he was definitely leveling with me," Russell declares. "But I'm going to wait and see. Hear what they all have to say. Then decide. Try not to be pressured. Just take it one day at a time." Russell's initial comments after a recruiting session often mimic the solemn coach-speak to which he is subjected every day. So many people—high-school and college coaches and free-lance street agents—want a piece of Russell and try to influence where he will sign that it often takes him a while to locate his own thoughts. "They say it's the second-biggest decision I gotta make in my life—after I pick my wife." He looks around the field, swatting imaginary flies. "But I'm doing good, I'm handling it." He locates some gum on the bottom rung of the bleachers, picks it free, rolls it between two fingers, and flips it onto the grass. "It's normal to be confused, right?" Now the elastic of his right sock receives his complete attention as he performs a series of micro-adjustments to get the folds just right. "That's only human, isn't it?" He takes one more look around and, finding nothing else to distract him, falls silent.

The recruiting circus has been a fact of life for Russell and his friends ever since they were in junior high. Directly across the street from Lincoln sits William Grady Tech—another powerhouse PSAL team—and the two schools compete zealously for the pool of talent coming out of the Coney Island projects. Lincoln players often refer to Grady as "the best team money can buy." Grady players claim that Lincoln tries to lure them away with sneakers and promises to "pass them along" in their classes. Coaches at both schools deny such allegations, but it is a fact that thirteen-year-old Coney Island athletes are encouraged to shop for high schools the way the seniors pick colleges—according to which school will give them the most playing time, the best chance to win a city title, and the exposure to get recruited to the next level.

25   The pressure of playing basketball in Coney Island affects Russell in mysterious ways. One time last year he snuck out the back door of the locker room to avoid a postgame team meeting, leaving everyone wondering whether he was angry at himself for his performance or angry at his teammates for not passing him the ball. Probably both. This year, knowing how much is at stake, Russell has struggled to change. He does this in small ways. Over the summer he told me he was planning a new image for himself. I waited to see what he meant. The first day of school he arrived wearing penny loafers, just like the coaches. The next day, building from the bottom up, he had added pleated pants. Then suspenders. A paisley tie. Finally he topped off the look with a pair of non-prescription wire-rimmed glasses—"because they make you look educated. You know, the professor look."

But today Russell seems agitated in the old way, restless with an emotion he can't identify. "You know, I used to say that I couldn't wait to be a senior," he says. "But I got to worry about classes, the season, recruiting, the SATs. That's *a lot* of pressure." According to NCAA rules, students who want to play sports at a four-year, Division I school, those with the nation's top athletic programs, must enter college having maintained at least a 70 average in high school and having received a combined score of 700 on the math and verbal sections of the SATs—the last an insurmountable obstacle to many black players with poor educations and little experience taking standardized tests. Failing that, a player must earn a two-year degree at a junior college before moving on to a four-year school. Many Division I coaches, however, refuse to recruit junior-college players, considering them damaged goods. So players who don't go directly to a four-year school often never get to play top college ball or earn their bachelor's degrees.

The first time Russell took the SATs, he received a combined score somewhere in the mid-500s. (You receive 400 points for signing your name.) This year he gave up his lunch period to study, and lately he's been carrying around a set of vocabulary flash cards, which he pulls out whenever there isn't a basketball in his hands. By dint of tremendous effort, Russell had also brought his average up to 78—the highest on the team. These are extraordinary developments for someone whose schooling over the years has been so bad that he had never, until recently, finished a book or learned the fundamentals of multiplication, even as he was being called upon to answer reading-comprehension and algebra questions on the SATs. "I used to think there were smart people and dumb people, but that's not true," Russell says forcefully. "Everybody's got the same brain. They say a human mind can know a thousand words—it's like a little computer! But you got to practice." He pauses. "But how come it's always the guys who don't study who get their 700s? Seems like the guys who work hard always get screwed. But oh, well." …

OCTOBER

After practice the players all tumble down the school's front steps. Stephon walks up to me and says, "Take me to Mickey D's. I'm hungry. I could eat three Big Macs. You got any cash?" I've already agreed to drive Russell and Corey home, so I tell Stephon to hop in. "This is your ride?" Stephon stares slack-jawed at my ten-year-old Toyota. "When I get to college, I'm gonna get me a white Nissan Sentra—that shit is *milk!*"

"Just get in the damn car," Russell says. In the last few weeks, some schools that had recruited Russell aggressively in September have backed off, and Russell is taking it hard. No sooner had Russell made up his mind to sign with Cal-Irvine than Coach Baker called to say they were no longer interested—the guard they thought was leaving decided to come back. Meanwhile, other schools seem convinced that Russell won't ever pass his SATs. (Coaches somehow learn of Russell's test scores before he's even had time to show them to his mother.) With every school that courts and then abandons him, Russell goes through the full cycle of infatuation, falling in love, rejection, and recuperation; each time he survives with a little less of the spirit to forge on with the school year. Stephon wants the front seat of my car, but Russell says gruffly, "Six foot three gets the front. Five foot nine goes in back." Corey wisely stays out of it. He puts his Walkman on, pops the hatch, and climbs in the far back, draping his legs over the bumper.

Autumn is arriving quickly this year. For weeks now the sky has been a study in gray, and the trees along Ocean Parkway are already bare. On the drive to McDonald's we splash through piles of fallen leaves. "If you crash and I get injured, Coach is gonna kill you," Stephon advises me. Then he announces, to no one in particular, "When I go to college, I'm going to Syracuse or Georgia Tech."

"How come?" I ask.

"Because at Syracuse you play in front of 32,820 people every home game—it's crazy-loud in there," he says, meaning the Syracuse Carrier Dome. "And because Georgia Tech knows how to treat its point guards." Stephon is no doubt thinking of Kenny Anderson—the player he is most often compared with—who left Georgia Tech after his sophomore year to sign a five-season, $14.5 million contract with the NBA's New Jersey Nets. Anderson's salary is a figure Stephon knows as precisely as the seating capacity of the Carrier Dome.

Driving along, we pass beneath the elevated tracks over Stillwell Avenue, where four of New York City's subway lines come to an end. The Coney Island peninsula begins here; beyond the tracks are the projects. Few store owners will risk doing business out there, and the McDonald's near Stillwell is the last outpost of junk food before the streets plunge into the shadow of the high rises. We order our food to go and pile back into my car. Stephon, hungrily consuming his first burger, wedges himself between the two front seats in order to speak directly into his friend's ear. "So, Russell. What are they offering you?" Russell snatches his head away and stares out the window. "You mean you're just gonna sign?" Stephon goes on. "And then when you get to campus and see all them players driving those nice white Nissan Sentras, what are you gonna say to yourself? 'Oh well, I guess they got them from their *mothers*'?"

We ride along in hostile silence. As we drive down Mermaid Avenue toward the projects, the trees, shops, and pedestrians become scarcer, block by block. During the urban-renewal years, the city knocked down storefronts all along this stretch, but it abandoned much of its commercial-redevelopment plan after moving tenants into the projects. Now the only signs of life along some blocks are the drunks leaning against the plywood of boarded-up buildings and the mangy dogs scavenging vacant lots.

35   Russell says, "By the way, Stephon, the NCAA does *not* allow players to get cars."

"Ha! You think the NCAA gives a fuck about *cars*?" Stephon, still with his head next to Russell's, gives a shrill little laugh. "Why do you think the best players go where they go? 'Cause the schools promise to take care of them and their families. They say the magic word: *money.*" …

NOVEMBER

Heading toward Thanksgiving, Lincoln could not have asked for greater success. The team was undefeated, making headlines in all the major New York City dailies, and had received an invitation to play in San Diego in a Christmas tournament of the country's top high-school teams. Lincoln didn't just win its games either; the team routed its opponents by such lopsided scores that opposing coaches often shook their heads and remarked, "Those guys were *high-school* players?" Russell was scoring at will—in the team's first scrimmage he turned in an outrageous 46-point performance, missing only three of twenty-four field-goal attempts, then kept to that pace for the next several games. *The Hoop Scoop,* a recruiting newsletter, ranked him the sixth-best player in New York City, and he earned an honorable mention in the magazine *Street & Smith*'s nationwide basketball roundup.

Meanwhile Stephon was getting his burn, and then some. He started the season's first game (fifteen points, twelve assists) and every one thereafter. *New York Newsday,* under a half-page picture of the Lincoln team holding their smiling young point guard in their arms, announced the beginning of "the era of Stephon Marbury." Scouting reports were giving Stephon their top rating, and an assistant from Providence College showed up in Coney Island to watch Stephon practice one day, waving discreetly to the freshman—violating the intent, if not the letter, of NCAA rules designed to protect underclassmen from recruiters. "It's never too early to start showing interest," the coach whispered. Word of Stephon's prowess even reached a TV production company, which contacted Stephon about making a commercial, though when the NCAA informed the Marburys that accepting a fee might violate its rules, his father declined.

Off the court, however, there were some unwelcome developments. Stephon was working hard in his classes, hoping to break the pattern of academic failure set by his brothers, but his teachers were noticing that his book reports rarely included a period or a capital letter—not a good omen for the verbal portion of the SATs. As for Russell, he was scoring well on practice SAT exams, but when test day arrived he would panic and forget all his last-minute cramming, shaking his faith that hard work would eventually win the day. Years of bad schooling are coming back to haunt Russell just when he needs his education the most. Leaving the school building now, he looks exhausted, defeated, like a sullen factory worker at the end of a long shift.

40   Russell took the SATs yet again last weekend. Terry was planning to treat him to a celebratory dinner after the test. As we walk down the school steps, I ask how his date went. "I dissed her good. You should have seen it. Tell him, Corey." Corey says nothing, so Russell goes on. "She came up to me all nice and sweet, and I said, 'Get out of my sight! Don't bother me no more!'"

I'm stunned by this development. The last time I saw them together, Terry was sitting on Russell's lap in study hall, feeding him a bagel bite by bite. "What were you fighting about?"

"I don't know. I guess I was just in a bad mood because of the SATs." Russell drapes his arm over my shoulder. "Never let a girl see you sweat. Didn't your mother ever tell you that?" Russell emits a peculiar mirthless laugh. I look at Corey. He shrugs and traces a circle around his temple with his index finger.

The days are getting shorter now. By the time practice is over, the sun has long since dropped into its slot behind the Verrazano Narrows Bridge and the sky at twilight is covered with brooding clouds. Corey's older brother Willie owns a barbershop just off Flatbush Avenue in central Brooklyn, twenty minutes away. After practice Russell, Corey, and Stephon like to hang out there, and I usually give them a lift on my way home. As we drive past the brightly lit bodegas and rice-and-beans joints on Flatbush Avenue, fires rage out of metal drums, circled by hooded men trying to keep warm. Corey looks out the window and says in a high, fragile voice, "Oh no. I just *hate* it when the Negroes wear those hoods. Scary! Oh! So scary!" Everyone laughs and Corey lifts his own hood over his head. He knows that when he too walks around like that, cops will stop him and pedestrians will turn away from him in fear. "Only in America," he says.

I have yet to hear Corey talk much about colleges, so I ask him where he wants to play. "Oh, I'm thinking about some southern schools: Florida State, North Carolina, maybe Virginia. I hate it when it gets sharp and brisk out like this. My one rule is, I won't go anyplace where I got to wear one of them Eskimo coats." Corey's recruiting hasn't even begun, but he's already established the proper hedonistic frame of mind.

45   "Still got to pass those SATs," Russell warns.

"I'm not scared," Corey replies. "I do well on tests. Anyway, this should be our year to relax."

"That test is *hard*," says Stephon from the backseat. "I looked at it once and almost fainted. I read somewhere that David Robinson got a 1300. Is that possible?"

"I heard there are players who get other guys to take the test for them," Russell says. "How do they get away with that? Find someone who looks like them?"

This is not a good sign. One of Russell's friends at Grady, who had scored lower than he on practice tests, suddenly got his 700 and signed with a top program. Some Lincolnites have begun wondering whether Grady players are using stand-ins to take the test.

50 The NCAA and the college basketball industry have done much soul-searching in recent years over the SAT requirement, as well they should. A combined score of 700 may not seem like a terribly rigorous standard, but given the quality of the Lincoln players' schooling, it's not surprising that they don't know a synonym for *panache* or how to make the most of what they do know; they've never been told, for example, to avoid guessing and answer only the questions they're sure of—the kinds of test-taking tips suburban kids learn on their first day in a Stanley Kaplan review course. Russell's school average, now over 80, says a lot more about his determination to succeed, but that alone will get him nowhere.

DECEMBER

A few nights later, Russell, Stephon, Corey, and I are all in my car, making the usual rounds to Willie's. Stephon announces that he's going to get an X shaved into the back of his scalp. Russell is considering a center part like Larry Johnson's, the star of the Charlotte Hornets. As we approach the barbershop Corey says, "Don't be wasting time, all right?" When I ask why, he tells me a gang from a nearby project has been roaming lately. Last week a woman was hit by a stray bullet right outside the shop, so they all want to get their cuts and be gone.

To me, Coney Island's desolate project walkways and stairwells have always seemed more threatening than the raucous street life here along Flatbush Avenue. And, in fact, the few Lincoln players who live "across town"—Flatbush or Crown Heights or East New York—won't be caught dead in the Coney Island high rises ever since one of them spent the night at Corey's apartment and someone blew up a car right outside his window. But I am given to understand that in the patchwork of highly distinct neighborhoods that make up Brooklyn, a group of black teenagers will always be at risk outside their own turf. Wherever they go, the three are always scanning to see who might be coming up to them. One of their teammates was shot in the hand a few months ago. Another classmate was stabbed at a party recently; he's still in intensive care. "Something's happening, boy, every day, every day," says Russell.

As planned, they're in and out of Willie's in a flash and happy to be heading home in my car. Russell has been unusually quiet all evening. When I ask if something is bothering him, he tells me his mother has forbidden him to speak to me anymore. Apparently, she doesn't think it wise for him to talk to a reporter while his recruiting hangs in the balance. I tell Russell that this story won't appear until he's already off to college, but he says, "You don't understand. My mother's *crazy!*"

Stephon pipes in with some advice for me. "Just greet her at the door and hit her with a hundred. She'll change her mind." He snickers knowingly. "She's no different than my father. He wants to make sure he gets some loot." Lately, Mr. Marbury has been threatening to keep Stephon from talking to me unless I cut him a deal.

55 At first I think Stephon is missing the point—that Mrs. Thomas's suspicion of me and her desperation to get Russell out of Coney Island are entirely different from Mr.

Marbury's demand for money. But Corey sees the connection: "Damn," he says, "your parents must have had a hard life."

"Still do," Stephon replies. "Your father got himself a whole plumbing business. My father and Russell's mother got nothing." Stephon looks at me out of the corner of his eye and says, "You're thinking, *What a bunch of niggers*, right?"

The word just hangs in the air. I can't think of a thing to say. Over the last five months, I realize, I have tried to ignore our racial differences in an attempt at some broader understanding. Stephon's comment may be his way of telling me that understanding *begins* with race. "You got to think like a black man," he goes on, "got to learn how to say, 'Fuck it, fuck everybody, *fuck the whole damn thing.*' Now *that's* life in the ghetto."

"It's true!" Russell exclaims, his mood improving for the first time all evening. "My mother is a nigger! She's a black woman who does not give a damn."

"Man, I'm *tired* of all this shit!" Stephon slams his hands down hard on his book bag. "Somebody's got to make it, somebody's *got* to go all the way. How come this shit only happens to us Coney Island niggers?" He shakes his head wildly and laughs. "My father and Russell's mother—yeah, they're crazy, but it's about time there was a little something for the niggs."

60   "Something for the niggs!" Russell repeats the line with a hoot. "Yeah, Steph! Time to get outspoken!"

"You got it," Stephon says, and laughs again. Then Corey joins in. And they're all three whooping and slapping their knees—laughing at their parents and also, I imagine, at the absurdity of this whole situation.

Here they are, playing by all the rules: They stay in school—though their own school hardly keeps its end of the bargain. They say no to drugs—though it's the only fully employed industry around. They don't get into trouble with the NCAA—though its rules seem designed to foil them, and the coaches who break the rules go unpunished. They even heed their parents' wishes—and often pay a stiff price.

Of course none of them is perfect: Russell panics about his SATs and the choices he must make, and has trouble owning up to it; Corey won't apply himself and kids himself into thinking it won't matter; Stephon has—what shall we call it?—an attitude that needs some adjustment. But they operate in an environment that forgives none of the inevitable transgressions of adolescence and bestows no second chances.

Which makes this process of playing for a scholarship not the black version of the American dream, as some would suggest, but a cruel parody of it. In the classic parable you begin with nothing and slowly accrue your riches through hard work in a system designed to help those who help themselves. Here you begin with nothing but one narrow, treacherous path and then run a gauntlet of obstacles that merely reminds you of how little you have: recruiters pass themselves off as father figures, standardized tests humiliate you and reveal the wretchedness of your education, the promise of lucrative NBA contracts reminds you of what it feels like to have nothing in this world.

65   Jou-Jou, Silk, Chocolate, Spoon, Spice, Ice, Goose, Tiny, T, Stretch, Space, Sky: all of them great Coney Island players, most of them waiting vainly for a second chance, hanging out in the neighborhood, or dead. And here come Russell, Corey, and Stephon in my car, riding down Mermaid Avenue in the bone chill and gloom of this December night, still laughing about "the niggs," hoping for the best, and

knowing that in this particular game failure is commonplace, like a shrug, and heartbreak the order of the day.

EPILOGUE: WINTER 1993

In the spring of 1992, near the end of his senior year, Russell signed with Philadelphia's Temple University, whose team in recent years has regularly been among the nation's top twenty. But on his final SAT attempt, his score went down and Temple withdrew its scholarship offer. Rob Johnson brokered Russell into a Texas junior college known on the street as a "bandit" school, where his teammates seemed to carry more guns than schoolbooks. Desperately unhappy, Russell transferred after a week to a junior college near Los Angeles. There, this past winter, he was averaging twenty-six points per game and hoping that after two years he would be recruited by a four-year school and earn his degree.

Corey fell short' of a 700 on his SATs by ten points. He planned to spend a year at a prep school to brush up on his academics but filed his application for financial aid too late. He went to another junior college in Texas. Away from his girlfriends, Corey earned four B's and two A's in his first semester. He hopes to move on to a four-year school himself.

Stephon is now in his sophomore year. In the summer of 1992, he was among the four youngest players invited to the Nike all-American camp, an all-expenses-paid jamboree in Indianapolis for the 120 top high-school stars in the country. His play, before every Division I coach in the country, looked like a highlight film. Now four inches taller and dunking the ball, he is dominating the PSAL and should have his pick of top programs in his senior year, provided he can score 700 on the SATs and that neither he nor his father violates any recruiting rules.

And at the Garden, some of Coney Island's elders have organized nighttime shooting drills for the neighborhood's schoolchildren—eight years old and up—to prepare them for the road ahead.

Notes

1. Some New York City newspapers withheld Russell's name when reporting this incident. In keeping with the practice of withholding the names of minors involved in suicide threats or attempts, *Harper's Magazine* has changed Russell's name and the name of his mother in this article. No other names have been altered.

Rereading Actively

1. In a small group, summarize the essential character traits of Russell, Corey, Stephon, and the narrator, Frey. Write short descriptions of each in your journal.

2. What patterns does Frey find in the attitudes of Russell, Corey, and Stephon toward college? How do you respond to their attitude?

3. With a partner or in a small group, discuss what you take to be Frey's overall point.

4. Frey followed these young men for a year. With a partner, pick two passages where he reveals his feelings about them, and discuss how these passages help to develop Frey's overall point.

5. How do Frey's final paragraphs and his discussion of the success and failure of his subjects, and the continued emphasis of their neighborhood on basketball, affect your reading of his narrative?

Exploring Your Responses

6. In a page or two in your journal, recall the decision-making process you went through in choosing to go to college, touching on how you gained entrance, what obstacles you had to overcome, what talents you brought, and how the school responded to you.

7. With two or three classmates, discuss the way higher education treats students. Start by talking about the experience of student athletes that is outlined by Frey; then, move on to discuss how universities treat other student assets like brains, money, ethnicity, creativity, and so on. Evaluate the exchanges that students and colleges make with one another.

8. In a freewrite, compare and contrast your view of college with that of one of the central characters.

WHY YOUNG WOMEN ARE MORE CONSERVATIVE
GLORIA STEINEM

As co-founder of Ms. *magazine, Gloria Steinem is one of the best known American feminists. She has written broadly about the status of women in American society, frequently talking about how a consumer culture—through advertising, entertainment, and the defining characteristics of the consumer—maintains conservative, patriarchal roles for women. This essay appeared in* Ms. *in 1979 with the title, "The Good News Is: These Are Not the Best Years of Your Life." It was revised for the first edition of* Outrageous Acts and Everyday Rebellions *(1983), and updated for the second edition (1995). Surprised by the relative conservatism of the female college students she met in the late 1970s, Steinem—a writer committed to activism—looks for reasons and concludes that while women may study harder in college than men, they don't learn to challenge the limits their society imposes on them.*

If you had asked me a decade or more ago, I certainly would have said the campus was the first place to look for a feminist or any other revolution. I also would have assumed that student-age women, like student-age men, were much more likely to be activists and open to change than their parents. After all, campus revolts have a long and well-publicized tradition, from the students of medieval France, whose "heresy" was suggesting that the university be separate from the church, through the anticolonial student riots of British India; from students who led the cultural revolution of the People's Republic of China, to campus demonstrations against the Shah of Iran. Even in this country where there is far less tradition of student activism, the populist movement to end the war in Vietnam was symbolized by campus protests and mistrust of anyone over thirty.

It has taken me many years of traveling as a feminist speaker and organizer to understand that I was wrong about women; at least, about women acting on their own behalf. In activism as in so many other things, I had been educated to assume that men's cultural pattern was the natural or the only one: if student years were the peak time of rebellion and openness to change for men, then the same must be true for women. In fact, a decade of listening to every kind of women's group—from brown-bag lunchtime lectures organized by office workers to all-night rap sessions at campus women's centers; from housewives' self-help groups to campus rallies—has convinced me that the reverse is more often true. Women may be the one group that grows more radical with age. Though some young feminists are big exceptions to this rule, women in general don't begin to challenge the politics of our own lives until later.

Looking back, I realize that this pattern has been true for my life, too. My college years were full of uncertainties and the personal conservatism that comes from trying to win approval and fit into the proper grown-up and womanly role, whether that means finding a well-to-do man to be supported by or a male radical to support. Nonetheless, I went right on assuming that brave exploring youth and cowardly conservative old age were the norms for everybody, and that I must be just an isolated and guilty accident. Though every generalization based on female culture has many exceptions and should never be used as a crutch or excuse, I think we might be less hard on ourselves and other students, feel better about our potential for change as we grow older—and educate reporters who announce feminism's demise because its red-hot center is not on campus—if we figured out that for most of us as women, the traditional college period is an unrealistic and cautious time. Consider a few of the reasons.

As students, women are probably treated with more equality than we ever will be again. For one thing, we're consumers. The school is only too glad to get the tuitions we pay, or our families or government grants pay on our behalf. With population rates declining because of women's increased power over childbearing, that money is even more vital to a school's existence. Yet unlike most consumers, students are too transient to have much power as a group. If our families are paying our tuition, we may have even less power.

5   As young women, whether students or not, we're also still in the stage most valued by male-dominant cultures: we have our full potential as workers, wives, sex partners, and childbearers.

That means we haven't yet experienced the life events that are most radicalizing for women: entering the paid-labor force and discovering how women are treated there; marrying and finding out that it is not yet an equal partnership; having children and discovering who raises them and who does not; and aging, still a far greater penalty for women than for men.

Furthermore, new ambitions nourished by the rebirth of feminism may make young women behave a little like a classical immigrant group. We are determined to prove ourselves, to achieve academic excellence, and to prepare for interesting and successful careers. More noses are kept to more grindstones in an effort to demonstrate newfound abilities, and perhaps to allay suspicions that women still need more and better credentials than men. This doesn't leave much time for activism. Indeed, we may not yet know that it is necessary.

In addition, the very progress into previously all-male careers that is revolutionary for women may be interpreted as conservative and conformist by outside critics. Assuming male radicalism to be the measure of change, they assume any concern with careers is evidence of "campus conservatism." In fact, "dropping out" may be radical for men, but "dropping in" is radical for women. Progress lies in the direction we have not been.

Like most groups of the newly arrived, our faith in education and paper degrees also has yet to be shaken. For instance, the percentage of women enrolled in colleges and universities has been increasing at the same time that the percentage of men has been decreasing. Among students entering college in 1978, women *outnumbered* men for the first time.[1] This hope of excelling at the existing game is probably reinforced by the cultural pressure on young females to be "good girls" and observe somebody else's rules.

10   Though we may know intellectually that we need to have new games with new rules, we probably haven't quite absorbed such facts as the high unemployment rate among female Ph.Ds; the lower average salary among female college graduates of all races than among their male counterparts who graduated from high school or less; the middle-management ceiling against which even those eagerly hired new business-school graduates seem to bump their heads after five or ten years; and the barrier-breaking women in nontraditional fields who become the first fired when recession hits. Sadly enough, we may have to personally experience some of these reality checks before we accept the idea that lawsuits, activism, and group pressure will have to accompany our individual excellence and crisp new degrees.

Then there is the female guilt trip, student edition. If we're not sailing along as planned, it must be *our* fault. If our mothers didn't "do anything" with their educations, it must have been *their* fault. If we can't study as hard as we think we should (because women still have to be better prepared than men), and have a substantial personal and sexual life at the same time (because women are supposed to need relationships more than men do), then we feel inadequate, as if each of us were individually at fault for a problem that is actually culture-wide.

I've yet to be on a campus where most women weren't worrying about some aspect of combining marriage, children, and a career. I've yet to find one where many men were worrying about the same thing. Yet women will go right on suffering from the terminal guilt of this double-role problem until men are encouraged, pressured, or otherwise forced, individually and collectively, to integrate themselves into the "women's work" of raising children and homemaking. Until then, and until there are changed job patterns to allow equal parenthood, children will go right on growing up with the belief that only women can be loving and nurturing, and only men can be intellectual or active outside the home. Each half of the world will go on limiting its full range of human talent.

Finally, there is the intimate political training that hits women in the teens and early twenties: the countless ways we are still brain-washed into assuming that women are dependent on men for our basic identities, both in our work and our personal lives, much more than vice versa. After all, if we're going to enter a marriage system that's still legally designed for a person and a half, submit to an economy in which women still average about fifty-nine cents on the dollar earned by men,[2] and work mainly as support staff and assistants, or *co*-directors and *vice*-presidents, then we have to be convinced that we are not whole people on our own.

In order to make sure we will see ourselves as half-people, and thus be addicted to getting our identity from serving others, society tries hard to convert young women into "man junkies"; that is, into people who are addicted to male-approval and presence. Both professionally and personally, we need a man standing next to us, actually and figuratively, whether it's at work, on Saturday night, or throughout life. (If only men realized how little it matters *which* man is standing there, they would understand that this addition depersonalizes them, too.) Given the danger to a male-dominant system if young women stop internalizing this political message of a derived identity, it's no wonder that those who try to kick the addiction—and, worse yet, to help other women do the same—are likely to be regarded as odd or dangerous by everyone from parents to peers.

15   When all that pressure combines with little experience, it's no wonder that younger women are often less able to support each other. Even young women who espouse feminist goals as individuals may refrain from identifying themselves as "feminist": it's okay to want equal pay for yourself (just one small reform) but it's not okay to want equal pay for women as a group (an economic revolution). Some retreat into individualized career obsessions as a way of avoiding this dangerous discovery of shared experience with women as a group. Others retreat into the safe middle ground of "I'm not a feminist but...." Still others become politically active, but only on issues that are taken seriously by their male counterparts.

The same lesson about the personal conservatism of younger women is taught by the history of feminism. If I hadn't been conned into believing the masculine stereotype of youth as the "natural" time for freedom and rebellion, a time of "sowing wild oats" that is made possible by the assurance of power and security later on, I could have figured out the female pattern by looking at women's movements of the past.

In this country, for instance, the nineteenth-century wave of feminism was started by older women who had been through the radicalizing experience of getting married and becoming the legal chattel of their husbands (or the equally radicalizing experience of *not* getting married and being treated as spinsters). Most of them had also worked in the antislavery movement and learned from the political parallels between race and sex. In other countries, that wave was also led by women who were past the point of maximum pressure toward marriageability and conservatism.

Looking at the early years of this second wave, it's clear that feminist activist and consciousness-raising groups were organized by women who had experienced the civil rights movement, or homemakers who had discovered that raising kids and cooking didn't occupy all their talents. While most campuses were still circulating the names of illegal abortionists privately (after all, abortion could damage our marriage value), slightly older women were holding press conferences and speakouts about the reality of abortions (including their own, even though that often meant confessing to an illegal act) and demanding reform or repeal of anti-choice laws. Though rape had been a quiet epidemic on campus for generations, younger women victims were still understandably fearful of speaking up, and campuses encouraged silence in order to retain their reputation for safety with tuition-paying parents. It took many off-campus speakouts, demonstrations against laws of evidence and police procedures, and testimonies in state legislatures before student groups began to make demands on campus and local cops for greater rape protection. In fact, "date rape"—the common campus phenomenon of a young woman being raped by someone she knows, perhaps even gangraped by several students in a fraternity house—is still being exposed. Marital rape, a more difficult legal issue, was taken up several years before. As for battered women and the attendant exposé of husbands and lovers as more statistically dangerous than unknown muggers in the street, that issue still seems to be thought of as a largely noncampus concern, yet at many of the colleges and universities where I've spoken, there has been at least one case within current student memory of a young woman beaten or murdered by a jealous lover.

This cultural pattern of youthful conservatism makes the growing number of older women going back to school very important. They are life examples and pragmatic activists who radicalize women young enough to be their daughters. The campus is becoming a major place for such cross-generational connections.

20 None of this should denigrate the courageous efforts of young women, and the many changes they've pioneered. On the contrary, they should be seen as even more remarkable for surviving the conservative pressures, recognizing societal problems they haven't yet fully experienced, and organizing successfully in the midst of a transient student population. Every women's history course, rape hot line, or campus newspaper that is finally covering *all* the news; every feminist professor whose job has been created or tenure saved by student pressure, or male administrator whose consciousness has been permanently raised; every counselor who's stopped guiding women one way and men another; every lawsuit that's been fueled by student energies against unequal athletic funds or graduate school requirements—all those accomplishments are even more impressive when seen against the backdrop of the female pattern of activism.

Finally, it would help to remember that a feminist revolution rarely resembles a masculine-style one; just as a young woman's most radical act toward her mother (that is, connecting as women in order to help each other get some power) doesn't look much like a young man's most radical act toward his father (that is, breaking the father-son connection in order to separate identities or take over existing power).

It's those father-son conflicts at a generational, national level that have often provided the conventional definition of revolution; yet they've gone on for centuries without basically changing the role of the female half of the world. They have also failed to reduce the level of violence in society, since both fathers and sons have included some degree of aggressiveness and superiority to women in their definition of masculinity, thus preserving the anthropological model of dominance.

Furthermore, what current leaders and theoreticians define as revolution is usually little more than taking over the army and the radio stations. Women have much more in mind than that. We have to uproot the sexual caste system that is the most pervasive power structure in society, and this means transforming the patriarchal values of those who run the institutions, whether they are politically the "right" or the "left," the fathers or the sons. This cultural part of the change goes very deep, and is often seen as too intimate, and perhaps too threatening, to be considered either serious or possible. Only conflicts among men are "serious." Only a takeover of existing institutions is "possible."

That's why the definition of "political," on campus as elsewhere, tends to be limited to who's running for president, who's demonstrating against corporate investments in South Africa, or which is the "moral" side of some conventional revolution, preferably one that is thousands of miles away.

25 As important as such activities are, they are also the most comfortable ones for the young. They provide a sense of virtue without much disruption in the power structure of our daily lives. Even when the most consistent energies on campus are actually concentrated around feminist issues, they may be treated as apolitical and invisible. Asked "What's happening on campus?" a student may reply, "The anti-nuke move-

ment," even though that resulted in one demonstration of two hours, while student anti-rape squads have been patrolling the campus every night for two years, and women's studies are transforming the very textbooks we read.

No wonder reporters and sociologists looking for revolution on campus often miss the depth of feminist change and activity. Women students themselves may dismiss it as not political, not serious. Certainly, it rarely comes in the masculine style of bombing buildings or burning draft cards. In fact, it goes much deeper than protesting a temporary symptom—say, the draft or military spending—and challenges the paradigm for the right of one group to dominate another, which is the disease itself.

Young women have a big task in resisting pressures and challenging definitions. Their increasing success is a miracle of foresight and courage that should make us all proud. But they should know that they, too, may grow more radical with age.

One day, an army of gray-haired women may quietly take over the earth.

—1979

Postscript

Two more reasons for this cultural pattern have come to light in the past decade and a half—plus one stage that comes before such gender-role conservatism begins.

30   First, studies have now shown that the form and content of education itself often diminishes young women's self-esteem. Because females are so rarely honored in authority in textbooks—and in higher education, they are also less likely to be authorities in the classroom or administration—many young women come to believe that, though they may get good grades by memorizing what others have done and thought, they cannot achieve or create on their own.

Second, there is now a greater understanding of the prevalence and impact of child abuse in general, and sexual abuse in particular—in which two-thirds of the victims are females and nine-tenths of the victimizers are males. Powerlessness, guilt, shame, withdrawal, and a feeling of having no value other than a sexual one: all these are results that become more acute with the sexual awakening of teenage years. Yet confronting this abuse and healing its effects rarely begin until young women are no longer dependent on their families. If the abuse has been severe, this may require many years of distance and safety, or begin only after the death of the parent or other abuser.

For both these reasons, women may take longer to become active on our own behalf. But there are other new insights that may reduce the waiting time. Carol Gilligan's research has shown that there is often a stronger sense of self before eleven or twelve when the "feminine" role descends. If that voice could be supported and strengthened, the years of gender restriction could be shortened—not just at their end but before their beginning.

—1995

Notes

1. This was also because more older women than older men were returning for a higher education, a trend that has continued. By 1990, according to the National Center for Education Statistics, one-third of all women enrolled in institutions of higher learning were at least thirty years old—double the comparable proportion in 1970, before the impact of the women's movement.

2. By 1992, the latest year figures were available from the Bureau of Labor Statistics, women were up to seventy-five cents on the dollar.

Rereading Actively

1. In the opening paragraphs, Steinem identifies herself as a "feminist speaker and organizer" (¶ 2) and notes that her theory about college women was wrong. How does this introduction help her accomplish her purpose in this essay?

2. How does Steinem relate her topic to her own life, and how does that connection affect your reading of the essay? In a journal entry, summarize your sense of the writer of this essay.

3. With a partner or in a small group, review the article, discussing what issues Steinem places at the center of the college experience and how those issues affect women and men. Differentiate between the experience women have in college and the one she thinks they ought to have. Write a page or two in your journal describing your group's conversation.

4. In a small group, review Steinem's use of the terms "conservative" and "radical," discuss how you respond to these terms, and summarize the "reasons" (¶ 4–8) female college students tend to be more conservative, according to Steinem.

5. What surprises you about the contributions Steinem believes feminist activism has made to college education? Write a response to two contributions that caught your attention.

6. Summarize Steinem's 1995 postscript (¶ 29–32), and explain how it changes the impact of the 1979 essay.

Exploring Your Responses

7. Freewrite about what college education means for you as a man or woman, looking beyond the classroom to the personal and social experiences that go along with studying. Review your thoughts and compare them with Steinem's.

8. In a page or two in your journal, describe an activity that you engage in that reveals your conservatism or radicalism when it comes to gender roles.

9. In a same-sex group of three or four students, discuss and evaluate Steinem's analysis of gender relationships, noting points where you agree and disagree with her and with one another. Be prepared to tell the class how accurate your group finds her assessment and what points your group just can't agree about.

Is Education a Great Equalizer?
Ira Shor

Ira Shor is a teacher and a social activist who has been an important voice in the call for educational reform. The author of numerous articles and books on the subject, including Culture Wars *(1986),* Critical Teaching and Everyday Life *(1987), and* Empowering Education *(1992), Shor is widely recognized as one of the most important leftist educational theorists in the United States. Since 1971, Shor has taught in the City University of New York system. Often working with first-generation, working-class college students, Shor has drawn on the teaching theory of Paulo Freire to discover an approach to education that puts the student learner at the center of the process. In this excerpt from* Empowering Education, *Shor tries to analyze how education fits into the American exchange.*

It is worth looking closely to see if education, dominated by teacher-talk and Euro-centric culture, has been a great equalizer. Has society been made more equal by providing more traditional schooling? The record is not encouraging, especially if we focus on race. In recent decades, minorities dramatically narrowed the gap between themselves and whites in terms of high school graduation. For example, nonwhites from 25 to 29 years old have made impressive educational gains. Some 82 percent of them had gone through at least high school by 1986, up from 12.1 percent in 1940, almost equal to the 86.6 percent of whites their same age who also finished secondary education (Digest of Education Statistics, 1989). In addition, Mortenson and Wu (1990) found that from 1972 to 1989 African-Americans from 18 to 24 years old had improved their high school graduation rate from 64.2 percent to 72.6 percent, while the white rate had only inched up from 83.3 percent to 83.8 percent. As more African-Americans were finishing high school, more were also taking the Scholastic Aptitude Test (SAT) for college entry. Despite an *increasing* number of African-Americans taking the SAT, which tends to depress overall scores, these minority students managed to *raise* their composite SAT scores 64 points by 1991, narrowing the historic 258-point gap between them and their white counterparts, as white students' scores stagnated from the 1970s on (College Board, 1991). But despite an increasing high-school graduation rate and higher scores on the SAT, the National Assessment of Education Progress, and the American College Testing Program, African-American high-school seniors had less access to college and less change of staying in college and graduating than whites. In a study of this racial inequity, Mortenson (1991) observed:

> The college access rates for black high school graduates declined sharply between 1978 and 1983, the same period that white college access rates were increasing.... Baccalaureate degree attainment rates for white high school graduates have increased slightly during the 1980s, while the rate for blacks has dropped sharply. The failure of the black experience in higher education is all the more striking given the substantial improvement in preparation for college by blacks in elementary and secondary education. (vi)

Given the higher graduation rates and test scores of African-Americans and the flattened rates and scores for whites, Mortenson concluded that the increased access of whites and decreased access of African-Americans to college degrees was "the sharpest imaginable contrast." Greater achievement did not produce greater equality in higher education for this disadvantaged group.

Compounding racial inequality, lower family income also works against the collegiate aspirations of nonelite students. Schmitt (1989) found that only 6.8 percent of poorer high-school seniors from the 1980 class had graduated from college six years later. Mortenson and Wu (1990) further reported:

> In 1989 a student from the bottom quartile of the family income distribution ...had a 6 percent chance of graduating from high school, enrolling in college, and graduating by age 24. If the student came from the second family income quartile ...his or her chances doubled to about 12 percent. At the next income quartile... the student's chances doubled again to about 27 percent. And between the third and top family income quartile...the student's chances redoubled again to about 55 percent. (124)

In community colleges enrolling five million students in the United States, where poorer groups and minorities are overrepresented, less than 500,000 two-year degrees are awarded each year, suggesting that fewer than 20 percent of these collegians graduate within four semesters (American Council on Education 1990). According to Goodlad (1990), 55 percent of African-Americans and 51 percent of Latinos who enter college do not have a degree twelve years later, while the same figure for whites is 33 percent. As of 1988, 16.8 percent of whites from 25 to 29 years old had completed four years of college compared to 9.4 percent of African-Americans and 8.1 percent for Hispanics (*Digest of Education Statistics,* 1989).

Unequal access to college degrees means unequal access to the best-paying jobs, which require college credentials. But even college graduation cannot guarantee income equity. Meisenheimer (1990) reported that in 1979 the median income of African-American male college graduates was 84 percent of the white male incomes in the 25 to 64 age group; ten years later the income differential had slipped to 76 percent. For younger men, 25 to 34, the ten-year decline was a little steeper, from 89 percent of the whites' income to 79 percent, but younger African-American women in this age group were able to improve their income position vis-à-vis younger white women, from 76 percent to 89 percent in the ten-year period. Equally striking is the report that in 1987 the median income of African-American males over 25 who had graduated from college was about the same as whites who had only graduated from high school, approximately $26,550 (U.S. Census Bureau, 1989).

To see educational gains failing to translate into economic gains for discriminated groups, another place to look is the comparative unemployment rates of whites and minorities. Here, too, the evidence is not encouraging in terms of education being a great equalizer. The overall minority unemployment rate from the 1950s through the 1980s stayed virtually the same, in good times and bad, at about *twice* the unemployment rate of whites, despite the long-term advance in minority educational achievement (*Monthly Labor Review,* 1989).

5   If education is a strong equalizer, we could at least expect some employment equity over the decades, just as we could expect rising high-school achievement to produce higher rates of African-American college success. Some explanations for this declining college success rate could be found in government economic policy in the 1980s, which produced an increasing number of people below the poverty line, weakening the financial floor under people of color, who are disproportionately represented in lower income groups. Further, higher college costs, more restrictive entry exams, lower federal aid to schools and colleges, loan programs replacing grants and scholarships, more required remediation, and increasing racist incidents on campus in the 1980s are among the other factors that may have discouraged students of color from attending college or completing their course of study.

The rising educational achievement of African-Americans in particular and their failure to achieve equality of employment, income, and access to college degrees suggest that the causes of inequality are rooted in the system, not in personal or group deficits. Discriminated groups have been demonstrating higher educational achievement in school and on standardized tests, but society is not rewarding these gains. Educational gains apparently cannot wipe out economic and social inequality, though some determined individuals from discriminated groups can move up through the system. Schooling can at best offer personal success stories for some students who start out at the bottom, but it cannot by itself equalize society.

Personal Success and Systemic Failures

Despite the weakness of education in reducing inequality, some disadvantaged students do use schooling to move up. The standard syllabus works for them. Teacher-talk in traditional education can be thought of as a cultural donation that a few can use to personal advantage, but not something that whole groups can employ to improve their unequal position in school and society.

Academic knowledge, correct usage, and work discipline cannot be drilled into the *bulk* of students to make them academic achievers and job-market successes. Only some students from poor, minority, or working-class homes can break the standard language and knowledge codes. This is not because only some are intelligent. They all possess intelligence. But only a fraction experience a peculiar blend of circumstances that makes them the academic cream of the crop, positioned for upward mobility. The peculiar blend of conditions that siphons off-some for upward mobility includes access to the limited amount of excellent instruction available in poorly funded schools, a stable home that maintains a floor of support under a child selected for success, some extra resources or attention directed at the child's development, and a disposition in the child toward print materials and language learning, so that the child from a home where nonstandard English is spoken is oriented towards breaking the usage code and behavior rules favored by teacher-talk. (There are also exceptional children who will rise no matter how much *bad* is done *to* them or how little *good* is done *for* them.)

Individuals from minority groups and the lower classes who use teacher-talk and Eurocentric culture to climb up need bulldog stamina to tolerate the tedium of passive schooling, the indignity of surrendering their speaking idiom for an elite one, and the long delay in rewards from the job market. About this prolonged self-denial, McLaren (1989) wrote that "For many economically disadvantaged students, success in school means a type of forced cultural suicide, and in the case of minority youth, racial suicide" (215). He referred to anthropologist John Ogbu, who examined the plight of minority students trying to use school for upward mobility. Ogbu found that

> blacks and similar minorities (e.g., American Indians) believe that for a minority person to succeed in school academically, he or she must learn to think and act white. Furthermore, in order to think and act white enough to be rewarded by whites or white institutions like the schools, a minority person must give up his or her own minority-group attitudes, ways of thinking, and behaving.... That is, striving for success is a subtractive process: the individual black student following school standard practices that lead to academic success is perceived as adopting a white cultural frame of reference...as acting white. (Quoted in McLaren 1989, 212)

Students from minority, female, and working-class groups face special challenges and sacrifices when trying to "make it" through education. Many face the painful choice between allegiance to their roots or to success.

10   Upwardly mobile individuals make headway partly because of their tolerance for teacher-talk and their patience in awaiting future payoffs, and partly because the huge numbers of peers left behind *do not rise with them*, and thus do not overtax the limited

rewards in the job market. The successful lower-class student partly owes her or his success to the many who drop out of high school or don't go on to graduate from college—which is the vast majority.

Limited upward mobility helps maintain an unequal society. For the status quo to remain what it is, the economic system needs a *high* drop-out rate and a flow of *some* lower-class climbers up the ranks. If the situation were reversed, an unequal society like that of the United States would face a crisis. That is, a *low* dropout rate and a *high* graduation rate would create serious pressures. If masses of students succeeded in school and college, the economic system could not possibly meet their expectations. On the one hand, wealth is not distributed equitably to those who work for it. Only some college graduates enter professions with good starting salaries (engineers, lawyers, doctors). On the other hand, even in the best of times there are not enough good-paying jobs to reward a mass of high achievers. The traditional curriculum of one-way teacher-talk, pervasive tracking, standardized tests, basic skills drills, memorized information, standard usage, and dull commercial textbooks is a program structured to produce the high degree of failure that relieves the unequal economic system of the need to reward a mass of high-achieving graduates.

To maintain inequality, then, the system needs a limited number of individuals who climb up and are certified for success, along with a mass of people certified as mediocre and blaming themselves for their own failures. Low scores on literacy and placement tests, and *D*'s in English, provide apparently nonpolitical, scientific means for sorting out the gifted few (Clark 1960; Owen 1985; Meier 1989). Teacher-talk, a frontal pedagogy that denies student culture, contributes to depressing the achievement and aspirations of nonelite students.

Critical dialogue opposes all mechanisms for sustaining inequality. Dialogue has a *majoritarian* interest in the rights, voices, and potential of nonelite groups, not a philanthropic interest in the rise of a few individuals. It is a critical thinking curriculum for the majority who lack power, in a project oriented to questioning inequality in school and society.

Teaching for the Majority: Dialogue Against Inequality

Inequality has been an unstable arrangement throughout history, but some periods are more stable than others. The political fit of teacher-talk with regenerating inequality in each new generation can produce stability only as long as failing students tolerate lesser schooling, lesser jobs, and political disempowerment. The dilemma since the youth rebellion of the 1960s has been the refusal of many students to accept their own subordination. Some of their resistance to authority has included self-destructive drug and alcohol addictions, sexual license and teenage pregnancy, violence and reckless behavior, sabotage of teacher-talk and the official syllabus, defiant anti-intellectualism, and work alienation on the job. The disaffection of the young means that the high failure rate of education adds to social instability. But the contradiction is that the economic system requires a high failure rate to maintain inequality, making educational and social life unstable. Inequality in the economic system would have to be transformed to reward higher achievement in schools and colleges.

15   Teacher-talk cannot solve these problems. It creates problems. Teacher-talk generates underachievement and alienation. It will continue to do so until teachers and

students develop mutual dialogue. By itself, dialogic education cannot change inequality in society or guarantee success in the job market. But it can change the students' experience of learning, encouraging them to learn more and to develop the intellectual and affective powers to think about transforming society. The power to think critically and to act constructively; the power to study in depth, to understand school, society, work, politics, and our lives; and the power to feel hopeful about an equitable future—these are some of the goals embraced by dialogue when teachers and students accept the invitation.

REFERENCES

American Council on Education. 1990. *Community and junior colleges: A recent profile.* Washington, D.C.: American Council on Education.

Clark, Burton. 1960. The cooling-out function in higher education. *American Journal of Sociology* 65 (May): 569–76.

College Board. 1991. *College-bound seniors: 1991 profile of SAT and achievement test takers.* New York: College Board.

Digest of Education Statistics. 1989. Washington, D.C.: Department of Education.

Goodlad, John. 1990. *Teachers for our nation's schools.* San Francisco: Jossey-Bass.

McLaren, Peter. 1989. *Life in schools: An introduction to a critical pedagogy in the foundations of education.* New York: Longman.

Meier, Terry. 1989. The case against standardized achievement tests. *Rethinking Schools* 3 (January-February): 9–12.

Meisenheimer, Joseph R. 1990. Black college graduates in the labor market, 1979 and 1989. *Monthly Labor Review* 113 (November): 13–21.

Monthly Labor Review. 1989. Selected Issues, Washington, D.C.: Department of Commerce.

Mortenson, Thomas G. 1991. *Equity of higher educational opportunity for women, black, Hispanic, and low income students.* ACT Student Financial Aid Research Report series, no. 91-1, January 1991. Iowa City: American College Testing Program.

Mortenson, Thomas G., and Zhijun Wu. 1990. *High school graduation and college preparation of young adults, by family income and background, 1970–1989.* Report no. 90-3, September 1990. Iowa City: American College Testing Program.

Owen, David. 1985. *None of the above: Behind the myth of scholastic aptitude.* Boston: Houghton Mifflin.

Schmitt, Carl. 1989. *Changes in educational attainment: A comparison among 1972 and 1980 and 1982 high school seniors.* Report no. C589413, Office of Educational Research and Improvement, April 1989, Washington, D.C.: U.S. Department of Education.

United States Census Bureau. 1989. *Current population reports.* Series P-60, no. 162. Consumer income. February, Washington, D.C.: Department of Commerce.

Rereading Actively

1. Summarize Shor's argument about the failure of "traditional schooling" to act as an "equalizer" (¶ 1).

2. In the first half of this excerpt, Shor presents many statistics. Why does he do this, and how might all the numbers affect readers?

3. In a small group or with a partner, identify references to the term "teacher-talk," and discuss its meaning. Try to write a definition for the term. Does Shor use it consistently? Does the term seem to have a fairly concrete meaning, or is it kind of vague?

4. With a partner, discuss the most surprising claim Shor makes about teacher-talk education. Describe this claim in your journal, and explain your response to it.

5. Explain the purpose of education that is implied in Shor's final paragraph. How might a proponent of teacher-talk education respond to the final paragraph?

Exploring Your Responses

6. Freewrite a description of your life as a student in which you compare your own experience as a student with Shor's picture of school. Using his data and claims, describe your life as a student.

7. In an entry in your journal, explore your position on whether education should act as an equalizer, using your own experience as evidence.

8. With two or three classmates, discuss your experience with teacher-talk and dialogue in high school and college, noting which style was used when and what effect each has. Evaluate these two teaching styles and Shor's position on them.

CASE-IN-POINT ASSIGNMENTS

When people talk about the "college premium," they are referring to economic advantage that accrues to those who earn bachelor's degrees. According to W. Michael Cox and Richard Alm in *Myths of the Rich and Poor* (1999), college graduates can expect to earn an average of $16,500 more a year than high school graduates.

The case-in-point readings detail just how difficult it is to define "higher education" in a consumer culture. As an element in a culture of exchange, education functions according to supply and demand. Sellers try to attract buyers with ads and information that proclaim quality, reputation, and services, but also with discounts and subsidies; buyers consider value and quality, but are also attracted (and distracted) by brand names, styles, and loyalties. At a basic level, these educational institutions reinforce social stability, prepare well-trained workers (who will buy goods and services as well as create them), develop new technology, and discover new ways to manage information, all important components in a productive and open economy and culture. Picking up on terms like choice, core curriculum, cost/benefit analysis, and accessibility, these writers document how campuses fashion the educational experience and what students (and their parents) expect to get from the university. In the following writing assignments, you will have a chance to compare your experience as a college student with a set of stories, statistics, and trends that represent aspects of life on campus.

Making Connections

1. Drawing on the perspective of students described by Traub and Steinem, analyze your role as a customer at your college. Focus on how your choices, behavior, and success/failure are or are not those of a consumer. Use your conclusion to explore your feelings about the position you're in.

2. Traub and Shor talk about how faculty do and should negotiate the educational marketplace. Drawing on their ideas, narrate your experience with a professor and speculate about why they do the things they do.

3. Steinem and Frey talk about college as it is experienced from outside the mainstream. Brainstorm your own uniqueness as a student—no one is purely mainstream—and write an essay that explains your personal and social needs as a student and evaluates how well college is serving you.

4. Use Steinem's analysis of women's experience in college and Hedegaard's profile of a white, upper-middle-class male's experience to frame an exploration of how your gender and class are affecting your experience in school.

5. Write a profile of yourself as a college student. Short profiles center on a theme: for example, Steinem focuses on gender; Hedegaard, on socializing; Frey, on winning it big; Shor, on creating equality. So, start by brainstorming themes that define your experience as a student, from career goals to friendships to technology to athletics and beyond. Focusing on a theme, describe a week of your life, showing how your theme affects the college experience that you are buying.

6. Going to college for many of us means moving away from home—one of the most fundamental and sometimes difficult transitions we make as we pursue higher education. Even if we continue to live in our home places while attending school, we contend with the new surroundings and routines of our class schedules and campus. Using one or two readings from Chapter 9, "Our Places, Our Selves," reflect on your experiences of going to school, focusing on the transitions you have had to make in learning your way in new surroundings. In what ways has this side of your educational experience influenced your feelings about learning and the things you have learned?

Collaborative Exchanges

1. With two or three classmates, discuss the processes that brought you to college (parental guidance, personal ambition, apathy, test scores, tradition, and so on), noting similarities and differences. As a group, describe each of your paths as a category that students fall into—traditional college student, class jumper, party animal, and so on. Be prepared to share your categories with the class and to discuss their relative merits.

2. As a class, read Steinem and Hedegaard, and then in same-sex groups of three of four students, talk about how gender affects student life at your school. Be prepared to share a report of your discussion and to compare your experience with that described in the readings.

3. With two or three classmates, review the images of the modern university painted by Shor and Traub and deliberate on what a good education is and whether a school like the University of Phoenix can deliver one. Be prepared to debate the topic with other groups.

Net Approaches

1. Go to the home pages of a community college, a liberal arts college, and a public university and search each one for discussions of the connection between an education and a career. These discussions will appear in mission statements, in recruitment pitches aimed at students, in career service department pages, and in other places. Draft a brief report that compares

and contrasts the three positions. Be prepared to explain which kind of institution best fits your goals.

2. Visit the most recent *U.S. News and World Report* ranking of undergraduate institutions. (You can find the page by visiting the *U.S. News and World Report* Web site <www.usnews.com> and working your way in.) Once you've found the entry page to the ranking, take the URL to AltaVista and do a link search. To do this, go to AltaVista <www.altavista.com> and enter into the search box the string: *link:URL*. (Replace *URL* with the address of the ranking page.) Notice who makes use of this well-known ranking. Scroll through the hits and note five surprising ones. Then, return to the ranking page and see where your school ranks. Be prepared to share your discoveries with the class.

3. Go to <www.hotbot.com> and search the following string: *(university of phoenix) and criticism.* Visit five interesting hits and note what they have to say about the University of Phoenix; then, visit the University of Phoenix page <www.uophx.edu> and see whether the criticism seems to be justified. Be prepared to share with the class the URLs of the critics, a summary of their criticism, and your impressions of the actual University of Phoenix page.

WRITING PROJECTS

EDUCATION

Project 1

Likely Readings

Background Readings
- Carger
- Edmundson
- Tompkins

Case-in-Point Readings
- Frey
- Hedegaard
- Steinem

Task and Purpose

Use your experience as a student to analyze the health of contemporary education. First, read through your notes and journal writing for this unit and identify a set of principles that are at the center of the current discussion about education. Then, catalogue your experience as a student, writing down the issues that have defined your experience. As you look at these two lists, narrow your scope to one or two issues where your experience intersects with the principles developed in the reading, and brainstorm a set of situations in which you personally had to deal with these issues. Explain these experiences so that a reader can see how the principles really guide education.

Project 2

Likely Readings

Background Readings
- Edmundson
- Jones
- Meier
- Tompkins

Case-in-Point Readings
- Shor
- Steinem
- Traub

Task and Purpose

None of us study and work at a perfect campus; on the other hand, there are strong programs at every campus. Write an open letter to a policy maker at the school you now attend. This letter will ask your audience to implement a new program, continue an old program, or improve a program; you can complain, praise, encourage, or accuse. But since you don't know this person, your request will need to be reasonable and clear, doing careful evaluation and analysis. You will probably want to suggest that other writers have called attention to the same issues and arguments—pull together evidence from at least three of the readings. You will also have to decide whether the fact that you pay tuition counts for anything in this case.

Project 3

Likely Readings

Background Readings
- Meier
- Carger
- Jones
- Edmundson

Case-in-Point Readings
- Traub
- Steinem
- Shor

Task and Purpose

Look over your reading journal and do some analytical freewriting on the role of choice and what Meier calls the "virtues" and "vices" of the market in the education of a particular kind of student (e.g., elementary, high school, university, elite, nonelite, vocationally oriented, liberal arts oriented). Once you have pulled together your thoughts on the subject, write an evaluative report that explains your position to a policy maker at your campus, a think tank that is developing new approaches to education, or students deciding where to go to school. Make sure you refer directly to the reading you have done.

Project 4

Likely Readings

Background Readings
- Edmundson
- Jones
- Meier

Case-in-Point Readings
- Shor
- Traub

Task and Purpose

Sort through your reactions to the background readings, and select an assessment of the current state of education that you find compelling (or repugnant). Then, look through the case-in-point readings, and sift through your own experience and identify a student or teacher attitude that is particularly interesting to you. Using principles from the background reading, do an evaluative analysis of that attitude.

Project 5

Likely Readings

Background Readings
- Carger
- Tompkins

Case-in-Point Readings
- Frey
- Hedegaard
- Shor
- Steinem

Task and Purpose

Look over your notes on the readings, and reflect on the consumer-like behavior that your peers and you yourself engage in. Decide what you think about this behavior, and then use evidence and arguments from the readings to defend and/or critique your behavior.

CHAPTER 8

Identity in Black and White: Negotiating Personal and Public Selves

The myth of America as a melting pot in which people from many nations become as one has guided the highest aspirations of this 250-year-long experiment in democracy and freedom. The reality of racist oppression—of a nation built on the labor of African slaves, on land stolen from hundreds of Indian tribes—stands alongside the myth of the melting pot as a reminder of the gap between this nation's aspirations and its real achievements. In the quest for a free and democratic society, race, especially the relationship between black and white Americans, remains one of the most difficult obstacles standing in the way. Calling for a year-long national conversation on race and racism in his second term in office, President Clinton recognized the need to address the work that remains unfinished.

Seeking to measure progress, we look back to the civil rights movement of the 1960s, to the landmark desegregation ruling in the *Brown* v. *Board of Education of Topeka, Kansas* Supreme Court case in 1954. We observe the integration of the armed forces at the end of World War II and the long service of black Americans on the fields of battle in both world wars. At the turn of the century, we see lynch mobs and Jim Crow laws; before them, we see the promise of the Reconstruction amendments to the Constitution, and the steady erosion of the rights and protections they offered to black Americans in the late nineteenth century. We observe the heroic efforts of the abolitionists and of spokespersons for freedom such as Frederick Douglass and Harriet Jacobs. This history looms closer to today than some of us appreciate. Only a few generations stand between us and the days and times we think of as long ago, and living memory binds us still to the burden (and the hope) of this legacy.

Our identity—our sense of ourselves, the person society perceives us to be—is shaped in intimate ways by this history. Black or white (or any other of the familiar categories the U.S. Bureau of the Census uses to divide the population), people inherit roles in a social system, roles that have been shaped over time. It is also true that we understand our lives are complex; racial labels do not easily pin down who we are. There are other aspects to our identity that matter a great deal. There are avenues available in our culture that allow us, to some extent, to shape the roles that history and society have set before us, to conform them to the special genius of our own place in time. We live in this exchange between public roles and the personal nuances we find in them.

This unit begins at this crossroads, where the personal and public aspects of racial identity intersect. Anticipating a focus on the crossover of hip-hop into mainstream commercial culture, the background readings present a variety of inquiries into race and identity. In different ways, they illuminate the ways black people and white people live with and work against the identity categories to which they are assigned. Each reading sheds light on some of the tensions, the complexity, and the mixed emotions that arise when we look at who we are. Together, the readings open up questions that lie at the core of our study of this culture of exchange we inhabit. How do we know who we are? To what degree is our identity given to us by society? To what degree are we able to evade, resist, or embrace this identity? To reshape its fundamental definition?

BACKGROUND READINGS

RACE RIGHT NOW

FARAI CHIDEYA

Farai Chideya is a correspondent for ABC news and has been a contributor to publications such as Time *and* Vibe *magazines as well as to MTV news. She has also worked as a CNN analyst and a reporter for* Newsweek. *Chideya is the author of two books—*Don't Believe the Hype *(1995) and* The Color of Our Future *(1999), from which this excerpt is taken. Focusing on racial identity, Chideya examines the younger generation of Americans for what they can show us about attitudes toward race and about mixed-race identities. "Americans in their teens and twenties see firsthand evidence…that America is becoming less white and more racially mixed," Chideya states. Throughout the book, Chideya shows evidence of the ways in which the predominant racial divide—black and white—is being replaced by a mosaic of ethnicities.*

America is a chameleon. A land populated by hundreds of Indian tribes became home to European settlers seeking religious freedom and economic opportunity. As the number of those settlers grew, the Native American population shrank—plagued by new diseases and pushed by the immigrants to ever-smaller plots of land. The European immigrants reinvented themselves as a nation, calling themselves Americans, and setting themselves and their country apart from their European forebears. These European Americans introduced yet another population to this land: the Africans who came—not all, but nearly so—as slaves.

When America was formally founded in 1776, it was already a multiracial nation, though few at the time would ever have thought to call it that. America is fundamentally different from most other cultures. For centuries, Europe had its nation-tribes: the Germans, the French, the Celts. So did Africa and Asia, where today's societies have grown out of ones that have existed for millennia. America was not homegrown but born out of the arrival of different peoples on an already-populated continent. The interactions between English and French settlers, blacks and whites, whites and Native Americans made America what it is today. We can't understand America without first understanding it as a cross section of cultures.

Over time, the blood of many whites, blacks, and Native Americans mingled. And the Mexicans who settled the West and Southwest had already formed their own mixture as well, Spanish and Indian blending into mestizos. As America took control of Mexican lands in California, Texas, and the Southwest, the nation became even more diverse. The thousands of Chinese immigrants who came to the United States in the mid-1800s to build the transcontinental railroad eventually settled in West Coast cities like San Francisco, though Chinese immigration was later curtailed by law. And on the East Coast, the turn of the century saw a great wave of European immigration, itself quite diverse: Jewish, Greek, Russian, Polish, Irish, Italian.

Trying to encapsulate America's history is probably foolish, and always controversial. But in order to understand where we are today, we have to try to find some common understanding of the past. America's "founding fathers" may have been white, but this nation never was populated or built by just one race. It's more critical than ever that we remember this, given the massive transformation our society is about to undergo.

5   America the chameleon is changing colors once again. Today, thanks to demographics, we can gaze into our future—one far different from our racial past. According to the U.S. Bureau of the Census, we're entering a century in which race in America will be turned upside down. By the middle of that century, whites will be a minority, and minorities will be in the majority.

A "Majority-Minority" America

In 1950, America was nearly 85 percent non-Hispanic white.[1] Today, this nation is 73 percent non-Hispanic white, 12 percent black, 11 percent Hispanic, 3 percent Asian, and 1 percent Native American.[2] (To put it another way, we're about three-quarters white and one-quarter minority.) But America's racial composition is changing more rapidly than ever. The number of immigrants in America is the largest in any post–World War II period. Nearly one-tenth of the U.S. population is foreign born.[3] Asian Americans, the fastest-growing group in America, have begun to come politically of age in California and the Pacific Northwest (where a Chinese American is governor of Washington State).[4] And the Census Bureau projects that the number of Latino Americans will surpass blacks as the largest nonwhite group by 2005.[5]

There's a much larger change looming for America. Around the year 2050, whites will become a minority.[6] This is uncharted territory for this country, and this demographic change will affect everything. Alliances between the races are bound to shift. Political and social power will be reapportioned. Our neighborhoods, our schools and workplaces, even racial categories themselves will be altered. Any massive social change is bound to bring uncertainty, even fear. But the worst crisis we face today is not in our cities or neighborhoods, but in our minds. We have grown up with a fixed idea of what and who America is, and how race relations in this nation work. We live by two assumptions: that race is a black and white issue, and that America is a white society. Neither has ever been strictly true, and today these ideas are rapidly becoming obsolete.

Our idea of "Americanness" has always been linked with "whiteness," from tales of the Pilgrims forward. We still see the equation of white/American every day in movies and on television (where shows like *Mad About You,* set in majority-minority New York, have no nonwhite main characters). We witness it in the making of social policy. (The U.S. Senate is only 4 percent nonwhite—though over 20 percent of the country is.)[7] We make casual assumptions about who belongs in this society and who is an outsider. (Just ask the countless American-born Asians and Latinos who've been complimented on how well they speak English.)

"Whiteness" would not exist, of course, without something against which to define itself. That thing is "blackness." Slavery was the forging crucible of American racial identity, setting up the black-white dichotomy from which we have never broken free. The landmarks of American history are intimately intertwined with these racial conflicts—the Civil War, Jim Crow, the Civil Rights movement. But today, even as America becomes more diverse, the media still depicts the world largely in black and white. The dramas and sitcoms we watch are so segregated that the top ten shows in black households and the top ten shows in white house-holds barely overlap.[8] Or examine the news media. The three-year-long coverage of the O.J. Simpson trials portrayed a nation riven by the black/white color line. And when *Nightline* did a first-rate series on race, it still didn't cover the true range of diversity but "America in Black and White." Race is almost always framed as bipolar—the children of slaves versus the children of slaveowners—even when the issues impact Asians, Latinos, and Native Americans as well. School segregation, job integration—they're covered in black and white. Political rivalries, dating trends, income inequalities—they're covered as two-sided dilemmas as well. For all the time we spend talking about black and white, the only thing we can agree on is that we disagree. Affirmative action: equal opportunity or reverse racism? Afrocentrism: black pride or hatred of whites? The entire race debate becomes nothing more than a shouting match, a sort of *McLaughlin Group* gone awry.

10   Everyone gets exposed to media images of race. Americans who have never met an immigrant from China or Mexico will doubtless have seen their images on the nightly news and formed an opinion about immigration from those images. Kids who have never met an African American will learn about slavery in school, listen to rap or R & B, and read an article on welfare reform or the NBA. It's only human nature to put together those pieces and try to synthesize an idea of what it means to be black. The media and pop culture have such a tremendous power in our society because we use them to tell us what the rest of the society is like, and how we should react to it. The problem is that, too often, the picture we're getting is out of kilter.

If you're not black and not white, you're not very likely to be seen. According to a study by the Center for Media and Public Affairs, the proportion of Latino characters on prime-time television actually dropped from 3 percent in the 1950s to 1 percent in the 1980s, even as the Latino population rapidly grew.[9] Asian Americans are even harder to find in entertainment, in the news, or on the national agenda, and Native Americans rarer still. How we perceive race, and how it's depicted in print and on television, has less to do with demographic reality than our mind-set. In the basest and most stereotypic terms, white Americans are considered "true" Americans; black

Americans are considered inferior Americans; Asians and Latinos are too often considered foreigners; and Native Americans are rarely thought of at all.

America can't move into the future if we as a society don't acknowledge who we are. But I can't chastise people for buying into the vision of a black and white America—after all, that's where I grew up....[10]

Some of the best stories about race in America are about America's youth as well. And the young Americans I have interviewed illustrate a fault line in the race debates that most of us don't even think about: a massive generation gap. On the one hand, America is led by baby boomers and people from the generations that came before them. These movers and shakers in government and industry came of age before and during the Civil Rights era, while America was dealing with (and reeling from) the struggles of blacks to gain legal equality with whites. But Americans in their teens and twenties see firsthand evidence in their own schools and neighborhoods that America is becoming less white and more racially mixed. America's pop culture today is infinitely more likely to show blacks as well as whites (though other races often remain unseen). The billion-dollar hip-hop industry, produced by blacks but driven by sales to young fans of all races, is one indicator of the cultural shift. Even more significant, 80 percent of teens have a close friend of another race.[11]

That's not to say that everyone in this generation lives a cookie-cutter version of life in an ethnically diverse America. Quite the contrary: how (and how much) we each experience diversity varies widely, and it depends on everything from geography to income. But there is a fundamental difference between this generation and the ones which came before. Until laws were revised in 1965, the United States accepted few immigrants besides Europeans. In most of the country, especially the East and Midwest, the vision of America as a black and white country largely held true. Today, especially for Americans younger than my twenty-nine years, the issue of race can no longer be described as a dichotomy. In many cases, "race" alone doesn't do justice to the issue; ethnicity and socioeconomics are just as important in the new America. There are more and more American kids who look like one "race" (say, Asian) but whose "ethnicity" is something entirely different (like the many Asian Latinos raised in Latin America). How does their history, their identity fit into the American agenda? My own life is a small example. Racially, I'm black. Ethnically, I'm half African (Shona, to be exact), though I was raised in America and identify as black American. Socioeconomically, I was raised as middle-*class*, even though we didn't have a lot of money. Anytime we reduce someone to just a race, we miss out on all these complexities.

15   It's difficult to define race, let alone quantify it. In many ways, it is a figment of our collective imaginations more than a biological phenomenon. For the purposes of this book, I treat black, white, Native American, Asian, and Latino as races. The U.S. Census doesn't. Its categories include black, white, Native American, and Asian/Pacific Island. The Census Bureau classifies Latinos/Hispanics as an ethnicity, not a race. The Merriam-Webster dictionary defines an ethnicity simply as an "ethnic quality or affiliation," and defines an "ethnic" person as "a member of a minority group who retains the customs, language, or social views of the group."[12] Latinos are definitely an ethnicity, and can be of any race. But Latinos are treated as a race in most sociopolitical contexts (for example, when describing the constituency of a politician or describing a mixed marriage between a Latina and a white man). Black Americans, on the other hand, have been seen as a race almost without ethnicity. Most black Americans are the

descendants of slaves, who were forced to discard their language and their customs here in the United States. But as more blacks immigrate to America from around the world, ethnicity is becoming a factor along with race.

Living in New York City, I see glimpses of the future of race every day. Here, the black community is no longer one but many. A child with brown skin and kinky hair may speak American-accented English—or Spanish, or Senegalese French, or Haitian Creole, or English with a Caribbean lilt. A man speaking fluent Spanish to his children on the subway one moment may switch to fluent, American-accented English the next. At a chic downtown club, a female DJ spins bangra for a multiracial crowd. That's a taste of young New York's diversity, but here, like other places, whites are often the most self-segregated. New York's public school system is disproportionately black, Latino, and Asian, while many white parents send their kids to private schools. This city of eight million people includes many racially and socioeconomically discrete neighborhoods. Some, like Chinatown, seem to welcome visits by outsiders; others, like Bensonhurst, have been the site of vicious racial incidents. Of course, New York is unique in how many cultures it encompasses. But the reality about race is this: every day America's heartland looks more and more like New York and Los Angeles, not the other way around.

I mean this literally, of course—there are more and more nonwhites in virtually every region and area of the country. But I'm also talking about the way ethnic culture permeates even the smallest, whitest towns. Consider another town I visit in the book. Delphi, Indiana, is a farming and industrial community of two thousand residents, almost all of them white. But most of the local teens listen to rap music as well as—sometimes instead of—rock and country. They spend countless afternoons watching hip, black kids on MTV and in sitcoms. They have the same albums, clothes, and shoes that inner-city kids do. And they're hungry for more. Says eighteen-year-old B. J. Bushnell, who moved to Delphi from Los Angeles: "It bothers me—but it's kind of hilarious—that some people will report at school that they saw a black person over the weekend…. They'll come up to me and say"—he feigns excitement—"'They dress just like they do on TV!'" You can't help but laugh, nervously, at the idea of white kids getting a buzz over seeing a real, live black person—but it shows how "minority" culture has shifted from the sidelines to the center. Today, rap music regularly tops the pop charts, and 60 percent of rap album sales are to whites.[13] Even in the heartland, American culture *is* multiracial culture.

NOTES
1. Bureau of the Census. *Census of Population: 1950.* Vol. II, Pt. 1. U.S. Summary. Table 38, pp. 90–91, and Table 61, pp. 109–11, and *U.S. Census of Population: 1950*, Special Reports, "Nonwhite Population by Race," Table 2, p. 16; Table 3, p. 17; Table 4, p. 18; and Table 5, p. 19.
2. Bureau of the Census, *Statistical Abstract of the United States 1997*, Table 22, pp. 22–23.
3. Kristen A. Hansen and Carol S. Faber. "The Foreign-Born Population: 1996" (P-20–494) (Washington, D.C.: Bureau of the Census Public Information Office, 1997); CB95–155, Bureau of the Census, "Foreign Born Residents Highest Percentage of U.S. Population Since World War II," 29 August 1995. (Immigration accounted for 30 percent of U.S. population growth in 1994. However, only Asian Americans had a higher rate of international immigration than "natural increase," or births in the United States.)
4. *Post-Intelligencer* Staff News Services, "Clinton Hails Locke as a National Symbol," *Seattle Post-Intelligencer,* 5 February 1997.
5. Bureau of the Census, Current Population Reports, "National Population Projections Resident Population of the United States: Middle Series Projections, 2001–2005, by Sex, Race,

and Hispanic Origin, with Median Age"; "Hispanic Population on Rise," *News & Observer* (Raleigh, N.C.), 7 August 1998, p. A-10.

6. Bureau of the Census, Current Population Reports, "National Population Projections Resident Population of the United States: Middle Series Projections, 2035–2050, by Sex, Race, and Hispanic Origin, with Median Age" (Washington, D.C., 1996).

7. Special Report, "Minorities in Congress," *Congressional Quarterly,* 4 January 1997, p. 28.

8. PR Newswire, "BBDO's 13th Annual Report on Black TV Viewing Finds Greater Disparity Between Viewing Preferences of Black and Total Households," 26 March 1998.

9. Clara E. Rodriguez, "Where Are Latinos? They're a Sizable U.S. Minority, but on TV They're Mostly Invisible," *Boston Globe,* 30 November 1997, p. D-4.

10. Robert Entman, "Representation and Reality in the Portrayal of Blacks on Network Television News," *Journalism Quarterly* 71, no. 3 (Autumn 1994): 509–20.

11. Nick Charles et al., "Rap Inc.: A Hip Hop Connection from the Bronx to the World," *New York Daily News.* 1 April 1997, p. 6; People for the American Way, *Democracy's Next Generation II: A Study of American Youth on Race* (Washington, D.C.: People for the American Way, 1992).

12. *Merriam-Webster's Collegiate Dictionary,* 10th ed. (Springfield, Mass.: Merriam-Webster Inc., 1993), p. 398.

13. Nick Charles et al., "Rap Inc.: A Hip Hop Connection from the Bronx to the World," *New York Daily News,* 1 April 1997, p. 6.

Rereading Actively

1. Review the article, identifying its major sections: Note where Chideya provides a historical background of race relations in the United States, and where the idea of a "majority-minority" society is introduced.

2. Chideya begins with the metaphor, "America is a chameleon." In a journal entry, explain what Chideya means by this. Pick two or three facts or statistics from the article that seem to illustrate this metaphor.

3. Chideya emphasizes the "generation gap" (¶ 13) that separates Americans according to their perceptions of race. Discuss this generational difference with a partner or in a small group, and then write a short journal entry that summarizes your discussion, explaining what Chideya means.

4. With a partner or in a small group, review the passage in which Chideya states that "80 percent of teens have a close friend of another race" (¶ 13). Discuss whether this claim seems congruent with your own experience. Do you have a shared definition of who a "close friend" is? Reflect on your discussion in a journal entry.

5. What is Chideya's interpretation of the definition of race?

Exploring Your Responses

6. In a page or two in your journal, play off Chideya's remark that living in New York, she sees "glimpses of the future of race every day" (¶ 16). What glimpses of the future of race do you see in the place you grew up, or on your campus?

7. Do you see evidence of different groups "self-segregating" on your campus? In a small group, discuss what evidence of self-segregation you have noticed. Write a page in your journal describing your group's observations.

8. What mix of races, ethnicities, or other heritages do you claim for yourself? Put another way, ask yourself how closely you identify with the racial or ethnic labels society categorizes you with. Reflect on this topic in a page in your journal.

IT'S THE LITTLE THINGS

LENA WILLIAMS

Lena Williams is a reporter for the New York Times *whose primary beat includes basketball—recently, she has done numerous stories on the WNBA as well as college ball. This article, published in the* Times *in 1997, is a departure from her usual subjects. It describes everyday behaviors that generate friction between blacks and whites. Responding to a question from a white colleague, Williams pursued this story, structuring her article as a catalogue of examples of "the little things" white people do that she says black people find insensitive or insulting. Williams also gives attention to the other side of this story, cataloguing some of the themes sounded when whites were asked if there were things black people did that they found insensitive or insulting. As a reporter, Williams documents some features of this interracial interaction, showing sources of tension that are subtler than the overtly bigoted behavior usually associated with racial divisions in society.*

The chic woman threw back her head and ran her fingers through her long flaxen hair on a crowded elevator in Macy's.

"I hate it when they do that," my brother-in-law whispered. I nodded in agreement.

"If she does it again," he said, "I'm going to tell her about it!"

He sounded agitated, and I gently patted his hand. The woman, still fingering her golden locks, got off on the next floor.

5   Later, I couldn't help wondering why such an inconsequential gesture had provoked such a strong response in both of us.

My brother-in-law, a soft-spoken, reserved black man of 62, has seen the best and worse life has to offer. Unlike me, a 40-something recovering black nationalist, he has been a staunch integrationist.

Yet, here we were, philosophical and political opposites, feeling a shared sense of indignation over a white woman shaking her hair. What may have seemed to be a petty annoyance aroused long simmering memories of racial slights that have yet to heal.

As blacks, we understood instinctively the role hair texture has played in perceptions of beauty and privilege in America. All our lives we've been bombarded with the images of white movie stars, models and other beauty icons with long flowing hair, which has been beyond our reach. For that brief moment in Macy's, we both saw a white woman flaunting a symbol of preference.

Neither my brother-in-law nor I are alone in our perception. When I shared the incident with black friends of various ages, classes and regions, they immediately understood. We knew the woman meant no harm. She was doing what came naturally.

10   But at a time when the discussion of race has entered new realms of political and scholarly debate and an emerging body of literature is re-examining the significance of race, it is a good time to look at the simple things in life—a look or stare at a store counter, a gesture on a crowded elevator, a maneuver on a sidewalk—that can turn moods red and unleash old emotions that sweep away rationality.

President Clinton has called for a year–long "great and unprecedented conversation about race." But you can't legislate frank discussions. Too much still remains unsaid, and too much assumed, imagined or inferred. Blacks, as well as whites, are guilty of making false assumptions about the other group's motives. Indeed, resentments over seemingly small slights are felt on both sides of the black-white divide.

So when asked recently by a white male colleague whether there were ordinary things that white people did and said that blacks found offensive, I was more pleasantly surprised than taken aback.

Racially sensitive exchanges seldom take place in mixed groups over coffee and danish in the office. They do happen over drinks at a corner bar among people of the same group, at dinner tables in Harlem apartments and in Upper East Side town houses, under hair driers in beauty salons and in small social settings where people's words are likely not to come back to haunt them.

I told my white colleague about the incident involving my brother-in-law, about blacks who refused to relinquish an inch to whites on narrow city sidewalks because it smacked of the bygone days of Jim Crow, about black men who felt that it was the height of condescension for white men to address them by their first names.

15   I recalled parties that were dead on arrival the minute the words "so what do blacks think about…" were uttered, and job offers that were rejected on the spot because a white interviewer used the adjective "articulate" for a well-spoken black applicant.

Almost across the board there are things blacks find irritating, if not sometimes downright insulting, in their day-to-day dealings with whites.

The Invisible Black Man Or Black Woman

A black person has been standing in line in, say, a restaurant or at a movie or at Bloomingdale's cosmetic counter. A white person arrives and cuts the line with not so much as an "excuse me," completely ignores the black person, asks the maitre d'hotel how long the wait will be for a table and then responds to the black's objections by "innocently" saying something like, "Oh, were you waiting for a table?"

Whites might view these incidents simply as New Yorkers behaving badly. But many blacks see them as the actions and typical attitudes of a people that still believes, as the Supreme Court declared in its 1857 Dred Scott ruling, that "a black man had no rights that a white man was bound to respect."

It may be "history," "the past" and "a different time and place" to whites, but for many blacks, some too young to remember, others too old to forget, some changes are slow to develop.

20   "Blacks tend to see history as currently relevant and echoing into the present," David K. Shipler, a former colleague, who is white, and author of "A Country of Strangers: Blacks and Whites in America" said when I queried him on the subject. "Whites tend to see history as the past and therefore irrelevant and not governing the present at all. That is one of the major fissures between blacks and whites, and it results in lots of misunderstandings."

Sometimes bottled-up despair and anger uncorks bad behavior by blacks. Just the other day, the present and past collided on a crowded Manhattan sidewalk when a well-dressed middle-aged black man pushed through a group of whites with such force that he nearly knocked one of the women into the gutter. The group looked dumbfounded and probably dismissed the close encounter as just another rude "only in New York" occurrences. I, however, saw a brother fed up with eating crow, as in Jim.

In the days of Jim Crow, blacks were suppose to "stay in their place," which was the back of the bus, the back door and clear of whites on sidewalks. Although such laws were abolished in the 1960's, for many blacks humiliation reverberates even now.

"White people still expect us to step aside, like they own the world," said Sharon Brailesford, a retired social worker who, a child in the 1940's, remembers "Colored Only" signs in her hometown, Newport News, VA. "They seem to have this innate sense of entitlement that has been passed down for generations like a precious family heirloom."

Mistaken Identities

We've all done it—call an acquaintance, colleague or classmate by someone else's name. Yet, black Americans are more likely to become agitated than others when whites call them by another's name, because they are convinced the mistake rests on the racial stereotype that blacks "all look alike."

25 "We have gradations in skin color and hair texture, but white people don't seem to make those distinctions," said Cassandra Woods, a thin, dark-skinned black in her 40's. A former bank teller, Ms. Woods recalled countless times when regular customers mistook her for another black teller who was lighter in complexion, heavier in build and 10 years her junior.

"It was bad enough when regular customers did it," she said. "But even some of my longtime colleagues would make the same mistake."

Worse, many blacks will tell you, are whites who tend not to recognize blacks outside their usual surroundings.

"Don't be out of context" said Ronald Prince, a black hair stylist, to the raucous laughter and nods of agreement among his black clients at Styles Hair Salon on West 46th Street in Manhattan. "As long as you're at your desk in the office, or in the classroom or doing your professional thing, they know you. The minute you're one of the masses, or someplace they think you shouldn't be, you become this faceless blur of blackness."

Truth be told, some blacks, myself included, have jokingly played the stereotype to their advantage. A black lawyer at a prominent midtown Manhattan law firm recalled playing hooky from his job to attend a Yankee game with a white colleague.

30 "He was so worried somebody would spot him in the crowd, and couldn't understand why I was acting so nonchalant," he said. "I told him, 'You know what they say: "We" all look alike. So what's to worry about?'"

First-Name Basis?

Among my people, familiarity often breeds contempt. While most Americans enjoy the informality of using first names, many of my black acquaintances, especially men, turn a deaf ear when they are not addressed by their surnames.

"I simply don't respond," said Otis Jenkins, a proud man with an old-fashioned sensibility of right and wrong. Mr. Jenkins, who works as a stylist at the Styles salon, says the "name thing" was about "respect denied." He continued: "We're old enough to remember white men referring to black men twice their ages by their first names or any name. I saw it done to my father, and his father before him, and I refuse to let them do it to me."

Dr. Alvin Poussaint, a professor of clinical psychiatry at Harvard Medical School, has also felt the sting of familiarity. "When I hear my first name, I immediately react as a black person," he said. "What is this person doing calling me Alvin? They may feel they're being friendly, but you get this emotional reaction."

Roger Wilkins, a former assistant United States Attorney General and currently a professor of history at George Mason University in Fairfax, Va., says that historically white people have used first names with blacks to establish superior-inferior relationships.

35 In order to get "their due," Mr. Wilkins told David Shipler, black people started giving their children names that required white people to address them with respect. "They'd name their kids Major or General," he said.

The Curiosity Factor

It is conveyed through such phrases as these: "Do you get sunburned?" "So what do you do for a living?" And it is sometimes acted out by touching a black's hair or skin.

"Don't forget the conspiracy theory," said Tyrone Greene, a longtime friend. "You know three blacks can't gather at one time in one place without some white person asking, 'So what are you guys up to?' Or, 'What are you all conspiring to do?' "

When a white woman saw Barbara George, a black woman with smooth chestnut-brown skin, applying sunscreen to her skin, the woman "had the audacity to ask why I was putting on suntan lotion."

"Do you sunburn?" Ms. George recalled her asking. Whites have also asked Ms. George whether her pug nose, high cheekbones and almond-shaped eyes are God-given or the work of plastic surgery.

40 "I guess us black folks are all supposed to have thick lips and wide noses," Ms. George said. "You know, the authentic Negro."

Andrew Hacker, a Queens College sociologist, author of "Two Nations: Black and White, Separate, Hostile, Unequal" and a white man who has spent decades studying human behavior, says blacks are more aware of the subtleties of race because they've been watching whites for centuries.

"Even the most liberal whites believe they understand blacks—what they want," he said. "We have already framed our perception, so we stop listening or watching behavior which might make our knowledge deeper. The 'hair thing' doesn't occur to us. We don't think about it."

Is This a Party or What?

Shelby Steele, a black scholar at the Hoover Institution in California, once talked about parties he'd attended that died from a "lethal injection of the American race issue." I, for one, like my parties like my wine: light and lively. To be cornered and peppered with questions about how "the race" feels about this or that is not my idea of a party, whether the setting is the office or the China Club. Anytime we are asked to speak on behalf of the 15 million to 20 million blacks in America it's off-putting, especially when one's mouth is stuffed with crudites.

Brenda Canty, a black woman who doesn't think twice about speaking her mind, says she has learned to respond to the question with a question. "I ask, 'So what do whites feel about so and so?' "

"The Look"

45 It starts with an expressionless stare. The eyes begin to squint. The mouth opens slightly. And you know you're being analyzed or sized up. It is a look whites often give

blacks who don't fit the composite notion of a Negro. If you're black, and you've lived long enough, you know the look when you see it. Often it comes right after you say what you do professionally.

"Really! So how long have you worked for…."

Sometimes "the look" appears when blacks say they have attended a college or university that is not an historically black school.

"*You* went to Harvard?"

"I've been at parties and had white people ask me what high school I attended," Dr. Poussaint recalled. "It's disconcerting, especially at my age, because you know they're asking to find out your history and how you arrived at this point."

50   I've jokingly told black friends that "the look" means "you don't compute"—in other other words, the sum of your life doesn't quite add up to the parts: black, American, minority member, second-class citizen. And now you say you do *what*! Blackness as an aberration.

For years, Cynthia Jones says, she got "the look" whenever she told whites she was reared on the Upper West Side of Manhattan, attended private schools, graduated from Oberlin College and received her law degree from the Benjamin N. Cardozo School of Law at Yeshiva University.

"*You* went to Oberlin?" Ms. Jones said. "Or, they'd say to my mother, 'Your daughter goes *there*?' "

What's Up with That?

Phrases often used by whites that blacks hear as racially loaded. "Isn't she articulate!" "I don't see color." Whenever whites try to talk black slang: "Homie!" "My man!" "Girlfriend."

Why? Blacks often find these remarks patronizing or attempts by whites to show they are not prejudiced or that some of their best friends are black.

55   If I counted the times a white person, whether a television commentator, journalist or employer, used "articulate" to refer to blacks who use proper diction or English in expressing themselves, I might be left with little else to do.

"Oh, isn't Michael Jordan articulate?"

Of course. He's being paid millions of dollars in endorsements and promotional fees because he's articulate and good-looking.

Over the years, I've learned to live with perceived racial slights. I refuse to let them define a life of success and achievement. I know better than to judge the actions of all whites by those of a few. Yet the cumulative effect of a lifetime of emotional nicks and scrapes exacts a toll on one's psyche.

"Psychiatrists refer to them as micro-aggressions," Dr. Poussaint explained. "They're the things you experience every day that then add up and take a toll. They may seem to be minor, but white people don't know how much this society makes blacks people constantly think about being black.

60   "These many slights and ways of interacting are things whites don't know they're doing," he continued. "It's not like using a racial slur. They're doing it in an intuitive way when they respond to the color of your skin. And they don't know enough about us, as a people, to know that we perceive things differently than they do."

Every time a taxi passes me on Eighth Avenue to pick up a white fare, every time I'm seated at a table near the kitchen in an exclusive restaurant, every time I get *that look* when I say I'm Lena Williams from The New York Times—every time, I briefly suffer a tinge of indignation.

In time, it passes. It must. I cannot afford to let it to fester like a sore. I have work to do, people to meet, places to go, a life to get on with.

Everyday Slights: The White Take

In no way is this a one-sided issue.

I spoke to whites who said there were things blacks often did and said that whites found racially offensive or insensitive. In fact, they were not at a loss for words or examples of ordinary interactions with blacks that left them feeling slighted.

65 Some did not want their names used, concerned that their perceptions, though valid, might be misconstrued as racist.

Here are themes that came up often:

The Macho Factor: A white man in his late 40's talked about black men who usurped space on subway cars by sitting wide-legged, causing others to be sardined on their seats. "They sit there defying you to ask them to move over, as if their manhood is at stake," he said.

Another white male said he resented inferences often made by black men that they were somehow more masculine or macho than whites.

A "Black Thing": "It's a black thing, you wouldn't understand," was the slogan of a popular T-shirt a few years back. Many whites took offense because the slogan implied that whites lacked a level of understanding about African-Americans.

70 "It's not important whether it was intended to hurt, but how it's perceived," said Max Weisman, an 18-year-old senior at Spring Valley High School in Rockland County. Mr. Weisman, who volunteers as a peer counselor for the Anti-Defamation League, said that if the noun were changed to "white" or "male" or "female," it wouldn't be difficult to understand why those not in that group might take offense.

Being Hopelessly Uncool: The idea that whites don't have rhythm, can't dance or just aren't as hip as blacks has long been a source of irritation to many whites, especially those of a younger generation.

"It's as if blacks have a monopoly on hipness," said Susan, a 15-year-old from Forest Hills, Queens. What hurts even more, a few whites indicated, are the suggestions that whites who do appear to be on the cutting edge are "acting black."

"Just the other day, a white male friend of mine wore an Afrocentric shirt to school, and some of the black kids said, 'Why are you trying to be black?' " said Rachel Weiss, a 16-year-old junior at South Shore High School in Brooklyn. Miss Weiss, who is also a peer counselor on race relations for the Anti-Defamation League, said she responded with a question of her own: "Why can't he wear it?"

As if blacks own red, black and green.

75 **Talking Out Loud:** Sylvia Lewis, a white woman in her 50's who lives in Queens, says she is not one for generalities, but...

"Blacks talk out loud in the movies, and that really annoys me," she said. "What they do is talk back to the screen. They'll just provide the dialogue or react to something they've seen."

Ms. Lewis, who asked to be identified by her maiden name, said she believed that blacks who behaved that way were "flouting the rules of white etiquette."

The Race Thing: Many whites said they simply hated it when blacks turned innocuous things into a racial guilt trip.

"I remember once, a black friend complained about a white sales clerk in a grocery store putting his change on the counter instead of in his hand," Ms. Lewis said. "When I said, 'She did that to me, too,' he said it wasn't the same thing and stormed off."

80   Sometimes it has nothing to do with race, but no one believes that, she concluded.

Rereading Actively

1. Study the article, noticing especially places where Williams describes how she gathered information for this story. What was her research method?

2. What does Williams mean by "the little things"?

3. The strategy in this story is to enumerate examples of insensitive or insulting behavior. Of the several examples Williams provides, which seem to you to be the most compelling? Why? Pick one example and comment on it in your journal.

4. With a partner or in a small group, discuss the effect of Williams's focus on negative behavior, focusing on three striking examples. Does it seem to you that her focus on disagreeable negative behavior is useful in getting her readers closer to the goal of interracial sensitivity? Why or why not? In your journal, write a page or two describing your discussion of this question.

5. In a small group or with a partner, discuss whether Williams does an effective job as a reporter. Does she maintain an objective stance toward her subject, in your opinion? Is she fair? Does she let the facts that she reports speak for themselves? Reflect on your discussion in a journal entry that draws on evidence to back up your evaluation.

6. The story concludes with a statement that Williams attributes to a white woman, Ms. Lewis: "Sometimes it has nothing to do with race, but no one believes that." Does it seem to you that Williams wishes her readers to agree with Ms. Lewis, or to disagree with her, that "sometimes it has nothing to do with race" and that "no one believes that"? Discuss this closing statement with a partner or in a small group, focusing on how you think Williams intends her readers to interpret it.

Exploring Your Responses

7. In your journal, freewrite a response to "It's the Little Things." Describe how the article hit you on a gut, emotional level. Did you feel challenged by it? Did you catch glimpses of recognition in the behaviors it describes? Or did it seem distant from your experience?

8. Underlying this article is an assumption that it is in the "little things" that the hardest work needs to be done in improving race relations. Having read this article, are you persuaded that Williams is correct in this assumption? Why or why not?

9. Many of the offensive behaviors depicted in this article are likely not intended to be offensive to members of another race. For example, the "chic woman"

who flips "long flaxen hair" (¶ 1) in the elevator at Macy's was probably oblivious to the negative meanings attributed to her act. Think about the nature of the problem here of unintended negative consequences of ordinary, "natural" behavior. Discuss this point with a partner or in a small group, and write a page or two in your journal reflecting on your discussion.

DIARIES AT AN ARTISTS COLONY

TOI DERRICOTTE

Toi Derricotte is a poet and teacher who has published four collections of poetry. Born in Detroit, Derricotte's book The Black Notebooks *(1997) explores her relationship to her own black identity: "All my life," she writes, "I have passed invisibly into the white world, and all my life I have felt that sudden and alarming moment of consciousness there, of remembering that I am black." This essay, "Diaries at an Artists Colony," addresses these subjects, recording Derricotte's encounters with other artists and writers to whom she reveals her black identity. Through the prism of her own experience, Derricotte analyzes the ways race weaves itself into the most casual of relationships; in doing so, she complicates the simple conceptions people usually hold about racial identity.*

Arriving for a stay of a few weeks, I was happy to find another black artist—who, unfortunately, was leaving on the day after I arrived. Coincidence? Or were we "tokens"? That question colored the rest of my time there. And another black artist arrived on the day I was leaving.

Black Arms

A group of us are sitting around the TV room. Bill, a painter from the South, is talking about how hard his mother works. He says, "I told her all you need is a pair of good black arms." The others snicker.

I am new here. All I want to do is get along. I say nothing, though now I know there is a part of me that is a joke to this man—my washerwoman great-grand-mother, my cook grandmother.

I will be silent. I want him to like me. I want to tell him how he hurts. But then the colonists will say, "You know how sensitive they are." I will be labeled. For six weeks, the only black person, I will never sit at the table without "Black Arms."

Dinnertime

Last night at the dinner table, John, a man who didn't know I'm black, noticed the book of women's diary writing that has a section of *The Black Notebooks* in it.

5   He asked to see the book, and when he took it I could see he wasn't going to skim over the table of contents. He went directly for my story, putting down his fork, and began to read. I felt a coldness, like a breeze ruffling a curtain on a line. The other dinner tables were quiet; many of the colonists don't know I'm black. I could just hear him blurt out, "I didn't know you're black. You don't look black. How did you get that color?"

I don't like to lose control that way. I fear being questioned or attacked, like an animal in a cage, prodded and poked by onlookers.

The man, fortunately, limited his comments to the quality of the work. "This is great. It sent a shiver up my spine. It's dramatic."

The other people at the table didn't know the content. Not that I mind every person at the colony knowing I'm black. I don't care, and I am proud of my work. But when several come at me from all sides, I don't know which way to turn. And heaven help me if I should show anger or be defensive.

John wouldn't let it alone. Later, when several of us were sitting around the fireplace, he said, "You should read this article in the *Times.* You'll like it. It reminds me of your book." I hadn't seen the article, but I knew it must be about black people. As soon as he knew I was black, I became a category, and now anything he reads by or about a black person reminds him of me.

10   A Chinese man who has also read my book said, "This article is nothing like the writing in Toi's book." I was glad he spoke, defending the uniqueness of my experience.

Later, John was playing pool. I was sitting twenty feet away and noticed him staring at me. I thought he was thinking I was attractive and was beginning to feel flattered. Suddenly he yelled across the room. "You really should read that article. You'll find it interesting, really timely."

"What's it about?" another man called out.

"Racism," he yelled back.

The people in the room looked up. I felt the conversation go out of my hands.

15   The other man said, "That isn't timely. It's ongoing and eternal."

I was glad somebody spoke. And it wasn't me.

The Testimony of Innocence

Last night I went over to Emily's studio to share my work. She read my diary entries and I read her poems. She said my diary entries were extremely important. She asked whom they were addressed to, and I read her the entry that described my audience: "… all the people in my past, black and white, who represent the internalized process of racism within me."

When I began writing *The Black Notebooks,* I wrote mainly for myself, although at the back of my mind was an idea that maybe I would find the courage to make it public. I wanted to tell the truth, however painful, but also to write for the larger human community—the world. I know that sounds ridiculously grandiose, but I felt an honest confession would have merit. My negative self-concept made me trust myself more than writers whose descriptions of racism are testimonies of their own innocence. I have always distrusted that, both from whites and blacks.

My skin color causes certain problems continuously, problems that open the issue of racism over and over like a wound. These openings are occasions for reexamination. My skin keeps things, literally, from being either black or white.

20   I know where I would like this all to end. I would like to be done with shame, to know I love myself and my own people, to believe that I have something positive to offer, that I am not unlovable, not because I am black, but because I am weak of character and disloyal, because there is something intrinsically wrong with me. I want it to end with some answer, some illumination that makes me see myself and the world in a new way. Then I will put the triumphant closing chapter on the diary and publish it, with pity, even disdain, for that woman who had written it.

I'll publish. I'll make a name for myself. I'll make money. I'll win the love of my relatives and get a full professorship at a university. I'll win a movie contract and play the heroine of my own story. It seems awful to hope that success will come from this.

Not to worry, my friend Cherrie says, writing about racism doesn't make you successful, it makes you ignored.

Coming Out

I still have not said anything to the painter from the South, though last night he said something about running off with a Puerto Rican woman. I am afraid to come out as a black person, to bear that solitude, that hatred, that invisibility. But I am also holding back something, a gift. I don't want to be a rejected gift, a piece of shit. Yet I can't expect love. I give myself because giving is right, because I make myself strong.

Bill

After breakfast I saw him lumbering toward his Jeep. He looked a little lost; several of his close friends have left. I had heard him say another gem this morning: "I wish I had ten little black women to sew the holes in that canvas...."

25   Every time the opportunity comes to talk to him, the time doesn't seem right. Either other people are around or there's another problem. After his art show last night, I stayed longer than anyone, but he seemed depressed by people's reactions. It would have been piling shit on top of shit if I had tried to talk to him; and I don't think he would have heard what I was saying. I found myself listening to his worries, reassuring him, and kicking myself for being a coward.

But this morning was perfect. I know he often goes into town for donuts. I had been on my way to my studio, but I turned in my tracks.

Sitting in the donut shop, the comforting cups of coffee were placed before us. He lit a cigarette. "There's something I have to tell you," I said. "I'm black, and last week when you made that comment about black arms, it made me feel bad. And this morning you said something about little black women sewing up holes in canvas." I didn't say it in a mean voice, just a human voice, one on one. (Inside, I'm saying, *Why can't I just blurt it out? Why do I have to be so careful?*)

I tried not to look at his face so I could get my words out, but I caught a glimpse and saw a muscle twitching in his cheek; his mouth was slightly open, and he was listening intently. I went on, "You see, I wanted to say something when this happened last week, but I didn't want to say something that would make people look at me as if I'm different. Sometimes when people find out I'm black, they treat me differently. So when people say things that hurt, I don't know what to do. I want to tell them. But at the same time, I'm afraid I'll be hurt even more."

He started to explain, "When I said that about 'black arms,' I was repeating something my mother-in-law said, and I was repeating it because I was horrified. What you feel must be similar to what I feel at my wife's house, because I am the only goy." I was happy he was identifying, but I hate it when, after I let a white person know they've said something racist, I end up having to listen for hours to the story of their life. "Please, I don't want to put you on the spot. I just want you to understand my feelings. Do you understand? What do you hear me saying?" He said, "I hear you saying that certain comments which other people make without sensitivity have great poignancy to you because you are black." That wasn't exactly what I was saying, but it seemed close. Besides, it had taken all the bravery I could muster to come this far, I couldn't press him further.

30   In the past, I have left conversations like this empty, not getting what I wanted. I thought it was rage I wanted to vent. But today, because he listened, because I waited for the right moment and asked for what I wanted, I thought, maybe I've found the answer. From now on, if I just wait, talk about my feelings honestly, if I don't expect the person to say something to take my pain away, if I just ask him or her to repeat back what I've said until they've understood, then everything will be fine.

    I want so much to find a formula! Of course, there is none. Sometimes it will come out OK, and sometimes I will walk away with a hole in my heart which all the black women in the world cannot sew up.

Saturday Night

Several colonists sat around trying to have fun on a Saturday night. We miss New York, movies, Chinese restaurants. We talked about feminism, about how, these days, many of the young girls have babies while in high school.

    A Southern lady said, "That's what black girls have been doing for years. They have babies and their families raise them. Maybe it's catching up with white girls."

    This is the same woman who three days ago was talking about how black people have "funny" names. "They name their kids the strangest things." I thought about the twins in New Jersey whose mother had honored the doctor who had delivered them by giving them the names he had suggested: Syphily and Gonorra.

35   This woman loves to talk about black people. She's our resident expert. She said, "There aren't any black people here. I haven't seen any."

    "Yes there are," I said, smiling.

    "Who?"

    "You're looking at one."

    "You're not really black. Just an eighth or something."

40   "I don't know how black I am, but I am black."

    "Was your mother black?"

    "My mother, my father, my grandparents. They are black, and they look just like me."

    "How do you know you're black?"

    "I'm black because the first people I touched and loved were black."

45   A woman at the table said, "Did you read the article in *The New York Times* that said if they were strict about genetics, sixty percent of the people in the United States would be classified as black?"

    I looked around the table; I was laughing. The others were not. They were worried about how black I was and they should have been worrying about how black *they* were.

    I thought of all the little white children, the light of their mothers' and fathers' eyes, in Montana, in flat Wyoming, in Idaho, in lakey Michigan; I thought of that "funny" blackness inside of them, a kernel in each little heart put there, somehow, in the night, like a visit from the tooth fairy. Somewhere babies are popping out of women and no one understands where they come from.

    I smile at that heart of darkness in sixty out of a hundred babies, the drop of blood that can't lie to statistics, that will be bled out, measured, and put in a crystal tube. That blood gives those little ones a special light. Wherever I look I see brothers, sisters, who want to break out of their cramped skins, singing with love.

That

Emily said yesterday she was surprised that Pat had called the colony a "white establishment," and said she was uncomfortable with some of the people. Emily hadn't noticed any of "that." Had I noticed any of "that"?

50   I was on guard. So many times if a black person admits discomfort, the white person then says that the black person must be "sensitive—paranoid"—responding not to the present environment, which is safe and friendly, but to something in the past. They want to hear that the white people in this environment (themselves) are fine. It's the black person who is crazy.

I said, "It's not something that is done consciously; but most of the white people here have had limited exposure to blacks; there are bound to be great problems in communication. There are some people who hate and fear blacks and don't want to be under the same roof. For example, Jan told me Sandra said, when she saw no black people in the dining room; 'Good. I'm glad there are no black people. After New York, this is refreshing.'"

Emily said sometimes when she is with black people, she doesn't know what to do; no matter what she does, it seems to be the wrong thing. She had invited a black woman, a lawyer, over to her house for dinner, and during the dinner conversation the guests at the table started talking about Arabs raising the price of everything in England. Emily said she didn't think they were saying anything racist, and even if they were, what did the Arabs have to do with this black woman? But the woman stood up from the table and said, "I'm sorry, I find this conversation extremely embarrassing." Emily asked me, did I think the woman was right?

I told her, "Emily, frequently white people who have been made uncomfortable by something a black person says or does go to another black person to try to ease the pain, to feel vindicated. First of all, I wasn't there, I don't know what she responded to. Secondly, there would be no way to find out unless both of you could sit down and talk to each other."

Emily said, "That will never happen because she has never asked me out, and when I called her she was cold."

55   "Black people don't like pain either."

There are so few friendships between whites and blacks in which the people are really themselves. Even when white people try, they are often operating on stereotypes, and though the black person might want to accept them, the only way to break the stereotypes is to tell the truth, which causes pain. A black person and a white person are not just two individuals who have to decide whether they like each other, but representatives carrying huge expectations, beliefs that they must scale like dangerous mountains trying to reach each other.

Gale's Studio

I visited Gale yesterday. I went there feeling greatly honored that she had asked me, since artists prize their time alone and don't want to be disturbed. I had just come into her room, sat down on the mattress, and received a cup of tea when she took off Mozart and asked me if I wanted to hear one of her favorite records, a record about the New York prison Attica. The hair on the back of my neck stood up. What connection had she made between me and Attica?

Give her a chance, I thought, calming myself, maybe it's just a coincidence.

It was atrocious. A white band had taken the departing words of a prisoner and repeated them over and over, as if to make certain that we caught the significance. Atonal music in the background, everything got louder and crashed to an end.

60   I sat there embarrassed, feeling the need to receive her gift with enthusiasm. She waited. The only word that came to my mind was "interesting."

She started flipping through her collection of classical music to find something else especially for me. "I have a record of Paul Robeson. Would you like to hear that?" *Oh God, it wasn't a coincidence!*

"No, thank you."

She seemed puzzled and at a loss. Finally, she asked, "There is a picture around here of a black man I liked. I slept with him. Would you like to see that?"

I gaped at her innocent face: Gale, the woman I head for at dinnertime because she is not pompous or intimidating, one of the only people I feel comfortable with.

65   I told her that just because I am black doesn't mean I am one-dimensional. I told her that I am interested in many things. I like classical music and know quite a bit about it. She said, "But my other black friends like it when I play those records." She looked genuinely hurt.

I told her all black people are different. She said, "But I've tried so hard. I'm tired of always trying to please them." She looked at me in anger. I was one more proof of her inadequacy, as if I should have taken whatever was offered and let her feel generous and good.

I left abruptly, sorry for my anger, sorry for what I had learned about her, sorry that she had lost her feeling of closeness, however illusory, to black people—sorry, sorry, sorry—and somehow to blame. I had felt close to her; now I distrusted my instincts and dreaded an isolation deeper than any I had experienced before.

Jazz

Now that I am the "known" black, everything with a tinge of blackness on it is delivered to me.

Mark, the composer, who has been talking about Mozart at the dinner table for days, comes running up to me this afternoon when he sees me on the path, his face lit like a beacon. He doesn't even bother with a greeting.

70   "Guess what I've been doing today?" he blurts.

I can't imagine.

"I've been writing JAZZ," he presents, as if it were a Cartier jewel on a silver platter.

What am I supposed to say? You must be a really nice white guy? Thanks for taking us seriously?

"Good for you," I answer, and walk on as quickly as possible.

Crazy Thoughts

75 How beautiful the view from my desk of wildflowers through the cathedral-tall window. I watch the lovely black birds. How kind the lunch on my doorstep, the vegetable torte with white cream sauce, the chocolate cake. How pleasing the flower on the table, the yellow Victorian sofa, the barn of colorful chickens. Kind and specific the words in the office, the locks on my doors. I am treated like a queen. But when the lights go off, I face my fears.

Why is my stomach in knots? Why do I fear that during the night I'll be smothered? I think poison gas will come out of the register. I think the people are monsters, not artists, and that during the night they will implant a small radio in my brain. How can I think this? The memory of my father being smothered by a pillow my grandmother put over his head when he was three? In the morning I am ashamed.

I try desperately to make friends, hoping I will actually feel that trust that makes the knots in my stomach loosen. I was terrified to come here; I always feel frightened, except when I'm near home. I trust no one—especially not myself.

I try to do my work. This is a perfect environment. No cleaning. No cooking. I needn't even go to get lunch; it is placed in a basket outside my door by a man on tiptoes. Wood is stacked. I make a fire. I sit in the sun. I want to be grateful. I am grateful. But the sickness backs up in my throat like phlegm.

In the kitchen the cook speaks softly. I want to sit by her all day and stay away from the roads on which I have been hurt by a word. But she is cooking and I don't want to bother her. Please, let me not bother anyone. Let me leave the tub without a hair. Let me not speak to those who turn their bodies slightly away. I must notice this.

80   No one can help. Only I, myself. But how can I let go? My face is a mask, like Uncle Tom's, my heart twisted with rage and fear.

After

After I came back I was sick for several weeks. I felt completely wrung out, run-down. I had left smiling, beaming, thanking everyone—the kitchen help, the office help, the yard help—for their kindness. My friend came to pick me up. The night before we were to drive home, I sat with her in the restaurant—the first black face I had seen in weeks—and for an instant, I felt my body falling under me, as if I had slipped under the wheels of a train. I had made it until the last minute, keeping a stiff upper lip, and here I was, so close to the end, finally about to lose it.

They were so sorry to see me go they offered me a stay of two more weeks. If I stayed, I would be proving my desperate bravery to myself. But I declined. I was tired of feeling frightened and wanted to go home, where I felt safe.

A Jewish activist friend returned shortly after and asked me to please write a letter telling them how hard it had been to be the only black person there. She had found the same token during her stay. I postponed it and postponed it. I didn't want to. I had been a success—I had gone someplace far from home and stayed four weeks without having a nervous breakdown. And they had tried to do everything to please me—cooked for me, cleaned up after me, put wood in my fireplace. I didn't have the heart to tell them I had been miserable and frightened the whole time. Besides, I wanted to be a "successful" black, a person they would ask back, a person who would ease the way for others. "See, we're not as bad as you thought."

The day my friend returned from the colony, she was full of news about how she had written a letter to the board, sent the names and addresses of black artists. The president had talked to her for a half hour about how pleased he was with her efforts. The next day she called me, despondent. Her editor had called from her large publishing house—they were remaindering her book. I felt so sorry for her. I told my husband about her efforts and how she had come home to this big disappointment. "I'm not surprised," he said. "Somebody from the colony must have gotten to somebody at her publishing house and they iced her." I looked at my husband angrily. "Oh, that's silly," I said. "One has nothing to do with the other." But I felt the ground under me sinking.

Rereading Actively

1. What is the most surprising information Derricotte reveals in this essay? Record your response to this revelation in your journal.

2. With a partner or in a small group, identify passages where Derricotte describes the way she is treated by others as a result of her being black. When others learn of her black identity, how does their behavior seem to change? Summarize your discussion in a page or two in your journal.

3. Derricotte narrates an incident in which she must answer the question, "How do you know you're black?" (¶ 43). Review this passage of the essay, noting the response she gives: Is her response persuasive to you in the context of the rest of her writing here? Why or why not?

4. With a partner or in a small group, identify passages where Derricotte reflects on her own perceptions and attitudes toward herself as a black woman. How does she describe and explain her feelings about herself? Write an entry in your journal that records your discussion of this point.

5. Derricotte asserts that "[a] black person and a white person are not just two individuals who have to decide whether they like each other, but representatives carrying huge expectations, beliefs that they must scale like dangerous mountains trying to reach each other" (¶ 56). With a partner or in a small group, review the article, identifying incidents that affirm or contradict this point.

Exploring Your Responses

6. Derricotte explains that once she becomes the "known" black at the artists colony, "everything with a tinge of blackness on it is delivered to me" (¶ 68). Freewrite a response to this: Have you ever observed this happening? Have you become the "known" black person, or gay person, or some other sort of "other" in a group? Have you been treated differently as a result? Write a page or two in your journal addressing this point.

7. With a partner or in a small group: After reading Derricotte's description of and reflection on her encounters with the other artists at the colony, discuss what inferences you can begin to draw about racial identity in relation to social interaction. For example, Derricotte could have continued to pass for white at the colony. Does this shed any light on your conceptions of "black" and "white" as readily identifiable categories?

8. In a page in your journal, begin to reflect on what you understand about Derricotte's own relationship to her blackness. What feelings does she express toward herself, and what do you understand about her sense of personal identity as a result of these feelings?

AN OVERVIEW OF IDENTITY NEGOTIATIONS THEORY
ROBERT BROOKE

Robert Brooke is a writing teacher and researcher whose work focuses on the social dimensions of writing and learning. The book from which this chapter is taken, Writing and

Sense of Self (1991), explores how students learn about writing in college. Addressing an audience of college writing teachers, Brooke draws on theorists from anthropology and sociology to interpret the behavior of students and teachers in college writing classrooms. Learning, says Brooke, is intimately involved in "identity negotiations." Brooke's work helps to show how identity is always in process and how we manipulate our places within social categories.

The problem of how self and society interact to form identity is a problem with a long history, and my version of identity negotiations theory emerges within a particular tradition of responses to the problem. This tradition is interdisciplinary, ranging from social psychology to anthropology and political science, and is widely accepted by researchers studying the formation of personality and social groups in various fields. Depending on the discipline, of course, this way of describing the self takes on a variety of forms. Cultural anthropologists like Clifford Geertz, for example, tend to emphasize the interpretive structures of culture in which the self emerges, while practicing therapists like R. D. Laing tend to emphasize the adaptive power of individuals in relating to the social contexts which surround them.

My version of this position is largely derived from three sources: (1) the social psychology of Erving Goffman, Erik Erikson, and R. D. Laing; (2) the political and cultural theories of educators such as Henry Giroux and Paulo Freire and feminists such as Adrienne Rich, Pamela Annas, and Mary Belenky; (3) and a tradition of interpretive anthropology described as "cultural critique" by George Marcus and Michael Fischer. While each of these writers approaches identity from somewhat different perspectives, all of them explore how the self is formed in interaction with society, only accumulating meaning and value from such interaction.

I have chosen to call my version of this position "identity negotiations" in order to highlight two important aspects of this theory: a focus on *identity*, a term often used to denote what is most central or important about the self, but a corresponding focus on the *negotiations* which create identity, a term which denotes attempts to mitigate the clash between opposing forces, to compromise between conflicting camps, to satisfy groups with different demands. The term *identity* is most often used in psychological studies, while the term *negotiations* is taken from political and social theory. The term *identity negotiations* therefore highlights the development of the self within a complex arena of competing social forces. From such a perspective, individual identity (at any point in time) is best seen as a dynamic construct which comes into being through mitigation or compromise with the social definitions of self surrounding the individual. A person's identity arises through negotiation with the many groups which provide these definitions.

Seen from this perspective, the central tension in identity formation is a tension between social and internal understandings of the self. In any given context, a person's bearing, past, and behaviors imply that the person is a given sort of individual, but this implied identity may or may not correspond to the person's internally felt sense of self. The problem of identity formation, thus, is how to deal with this ever-present distance between implied and felt identity.

5   As an initial description of the differences between implied and felt identity, Erving Goffman's taxonomy of three aspects of identity is helpful. In *Stigma*, Goffman distinguishes three meanings of the word identity, each of which relates social interaction to individual experience in a unique way. The first two meanings describe implied identity, while the last describes felt identity.

First, for Goffman, identity often refers to a person's social identity—that is, the classifications of individuals that others will make on the basis of first impressions. Clothes, bearing, accent, physical attractiveness, cleanliness, and the like all come into play here. A student who attends the first day of class wearing a Delta Delta Delta sweatshirt uses this aspect of identity to be seen as a certain sort of person. Obviously, different social groups assign an individual different social identities on the basis of the same appearances. On many state college campuses, for example, students affiliated with the Greek system and students who are independents hold rather rigid stereotypic opinions about each other. On the first day of class, consequently, the Delta Delta Delta student is likely to be judged stereotypically by Greeks and independents because of the sweatshirt, and such initial judgments may affect class interaction well into the semester.

Second, Goffman identifies *personal identity* as a meaning of the term *identity*. He defines personal identity as the sum total of physical and biographical information known or attributed to an individual in a given context. Unique physical attributes—a facial deformity, for example, or great beauty—are marks of personal as well as social identity. But more important for this category are the biographical records left by an individual's journey through life. These records take two forms: the official paper trail of birth certificates, school attendance, wedding licenses, and the like; and the informal memories other people have of the individual. Different social groups value different aspects of a person's personal identity, just as they value different aspects of social identity. The student in the Delta Delta Delta sweatshirt, for example, might have a police record for driving while intoxicated during her senior year of high school, and this fact, when known by others, might raise her social standing among some elements of the undergraduate community, while it might lower her social standing in the eyes of her sorority administration.

Taken together, these two aspects of identity define the sort of implied identity that a context is likely to assign an individual. Each social context will value certain kinds of immediate appearance (social identity) and certain kinds of information about an individual's past (personal identity). Given an individual's particular social appearance and known personal history, other people in that context will tend to conceive of that person as a particular sort of person.

Goffman's third meaning for identity leads beyond the identities that situations imply to the identities that people feel themselves to have. The alignments of individuals toward the groups that surround them define what Goffman calls "ego identity" (in Erikson's sense of the person's guiding self-conception). Individuals will, Goffman points out, be perceived as a member of some groups and as an outsider in others, largely as a consequence of their social and personal identities. How persons align themselves to these groups lets others know a great deal about the self they wish to be or project. The student who wore the Delta Delta Delta sweatshirt did so to assert her membership in the Greek system as a positive and important aspect of her identity. Other students affiliated with the Greek system will project different alignments to that subculture, perhaps by dressing Greek only at Greek functions, by taking anti-Greek positions during class debates, or by never letting on to those outside the system that they are in fact members of it. By such behaviors, individuals show their alignments to the groups they seem to belong to. The particular ways individuals align themselves to such groups show a great deal about how they conceive of themselves, about their felt identity.

10   In fact (though Goffman does not make this point), it is this sense of ego identity formed through group affiliation that largely guides the choices individuals make
about how to present their social and personal identities. How people choose to appear
and behave (social identity) is a consequence of what sort of individuals they want to
be classified as. Similarly, what people choose to tell about themselves (personal identity) is influenced by how they want others to understand their relationships to the
groups surrounding them....

To summarize, identity negotiation theory rests on two assumptions about the
structures of social interaction and the self:

1. Each social interaction carries with it expectations for contextually appropriate and inappropriate behavior which produce a range of roles a person
   might take. Each social group, however, has its own expectations for what
   roles its members will play in different contexts, sometimes advocating
   roles contextually appropriate to the situation and sometimes advocating
   other roles as a way of rejecting the situation's structure. Thus, whenever
   individuals engage in social interaction, their particular history surrounds
   them with expectations which delimit the range of roles they might fill in
   that interaction and the values of those roles for the groups that are important to them.

2. At any given point in time, our identity structure, both as we ourselves and
   others understand it, is composed of the conglomerate of stances we take
   towards the role expectations that surround us. By complying with some
   role expectations, we identify ourselves with various groups and their values; by resisting other roles, we separate ourselves from other groups. In
   any given identity structure at any given point in time, the processes of
   compliance and resistance are mutually important, for it is in their pattern
   that a unique identity emerges. To comply with or resist role expectations,
   moreover, we must act. Behavior thus forms a system of information by
   which we show our stances towards the social world. Through our behavior, we show both our intent to belong to certain social groups as well as
   our ability to belong.

These assumptions form the basis of identity negotiations theory. Taken together,
they describe the social world as a plurality of interactions and groups (each carrying
its own expectations) and identity as formed through the negotiations in which individuals work out their own stances towards those expectations....

Social Interaction and Role Expectations

Expected activity in [an] organization implies a conception of the actor and an
organization can therefore be viewed as a place for generating assumptions about
identity.... To engage in a particular activity in the prescribed spirit is to accept being
a particular kind of person who dwells in a particular kind of world.

(Goffman, *Asylums* 186)

Individuals develop their identities in context, through interacting with the social groups
that surround them. The social contexts surrounding individuals, however, are plural.
There are many of them: a given individual is surrounded, for example, by family, peers,

schools, political parties, religious organizations, and so on. There is no such thing as a single, unified social context surrounding the self. Instead, each person lives her or his life within interlapping contexts, each of which requires different practices.

15   At a general level, the differences among such contexts seem obvious. How teenagers act at home, out with friends, and at school are remarkably different—there are clearly different practices involved. But to distinguish among contexts is not always simple. Recently, sociologists like Goffman (*Frame Analysis*) and conversation analysis like Craig and Tracy (*Conversational Coherence*) have suggested that every single interaction we take part in, from waiting for an elevator with strangers to saying good-bye on the telephone, ought to be treated as a separate context because the rules of acceptable behavior in each case are distinct. Other thinkers would identify somewhat larger units of interaction as more crucial, as in Labov's studies of people's changing patterns of speech when the groups or social classes they are talking with change (*Language in the Inner City*). His work points out that similar kinds of practices hold for many different interactions, changing only when the social relationships between the speakers change.

    For our purposes, it is unnecessary to distinguish where one context begins and another ends or how big a unit of interaction a context is. What is important for identity formation is the more general point that each context carries with it implications about the participants. In sociology generally, these implications are called "roles," and different social settings are described as involving different roles for individuals. At school, for example, a young person is assigned a "student" role, and his behavior at school will be evaluated by others according to the expectations of that role. Hence, by doing well at his studies he can become a "good student," by doing poorly although trying to do well he becomes a "bad student," by resisting work and trying to disrupt the classroom he becomes a "discipline problem" or "disruptive student." The individual at school, in short, is able to develop any version of the student role he wishes, but he is not free to step outside the role altogether.

    In a writing classroom, similarly, certain roles are established for participants, and individuals will respond to these roles by developing particular versions of them. As in other classrooms, one set of such roles are student roles—writing classrooms share with other classrooms some general expectations about the way people will behave as students. But more importantly for our purposes, each writing classroom will, by its activities, establish a certain role for being a writer, a certain kind of behavior that is evaluated in that classroom as writerly behavior. When we study writing classrooms from an identity negotiations perspective, one important focal point is what the class establishes as writers' roles and what versions of these roles participants develop as the class progresses.

    In identity negotiations theory, it is a context's ability to delimit a range of roles for the individual that is crucial. Each context holds certain expectations for how individuals will act and evaluates the worth of individuals in relation to these expectations.

    What makes these role expectations a problem for identity development, of course, is the fact that different contexts value different practices, and hence evaluate individuals differently. And contexts overlap; they are hard to keep separate. A college student sitting in class, for example, operates in a plurality of overlapping contexts. She operates as a student in a classroom, as a member of her Greek or dorm social network, as a young woman aware of potential for dating and harassment, as a representative of a particular ethnic group, and so on. Her affiliation with each of these groups produces pressures for certain behaviors in the classroom—many of which conflict. As this individual matures beyond college, she will find herself living in an even larger range of social contexts, each of which defines her roles according to different and conflicting principles.

20   Labov (*Language in the Inner City*) gives a striking example of such conflict related to education. Describing the lives of adolescent gang members in New York, he points out the complete disjunction between linguistic behaviors valued by peer gangs and those valued by school officials. Consequently, when boys are in classrooms filled with gang members and teachers and other students, there is no way of behaving that can please all the role expectations there. To be obedient and deferential to the teacher would assign a boy a "good student" role for school officials, but would also assign him a "lame" role for other gang members, who value creativity with insults and bravery or defiance in the face of authority. In such a situation, an individual must negotiate between roles, either choosing to reject one role and embrace another or to mitigate the conflict somehow.

REFERENCES

Craig, R. and K. Tracy, eds. *Conversational Coherence: Form, Structure, and Strategy.* Beverly Hills, CA: Sage, 1983.

Goffman, Erving. *Asylums: Essays on the Social Situation of Mental Patients and Other Inmates.* Chicago: Aldine Publishing Company, 1961.

———. *Frame Analysis: An Essay on Face to Face Behavior.* New York: Pantheon, 1967.

———. *Stigma: Notes on the Management of the Public Order.* New York: Harper and Row, 1971.

Labov, William. *Language in the Inner City.* Philadelphia: Pennsylvania University Press, 1972.

Rereading Actively

1. In a journal entry, summarize what Brooke means by the term "identity negotiations."

2. With a partner, review the article, identifying passages in which Brooke gives concrete examples to illustrate the concept of identity negotiations. In your journal, list these passages in the order that they appear, and suggest how they work together to develop his argument.

3. Experiment with applying the concept of identity negotiations to observations you make. With your partner, brainstorm examples of incidents in which the process of identity negotiation seems evident. To what extent do you negotiate your identity?

4. Brooke summarizes three meanings of "identity" that Erving Goffman provides. List each in your journal, and draft in your own words a brief definition for each meaning.

5. Brooke discusses the idea of context in relation to identity. Review this section of the article with a partner, and explain in your own words what this relationship is. How does context influence identity?

Exploring Your Responses

6. With a partner, brainstorm examples that illustrate differences in your behavior that relate to different contexts. Think of various contexts in which you operate. What are some things you might do or say in one context that you would not do or say in another?

7. Home, neighborhood, school, workplace—each is a different context that brings varying expectations to you about dress, behavior, speech, and so on. With a partner or in a small group, brainstorm and discuss incidents you have observed where you see conflict between the expectations of a given context and the behavior of an individual. In your journal, describe some of the incidents that your group discussed.

8. Peer pressure and pressure from authority figures can pull us in opposite directions. Think of a time in school when you were faced with a conflict between what would earn you the esteem of your peers and what would earn you the esteem of a teacher or coach. In a page or two in your journal, identify what the conflict was about and how you responded to it.

BACKGROUND ASSIGNMENTS

The readings in this section approach the question of race and identity. In different ways, they show how our interactions with others influence our sense of who we are. Similarly, our deepest sense of our selves affects the way we relate to others. The interaction between self and other is complex, and it can become more emotionally charged when race is an element in the exchange. Each of us lives with the burden of the history of slavery in the United States, a legacy that includes oppression and fear as well as strength and survival. This legacy "colors" many of the most intimate dimensions of our ordinary experiences. Each of us—whatever our race—also lives in a kind of balancing act of identity as we accept, resist, or reshape the roles and identities our families, communities, and society offer us.

Making Connections

1. Using the form of Toi Derricotte's *"Diaries at an Artists Colony"* as a model, compose a series of episodes in which you are challenged by the expectations or prejudices of others. In each episode, describe what happened, and explore your reaction to the incident. To the extent that each helps you articulate your reactions, draw on Robert Brooke's discussion of identity negotiations or Lena Williams's descriptions of the "little things" that generate friction between members of different groups.

2. Farai Chideya argues that for young people today, identity is not easily defined in racial terms because race, ethnicity and socioeconomic class are all likely to play important parts in shaping who we are (¶ 14–15). Using Chideya's ideas as a framework along with Robert Brooke's discussion of the "tension between social and internal understandings of the self" (¶ 4), write an essay in which you consider the fact that racial categories are a fundamental part of our everyday lives even while they may be misleadingly simplistic.

3. Who are you? Using Robert Brooke's theory of identity negotiations, develop a profile of yourself. Describe the categories or roles that you feel most closely identified with, along with those that others may put you in against your preference. How do you "negotiate" your identity in these situations? (You might, for example, compare or contrast your experience to that of Toi Derricotte.) Do you see yourself as others see you? Why or why not?

4. Lena Williams and Toi Derricotte focus on the difficulty of communicating across the racial boundary that separates black people from white. Farai Chideya has a more positive view of racial mixing and the future of multi-cultural society. Using these writers' ideas, analyze your own community's progress toward inclusiveness and respect for other people.

5. Robert Brooke and Toi Derricotte suggest how our sense of ourselves can be upset when we enter alien surroundings or interact with strangers. In his discussion of neighborhood, Yi-fu Tuan (Chapter 9) makes an explicit connection between our feelings of comfort and the territories we enter in the course of a day, e.g., home, school, or work place. Drawing on these writers' ideas, analyze the changes you go through as you move through different places in your day.

Collaborative Exchanges

1. Though racial identity seems self-evident, as the background readings suggest the situation is anything but simple. In a small group, explore the question of racial identity by focusing on "whiteness." Take the task in two steps. First, ask what it means to be white. How do white people act or appear as "white"? Brainstorm images of whiteness that come from the media—television shows and movies, popular songs, advertising, and so on. Create a list of examples, images, or stereotypes of white identity. Second, reflect on this process, discussing whether you succeeded in defining white identity, and what feelings you experienced as you tried to define it.

2. Elsewhere in *The Black Notebooks,* Toi Derricotte describes an experience she had exchanging journal entries with a white woman. Each of them wrote accounts of incidents in their childhood that reflected confrontations with racism. Together, each woman tried to make a document that traced black and white encounters on the color line. Draw on this as a model. Working with a partner with whom you share some comfortable difference (or some difference that makes you a little uncomfortable), create an exchange of journal entries. Each of you should write an entry that relates some encounter you have had with this difference you share, describing what happened, how you reacted, and your thinking about that incident now. Exchanging your entries, you each should write a response to your partner's account. Finally, working together, compose an interpretation of your exchange.

Net Approaches

1. Visit a local or regional magazine, newspaper, or other searchable online news site and perform the following search: *race and identity.* (You may decide to use the AJR Newslink <ajr.newslink.org> to help you find an online news

site.) Scroll through articles this search turns up, going back about six months. Make note of references to themes mentioned in the reading for this unit, and freewrite your own sense of the state of race in the local news.

2. Point your browser to <www.liszt.com> and search for listservs that deal with race. Follow the liszt.com instructions and subscribe to a listserv that catches your eye. Listen in for a week, participating if it makes sense. Generate a report that explains the issues and perspectives participants have, and connections between their postings and the reading you have done in this unit. Follow liszt.com instructions to unsubscribe when you are finished.

3. Go to <www.hotbot.com> and run the following search: *race and racism.* Scroll through at least fifty hits, noting in your journal the kinds of pages you see. Visit at least one page. Then, tie the term "identity" into the same search (*race and racism and identity*). Again, scroll through a couple of dozen hits, visiting at least one page. Be prepared to participate in a class discussion of race on the web and the significance of the term "identity."

CASE-IN-POINT READINGS

Hip-Hop Crossover: The Inner City Comes to Suburbia

Crossover—the adoption by one group of the customs, crafts, and styles identified with another—is probably inevitable when cultures live in contact with one another. However, the means by which crossover occurs and the meanings assigned to the cultural goods that cross over are important points to examine. The readings here look at the crossover of hip-hop into mainstream commercial culture. Emerging in the late 1970s in the South Bronx (which Tricia Rose in *Black Noise* (1994) identifies as "the home of hip-hop culture"), hip-hop became its own kind of cultural melting pot, including Puerto Ricans (such as the graffiti artist Futura and the breakdancer Crazy Legs), Jamaicans and other Caribbean people, and African Americans (DJs and rappers, such as Grandmaster Flash and Red Alert). By the early 1990s, hip-hop had become one of the most widely traded commodities in the pop culture industry and included rap music and fashion. The commercial success and visibility of hip-hop that has resulted from its embrace by white suburban teenagers becomes the occasion for the readings gathered here. Each looks at the phenomenon of hip-hop crossover, considering its commercial success in relation to black and white identity.

MARKETING STREET CULTURE:
BRINGING HIP-HOP STYLE TO THE MAINSTREAM
MARC SPIEGLER

Marc Spiegler wrote this article for American Demographics *in 1996. (*American Demographics, *published by Dow Jones and Company, draws together population studies, data from the U.S. Bureau of the Census, and consumer trends.) The article describes the adop-*

tion of hip-hop style in mainstream retailing: driven by the quest for higher sales, retailers repackage elements of hip-hop—clothing, music, and language—for teenagers who live far from the inner cities where hip-hop was born. In addition to focusing on the selling process by which hip-hop becomes commercialized, Spiegler also tries to discern the motivations of the buyers, the white teenagers whose spending drives the market.

The Scene: Martha's Vineyard, Massachusetts, a bastion of the white East Coast establishment. A teenaged boy saunters down the street, his gait and attitude embodying adolescent rebellion. Baggy jeans sag atop over-designed sneakers, gold hoops adorn both ears, and a baseball cap shields his eyes. On his chest, a Tommy Hilfiger shirt sports the designer's distinctive pairing of blue, red, and white rectangles.

Four years ago, this outfit would have been unimaginable to this cool teen: only his clean-cut, country-club peers sported Hilfiger clothes. What linked the previously preppy Hilfiger to jeans so low-slung they seem to defy gravity? To a large extent, the answer lies 200 miles southwest, in the oversized personage of Brooklyn's Biggie Smalls, an admitted ex-drug dealer turned rapper.

Over the past few years, Smalls and other hip-hop stars have become a crucial part of Hilfiger's open attempt to tap into the urban youth market. In exchange for giving artists free wardrobes, Hilfiger found its name mentioned in both the rhyming verses of rap songs and their "shout-out" lyrics, in which rap artists chant out thanks to friends and sponsors for their support.

For Tommy Hilfiger and other brands, the result is *de facto* product placement. The September 1996 issue of *Rolling Stone* magazine featured the rap group The Fugees, with the men prominently sporting the Tommy Hilfiger logo. In February 1996, Hilfiger even used a pair of rap stars as runway models: horror-core rapper Method Man and muscular bad-boy Treach of Naughty by Nature.

5   Threatened by Hilfiger in a market he had profited from but never embraced, it hardly seems coincidental that Ralph Lauren recently signed black male super-model Tyson to an exclusive contract. Even the patrician perfumier Esteé Lauder recently jumped on the Hilfiger bandwagon, launching a new cross-promotion series with the clothing company. The name of one of Lauder's new perfumes says it all. "Tommy Girl" plays on both Tommy Hilfiger's name and the seminal New York hip-hop record label Tommy Boy. Hilfiger also launched a clothing line for teenaged girls in fall 1996, projected by the company to gross $100 million in its first year on retail racks.

On the surface, it seems Hilfiger and others are courting a market too small and poor to matter. The majority of true hip-hoppers live in inner cities, although not all urban youths embrace the culture. About 5 million U.S. teens aged 15 to 19 lived in central cities in 1994, or 28 percent of all people that age. Inner-city blacks aged 15 to 19 are an even smaller group. At 1.4 million, they are only 8 percent of all teens. They also have significantly lower incomes than their white suburban counterparts. The numbers of 20-to-24-year-olds and black 20-to-24-year-olds in central cities are also small, at 6.5 million and 1.6 million, respectively.

So why are companies pitching products to the hip-hop crowd? Because for most of the 1990s, hordes of suburban kids—both black and white—have followed inner-city idols' in adopting everything from music to clothing to language. The most prominent examples are in evidence at suburban shopping malls across the country: licensed sports apparel, baseball caps, oversized jeans, and gangster rap music.

Scoring a hit with inner-city youths can make a product hot with the much larger and affluent white suburban market. But to take advantage of this phenomenon, you have to dig into how hip-hop culture spreads from housing projects to rural environs, understand why hip-hop is so attractive to suburban whites, and discern the process by which hip-hoppers embrace products.

Hip Hop Hits the Mainstream

In its early years, MTV drew jeers for being too "white," for shying away even from vanilla-flavored black pop stars such as Michael Jackson. Yet most pop-culture watchers agree that the cable channel's launching "Yo! MTV Raps" in 1992 was the pivotal event in the spread of hip-hop culture. Running in a prime after-school spot, and initially hosted by graffiti artist and rapper Fab Five Freddy, the show beamed two daily hours of inner-city attitude at adolescent eyeballs in even the most remote Iowa corn country.

10   "There's no question—'Yo! MTV Raps' was the window into that world for Middle America," says Janine Misdom of Sputnik, a Manhattan-based firm that tracks youth trends for clients such as Levi-Strauss, Reebok, and Pepsi. Other video-oriented media soon followed. Within a few years, an all-day viewer-controlled channel called The Box supplied a steady stream of harder-edged hip-hop to any kid within the viewing area of a major metropolis. In 1993, about a year after "Yo! MTV Raps" hit cable, more than six in ten teens aged 12 to 19 rated hip-hop music as "in," according to Teenage Research Unlimited (TRU) of Northbrook, Illinois.

Music and fashion went hand in hand, as teens adopted the looks sported by rappers. Most Americans first saw baggy jeans in music videos sagging around the hips of white rap star Marky Mark. Teens also got an eyeful of Mark's boxers-exposed backside in his beefcake ads for Calvin Klein jeans. By spring 1993, 80 percent of teens favored the style, up from two-thirds six months earlier. And the look has staying power. Seventy-eight percent of teens still say baggy clothes are "in," according to TRU's Spring 1996 survey, although the style's popularity may be waning slightly.

Today, elements of hip-hop culture appear in the mainstream media, from commercials using rapped slogans to hit films such as *Menace II Society* and *Boyz N the Hood.* Suburban record stores stock relatively extensive hip-hop sections, and with good reason. Among consumers aged 12 to 17, almost three in five (58 percent) either "like" or "strongly like" rap, according to SounData of Hartsdale, New York, which tracks sales and other trends for the music industry. The 1996 figure is equally high among 18-to-20-year-olds. And even among the solidly adult 21-to-24-year-old age group, almost two-fifths favor the genre. Not surprisingly, it has now become a music-industry maxim that for a rap record to go platinum, it must sell strongly among white youths.

What draws white teens to a culture with origins so strongly linked to the inner city, and so distant from their suburbia's sylvan lawns? Clearly, rebellion is a big factor. "People resonate with the strong anti-oppression messages of rap, and the alienation of blacks," says Ivan Juzang of Motivational Educational Entertainment, a six-year-old Philadelphia firm specializing in targeting urban youth. "All young people buy into rebellion in general, as part of rebelling against parental authority."

Embracing Fear

Gangster rap artists such as the late Tupac Shakur and Dr. Dre represent only the latest link in a long chain of anti-establishment American icons (Shakur was wounded in a drive-by shooting in Las Vegas in September 1996 and died a week later). Amer-

Who's Got the Beat

**Percent of teenagers and adults aged 12 and
older who like or strongly like rap music, by age, 1996**

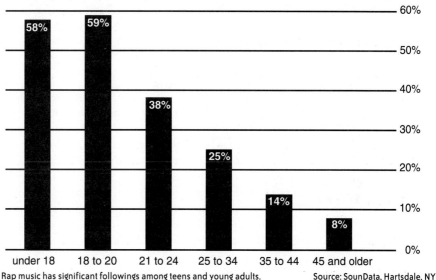

Rap music has significant followings among teens and young adults.   Source: SounData, Hartsdale, NY

ican teens have always been fascinated with outsider heroes, who score money and
fame without being cowed by societal strictures. Such idols run from John Dillinger
and Dennis Rodman, to Marlon Brando's fictional biker in *The Wild One* to James
Dean's *Rebel without a Cause*.

15   Yet many argue that hip-hop's attractiveness transcends mere rebellion, placing
it in a different category from past teen trends. For instance, punk, with its body piercing and mohawked heads, was often rebellion for rebellion's sake. Based on the urge
to shock, it constructed a new reality for its adherents outside of societal norms. In
contrast, hip-hop springs from the experiences of young blacks living in cities. It's
based on a real culture, giving it more permanence than earlier teen trends. People
who want a part of hip-hop culture always have something new to latch onto, because
the culture is always evolving.

          But perhaps more important to white teens, embracing hip-hop fashion, lan-
guage, and music lets them claim to be part of black, inner-city culture. "By entering
into the hip-hop sphere, I felt like I was opening a whole world that was closed to me
before—it gave me a basis to meet all these people I had been scared of, whose main
context for me was that they stole my bikes," says white 23-year-old William "Upski"
Wimsatt, author of the memoir *Bomb the Suburbs*. The book in part details his trajectory from University of Chicago faculty brat to graffiti artist and journalist covering the rap music scene.

          The attraction, he says, is part admiration, part fascination, and part fear. "A lot
of white kids suspect they wouldn't make it through what inner-city blacks do, so
there's an embedded admiration that's almost visceral," Wimsatt says. "Fear is one of
our strongest impulses, and poor black men are the greatest embodiment of that fear."

Skateboarders, snowboarders, and other practitioners of nontraditional sports were among the first white teens to adopt the accouterments of hip-hop culture. Yet they are also some of the culture's least devoted adherents. "Most of them don't really understand hip-hop," says Chicagoan Tim Haley, a Midwest sales representative for snow-boarding gear. They want to come off as being bad ass, pumping their stereo around town," he says. "So you'll see a bunch of white kids in Podunk, Michigan, trying to dress 'hip-hop,' but really they're just jocks with rich parents."

Got to Be Real

Turning teens like these on to hip-hop styles begins with a much smaller group—hardcore hip-hoppers. "If we develop the hardest core element, we reach middle-class blacks, and then there's a ripple effect," says Juzang of Motivational Educational Entertainment. "If you don't target the hard-core, you don't get the suburbs." For example, marketers for the 1995 Mario Van Peebles film *Panther* misfired by casting it "as *JFK* for African Americans," Juzang says. The flick bombed. Soon after, the comedy *Friday* came out, pitched as a straight-up ghetto laugh-fest, and scored big both inside and outside city borders. The lesson here: core hip-hoppers display an almost fanatical obsession with authenticity. Sanitizing any element of hip-hop culture to make it more palatable for middle-class suburban whites is likely to result in failure, because the core hip-hop audience will reject it. And other groups look to this core for their cues. This wasn't always the case. The pop-music audience was responsible for the commercial success of artists such as faux rapper Vanilla Ice and thinly disguised pop star MC Hammer. Both scored major hits by unimaginatively sampling 1980s pop songs and rapping bland rhymes over them. But now, even peripheral hip-hop consumers have grasped the difference between real and rip-off. If white kids realize a product has been toned down in a bid to make it "cross over," they'll avoid it. Instead they go for music with a blunt, urban sensibility—the harder-edged stuff Chuck D of the rap group Public Enemy once described as "CNN for black America." Soundscan sales statistics bear this out. In 1994, three-quarters of hard-core rap albums were sold to white consumers.

The Inner and Outer Circles

20   The hip-hop market encompasses consumers with varying levels of commitment to the culture. Millions of people buy rap records, but can hardly be called hard-core. Strictly speaking, a person must do at least one of three things to qualify: rap or be a disc jockey; breakdance; or paint graffiti.

Few white-teenagers meet these criteria. Some are afraid to venture into inner cities or cities at all, many are restricted by their parents, and others are content to absorb hip-hop culture through television and other media. "Lots of kids' parents won't let them cross certain borders. So they're watching videos to see how to dress, how to look, how to talk," says black urban-sportswear designer Maurice Malone. "They can visualize the inner city. But they don't go there, so they can't fully communicate with the heart of the hip-hop movement."

Wimsatt, the Chicago hip-hop writer, sees the white parts of the "hip-hop nation" as a series of concentric attitudinal rings. At the center lie those who actually know

Music Video Generation

Percent of hip-hoppers* and all blacks aged 16 and older who watch selected types of television programs at least once a week, 1995

	Hip-hoppers	Bourgeois/Mercantile
Game Shows	44%	40%
Music Video Shows	42	34
Weekday Morning News	37	37
Dramas	36	40
Award Shows	35	29
Nighttime Comedies	31	32
Late-night Entertainment	29	24

*Hip-hoppers are young, urban blacks as defined by Yankelovich Partners
Source: Yankelovich Partners Inc. Norwalk, CT.

blacks and study the intricacies of hip-hop's culture. "These people tend to consider themselves the racial exception," says Wimsatt. "They have a very regimented idea of what's cool and what's not."

Next is a group that has peripheral contact with the culture through friends or relatives, but doesn't actively seek "true hip-hopper" status. They go to shows, but don't rap, spray-paint, or breakdance. "After that, you have people who play hip-hop between other types of music," Wimsatt says. "They're sort of free-floating fans." Most white suburban teens probably fall into this category, listening to accessible acts such as Tribe called Quest and De La Soul.

Finally, the people in the outermost circle are those Wimsatt documented in a controversial 1993 article for hip-hop's *Source* magazine. Touring America, he met rural "wiggers" who avoided cities, thought blacks complained too much about their societal lot, and spouted phrases such as, "We wear a lot of pro-black clothes." To Wimsatt, such kids "are pure consumers—they're really into rap, but don't know much, so they're easily manipulated."

Unlocking the Door

25 As hip-hop has made its mark on the mainstream, all but the most gullible fans have spotted a flurry of laughable bids to capitalize on the trend. Anybody with a drum machine and a rhyming dictionary, it seemed, could be presented as a true hip-hopper. "The history of semi-insiders trying to exploit hip-hop is an incredible comedy of errors," Wimsatt says. "I've seen so many commercials with some sort of hip-hop theme that are just transparent. You can almost see the creatives looking around the office and saying, 'Hmm… who do we know who's black and has a teenage cousin? Maybe that cousin raps…'" If you're trying to reach the hip-hop crowd, he says, take the time to find and hire legitimate hip-hop players. Good places to start tracking down insiders include record stores, music venues, and recording studios. National magazines such as *Vibe, RapPages,* and *The Source* may also mention local players on their pages.

Sprite evidently did its homework. For a series of NBA-game commercials, Coca-Cola Company (makers of Sprite) hired two of hip-hop's legendary "MCs," wordsmiths KRS-One and MC Shan. Even better they had them face off in the sort of extemporaneous "freestyle battle" seen as any rapper's truest test of verbal skills and mental agility. The spot was roundly acclaimed, both inside and outside the rap world.

In the clothing arena, it's the same game. Mainstream designers such as Hilfiger and Lauren have scored. But smaller "underground" lines can also flourish in both city and suburb, says Misdom of Sputnik. "Even in places like [Minnesota's] Mall of America, you'll see kids who dress 'hip-hop' wearing grass-roots brands like Mecca, Boss Jeans, and Phat Farm," she says. "They are embracing these brands because they are seen as 'true.'"

Not every company that wants to sell to the inner-city crowd has grasped this wisdom. Malone cites two design prototypes making the rounds recently. Both try to emulate the boxers-exposed-by-sagging-jeans look. One pair of pants sports an underwear-like band of cloth sewn directly into the jeans waist, to peek out in a risk-free risqué style. Another features two waists—the first hangs at pelvis height giving the impression of disdain for belts, the second sitting traditionally on the hips. Both models have yet to make any splash. As Malone points out mockingly,

"The most successful crossovers don't try. People will cross over to you if you don't try to play to them."

Rappin' on the Web

Hip-hop enthusiasts maintain dozens of internet web sites. These are good sources of information on language, art, music, and figures in hip-hop. The following is a sampling. Most have links to other rap and hip-hop sites.

The Rap Dictionary
http://www.rapdict.org
Vibe magazine
www.vibe.com
The Source
www.enews.com/magazines/source
DaSewaSide
http://www.users.interport.net/~gbishop/
Fresh Out the Box
http://www.holo.com/fresh/
Yahoo!'s list of rap and hip-hop sites
http://www.yahoo.com/Entertainment/Music/Genres/Rap_and_Hip_Hop/
The Krib
http://www.trader.com/users/5013/1723/krib.htm

An Ever-Changing Scene

There's another reason the phony jeans may have failed. In hip-hop, the baggy jeans look has started to fade, following the lead of the skate-boarding subculture that abandoned drowning in denim for a "cleaner," tighter look in 1995. Baggy clothes of all kinds reached their peak in popularity in Fall 1993 and Spring 1994, when 82 percent of teens aged 12 to 19 said baggy clothes were in. That share slipped to 78 percent in spring 1996, according to Teenage Research Unlimited.

30   Hip-hop culture is constantly evolving, partly because of the commercial success of some of its elements. As Don DeLillo wrote in his novel *America*, "as soon as Madison Avenue breaks the code, Harlem devises a new one." But hip-hop music, language, and fashion also change because looking good and sporting the latest styles are very important to core members of the culture.

The 1995 Yankelovich African-American Monitor clusters black consumers into six segments based on attitudes and income. Its "hip-hopper" segment includes 27 percent of U.S. blacks. These single, urban blacks probably include members who are not authentic hip-hoppers. But their attitudes are telling, nonetheless. More than half of Yankelovich's hip-hoppers strongly agree that they feel the need to be fashionably dressed, compared with only 33 percent of all blacks aged 16 and older. These hip-hoppers are twice as likely as all blacks to strongly feel the need to keep up with new styles, at 42 percent.

To Sputnik's Misdom, hip-hop culture's emphasis on innovative fashion counts among its strongest selling points for teens, who demand a never-ending slew of status symbols to define them against both their peers and parents. "All the rock and

Hip-Hop Stuff

Percent of teens aged 12-19 who say selected things are "in," 1996

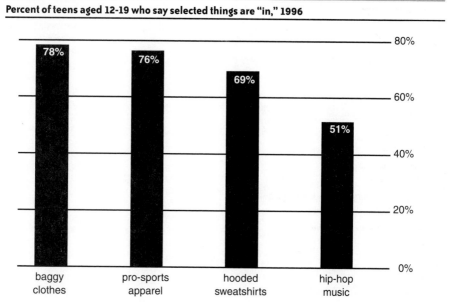

Gravity-defying pants are firmly entrenched with U.S. teens.   Source: Teenage Research Unlimited, Northbrook, IL

Hip-Hop 101: The Placement Test*

Although hip-hop's media prominence has risen, the culture's slang, dress and music evolve so quickly that it's hard to track. Below, a little test of how much hip-hop knowledge has come your way over the years, broken down into three levels of difficulty.

Easy

1. When Will Smith was "The Fresh Prince," who was his partner?
A. Jazzy Jeff
B. Schooly D
C. Big Daddy Kane
D. Queen Latifah

2. Which of the following terms means, or used to mean "cool" in hip-hop slang?
A. "Dope"
B. "Fat"
C. "Stupid"
D. All of the above

3. For hip-hop fans, the term "sampling" refers to:
A. Any poll-taking method
B. Reusing sections of an older song
C. Shoplifting "gear" from malls
D. Using rhymes from other artists

4. Deliberately "scratching" a record yields
A. An angry record owner
B. A broken record needle
C. New sounds for a musical mix

5. Run-DMC's lyrics promoted which shoe company?
A. Nike
B. Adidas
C. Pony
D. Converse

Moderate

6. The Beastie Boys started as:
A. A breakdancing group
B. Art school students
C. A 3-on-3 basketball team
D. A hardcore punk band

7. Two of the following pairs were partners. Two had famous feuds. Which are which?
A. Scott LaRock & Kris Parker
B. Canibus & LL Cool J
C. Puff Daddy & Suge Knight
D. Q-Tip & Phife

8. Which of the following white rappers are generally considered "legit" by their black peers?
A. Eminem
B. Marky Mark
C. Vanilla Ice
D. Everlast

9. "Freestyling" refers to:
A. Impromptu breakdancing
B. Spontaneous rapping
C. Drawing graffiti without stencils

10. For Tupac Shakur, conviction and imprisonment on sexual-assault charges meant:
A. The end of a budding career
B. A temporary hiatus
C. A huge boost in popularity
D. A religious conversion

Harder

11. In 1999, which NBA team had two players who are rap recording artists?
A. L.A. Lakers
B. Chicago Bulls
C. New York Knicks
D. Boston Celtics

12. In hip-hop slang, the term "bombing" refers to:
A. Artistry
B. Terrorism
C. Insect extermination

13. Dr. Dre is:
A. The ex-NWA member who scored a huge hit with "The Chronic"
B. A movie actor and VJ on MTV
C. The man charged with recruiting dancers for 2 Live Crew videos

14. A "B-Boy":
A. Plays basketball well
B. Wears baseball caps
C. Breakdances
D. Works as a bouncer at rap shows

15. Which of the following brands has never been embraced by hip-hop's fashion mavens?
A. Teva   F. North Face
B. Nike   G. Stetson
C. Timberland H. Kangol
D. Bass shoes I. Gucci
E. Polo   J. Ferragamo

Answers

1. A
2. D
3. B
4. C
5. B. The 1986 song "My Adidas" counts among the earliest or rap's frequent product "shout-outs."
6. D. (Kate Schellenbach, of Luscious Jackson, was their drummer)
7. The allies: A, as Boogie Down Productions; and D, in A Tribe Called Quest. The enemies: B and C.
8. A, D. In 1999, Dr. Dre oversaw production of Eminem's hit record "Slim Shady." Everlast was featured on Prince Paul's critically acclaimed "Prince Among Thieves."
9. B
10. C. Shakur scored a No. 1 song while behind bars with "Dear Mama."
11. A. Shaquille O'Neal has cut several records, while Kobe Bryant rapped on R&B star Brian McKnight's 1998 single "Hold Me."
12. A. The "bomb" involved is an aerosol can used by graffiti artists.
13. B. The DJ and Producer is Dr. Dre. And, yes, it's a trick question.
14. C
15. A, D, G, J

* Marc Spiegler revised and updated The Placement Test for this book.

Figure 8.3

grunge styles have stayed the same," she says. "But hip-hop always has a lot of styles coming out." Already her studies project a shift away from the preppier Hilfiger style toward "uptown," high-end designer labels such as DKNY, Versace, and Dolce & Gabbana. Garments bearing these labels have a sleeker, more European look than brands such as Hilfiger. They also have higher price tags.

Recent rap videos support her observations. "Roughneck" styles featuring hunting and fishing apparel are on the wane. Another emerging hot style uses high-tech fabrics and styles that resemble those worn by scientists at the South Pole and by mountain climbers. Last summer, designer Donna Karan dressed many of New York City's fashionable young in DKNY Tech. This lower-priced line of clothing featuring high-tech fabrics represents the designer's nod to the trendsetting power of urban teens.

Hip-hop culture is in some ways the next page in the decades-long book of teenagers embracing the forbidden. Yet it's also more lasting, because it is based on the day-to-day experiences of millions of inner-city teens. Targeting this relatively small group of teens may open the door to the larger, more affluent, white, suburban market. But the niche has countless pitfalls. Companies that have successfully negotiated them know a fundamental truth of hip-hop culture: For a product to appeal to a rapper in south central L.A. or a white mall crawler in Des Moines, it's got to be real.

Rereading Actively

1. In a small group, review the article, focusing on some of the reported facts and statistics that you find surprising or especially striking. Discuss what seems significant to you about these facts or statistics. Then, in your journal, describe your group's conversation, noting some of the striking information you found in the article.

2. Spiegler states that hip-hop has hit the mainstream. But how did it get there? With a partner, review the section discussing the role of MTV in the crossover of hip-hop. Then, summarize the role MTV played in an entry in your journal.

3. What are some of the motivations Spiegler attributes to white teenagers who adopt hip-hop style?

4. What are "the inner and outer circles" of hip-hop?

5. Hip-hop's emphasis on innovation is one of its strongest selling points for teens. Explain how this fact is illustrated by the example of baggy jeans that Spiegler focuses on near the end of the article.

Exploring Your Responses

6. In a page or two in your journal, reflect on the marketing process that Spiegler describes: Does the selling of hip-hop style in the "mainstream" seem like a positive thing to you? Why or why not?

7. In a small group, take the quiz ("Hip-Hop 101: The Placement Test"). Compare your scores and discuss the results. Who is "stupid"? Who isn't? In a journal entry, evaluate your knowledge of hip-hop.

8. Reflect on the idea that purchasing hip-hop clothing or music can let suburban white teenagers participate in black life. ("[I]t gave me a basis to meet all
these people I had been scared of" (¶ 16), one youth is quoted as saying.)
Write a page or two in your journal commenting on this: Does this youth take
a meaningful step toward a different culture? Draw on your own experience
if it applies.

IMITATION OF LIFE

JAMES LEDBETTER

James Ledbetter is the New York Bureau Chief for the Industry Standard, *a weekly magazine covering the Internet economy. In addition, he is the author of* Made Possible By:
The Death of Public Broadcasting in the United States *(1997). His essay, "Imitation of
Life," was published in 1992 in the premier issue of* Vibe, *a multicultural journal founded
by the musician Quincy Jones, which is aimed a young, urban audience. Ledbetter was
one of the first to interrogate the adoption of hip-hop style by millions of whites. Ledbetter borrowed the title, "Imitation of Life," from a 1933 novel of "passing" for white by Fan-
nie Hurst, and the original version of this essay begins with lyrics from a Lou Reed song,
"I Wanna Be Black," a scathing satire of the fetishization of black street culture which
appears on Reed's album,* Street Hassle *(Arista Records, 1978). Omitted from this reprint
because their sensational language might be offensive to many people, these lyrics are
alluded to in (¶ 5) and in (¶ 11).*

In 1989, Madonna gushed to an interviewer: "When I was a little girl, I wished I was
black.... If being black is synonymous with having soul, then, yes, I feel that I am."
In concert, the Beastie Boys strut around the stage in an exaggerated "black" walk and
chant a street dialect somewhere between an imitation of black speech and a bad translation of it. Radio clown Howard Stern has said of his childhood: "I remember for the
longest time wanting to be black." A 16-year-old white Pennsylvanian says his high
school is full of "wiggers," whites so desperate to adopt black modes of dress and conduct that they end up being parodies. Call 'em wanna-be's, call 'em rip-offs, call 'em
suckers, but they're everywhere—white folks who think they're black, or wish they were.

The arrival of hip-hop as a leading musico-cultural force has created an entire
subclass of these wanna-be's. Following the Beasties' lead, there was 3rd Bass, white
rappers who, until their recent breakup, expressed an almost painful identification
with New York blacks. Then came House of Pain, an Irish-American rap group whose
video cuts from black-styled hip-hop dancing to marching bagpipe players. Now
there's A.D.O.R., a hard-core white rapper whose name means Against Discrimination of Race and a Definition of Real. Perhaps most extreme are Young Black
Teenagers, an all-white and not very good rap group whose strut and postures are
"blacker" than most of their fans, even more so than most blacks. What's more, millions of white fans of black rappers have adopted modes of dress, speech, and style
that they consider black.

The phenomenon isn't new. American writers, sociologists, and armchair sociologists have long spotlighted black wanna-be's, arguing that their desire to be black has
some tenuous connection to African-American social oppression. Norman Mailer, in

his prescient, bizarre, and overwritten 1957 essay "The White Negro" asserted that "it is no accident that the source of Hip is the Negro for he has been living on the margin between totalitarianism and democracy for two centuries." Nor is it new that attempted race bending expresses itself musically, with earlier examples ranging from minstrel shows, a dominant Southern entertainment form through the mid-20th century, to Janis Joplin, who a generation ago told a reporter: "Being black for a while will make me a better white."

It's a curious spectacle, and one that pisses off a lot of people, both black and white. Americans take their segregation very seriously, and not just the de facto racial separation of housing, education, and income, but our cultural apartheid as well. America reacts dramatically, even violently, to cultural expressions that suggest racial admixture—the original 1952 rock 'n' roll riot in Cleveland was due not only to an oversold show, but also, some say, to the fact that inside the Cleveland Arena ballroom, blacks and whites were dancing together to the same music.

5   In part, the disgust with wanna-be's comes from the sheer vulgarity of the white who cavalierly adopts the black mantle without having to experience life-long racism, restricted economic opportunity, or any of the thousand insults that characterize black American life. (Similar ridicule was aimed at an earlier generation's purveyors of radical chic.) And, as depicted in Lou Reed's outrageous lyrics, whites' interpretation of what it means "to be black," even when they're attempting to "understand" or "empathize with" victims of racism, often results in a version that looks an awful lot like racism itself. Finally, whites have been riffing off—or ripping off—black cultural forms for more than a century and making a lot more money from them. Whether it's Al Jolson, Elvis, the Rolling Stones, Blues Brothers, Commitments, New Kids, or Beasties, it's impossible to deny that, as a rule, the market responds much better to a black sound with a white face.

There are two crucial factors separating the minstrel of past generations from today's racial flaneurs. The first is easily identified: the market. In Mailer's essay, for example, the white hipster was necessarily on the margins; Mailer even identified him with the psychopath. The white Negro, with his lust for jazz and grass, was a threat to the American way of life, a figure whose existential insight was contingent on his isolation from society. Today, the inverse is true: There are a number of intersecting multi-billion-dollar American industries (music, advertising, television, sports) whose survival at current profit levels depends on the existence of a massive audience of white Negroes.

Take *Saturday Night Live's* fall 1991 premiere, hosted by Michael Jordan, with musical guest Public Enemy and cameo appearances by Spike Lee and Jesse Jackson. It was punctuated by Gatorade ads featuring white and black kids singing "If I Could Be Like Mike." Coincidentally, it aired the night Miles Davis died and thus the live program carried several allusions to the jazz legend. The resulting episode was the highest-rated *SNL* season opener ever. It wasn't just black viewers who made those Nielsens jump, but whites who, as fans of basketball, hip-hop, jazz, and Lee's movies, have become more or less integrated into a black ethos. Rap music may be, as Chuck D says, black people's CNN, but there are a lot of white folks tuning into that signal too.

And where such black-oriented whites do not exist, they must—through advertising, fashion, MTV, and magazines such as this one—be created. Somewhere in the mid-Black Power period, America's culture industry discovered that, instead of being polarizing and threatening, black slang, music, and energy could be harnessed for immense profits. (My earliest memory of this co-optation was the slogan "Write on, Bros., write on," used to sell 19-cent Write Bros. pens.) Just as on the record charts, hip-hop and its derivatives have taken over this promotional agenda; its beat and style are today used to hype not just hip-hop artists, but also television shows, children's clothing, bubble gum—even hair-care products for whites. This guarantees thousands, even millions more hipsters than Mailer could ever have imagined, but their value is accordingly debased. If a white can become "hip" simply by buying the right shampoo or CD, then the control of "hip" has been passed from society's rebels to its representatives.

The second factor differentiating the contemporary wanna-be is more obscure, and not as powerful as the market, though its rise also corresponds to the development, beginning in the mid-1960s, of a more militant black agenda. There exists today a limited (but nonetheless quasi-institutionalized) school of music critics, artists, record industry honchos, intellectuals, and activists whose tolerance for the white Negro has more or less expired. This isn't to say that, in the past, white beatniks or hippies were universally embraced by the blacks they emulated. But there has been a shift in the balance of power: Whereas black jazz musicians in the 1940s had to shrug (or innovate further) when whites copied their musical styles, today the more exploitative wanna-be's—Vanilla Ice is the best example—are called out as the frauds they are. Armed with a body of criticism that extends from LeRoi Jones through Greg Tate, and with an ideology that draws strength from Afrocentrism (even while rejecting portions of it), rappers and writers today regularly dis wanna-be's in public as opportunists or racists or both. One of the more extraordinary developments is that even the contemporary white hipster must go through this ritual of denouncing a fellow wanna-be as somehow being less authentic. Both 3rd Bass albums, for example, seem almost obsessed with denouncing Vanilla Ice, as if his downfall would inflate their "genuine" attachment to blacks and to rap.

10   The authenticity argument gets even blurrier when rappers rank on Hammer, thus far their most commercially successful colleague. To say, as so many have, that Hammer can't rap or has sold out introduces the idea of the Oreo, the inauthentic black, cousin to the wanna-be (and a target of equally vehement criticism from many black artists and critics, notably Ice Cube in "True to the Game" on *Death Certificate*). It also breaks down the simple dichotomy under which both wanna-be's and some black artists and critics operate; it admits the possibility that blackness is a quality other than pigmentation, even other than a social condition, since Hammer's upbringing wasn't radically different from those considered true black rappers. This is the direction in which a number of intellectuals, notably Stuart Hall and Paul Giroy, have been heading, insisting that "blackness" is too complex, too amorphous a code to be reduced to a simple question of color or even class.

In a way, the very existence of the wanna-be implies this complexity. Because while the Vanilla Ices of the world can be explained as mere economic exploiters, the 1990s white suburbanite gets no money from listening to Public Enemy. And at least he or she gets out of it some exposure to a black urban reality—which is more than Beaver Cleaver ever got. Janis Joplin's comment, sincere as it was naïve, speaks to the multiple motivations behind youth's racial switcheroo—it's intended to resolve a racial gap that the white kid doesn't feel responsible for. Lou Reed's offensive, funny lyrics are a frank expression of the self-emptiness that makes some renegade whites want to be "black" (and, at the same time, a vicious parody of that desire). Later in the song, Reed sings of wanting to be shot like Martin Luther King and wanting to be like Malcolm X. Those lyrics, as nasty as they are, speak to a genuine yearning: There is, for young American whites, no white leader in recent memory who invokes such a powerful self-identity and moral force. The closest for them may be artists and rock stars (including Reed), but they never achieved anything approaching the status and power those men had. That both were gunned down only enhances, for black and whites, their embodiment of authenticity and unapologetic rebellion.

By listening to rap and tapping into its extramusical expressions, then, whites are attempting to bear witness to—even correct—their own often sterile, oppressive culture. Cornel West has referred to this as the Afro-Americanization of American youth, a potent thought since this country is fast headed toward a non-white majority for the first time since its colonization. If current population growth trends hold, with Asian, Latino, black, and other nonwhite segments growing at much higher rates than white, the U.S. will be a "minority majority" nation within the next century. Wanna-be's, in that sense, are harbingers of America's multicultural future.

Intentions, though, aren't enough, today or ever. The most difficult (and almost always unasked) question for wanna-be's, particularly those with access to airwaves and media, is: Does their identification with what they view as black culture extend to taking concrete steps to end America's political and cultural apartheid? Are they at the very least willing to renounce, up front, the systemic abuses of the white order, from which, regardless of their implicit dissent, they have doubtlessly benefited? It accomplishes nothing to play at being black and ignore the society that made you want to do it. Indeed, the wanna-be is at great risk of using black posturing solely as a way to assuage his or her conscience.

The challenge for the wanna-be is to make the critique of America more explicit. There are very clear analogies in politics. Whites would find themselves on the defensive a lot less if they stopped ignoring those political causes that seem to affect blacks almost exclusively. For example, where are the white political leaders willing to put themselves on the line to oppose the Bush Administration's unconscionable wholesale repatriation of Haitian refugees, announced not coincidentally in an election year? More shocking is that even after a willingly slumbering nation was awakened by the videotape of white cops bashing Rodney King, no prominent white leader has announced that police brutality against people of color is an outrage that must be stopped. If America's wanna-be's wanna be taken seriously, they ought to be adopting such issues. For white hip-hop artists, this means using the music as a vehicle to discuss segregation and economic blight, rather than simply as a way to provide one more commercial distraction. For the far more numerous white fans, it means screaming out that you accept the criticism of the American system offered by the likes of Ice Cube and Public Enemy, and you want the society to do something more than buy and sell their records.

Rereading Actively

1. With a partner or in a small group, make a list of the performers past and present whom Ledbetter names in this article and who represent different aspects of the crossover of black culture into white America.

2. Ledbetter identifies an economic factor that distinguishes hip-hop from other examples of crossover in the past. In a journal entry, explain the role Ledbetter attributes to "marketing."

3. The issue of "authenticity" becomes a social factor Ledbetter links to those white artists who would adopt black styles. What does "authenticity" seem to mean in critiques of white performers who have formed rap acts?

4. Ledbetter discusses psychological factors that may explain why whites are interested in borrowing from black culture. With a partner, review this section of the article, and write a brief, collaborative summary of Ledbetter's psychological explanation of the motives of "wanna-be's."

5. What "challenge" does Ledbetter feel "wanna-be's" ought to face? Describe this challenge in an entry in your journal.

Exploring Your Responses

6. Do you agree with Ledbetter that white hip-hop artists should be using their music as "a vehicle to discuss segregation and economic blight" (¶ 14)? (Is he correct in assuming in 1992 that these remain real issues? Do they remain issues today? Do white hip-hop artists have an obligation to address them?)

7. Ledbetter speculates that white male teenagers can find few if any white leaders who compare, in their power of self-identity and moral force, with Dr. Martin Luther King, Jr., or Malcolm X. Do you agree with Ledbetter's assessment? Why or why not? Does this seem like a persuasive explanation of the crossover of hip-hop into white culture?

8. "[A]s a rule," Ledbetter argues, "the market responds much better to a black sound with a white face" (¶ 5). Does that seem true to your observations and experience?

9. In a page or two of your journal, explore the contradictions Ledbetter identifies in both "the white who cavalierly adopts the black mantle without having to experience life-long racism" (¶ 5) and in whites' problematic interpretations of "what it means 'to be black'" that end up looking "an awful lot like racism itself" (¶ 5).

10. An argument can be made that a faithful reprint of this article would include the lyrics from the Lou Reed song. We chose to omit them, fearing they would offend some people, or that some would deem them rhetorically inappropriate for a college text book. (Again, we refer you to Reed's album if you wish to see the lyrics.) What situations cause you to place limits on your own speech or writing? Do you feel that the most important part of your message gets lost as a result of self-censorship, or do you find other ways of expressing your ideas?

"THEY DONE TAKEN MY BLUES AND GONE": BLACK TALK CROSSES OVER

GENEVA SMITHERMAN

Geneva Smitherman is a professor of sociolinguistics at Michigan State University and one of the most important scholars of Black English in the world. Her 1977 book, Talkin and Testifyin, *is among the most comprehensive descriptions of the language system known and used to some extent by most black residents in the United States. Black Talk, the book from which this excerpt is taken, appeared in 1994. It is a dictionary of Black English that includes the origins and history of hundreds of words from the Black English lexicon. "They Done Taken My Blues and Gone" focuses specifically on the crossover of elements of Black culture, with particular emphasis on language.*

> A 16-year-old white Pennsylvanian says his high school is full of "wiggers," whites…desperate to adopt black modes of dress and conduct…. Call 'em wanna-bes, call 'em rip-offs, call 'em suckers, but they're everywhere—white folks who think they're black…. Whites have been riffing off—or ripping off—black cultural forms for more than a century and making a lot more money from them…. [Whites] cavalierly adopt …the black mantle without having to experience life-long racism, restricted economic opportunity, or any of the thousand insults that characterize black American life…. It's a curious spectacle.
>
> —White journalist James Ledbetter, in "Imitation of Life," Fall 1992,
> *Vibe* Magazine

In the nineties U.S.A., the "curious spectacle" is everywhere. White males HOOP on courts in Great Falls, Montana, Oak Park, Illinois, Orange County, California, and Brownsville, Tennessee, HIGH-FIVin it and TALKIN TRASH, often without the slightest inkling that they are doing a BLACK THANG. And they think nothing of donning X caps, wearing them sideways or backwards as is fashionable in the HOOD. White females sport TUDES of twenty-first century assertive womanhood as they RAP "Fly Girl" from Queen Latifah's 1991 album *Nature of [A] Sista:*

> I always hear "Yo, Baby." …
> No, my name ain't "Yo,"
> And I ain't got yo "baby."

Coming into their own, white girls issue ultimatums to their WIGGAS, DROPping SCIENCE from Mary J. Blige's 1991 title cut, "What's the 411?":

> The same ol shit you pulled last week on Kim,
> I'm not havin that….
> So come correct with some respect.

A 1993 article by a European American used the title "A New Way to TALK THAT TALK" (small capitals added) to describe a new talk show. *The American Heritage Dictionary,* Third Edition, lists BUG and GRAPEVINE as just plain old words, with no label indicating "slang"or "Black." Merriam-Webster's latest (tenth) edition of its Collegiate Dictionary lists BOOM BOX the same way. A lengthy 1993 article in the *New York Times Magazine,* entitled "Talking Trash," discussed this ancient Black verbal tradition as the "art of conversation in the N.B.A." And in his first year in office, the nation's new "baby boomer" President was taken to task for "terminal HIPness."

The absorption of African American English into Eurocentric culture masks its true origin and reason for being. It is a language born from a culture of struggle, a way of talking that has taken surviving African language elements as the base for self-expression in an alien tongue. Through various processes such as "Semantic Inversion" (taking words and turning them into their opposites), African Americans stake our claim to the English language, and at the same time, reflect distinct Black values that are often at odds with Eurocentric standards. "Fat," spelled *phat* in Hip Hop, refers to a person or thing that is excellent and desirable, reflecting the traditional African value that human body weight is a good thing, and implicitly rejecting the Euro-American mainstream, where skinny, not fat, is valued and everybody is on a diet. Senior Blacks convey the same value with the expression, "Don't nobody want no BONE." By the process of giving negative words positive meanings, BAD means "good," STUPID means "excellent," and even the word DOPE becomes positive in Hip Hop, meaning "very good" or "superb."

The blunt, coded language of enslavement SIGGed ON Christian slaveholders with the expression, "Everybody talkin bout Heaven ain goin there." Hip Hop language, too, is bold and confrontational. It uses obscenities, graphic depictions of the sex act, oral and otherwise, and it adheres to the pronunciation and grammar of African American English (which the uninformed deem "poor English"). Thus B-BOYS and B-girls snub their noses at the European American world and the EUROPEAN NEGRO world as well. About the former, European American journalist Upski, writing from the "front lines of the White Struggle" (in *The Source,* May 1993), says:

> Even lifetime rap fans…usually discount a crucial reason rap was invented: white America's economic and psychological terrorism against Black people—reduced in the white mind to "prejudice" and "stereotypes," concepts more within its cultural experience.

About the latter, Armond White, reviewing the 1993 film *CB4* (in *Emerge,* May 1993), writes:

> *CB4* offers an unenlightened view of rap….It panders to…the black bourgeois fear that only "proper" language and "civilized" attitudes are acceptable means of addressing politics or articulating personal feelings.

5   But back to the lecture at hand, as Dr. Dre would say—the crossover of African American Language and Culture. Bemoaned by Black writer Langston Hughes ("they done taken my blues and gone"), reflecting on the out-migration of Black Culture during the Harlem Renaissance era of the 1920s when the "Negro was in vogue"…analyzed by white writer Norman Mailer in 1957 in his discussion of the "language of Hip" and "white Negroes"…resented, even as I write, by BOO-COOS African Americans, like twenty-two-year-old Jamal, in my survey of Black opinion on the WIGGA phenomenon:

> White folk kill me tryin to talk and be like us; they just want the good part. But it don't go like that; you got to take the bitter with the sweet.

Actually, as I said to the BROTHA, there's plenty of bitter to go around. Contrary to popular Black stereotypes, white folks' life is not all sweetness and light. Despite European Americans' higher material circumstances, it really is true that neither man nor woman can live by bread alone. European Americans live "lives of quiet desperation" too; it's just a different kind of desperation. Which is exactly why Black Talk continues to cross over, doing so today on an unprecedented scale because of the power of post-modern technology.

The dynamism and creativity in African American Language revitalizes and re-energizes bland Euro-talk. There's electricity and excitement in PLAYERS and FLY girls who wear GEAR. The metaphors, images, and poetry in Black Talk make the ordinary ALL THAT, AND THEN SOME. African American English is a dramatic, potent counter-force to verbal deadness and emptiness. One is not simply accepted by a group, one is IN LIKE FLIN. Fraternities and sororities don't merely march; they perform a STEP SHOW. And when folk get AMP, they don't fight the feeling, they TESTIFY. For whites, there is a certain magnetism in the African American use of English because it seems to make the impossible possible. I bet you a FAT MAN AGAINST THE HOLE IN A DOUGHNUT....

For *wiggas* and other white folk latching onto Black Talk, that's the good news. The bad news is that there's a reality check in African American English. Its terms and expressions keep you grounded, catch you just as you are taking flight and bring you right back down to the NITTY GRITTY of African American Life. There are rare flights of fancy in this poetry, no chance of getting so carried away that you don't know yo ASS FROM A HOLE IN THE GROUND. Unh-unh. Words like NIGGA reinforce Blackness since, whether used positively, generically, or negatively, the term can refer only to people of African descent. DEVIL, a negative reference to the white man, reminds Blacks to be on the lookout for HYPE. RUN AND TELL THAT, historically referring to Blacks who snitched to white folks, is a cultural caution to those planning Black affairs to be wary of the Judases among them. Such words in the Black Lexicon are constant reminders of race and the Black Struggle. And when you TALK THAT TALK, you must be loyal to Blackness, or as Ice Cube would say, be true to the GAME.

There are words and expressions in Black Talk like TWO-MINUTE BROTHA, describing a man who completes the sex act in a few seconds, and it's all over for the woman. Both in RAP and in everyday talk, the words B (bitch) and HO (whore) are generic references to Black women. GOT HIS/HER NOSE OPEN describes a male or female so deeply in love that he or she is ripe for exploitation. Terms like these in Black Language are continuing reminders that, despite all the talk about Black passion and SOUL, despite all the sixty-minute-man myths, despite all the WOOFin and TALKin SHIT, at bottom, the man-woman Thang among African Americans is just as problematic as it is among other groups.

10   Some African Americans see crossover as positive because of its possibilities for reducing racial tension. Fashion journalist Robin D. Givhan, writing in the *Detroit Free Press* (June 21, 1993), asserts that she is "optimistic about wiggers":

> Appreciating someone else's culture is good. An increased level of interest among whites in what makes some African Americans groove can only be helpful to improved race relations.

Yet the reality of race, racism, and personal conflicts, which are often intensified by racism, does make crossover problematic. Whites pay no dues, but reap the psychological, social, and economic benefits of a language and culture born out of struggle and hard times. In his "We Use Words Like 'Mackadocious,'" Upski characterizes the "white rap audience" thus: "When they say they like rap, they usually have in mind a *certain* kind of rap, one that spits back what they already believe or lends an escape from their limited lives." And Ledbetter's "Imitation of Life" yields this conclusion: "By listening to rap and tapping into its extramusical expressions, then, whites are attempting to bear witness to—even correct—their own often sterile, oppressive culture." Yet it is also the case that not only Rap, but other forms of Black Language and Culture, are attractive because of the dynamism, creativity, and excitement in these forms. However one accounts for the crossover phenomenon, one thing is certain: today we are witnessing a multi-billion-dollar industry based on this Language-Culture while there is continued under-development and deterioration in the HOOD that produces it. In Ralph Wiley's collection of essays *Why Black People Tend to Shout,* which contains his *signifyin* piece, "Why Black People Have No Culture," he states: "Black people have no culture because most of it is out on loan to white people. With no interest."

From Home to Homey

> You're the kind of girl I wanna get closer to
> Become the most to you
> Like lovers suppose to do
> Cause I fell straight into your trap
> And since they say love is blind
> I'm the Ray Charles of rap
> And I'm waitin for you to put me in ya mix
> Because you got my nose open like a jar of Vicks.
>
> > —Rapper Big Daddy Kane, "Very Special,"
> > from his 1993 album *Looks Like A Job For …*

Ray Charles, singer, musician, founder of a seven-piece Rhythm and Blues band…born in 1932…blind since age six…released his first LP in 1957…soulful style blends Gospel, jazz, blues, and funk…height of popularity, the 1960s. Thus Big Daddy Kane and other HIP HOP artists pay tribute to their musical elders and seek to root themselves in The Tradition.

The Mary J. Blige TIP is a soulful blend of Rhythm and Blues, Hip Hop, and 1960s MOTOWN era sounds. This twenty-one-year-old DIVA says that her work "brings people back to those good Old School music days…Otis Redding, Gladys Knight, Al Green, Donny Hathaway, the Staple Singers." Guru (gifted/unlimited/rhymes/universal), of the RAP group Gang Starr, had long wanted to JAM with the "old cats." His 1993 album *Jazzmatazz,* which he calls "an experimental fusion of Hip Hop and live jazz," featured Donald Byrd, Roy Ayers, Branford Marsalis, and other jazz greats. Guru kicks the ballistics in "Cool Like Us" (*Details,* July 1993):

> This is fusion we're doing here. But it's also some gangsta shit. These old cats, they all made records reflecting street life. That's why rappers sample their shit.

Ice Cube's popular JAM "It Was A Good Day" (on his 1992 album *The Predator*) contains samples from the Isley Brothers' "Footsteps in the Dark," on their 1977 album, *Go For Your Guns.* Divas En Vogue went gold with their single "Something He Can Feel," a Curtis Mayfield JAM recorded by Aretha Franklin in the 1970s. Rapper Ice-T paid homage to history when he sold "dope beats and lyrics, no beepers needed" in his "I'm Your Pusher" duet with Mayfield based on Mayfield's 1972 *Superfly* movie soundtrack. Public Enemy (P.E.), always political, protested Arizona's refusal to honor Dr. Martin Luther King, Jr.'s birthday in "By The Time I Get To Arizona" (on their 1991 album *Apocalypse 91: The Enemy Strikes Black*), a Rap that recalls Isaac Hayes's talk-singing jam, "By The Time I Get to Phoenix," on his 1969 *Hot Buttered Soul* album.

SIGNIFYIN, LYIN, TALKIN TRASH, PLAYin THE DOZENS, and other old forms of Black Talk are all over the place today, from GANGSTA Rapper Schooly D's early jam, "Signifyin Rapper," to the recently released HYPE rhymes of Mary J. Blige's "4 1 1" duet with Rapper Grand Puba. Reaching back to Blackness untainted by wannabe vibes and the crossover explosion that the 1960s Black Movement set in motion…coming correct, with all due respect…engaged in a conscious return to The Source…making their way toward an African identity for the twenty-first century…these HOMEYS are in search of home.

15   Nor is today's generation the first to look for home. Forcibly removed from their native land, homeless Africans in America have been on a continual quest for home since 1619. After Emancipation, they thought they could make home the rich, fertile land of the South. But Reconstruction ended, and the Federal Government abandoned them, forcing them to survive amidst lynch mobs and the Ku Klux Klan and leaving them to fend for themselves as sharecroppers trapped in a new form of enslavement. African Americans began to leave their Southern home in droves, migrating to urban metropolises during and after World Wars I and II. Senior BLOODS and their children of the 1950s and 1960s searched for home in the PROMISED LANDS of the North. But what they found was urban blight, poor housing, inadequate schools, police brutality, and other social problems of the "inner city."

The "deferred dreams" of previous generations exploded in the REBELLIONS of the 1960s. The source of much of Hip Hop's language and many of its cultural forms is the generation that produced these rebellions during the Black Freedom Struggle of the 1960s and 1970s. TLC, the name of a popular female Rap group, is the abbreviation for "tender, loving care"; both the phrase and the abbreviation date back at least to the 1960s and can still be heard in the conversations of those who came of age during that time. Phrases from the 1960s and 1970s, such as BAD *self* and GIT IT ON, are frequently heard when Rappers like P.E. are IN THE HOUSE. Words like JAM and FUNKY are as common in Hip Hop as they were during the 1950s. And when B-BALL star "Sir Charles" Barkley and filmmaker Spike Lee are proudly characterized as "nineties NIGGAZ" (a phrase Barkley himself coined), we are reaching way back to enslavement, when the BAD NIGGA was born. Bad niggaz dared to buck Ole Massa, they didn't TAKE NO SHIT from Blacks or whites, and some of them even lived to tell about it.

Bridging generations, a good deal of Hip Hop lingo recycles either the same word or a variation of an older term. Words like PAD, IG, FRY, and SALTY appeared in Cab Calloway's 1938 *Hepster's Dictionary* and are still current today. Would you prefer to BIG-TIME IT (1960s/1970s) or to LIVE LARGE (1990s)? Answer: either, since both refer to SERIOUS material possessions and living the Good Life. But neither the sixties nor the nineties generation has anything on seniors who convey the same meaning with their colorful expression LIVIN HIGH OFF THE HOG, that is, living as though you're eating the upper parts of the hog, such as ribs or pork chops, rather than the lower parts, such as pig feet or CHITLINS. The PIMP WALK of the 1960s/1970s, the male strutting style of walking with a slight dip in the stride, is essentially the same as the GANGSTA LIMP of the 1990s; both expressions can be heard today. And though neither is identical to the CAT WALK of earlier years, what is important in all of this is the VIBE, the concept of a style of walking that projects a self-assured, TOGETHA, confident, even cocky man-image. Like walking with ATTITUDE…like by your walk conveying the message that you GOT IT GOIN ON.

Basic in Black Talk, then, is the commonality that takes us across boundaries. Regardless of job or social position, most African Americans experience some degree of participation in the life of the COMMUNITY—they get their hair done in African American BEAUTY SHOPS, they worship in Black churches, they attend African American social events, and they generally PAR-TAY with Blacks. This creates in-group crossover lingo that is understood and shared by various social groups within the race—words like KINKY and NAPPY to describe the texture of African American hair; HIGH YELLUH to refer to light-complexioned Blacks; CHITLINS to refer to hog intestines, a popular SOUL food; and a ready understanding of the different meanings of the N-WORD.

As stated, the closest connection between generations in Black Talk, as in today's music, is between Hip Hop and the 1960s/1970s. In addition to the terms given above, other examples of parallel expressions include COOL OUT (1960s/1970s) and CHILL (1990s), meaning, to relax, take it calm and easy; DOIN IT TO DEF (1960s/1970s) and DEF (1990s), to describe something that is superb or excellent; RUN IT DOWN (1960s/1970s) and BREAK IT DOWN (1990s), meaning, to explain and simplify something, make it plain; BLOCK BOY (1960s/1970s) and BANJY BOY (1990s), referring to a gay male in FLY culture who dresses like straight males; ALL THE WAY LIVE (1960s/1970s) and LIVE (1990s), to describe an exciting, desirable event, person, place, or experience; and ACE BOON COON (1960s/1970s) and ACE KOOL (1990s), to refer to your best friend.

20 Another feature of Black Talk is the coining of words that capture unique characteristics of individuals. The older term BOGARD (to aggressively take over something) was based on the style of film star Humphrey Bogart, who typically played strong-arm, tough guy roles. Today's generation has contributed OPRAH to the Lexicon, after talk show personality Oprah Winfrey, to refer to the art of getting people to reveal intimate facts about themselves, as Oprah skillfully manages to do on national television.

African American English had its genesis in enslavement, where it was necessary to have a language that would mean one thing to Africans but another to Europeans. Forced to use the English of Ole Massa, Africans in enslavement had to devise a system of talking to each other about Black affairs and about THE MAN right in front of his face. Because of continued segregation and racism, this necessity for a coded form of English persisted even after Emancipation, and it underlies the evolution of Black Language. Black Talk's origin in enslavement and the still-unresolved status of Africans in America account for the constant changes in the Lexicon. If and when a term crosses over into the white world, it becomes suspect and is no longer considered DOPE in the Black world. A new term must be generated to take its place. There is a certain irony here because in this cultural circumstance, imitation is not considered flattery. The same lingo generated by the creative juices of the community and considered DEF today can tomorrow become WACK and suitable only for LAMES if it gets picked up by whites. Of course a lot of African American Talk does get picked up by European Americans, especially in this post-modern nineties era, with MTV, BET, "Def Comedy Jam," and the power of the media to spread culture and language rapidly throughout the nation. Nonetheless, the pattern persists: once phrases and terms are adopted by whites, Blacks scramble to come up with something new.

On the other hand, language that does not cross over, regardless of how old it is, continues to be used in the community and to remain HYPE. Examples include most of the vocabulary of the Traditional Black Church and many of the terms referring to male-female relations. For example, "YOU GOT MY NOSE OPEN" is at least half a century old and was used in Big Daddy Kane's 1993 "Very Special" jam. Another example is WHAM BAM, THANK YOU, MAM! (also BIP BAM, THANK YOU, MAM!), used especially by women to refer to a man who completes the sex act in a matter of seconds; this signifyin expression is also at least fifty years old and was used by Mary J. Blige in her 1992 "411" jam. Other terms that don't cross over are words for whites, such as ANN, HONKY, CHARLIE; terms referring to Black hair and other physical features, such as ASHY, LIGHT-SKIN, DARK-SKIN, KITCHEN; and other words that describe Blacks only, such as OREO, COLOR STRUCK, TOM.

Though often misunderstood (and even damned) for their NITTY GRITTY language, especially the MUTHAFUCKAS, HO'S, and NIGGAZ, the Hip Hop generation is coming straight outa the Oral Tradition. In that Tradition, language is double-voiced, common English words are given unique Black meanings, and a muthafucka is never a person with an Oedipus complex.[1] Rather than breaking with the Black past, as some members of the previous generation have tried to do, Hip Hoppers seek to connect with past verbal traditions and to extend the semantic space of Black lingo by adding a 1990s flavor. They are not merely imitating and reproducing the past, but grounding themselves in it as they seek to stamp their imprint upon the GAME. Any time you venture beyond the tried and true, errors BIG-TIME, painful distortions, and horrific extremes are likely to result. Experimentation breeds failures as well as successes. The violent antagonism toward and brutalization of women by male Rap groups, such as Los Angeles's NWA (Niggaz With Attitudes), is a case in point. But it was also NWA who early on, in their 1989 jam "Fu[ck] the Police," HIPped us to the brutality of the Los Angeles Police Department, which should have prepared us for the Rodney King tragedy had we listened.

This is a historical moment in which Rap and other forms of Black Talk and Culture are used to sell everything from Coca-Cola and Gatorade to snow blowers and shampoo for white hair. When you factor in profits from music, television programming, sports, clothing, and advertising, it is clear that America's corporate economy is capitalizing on Hip Hop, making it a booming billion-dollar industry. However, while Black *Talk* has crossed over, Black *people* have not, as is excruciatingly evident from the staggering unemployment and economic deterioration of the HOOD, reemerging racism (even on college campuses), and open physical attacks on African American males by the police as well as by ordinary white citizens. Recognizing WHAT TIME IT IS, homeys are in search of authentic Black Language and Culture, an unapologetic African American Self, and a way to resolve the unfinished business of being African in America. Their quest has led them to the ruins of the 1960s. There HOME-BOYS and HOMEGIRLS found folk like Rudy Ray Moore's "Dolemite," with his hilarious, pornographic talk and, yes, his put-downs of women. But there they also found the "do-rag lover and revolutionary pimp"[2] Malcolm X.

NOTES

1. The Oedipus complex derives from the work of Sigmund Freud (1856–1939), the Austrian physician who founded psychoanalysis. This theory of human behavior argues that psychological problems are traceable to infancy and childhood and the individual's failure to resolve childhood sexual conflicts and fantasies, which should come about naturally with maturity. One such conflict is the sexual desire of a male child for his mother and subsequent hostility toward

his father, who is enjoying the sexual pleasures denied the child. This problem was named the "Oedipus complex" after the character Oedipus in Greek mythology. He was abandoned at birth and wandered to and fro until adulthood, when fate led him to Thebes, where he killed the king and married the queen, who, unbeknownst to Oedipus (or them), were his parents.

2. From the poem "Malcolm Spoke/who listened? (this poem is for my consciousness too)," by Haki Madhubuti, from his collection *Don't Cry, Scream,* published in 1969, when he was Don L. Lee.

Rereading Actively

1. Smitherman presents differing views on the crossover of African-American culture. With a partner, review the article, identifying passages where these different views are presented. Discuss each view, and summarize them in an entry in your journal.

2. Smitherman documents several examples of hip-hop language and culture bridging generations, reaching back to the 1960s and beyond as it recycles slang terms. Identify several examples of this recycling.

3. Smitherman touches on "crossover" within the African-American community. Explain what she means by this, identifying some examples of "in-group crossover lingo" (¶ 18).

4. According to Smitherman, what are the origins of African-American English? Summarize her explanation in a journal entry.

5. What are some of the attractions that African-American language offers to European Americans?

Exploring Your Responses

6. Discuss Smitherman's writing style with a partner or in a small group. What effect does it have on you as a reader? Does it seem to help Smitherman explain her case? Describe the reactions of the members of your group in a journal entry.

7. Does Smitherman's account persuade you that African-American English can re-energize "bland Euro-talk" (¶ 7)? Why or why not?

8. In a page or two in your journal, respond to Smitherman's discussion of differing views of crossover. Is crossover problematic to you? Why or why not?

REBIRTH OF THE COOL
ALLISON SAMUELS AND JOHN LELAND

Reporters Allison Samuels and John Leland cover topics that include black arts and entertainment. Their focus in this 1997 Newsweek *article is the alternative side of the hip-hop scene. Beyond the commercial visibility of gangsta rap, they link the underground scene they describe here to a "bohemian" anticommercial tradition of poetry and jazz that is culturally eclectic while espousing views of racial uplift and self-love.*

It took Cora Spearman more than three weeks before she braved the Lit X stage, but now here she is, all Saturday-night nerves and hip-hop bravado. It is still early evening in Chicago's funky Wicker Park neighborhood, and the club—the dimly lit basement of an African-American bookstore—is packed with twentysomething hip-hoppers in baggy jeans and African accessories, puffing cigars or joints beneath Bob Marley posters and paintings by black artists. Cora is 19, a sophomore at Antioch College; she wandered into the poetry nights at Lit X for the vibe: part rap jam, part group-therapy session. "Hip-hop now has so many negative images," she says, "that there was nowhere else to go but positive." Under a cloud of incense, she takes the stage, her short perm just starting to grow out. Some of the earlier poets were accompanied by hand drums, flute or the staccato sputtering of a "human beat box," but Cora brings only herself and her metaphors. "You are like my afro," she calls, "something I want but don't have yet."

This is the hip-hop culture nobody sees. Beyond the commercial tsunami of gangsta rap, hip-hop has always harbored a more reflective, alternative edge. Now, as the rap scene reels from the murders of Tupac Shakur and the Notorious B.I.G., the bohemian hinges are starting to bloom. This spring's unsung gem, the romantic comedy "love jones," showcased the Chicago poetry scene, turning hip-hop-generation lovers loose in a boho playground of John Coltrane LPs, Gordon Parks photos and sexy raindrops. On urban radio, the million-selling Erykah Badu channels the fragile heartache of Billie Holiday. Her head wrapped in African cloth, her conversation laced with talk of "spirituality" and "consciousness," she is a compendium of bohemias past, all tightened with contemporary hip-hop torque. Singers like Maxwell, Eric Benet, Me'Shell NdegeOcello and Dionne Farris reprise jazzy soul moves. What's a gangsta to do? "Rapping about one brother killing another brother is just not where I am coming from these days," says producer and rapper Dr. Dre, the musical architect behind gangsta rap. "And I think with the recent deaths no one should. The new vibe out there reflects that."

It has been called alternative soul, ebony nouveau or hip-hop renaissance, an efflorescence still in search of a name. It is a blip compared to gangsta, and sometimes dopey in its earnestness. In sweaty spots like Lit X, or its better-known equivalents—the Nuyorican Poets Cafe in New York, the Lyrical Café in Los Angeles—it is as hiphop as Snoop Doggy Dogg, but without the cussing and cartoon machismo. For a generation now passing out of its teens, you could call this the rebirth of the real. "This is a movement that's said that black life doesn't end at age 25," says Branford Marsalis, who combines rap, jazz and poetry in his group, Buckshot LeFonque. Spend a Saturday night at Lit X and you'll pick up an earful: about Ricki Lake and Jimi Hendrix, about slave auctions and drive-by shootings, about the vulnerable side of male love. "To me hip-hop had become too commercial," says James Williams, just off the Lit X stage. "Rappers [started rhyming] about what they thought mainstream America wanted to hear. At Lit X we get back to what hip-hop was supposed to be. It isn't about posturing or trying to fit a mold. It's about self-love and uplifting the race."

In an early seduction scene in "love jones," Larenz Tare plays an old vinyl album for Nia Long. As the room fills with a melancholy alto sax, she says, "Charlie Parker. I've never heard this particular [version]." It is a line of dialogue out of a dream, or at least not out of contemporary black Hollywood. But it could be a signature for the new bohemia. Like the scene at Lit X or the retro grooves of Erykah Badu, the film serves up a banquet of black respect: for the past, for the culture, for each other. The good vibes can feel forced, but never faked. To fans like Latisa Collins, 21, a senior at Spelman College, who saw the movie "about seven times," the note rang both true and overdue. "'Waiting to Exhale' wasn't my reality, nor was 'Booty Call,'" she says. With "love jones," though, "there is finally a feeling out there that I feel."

5   This nostalgia is something new. The great jazz drummer (and MacArthur Fellow) Max Roach once argued that black culture didn't romanticize the past, because the past held only injustice. It was an article of racial progress to keep on pushing, the engine that kept African American expression so fresh. But in an era of economic backsliding, the nostalgia of "love jones" or Lit X plays less as escapism than idealism—a new drink from an old wellspring. "Blacks have always celebrated their history," contends director Ted Witcher. "We've just always had to pick and choose what to keep and discard. 'love jones' embraces both the past and the present, because the present must learn from the past to continue."

On a Monday night at the House of Blues on L.A.'s Sunset Strip, Badu invites her audience across this cultural span. Where Lit X and "love jones" are relatively marginal, Badu is a force; her album, "Baduizm," hit No. 1. The stage is lit with candles, bathed in the smoke of incense—the kind of Afrocentric trappings often mistakenly tagged as hippie. Badu used to rap, and still writes rhymes; in a regal mint green African dress, she brings Brooklyn swagger and a message of renewal. The crowd, mostly in their 20s and 30s, wants to join her, but they are only halfway there, still dressed in their office attire. But they are singing, and to *every song.* "Thank you for being a part of the birthing process," she says. "I'm the midwife, but you're a part of the process, too."

In the audience, supermodel Tyra Banks nods in recognition, and director John Singleton. And captivated by the sound is Dr. Dre, not a gangsta air about him. He, too, is growing out his afro, thinking about his next move. "Hip-hop has to continue to evolve if it wants to survive," he says, "and part of that evolving is getting back to the positive." These are soft words, as mollifying as Badu's seductive plaint. As the drums pad gently behind her, the man who gave you "F--- tha Police" joins a roomful of other successful young African-Americans, lost in a retro swing that may be his future.

Rereading Actively

1. With a partner or in a small group, discuss the possible meanings and associations that are given in the article for the word "bohemian." In your journal, describe your conversation, and then look up this word in a dictionary. How does the scene that Samuels and Leland describe fit the definitions you find in your dictionary?

2. "Retro" names one theme running through this article. With a partner, review the article, identifying passages that address this idea of "retro" as a return to roots, and a reckoning of history. Why is "retro" cool?

3. The article is replete with references to hip-hop artists from the mainstream as well as artists who represent this retro scene. In your journal, make a list of the artists mentioned for each category and write a one-sentence evaluation of any artist with whom you are familiar.

4. How does the black bohemian hip-hop scene differ from the gangsta rap scene, according to this article?

Exploring Your Responses

5. Are you familiar with the artists and work the writers describe here? If so, would you agree with their characterization of it as representing a "rebirth of the cool"? If you are not familiar with it, do you get a clear sense of what this movement seems to be about?

6. The writers quote one hip-hop performer saying, "Rappers [started rhyming] about what they thought mainstream America wanted to hear" (¶ 3). Who do you suppose this "mainstream" is? Is this a way of talking about white people? Or, in the context of an audience for this bohemian side of hip-hop, is race not relevant to defining the "mainstream"?

7. Are you persuaded that this scene (which seems to include Dr. Dre, the super-model Tyra Banks, and number one recording artist Erykah Badu) is really "alter-native"? Or does it seem to you to be just another avenue of commercialism?

OFF THE CHARTS, OFF THE COVERS: FOR HIP-HOP ACTS THAT BOOM, THE MEDIA HAVE NO ROOM

ARMOND WHITE

Armond White reports here on the mismatch between the commercial success of hip-hop acts and the coverage given to artists and performers in the music media. White points out that the Top 10 charts are typically dominated by black music acts, but African-American performers are slighted by media coverage that focuses on white acts. Backing up his claims with facts, White analyzes coverage given to black and white performers in pop music and general-interest mainstream publications. White is the author of The Resis-tance: Ten Years of Pop Culture that Shook the World *(1995), and* Rebel for the Hell of It: The Life of Tupac Shakur *(1997). This article first appeared in 1997 in the* Nation, *one of the most important liberal journals published in the United States. The journal's editorial view takes a leftist, critical view of the social and economic mainstream.*

Calling out around the world, Jim Farber, a music reporter for New York's *Daily News,* broke a story earlier this year that no one wanted to dance to. He called out the factionalism that splits American popular culture, separating music into black or white and segregating pop aesthetics. Noting the difference between recording artists' commercial success and media coverage, he reported a sad fact that has long been sup-pressed: The culture is going in one direction while the critical community and the press are going in another. Examples are annoying and frequent: female libertine rap-per Li'l Kim being judged from the *Chicago Reader* to *The Village Voice* as a sex worker rather than an artist with little mention that her image came from a conscious creative collaboration with the late rapper Biggie Smalls; celebrations of the white Midwest-ern trio Hanson that avoid the group's imitation of the Jackson Five and hip-hop pro-duction styles; Spice Girls promotion that neglects the British quintet's imitation of the hip-hop girl group T.L.C.

The charts, Farber learned, showed a fount of racial favoritism and prejudice in journalistic practice that presumably serves the music biz. It exacerbates the differences in the way white and black Americans experience the musical culture and fosters a biased sub-industry, validating who gets on magazine covers. Even cross-fertilized, supposedly democratic American pop fractures record company departments into race-based camps, and eventually determines the apportioning of significance in cultural studies.

"We're like a big archeology dig," said a black music publicist, summing up how black musicians are treated in cultural journalism. "Black acts don't get discovered until their shelf lives are over, then critics look back and see all this creativity that at the time was completely overlooked." Her job, getting press and media attention for a label's black acts in the mainstream media, is so frustrating that she keeps her résumé updated. Like many of the publicists interviewed for this piece, she insisted on anonymity.

Publicists are a substratum of the music industry but essential to its operations—the volume control of the biz's voice. Thus, the protection of one's identity for fear of retaliation indicates the powerful connection between record companies and media—in rap lingo, a crucial conflict. There's a secret understanding that how contemporary media tell the story of popular music culture isn't just reporting—it contributes to current and future cultural perception. When it comes to telling the story of black artists' influence on the industry and on the culture, reportage goes wack, and cultural history gets distorted.

5   Since the 1991 implementation of SoundScan, the system of tracking record sales reported in *Billboard's* weekly charts, there has been conclusive evidence that popular musical developments are not being accurately reflected in the mainstream media. As the *Daily News* noted, "album charts in the past year have seen hard-line r&b acts like New Edition and R. Kelly outsell big rockers like R.E.M., Sheryl Crow and even Van Halen." Rarely has there been a week in which the Top 10 charts did not show black acts (i.e., identified as r&b or rap or dance) occupying at least seven of the ten positions—usually no fewer than eight.

But the coverage in leading pop music publications—*Rolling Stone, Spin*—and mainstream general-interest publications that emphasize pop music in their arts coverage, like *The New York Times* and *The Village Voice*, inverts the sales ratio. A look at *Rolling Stone* and *Spin* cover stories alone demonstrates this incongruity. Just one example: At the time Boyz II Men broke Elvis Presley's chart-topping record, no cover story announced the shift in pop taste. In any one year, of those magazines' covers, two might feature a best-selling black act. It makes a black publicist's life hell, but worse, it distorts the picture of how popular music thrives.

"Oh, it's a big lie," one of the few black male publicists admitted. "U2 [frequent *Rolling Stone* cover stars] isn't really that important to people. *Billboard's* charts prove it, sales prove it. But magazines say otherwise." Another journeywoman who has worked at several different record labels clarifies: "I don't think it's outright misinformation or a conspiracy or anything. It's the nature of people's different tastes. The people editing music magazines don't represent the larger public, they represent themselves and they put their tastes before the public." The disparity is not just because of the biases in taste of the gatekeepers of the music world (record execs and critics); it's also due to differences in how white and black Americans experience culture.

Such media biases construct a dangerously "alternative" view of whatever changes, advances and regressions occur in pop music. When "urban" music—an industry euphemism for black-created music—came to be mostly identified as rap (peaking in the late eighties and early nineties), "alternative" was the industry's answer. The term resonates: White rock and roll, emerging this time from America's white fringes, became the mainstream media's preferred alternative to rap. And the music industry itself followed suit, signing "grunge" acts like Nirvana, Pearl Jam and Alice in Chains with the same hunger they had shown for rap several years earlier. The white alternative reasserted a type of cultural domination, a virtual return to Jim Crow.

Editors offer a variety of excuses for their lack of coverage of black acts. One publicity executive relates a typical refusal: "'This artist isn't right, that artist is not appropriate, I don't know if our readers are interested in that,' they'll say. There's been a resurgence of r&b, but you'd never know it from magazines. It's because the white men who edit these publications don't get it. That's not always in *Rolling Stone*: it could be in *Vibe*," a monthly devoted to r&b and rap.

10   "If Teddy Riley [performer-songwriter and producer of Blackstreet and other acts] was treated like a white artist, he'd be Mr. Everything," artist/manager Barry Hankerson told Farber. Hankerson represents R. Kelly, the multimillion-selling r&b singer one publicist recalls strenuously pitching "long after he sold a million records." One critic complained, "You expect that at some level at *Rolling Stone*; you don't expect it at *Vibe*." Alan Light, the recently demoted editor of *Vibe*, defended the magazine's controversial slant by saying that r&b music "is the hardest sell to the mainstream media. It's the least respected genre out there."

This frustration over what a publicist called "a taste thing" goes to a key point, the rock magazines' proprietorship of U.S. culture. A West Coast publicist views the mainstream media's attitude as one in which "people only care about black artists when it involves scandal—when they're shot, naked or something sexual. If they've done anything scandalous, they've got a chance for mainstream press." That explains the disproportionate attention given to rappers who've had run-ins with the police.

Unlike *Billboard*, a trade magazine serving the industry, pop music magazines exist to create an interest in selected aspects of the culture; they boost favored artists and ideas while ignoring or debunking others. Publications, like flags, carry an ideology; pop mags promote the agreed-upon interests of the whites who own them (and read them), and this is a more consistent, if subtle, mandate than the blather about rebellion and genius. Proof is in the steady praise conferred upon white artists and denied to black artists, with critical attribution of intellect to whites, sexuality to blacks. No better example of this injustice exists than *The New York Times's* campaign against Michael Jackson, criticism apart from the news reports of his legal hassles. In the past three years, the *Times* has repeatedly run disparaging stories, each a bitter critique of the latest aspect of his career. This close inspection contradicts the implicit point: Jackson's strangeness, inconsequence and—in the United States—his "unpopularity." Hammering home this message suggests an effort to destroy the artist without regard to Jackson's interest as a development in the advancement of black pop. It reflects an agenda: *The New York Times* (or the class it represents) wants him finished. They've made it uncool to buy Michael Jackson. Jackson gets castigated for his disturbing cultural impact—he's had no *Rolling Stone* covers since his *Thriller* album of the early eighties, while the same magazine has declared, "Never has there been a rock star as complex as Marilyn Manson."

Even when editors use the alibi that a black act isn't selling, it still rankles. "Maybe they're not but neither is fuckin' U2," the West Coast publicist says. "There's not a publication that takes a lot of chances these days. Most of them want big-name acts now. There's so much competition and so many publications. They're after the 'It' band of the moment, and who that is is very cyclical—it helps if there's a curvy white girl involved. TV actresses Jennifer Aniston, Jenny McCarthy or any blond bimbo who has nothing to do with music gets press attention. And it's not even a discussion."

Industry wisdom says all those millions of records aren't being sold just to a black audience. And yet the media's tacit restriction persists. Even the publications' annual awards issues convert prejudice into arbitrary qualitative measurements. From *Entertainment Weekly* to *Rolling Stone*, no black artist's album has ever been chosen the best of the year. Whites PJ Harvey, Liz Phair and Courtney Love won the *Village Voice* critics' consensus in years that blacks Whitney Houston, Janet Jackson and Mary J. Blige made their most popular and significant albums. "There's this whole appreciation of pseudo-soul: All these white girls who want to be black girls are huge, yet all these huge black girls are not huge," said one publicist. "It's like someone has set the idea of what a rock critic is supposed to like."

15   Indeed, a philosophy has developed around the idea of pop music. Rock, historically an outgrowth of r&b, is now institutionalized by major press outlets and the weight of a thirty-year tradition as something distinctly different—a way for white artists and audiences to remain isolated in their self-appraisal and self-aggrandizement. "It's the 'pop music' thing," one P.R. professional said. "And I don't think they want to include contemporary black artists—they let in the old guys, Bo Diddley and those kinds of guys, but they don't want pop music to encompass hip-hop. Rap acts are not included in their concept of pop music; it's still Other. But in popular culture, it's totally consumed. Boyz II Men have had to become hugely popular to get any coverage at all. They just don't care because rap's not pop music to them, and that critic's thing justifies it, makes it less pop music for them."

When editors do put a black person on the cover, more problems concerning perception and respect arise: "When they get a photographer who never shot a black person, it's not flattering," an East Coast artist manager complained. When this half-gesture occurs after the record has peaked, "It may not be a good-selling magazine based on that cover. The artist is not hot anymore, they waited too long, the artwork is horrible. Maybe it would work if you put edgy black folks on the cover, took fly photographs people would want to see." But weak responses to these rare, halfhearted efforts end up justifying the editors' reluctance: "Then they can say black people can't sell a magazine."

Just like the magazines, TV talk shows neglect black acts and favor white groups. Analyzing logs from late-night programs, Farber reported in the *Daily News* a huge discrepancy between black and white musical appearances. Another industry journalist explained that TV producers look to "a review in *Rolling Stone* or *The Village Voice* to see who's worthy." A publicist agreed: "At late-night TV, it's on the host. Letterman doesn't like rap so there's none on his show. This is the fact unless record companies make a stink [i.e., threaten not to advertise]. A label president will make a phone call on white artists; rarely do they do that for black artists."

The rock press operates in ways that contradict the idea of pop as rebellion or open expression. It's a new form of the old racist hierarchy. The (mostly) white men in charge of mainstream music media limit themselves to their personal taste and thereby have created a spurious pop music aesthetic that prizes such things as rebellion and aggression over other human motivations. The black cultural tradition that perpetuates a spiritual or sexual approach to social activity is often misunderstood by others who diminish it through a new form of hierarchy—turning rockism (the preference for guitar-oriented up-tempo music) into racism.

Some black acts have adopted this mainstream perspective on pop—as in the macho rebellions of rap, which are a derivation of rock (white male) aesthetics—but it's done them little good in breaking the media's barriers. Public Enemy, famous for its lyric "Your general subject—love—is minimal! It's sex for profit," has partially adhered to a rockist idea. P.E. caused a revolution in the way rap was perceived by black and white audiences. Their politically informed pop sold two platinum and four gold albums without their once gracing the cover of *Rolling Stone*.

20   In the elusive moods impelling editorial fiat, ideas about significance and merit get tangled with subjective notions of taste. Do the mainstream media cover an artist because she or he has proven popular through sales, or because editorial judgment deems an artist worthy of attention? If the former, magazine coverage of pop would be governed by the sales charts—but it isn't. The latter holds sway, and though rarely consonant with popular sales, it is consistent with a tradition of cultural bias that's so widely held it seems natural and is never questioned. Since the advent of SoundScan, the pop world has learned to live with the paradox of big sales/little coverage, few sales/big coverage, because it's part of the way America has traditionally segregated its attention span and its genuine interest. Our bifurcated cultural approbation, separating respectable art from art that gives instinctual pleasure, reflects society's racial and sexual segregation.

Originating among the literate and empowered classes that sustain social biases, music reporting and criticism submits to cultural intolerance and restriction. Pop journalism is neither impartial nor innocent. By re-explaining music, it has corrupted our humanities.

Rereading Actively

1. In a small group, review the article, identifying the evidence that White presents to support the contention that white pop acts get disproportionate coverage in the media. (Focus on the issue of record sales.) Summarize the facts in a journal entry.

2. What are some examples White gives of cover stories that seem to reflect the media bias against black performers?

3. What reasons does White present to explain why magazines like *Spin* and *Rolling Stone* might favor white acts over coverage of black performers? List his arguments, and offer a one- or two-sentence evaluation of each one.

4. White presents an interpretation of the emergence of "alternative" rock in the early 1990s. Discuss this passage with a partner, and then explain White's interpretation in a journal entry.

5. White focuses on the coverage given to Michael Jackson's career as an important example of mainstream media bias against a black performer. Write a brief summary of White's interpretation of the Michael Jackson case.

Exploring Your Responses

6. The rock press, White asserts, is "a new form of the old racist hierarchy" (¶ 18). Based on the evidence he presents in this article, do you agree? Why or why not?

7. White presents the editors of pop music magazines as "gatekeepers" (¶ 7) whose personal tastes lead them to give slight coverage to black artists. Assuming White's assessment is accurate, should these editors set aside their own preferences in deciding which artists to give attention to?

8. Pick two records by artists referred to here—one by a black artist, one by a white, for example, PJ Harvey and Mary J. Blige. In a small group, evaluate the recordings, and discuss how you approached this evaluation: Can you determine that one recording is "better" than the other? In a page or two in your journal, describe your group's conversation and consensus (or lack of consensus) about the recordings you evaluated.

Hip-Hoppreneurs
Eric L. Smith

Eric L. Smith is the Business News Editor at Black Enterprise Magazine, *a business journal with a circulation of approximately 350,000 nationwide. Smith's articles cover business and economic news trends as well as political issues that affect African-American business owners. In "Hip-hoppreneurs" (1997), Smith reports on the move of hip-hop artists and musicians into other business ventures such as fashion design, clothing retail, nightclubs, footwear, spas, and others. In reporting this trend, Smith composes a series of profiles of prominent hip-hop artists who have made the move. In approaching the story this way, the article presents the crossover of hip-hop into other enterprises as the result of the hard work and ingenuity of the hip-hop artists themselves.*

It's the twilight of summer in Los Angeles and Russell Simmons is in cruise control. Motoring down Wilshire Boulevard in a coal black convertible Benz, the 40-year-old CEO of Rush Communications lets it casually slip that he just recently learned to drive. But that doesn't discourage him from furiously working the car cell phone with one hand while gingerly grasping the steering wheel in the other.

Simmons is coordinating last-minute celebrity contributions to his annual Rush Philanthropic Arts Foundation celebrity auction, which focuses primarily on the needs of inner city youth. So far, the donated items include an autographed poster and watch from the Will Smith movie *Men in Black*, a pair of size 22 Reeboks signed by Shaquille O'Neal, and an autographed copy of the Sidney Poitier film *To Sir with Love*. Now Simmons is after his next target.

"I need Maria's number," Simmons barks into the phone. "Not the office—the number at home. Did we get anything back from her or Arnold for the auction? The least we should be able to get is a signed *Terminator* poster." These days, the BE 100s CEO can not only make such demands on Hollywood's elite but also expect a prompt response. (Schwarzenegger ultimately donates a leather Planet Hollywood jacket autographed by himself and wife Maria Shriver.) If nothing else, it is a testament to the prestige Simmons wields among Hollywood's upper echelon.

If Simmons is considered influential by those within the urban music industry, it's not only because of these accomplishments; it is also because he is the forerunner of the "Hip-Hopprenuer." Many in the industry credit Simmons for setting the standard for rap artists and executives who've risen through the urban music ranks to realize that the key to sustained success and wealth doesn't end after making a few hit singles. Far from your stereotypical Brooks Brothers-wearing corporate executives, a swelling group of artists, including such top selling acts as The Wu-Tang Clan and Spindarella of Salt N' Pepa, are leveraging their celebrity in the music industry to spin into different business enterprises. Their concerns run the gamut from down-low street fashion to high-comfort spas. These Gen Xers have propelled themselves onto a different stage by realizing that name branding and business ownership is the real secret to success.

5   Although a corporate executive and not an artist, Simmons is the perennial example of a true player in the hip-hop industry. Since founding Def Jam Recordings in 1985—the largest subsidiary of Rush Communications—Simmons has methodically spread his reach from hip-hop across the entertainment arena into fashion, film and advertising. In 1997, Phat Farm—Rush Communications' wholesale and retail clothing company—is projected to gross sales of $10 million. With the success of films like the late Tupac Shakur's *Gridlock'd* and Def Jam's *How To Be a Player* (starring Bill Bellamy), Def Pictures will tout gross box office sales of over $25 million this year. And, with prized accounts from Coca-Cola and other clients, newly formed Rush Media projects gross billings of over $1 million in this, its first full year.

Second only to BET Holdings Inc., Rush Communications (No. 54 on the BE INDUSTRIAL/SERVICE **100** list) is now the second largest black-owned entertainment company in the United States. But there's a host of young, hungry hip-hoppers eager to follow in Simmons' entrepreneurial tracks. Whether they succeed will not depend on how well they rap or rhyme, but how well they manage the bottom line.

Wu-Tang Treks the Entrepreneurial Path

The midtown Manhattan office of Razor Sharp Records is used to a frenetic pace. It's where the Wu-Tang Clan work. Earlier this year, the multi-platinum-selling act released their sophomore album, Wu-Tang Forever. Despite weak radio airplay, album sales had topped $4 million by late September.

This particular evening the group will introduce several acts at Radio City Music Hall for the MTV Music Awards. Various members of the nine-member Clan are rushing in and out of Razor Sharp getting their artist credentials for the evening and going over last-minute routines. In the midst of the confusion, Clan member Lamont Hawkins, a.k.a. U-God, says while Wu-Tang may be the flavor of the moment among rap music fans, each member is very aware of the need to think beyond the moment.

"Everyone here is concerned with getting into something more than rhyming because we realize that what we have here is a vehicle that gets you from one step to the next," says Hawkins. "This is a business where one day you might be in and the next day you're out. So it's up to you to take it to the next level."

10   The first sign that Wu-Tang wasn't your run-of-the-mill rap group came in the innovative way the Clan structured its individual projects on separate music labels. Spearheaded by group member Robert Diggs/RZA, most members have distinct solo deals including Clifford Smith/Method Man (Def Jam), Russell Jones/Ol' Dirty Bastard (Elektra), Corey Woods/Raekwon (Loud Records), Gary Grice/GZA (Geffen) and Dennis Coles/Ghostface Killah (Razor Sharp/Epic). Each has a 50% partnership deal with Wu-Tang Productions, and a solo deal also contributes 20% of their earnings to

Wu-Tang Productions. Their arrangement is a feat nearly unprecedented because it gives the group ties to nearly every major label in the music industry.

But that was just a start. The Clan's first vehicle to extend their brand name beyond hip-hop has been the apparel industry. As with Simmons' Phat Farm, the Clan sees a synergy between hip-hop music and clothing. With start-up costs of $50,000 for a storefront and merchandise, the group launched its apparel line, Wu-Wear, and opened its first Wu-Wear clothing store in Staten Island, New York, in 1995. The clothing, produced abroad in China and domestically in Massachusetts, is made at Wu Manufacturing L. L. C.

The Clan is targeting urban teens and college students ages 12–28. Wu-Wear apparel includes sweatshirts, headwear, socks, underwear, bags, wallets and mugs. After the designs for Wu-Wear are approved for different clothing, product samples are made. Following the Clan's approval of the actual product, inventory is ordered for the flagship store in Staten Island. Samples are sent to wholesale and mail order reps, and catalog sheets are prepared.

By all indications, the line is thriving. The flagship store had sales in excess of $1 million its first year. Now with two additional stores in Norfolk, Virginia, and Atlanta, and a thriving mail order operation, Wu-Wear president and CEO Oli Grant is projecting year-end sales for all three outlets to exceed $5 million. Approximately 40% of 1997 revenues will come from the three retail outlets. Fifty percent comes from Wu-Wear's wholesale operation. Last spring, the group inked a deal with retail giant Federated Department Stores, owners of Macy's, Bloomingdale's, Bon Marché and Rich's. The clothing is also found in smaller retail chains such as Dr. Jays and Gadzooks. The final 10% comes from the group's mail order operation.

"At Federated, we're always interested in the newest product for our stores," says Allen Zwerner, group senior vice president for men's, young men's and kids' merchandise. "It certainly doesn't hurt if there is additional exposure to the customer through their music. However, the product must be right for the fashion market. Currently, our stores are carrying their T-shirts, and as we move into spring 1998, they will be expanding their line into a full-blown sportswear line, and we feel good about giving them a shot," adds Zwerner.

15   Illustrating the synergy between their music and clothing, Wu-Tang provides mail order information for its apparel inside each CD jacket. In a moment of marketing inspiration, the group released the single and video "Wu-Wear," featuring RZA, Method Man and Cappadonna. The song urged listeners to abandon their current clothing in favor of—what else—Wu-Wear.

Mitchell Diggs, CEO of Wu-Tang Productions, is responsible for managing all of the separate and group projects for the Clan. He says once the group attracted mass attention and various offers for projects or investments came along, the decision was made to cut out the middleman and explore business opportunities for themselves. "You start listening to these deals and hearing what they're trying to offer and you start thinking, 'Hey I have access to that same type of money. Why not look and see what we can do for ourselves?' A lot of artists might get caught up in the hype of it. But we can't be rappers all of our lives and the show doesn't pay the rent forever," he adds. So Diggs says he and members of the Clan decided to make their own deals. "Now we explore all avenues. Instead of always giving the deal to someone else and making them rich, why not keep it for ourselves?"

What's next for the Wu? Grant says a fourth Clan store is under construction in Philadelphia and plans for a Wu-Mega store in the Melrose area of Los Angeles are in the works for next year.

But can Wu-Tang sustain its momentum? A hot name alone isn't enough. The inherent dangers in both music and fashion are the relative youth and fickleness of these industry's consumers. And the transition from music to fashion, say insiders, is a difficult one since the audience for both is often looking for the next fad or trend.

But the fashion industry is attractive to hip-hop artists wanting to branch out because it can be a gold mine, says Alan Millstein, editor and publisher of the *Fashion Network Report*. According to Millstein, the average life span of most clothing lines is five years or less, but "if you hit, there's a ton of money to be made." Designers such as Tommy Hilfiger, Calvin Klein and BE 100s CEO Karl Kani have long embraced and financially benefited from hip-hop's influence on fashion. Touted in rap lyrics for the past decade, these designers have reaped millions off the urban hip-hop market. According to a recent report in *Forbes* magazine, Tommy Hilfiger reported a 40% jump in sales to $491 million as of its current fiscal year with earnings climbing 47% to $64 million. How much of that increase can be directly attributed to the hip-hop market is unclear, but many black artists believe the time is overdue to start going after that market for themselves.

20　　Carl Williams, CEO of Karl Kani Infinity Inc., believes Wu-Wear has found the right niche to hit by attacking the urban market. "The fact that groups like Wu-Tang have the ability to sell a million albums means something. There are people out there listening to them, watching them. And a lot of the kids who see their videos are going to want to dress like them," says Williams. "Marketing their clothing through their music and CDs is creative and unique. And it won't hurt the sales of their next album to have everyone walking around with a big Wu symbol on their backs," he adds.

Diggs says the group is simply trying to take control of their own image and marketability. "It's really just understanding what makes money from you," he says. "You have to understand how your product makes the larger industry so successful and make sure that you get more than just a penny of the proceeds."

Can Music Success Translate into Business Enterprises?

The main problem is most artists' general lack of knowledge about the fashion industry. "Most musicians are simply naive about the production cycles and complexities of design," says Millstein. "Apparel is a totally different world from being in the production studio and making a CD."

But not all rappers with outside business interests are into apparel. Percy Miller, a New Orleans native who goes by the handle "Master P," purchased a Tenneco Gas Station and signed on as an Athlete's Foot franchisee earlier this year. Miller, who's also owner and president of No Limit Records, says the start-up costs for both of his Baton Rouge-based concerns ($500,000 for Tenneco and $250,000 for the Athlete's Foot) are expenses well spent, as he plans to branch out into the business arena. "When you get in this business, you have to think ahead if you want to stay around. You don't want to just get a few dollars, and next year there's nothing happening," Miller says.

"With Tenneco, I look at it as a great investment because it's obviously something everybody needs," says Miller. "We're right off the interstate at a rest area, so it's accessible. There's less manual work involved because we have computerized pumps installed. And it's a 24-hour operation, so it's always making money." Miller is projecting revenues at his Tenneco station of $1.5 million by year's end.

25   The Athlete's Foot outlet, which will be located in a mall currently under construction, is expected to be open early next year. Among the other shoes and clothing the store carries will be—you guessed it—'Bout It apparel, Miller's own clothing line. "I feel like if you're really an entrepreneur, you should buy a business every chance or opportunity you get," he says. "Not to the point where you spread yourself thin, but where you can control all of your interests. That's what helps you grow."

Nelson George, a former *Billboard* editor and longtime music critic, notes the growing number of artists trying their hand at entrepreneurship. He says the movement really dates back to figures like Simmons and filmmaker Spike Lee. "They became very big entrepreneurial role models with the success of businesses like Def Jam and 40 Acres, and they both became multi-media. Spike had his books and clothing store. Russell had Def Comedy Jam and his own clothing line," says George. "These are the people who originally took the idea of having success in one particular medium and then flowing into different arenas."

With the storied successes, it's still an arena laden with pitfalls. And the challenge is even greater for artists with little or no business experience. James Walker, an attorney with the Hartford, Connecticut-based entertainment law firm Robinson & Cole, says the hazard most artists face is entrusting family or friends with little business expertise to manage their affairs. "These ventures typically fail because artists often have a friend they grew up with or someone in their inner circle running things," he says. "The key is to surround yourself with professionals who understand how business works and not entertainment groupies."

Miami-based rapper/entrepreneur Luther Campbell knows all about that mistake. He gained a fortune and worldwide notoriety in the late '80s as the lead bad boy of 2 Live Crew. His risqué 1989 album, *As Nasty As They Wanna Be*, sparked a national debate over censorship while lining Campbell's pockets with millions. With his wealth, Campbell created his own production company, Luke Records, and opened several nightclubs in Hialeah and Miami Beach. He also had a construction company, Luke Development. Published reports placed Campbell's assets at $11 million in 1989.

But by 1994, Campbell had filed for bankruptcy following a legal suit over royalties due to another artist. Campbell, however, blames most of his financial troubles on trusting the wrong individuals with his money.

30   "The trap I fell into was hiring all my boys and people I grew up with who I thought I could trust to handle my affairs," Campbell says. "You get into situations where signatures are required and money is being spent and it's hard to keep track of what's going on." At one point, Campbell says, a co-worker embezzled $600,000 from one of his businesses. "If I learned one thing, it's that you never totally trust any one person, no matter how well you think you know them."

Attempting to climb back up from bankruptcy, Campbell is now focusing on his production company and expects to turn a modest six-figure profit this year.

Taking a Different Spin

Deidra Roper has been a staple of the hip-hop industry for well over the past decade. Better known by the moniker "Spindarella," Roper is the disk jockey for the Grammy Award-winning group Salt N' Pepa, arguably the most popular and longest-lasting female rap group ever to hit the airwaves. And after a dozen years in the industry, Roper is working to complete her first solo album, *Spindarella's Ball*

But she wanted more. So in January, the East New York native started her own business. The She Things Salon/Day Spa opened its doors in early January in Laurelton, Queens. The two-story enterprise covers 3,200 sq. ft. and employs 18 staffers. Among the services the spa offers are hair care, manicures, pedicures, facials, massages and aromatherapy. The spa also sells Ascend, Roper's new skin care line. The products range in price from $10 to $30 for cleansers, toners, day creams and body gels, and accounted for nearly $25,000 in sales in She-Things' debut year.

Roper says when deciding what type of business to start, she realized it was important not to key in on anything faddish. "The one sure thing in life is that women are always going to want their hair and nails done. That's not a trend," Roper says. "I've been on the road for so many years with the girls, I already knew about hair, nails and what it took to take care of my body and makeup. And I know a lot of women who work very hard every day but aren't introduced to things like aromatherapy, pedicures, facials, wraps or full body massages."

35   The spa packages run from $129 for "The Eden," which includes a half-hour facial, massage and pedicure, to "The Retreat," which also includes deep tissue aromatherapy, a manicure, champagne and flowers for $236. According to Desiree Roper, manager of She-Things (and Deidra's sister), the salon services about 70–75 clients a day. About 40% come in for hair care, while another 35% come in for the assorted spa services. The rest is made up of walk-in customers purchasing retail items like the skin care line.

"Starting her own business was something I'd been pushing Deidra to do for years," says big sister Desiree. "The music business isn't something you can count on every day. But a business, if it's run right, is something she can pass down to her children."

With start-up costs of approximately $180,000, Desiree is projecting first-year revenues of $300,000 by year-end. With the addition of a wet room and additional spa features, projections of $500,000 are being made for 1998.

"We've been very fortunate with our longevity. And in the rap industry where there's a lot of money, we have the opportunities to open businesses and do things with our money, and not just flash and buy cars," says Deidra. "It should be about putting some money away and starting something of your own, so you won't be dependent on other people."

So what does Russell Simmons think of the movement he's helped to create? Ironically, he's skeptical of artists attempting to move too far away from their core music business to focus heavily on business enterprises. "It's hard for any artist to be more than an artist and be very successful," says Simmons. "If you want to put your artistry on the back seat, that's one thing, but you can find someone better than you to run your clothing company. You can't find someone to do your music."

40   Says Vernon Slaughter, an entertainment attorney with Atlanta-based Katz, Smith & Cohen: "The number one task for these artists is having a basic understanding of business principles. Although a lot of these kids are often very smart, they are still inexperienced in basic business principles."

Slaughter, whose firm represents a host of hip-hop artists including Bobby Brown and Michael Bivins, TLC's Lisa Lopez and Tionne Watkins, and rappers Too Short and Bone Thugs-N-Harmony, says artists venturing into entrepreneurship should reach out to experienced business figures. "You really have to learn how to build a team around you of qualified individuals. And the qualifications have to be more than they share the same last name as you or because that's your boy," he says. "That's not a dilemma that's specific to hip-hop or even race specific. It's a dilemma all small businesses have to deal with."

Adds Slaughter: "The most successful of these ventures will be the ones that marry the enthusiasm and creativity of hip-hop with the wisdom and experience of those that understand the business sector."

Rereading Actively

1. With a partner, review the artists profiled here, and list the different businesses each has ventured into.

2. What similarities do there appear to be among the experiences of the "hip-hoppreneurs" profiled here? Look back at your findings in the previous exercise and draft a paragraph that notes shared experiences.

3. Can you detect something that might be the secret of success for these hip-hoppreneurs? Based on what you have learned from the article, how would you say they have managed to do as well as they have?

4. In a small group, discuss the article overall: What does it tell you about the crossover of hip-hop into other avenues of production? Can you make any generalizations based on what you read in the article about the future of these businesspeople or the future of hip-hop culture in the mainstream economy?

5. What risks seem to endanger the success of these business ventures? Review the article with a partner or in a small group, and briefly describe the problems these entrepreneurs are likely to encounter.

Exploring Your Responses

6. This article appeared in a business-oriented journal. It describes the successes that are possible when hip-hop artists venture into other enterprises. Does it raise concerns about commercialization or "selling out"?

7. People usually do not identify great artists as great businessmen or businesswomen. But here we find several examples of people who succeed in both worlds. How do you react? Are you surprised? Curious? Proud? Reflect on your reactions in a journal entry.

CASE-IN-POINT ASSIGNMENTS

Early in the twentieth century, the revered African-American scholar, writer, and editor W. E. B. Du Bois identified the monumental social problem that faced America. It was the problem of the "color line," he said, naming the racial division that separated people. With the advent of the twenty-first century, we might reflect on Du Bois's diagnosis, considering progress that has been made and promises that remain unfulfilled.

Things are different now, of course, and in ways Professor W. E. B. Du Bois seems not to have predicted: Demographic trends point toward a future, not too far away, in which white people are a minority in an ever more diverse population. What was undoubtedly the defining racial divide in this country's first 250 years has begun to give way to a mosaic of cultures and a mixture of identities that are not adequately summed up by the old labels. Still, in spite of these trends, a racial divide persists. In this context, the crossover of hip-hop into the cultural mainstream may be regarded as a harbinger of an invigorating multicultural future. At the same time, the commercial forces that have combined to popularize and disseminate hip-hop might be looked at as contributing something less than real racial reconciliation: some might argue that they offer instead another instance of racial disconnection, where association with products associated with black identity takes the place of association with people who are black.

Making Connections

1. Compare the discussion of hip-hop slang and Black English crossover offered by Spiegler and Smitherman. What relationship is suggested between language and identity in these readings? Does slang (hip-hop or otherwise) play an important part in your interactions with your friends? Does slang provide you with a language that expresses something essential about your identity?

2. Think about the contemporary state of relationships between blacks and whites. Write an analysis of how hip-hop may be transforming that relationship within the dynamics of a consumer culture (for better or worse). You'll need to draw on case readings that explain the marketing of hip-hop, as well as those that raise questions about hip-hop's crossover. (Spiegler and Smith talk about the former, Ledbetter and Smitherman the latter.)

3. Allison Samuels and John Leland describe a revival of black bohemia in the hip-hop scene, a revival that seems to be a reaction against the mainstream commercial success of other segments of the hip-hop industry. Respond to the scene Samuels and Leland describe: What can we learn about Black and white identity from the "rebirth of the real" (¶ 3) that they report? How do the sentiments that they describe align with the views depicted in White or Ledbetter?

4. Armond White reports that the pop music press gives too little or the wrong kind of coverage to hip-hop artists. James Ledbetter is critical of (or at least skeptical of) the motives of white people who, like Madonna, wish they were black. Together, these writers raise questions that cut at the promise of racial melding that hip-hop may represent. Their pessimistic message seems to be that underneath its successes in the white mainstream, hip-hop is entangled in the old struggles along the deepest of America's racial fault lines. Respond to the point of view represented by White and Ledbetter, agreeing or disagreeing with the positions they take, and suggesting, if it is possible, an optimistic alternative view.

5. Use Samuels and Leland, Spiegler, or Smith to write an essay that explores the place that hip-hop plays in your day-to-day life.

6. Write an essay that uses McCloskey's discussion of the middle class to analyze and explain the business successes described by Eric L. Smith. Is there a place for hip-hop in the middle class (or vice versa)?

Collaborative Exchanges

1. In a small group, develop a slang dictionary, recording and defining current terms that you and your peers use. For each term, try to track down its origins: Where did you first hear it? Who among your peers seems to have introduced it into your daily dialogue? Bring your dictionary to a close with an overview, evaluating the function that this slang seems to play in your peer group.

2. In a small group, investigate the evidence of hip-hop in the school community around you. Spend time observing others, noting hip-hop clothing, music preferences, style, and so on. To what degree has hip-hop penetrated the social environment at your school? What seem to be the most common hip-hop elements? Can you discern a difference between authentic hip-hoppers and hip-hop "wanna-be's"? Be prepared to report your observations and conclusions to the rest of your class.

Net Approaches

1. Visit a national news magazine, newspaper, or other online news site and search for the term "hip-hop" in articles published in the past year. (You may decide to use the AJR Newslink <ajr.newslink.org> to help you find an online news site.) Scroll through thirty references to get a feel for the topic. Then, turn to a local news site and do the same search, but this time sort the first thirty articles into the following categories: artists, culture, fashion, business, crossover, or other. Comment on one article from each category. Sketch some generalizations about the local representation of hip-hop.

2. Point your browser to <www.liszt.com> and search for listservs or newsgroups that deal with hip-hop. Follow the internal instructions and subscribe to a list or group that looks interesting to you. Listen in for a week and browse archived postings, participating if it makes sense. Generate a report that explains the issues and perspectives participants have, and connections between their postings and the reading you have done in this unit. Follow the Liszt.com instructions for unsubscribing to a list or group when your are finished with the project.

3. Go to <hotbot.com> and run the following search: *hip-hop and identity*. Visit five interesting hits and note what they have to say. Be prepared to share with the class the range of positions on hip-hop identity and the way those positions are represented online.

4. Go to <altavista.com> and do a link search on <http://www.defjam.com>. To do this, type the following string in the search box: *link:http://www.defjam.com*. Visit one personal page and one commercial page that are linked to the DefJam site. Describe and summarize them, and compare them with each other; then, evaluate the motivation of each link to DefJam.

WRITING PROJECTS

IDENTITY IN BLACK AND WHITE

Project 1

Likely Readings

Background Readings
- Brooke
- Williams
- Chideya

Case-in-Point Readings
- Spiegler
- Smith
- White

Task and Purpose

Consider the background readings listed above, and locate an idea, principle, or theme that is interesting to you that connects them to each other. With this idea in mind, turn to the work of one of the case-in-point readings listed above, focusing on the motivations and the processes by which white young people adopt hip-hop style. Use the background readings about identity and black–white interactions to analyze this crossover. Draw some conclusions about American consumer culture, and the role that commercialization seems to be playing in bringing people closer together (or driving them farther apart).

Project 2

Likely Readings

Background Readings
- Derricotte
- Chideya

Case-in-Point Readings
- Ledbetter
- Samuels and Leland
- Spiegler
- Smitherman

Task and Purpose

The readings above raise questions about "authenticity" in black identity. "What makes you black?" Toi Derricotte is asked. How close to something that might be an "authentic" Black experience is available to white hip-hoppers? Consider these questions and synthesize a position on the question of "authenticity."

Project 3

Likely Readings

Background Readings
- Williams
- Derricotte
- Brooke

Case-in-Point Readings
- Spiegler
- Samuels and Leland
- Smitherman

Task and Purpose

As a commercial phenomenon, hip-hop sells things, but as a (multi)cultural phenomenon, it also becomes a way to redefine people's perceptions and relationships to one another. Using Brooke's, Williams's or Derricotte's ideas as a backdrop and the case-in-point readings as examples, describe the local hip-hop scene so that your readers understand how identities are being negotiated there.

Project 4

Likely Readings

Background Readings
- Chideya
- Derricotte

Case-in-Point Readings
- Smitherman
- Smith
- Samuels and Leland
- Spiegler

Task and Purpose

These readings suggest a variety of ways that socioeconomic class might intersect with hip-hop culture in redefining black and white identity. Write a paper in which you examine tensions that seem evident in some of these readings, tensions that see racial identity and middle-class identity pulling against one another, or reacting synergistically with one another.

CHAPTER **9**

Our Places,
Our Selves:
Where We Come from,
Who We Are

I n her book *Mules and Men* (1935), writer and ethnographer Zora Neale Hurston described what it's like to return to a place we used to know well. Traveling from New York to her hometown of Eatonville, in rural Florida, Hurston began to see the way her childhood had been shaped by the culture of that community: "[I]t was fitting me like a tight chemise," she said. "I couldn't see it for wearing it. It was only when I was off in college, away from my native surroundings, that I could see myself like somebody else and stand off and look at my garment." Having grown up inside it, Hurston returned as an outsider to study her childhood home, an act that lit up a part of her life that had been almost invisible.

We know we live in a mobile society. Very, very few of us can expect to grow up, start careers, and raise families in one "hometown." Lots of us will move, perhaps six or eight times or more, in the course of time—and this doesn't necessarily count the summer sublets we jump into, the dorms, the fraternity or sorority houses. So what does it mean to talk about places we live? Do we mean the housing we occupy? Do we mean the neighborhood where this housing is located? We may answer the question, "Where are you from?" by naming the town or the city we live in, but do we think of the whole city or town as our home? When we think about where we come from, do we think of a place? A community of people? Does that thing we call home have a literal spatial location, or is home a "state" of mind, composed of our feelings and perceptions?

The readings in the first part of this unit present ways of thinking about the places we live. To start with, these writers share the assumption that there are useful ways of looking at and conceptualizing space. They recognize there is much to learned in studying

541

how the land (the "untrammeled wilderness," or the "trackless waste," as it used to be called) becomes the "built landscape," a jumbled terrain of roads and buildings, parking lots, stores and factories, and parks and houses. In the built landscape we inhabit today, these writers read as if from a history book the expressions of past human desires and designs. Second, these writers are interested in how consumer culture produces space, the recognizable divisions that fill the horizon. We can see what they are talking about as we picture the enormous, empty landscapes of the western plains, a vastness onto which were projected the visible markers of invisible networks of commerce and property: barbed wire fences, telegraph lines, the railroads. Now, of course, this division of space is more encompassing: think of controlled "air space," or the "cells" used by mobile phone services. And we see how the places we live are divided and organized by the private property of the family home, the retail site or the office park, the accommodations we make for automobiles, and the expressions, evident in neighborhood boundaries, of divisions reflecting class, race, or ethnicity. A third common theme in these readings is that there is an intimate link between our places and our selves, between who we are and where we are from. In different ways, the writers assume the importance of recognizing the relationships that link our personal lives and experiences to concrete geographical locations. Through our attachments to a place, we become related to other people and to the diverse histories that surround and enfold our individual experiences.

In short, these readings offer methods or models for looking at, thinking and talking about the places we live. They lay groundwork for the case-in-point readings that focus on "borders," especially in the West and Southwest. While the examples provided by the case-in-point readings have their own specific implications, the themes that surface in them reflect issues we all contend with as we look to the future.

BACKGROUND READINGS

CONSERVATION AND LOCAL ECONOMY
WENDELL BERRY

Wendell Berry is a writer and teacher who has published dozens of books of poems, essays, and fiction. A resident of the tiny farm crossroads community of Port Royal, Kentucky, Berry's abiding passion is the ethical and spiritual ties that bind humans to the land. "Conservation and Local Economy" expounds on this theme. From his book, Sex, Economy, Freedom and Community *(1992), the essay opens with seven propositions, the implications of which Berry then amplifies as he moves to articulate an alternative to the economic system that he says damages the land and the human communities that live upon it. Berry's strategy as he engages the issues of consumption and conservation is to frame his case in "terms and limits set not by anyone's preference but by nature and by human nature."*

In our relation to the land, we are ruled by a number of terms and limits set not by anyone's preference but by nature and by human nature:

I. Land that is used will be ruined unless it is properly cared for.

II. Land cannot be properly cared for by people who do not know it intimately, who do not know how to care for it, who are not strongly motivated to care for it, and who cannot afford to care for it.

III. People cannot be adequately motivated to care for land by general principles or by incentives that are merely economic—that is, they won't care for it merely because they think they should or merely because somebody pays them.

IV. People are motivated to care for land to the extent that their interest in it is direct, dependable, and permanent.

V. They will be motivated to care for the land if they can reasonably expect to live on it as long as they live. They will be more strongly motivated if they can reasonably expect that their children and grandchildren will live on it as long as they live. In other words, there must be a mutuality of belonging: they must feel that the land belongs to them, that they belong to it, and that this belonging is a settled and unthreatened fact.

VI. But such belonging must be appropriately limited. This is the indispensable qualification of the idea of land ownership. It is well understood that ownership is an incentive to care. But there is a limit to how, much land can be owned before an owner is unable to take proper care of it. The need for attention increases with the intensity of use. But the *quality* of attention decreases as acreage increases.

VII. A nation will destroy its land and therefore itself if it does not foster in every possible way the sort of thrifty, prosperous, permanent rural households and communities that have the desire, the skills, and the means to care properly for the land they are using.

In an age notoriously impatient of restraints, such a list of rules will hardly be welcome, but that these *are* the rules of land use I have no doubt. I am convinced of their authenticity both by common wisdom and by my own experience and observation. The rules exist; the penalties for breaking them are obvious and severe; the failure of land stewardship in this country is the result of a general disregard for all of them.

As proof of this failure, there is no need to recite again the statistics of land ruination. The gullies and other damages are there to be seen. Very little of our land that is being used—for logging, mining, or farming—is being well used. Much of our land has never been well used. Those of us who know what we are looking at know that this is true. And after observing the worsening condition of our land, we have only to raise our eyes a little to see the worsening condition of those who are using the land and who are entrusted with its care. We must accept as a fact that by now, our country (as opposed to our nation) is characteristically in decline. War, depression, inflation, usury, the attitudes of the industrial economy, social and educational fashions—all have taken their toll. For a long time, the news from everywhere in rural America has been almost unrelievedly bad: bankruptcy, foreclosure, depression, suicide, the departure of the young, the loneliness of the old, soil loss, soil degradation, chemical pollution, the loss of genetic and specific diversity, the extinction or threatened extinction of species, the depletion of aquifers, stream degradation, the loss of wilderness, strip mining, clear-cutting, population loss, the loss of supporting economies, the deaths of towns. Rural American communities, economies, and ways of life that in 1945 were thriving and, though imperfect, full of promise for an authentic human settlement of our land are now as effectively destroyed as the Jewish communities of Poland; the means of destruction were not so blatantly evil, but they have proved just as thorough.

The news of rural decline and devastation has been accompanied, to be sure, by a chorus of professional, institutional, and governmental optimists, who continue to insist that all is well, that we are making things worse only as a way of making things better, that farmers who failed are merely "inefficient producers" for whose failure the country is better off, that money and technology will fill the gaps, that government will fill the gaps, that science will soon free us from our regrettable dependence on the soil. We have heard that it is good business and good labor economics to destroy the last remnants of American wilderness. We have heard that the rural population is actually growing because city people are moving to the country and commuters are replacing farmers. We have heard that the rural economy can be repaired by moving the urban economy out into the country and by replacing rural work with work in factories and offices. And all the while the real conditions of the rural land and the rural people have been getting worse.

5   Of the general condition of the American countryside, my own community will serve well enough as an example. The town of Port Royal, Kentucky, has a population of about one hundred people. The town came into existence as a trading center, serving the farms in a few square miles of hilly country on the west side of the Kentucky River. It has never been much bigger than it is now. But whereas now it is held together by habit or convenience, once it was held together by a complex local economy. In my mother's childhood, in the years before World War I, there were sixteen business and professional enterprises in the town, all serving the town and the surrounding farms. By the time of my own childhood, in the years before World War II, the number had been reduced to twelve, but the town and its tributary landscape were still alive as a community and as an economy. Now, counting the post office, the town has five enterprises, one of which does not serve the local community. There is now no market for farm produce in the town or within forty miles. We no longer have a garage or repair shop of any kind. We have had no doctor for forty years and no school for thirty. Now, as a local economy and therefore as a community, Port Royal is dying.

What does the death of a community, a local economy, cost its members? And what does it cost the country? So far as I know, we have no economists who are interested in such costs. Nevertheless, when you must drive ten or twenty or more miles to reach a doctor or a school or a mechanic or to find parts for farm machinery, the costs exist, and they are increasing. As they increase, they make the economy of every farm and household less tenable.

As people leave the community or, remaining in the place, drop out of the local economy, as the urban-industrial economy more and more usurps the local economy, as the scale and speed of work increase, care declines. As care declines, the natural supports of the human economy and community also decline, for whatever is used, is used destructively.

We in Port Royal are part of an agricultural region surrounded by cities that import much of their food from distant places. Though we urgently need crops that can be substituted for tobacco, we produce practically no vegetables or other foods for consumption in our region. Having no local food economy, we produce a less and less diverse food supply for the general market. This condition implies and virtually requires the abuse of our land and our people, and they are abused.

We are also part of a region that is abundantly and diversely forested, and we have no forest economy. We have no local wood products industry. This makes it almost certain that our woodlands and their owners will be abused, and they are abused.

10   We provide, moreover, a great deal of recreation for our urban neighbors—hunting, fishing, boating, and the like—and we have the capacity to provide more. But for this we receive little or nothing, and sometimes we suffer damage.

In our region, furthermore, there has been no public effort to preserve the least scrap of land in its pristine condition. And the last decade or so of agricultural depression has caused much logging of the few stands of mature forest in private hands. Now, if we want our descendants to know what the original forest was like—that is, to know the original nature of our land—we must start from scratch and grow the necessary examples over the next two or three hundred years.

My part of rural America is, in short, a colony, like every other part of rural America. Almost the whole landscape of this country—from the exhausted cotton fields of the plantation South to the eroding wheatlands of the Palouse, from the strip mines of Appalachia to the clear-cuts of the Pacific slope—is in the power of an absentee economy, once national and now increasingly international, that is without limit in its greed and without mercy in its exploitation of land and people. Between the prosperity of this vast centralizing economy and the prosperity of any local economy or locality, there is now a radical disconnection. The accounting that measures the wealth of corporations, great banks, and national treasuries takes no measure of the civic or economic or natural health of places like Port Royal, Kentucky; Harpster, Ohio; Indianola, Iowa; Matfield Green, Kansas; Wolf Hole, Arizona; or Nevada City, California—and it does not intend to do so.

In 1912, according to William Allen White, "the county in the United States with the largest assessed valuation was Marion County, Kansas.... Marion County happened to have a larger per capita of bank deposits than any other American county.... Yet no man in Marion County was rated as a millionaire, but the jails and poorhouses were practically empty. The great per capita of wealth was actually distributed among the people who earned it." This, of course, is the realization of that dream that is sometimes called Jeffersonian but is really the dream of the economically oppressed throughout human history. And because this was a rural county, White was not talking just about bank accounts; he was talking about real capital—usable property. That era and that dream are now long past. Now the national economy, which is increasingly a global economy, no longer prospers by the prosperity of the land and people but by their exploitation.

The Civil War made America safe for the moguls of the railroads and of the mineral and timber industries who wanted to be free to exploit the countryside. The work of these industries and their successors is now almost complete. They have dispossessed, disinherited, and moved into the urban economy almost the entire citizenry; they have defaced and plundered the countryside. And now this great corporate enterprise, thoroughly uprooted and internationalized, is moving toward the exploitation of the whole world under the shibboleths of "globalization," "free trade," and "new world order." The proposed revisions in the General Agreement on Tariffs and Trade are intended solely to further this exploitation. The aim is simply and unabashedly to bring every scrap of productive land and every worker on the planet under corporate control.

15   The voices of the countryside, the voices appealing for respect for the land and for rural community, have simply not been heard in the centers of wealth, power, and knowledge. The centers have decreed that the voice of the countryside shall be that of Snuffy Smith or L'il Abner, and only that voice have they been willing to hear.

"The business of America is business," a prophet of our era too correctly said. Two corollaries are clearly implied: that the business of the American government is to serve, protect, and defend business; and that the business of the American people is to serve the government, which means to serve business. The costs of this state of things are incalculable. To start with, people in great numbers—because of their perception that the government serves not the country or the people but the corporate economy—do not vote. Our leaders, therefore, are now in the curious—and hardly legitimate—position of asking a very substantial number of people to cheer for, pay for, and perhaps die for a government that they have not voted for.

But when the interests of local communities and economies are relentlessly subordinated to the interests of "business," then two further catastrophes inevitably result. First, the people are increasingly estranged from the native wealth, health, knowledge, and pleasure of their country. And, second, the country itself is destroyed.

It is not possible to look at the present condition of our land and people and find support for optimism. We must not fool ourselves. It is altogether conceivable that we may go right along with this business of "business," with our curious religious faith in technological progress, with our glorification of our own greed and violence always rationalized by our indignation at the greed and violence of others, until our land, our world, and ourselves are utterly destroyed. We know from history that massive human failure is possible. It is foolish to assume that we will save ourselves from any fate that we have made possible simply because we have the conceit to call ourselves *Homo sapiens*.

On the other hand, we want to be hopeful, and hope is one of our duties. A part of our obligation to our own being and to our descendants is to study our life and our condition, searching always for the authentic underpinnings of hope. And if we look, these underpinnings can still be found.

20   For one thing, though we have caused the earth to be seriously diseased, it is not yet without health. The earth we have before us now is still abounding and beautiful. We must learn again to see that present world for what it is. The health of nature is the primary ground of hope—if we can find the humility and wisdom to accept nature as our teacher. The pattern of land stewardship is set by nature. This is why we must have stable rural economies and communities; we must keep alive in every place the human knowledge of the nature of that place. Nature is the best farmer and forester, for she does not destroy the land in order to make it productive. And so in our wish to preserve our land, we are not without the necessary lessons, nor are we without instruction, in our cultural and religious tradition, necessary to learn those lessons.

But we have not only the example of nature; we have still, though few and widely scattered, sufficient examples of competent and loving human stewardship of the earth. We have, too, our own desire to be healthy in a healthy world. Surely, most of us still have, somewhere within us, the fundamental human wish to die in a world in which we have been glad to live. And we *are*, in spite of much evidence to the contrary, somewhat sapient. We *can* think—if we will. If we know carefully enough who, what, and where we are, and if we keep the scale of our work small enough, we can think responsibly.

These assets are not the gigantic, technical, and costly equipment that we tend to think we need, but they are enough. They are, in fact, God's plenty. Because we have these assets, which are the supports of our legitimate hope, we can start from where we are, with what we have, and imagine and work for the healings that are necessary.

But we must begin by giving up any idea that we can bring about these healings without fundamental changes in the way we think and live. We face a choice that is starkly simple: we must change or be changed. If we fail to change for the better, then we will be changed for the worse. We cannot blunder our way into health by the same sad and foolish hopes by which we have blundered into disease. We must see that the standardless aims of industrial communism and industrial capitalism equally have failed. The aims of productivity, profitability, efficiency, limitless growth, limitless wealth, limitless power, limitless mechanization and automation can enrich and empower the few (for a while), but they will sooner or later ruin us all. The gross national product and the corporate bottom line are utterly meaningless as measures of the prosperity or health of the country.

If we want to succeed in our dearest aims and hopes as a people, we must understand that we cannot proceed any further without standards, and we must see that ultimately the standards are not set by us but by nature. We must see that it is foolish, sinful, and suicidal to destroy the health of nature for the sake of an economy that is really not an economy at all but merely a financial system, one that is unnatural, undemocratic, sacrilegious, and ephemeral. We must see the error of our effort to live by fire, by burning the world in order to live in it. There is no plainer symptom of our insanity than our avowed intention to maintain by fire an unlimited economic growth. Fire destroys what nourishes it and so in fact imposes severe limits on any growth associated with it. The true source and analogue of our economic life is the economy of plants, which never exceeds natural limits, never grows beyond the power of its place to support it, produces no waste, and enriches and preserves itself by death and decay. We must learn to grow like a tree, not like a fire. We must repudiate what Edward Abbey called "the ideology of the cancer cell": the idiotic ideology of "unlimited economic growth" that pushes blindly toward the limitation of massive catastrophe.

25   We must give up also our superstitious conviction that we can contrive technological solutions to all our problems. Soil loss, for example, is a problem that embarrasses all of our technological pretensions. If soil were all being lost in a huge slab somewhere, that would appeal to the would-be heroes of "science and technology," who might conceivably engineer a glamorous, large, and speedy solution—however many new problems they might cause in doing so. But soil is not usually lost in slabs or heaps of magnificent tonnage. It is lost a little at a time over millions of acres by the careless acts of millions of people. It cannot be saved by heroic feats of gigantic technology but only by millions of small acts and restraints, conditioned by small fidelities, skills, and desires. Soil loss is ultimately a cultural problem; it will be corrected only by cultural solutions.

The aims of production, profit, efficiency, economic growth, and technological progress imply, as I have said, no social or ecological standards, and in practice they submit to none! But there is another set of aims that does imply a standard, and these aims are freedom (which is pretty much a synonym for personal and local self-sufficiency), pleasure (that is, our gladness to be alive), and longevity or sustainability (by which we signify our wish that human freedom and pleasure may last). The standard implied by all of these aims is health. They depend ultimately and inescapably on the health of nature; the idea that freedom and pleasure can last long in a diseased world is preposterous. But these good things depend also on the health of human culture, and human culture is to a considerable extent the knowledge of economic and other domestic procedures—that is, ways of work, pleasure, and education—that preserve the health of nature.

In talking about health, we have thus begun to talk about community. But we must take care to see how this standard of health enlarges and clarifies the idea of community. If we speak of a *healthy* community, we cannot be speaking of a community that is merely human. We are talking about a neighborhood of humans in a place, plus the place itself: its soil, its water, its air, and all the families and tribes of the nonhuman creatures that belong to it. If the place is well preserved, if its entire membership, natural and human, is present in it, and if the human economy is in practical harmony with the nature of the place, then the community is healthy. A diseased community will be suffering natural losses that become, in turn, human losses. A healthy community is sustainable; it is, within reasonable limits, self-sufficient and, within reasonable limits, self-determined—that is, free of tyranny.

Community, then, is an indispensable term in any discussion of the connection between people and land. A healthy community is a form that includes all the local things that are connected by the larger, ultimately mysterious form of the Creation. In speaking of community, then, we are speaking of a complex connection not only among human beings or between humans and their homeland but also between the human economy and nature, between forest or prairie and field or orchard, and between troublesome creatures and pleasant ones. *All* neighbors are included.

From the standpoint of such a community, any form of land abuse—a clear-cut, a strip mine, an overplowed or overgrazed field—is as alien and as threatening as it would be from the standpoint of an ecosystem. From such a standpoint, it would be plain that land abuse reduces the possibilities of local life, just as do chain stores, absentee owners, and consolidated schools.

30   One obvious advantage of such an idea of community is that it provides a common ground and a common goal between conservationists and small-scale land users. The long-standing division between conservationists and farmers, ranchers, and other private small-business people is distressing because it is to a considerable extent false. It is readily apparent that the economic forces that threaten the health of ecosystems and the survival of species are equally threatening to economic democracy and the survival of human neighborhoods.

I believe that the most necessary question now—for conservationists, for small-scale farmers, ranchers, and businesspeople, for politicians interested in the survival of democracy, and for consumers—is this: What must be the economy of a healthy community based in agriculture or forestry? It *cannot* be the present colonial economy in which only "raw materials" are exported and *all* necessities and pleasures are imported. To be healthy, land-based communities will need to add value to local products, they will need to supply local demand, and they will need to be reasonably self-sufficient in food, energy, pleasure, and other basic requirements.

Once a person understands the necessity of healthy local communities and community economies, it becomes easy to imagine a range of reforms that might bring them into being.

It is at least conceivable that useful changes might be started or helped along by consumer demand in the cities. There is, for example, already evidence of a growing concern among urban consumers about the quality and the purity of food. Once this demand grows extensive and competent enough, it will have the power to change agriculture—if there is enough left of agriculture, by then, to be changed.

It is even conceivable that our people in Washington might make decisions tending toward sustainability and self-sufficiency in local economies. The federal government could do much to help, if it would. Its mere acknowledgment that problems exist would be a promising start.

35   But let us admit that urban consumers are not going to be well informed about their economic sources very soon and that a federal administration enlightened about the needs and problems of the countryside is not an immediate prospect.

The real improvements then must come, to a considerable extent, from the local communities themselves. We need local revision of our methods of land use and production. We need to study and work together to reduce scale, reduce overhead, reduce industrial dependencies; we need to market and process local products locally; we need to bring local economies into harmony with local ecosystems so that we can live and work with pleasure in the same places indefinitely; we need to substitute ourselves, our neighborhoods, our local resources, for expensive imported goods and services; we need to increase cooperation among all local economic entities: households, farms, factories, banks, consumers, and suppliers. If we are serious about reducing government and the burdens of government, then we need to do so by returning economic self-determination to the people. And we must not do this by inviting destructive industries to provide "jobs" in the community; we must do it by fostering economic democracy. For example, as much as possible of the food that is consumed locally ought to be locally produced on small farms, and then processed in small, non-polluting plants that are locally owned. We must do everything possible to provide to ordinary citizens the opportunity to own a small, usable share of the country. In that way, we will put local capital to work locally, not to exploit and destroy the land but to use it well. This is not work just for the privileged, the well-positioned, the wealthy, and the powerful. It is work for everybody.

I acknowledge that to advocate such reforms is to advocate a kind of secession—not a secession of armed violence but a quiet secession by which people find the practical means and the strength of spirit to remove themselves from an economy that is exploiting them and destroying their homeland. The great, greedy, indifferent national and international economy is killing rural America, just as it is killing America's cities—it is killing our country. Experience has shown that there is no use in appealing to this economy for mercy toward the earth or toward any human community. All true patriots must find ways of opposing it.

—1991

Rereading Actively

1. With a partner, scan the essay and observe its organization: Talk about how you might divide the essay into two or three sections, each addressing a major point. Mark the section boundaries in the essay itself and write a short explanation of your work in your journal, naming the sections and the major point you believe each contains.

2. In a small group, review the seven propositions that open this essay. Discuss your understanding of them, restating them in your own words. What is the effect of opening an essay with claims like these?

3. Identify which among the seven opening propositions you react to strongly— either favorably or unfavorably. In a journal entry, explain your reaction.

4. Review the essay, identifying passages that address the topic of the future— what does Berry foretell of future community relationships to the land? Write a brief restatement of Berry's predictions for the future.

5. With a partner, review the essay, identifying passages that address the changes that Berry calls for. What kinds of changes in thinking and behavior does Berry want people to make? Write a brief summary of these recommendations in your journal.

6. With a partner, review the essay, identifying passages that address the issue of the "health" of a community. What does Berry say must be included in a definition of a healthy community? Write a short explanation of Berry's view in your journal.

Exploring Your Responses

7. Among the points that Berry raises, forging connections between local food producers and local consumers becomes a key strategy. Reflect on your experience as a consumer: Where does the food you eat come from? Do you have access to locally grown produce or other products? In your journal, record what you ate yesterday; for each item, record where it came from, or that you don't know its origins. Reflect in your journal on the results of this inventory: Does it raise any questions for you? Are you interested in how much or how little you know about where the food you eat is produced?

8. Berry challenges our faith and optimism in economic expansion based on pursuing the interests of business and the development of new technologies (a view expressed, for example, by Sagoff in Chapter. 3). Respond to his views on this topic, stating whether you agree or disagree with his position, and why.

9. In a small group, brainstorm an inventory of your locality, listing areas that appear to be victims of "land abuse" (¶ 29), as well as areas that appear still be "abounding and beautiful" (¶ 20). Does the balance of your survey tip toward the former or the latter? What signs of hope for the future health of your locality do you see? In a journal entry, describe what your group came up with, what it decided in terms of sources of hope for the future.

NEIGHBORHOOD

YI-FU TUAN

Yi-fu Tuan is a world-recognized geographer whose work is widely cited by land-use plan-ners and scholars interested in the interaction of people and place. Among his dozens of publications are Escapism *(1998) and* The Good Life *(1986). This piece comes from* Topophilia *(1974), in which Tuan explores our feelings for and perceptions of places we inhabit. Undertaking an analysis of the idea of the neighborhood in cities in the United States, Tuan examines people's evaluations of the physical and social features of the places they live. In this excerpt, he explains the varied ways we think about neighborhood, offer-ing a complex and subtle definition of this seemingly familiar concept.*

Recognition

"Neighborhood" and "community" denote concepts popular with planners and social workers. They provide a framework for organizing the complex human ecology of a city into manageable subareas; they are also social ideals feeding on the belief that the health of society depends on the frequency of neighborly acts and the sense of com-munal membership. However, Suzanne Keller has shown that the concept of neigh-borhood is not at all simple.[1] The planner's idea of neighborhood rarely coincides with that of the resident. A district well defined by its physical characteristics and given a prominent name on the city plan may have no reality for the local people. The words "neighborhood" and "district" tend to evoke in the outsider's mind images of simple geometrical shape, when in fact the channels of neighborly act that define neighbor-hood may be extremely intricate and vary from small group to small group living in close proximity. Moreover, the perceived extent of neighborhood does not necessarily correspond with the web of intense neighborly contacts. "Neighborhood" would seem to be a construct of the mind that is not essential to neighborly life; its recognition and acceptance depend on knowledge of the outside world. The paradox can be put another way: residents of a real neighborhood do not recognize the extent and uniqueness of their area unless they have experience of contiguous areas; but the more they know and experience the outside world the less involved they will be with the life of their own world, their neighborhood, and hence the less it will in fact be a neighborhood....

Neighborhood is the district in which one *feels* at home. Another more abstract sense of neighborhood is that it is the district one knows fairly well both through direct experience and through hearsay. Most West Enders claim familiarity with a large part or most of West End; and many have knowledge of contiguous areas. A quarter of the people interviewed report familiarity with some distant sector of the Boston region. In other words, many residents are aware of an inner world of the West End, sur-rounded by a somewhat hostile outer world. We should not expect the West Enders to be able to delimit the boundaries on maps, nor that their inner worlds be much alike. They have experienced certain differences between their world and what lies beyond, and their consciousness of these differences is intensified by their perception of the outside world as not only rich and powerful, cold and lonely, but threatening. In the mid-fifties the vague sense of threat turned into reality when plans for redevel-opment were announced. For a time West Enders became fully conscious of the unique character of their district, but...with the exception of a few intellectuals and artists, their concern for the survival of West End sufficed to generate only an occasional flurry of uncoordinated protests.

Neighborhood Satisfaction

By and large people are satisfied with their residential area. For those who have lived at a place for many years, familiarity breeds acceptance and even attachment. Newcomers are more prone to voice discontent; on the other hand, people may express contentment with their new neighborhood despite their real feelings, because it is difficult for them to admit that by moving for economic gain they have in fact made fools of themselves. People of high income most often express satisfaction, which is hardly surprising since they are where they are by choice, and they have the means to improve the quality of their neighborhood. Less affluent people are less enthusiastic: the reasons given for why they like their area tend to be general and abstract, whereas those given for disliking it are more specific and concrete. Satisfaction seems a rather weak word: it may mean little more than the absence of persistent irritations.

It is often difficult to know how to interpret "liking" or "attachment" when it is verbally given. Liking a district does not necessarily commit a person to stay in it or even to patronize predominantly its facilities and services. Keller writes:

> In one racially mixed area of Philadelphia both white and Negro residents appreciated the area for its cleanliness, quietness, convenient location, well-maintained property, and even pleasant people. However, the white residents went outside the area for shopping and recreation and refused to participate in the single community organization, thus staying in the area physically but not in spirit.[2]

Satisfaction does not mean strong attachment. In the study of residential areas in West Philadelphia, most of those interviewed considered their area as a "fairly good" place in which to live, but fully three quarters could imagine living elsewhere. Seventy-five percent of the residents of Boston's West End, before its redevelopment, said that they liked the district or liked it very much, and fully 71 percent named the West End as their real home. Yet for a large group the West End as home seems to have meant little more than a satisfying base for moving out into the world and back. Indeed many showed greater appreciation of the home base's accessibility to other places than with the home base itself.[3] Despite the claim to liking the neighborhood, including its densely built tenements and the visual and aural closeness of people, many West Enders indicated that they would gladly move to a new house in the suburb under two conditions: that the suburb be one of the older kind scattered around Boston city, and that they could move together, maintain the old social ties and the old social climate.

5   City dwellers put a higher value on the quality of their neighborhood than on either the conveniences of the city or on the quality of their home. In a study of two southern cities (Durham and Greensboro, N.C.), the researchers found that by far the greater portion of the residents, from both the central districts and the fringes and from both high- and low-income groups, expressed satisfaction with their city as a place to live in; and that their attitudes toward the city tended to parallel their attitudes toward the neighborhood. But people also showed a greater readiness to give an opinion of their neighborhood and were far more critical of it than they were of the

general environment of the city. When discussion centered on the city the residents displayed much interest in roads and streets and in mobility. However, when they had to choose between "a very good but inconveniently located neighborhood" and "a less desirable but conveniently located neighborhood," the residents were three to one in favor of the good neighborhood: accessibility to other parts of the town mattered less. In both Greensboro and Durham, higher value was placed on neighborhood than on house. When the choice was between "a very good house in a less desirable neighborhood" and "a less desirable house in a good neighborhood," six to one of the people interviewed were in favor of the neighborhood over the house.[4] Middle-class residents want a good house but most would settle for a lesser one if they could have the real advantage as well as the prestige of the good neighborhood. Working-class people also attached greater importance to the neighborhood than to the dwelling but for somewhat different reasons. In the first place, low-income working people rarely enjoyed the option of selecting between "a very good house" and "a less desirable one." They also showed less concern with the symbolic status of suburbia than did members of the lower-middle class who strove consciously to better themselves. The measure of working-class preferences requires a negative scale expressing relative states of dissatisfaction. For the working class, dissatisfaction with dwelling does not necessarily mean dissatisfaction with neighborhood. For example, although half of the Puerto Rican immigrants in New York City were dissatisfied with their living quarters, only 26 percent were dissatisfied with their neighborhoods.[5] This attitude is compatible with an oft-observed tendency among working-class people: that they do not restrict their social lives to their immediate dwellings as middle-class people tend to do, nor to differentiate private from public space quite so sharply.

Satisfaction with neighborhood depends more on satisfaction with neighbors—their friendliness and respectability—than on the physical characteristics of the residential area. Complaints about inadequate housing or unsafe streets often turn out to be complaints about the habits and standards of neighbors. Social relations seem to determine how a people will respond to the adequacy of their dwellings and facilities, whether they will stay or move, and how they cope with overcrowding and other inconveniences. West Enders of Boston…were quite willing to move if they could do it together and maintain the old social ambiance. They were content with their district because they liked the close group experience. They did not see their area as a slum and resented the city's labelling it as such. In Greensboro, North Carolina, contentment with urban living was related to the amount of participation in church activities. The proportion of highly satisfied men who were affiliated with the church was 12 percent greater than the proportion of highly satisfied men who were not affiliated, and for women the difference was 20 percent. Similar results were obtained in Durham. The dissatisfied, who made up only a tenth of the total sample, complained about the poor shopping and transportation facilities, but it was not primarily economics that distinguished the dissatisfied from the satisfied. It was rather social relationships. The dissatisfied griped about the lack of contact with friends, with the church, and about the kind of people they had to associate with, at least twice as often as among the satisfied. Women, expectedly, put greater value on friendly and suitable neighbors than did the men. They were more attached to the neighborhood and showed greater reluctance to leave it. For both men and women general satisfaction correlated with whether expectation was frustrated or fulfilled. Thus, people with less than a high school education had few aspirations and consequently few dissatisfactions. The college educated had high aspirations but these they could fulfill in large measure; they too tended to be satisfied with their neighborhood. Discontentment reached highest proportion with people possessing a high school diploma; they had had their sights raised but they lacked the means to achieve them in adequate measure.[6]

Notes

1. Suzanne Keller, *The Urban Neighborhood* (New York: Random House, 1968).
2. Keller, Urban Neighborhood, p. 110.
3. Marc Fried and Peggy Gleicher, "Some Sources of Residential Satisfaction in an Urban Slum," *Journal of the American Institute of Planners*, 27, No. 4 (1961), p.307.
4. Robert L. Wilson, "Livability of the City: Attitudes and Urban Development," in F. Stuart Chapin, Jr. and Shirley F. Weiss (eds.), *Urban Growth Dynamics in a Regional Cluster of Cities* (New York: Wiley, 1962), pp. 380–81.
5. N. Glazer and D. McIntire, *Studies in Housing and Minority Groups* (Berkeley and Los Angeles, University of California Press, 1960), p. 163.
6. J. Gulick et al., "Newcomer Acculturation in the City: Attitudes and Participation," in Chapin and Weiss, *Urban Growth Dynamics*, pp. 324–27.

Rereading Actively

1. Review the article with a partner, discussing the initial observation that "[a] district well defined by its physical characteristics … may have no reality for the local people" (¶ 1). Write a short explanation of this point in your journal.

2. Continue your review of the article with your partner, discussing the observation that "the channels of neighborly act that define neighborhood may be extremely intricate and vary from small group to small group living in close proximity" (¶ 1). Write a short explanation of this point in your journal.

3. In a small group or with a partner, discuss the style of writing you encounter in this article. Write a short response to this style in your journal.

4. Underline passages in the article that explain how social relationships affect people's satisfaction with their neighborhood. Write a short summary of Yi-fu Tuan's explanation of the influence of social relationships on satisfaction.

5. Note passages in the article that address the effect location has on people's satisfaction with their neighborhood. Write a short explanation of the ways location influences satisfaction.

Exploring Your Responses

6. In your journal, jot down some physical features (parks, streets, buildings) that are symbols people in your area associate with the neighborhood in which you live.

7. When you think about the neighborhood in which you live, do you think mainly in terms of a human community or do you think in terms of the built environment? Reflect on your thinking in an informal entry in your journal.

8. Do you feel "attached" to the place you live? Are you satisfied with it? What are the sources of your attachment, or conversely, the sources of your dissatisfaction? Freewrite a response to these questions in your journal.

9. With a partner or in a small group, discuss your responses to the previous question, focusing on the sources and kinds of your satisfaction. Follow up your discussion with an entry in your journal describing others' responses to their neighborhoods.

THE ACCESSIBLE LANDSCAPE

JOHN BRINCKERHOFF JACKSON

John Brinckerhoff Jackson was a foremost scholar of landscape studies in the United States. The author of dozens of articles and numerous books, including Discovering the Vernacular Landscape *(1984) and* The Necessity for Ruins *(1980), Jackson was interested in the interaction between human activities and the natural world—that is, the patterns of human use that are impressed on the land. "The Accessible Landscape" originally appeared in the* Whole Earth Review *(1988). Drawing on the work of other researchers, Jackson discusses the reasons humans shape the places they live into territories, using different kinds of boundaries to regulate access to one another.*

About fifty years ago Americans of my generation had the kind of experience that comes once in a lifetime and, overnight, changes the way we view the world. What happened was that with the coming of commercial aviation we were all able to take to the air and fly across America. We thereby discovered a new way of seeing and interpreting the landscape.

To the present generation this is an old story. But until some time in the 1930s we had always seen our country on foot or when we rode in a car or a train. We had seen it as an evolving sequence of views. To cross the continent in those days was a serious undertaking, and we said harsh things about the monotony of Kansas and the emptiness and dust of Texas. Then, in the course of a few years, we learned to see America from twenty or thirty thousand feet in the air.

We saw it first of all as a marvelous multicolored map, a vast, rectangular pattern: fields, orderly towns, white farmsteads strung out along straight white roads. In the background was a river winding through wooded hills. It took time for us to perceive the national grid system, which few of us had heard about. But eventually we recognized that it was the product of a national land policy whereby millions of Americans became landowners and farmers. This meant that we could interpret the enormous panorama of stripes and squares and rectangles reaching out of sight in every direction as being composed entirely of small, individual properties. Even the close-packed blocks of houses in towns could be seen as clusters of independent domains. Confronted, as we were for hours at a time, with the monotony of the grid beneath us, we sought some variation in the pattern, some individual feature to focus on. It was a relief to single out the freestanding, lonely farm house in the countryside. It was only when we could divide and subdivide it into a million small private spaces, each clearly bounded and protected by fences and hedges and rows of trees, that the monolithic landscape acquired a human scale.

Thus the aerial perspective reinforced our modern tendency to analyze and reduce phenomena to their smallest components. The more extensive our view, the more we concentrate on details, and for many Americans, especially those involved in environmental studies, the landscape as a composition has almost ceased to exist. Fragments of the whole—studies of microecosystems, isolated structures and spaces of little significance—are all that matters.

There is nothing wrong in concentrating on small-scale variations in the landscape. Variety is essential not only as a source of delight and inspiration; biologically and socially, it is essential to our well-being. No one questions that. What we *can* question is how these highly specialized structures and spaces relate to their wider workaday setting. Should the wilderness area, the traditional farming landscape, the historic urban district be preserved forever, fenced off and protected from change? Should they be assimilated? We can only give an answer when we have defined their function.

5   Several years ago a book called *The Territorial Imperative,* by Robert Ardrey, enjoyed wide popularity. Ardrey was not a scientist, but he wrote extremely well and persuasively. His thesis was that the impulse, which all human beings and all animals have, to organize their own private space or territory was based on a universal, biologically determined need to establish boundaries and defend them against all intruders. "The territorial principle," Ardrey wrote, "has been evolution's most effective implement in the distribution of animal space. And if Man is a being biologically equipped with territorial patterns then at least we have a premise to work from. Urbanization is deterritorialization in the classic sense of denial of land. But perhaps there may be conceptual substitutes or symbolic channels that will preserve our biological sanity. We may be sure, however, that we must somehow preserve NO TRESPASSING signs."

Ardrey had no special ideological axe to grind. All that he wanted to prove was that human behavior is determined more by biological than by cultural factors, and that the territorial instinct was to be taken into account in every aspect of our life, from family relationships to relationships between nations.

But the reader is likely to be repelled by his persistent references to defense and privacy and the sanctity of boundary lines. The world he depicts is just as fragmented as the one so many scholars now see, and more secretive. My own reaction is that the territorial imperative he describes is by no means as universal or as innate as he claims. Indeed, I believe it is a relatively modern development, not more than two or three hundred years old, and, as I see it, already on its way out.

Another explanation of that impulse to create exclusive defensible spaces was recently proposed by an American geographer, Robert Sack. He rejected the biological basis of territoriality and suggested that it was a political or economic device. "Territoriality," he said, "is the attempt by an individual or a group to affect, influence, or control people, phenomena, and relationships by delimiting and asserting control of a geographical area.... [It] is a strategy to establish different degrees of access to people, things, and relationships." There is in consequence a history of human territoriality—and indeed that is the title of his book. He illustrated his thesis by describing the political divisions within the United States, the bureaucratic divisions within the Catholic church, and the architectural divisions within a modern factory as various ways of acquiring political or economic power and control.

Both Ardrey's and Sack's books give us an informed way of looking at the landscape. When we glance down from the plane, we can interpret what we see either as a composition of private, jealously defended territories, protected by laws and topographical barriers, or else as the diagram of a long-range plan for economic or political exploitation by a powerful minority.

10   I was an early advocate of studying landscapes from the air. At one time I had a large collection of aerial views. But when flying became increasingly unpredictable I gave it up, and I recently drove from New Mexico to Illinois and Iowa in my pickup truck. It was a long trip with many monotonous hours, but I do not regret it. It broke the spell cast by the air-view of the grid system and reminded me that there is still much to be learned at ground level. What goes on *within* those beautifully abstract rectangles is also worth observing.

Almost everything I saw on my way east was familiar. I was glad to refresh my memory of the midwestern landscape and at the same time to note the changes which had taken place over the past decade. In retrospect, all the towns I passed through seem to merge into one image of an archetypal American town or small city. Main Street has lost much of its earlier vitality and has become, particularly in the center of town, a kind of skid row minus the drunks and tattoo parlors; a shabby corridor between decaying buildings with empty store windows, cars parked every which way in the vacant lots. But where it extends out into the new part of town it recaptures its style. It is bordered by used-car lots decorated with pennants and flags, motels and ethnic restaurants, and it passes a vast shopping mall with a skating rink. There are rows and rows of parked cars and beyond the mall is a new low-cost housing development. It too has pennants and flags, and pickups are already parked on some of the new driveways. In the past I had been attracted by the strip. It seemed new and full of promise, and not yet integrated into the fabric of the town. Now I discovered that its drive-in facilities, once so novel, had become commonplace throughout the city, at least along the wider commercial streets. The houses had been taken over by small businesses catering to daily needs, and each, from the doctor's office to the beauty parlor and laundromat, had its miniature front parking lot and its own conspicuous sign. A great deal of writing and photography is currently being produced about the strip and its architecture: it has become a favorite topic with many students of American vernacular culture, but I suspect they run the risk of already being out of date. The strip is in disarray, and the relationship it once established between business and street, and its once distinctive jumble of signs and drive-ins and parking facilities and commercial facades, are now best seen in the downtown section.

Downtown has sprouted a half-dozen medium-size glass high-rise office buildings with underground parking garages and stylish lobbies. The oldest and once the best hotel in town, with an ornate ballroom and a uniformed doorman, now accommodates a modest population of senior citizens. The railroad station, long since abandoned, has been restored, painted in bright colors, and converted to a popular eating place, "The Chew-Chew Train," and the ornate nineteenth-century city hall has been torn down to make way for a metered parking lot. There is an old-fashioned factory or brick warehouse, once identified with the railroad tracks, made over into apartments and boutiques, and the elegant old mansions on tree-lined streets are occupied by law offices or the offices of insurance companies, the front lawn turned into a tastefully designed parking lot. Abruptly, in the midst of what was formerly a blue-collar neighborhood of bungalows and shabby houses with wide porches, there emerges an ethnic community with spray-can graffiti in an unknown tongue.

There is much to be learned from reading the local newspaper and watching the local "eyewitness" news. That was how I found out that the public library was being invaded every day by street people looking for a place to sleep, and that the art museum had been the scene of a fashionable fundraising dinner followed by dancing. That was how I learned that the mayor and the city council were at odds about the location of a new super-convention center: should four blocks of low-quality downtown housing be razed, or should the site be out where there was an important interchange on the interstate highway?

I made notes of these random sights and events because each of them, in one way or another, seemed to indicate that a number of changes under way in the city could tell me more about the contemporary American scene. Many were of an almost predictable kind: age and decay meant that some buildings had outlived their usefulness and had to be replaced; growth and prosperity demanded large spaces, and more of them. A common spectacle across the country are the cars, three abreast and ten deep, waiting at an intersection and watching the intricate choreography of the traffic lights overhead—then surging away to travel miles across open country between billboards and auto junkyards, to some satellite industrial suburb. Automobiles, in fact, account for more changes than anything else, and denouncing automobile culture is one way of denouncing the American city. But I admit that I was unable to pass coherent judgment on the city as a landscape. Was it handsome? Was it healthy? Was it a good place to live? Was all that growth and change headed in the right direction—was it in fact headed in any direction at all? The scattered observations I collected were vivid enough, but added up to very little. I was suffering (like many other commentators on the landscape) from that myopic vision, the environmentalist's inability to see the forest for the ecosystems, the inability to see the city as an entity. Much writing on the American city tells of its fragmentation, but often that writing comes from our predilection to *see* fragmentation; to see territories isolated from their setting, and to lament their disappearance.

15   There is clearly such a thing as a middle- or upper-class American way of perceiving and creating a landscape. It comprises those spaces and structures and relationships which people of those classes are familiar with and find pleasant as a setting for their way of life. It is a spacious rural (or semirural) landscape of woods and green fields (plowed fields are suspect, hinting at mechanization or, worse yet, commercialized farming). It is a landscape of private territories, admission to which is by invitation only. The houses, substantial and usually architect-designed, are self-sufficient and somewhat withdrawn from too close a contact with their neighbors, and are surrounded by a buffer zone of lawns and shrubbery and trees. Not far away is a small forest or miniature wilderness area, tacitly recognized as the exclusive playground of the local families. Life proceeds according to a fixed schedule from one territory to another: from private house to private tennis club to parish church and private school. To pass through a gate, a portal, or a front door, or to park in a private driveway is more than merely entering: it affirms membership in a well-established group. As in a Jane Austen novel, nothing of significance happens in the public realm, and with little traffic and no sidewalks, the streets are like country roads all eventually leading to privacy and home.

The urban version of this middle-class landscape has seen its best days. We do what we can to preserve and even restore its few remnants: the Victorian mansion, the early factory or mill, the romantic Olmsted park and the old-style neighborhood of row houses, however impoverished and dilapidated it may be. By holding on to these landmarks and giving them a special status, we are underscoring their isolation, their out-of-date territoriality, but we are preserving some of the variety of the urban landscape.

Whenever I could, I made a detour (as I passed through towns) to visit these so-called historic areas, and I enjoyed seeing them. But inevitably I found myself returning to the more active part of town and the through streets, leaving behind those quiet residential streets, similar in atmosphere to the streets in small towns—little used and almost rural in their profusion of trees and lawns. I could sense that the nearby urban streets were beginning to take over; streets which were like turbulent streams flooding their banks and drowning what was left of the old boundaries, the old privacy and autonomy. In the end the driver's perspective saw all those changes and adaptations, all that destruction and leveling as elements in a battlefield. Two concepts of how to organize and use space were meeting head-on: privacy and security and permanence as symbolized by those established territories or domains versus a vernacular impulse toward accessibility and freedom of movement.

The traveler who, like myself, rarely gets out of his car is more likely to be more aware of the roadway ahead of him than of the spaces and buildings on either margin. But if you have had, as I have had, the experience of driving fifty or more years ago, you cannot fail to be struck by how the street in the average American town or city has been transformed, how it dominates its immediate environment, how complex it is in design, how many functions it now serves, and how it constantly creates new ancillary spaces and structures: parking garages, underground parking, parking lots, drive-in facilities and skyways and overpasses and interchanges and strange little slices and islands of greenery. In its most inclusive sense, the street has taken over the role of making landscapes, changing them and destroying them. In the old days, roads were cautiously planned and built solely to reach a specific destination. Now we build highways hundreds of miles in length to open a whole region to development, and even a new street cut across a vacant suburban area promptly produces house after house along its margin, the way the branch of a tree produces leaves in spring. In the hands of a skilled planner or traffic engineer, a street becomes a versatile tool: outlawed parking, limited speed, one-way traffic, and a succession of traffic lights can either ruin the social and economic life of a neighborhood or cause it to flourish.

Sometimes, it is true, the scale and complexity of this highway environment can make a driver break out in a cold sweat. In town after town I have found myself enmeshed in a tangle of interchanges and overpasses and ramps, and have been reduced to total helplessness, timidly seeking to follow signs and numbers and arrows, and to obey the commands and warnings painted on the surface of the road in front of me.

20   Still, it is easy to exaggerate how sensitive we are to the modern highway environment. Without our always admitting it, we are at home, we know what to expect, when we drive for block after block between a succession of drive-ins, parking lots, used-car lots, garages, and gas stations. We are not simply in a commonplace, often unsightly part of town, we are in a new organization of urban space, one designed for

work, for accessibility, and for the satisfaction of short-term essential needs—all based on the presence of the automobile.

Automobile culture is a topic far too complicated for me to discuss. Let me merely say that I think we can begin to understand it when we overcome two deep-rooted middle-class prejudices. The first is that "automobile" means passenger car; not truck or van or pickup, but the automobiles that we see advertised and buy. The second prejudice is that the automobile, thus defined, is a vehicle used for going to work in the morning, parked during the work hours, then used for going home, for paying visits, and over the weekend for driving in the country, as remote as possible from other automobiles. I would hazard a guess that for three-quarters of the American public the automobile (in its widest definition) is seen primarily as essential to the process of making a living. It not only takes us to work, it is part of work itself: it collects, hauls, distributes; it carries people and equipment and materials. It is part of every industrial enterprise, every service, every job, and it intrudes on every work site. That is why the working automobile demands accessibility even in the private realm, and that in turn is why its impact on the older and more densely built-up parts of town has been so destructive. The harmonious street perspective, the homogeneous neighborhood of spacious private territories, the last traces of established boundaries, have all been destroyed by the piecemeal and unplanned introduction of a new ordering of space.

Yet one reason the auto-oriented street is so intrusive is that the nineteenth century, unlike previous centuries, failed to provide any transitional zone between the private realm and the street. The territorial imperative of the period refused to admit any dependence on the outside mobile world—hence the forbidding facades, the awe-inspiring doorways, locked and bolted, hence the "no trespassing" signs which Ardrey considered essential. The city was not always so exclusive, so determined to defend its boundaries. In earlier times the landscape, rural as well as urban, always contained a variety of spaces and structures which the public, no matter how humble, could occupy and use on a strictly temporary basis. The origin of these common spaces and of the right to use them is obscure, but their effect on the social order was good. They brought classes together and allowed people to work and come together without competitiveness and suspicion. This tradition of common spaces and structures directly contradicts Ardrey's theory that the basic spatial division is one of defensible private territories. But it is also at variance with the theory proposed by Sack: that territoriality is a means of establishing control over people and things.

The nineteenth century helped do away with most of those customary rights and spaces, but our own century has seen the beginning of their return. A social historian could establish within a decade or two when a reaction set in against autonomy and toward greater accessibility—accessibility not only *to* work and the public realm but also *from* the street to the house.

I am tempted to dwell on the importance of the parking lot. I enjoy it as an austere but beautiful and exciting aspect of the landscape. I find it easy to compare it with such traditional vernacular spaces as the common: both are undifferentiated in form, empty, with no significant topographical features to determine use, both easily accessible and essential to our daily existence. But on another level, the parking lot symbolizes a closer, more immediate relationship between various elements in our society: consumer and producer, public and private, the street and the dwelling.

25   I am very much aware of the excesses of accessibility, of the confusion and squalor of the environment often created by the rejection of the traditional private organization and use of space. I wish there were fewer cars. I wish distances were not so great. I wish the pursuit of accessibility, the constant striving for the attention and good will of the mobile consumer did not often mean lack of dignity and individuality. And I have dark moments when I foresee that the American city will in the future come to resemble those immense and formless cities of the third world.

That may be what happens. In the meantime, we should perhaps remind ourselves that behind this new way of building and planning and incessantly moving about is a basic universal urge: not to withdraw into a private domain of our own but to participate in the world and to share it with others. Ours is a society where vernacular values are taken seriously. However extravagant and unsightly much of the contemporary urban scene may be, it is essentially vernacular in that it offers the public, and particularly the working public, an easy and presumably attractive way of satisfying the needs of everyday existence.

Ardrey and his followers taught us how to distinguish one space from another and how each had its own unique character. What Sack, in his book *Human Territoriality,* taught us was how these various spaces were related to one another and how they often compete. Perhaps we can go one step further and see how in the vernacular world we are learning to *share* spaces, learning how to use them in a temporary way in order to overcome both the old-fashioned biological exclusiveness and the more modern overemphasis on competition and control.

Rereading Actively

1. Jackson's chapter progresses through three or four major topics. Working with a partner, review this piece, identifying boundaries where one topic seems to give way to the next. Mark these boundaries.

2. Discuss the section divisions you identified with your partner. Together, develop a one- or two-sentence explanation of what each section is about, and then explain the function each section seems to perform in the piece as a whole.

3. Two key words in this essay are "accessibility" and "territoriality." Review the article, identifying passages that offer various explanations of these terms, and then, in your journal, develop definitions for each term.

4. Jackson applies the concepts of accessibility and territoriality to his observations of American towns. With a partner or in a small group, identify what Jackson concludes about accessibility and territoriality based on his observations. Write a short summary of his conclusions in your journal.

5. The automobile becomes an important element in Jackson's study of "the accessible landscape." In a small group or with a partner, identify Jackson's conclusions about the role of the automobile in relation to "accessibility." Record your discussion in a journal entry.

6. Jackson describes what he says is a typical "middle- or upper-class American way of...creating a landscape" (¶ 15). What are some of its attributes, according to Jackson? Explain in your own words his description of a typical example of this sort of landscape.

Exploring Your Responses

7. With a partner or in a small group, visit a locale that is nearby and observe it as Jackson might, looking at it in terms of "accessibility" and "territoriality." Do you see evidence of boundaries that seem intended to regulate human interaction? Write a journal entry in which you reflect on your observations of this place, describing the evidence of territoriality and accessibility you noticed.

8. Jackson is interested in changes in the landscape brought about by automobile culture. He notes, for example, that the mobility of this culture has loosened the tight controls on territory that the nineteenth century city featured—the "forbidding facades, the awe-inspiring doorways, locked and bolted" (¶ 22). According to Jackson, more "transition zones" (¶ 22) between public and private realms are evident in the landscape now. In a small group, brainstorm a list of some "transition zones" you are familiar with.

9. Jackson says that recent changes in the landscape reflect a "universal urge: not to withdraw into a private domain…but to participate in the world and to share it with others" (¶ 26). Freewrite a response to this, evaluating whether Jackson's claim applies to your own preferences.

Urban Landscape History: The Sense of Place and the Politics of Space

Dolores Hayden

Dolores Hayden is a Yale professor of architecture, urbanism, and American studies. She has published several books, ranging from Seven American Utopias *(1976) to* Playing House *(1998). Hayden brings a feminist and historicist perspective to her work.* The Power of Place: Urban Landscapes as Public History *(1995), from which this selection is drawn, recognizes that the histories of women and minorities are contained in the landscapes of tenement houses, workplaces, scenes of labor struggles, ethnic festivals, and neighborhood community arts. To make these histories visible, Hayden created a project called "The Power of Place" in Los Angeles, overseeing the design and construction of public displays that tell these stories. The excerpt here introduces the idea that urban landscapes contain public history that must be preserved and transmitted to future generations, and it begins to enumerate some useful methods for gathering urban public history—that is, "a way to frame the social history of urban space."*

Authentic knowledge of space must address the question of its production.

Henri Lefebvre, *The Production of Space*

Layered with the traces of previous generations' struggles to earn a living, raise children, and participate in community life, the vernacular landscape, as John Brinckerhoff Jackson writes, "is the image of our common humanity—hard work, stubborn hope, and mutual forbearance striving to be love."[1] His definition carries cultural geography and architecture straight toward urban social history. At the intersection of these fields lies the history of the cultural landscape, the production of space, human patterns impressed upon the contours of the natural environment. It is the story of how places are planned, designed, built, inhabited, appropriated, celebrated, despoiled, and discarded. Cultural identity, social history, and urban design are here intertwined.

Indigenous residents as well as colonizers, ditchdiggers as well as architects, migrant workers as well as mayors, housewives as well as housing inspectors, are all active shaping the urban landscape. Change over time can be traced in incremental modifications of space as much as in an original city plan or building plan. This chapter sketches a way to frame the social history of urban space, a scholarly terrain where many fields overlap. It combines an approach to aesthetics (based on work dealing with the sense of place from the humanities, architecture, and landscape traditions in geography and environmental psychology) with an approach to politics (based on work on space in the social sciences and economic geography) and suggests how both apply to the history of urban landscapes.

"Place" is one of the trickiest words in the English language, a suitcase so over-filled one can never shut the lid. It carries the resonance of homestead, location, and open space in the city as well as a position in a social hierarchy. The authors of books on architecture, photography, cultural geography, poetry, and travel rely on "sense of place" as an aesthetic concept but often settle for "the personality of a location" as a way of defining it. Place for such authors may engage patterns in the mellow brick of an eighteenth-century building, the sweep of the Great Plains, the bustle of a small harbor full of sailboats, but such images can easily become cliches of tourist advertising. In the nineteenth century and earlier, place also carried a sense of the right of a person to own a piece of land, or to be a part of a social world, and in this older sense place contains more political history. Phrases like "knowing one's place" or "a woman's place" still imply both spatial and political meanings.

People make attachments to places that are critical to their well-being or distress. An individual's sense of place is both a biological response to the surrounding physical environment and a cultural creation, as geographer Yi-Fu Tuan has argued.[2] From childhood, humans come to know places through engaging all five senses, sight as well as sound, smell, taste, and touch.[3] Extensive research on perception shows the simultaneous engagement of several senses in orientation and wayfinding. Children show an interest in landmarks at three or earlier and by age five or six can read aerial maps with great accuracy and confidence, illustrating the human ability to perceive and remember the landscape.[4]

5   As social relationships are intertwined with spatial perception, human attachment to places attracts researchers from many fields. Environmental psychologists Setha Low and Irvin Altman define "place attachment" as a psychological process similar to an infant's attachment to parental figures. They also suggest that place attachment can develop social, material, and ideological dimensions, as individuals develop ties to kin and community, own or rent land, and participate in public life as residents of a particular community.[5] (Some earlier sociological studies of the aftermath of urban renewal, those that convey the process of mourning for a lost neighborhood, have utilized attachment theory as well[6] to explain the power of human connections to places that may no longer exist physically.)

Cultural landscape studies, as geographer Carl Sauer developed them, focused on the evolution of places and included the "combination of natural and man-made elements that comprises, at any given time, the essential character of a place."[7] Cultural landscape has much more specific meanings than place. Yet the earliest cultural land-scape methods for studying places, and people's shaping of them and attachments to them, were not adequate to convey their political dimensions. Unlike social history, which developed in the 1960s with an urban bias, cultural geography from the 1940s on leaned to the study of rural, preindustrial landscapes, rather than the complicated urban variety, mapping ethnicity along with vernacular house types or patterns of cultivation, considering ecology but avoiding issues of political contestation....[8]

At the heart of Carl Sauer's definition of the cultural landscape was "the essential character of a place." It has often proved easier to study either the natural or the built components of a cultural landscape than to wrestle with the combination of the two in the concept of place. In recent decades, as geographers John Agnew and James Duncan have shown, social scientists have frequently avoided "place" as a concept, and thus have sidetracked the sensory, aesthetic, and environmental components of the urbanized world in favor of more quantifiable research with fewer epistemological problems.[9] Some have argued for the importance of an increasingly "placeless world," or a "non-place urban realm," but speaking critically of bad places is more effective than dismissing them as places.[10] The process that transforms places demands analysis. As a field of wildflowers becomes a shopping mall at the edge of a freeway, that paved-over meadow, restructured as freeway lanes, parking lots, and mall, must still be considered a place, if only to register the importance of loss and explain it has been damaged by careless development. Places also suffer from clumsy attempts to market them for commercial purposes: when small towns in Iowa that once seemed to embody everyday life in the Midwest developed "themes" to make them more attractive to tourists, the places became caricatures of themselves.[11]

If place does provide an overload of possible meanings for the researcher, it is place's very same assault on all ways of knowing (sight, sound, smell, touch, and taste) that makes it powerful as a source of memory, as a weave where one strand ties in another. Place needs to be at the heart of urban landscape history, not on the margins, because the aesthetic qualities of the built environment, positive or negative, need to be understood as inseparable from those of the natural environment.[12] Together these two provide the basis for considering the history of the American urban landscape.

The Production of Space

Henri Lefebvre, the French sociologist who began writing about the "production of space" over two decades ago, provides a framework that can be used to relate the sense of place encountered in cultural landscape studies to the political economy. Lefebvre argues that every society in history has shaped a distinctive social space that meets its intertwined requirements for economic production and social reproduction.[13] In terms of production, Lefebvre would be close to cultural geography in identifying spaces or landscapes shaped for mining, manufacturing, commerce, or real estate speculation. Most original is his analysis of the space of social reproduction, which ranges over different scales, including the space in and around the body (biological reproduction), the space of housing (the reproduction of the labor force), and the public space of the city (the reproduction of social relations). Here he links the physical to the social in decisive ways. (More speculative are his analyses of the role of artists' representations of space, and the role of popular political movements in creating "counter-space" in opposition to existing political structures.) Cultural critic Fredric Jameson, in *Postmodernism*, assessed Lefebvre's importance: he "called for a new kind of spatial imagination capable of confronting the past in a new way and reading its less tangible secrets off the template of its spatial structures—body, cosmos, city...."[14]

10   Lefebvre suggests that the production of space is essential to the inner workings of the political economy. A small factory on a stream near a waterfall, with a boarding house and a couple of workers' cottages, announces New England in the earliest stages of textile production; a vast aerospace complex next to a suburban tract of ten thousand identical houses exemplifies defense industries and their work force one hundred and fifty years later. But Lefebvre also sees commonalities between the tract houses, the identical suites in corporate skyscrapers, and the identical shops in malls, suggesting that a quality of late capitalist space is the creation of many identical units—similar but not "placeless" places—by the large commercial real estate market that has become, in itself, a distinguishing feature of the economy. And just as analysts begin to count the environmental costs that this production of endless units of salable space may entail, so the cultural costs in terms of identity, history, and meaning can be weighed.[15]

Lefebvre's approach to the production of space can provide a framework for constructing some specific social histories of urban places. Depending on the kinds of arguments historians want to make (and the resources available in oral histories, social histories, and buildings), research might explore working landscapes, territorial histories of groups in the population, or political histories of building types. The first focuses on economic production as it is tied to social reproduction, the others make social reproduction the major theme.

Working Landscapes

The production of space begins as soon as indigenous residents locate themselves in a particular landscape and begin the search for subsistence. The place may grow into a town, inhabited by new waves of settlers. Many cities begin with farming, mining, fishing, or trading rather than manufacturing. The farm laborers, the miners, the fishermen, or the stall holders in the market, and their families, are the earliest builders of the economic enterprise that eventually becomes a city. Space is shaped for both economic production—barns, or mine shafts, or piers, or a factory—as well as for social reproduction—housing for the workers, managers, and owners, a store, a school, a church. As the town grows, configuring streets and lots formalizes the earliest uses of land and path systems. This leads to infrastructure such as paved roads, bridges, water systems, streetcars, and railroads, all of which have substantial environmental effects.

All of these different kinds of private and public planning activities and public works have a social as well as a technological history.[16] People fight for and against them. People also construct and maintain them (figure 9.1). The ditchdiggers and piledrivers, the streetcar workers and the railroad mechanics, the canal drivers and crane operators represent class, ethnic, and gender history shaping the landscape in ways that have barely been studied. As environmental historian Patricia Nelson Limerick has observed, "Workers, often minority workers, provided the essential labor of environmental change, and members of minority groups often absorbed a disproportionate share of

Figure 9.1 Workers' landscapes.

Chinese American railroad workers on the tracks, next to an Anglo American supervisor, near Lang, California, 1876. (Security Pacific Collection, Los Angeles Public Library.) [Note: This is the attribution from the original source.]

645—Chinamen going to work on the Oregon and California R. R.

undesirable environmental impacts…yet environmental history and ethnic history have been very separate enterprises."

The history of the railroad in the nineteenth century offers just one of many possible examples. One can understand the railroad in engineering terms, as the history of trains and tracks, or in architectural terms, as stations and freight yards, or in urban planning terms, as the right and the wrong side of the tracks, without fully capturing its social history as the production of space. Limerick notes that twenty-nine Chinese workers died while building Wrights Tunnel for the South Pacific Coast Railroad through the Santa Cruz Mountains in California in 1879, and dozens more were injured. Other historians have commented that the Chinese "contributed" to California's economic development. Limerick goes farther: the "'price of progress' had registered in the smell of burnt human flesh."[17] She concludes, "In our times the rediscovery of the landscape hinges on just such recognitions as this one." One could add that coming to terms with ethnic history in the landscape requires engaging with such bitter experiences, as well as the indifference and denial surrounding them.

15   Like the dwelling, which may be typical of the way millions were sheltered, something as basic as a railroad or streetcar system changes the quality of everyday life in the urban landscape, while marking the terrain.[18] For some it provides jobs

in design, or construction, or operation, or maintenance; for others, it makes a journey to work through the city possible; for a few, it may bring profits as an investment. John Stilgoe has shown how to study the clustering of different vernacular building types along railroad lines, and the concept of the space of the railway as a "metropolitan corridor."[19] As Limerick shows, there is also an important underlying story to tell about the work force and the social space of the metropolitan corridor, from the people who blasted the tunnels and drove the trains right down to the workers who kept the cars clean and emptied the trash. From the perspective of social history, it is this story about the work force that can turn an abandoned set of railroad tracks or a decaying freight shed into a potential resource for projects concerned with larger public meanings in the urban landscape.

Territorial Histories of Cities Based on Race and Gender

Lefebvre emphasized the importance of space for shaping social reproduction. One of the consistent ways to limit the economic and political rights of groups has been to constrain social reproduction by limiting access to space. For women, the body, the home, and the street have all been arenas of conflict. Examining them as political territories—bounded spaces with some form of enforcement of the boundaries—helps us to analyze the spatial dimensions of "woman's sphere" at any given time.[20] And just as gender can be mapped as a struggle over social reproduction that occurs at various scales of space, the same is true of race, class, and many other social issues.

As Michael Dear and Jennifer Wolch have written, the interplay between the social and the spatial is constant: "Social life structures territory…and territory shapes social life."[21] Ghettos and barrios, internment camps and Indian reservations, plantations under slavery and migrant worker camps should also be looked at as political territories, and the customs and laws governing them seen as enforcement of territory.[22] The territories of the gay and lesbian communities can be mapped. So can those of childhood or old age. The spatial dimensions of class can be illuminated by looking at other boundaries and points of access.[23] Since many of these categories interlock, studying how territories defined by gender, class, race, ethnicity, sexual preference, or age affect people's access to the urban cultural landscape can be frustrating.

How can one find evidence about social groups' experiences of these overlapping territories? Frequently observations about urban space are ignored by historians because the comments appear to be spatial description rather than social analysis, but they can form the basis of a territorial history focusing on access to the public spaces of the city. For example, Loren Miller, Jr., an African American lawyer who grew up in a middle-class family in Los Angeles in the 1940s, didn't see a segregated movie house until he went to Kansas in 1948. He could go to the beach any time on the streetcar. But he observed, "As teenagers, we knew not to drive into Compton, to Inglewood, not to drive into Glendale 'cause you would just be out, with your hands on top of the car,… LAPD did the same thing. You got too far south on Western, they would stop you." This man also remembered, as a child, having Japanese American neighbors interned, going to visit them in temporary quarters at the Santa Anita race track, and finding that "soldiers with guns wouldn't let me go on the other side of the table, and they wouldn't let me play with my friends."[24] This is one individual account of spatial barriers about race. Another writer, Lynnell George, comments on this city in the 1940s, "Off-limits for people of color in Los Angeles ran the gamut … not West of Main, not Glendale after dusk, never ever Fontana and its dusty flatlands dotted with burning crosses."[25]

Accounts like these begin to make it possible to map spatial segregation for the larger African American community: not only streets and neighborhoods, but schools, hotels, stores, fire stations, swimming pools, and cemeteries would be some of the places to examine. Photographs often convey territorial history as well, documenting both residential segregation and communities' struggles against territorial exclusion (Figures 9.2, 9.3).[26] In images of public space from the 1940s, a small cafe has different entrances for "White" and "Colored" labeled over the doors, while a movie theater has a large arrow painted on the side of the building, pointing "Colored" to an exterior stair leading to a balcony. Documentary photography, newspaper photography, commercial photography, and amateur snapshots all reveal different sides of a city. It can be revealing to consider the gender and ethnic background of the photographer as well as the architectural subject selected for the picture.

Figure 9.2   Territorial histories.
Exclusion of Japanese Americans from a residential neighborhood in Hollywood, California, took the form of signs as well as deed restrictions, 1920s. (Visual Communications.)

Figure 9.3   Territorial histories.
Segregated tract, with African American observer, Los Angeles County, early 1950s. (Southern California Library for Social Studies and Research; the original source is possibly the California *Eagle*, Charlotta Bass Collection.)

20   A territorial history based on limitations of gender in the public spaces of the city would use similar sources and would put buildings or parts of them off limits, rather than whole neighborhoods.[27] In the twentieth century, spatial segregation includes private men's clubs, university faculty clubs, programs in higher education, and numerous other spaces. The segregation need not be absolute—women might be permitted to attend a class, but sit separately, or they might be allowed to enter a club as men's guests, provided they remained in a special room reserved for ladies, and so on. In the nineteenth century the list would be longer, and forbidden activities might include voting, entering a public saloon, or sitting in the main body of an assembly hall rather than the more restricted balcony. To understand the intersecting segregation of race, class, and gender, the spatial dimensions of traditional "woman's sphere" have to be studied in combination with the spatial limits imposed by race or class. Because white women's clubs, charities, and suffrage organizations were often segregated, African American women sometimes formed their own parallel groups, with their own meeting places, to help working women and girls in their own communities.[28] Or, to take another example, one photograph of a class at a state university open to women in the 1890s shows the men and women sitting separately. It is equally important to ask if there appear to be people of color present, segregated by gender and race, sitting at the very back of each group (Figure 9.4).

Figure 9.4 Territorial histories.
Male and female students sitting separately at a lecture on physics, University of Michigan Medical School, late 1880s. (Bentley Historical Library, University of Michigan.)

1. John Brinckerhoff Jackson, *Discovering the Vernacular Landscape* (New Haven: Yale University Press, 1984), xii.
2. Yi-Fu Tuan sees both biology and culture forming the human connection to place, in *Space and Place: The Perspective of Experience* (Minneapolis, Minn.: University of Minnesota Press, 1977), 6. He also notes that these terms may be elusive: "Architects talk about the spatial qualities of place; they can equally well talk about the locational (place) qualities of space." Tuan describes place as a pause in the flow of time: "If we see the world as a process, constantly changing, we should not be able to develop any sense of place." He argues that the experience of place engages all five senses in seeing, smelling, feeling, hearing, and tasting the essence of places.
3. Cross-cultural studies reveal heightened sensitivities to certain kinds of places. The Aivilik of northern Canada can describe many kinds of snowy landscapes; the Puluwat Islanders of the Pacific can read minute variations in ocean currents. Yet it would be wrong to say that sense of place is primarily determined this way. Among the Aivilik gender accounts for marked differences. Settlements and trading posts appear on cognitive maps drawn by women, while coastline is the key to those made by men, according to Tuan, *Space and Place,* 79–84.
4. Tuan, *Space and Place,* 30, 79–84.
5. Irwin Altman and Setha M. Low, eds., *Place Attachment* (New York: Plenum Publishing, 1992). Also see Denise L. Lawrence and Setha M. Low, "The Built Environment and Spa-

tial Form," *Annual Review of Anthropology* 19 (1990), 453–505, a review essay covering several hundred works.

6. Herbert J. Gans, *The Urban Villagers: Group and Class in the Life of Italian-Americans*, 2d ed. (New York: Free Press, 1982); Peter H. Marris, *Family and Social Change in an African City* (Evanston: Northwestern University Press, 1962); Peter H. Marris, *Loss and Change*, 2d ed. (London and New York: Routledge and Kegan Paul, 1986).

7. Sauer said: "Culture is the agent, the natural area is the medium, the cultural landscape is the result." See "Landscape," in Robert P. Larkin and Gary L. Peters, eds., *Dictionary of Concepts in Human Geography* (Westport, CT: Greenwood Press, 1983), 139–144. Among the scholars who have helped shape cultural landscape studies are John Brinckerhoff Jackson and Donald Meinig. See Jackson's essays in *Landscapes* (Amherst: University of Massachusetts Press, 1980). *Discovering the Vernacular Landscape* (cited above), and *A Sense of Place, a Sense of Time* (New Haven: Yale University Press, 1994); and Meinig's edited volume, *The Interpretation of Ordinary Landscapes* (New York and Oxford: Oxford University Press, 1979) as well as his *The Shaping of America*, 2 vols. (New Haven: Yale University Press, 1986 and 1993). More recent edited volumes include Dell Upton and John Michael Vlach, eds., *Common Places: Readings in American Vernacular Architecture* (Athens, Georgia: The University of Georgia Press, 1986) and Michael Conzen, ed., *The Making of the American Landscape* (New York: HarperCollins, 1990), both with extensive bibliographies. Conzen's is the more urban of the two, and the broader in focus. Also see Wayne Franklin and Michael Steiner, eds., *Mapping American Culture* (Iowa City: University of Iowa Press, 1992). Landscape architect Anne Whiston Spirn, in a forthcoming book, *The Language of Landscape*, will provide a more thorough grounding in aesthetics and environmental science for landscape studies and design. See her articles "From Uluru to Cooper's Place: Patterns in the Cultural Landscape," Orion 9 (Spring 1990), 32–39, and "The Poetics of City and Nature: Towards a Now Aesthetic for Urban Design," *Landscape Journal* 7 (Fall 1988), 108–127.

8. Two collections of essays on ethnic spatial patterns and vernacular architecture in the American rural landscape exist, but there is nothing comparable focusing on vernacular building in urban ethnic places: Allen G. Noble, ed., *To Build in a New Land: Ethnic Landscapes in North America* (Baltimore: Johns Hopkins University Press, 1992); Dell Upton, ed., *America's Architectural Roots: Ethnic Groups That Built America* (Washington, D.C.: The Preservation Press, 1986).

9. John A. Agnew, "The Devaluation of Place in Social Science," examines the way that ideas about class and community have become more central to social science research than ideas about place, in Agnew and Duncan, eds., *The Power of Place*. Also see David Ley, "Modernism, Post-Modernism, and the Struggle for Place," in the same volume, 44–65.

10. Edward Relph, *Place and Placelessness* (London: Pion, 1976), promoted the term "placeless," which is misleading since he really meant bad place. Melvin Webber, an urban planner, used "non-place urban realm" earlier in a way that was neither positive nor negative but referred to the decline of face-to-face activities and the rise of telephone, television, etc. More recent commentators stress the "information highway" as a non-place.

11. Mira Engler, "Drive-Thru History: Theme Towns in Iowa," *Landscape* 32 (1993), 8–18; Patrick Wright, *On Living in an Old Country* (London: Verso, 1985).

12. But terminology is in flux. Alexander Wilson describes his *The Culture of Nature: North American Landscape from Disney to Exxon Valdez* (Cambridge, Mass.: Blackwell, 1992) as "a cultural history of nature in North America," 12.

13. Henri Lefebvre, *The Production of Space*, tr. Donald Nicholson-Smith (Oxford, England, and Cambridge, MA: Basil Blackwell, 1991).

14. Fredric Jameson, *Postmodernism, or, The Cultural Logic of Late Capitalism,* (Durham: Duke University Press, 1991), 364–365.

15. For a more complex look at these issues, see Gregory, *Geographical Imaginations,* and David Harvey. *The Condition of Postmodernity* (Cambridge, MA, and Oxford: Blackwell, 1989), especially Table 3.1.

16. To list just a few examples of works that deal with political contestation: on city plans, Gwendolyn Wright, *The Politics of Design in French Colonial Urbanism* (Chicago: University of Chicago Press, 1991); and on parks, Galen Cranz, *The Politics of Park Design* (Cambridge, Mass.: MIT Press, 1982), and Roy Rosenzweig and Elizabeth Blackmar. *The People and the Park* (Ithaca: Cornell University Press, 1992).

17. Patricia Nelson Limerick, "Disorientation and Reorientation: The American Landscape Discovered from the West," *Journal of American History* 79 (December 1992), 1031–1034.

18. Denis Wood's atlas of the Boylan Heights neighborhood of Raleigh, North Carolina, is a wonderful example of the evocation of an entire urban neighborhood, achieved through drawings that record the contours of its landscape and the patterns of its roads, alleys, bridges, sewers and water mains, manhole covers, street trees, street signs, and stop signs. Denis Wood, *Dancing and Singing: A Narrative Atlas of Boylan Heights,* proof copy from the author, 1990, School of Design, North Carolina State University. A basic text that explores some of these materials for teachers undertaking school projects is Gerald Danzer, *Public Places: Exploring Their History* (Nashville, Tenn.: Association for State and Local History, 1987.)

19. John Stilgoe, *Metropolitan Corridor: Railroads and the American Scene* (New Haven: Yale University Press, 1983).

20. At the scale of bodily space, in the middle third of the nineteenth century, some middle-class women fought for dress reform and access to birth control, while African American women fought slavery as a system that required them to bear children as a source of new wealth for their owners. At the scale of housing space, by the last third of the century, some middle-class women, who were usually political activists and housewives, were looking for ways to reorganize the home economically as a domestic workplace. In the same period, some African American women, who were employed as domestics, organized a major strike of household workers in Atlanta in 1881. At the scale of urban space, in the late nineteenth and early twentieth centuries, middle-class white women's movements for "municipal housekeeping" challenged corrupt government by men; suffrage also brought broad coalitions of women, across lines of class and race, into public space to demand this right. At the same time, while African American women participated in these wider movements, they would have experienced more limited access to space in the city. Dolores Hayden, *The Grand Domestic Revolution: A History of Feminist Designs for American Homes, Neighborhoods, and Cities* (Cambridge: MIT Press, 1981); Mary P. Ryan, *Women in Public: Between Banners and Ballots, 1825–1880* (Baltimore: Johns Hopkins University Press, 1990).

21. Dear and Wolch, *The Power of Geography,* 4.

22. For example, Rina Swentzell, "Conflicting Landscape Values," *Places* 7 (Fall 1990), 19–27; Dell Upton, "Black and White Landscapes in Colonial Virginia," in Robert Blair St. George, ed., *Material Life in America 1600–1860* (Boston: Northeastern University Press, 1988), 357–369; Manuel Castells, "Cultural Identity, Sexual Liberation and Urban Structure: The Gay Community in San Francisco," *The City and the Grassroots* (Berkeley: University of California Prass, 1983), 138–172; George Chauncey, *Gay New York: Gender, Urban Culture and the Makings of the Gay Male World, 1890–1940* (New York: Basic Books, 1994).

23. For example, Allen Scott and Michael Storper, eds., *Production, Work, and Territory: The Geographical Anatomy of Industrial Capitalism* (London: Allen and Unwin, 1986); Dear and Wolch, eds., *The Power of Geography.*

24. Interview with Loren Miller. Jr., in Charles Perry. "When We Were Very Young," *Los Angeles Times Magazine* (February 4, 1990), 13–14.

25. Lynell George, *No Crystal Stair: African Americans in the City of Angels* (London and New York: Verso, 1992), 222–223.

26. Such photographs are often surprisingly difficult to locate since only certain archives are willing to preserve them. Lonnie G. Bunch's *Black Angelenos* includes a good selection (Los Angeles: California Afro-American Museum, 1989).

27. For a sociological look at these spatial issues in world perspective, see Daphne Spain, *Gendered Spaces* (Chapel Hill: University of North Carolina Press, 1992).

28. Miller, in Perry, "When We Were Very Young," 13, includes a photograph of an African American women's social club his mother belonged to in Los Angeles in the 1950s.

Rereading Actively

1. With a partner, scan the excerpt and observe its organization: Talk about how you might divide the piece into two or three sections, each addressing a major point. Mark the section boundaries in the excerpt itself, and write a short explanation of your work in your journal, naming the sections and the major point you believe each contains.

2. Hayden identifies several meanings of the word "place," and she links them in her approach to urban social history. Summarize in your journal the several meanings of "place" as Hayden explains them.

3. In a small group, review the excerpt, identifying two or three passages that seem clear to everyone in the group. Discuss these passages, formulating your own explanation of their meaning.

4. Identify two or three passages that are unclear to members in your group, discussing some possible meanings for them. Write the results of this discussion in your journal, stating what questions you had and what tentative answers you developed.

5. Review the piece with a partner or in a small group, identifying passages that talk about methods you might use to collect information and frame the social history of the place you live or of a place you are familiar with. List these methods in your journal, with a brief explanation of Hayden's comments about each one.

Exploring Your Responses

6. Hayden begins with a reference to the traces of previous generations visible in the "vernacular landscape" (¶ 1) (the ordinary world of everyday communities—the dwellings and yards, the marketplaces and streets of ordinary places.) Visit a neighborhood or locale you are familiar with and describe what you see.

7. Since our connection to place is formed through the senses, add to your description of the previous exercise details of sight, sound, smell, touch, and taste.

8. Reflect on your description of questions 6 and 7, identifying in your journal any evidence of the presence of past generations.

BACKGROUND ASSIGNMENTS

The readings here offer approaches to seeing, in place, our relationships to communities—networks of personal relationships and exchanges that are built into the streets, neighborhoods, marketplaces, and public spaces we inhabit. Each of the readings offers a way of looking at the scenes of our daily routines, discerning patterns in them that shed light on otherwise hidden histories or that point to uncertain futures. Focusing on our sense of place, of "home," of community, the authors give us tools—concepts, questions—to see, think, and talk about the places we live.

Making Connections

1. What happens when you venture into unfamiliar places, a new environment? Think about how principles from some of the background readings may allow you to analyze your experience of feeling "out of place." For example, you might apply Tuan's discussion of the subjective aspects of home or neighborhood, or Jackson's comments on territoriality and accessibility. Identify a principle, using it to analyze your subjective experience of new or unfamiliar places, e.g., relocating, immigrating, or going to college.

2. Use the concepts and methods described by Tuan and Hayden to create a history of your neighborhood. For example, gather photographs and interview neighbors in order to locate intersections between autobiography and community history: Your goal should be to illuminate the meaning of events in your own life by relating them to larger events in your community or in society in general.

3. Berry, Hayden, and Jackson each approach the issue of public (communal) and private (personal) space. Write an essay in which you synthesize their views about the need for a responsible consideration of the relationship between public and private space in our consumer society.

4. Many people today are concerned about the social and ecological dangers associated with sprawl the constant movement of residential and commercial away from city centers into undeveloped places. Though neither author explicitly emphasizes this topic, both Berry and Tuan draw our attention to the intimate and fragile connection between place and community. Write an essay about sprawl, using Berry's and Tuan's ideas as framework to examine the social and ecological implications of this kind of development.

5. Identify a theme that appears in several of these background readings, and apply it to an analysis of shopping malls. For instance, you might define the idea of "community" by drawing in different ways on Berry, Tuan, and Jackson, and apply the idea of community they seem to share to questions raised by Guterson (Chapter 3) of whether shopping malls create real communities or not.

Collaborative Exchanges

1. The use of public space is a theme percolating through these readings. With two or three classmates, review the readings, focusing on this theme of public space. Individually or as a group, visit and assess locations near you: Do you find formal and informal public gathering places? Who uses them? How are they defined? Once you have done this work, meet as a group, compare your observations, and draft a collaborative analysis of how the locations you visited serve as the setting for public gatherings.

2. With two or three classmates, review what Berry and Tuan have to say about the relationships between people and the places they live. Discuss the important relationships you have with people, and how these relationships are affected by place. Does your circle of relationships exist within a specific place, or is it dispersed through many places? Does your "neighborhood" exist in one clearly bounded space? Develop a collaborative description of how your relationships with others are mediated or influenced by place.

3. Jackson talks about seeing in the forms of buildings, streets, and parking lots expressions of territoriality and accessibility. Hayden talks about seeing "cultural identity, social history, and urban design" in the "the production of space" of urban neighborhoods. With a small group, take a field trip to a place you all agree is perfectly ordinary. Train your observations on it, and write descriptions that, as Hayden says, engage "all five senses, sight as well as sound, smell, taste, and touch." Generalize from your observations, identifying your dominant impressions of the place by focusing on its expression of territoriality and accessibility.

 ## Net Approaches

1. A ready application of the themes in these readings is the issue of sprawl. Visit a local magazine, newspaper, or other online news site and look for articles on sprawl. (You may decide to use the AJR Newslink <ajr.newslink.org> to help you find an online news site.) Make note of what articles seem to focus on. Then, in your journal, freewrite about the local concern with sprawl and draft a comparison between local concerns and the themes mentioned in the reading for this unit.

2. Point your browser to <www.liszt.com> and skim through newsgroups associated with the following terms: land use, urban development, urban, suburban, and rural. Following the internal instructions, subscribe to one of the newsgroups you discover and listen in for a week, participating if it makes sense. Generate a report that explains the newsgroup, the issues and perspectives participants have, and connections between their postings and the reading you have done in this unit. Cancel your subscription to the newsgroup when you are finished with the project.

CASE-IN-POINT READINGS

The Future Is a Border: Crossing a Map of Contested Terrains

The "border" is a theme that has received a great deal of attention lately. Scholars have used the term to describe social spaces where different cultures meet and overlap. Others see the word in its more literal sense, focusing on neighborhood and national security to be achieved by defending physical borders. To conceive of the future as a border may seem to take a leap of imagination, yet we speak of it as a place when we say we "move into" the future. Indeed, our thinking about the future and our thinking about the places we live seem very closely intertwined: where will we be as a nation in twenty-five years, we ask. Furthermore, in the frontier mythology that profoundly shapes our experiences, we learn to anticipate the future as the promise of new territory: we look for our chance, and we break for the openings, the new beginnings where alternative arrangements can be made. The readings here examine sites where the future is fast dawning upon us, where the territory of the new century is being shaped, where Americans are negotiating their future society. Underlying each of the cases are abiding questions of community: What can it mean that we may live together? What can it mean that we may live apart? Freedom and security contend with one another in these cases. Opportunity and tradition also clash, as patterns of community we inherit from the past weigh on our actions as we invent the future.

HUE AND CRY: WRITER'S PURPLE HOUSE HAS CAUSED A STIR IN SAN ANTONIO
DAVID MCLEMORE

David McLemore is a reporter for the Dallas Morning News. *This article (a story that was picked up by other national newspapers) describes a controversy surrounding a woman and her dispute with the San Antonio Historical Review and Design Commission. At the center of the controversy is Sandra Cisneros, the owner of the purple house and the author of many books, including a widely acclaimed book,* The House on Mango Street *(1985). This article explains the sides of the controversy—Cisneros's perspective on the traditional roots of the vibrant colors of her house, and the commission's view of the need for preserving uniformity in the appearance of the houses in the King William district of San Antonio.*

San Antonio—Cars meander down Guenther Street, slowing for a longer look at the purple house nestled in a sea of sage, cactus and sweet-smelling vines. Some visitors stop to take souvenir photos or drop notes into the straw basket at the gate.

"It's like tourists at the Alamo. I feel like they're paying homage," said Sandra Cisneros, novelist and proud first-time homeowner. "I'll sometimes stand at the porch and wave, and they smile and wave back. I like to think my casita makes their day happier."

The two-story 1903 Victorian cottage rises in a cloud of color amid its more conventionally gray, brown or off-white neighbors in the city's King William district—a collection of restored turn-of-the-century homes that range from towering mansions to more modest gingerbread cottages.

Last October, Ms. Cisneros began painting her home a dark purple, trimmed in a lighter purple to reflect, she said, her own Latina roots and to celebrate San Antonio's connection to the vivid colors of Mexico.

5 Her color scheme definitely hasn't brought joy to the San Antonio Historical Review and Design Commission, charged with approving changes in the city's 16 historic districts. Nor to city historic preservation officer Ann McGlone, who has deemed Ms. Cisneros' periwinkle purple "inappropriate" to the King William Historic District.

The city issued a citation in June for noncompliance with rules governing historic homes. Ms. Cisneros decided to fight City Hall. She began researching the history of the homes in her neighborhood. She visited the San Antonio Conservation Society library, expecting to find ample documentation of vibrant color in San Antonio's homes.

Instead, she found that the preferred colors for historic properties were whites and such approved colors as Plymouth Rock Grey and Union Blue.

"It broke my heart," she said. "Where were the Tejano traditions of walls of mango yellow or rosa mexicana? The visual record of the people who have lived in this city for nearly 300 years had been allowed to disappear."

Ms. Cisneros is widely known beyond City Hall. Her novels and poetry depict the struggles and joys of contemporary Latino life.

10 She has emerged as "an essential" American writer, according to The New York Times Review of Books. Two years ago, she received a $225,000 "genius" grant from the MacArthur Foundation.

In her writings, particularly her 1985 novel "The House on Mango Street," the house is a deeply personal icon, signifying both the shame of growing up poor and the triumph of rising above poverty.

"Growing up in third-floor walk-ups in Chicago, poverty was, for me, an ugly door, a peeling wall," she said. "My mother stressed keeping inside clean and bright. I always dreamed of the day when I could make the exterior a reflection of who I am."

On Wednesday, she defended her home before the 11-member commission with a heartfelt manifesto for bright hues and a wider palette of culture in the city's landscape. On hand to applaud Ms. Cisneros and yell encouragement were about 30 friends, neighbors and local artists.

The meeting room rapidly filled with TV cameras, reporters and bewildered architects accustomed to more sedate commission hearings.

15 Ms. Cisneros, wearing a red dress, a brilliant green scarf and cowboy boots decorated with cactus, presented an eight-page history of her house and the changes she's made in it. She included a photo album documenting the house's transformation from a pleasant if bland dwelling to the hard-to-miss purple. The album is complete with handwritten notes of her thoughts and feelings about the house.

Ms. McGlone, the preservation officer, said she had no objection to bright colors for homes in the historic district.

"There just isn't any evidence or documentation that these colors were ever used in the King William area," she said.

"Appropriate paint colors in historic districts should be based on historic evidence of colors actually used on that house, that neighborhood or the era."

When told by commissioners that the city had given her due process and proper notice and that she should have known that purple was not a historic color in her neighborhood, Ms. Cisneros fired back: "According to my history, purple is a historical color, and I want my house to reflect the traditions of the city's Tejano past. Why is that being excluded?"

20 The first skirmish with the review board ended in a compromise.

Ms. Cisneros admitted her error in beginning the paint job last year without seeking commission approval. She also said she would be willing to repaint her house red with pink trim, colors that she said had been documented in the neighborhood.

In turn, the commission agreed to take no action and asked Ms. McGlone to review what other colors of a wider palette may be appropriate for Ms. Cisneros' neighborhood.

A few days later, over a lunch of tacos and Mexican-style coffee, Ms. Cisneros said she wasn't so sure she was willing to compromise.

"The issue has moved beyond my house or the color purple. What these people are saying is that the visual history of the Mexican people is not valuable, that it doesn't count," she said.

25 "I'm not sure I will change the color, not even to another Mexican color," she said. "I plan to collect the testimonials of those who live in this neighborhood and elsewhere in San Antonio, to invite in students to do a history of the cultural colors that made up the city and allow the palette of the city to broaden."

One of seven children of a Mexican-born father and a Mexican-American mother, Ms. Cisneros grew up in Chicago. She moved to San Antonio about a decade ago because of its unique mixture of Mexican and American cultures.

"I made a conscious choice to move to Texas a few years ago precisely because I realized, My God! This is what I grew up with in my house in Chicago, and I hear it everywhere, and I need to live here because this is where I'm going to get the ideas for the things I need to write about,'" she said in a 1992 interview. "To me, San Antonio is where Latin America begins, and I love it."

She bought her home on Guenther Street in 1992 and began immediately to reshape it to her image. Artist friends painted the walls magenta, mango and the colors of sand and lime green.

Contemporary paintings vie for space with Mexican folk art along walls painted with murals of maguey plants and jungle scenes.

30 Outside, the conventional rectangle of lawn has been converted into a landscape of maguey and Spanish dagger plants, sage and other native plants—counterpoint to the graceful arabesque of an ancient mesquite tree.

"I am not arguing against the preservation laws. I have great respect for the preservation of all cultures," she said. "I walk along my neighborhood and truly admire the old homes painted in the grays and browns and beige tones that fit them quite nicely.

"I just want to expand the definitions of what we consider acceptable and appropriate," she said. "Who are they to say bright Mexican colors don't fit on the palette for a city named San Antonio?"

Rereading Actively

1. With a partner, review the article, analyzing the arguments that Cisneros and the commission make. In your journal, draw a vertical line down the middle of the page, and list Cisneros's points on one side and the commission's points on the other.

2. Restate in your own words the significance of the colors Cisneros elected to use on her house. Why did she insist on painting her house those colors?

3. Cisneros is quoted as saying, "Who are they to say bright Mexican colors don't fit on the palette for a city named San Antonio?" (¶ 32). Explain in your own words the point Cisneros is making here: what is significant about the fact that the name of the city is San Antonio?

Exploring Your Responses

4. Which side of this dispute do you take? Why? Write a statement explaining your position in your journal.

5. What metaphorical meaning can you make out of this dispute over approved colors? In your thinking, does this case appropriately symbolize the changing demographics of the United States?

6. Cisneros failed to gain commission approval prior to painting her house purple. Was she justified in bypassing the commission, or should she have worked with them toward a compromise in the first place? Why?

THE RUSTED IRON CURTAIN
ROBERT KAPLAN

Robert Kaplan is a contributing editor for Atlantic Monthly *and the author of several books, including* Balkan Ghosts: A Journey Through History *(1993),* The Ends of the Earth *(1996), and* Empire Wilderness: Travels into America's Future *(1998). This excerpt is from one in a series of articles that Kaplan wrote for* Atlantic Monthly *1998 focusing on regional zones of cross-cultural contact. In it, he examines the changing demographics in these zones, seeing in the shifting makeup of the population the social and economic patterns that are laying the foundation for America's future. Kaplan explores the border towns of Nogales—Nogales, Arizona, and Nogales, Sonora—recording his observations and comparing this border to other national boundaries, including the Great Wall of China and the Berlin Wall. Kaplan here builds on his contrasting observations in order to develop the motif of the "rusted iron curtain"—that is, a border we do not fully control.*

What we call "the border" has always been a wild and unstable swath of desert, hundreds of miles wide—a region that the Aztecs, cruel as they were, could not control, that the Apaches brutalized in eighteenth- and nineteenth-century raids, and where U.S. soldiers unsuccessfully chased the bandit revolutionary Pancho Villa.

My bus came around a low rise, and a long, narrow belt of factories and shanties stretched out almost to the horizon between brown hills studded with juniper and sagebrush. This was the border town of Nogales, a crowded warren of distempered stucco façades spray-painted with swastikas and graffiti, of broken plastic-and-neon signs, of garish wall drawings of the Flintstones and other television icons. Among the façades were the industrial *maquiladora* plants I had heard about—plants that attract blue-collar workers from throughout Mexico, who assemble American-made parts into products exported to the United States.

Not all the workers find jobs, and the migration has spawned shantytowns and violent crime, drug and alcohol abuse, class conflict, and the breakup of families. Both rape and car accidents are more common in the north than in the rest of Mexico. More than 2,000 companies opened factories in this region from the late sixties to the mid-nineties, resulting in what the American Medical Association has labeled a "cesspool" of polluted air, contaminated groundwater and surface water, unsanitary waste dumps, and other health and environmental problems associated with uncontrolled urban growth. The abandonment of subsistence farming by workers in search of better-paying manufacturing jobs is a latter-day gold rush—ugly upheaval and bright promise—but on a vast scale and likely to be permanent.

Many of our microwave ovens, televisions, VCRs, toasters, toys, and everyday clothes are made by Mexican laborers in border towns like this one. They earn three to five dollars a day—not an hour but a day!—and as Charles Bowden, an expert and writer on Mexico and the U.S. Southwest, notes, they work in conditions that are often dangerous because of pollution and toxic chemicals. American consumers are now in a tight political and economic relationship with Third World workers. This close relationship is also oligarchic, and not much different from that between the citizens of ancient Athens or Rome and their slaves.

5   I checked into a hotel and then walked toward the border, where I watched two boys kick a soccer ball made of rags until one of them kicked the ball onto a scrap-metal roof. When the ball failed to roll back down, the boys walked away. I saw a group of teenagers with hair cut in punk styles and dyed primary colors, wearing expensive leather belts, winter ski hats, and summer shorts—anything they could get their hands on. Their expressions were untamed. A hundred yards from the border began a concentration of scrap-metal storefronts, offering every manner of souvenir and after-hours activity, including off-track betting. Here were crowds of destitute people reeking of alcohol. Edward Gibbon wrote in *The History of the Decline and Fall of the Roman Empire* that the fifth-century Goths "imbibed the vices, without imitating the arts and institutions, of civilised [Roman] society." What I saw at the border is nothing new.

The actual border, on International Street, was at the time of my visit a twelve-foot-high, darkly rusted iron curtain, constructed by the American authorities from scraps of metal that the U.S. Army used in the Persian Gulf War. (It has since been partly replaced by a new wall.) Walking back from the border I saw the neat squares and rectangular roofs of houses high on the hills of the American side, where it was obvious that every joint fit and that every part was standardized, in contrast to the amateurish and inspired constructions all around me.

Though here, in the middle of a city, the border looked forbidding, out in the desert it ebbs to a few strands of barbed wire, which work to keep only cattle from migrating. Along the narrow Rio Grande in Texas, where there is no fence at all, or any natural obstruction, no mountain range or wide, surging river, the border is highly penetrable. The military radar used by U.S. border guards is like a penlight in a dark forest, as William Langewiesche has written (see "The Border," May and June, 1992, *Atlantic*). An artificial,

Figure 9.5 In Nogales, looking into Mexico

purely legal construct, the border has for several centuries been an unruly and politically ambiguous "brown zone" where civilizations—Spanish and Anglo, Athapaskan-speaking Indians from the Arctic and Aztecan Indians from southern Mexico—mingle.

The factors that have kept Mexico at bay—drug profits and the wages of illegal aliens—stem from the very activities that Washington claims it wants to stop. Without the drug trade and illegal migration the United States would face what it has always feared: a real revolution in Mexico and true chaos on the border. To deprive Mexico of its largest sources of income would hasten the collapse of its already weak central authority. Indeed, by supporting the Mexican economy, America's appetite for marijuana and cocaine protects against a further flood of immigrants from a contiguous, troubled, and ever more populous Third World country.

The unpalatable truth about Mexico is its intractability—the intractability of an ancient "hydraulic" civilization, like Egypt's, China's, and India's, in which the need to build great water and earth works (Mexico has both canal systems and pyramids) led to a vast, bureaucratic tyranny. Centuries of what Karl Marx called "oriental despotism" have imprinted the political culture, despite the influence of a great democratic civilization to the north. And it is not clear that our influence on Mexico is beneficial. Our appetite for drugs may be turning this ancient non-Western civilization into an amoral yet dynamic beast of the twenty-first century.

10   Meanwhile, integration proceeds irreversibly. Vectors of binationhood have emerged between Phoenix and Guaymas, Tucson and Los Mochis, Dallas and Chihuahua City, in which prosperous Mexicans and Americans commute back and forth by air. North America's geographic destiny may be no longer east to west but one in which the arbitrary lines separating us from Mexico and Canada disappear, even as relations between the East

Coast and Europe, the West Coast and Asia, and the Southwest and Mexico all intensify. Is our border with Mexico like the Great Wall of China—a barrier built in the desert to keep out Turkic tribesmen which, as Gibbon wrote, held "a conspicuous place in the map of the world" but "never contributed to the safety" of the Chinese?

"Ambos Nogales"

I had crossed the Berlin Wall several times during the Communist era. I had crossed the border from Iraq to Iran illegally, with Kurdish rebels. I had crossed from Jordan to Israel and from Pakistan to India in the 1970s, and from Greek Cyprus to Turkish Cyprus in the 1980s. In 1983, coming from Damascus, I had walked up to within a few yards of the first Israeli soldier in the demilitarized zone on the Golan Heights. But never in my life had I experienced such a sudden transition as when I crossed from Nogales, Sonora, to Nogales, Arizona.

Surrounded by beggars on the broken sidewalk of Mexican Nogales, I stared at Old Glory snapping in the breeze over two white McDonald's-like arches, which marked the international crossing point. Cars waited in inspection lanes. To the left of the car lanes was the pedestrian crossing point, in a small building constructed by the U.S. government. Merely by touching the door handle one entered a new physical world.

The solidly constructed handle with its high-quality metal, the clean glass, and the precise manner in which the room's ceramic tiles were fitted—each the same millimetric distance from the next—seemed a marvel to me after the chaos of Mexican construction. There were only two other people in the room: an immigration official, who checked identification documents before their owners passed through a metal detector; and a customs official, who stood by the luggage x-ray machine. They were both quiet. In government enclosures of that size in Mexico and other places in the Third World, I remembered crowds of officials and hangers-on engaged in animated discussion while sipping tea or coffee. Looking at the car lanes, I saw how few people there were to garrison the border station and yet how efficiently it ran.

I gave the immigration official my U.S. passport. She glanced up at me and asked how long I had been in Mexico. I told her several weeks. She asked, "Why so long?" I explained that I was a journalist. She handed back my passport. With her eyes she motioned me through the metal detector. The customs official did not ask me to put my rucksack through the machine. U.S. Customs works on "profiles," and I evidently did not look suspect. Less than sixty seconds after walking through the glass doors on the Mexico side, I entered the United States.

15   The billboards, sidewalks, traffic markers, telephone cables, and so on all appeared straight, and all the curves and angles uniform. The standardization made for a cold and alienating landscape after what I had grown used to in Mexico. The store logos were made of expensive polymers rather than cheap plastic. I heard no metal rattling in the wind. The cars were the same makes I had seen in Mexico, but *oh*, were they different: no chewed-up, rusted bodies, no cracked windshields held together by black tape, no good-luck charms hanging inside the windshields, no noise from broken mufflers.

The taxi I entered had shock absorbers. The neutral-gray upholstery was not ripped or shredded. The meter printed out receipts. As I sank into the soft upholstery for the ride to the hotel, I felt as though I had entered a protective, ordered bubble— not just the taxi but this whole new place.

The Plaza Hotel in Nogales, Sonora, and the Americana Hotel in Nogales, Arizona, both charged $50 for a single room. But the Mexican hotel, only two years old, was already falling apart—doors didn't close properly, paint was cracking, walls were beginning to stain. The American hotel was a quarter century old and in excellent condition, from the fresh paint to the latest-model fixtures. The air-conditioning was quiet, not clanking loudly as in the hotel across the border. There was no mold or peeling paint in the swimming pool outside my window. The tap water was potable. Was the developed world, I wondered, defined not by its riches but by maintenance?

As I walked around Nogales, Arizona, I saw a way of doing things, different from Mexico's, that had created material wealth. This was not a matter of Anglo culture per se, since 95 percent of the population of Nogales, Arizona, is Spanish-speaking and of Mexican descent. Rather, it was a matter of the national culture of the United States, which that day in Nogales seemed to me sufficiently robust to absorb other races, ethnicities, and languages without losing its distinctiveness.

The people I saw on the street were in most instances speaking Spanish, but they might as well have been speaking English. Whether it was the quality of their clothes, the purposeful stride that indicated they were going somewhere rather than just hanging out, the absence of hand movements when they talked, or the impersonal and mechanical friendliness of their voices when I asked directions, they seemed to me thoroughly modern compared with the Spanish-speakers over in Sonora. The sterility, dullness, and predictability I observed on the American side of the border—every building part in its place—were signs of economic efficiency.

20   Though the term *"ambos Nogales"* ("both Nogaleses") asserts a common identity, the differences between the two towns are basic. Nogales, Arizona, has only 21,000 residents, a fairly precise figure; nobody in Nogales, Sonora, has any idea how many people live there—the official figure is 138,000, but I heard unofficial ones as high as 300,000. Here the streets were quiet and spotless, with far fewer people and cars than in Mexico. Distances, as a consequence, seemed vast. Taxis did not prowl the streets, and thus I was truly stranded without a car. I had reached a part of the earth where business is not conducted in public, so street life was sparse.

When the English and other Northern European settlers with their bourgeois values swept across this mainly uninhabited land, they swept away the past; technology and the use of capital have determined everything since. Because subsequent immigrants sought opportunity, the effect of periodic waves of immigration has been to erase the past again and again, replacing one technology with another. Economic efficiency, as these streets in Nogales, Arizona, proclaimed, is everything in America. Liberals may warn against social Darwinism, but the replacement of obsolete technology and the jobs and social patterns that go with it are what our history has always been about, and immigrants want it that way. For them it means liberation: the chance to succeed or fail, and to be judged purely on their talents and energy and good fortune.

In Mexico the post offices looked as if they had just been vacated, with papers askew and furniture missing. In Nogales, Arizona, the Spanish voices in the post office were the last thing I noticed; what struck me immediately was the evenly stacked printed forms, the big wall clock that worked, the bulletin board with community advertisements in neat columns, the people waiting quietly in line, and a policeman standing slightly hunched over in the corner, carefully going through his paperwork, unlike the leering, swaggering policemen I had seen in Mexico.

The silent streets of Nogales, Arizona, with their display of noncoercive order and industriousness, cast the United States in a different light not only from Mexico but from many of the other countries I had seen in my travels. Nogales, Arizona, demonstrated just how insulated America has been—thus far, at least.

Rereading Actively

1. Kaplan's writing is dense with descriptive detail. Review the article, identifying details that seem particularly striking to you.

2. In a small group, identify descriptive details that best illustrate Kaplan's observations of Nogales, Mexico. Then, identify details that best illustrate his observations of Nogales, Arizona. In your journal, divide a page in half vertically, and on one side make a list of five or six distinguishing details that highlight the characteristics of one Nogales; then, make a list for the other Nogales on the other side.

3. The article moves through a progression of topics, loosely organized by the progress of Kaplan's journey as he crosses from Mexico into the United States. Working with a partner, divide the article into three or four major sections, and in your journal, tell what each section seems to focus on.

4. One writing strategy that Kaplan uses is to make comparisons between the Mexican–U.S. border and the Great Wall of China and the Berlin Wall. With a partner, review the passages that make these comparisons and write a short, collaborative explanation of them. What effect does Kaplan achieve by comparing these three famous borders?

5. The central image of the article is arguably in the title, "the rusted iron curtain." What does Kaplan seem to be trying to express about the U.S.–Mexican border through this image? What specific details that describe this border can you associate with the image of a rusted iron curtain?

6. Kaplan makes several provocative assertions in this article, including the point that illegal immigration and the drug trade between the United States and Mexico form an essential bulwark against the collapse of the Mexican economy. Review this passage, and write a short restatement of Kaplan's opinion about immigration and drugs.

Exploring Your Responses

7. Respond to Kaplan's assertions regarding the importance of illegal immigration and the drug trade to stable U.S.–Mexican relations. Do his ideas seem believable to you? Why or why not?

8. Reflect on Kaplan's position in this article. Does he seem to show bias in his writing? If so, what biases do you notice?

9. What favorable impressions do you gain of Nogales, Mexico, from reading this article? What unfavorable impressions do you gain?

10. What favorable impressions do you gain of Nogales, Arizona, from this article? What unfavorable impressions?

POCHO PIONEER
RICHARD RODRIGUEZ

Following the 1993 ratification of the North America Free Trade Agreement (NAFTA), the United States convened a meeting of governmental leaders from up and down the western hemisphere in a forum called the Summit of the Americas. Its purpose was to focus on issues like preserving democracies, promoting prosperity, eradicating poverty, and conserving the environment. As part of that first summit, cultural leaders were invited to an "encuentro" (encounter, meeting) to examine issues like state and civil society, diversity and difference, and the possibilities of a new world culture. "Pocho Pioneer" is a revised version of one speech Richard Rodriguez presented there. Along with the presentations and remarks of the other participants, it was published in a collection titled A New Moment in the Americas *(1994), which includes a Foreword by Al Gore. Rodriguez is an editor at Pacific News Service and the author of* Hunger of Memory *(1981), and* Days of Obligation *(1992).*

It is appropriate that I come to this distinguished encuentro as something of a naysayer. It is appropriate, though ironic, that I sound a sour note in the midst of all your talk about "a new moment in the Americas." As a child, I grew up in blond California where everyone was optimistic about losing weight and changing the color of her hair and becoming someone new. Only my Mexican father was dour and sour in California—always reminding me how tragic life was, how nothing changes, reminding me that everything would come to nothing under a cloudless sky.

Mexicans speak of "el fatalismo del Indio"—the sadness at the heart of Latin America. As a child, when I looked South, I shuddered at the Latin sensibility. I turned away from it, spent my childhood running toward Doris Day and Walt Disney.

You cannot imagine the irony with which I regard this meeting. My Latin American colleagues have travelled several thousand miles north to speak about the new democratic spirit in their countries, the new spirit of individualism. We of the north, by contrast, have become a dark people. We do not vote. We have lost our optimism. We are besotted with individualism and we have grown lonely. We, in California, now sound very much like my Mexican father.

I end up a "pocho" in the United States, reflecting on the tragic nature of life.

5 Clearly, I am a freak of history. I carry this Indian face; I have a Spanish surname; my first name is Richard (*Ree-cherd*, Mexico calls me). The great Octavio Paz, in *The Labyrinth of Solitude,* has a chapter concerned with the "pachuco"—the teenaged gangster in Los Angeles. For Paz the gang kids of California represent the confusion within the Mexican American—caught between two cultures. The child does not know where he belongs. The child has lost his address. The child no longer belongs to Mexico, neither does he fit into the United States. The Mexican American is a tragic figure, a pathetic one. Señor Paz is right about Mexican Americans, but he is also arrogant and wrong about us.

Consider these the reflections of a pocho…

You know, we sit here in this elegant room, talking about the new moment in the Americas as though the moment has just happened, today—November 12, 1994. We act as though we are the witnesses of its happening. In fact, the so-called moment, the discovery of the Americas by Americans, has been going on for nearly a century. But the discovery has been mainly by peasants. They were the first Americans who trespassed American borders.

I speak of the hundreds of thousands of migrant workers who have been coming to the United States since the turn of the century. The two largest groups: Puerto Ricans and Mexicans. Back and forth they went, across borders, time zones, languages, faiths. Between Puerto Rico and New York, between Los Angeles and Mexico.

The Puerto Ricans found themselves, at the end of the nineteenth century, suddenly part of the United States. The Mexicans found themselves in places like Arizona and California, which used to be part of Mexico. The Mexicans and Puerto Ricans were like no other immigrant group the United States had ever seen. There was something wrong with us.

10   And yet I would like to argue that we were the first Americans—Americans, that is, in the sense we are talking today. The peasants of Puerto Rico and Mexico were the first people who saw the hemisphere whole.

Oh, there is President Salinas de Gortari today with his Harvard degrees, as there are the new "technocrats" of Latin America with their Ivy League degrees. Business executives and government officials in the United States sigh with relief at meeting this new class of Latin Americans.

"At last, Señor Salinas, we understand you. You speak our language. You are our kind of Mexican. Let's talk business."

Do not listen to the flattery of the United States, Señor Salinas. I am sorry to have to tell you that you have been preceded North to the United States by several decades, by millions of peasants.

Mexican Americans, Puerto Ricans—we were a puzzle to the United States. We were people from the South in the east-west country. (The United States has written its history across the page, east to west. The United States saw its manifest destiny unfolding in the western migration.) Land was the crucial metaphor for possibility in the United States' scheme of things. As long as there was land, there was possibility. As long as you could move West, you had a future. As long as you could leave Maryland for Nebraska, then you could change the color of your hair, change your religion. As long as you could leave Kansas for Nevada, you could drop your father's name or shorten it. You could drop the embarrassing "ini" or "izzi" or "stein." You could become someone other than your father.

15   I am going to California to become Tab Hunter. Yes, I like that name, Me llamo Tab Hunter.

The crisis in California today is due to the fact that the United States has run out of land. The metaphor of the west has been exhausted. The end had been decades in coming. As early as the 1860s, there were premonitions of finitude in California. In the 1860s, when California was newly U.S. territory, environmentalists reached the coast with a sense of dread. John Muir stood at the beach in the 1860s and announced to the United States that he had come to the edge of possibility: America is a finite idea. We have to start saving America. We have to start saving the land. Conserving America. The message went back—west to east—back to the crowded brick cities of the East Coast.

I grew up in the 1950s when California was filling with people from Nebraska and Minnesota. People arrived from Brooklyn, or they came from Chicago. They came for a softer winter. They came to recreate themselves.

But shortly we ran out of land. Los Angeles got too crowded and needed to reinvent itself as Orange County. Then Orange County got too crowded and had to reinvent itself as north county San Diego. Then north county San Diego got too crowded. Now Californians are moving into the desert. We don't have enough room any more, we say.

Suddenly foreign immigrants are coming. They are pouring into California from the South. ("We are sorry to intrude, señor, we are looking for work.") They come from Latin America, talking of California as "el Norte," not the West Coast. El Norte is wide open. The West Coast is a finite idea. *Whose map is correct?*

20 There are planes landing in Los Angeles today, planes from Thailand, from Hong Kong, planes from Seoul and from Taiwan. People getting off the planes say about California, "This is where the United States begins." Those of us in the United States who believe in the western route to California say, "No, no. California is where the United States comes to an end." *Whose myth is true?*

People in the United States used to say, "Go West, young man." We meant, go West toward possibility. Now that we have hit against the wall of the coastline, we start talking about going East. "Go East, young man!"

"I'm leaving California; I'm going to Nebraska."

"I'm leaving California; I'm going to Colorado."

And, for the first time, today Californians speak of the North and the South. Not because we want to. Not because we are accustomed to looking North and South. It's only because the West is a finite idea.

25 "I'm going to get a condominium in Baja California. You know, there are condos throughout Baja where everyone speaks English. We're going to make Baja our national park."

Or, "I'm leaving California for Canada. I'm going to Vancouver. There are too many ethnics in California. I'm going to Canada where the air is cleaner."

Go North, young man.

Puerto Ricans, Mexicans—early in this century we were a people from the South in an east-west country. We were people of mixed blood in a black and white country. America's great scar, its deep tear, has always been the black and white division. Puerto Ricans and Mexicans tended to be of mixed race. Hard, therefore, for the United States to classify or even see.

For the last thirty years in the United States, Hispanics have impersonated a race. We have convinced bureaucrats in Washington—bureaucrats who knew nothing about us and cared less—that we constituted a racial group. It was essential, if the United States were ever to recognize us, that we be a racial group, people subject to "racial discrimination."

30 The only trouble is, Hispanics do not constitute a racial group. But what does the United States care? There we are in the ponderous morning pages of *The New York Times,* listed on a survey alongside black, white, Asian.

Puerto Ricans, Mexicans—we were Catholics in a Protestant country. And millions of us were Indians in a country that imagined the Indian to be dead. Today, Los Angeles is the largest Indian city in the United States. All around the city, you can see Toltecs and Aztecs and Mayans. But the filmmakers of Hollywood persist in making movies about the dead Indian. For seven dollars, you can see cowboys kill the Indians. We are sorry about it. We feel the luxury of regret from our swivel seats.

On the other hand, I remember a chic dinner party in Mexico City. (You know, rich Mexicans can be very polite when they say cruel things. It is their charm.) One Mexican, a drink in his hand, said to me, "You are a writer? Very interesting. Your work has been translated in Mexico?"

I replied, "Well, not much."

He said, "Well, we Mexicans are not going to know what to make of you as a writer." He said, "We're not accustomed to writers who look like you."

35   Seriously, let me apologize. I must *apologize* for not being able to speak to many of you in your own language. I suffer from this strange disability. I can understand spoken Spanish, can read it. But I can't speak Spanish with ease. I walk through Latin American cities like a sleepwalker, comprehending everything but unable to join the conversation.

How shall I explain my disability? Elena Castedo, in her wonderful essay on the United States, suggested that we in the United States are afraid of foreign languages. That is true, but not quite right. Better to say that we are obsessed with foreign languages. Most of us in this country are one or two generations from a grandparent who scolded us for losing her language. There is an enormous guilt in the American soul.

I want you to know that I have been haunted by Spanish for most of my life. I understand your jokes and your asides. I hear your whisperings. I smile feebly in response. I feel so guilty about not being able to join you. It is because I have taken this new lover, American English, this blond lover of mine has taken my breath away.

Hispanics in the United States turn into fools. We argue among ourselves, criticize one another, mock one another for becoming too much the gringo. We criticize each other for speaking too much Spanish or not enough Spanish. We demand that our politicians provide us with bilingual voting ballots, but we do not bother to vote. We are, as Señor Paz observed decades ago, freaks of history.

I have heard Mexicans of the middle class say to their children, when their children head for the United States to go to college, "Stay away from those Chicanos, whatever you do. Stay away from them because they're crazy. They think of themselves as 'minorities.'"

40   We are Mexico's Mexicans. Everything Mexico loathes about herself she hates in us. We lost our culture to a larger power. Mexico lost her tongue to Cortés. For us Cortés is Uncle Sam. If I go back to Mexico, Mexico comes closer to me, breathes in my ear. "Hijito, háblame en español," Mexico says.

I say, "Ay, Madre, no puedo. No más un poquito,"

"Un poquito. Un poquito. Tu propio idioma …!"

Then, POCHO.

Michael Novak was speaking last night about what unites the hemisphere. What unites us as Americans, he said, is our willingness to say goodbye to the motherland. We say to Europe, farewell. And there is bravery in that cry of goodbye.

45   The only trouble is that adiós was never part of the Mexican American or the Puerto Rican vocabulary. We didn't turn our backs on the past. We kept going back and forth, between past and future. After a few months of work in New York or Los Angeles, we would cross the border. We were commuters between centuries, between rivals. And neither country understood us.

Abuelita didn't understand us because our Spanish was so bad. On the other hand, people in the United States would wonder what was wrong with us. Why do you people need to keep going back home? (In a country that believes so much in the future our journey home was almost a subversion.) The United States said to us, "When my parents left Sweden, they didn't keep going back to Sweden. But you—you keep turning back. What's the matter with you? Are you a mama's boy?"

Pocho.

Someone said last night that the gringo had hijacked the word "American" and given it to himself with typical arrogance. I remember my aunt in Mexico City scolding me when I told her I was from America. Didn't I realize the entire hemisphere is America? Listen, my Mexican aunt told me, "People who live in the United States are norteamericanos."

Well, I think to myself—my aunt is now dead. God rest her soul—but I think to myself, I wonder what she would have thought when the great leaders—the president of Mexico, the president of the United States, the Canadian prime minister—signed the North American Free Trade Agreement. Mexico woke up one morning to realize that she's a norteamericana.

50   I predict that Mexico will have a nervous breakdown in ten years. She will have to check into a clinic for a long rest. She will need to determine just what exactly it means that she is, with the dread gringo, a North American.

Meanwhile, the peasants keep crossing the border. The diplomats keep signing the documents. But has anyone ever met a North American? Oh, I know. You know Mexicans. And you know Canadians. But has anyone met a North American?

I have.

Let me tell you about him, this North American. He's a Mixteco Indian who lives in the Mexican state of Oaxaca. He is trilingual. His primary language is the language of his tribe. He speaks Spanish, the language of Cortés, as a second language. Also, he has a working knowledge of U.S. English.

He knows thousands of miles of dirt roads and freeways. He commutes between two civilizations. He is preyed upon by corrupt Mexican police who want to "shake him down" because he has hidden U.S. dollars in his shoes. He is pursued as "illegal" by the U.S. border patrol. He lives in a sixteenth century village where his wife watches blond Venezuelan soap operas. There is a picture of La Virgen de Guadalupe over his bed. He works near Stockton, California, where there is no Virgin Mary but the other Madonna—the rock star.

55   This Mexican peasant knows two currencies. But he is as illegal on one side of the border as he is an embarrassment to his government on the other side of the line. *He is the first North American.*

People in the United States have always been wary of Mexican water. We love your beaches and your pre-Columbian ruins. But we are afraid to sing in the shower at the hotel. On the other hand, we have always trusted Canadian water. We drink gallons of it. We also assumed that Canadian water was clean.

But there is a virus in Canadian water called "multiculturalism" which is making its way into the United States' blood stream. The most interesting thing we think to say about one another now in the United States is that we are multicultural. But, of course, when people in the United States talk about multiculturalism, they mean, like the Canadians, culture to signify only race or ethnicity. In fact, culture means many other things, too.

Culture means region. What part of the world, what sky governs your life? I come from California.

Culture means age. The old man looks at the young boy with incomprehension.

Sex is culture—that great divide between the male and female, their delight and their frustration.

Religion. The United States is a Protestant country though we do not like to describe ourselves in that way.

We are a Puritan country.

A friend of mine, Pico Iyer, who writes of the confusion of cultures in the U.S. metropolis, speculates about the inevitable confusion that results when so many races, so many languages, altars, meet in modern Los Angeles. I think the more interesting dilemma for the post-modern citizen of the city is that she feels herself multicultural within herself: *How shall I reconcile the world within my own soul?*

My father remembers a Mexico that no longer exists. My father remembers a village. "Where is it, Papa? Show me where, in the state of Colima, you were a boy. Where?"

He explores the map with his finger. The city of Colima has swallowed up the village. The city has grown bloated, has larded itself over the countryside, obliterating the village.

"It is not there," he says.

We Mexican Americans end up like the British Columbians. If you go to British Columbia, you can visit houses and see the Queen of England on the wall. People use tea cozies in British Columbia. They remember an England that is nothing like the Britain of blue-haired soccer punks who beat up Pakistanis on Saturday nights. The British Columbians remember an England that exists nowhere on earth but on a faded post card.

My father remembers a Mexico that used to be a village.

A friend of mine, a European, was a hippie in northern Mexico during the 1960s. Recently my friend took his son back to Mexico to look for the villages where he was a bohemian.

My friend phoned me the other night with chagrin. He said, "Everything has changed. The little towns—no one hangs out anymore. All the Mexicans are working at the local maquiladora." And he says, "Thirty years ago, Mexicans used to walk around these small towns wearing guns. Now nobody wears guns."

I say to my friend, "If you want to see Mexicans wearing guns, go to East Los Angeles." My relatives in Mexico City, they watch ESPN. My niece in Mexico City is inordinately proud of her tee-shirt which proclaims HARD ROCK CAFE. My relatives in Mexico City have wandered away from Roman Catholicism in favor of Buddhism. My relatives in Mexico City are divorced.

At this moment, about this time in the afternoon, there are minibuses going South—Jehovah's Witnesses, Mormons. This is the great moment of conversion in the Mormon world. By the end of the century, half of the world's Mormon population will be Spanish-speaking, at which time what will we think of Salt Lake City? And of course, here come the evangelical Christians. They are converting Latin America. The great soul of Latin America is turning toward the Easter promise of Protestantism. "You are redeemed! You can change! You can become a new man! You can put away the old ways, become someone new, praise the Lord! Hallelujah!"

A Lutheran pastor I know in San Francisco works with immigrants from Central America. He often notices that, without even asking, without even thinking too much about it, the immigrants convert to Protestantism as they settle in the United States. The conversion becomes part of their Americanization. They seem to sense that in becoming Americans, they should also become Protestant.

On the other hand, the other day in Tijuana, Mexico, I met three boys from an evangelical church called Victory Outreach. (Victory Outreach works with kids who suffer from serious drug problems.) The kids said they are coming to the United States this year—502 years after Columbus—they are coming to the United States to convert us back to our Protestant roots. The youngest one said, "Those Americans are so sad."

75   Someone once asked Chou En-lai, the Chinese prime minister, what he thought of the French Revolution. Chou En-lai gave a wonderful Chinese response. He said, "It's too early to tell."

I think it may be too early to tell what the story of Columbus means. The latest chapter of the Columbus story might be taking place right now, as the Hispanic evangelicals head north. Who says ideas don't travel in both directions?

The kids on the line tonight in Tijuana, if you ask them why they are coming to the United States of America, will not say anything about Thomas Jefferson or notions of democracy. They have not heard about Thomas Paine or the *Federalist Papers*. They have only heard that there is a job in Glendale, California, at a dry cleaners.

They are going back to Mexico in a few months, they insist. They are only going to the United States for the dollars. They don't want to be gringos. They don't want anything to do with the United States, except for the dollars.

But then a few months will pass, and they will not go back to Latin America. What will happen, of course, to their surprise, is that the job in Glendale will make them part of the United States. (Work in the United States is our primary source of identity.)

80   People in this country, when they meet one another, do not ask about family or where you come from. The first thing people in the U.S. ask each other at cocktail parties is what the other does for a living.

The hemisphere, the story of the hemisphere, began with a little joke about maps and the fact that Columbus, our papasito, our father, got it all wrong. He imagined he was in some part of the world where there were Indians. He thought he had come to India.

We laugh today because papi didn't know where he was. But I'm not sure we know where we are, either. We are only beginning to look at the map. We are only beginning to wonder what the map of the hemisphere means.

The story of the Americas began with a cartographer's whimsy in the Renaissance: *Is the world flat?* And to the delight of the mapmaker, the explorer set out on the sea to discover the great human possibility of roundness.

Mexican Americans, Puerto Ricans—we ended up in the United States city. We are people from the village. We ended up with a bad knowledge of English, a failing knowledge of Spanish. Yet we were remarkable people. We travelled many thousands of miles, some of us on foot. We ended up cooking for the United States or making beds or gardening. We have become the nannies of North America. We take care of the blond children of Beverly Hills and Park Avenue—these children will become the next generation of Hispanics. We have subverted, invaded, the wealthiest homes in America.

85   The kids in East LA, the kids that Octavio Paz was talking about forty years ago, the pachucos have turned murderous against one another. Several months ago I was talking to some gang kids in Los Angeles about New York. The photographer working with me was from New York. I asked one of the gang kids, "Would you like to see New York some day?"

The littlest one piped in response, "Not me, man."

I said, "Why not? Don't you want to see where Joe, the photographer, comes from?"

"Not me, man! I'm Mexican. I belong here."

Here? This boy lives within four blocks. If he goes a fifth block he's going to get his head blown off because he doesn't use the right sign language or he is wearing the wrong color today. This Mexican kid couldn't even find his way to the beaches of Los Angeles.

90   The odd thing, the tragic irony, is that many times our fathers and grandfathers who were so brave, who travelled so many thousands of miles, trespassed borders, end up with grandchildren who become Chicanos, timid children who believe that culture is some little thing put in a box, held within four blocks.

One of the things that Mexico had never acknowledged about my father, I insist that you today at least entertain—the possibility that my father and others like him were the great revolutionaries of Mexico. They, not Pancho Villa, not Zapata, were heralds of the modern age. They went back to Mexico and changed Mexico forever. The man who worked in Chicago in the 1920s returned one night to his village in Michoacán. The village gathered around him—this is a true story—and the village asked, "What is it like up there in Chicago?"

The man said, "It's okay."

That rumor of "okay" spread across Michoacán, down to Jalisco, across Jalisco into Oaxaca, from village to village to village.

There are now remote villages in Latin America that have become the most international places in the world. Tiny Peruvian villages know when they are picking pears in the Yakima Valley in the state of Washington.

95   We talk about the new moment in the Americas. The moment has been going on for decades. People have been travelling back and forth.

I am the son of a prophet. I am a fool. I am a victim of history. I am confused. I do not know whether I am coming or going. I speak bad Spanish. And yet, I will tell you this: to grow up Hispanic in the United States is to know more Guatemalans than if I grew up in Mexico. Because I live in California, I know more Brazilians than I would know if I lived in Peru. Because I live in California, it is routine for me to know Nicaraguans and Salvadorans and Cubans— as routine as meeting Chinese or Greeks.

People in California talk about the "illegals." But there was always an illegality to immigration. It was a rude act, the leaving of home. It was a violation of custom, an insult to the village. A youthful act of defiance. I know a man from El Salvador who has not talked to his father since the day he left his father's village. (It is a sin against family to leave home.) Immigrants must always be illegal. Immigrants are always criminals. They trespass borders and horrify their grandmothers.

But they are also our civilization's prophets. They, long before the rest of us, long before this room, long before this conference was ever imagined, they saw the hemisphere whole.

Rereading Actively

1. Consider that "Pocho Pioneer" is a revised version of a speech. In what ways does this text seem to preserve the feeling of spoken language?

2. Reviewing the first thirteen paragraphs, identify the points where Rodriguez enacts his role as "something of a naysayer" (¶ 1). Whose points of view does he dispute?

3. With a partner or in a small group, identify the contrasts Rodriguez draws between the way the United States has conceived of its history and destiny, and the way it has been (and still is) viewed by pocho pioneers, or other immigrant groups.

4. With a partner or in a small group, discuss what Rodriguez seems to mean when he talks about "the Mexican peasant" who is "the first North American" (¶ 55).

5. How do the issues of place, language, religion, generation, and economics come together to define the identity of today's pocho pioneers?

Exploring Your Positions

6. How does style of this article, which bears the imprint of spoken language, affect your reading?

7. Through the use of the word "we," Rodriguez sometimes assumes the role of spokesperson for Mexican Americans and Puerto Ricans. Does he seem credible in this role? Why or why not?

8. Respond to the last several paragraphs, in which Rodriguez wraps up his remarks; does Rodriguez persuade you to see immigration (or migration) from the new perspective he urges here on his audience?

9. Think about Rodriguez's purpose in directing attention toward the millions of Mexicans and Puerto Ricans and other groups who for generations before NAFTA saw the continent whole, as a trade zone. Does Rodriguez succeed to any degree in changing the way you picture the borders of the place you live?

TRIBES RECLAIM STOLEN LANDS
GREG HANSCOM

Greg Hanscom is a reporter for High Country News, *a monthly newspaper that focuses on land-use issues and environmental politics in the Rocky Mountain west. The cover story of the issue in which it appeared, "Tribes Reclaim Stolen Lands" provides an in-depth look at the efforts of Indian tribes in western states to recover control and ownership of land that they argue has been improperly taken from them. There are economic and cultural ramifications to these land disputes. Economically, productive farmland on reservations may be leased to white farmers at below-market rates, depriving tribes of needed income. Culturally, tribes identify themselves with the land they occupy, so that regaining control of the places they live is in effect regaining a connection to their traditional past. Hanscom approaches his story from the point of view*

*of the important parties to the dispute, including the tribal activists and attorneys who
are litigating the cases and the white farmers whose livelihood depends in part on the
outcome of the litigation.*

Fort Hall, Idaho—The councilman's voice drones through the microphone, echoing off walls lined with nickel slots and joker poker games. The Shoshone and Ban-
nock people file into the bingo hall slowly, some wearing tight jeans and cowboy hats,
others sporting baggy gangsta pants and T-shirts rolled up at the sleeves. Children
chase each other through the aisles as parents settle into seats for the tribes' annual
meeting in May.

A hand shoots up in the crowd, and a woman stands. "This is not a council meeting," she yells, asking the elected official at the microphone to have a seat. "This is the
people's time to talk."

The people have plenty to say. When the meeting closes 10 hours later, they have
voted to fire the chairman of the tribal business council and the editor of the Sho-Ban
News, the reservation newspaper, and asked the tribal council to oust three local staff
members of the federal Bureau of Indian Affairs. The votes are only recommendations
and the council will make the final decisions later this summer. But a storm is brewing on the Fort Hall Reservation.

One of the forces behind the tumult is Ernestine Werelus, a 69-year-old Shoshone
woman who grew up raising cattle and quarter horses along the Snake River west of
town. She left the reservation for 30 years to work as a dentist with the Indian Health
Service. She returned to Fort Hall four years ago to retire.

5   But what Werelus found here wouldn't let her rest. Mormon potato farmers and
the Bureau of Indian Affairs were holding down the 4,500 Sho-Bans, she says. While
an acre of prime potato land off the reservation was going for $150 to $200 per year,
the Bureau was renting out Indian land for as low as $50. On a reservation of a half-
million acres, that amounted to millions of dollars lost each year–money that should
have gone to people whose unemployment rate swings from 20 to 50 percent with the
seasons, and who are lucky to make $8 an hour.

Werelus decided to act. She pulled together volunteers to run a nonprofit called
the Fort Hall Landowners Alliance, to teach people how to gain control of their land.
With the permission of the landowners, she bypassed the bureau officials who had
been negotiating the leases, and started driving hard deals with farmers who rent land
on the reservation. She and her team appealed leases they thought unfair.

Now, two years later, the alliance has 300 members, and a sample of 19 leases it
helped negotiate shows yearly rates jumping from between $55 and $80 per acre to as
high as $130. Over the five-year life of the sample leases, landowners will earn $4.7
million, almost twice what they would have made under their old leases.

"The tribe said, 'Your lease rates are too high,'" says Werelus. "'You're going to run
off these farmers.'" And in fact, a few farmers have backed out of deals, leaving land
fallow, but the rest have agreed to pay more.

The alliance's success has been a boost for the Sho-Bans. It also helped convince those
attending the annual meeting that they want several bureau officials out of Fort Hall.

10   The changes at Fort Hall are important of themselves. A group of Indians in Idaho
is moving step-by-step to take back control of their land. But Fort Hall is also impor-

tant because it is not unique. Across the West, Indian people are in the early stages of a long-term revolution.

This is not a revolution that attracts headlines, like the sit-ins and confrontations of the 1960s. Rather than armed takeovers and battle cries, this revolution is made up of soil surveys, changes in the laws governing land inheritance, the control of capital and negotiations over leases. The revolution is both political and economic, and it promises to change the face of Indian country.

A Legacy of Abuse

Between the Fort Hall tribal office building, where the Landowners Alliance does business, and the railroad tracks that carry trainloads of potatoes off the reservation, stands a low, mustard-yellow building. The structure is the headquarters of the local Bureau of Indian Affairs, the agency that critics say has stood between the Sho-Bans and their land for over a century.

"We try and inform them (landowners) as much as we can" about leasing land on the reservation, says the bureau's senior soil scientist Norman Bird. "We have an open door policy."

But Sho-Bans and other bureau staffers say Bird, a non-Indian and a Mormon from Blackfoot, Idaho, and other officials hold the door open for farmers, but not for Indians. They charge that the bureau has deprived Sho-Bans of millions of dollars by leasing Indian land for bargain-basement prices. They also charge that the agency has permitted farmers whose leases have expired to continue to farm, and allowed others to sublease land for more than they are paying its Indian owners.

15   It is no secret that the bureau has also allowed farmers to pass sweetheart deals on to their children and friends. Some land on Fort Hall is being worked by the third generation of the same non-Indian families.

"I've had farmers say to me, 'It's not your land. It belongs to the federal government,'" says Ernestine Werelus. "Some of these people think the land belongs to them."

There are bureau staffers who see the problems, too, but they will only speak anonymously. "We're supposed to get the best price for their ground," says one agency official. "But we're not doing it. We're looking out for the farmers and the Mormon church."

As an example, he points to a 10-year lease on 3,000 acres of potato land on the reservation. The original lease, signed with non-Indian farmer Chris Thompson in 1990 for $60 per acre each year, came up for review in 1994. A second farmer, Chris Drakos, offered the bureau $130 per acre for the land, apparently thinking the agency could drop its lease with Chris Thompson. But the bureau stuck with Thompson, raising the rate to just $70 an acre.

"It was a fair price" in 1990, says Thompson, who acknowledges Drakos made a higher offer. But Thompson says his lease still had five years to run. Drakos refused to comment on the lease, but bureau officials say the $130 offer never existed. "Chris Drakos did not submit a bid," says Superintendent Eric LaPointe. "There was no lease to be had."

20   But the anonymous agency staffer says the bureau knew it could get $130 for the land, and by refusing to raise the lease rate to reflect the land's value, the bureau lost landowners almost $1 million. "That's one farm. The people and the tribe are getting screwed out of millions and millions and millions," he says. "Every one of these Indians should be living high on the hog. They shouldn't be living in shacks."

In another instance, he points to a potato storage facility Chris Thompson leases for $3,000 a year. Thompson subleases the facility to another farmer, Dick Watt, pulling in up to $16,500 that should go to the Indians who own the land. Thompson says the profits go to maintaining the facilities, and that the bureau approved the sublease 15 years ago. Bureau Superintendent LaPointe says he can find no such approval in his records.

These and other problems have been pointed out numerous times by landowners and bureau officials, but reports have generally been "shoved under the blankets," according to staffers.

Eric LaPointe says that the bureau is doing all it can with limited resources. "I've got three staff members to cover a half-million acres, and Congress says that's enough," he says. "We rely on the tribe's staff to report abuses to us. We're just the referee."

The real problem, says the bureau's Norman Bird, is that farmers are reluctant to get into business in Indian country. "When (critics) say there's just a whole horde of people over here just waiting for the next bid," says Bird, "we just haven't seen that."

25   Under former Fort Hall superintendent Dennis Whiteman, the bureau updated its soil and crop yield information for the first time in three decades, so that farmers who had no experience with the land could make informed bids. The bureau also began advertising leases in local newspapers and farm stores. Last year, the agency started a new bidding process, and rent prices are rising.

But the alliance's ability to get more money for leases seems to show that the bureau could be doing more. "People are willing to pay good money for the land out here," says another agency staffer. "Even the (non-Indian farmers') hired help is driving new pick-ups. The Indians say, 'They're getting rich on our land and the Indians are just barely scraping the bottom of the bowl.'"

Change Hurts

"Yeah, I am driving a new truck. I am doing pretty well," says Garth VanOrden, a 23-year veteran of Fort Hall spud farming, as he wheels his pickup through fields of spring wheat and potatoes. But farming is no way to get rich, he adds.

As the spokesman for the Fort Hall Lease Holders, a group of 50 non-Indian farmers who work on the reservation, VanOrden is seen by many Indian landowners as the voice of the enemy. "Their mindset right now is, 'you're screwing us, you're screwing us,'" he says. "Sometimes I feel like I have to apologize for Columbus."

VanOrden acknowledges that there are farmers who abuse the system, but he says Indians need to realize that farming on the reservation is more expensive and time-consuming than it is elsewhere. Land on the reservation is not always equipped with irrigation systems provided on private land, and Indian land is usually owned by more than one individual. "When I lease land off the reservation, I'm dealing with one person," he says. "On the reservation, I'm dealing with tracts of land with over 100 owners."

30   When VanOrden puts $44,000 into a new center-pivot irrigation system, he and his bank need to know he will be able to use it for 20 years. But multiple owners and five-year leases lead to uncertainty. The tribes require the farmers to rotate potatoes with wheat at least every other year to keep the soil healthy, he says. That means that in a five-year lease, VanOrden may only have two years of spuds, his money-making crop.

"If it's so tough, why am I out here? It's good productive land and we've learned how to farm it," he says. "To be honest with you, it's the only thing I know how to do, and I have a shitload of money invested in it.

"It's in the landowner's best interest to have income and it's in the farmer's best interest to have satisfied landowners. That's just sound business," says VanOrden. "But it goes both ways."

Still, as Sho-Bans get more involved in managing their lands, they are going to shake things up on the reservation, and everyone—farmers, landowners and the bureau alike—had better be ready.

"Change is always scary," says VanOrden, "but in the end the result can be good. This is the Indian people's land and at some point they need to decide for themselves what they want from it."

The Dawes Act: Dismantling Indian Country

35   Control of the land has been beyond the reach of many Indians for over a century, thanks in large part to a grand plan by the federal government in the late 1800s to turn Indians into civilized landowners.

Under the original treaties and agreements signed with the federal government in the 1800s, reservations were owned communally. But Christian reformers, led by U.S. Sen. Henry Dawes of Massachusetts, saw the reservation system as racial segregation that reduced Indians to paupers. Their answer was to dissolve the reservations and distribute land to individual Indians. Private ownership, they reasoned, would also ensure Indians a place of their own, safe from encroachment by homesteaders and miners, who continuously tried to move in on Indian lands.

"If you will prepare the Indian to take care of himself upon this land that is allotted, you will find the solution to the whole question," Dawes told a gathering of the liberal Christian group Friends of the Indians in 1886. "He shall have a home and be a citizen of the United States, shall be one of us."

His centerpiece was the 1887 General Allotment Act, or the "Dawes Act," that authorized the president to survey Indian lands and assign farm plots to individual Indians. Married couples received a quarter-section, or 160 acres, single adults got 80 acres, and children 40 acres.

But instead of bringing Native Americans into contact with the land, the law drove them away from it. When reservations were divided, government agents gave some Indians land that could never be irrigated, much less farmed. Family members might be allotted tracts on opposite ends of reservations.

40   Once each Indian was given an allotment, the Interior secretary bought "surplus" reservation land—sometimes the most desirable land on the reservation—and opened it to non-Indian homesteaders or railroad companies. The practice led to "land runs," where white settlers lined up at reservation boundaries to wait for the official gunshot signifying the opening of new territory for settlement.

Accompanying the settlers' hunger for land was the fact that not all Indians wanted to be farmers. Within four years of the Dawes Act, the Department of the Interior, which held Indian land in trust, was leasing allotted lands to non-Indians. Over the years, many Indians sold their allotments to non-Indians. Others were cheated out of their land, creating islands of private "fee" land within reservation boundaries.

John Collier, Commissioner of Indian Affairs under President Franklin Roosevelt, ended the allotment system by convincing Congress to pass the Indian Reorganization Act of 1934. But much damage had already been done. When Congress passed the Dawes Act in 1887, there had been 138 million acres of Indian land in the United States. By 1934, that number had plummeted 65 percent, to 48 million acres.

A Promise Dissolves

The erosion of Indian land ownership didn't stop with the end of the allotment system. Because Native Americans had no written wills, the Dawes Act set up inheritance codes. When the owner of a piece of land died, the Bureau of Indian Affairs kept the land physically intact, but divided it on paper by giving each heir an "undivided" interest in it.

The inheritance rules were the undoing of Dawes' promise of private land and a home Indians could call their own. As Indians died and their property was passed on, the number of owners increased exponentially. Today, many parcels of land have hundreds of owners spread around the country. Intermarriage between tribes means Indians often inherit interest in land on several reservations.

45 With each passing generation, Indian ownership in land washes out like an arroyo in a spring flood. And as the gully between Indians and their land widens, Indian people depend more on the Bureau of Indian Affairs, which today acts as the trustee of the current 55 million acres of Indian land.

In order to grow potatoes, build a home or sell an interest in fractionated land, an individual needs permission from a majority of the others who own interest in the land. Consensus is tough when there are only a few owners, and nearly impossible when there are a hundred owners, whose addresses and phone numbers are kept secret from each other by the bureau under the Privacy Act.

"You basically can't do anything with Indian land without getting through a maze of federal regulations," says Theresa Carmody, a member of the Seneca tribe and an expert on Indian land tenure from Wagon Mound, N.M.

Critics say the system is designed to be abused. As fractionated ownership pushes Indians farther from their land, the bureau hears little from landowners, but plenty from the non-Indian farmers who lease the land. Naturally, the bureau tries to keep farmers and other lessees happy, says Carmody.

"The system is not in place to empower" Native American landowners, says Carmody, who has worked for the National Congress of American Indians in Washington, D.C. and the Boulder, CO-based Native American Rights Fund. "The system is in place to lease."

50 The numbers support her charge: Non-Indians lease 70 percent of all Indian agricultural land, according to a 1990 bureau report.

Because Indians are cut off from their land, most reservations remain economic colonies, where the Bureau of Indian Affairs manages land and resources, and non-Indians reap the profits.

One of the major problems is a lack of access to capital. Banks are reluctant to lend money to Indians on reservations, where clear title to land is rare, and where repossessing property may be impossible under tribal laws.

As a result, says John Halliday, director of economic development for the Muckleshoot Tribe in Washington, banks have given only 93 conventional home loans in all of Indian country in the last 15 years. Halliday calls the situation "organized poverty—the most violent kind of racism there is."

A Groundswell of Change

The federal government has tried several times to remedy fractionated ownership, but its solutions have strengthened tribal governments at the expense of individual landowners. One 1983 bill even declared interests of less than 2 percent of an allotment worthless, and turned them over to the tribes. The Supreme Court later found the "2 percent rule" unconstitutional.

55   But a growing community of Native Americans is not waiting for the federal government to solve its problems. Some, like Ernestine Werelus in Fort Hall, are tackling the bureau head on, fighting for a voice in the way land is managed and leased. Others are helping Indian people reduce the number of landowners by writing wills and by buying and trading fractionated interests. Some tribes have adopted codes that only allow tribal members to inherit land on their reservations, while others are pushing banks to start lending money in Indian country.

Scattered efforts like these have flared up in the past, but they never caught on at the national level. Now, the movement is spreading. Tribes are organizing, exchanging ideas and building viable economies on Indian reservations while trying to maintain their cultures and autonomy.

One of the pioneers is Helen Sanders, a member of the Quinault Tribe in Washington state. Sanders got involved in the fight over Indian land in the late 1950s, when her daughter inherited forest land. At the time, two non-Indian timber companies controlled logging on the reservation. Indians knew they were getting the short end of the deal, but few had the funds or the patience to do anything about it.

"It was common gossip among loggers that the Indians were getting beat out of their timber," says Sanders.

Rather than have the bureau sell the timber on her daughter's land, Sanders decided to go into the logging business. It took her years to navigate the bureaucratic obstacles, but she succeeded. With the help of a new bureau superintendent, she convinced the federal Small Business Administration to guarantee a start-up loan. Her daughter's land and that first loan were enough to get her business up and running, and from there she moved to other Quinault land. For 12 years, Sanders worked one allotment at a time, borrowing money to pay the lease and pull the timber off the land, and then repaying her loan with the proceeds.

60   In the process, Sanders discovered that the bureau had been selling off not just timber but Indian land as well. She took what she had learned from her business and put it to work for her people. With the help of the bureau superintendent, she stopped the sales to non-Indian timber companies, and in 1971, she sued the bureau for mismanaging the timber resources. Twenty years later, she settled out of court for $26 million, which went to her fellow landowners.

"It takes a lot of footwork and a lot of determination," says Sanders, now a leading voice for Indian lands on the national level. "Many of our people just don't know how to fight the battle. They get two doors closed on them and they give up."

Sanders had what most people lack: the fortitude to force her way past a dozen closed doors. Now, on the Umatilla Reservation in northeast Oregon, the tribal government is trying to open some of those doors for the people.

It's a huge job, akin to turning an omelet back into whole eggs. Twenty thousand people own interest in the 1,400 allotments on the Umatilla Reservation, and most owners belong to other tribes. Predictably, the bureau controls most of the land and it leases 95 percent of it to non-Indian wheat farmers. Most Indian landowners didn't even know where their property was or who their fellow owners were.

They would have been hard pressed to find out. Records showing who owned the land, who was leasing it, and what the land was capable of producing were scattered everywhere: in filing cabinets and computers of the Bureau of Indian Affairs, in tribal offices and in the Umatilla County courthouse.

65   Landowners could do nothing, because they knew nothing.

"We needed to get people information," says retired Indian rancher Bill Northover. "A lot of these people don't want to live in the projects (federally funded housing developments). They want to build themselves a home out there in the country (on land they own). They know that their land is worth something, and they want to get more information about what they own so they can get the most out of it."

In 1990, a foundation helped the tribes begin to pull together scattered land records and to put them in a computer database. Armed with additional money from a new casino, a golf course and a hotel, the tribes bought a geographic information system (GIS) computer program. Northover and the tribes' Land Acquisition Program are putting the tribes back in the driver's seat.

Indians who want to sell or trade interests for a piece of land all their own can now get up-to-date information quickly. The new computer system has also allowed the tribes to start buying back lands that were lost to homesteading and sales. Last year, they bought more than 7,000 acres.

"It's a very powerful tool," says Northover. "With GIS, we can go out and get our own data. We don't have to wait for the bureau."

70   Other tribes have caught on. In the Northwest, the Yakama, Warm Springs, Coeur d'Alene and other tribes are all working on geographic information system programs, and in the Dakotas, reservations such as Pine Ridge are jumping on board.

The key to success, says Northover, is to develop a good working relationship with the Bureau of Indian Affairs. "The BIA is a bastard. But it's a powerful bastard and we have to work with it."

Building Nations

The bureau doesn't need to have any part in it, says CloAnn Villegas, computer systems manager for the Salish and Kootenai Tribes on the Flathead Reservation in Montana. The Salish and Kootenai are miles ahead of most tribes in building a nation independent of the Bureau of Indian Affairs. They have developed a sophisticated legal system, and fought to protect water quality in Flathead Lake, as well as managing fishing and bird hunting cooperatively with the state of Montana.

For years, the tribes felt that the bureau and non-Indian farmers were managing the land without their consent. The agency had no data on what the soil could produce or how many cattle a piece of land could support. Officials didn't review leases regularly, and some farmers and businesses had been paying the same rates for 25 years.

In the 1980s, with coffers full from timber sales and a federal contract on a dam on Flathead Lake, the tribes decided they'd had enough of the bureau. They used the 1975 Indian Self Determination and Educational Assistance Act to take over management of the irrigation canal system on the reservation. In 1990, they contracted the bureau's real estate services, which include agricultural, weed and mineral management, as well as leasing and billing.

75　　　Last year, the tribes gathered up the title records to all their land. "We backed a U-Haul up to the Portland area office and took all of our title plans," says Villegas, an accountant by training and "a techie by default." Today, there are only two bureau officials left on Flathead.

After eight years, three computer programmers and $80,000, she has a remarkable new billing program and the groundwork laid for a geographic information system.

Despite the achievement, the Salish and Kootenai now realize they may have bitten off more than they can chew. They ousted one bureaucracy but had to create another.

Their beefed-up staff is putting the paperwork in order, an expensive task. At the same time, they have less money to work with because lease rates have dropped since the tribe took over. Says Villegas: Indians now get top priority on leases on the reservation, even if they can't pay as much as non-Indians.

The tribe instead of the bureau now compiles the environmental studies required under the National Environmental Policy Act, a time-consuming process that has reduced the amount of timber the tribes can sell.

80　　　"The (bureau) was always understaffed," says Villegas. "We've put the bodies in place. We just need to make sure we have the money to get the job done."

Looking Out for the Tribe

In South Dakota, the Rosebud Sioux are attempting to strike a different balance between Indian empowerment and cash flow, perhaps because the man leading the charge, Howard Valandra, once ran a national computing business.

Valandra is the uncompromising chairman of the Tribal Land Enterprise, which has survived for 55 years, with ups and downs, in the fourth poorest county in the nation, where kids often go to school just for the free meals.

When Valandra joined the board in 1993, the land enterprise already had control of roughly 700,000 acres on the Rosebud Reservation, but it wasn't getting rates much better than the bureau would have. Valandra and his team at the enterprise started raising lease rates. In response, farmers organized and started using "fear tactics," he says. "They said if you drive leases up, we're not going to lease your land."

Instead of giving in, the enterprise built up a war chest big enough to survive without leasing any land for two years. The board then told the farmers that if they didn't pay fair market value, the tribe would take its land out of circulation completely.

85　　　"Banks, production credit, the Small Business Administration would go broke. Anybody who has lent a penny to anybody in Indian country would feel it," he says. "Individuals (farmers) who think they need to be subsidized need to realize those days are dwindling fast."

The enterprise has been known to retaliate against farmers who speak out against the tribe at public meetings by raising their lease rates. It is common knowledge among farmers on Rosebud: now if you're going to do business here, you'll do it by the Indians' rules.

The enterprise buys between 5,500 and 6,000 acres each year. Individuals can also trade scattered interest in land for a parcel of tribal land where they can build a home. And staffers are working to allow Rosebud members who own interest on the nearby Pine Ridge reservation to trade with Pine Ridge residents who own interest on Rosebud.

But the enterprise is equally firm with its own people. When a landowner trades interest for a piece of tribal land, the land remains in tribal ownership so it can't be sold to non-Indians. And before a deal is final, the owner must name a single Rosebud Sioux heir to the land to stop fractionation.

Some landowner groups "look out for the individuals," says Valandra. "We look out for the tribe."

Points of Intersection

90 No one solution will work for every tribe, but a meeting held in Pendleton, OR, in 1991 started a collective push to address Indian land ownership on a national level. Helen Sanders, Theresa Carmody and Bill Northover were among 150 people from 36 tribes who showed up for the first annual Indian Land Consolidation Conference.

The ad hoc committee that grew out of the conference, now called the Indian Land Working Group and chaired by Howard Valandra, launched a national crusade to give Indian people the information and resources they need to regain control of their land. Made up of roughly 30 representatives of tribal governments and landowners alliances, and individual activists, the group is making waves around Indian country.

Its annual conferences are attended by hundreds of people, and it has a Web page, informational videos and a several thousand-member mailing list.

"We've developed a pretty strong network," says Theresa Carmody, the New Mexico Indian activist who is now the working group's secretary/ treasurer. "If something happens at Fort Hall, Rosebud, Quinault, we know about it."

In addition to its work on reservations, the group has put a bill before Congress to address fractionated ownership on the national level. The bill, introduced in the House in July, would provide funds to teach people about estate planning and assure their access to land records. It would also tear down bureaucratic barriers by allowing landowners to sell or exchange interest with other Indians without going through the bureau.

95 "The only restriction we want is if you're going to sell, sell to another Indian," says Carmody. "Other than that, let people buy, sell, anything they want to do." The bill also includes a strict inheritance code for tribes that haven't developed their own, preventing non-Indians from inheriting Indian land.

Like a similar bill put forth by the Interior department, the Working Group's bill would set up an acquisition fund to buy up interest in land and consolidate ownership. But where the government's bill would give the Interior secretary control over the fund, the working group's bill would provide loans to tribes and individuals and leave the decisions to them.

It is only by putting power back in the hands of individual Indians that Interior can bridge the chasm that has opened between Indians and their land, says Theresa Carmody. "As Indian landowners become more knowledgeable, they're going to demand that they can get involved.

"We see it happening gradually. The road is long and there are still some real barriers out there, but that's life," says Carmody. "It took 100 years to get this way and it's not going to change overnight.

"A sense within people of self-sufficiency and strength is coming back," she says. "We've hit bottom and now we're on the upswing."

Rereading Actively

1. In a small group, review the article, identifying the positions in the land claims controversy taken by the Indians, the farmers, and the government officials with the Bureau of Indian Affairs (BIA). Write a brief summary explaining each position in your journal.

2. With a partner or in a small group, review the article, focusing on the history of Indian land ownership as Hanscom reports it. Look closely, for example, at the section discussing the "dismantling" of Indian territory as a result of the General Allotment or Dawes Act. To what extent were you aware of this history prior to reading this essay?

3. With a partner or in a small group, discuss how the "erosion of Indian land ownership" (¶ 43) continued after the repeal of the Dawes Act.

4. Hanscom describes the "fractionalized" ownership of land in Indian country. What does he mean by this term? What are some of the economic difficulties that Indians face as a result of this kind of property ownership?

5. In a small group, identify the different tribes whom Hanscom describes, and discuss how each is addressing the issue of land claims. List the tribes in your journal, with a brief notation capturing their position in relation to land ownership.

6. Review the article, focusing on the exposure to losses that white farmers or businesses face as a result of Indian tribes' efforts to reclaim territory. In a brief journal entry, summarize the losses these people may incur.

7. In general, what is the state of Indian land ownership today, according to Hanscom?

Exploring Your Responses

8. In a page or two in your journal, respond to the issue of Indian land claims as Hanscom reports it. Where do you stand in relation to the claims the tribes are making? In relation to the losses that white farmers and businesses may face?

9. Do you see a workable solution to the conflict of land claims? Is there one outcome that is clearly just and equitable?

10. Group ownership of property does not always fit well within an economic system of banking, loans, and exchange—individual ownership of "private"

property is the norm. Have you ever been involved in any kind of group ownership of something? If so, is it something you would become involved with
again? If not, does it seem appealing to you? Why or why not?

EDGE CITY: LIFE ON THE NEW FRONTIER
JOEL GARREAU

Joel Garreau is a geographer and the author of a book, The Nine Nations of North America *(1981), in which he distinguishes nine distinct regional and cultural "nations" within
the territory of the United States. In the more recent book,* Edge City: Life on the New
Frontier *(1991), Garreau focuses on cities as the material reflection of the motives, values, and behaviors of people. In this excerpt, Garreau introduces the concept of "edge
cities" as the biggest change in our society and the built environment in 100 years. Drawing on extensive travels and thousands of hours of interviews, Garreau presents his argument about the meaning of this new form, and what it foretells of our future. An important
part of Garreau's purpose is to represent these areas in a positive light; contrary to prevailing opinion that laments the barren landscape of office parks and freeways, Garreau
is persuaded that these new forms are full of vitality and the spirit of the age.*

> But I reckon I got to light out for the Territory.
> —Huckleberry Finn, at the close of Mark Twain's novel, 1885

Americans are creating the biggest change in a hundred years in how we build
cities. Every single American city that *is* growing, is growing in the fashion of Los
Angeles, with multiple urban cores.

These new hearths of our civilization—in which the majority of metropolitan
Americans now work and around which we live—look not at all like our old downtowns. Buildings rarely rise shoulder to shoulder, as in Chicago's Loop. Instead, their
broad, low outlines dot the landscape like mushrooms, separated by greensward and
parking lots. Their office towers, frequently guarded by trees, gaze at one another from
respectful distances through bands of glass that mirror the sun in blue or silver or
green or gold, like antique drawings of "the city of the future."

The hallmarks of these new urban centers are not the sidewalks of New York
of song and fable, for usually there are few sidewalks. There are jogging trails
around the hills and ponds of their characteristic corporate campuses. But if an
American finds himself tripping the light fantastic today on concrete, social scientists know where to look for him. He will be amid the crabapples blossoming under
glassed-in skies where America retails its wares. We have quaintly if accurately
named these places after that fashionable tree-lined promenade created in the late
1600s—the Mall in London's St. James's Park. Back then, its denizens even had a
name for the hour when the throng of promenaders "giggling with their sparks"
was at its height. They called it High Mall. Pity we've not picked up that usage. We
have certainly picked up the practice, because malls usually function as the village
squares of these new urbs.

Our new city centers are tied together not by locomotives and subways, but by
jetways, freeways, and rooftop satellite dishes thirty feet across. Their characteris-

tic monument is not a horse-mounted hero, but the atria reaching for the sun and shielding trees perpetually in leaf at the cores of corporate headquarters, fitness centers, and shopping plazas. These new urban areas are marked not by the penthouses of the old urban rich or the tenements of the old urban poor. Instead, their landmark structure is the celebrated single-family detached dwelling, the suburban home with grass all around that made America the best-housed civilization the world has ever known.

5   I have come to call these new urban centers Edge Cities. Cities, because they contain all the functions a city ever has, albeit in a spread-out form that few have come to recognize for what it is. Edge, because they are a vigorous world of pioneers and immigrants, rising far from the old downtowns, where little save villages or farmland lay only thirty years before.

Edge Cities represent the third wave of our lives pushing into new frontiers in this half century. First, we moved our homes out past the traditional idea of what constituted a city. This was the suburbanization of America, especially after World War II.

Then we wearied of returning downtown for the necessities of life, so we moved our marketplaces out to where we lived. This was the malling of America, especially in the 1960s and 1970s.

Today, we have moved our means of creating wealth, the essence of urbanism—our jobs—out to where most of us have lived and shopped for two generations. That has led to the rise of Edge City.

Not since more than a century ago, when we took Benjamin Franklin's picturesque mercantile city of Philadelphia and exploded it into a nineteenth-century industrial behemoth, have we made such profound changes in the ways we live, work, and play.

10   Good examples of our more than two hundred new Edge Cities are:

- The area around Route 128 and the Massachusetts Turnpike in the Boston region that was the birthplace of applied high technology;
- The Schaumburg area west of O'Hare Airport, near which Sears moved its corporate headquarters from the 110-story Sears Tower in downtown Chicago;
- The Perimeter Center area, at the northern tip of Atlanta's Beltway, that is larger than downtown Atlanta;
- Irvine, in Orange County, south of Los Angeles

By any functional urban standard—tall buildings, bright lights, office space that represents white-collar jobs, shopping, entertainment, prestigious hotels, corporate headquarters, hospitals with CAT scans, even population—each Edge City is larger than downtown Portland, Oregon, or Portland, Maine, or Tampa, or Tucson. Already, two thirds of all American office facilities are in Edge Cities, and 80 percent of them have materialized in only the last two decades. By the mid-1980s, there was far more office space in Edge Cities around America's largest metropolis, New York, than there was at its heart—midtown Manhattan. Even before Wall Street faltered in the late 1980s there was less office space there, in New York's downtown, than there was in the Edge Cities of New Jersey alone.

Even the old-fashioned Ozzie and Harriet commute from a conventional suburb to downtown is now very much a minority pattern, U.S. Census figures show. Most of the trips metropolitan Americans take in a day completely skirt the old centers. Their journeys to work, especially, are to Edge Cities. So much of our shopping is done in Edge Cities that a casual glance at most Yellow Pages shows it increasingly difficult in an old downtown to buy such a commodity item as a television set.

These new urban agglomerations are such mavericks that everyone who wrestles them to the ground tries to brand them. Their list of titles by now has become marvelous, rich, diverse, and sometimes unpronounceable. The litany includes: urban villages, technoburbs, suburban downtowns, suburban activity centers, major diversified centers, urban cores, galactic city, pepperoni-pizza cities, a city of realms, superburbia, disurb, service cities, perimeter cities, and even peripheral centers. Sometimes it is not clear that everybody is talking about the same thing. My heart particularly goes out to the San Francisco reporter who just started calling whatever was seething out there, past the sidewalks, Tomorrowland.

The reasons these places are tricky to define is that they rarely have a mayor or a city council, and just about never match boundaries on a map. We're still in the process of giving each Edge City its name—a project, incidentally, that could use more flair. In New Jersey, for example, there is one with only the laconic designation "287 and 78." The reason there are no "Welcome to" signs at Edge City is that it is a judgment call where it begins and ends.

15   Take the traditional measure of urban size—population. The out-counties where Edge Cities now rise are almost by definition larger than the cores they surround. After all, these places we thought of until recently as suburbs are where the majority of Americans have been living for decades. Fairfax County, Virginia, is more populous than either Washington, D.C., or San Francisco. Ninety-two percent of the people in the New York metropolitan area do not live in Manhattan.

A more narrow, and I think more accurate, comparison is to take Edge City—that acreage where the huge growth in jobs and other truly urban functions is centered—and compare it with the old central business district, the old downtown. Even by that tight measure, Edge City is almost always more populous. How many people in America, after all, live right in the old downtown? Fewer than live within sight of that Edge City landmark—the office monument so huge it would have been unthinkable to build one anywhere but downtown only thirty years ago.

That is why I have adopted the following five-part definition of Edge City that is above all else meant to be functional.

Edge City is any place that:

- *Has five million square feet or more of leasable office space—the workplace of the Information Age.* Five million square feet is more than downtown Memphis. The Edge City called the Galleria area west of downtown Houston—crowned by the sixty-four-story Transco Tower, the tallest building in the world outside an old downtown—is bigger than downtown Minneapolis.

- *Has 600,000 square feet or more of leasable retail space.* That is the equivalent of a fair-sized mall. That mall, remember, probably has at least three nationally famous department stores, and eighty to a hundred shops and boutiques full of merchandise that used to be available only on the finest boulevards of Europe. Even in their heyday, there were not many downtowns with that boast.

- *Has more jobs than bedrooms.* When the workday starts, people head toward this place, not away from it. Like all urban places, the population increases at 9 A.M.

- *Is perceived by the population as one place.* It is a regional end destination for mixed use—not a starting point—that "has it all," from jobs, to shopping, to entertainment.

- *Was nothing like "city" as recently as thirty years ago.* Then, it was just bedrooms, if not cow pastures. This incarnation is brand new.

An example of the authentic, California-like experience of encountering such an Edge City is peeling off a high thruway, like the Pennsylvania Turnpike, onto an arterial, like 202 at King of Prussia, northwest of downtown Philadelphia. Descending into traffic that is bumper to bumper in *both* directions, one swirls through mosaics of lawn and parking, punctuated by office slabs whose designers have taken the curious vow of never placing windows in anything other than horizontal reflective strips. Detours mark the yellow dust of heavy construction that seems a permanent feature of the landscape.

20   Tasteful signs mark corporations apparently named after Klingon warriors. Who put Captain Kirk in charge of calling companies Imtrex, Avantor, and Synovus? Before that question can settle, you encounter the spoor of—the mother ship. On King of Prussia's Route 202, the mark of that mind-boggling enormity reads MALL NEXT FOUR LEFTS.

For the stranger who is a connoisseur of such places, this Dante-esque vision brings a physical shiver to the spine and a not entirely ironic murmur of recognition to the lips: "Ah! Home!" For that is precisely the significance of Edge Cities. They are the culmination of a generation of individual American value decisions about the best ways to live, work, and play—about how to create "home." That stuff "out there" is where America is being built. That "stuff" is the delicate balance between unlimited opportunity and rippling chaos that works for us so well. We build more of it every chance we get.

If Edge Cities are still a little ragged at the fringes, well, that just places them in the finest traditions of Walt Whitman's "barbaric yawp over the rooftops of the world"— what the social critic Tom Wolfe calls, affectionately, the "hog-stomping Baroque exuberance of American civilization." Edge Cities, after all, are still works in progress.

They have already proven astoundingly efficient, though, by any urban standard that can be quantified. As places to make one's fame and fortune, their corporate offices generate unprecedentedly low unemployment. In fact, their emblem is the hand-lettered sign taped to plate glass begging people to come to work. As real estate markets, they have made an entire generation of homeowners and speculators rich. As bazaars, they are anchored by some of the most luxurious shopping in the world. Edge City acculturates immigrants, provides child care, and offers safety. It is, on average, an *improvement* in per capita fuel efficiency over the old suburbia-downtown arrangement, since it moves everything closer to the homes of the middle class.

That is why Edge City is the crucible of America's urban future. Having become the place in which the majority of Americans now live, learn, work, shop, play, pray, and die, Edge City will be the forge of the fabled American way of life well into the twenty-first century.

25   There are those who find this idea appalling. For some who recognize the future when they see it, but always rather hoped it might look like Paris in the 1920s, the sprawl and apparent chaos of Edge City makes it seem a wild, raw, and alien place. For my sins I once spent a fair chunk of a Christmas season in Tysons Corner, Virginia, stopping people as they hurried about their holiday tasks, asking them what they thought of their brave new world. The words I recorded were searing. They described the area as plastic, a hodgepodge, Disneyland (used as a pejorative), and sterile. They said it lacked livability, civilization, community, neighborhood, and even a soul.

These responses are frightening, if Edge City is the laboratory of how civilized and livable urban American will be well into the next century. Right now, it is vertigo-inducing. It may have all the complexity, diversity, and size of a downtown. But it can cover dozens of square miles, and juxtapose schools and freeways and atria and shimmering parking lots with corporate lawns and Day-Glo-orange helicopter wind socks. Its logic takes a while to decode.

Will we ever be proud of this place? Will we ever drag our visiting relatives out to show off our Edge City, our shining city on the hill? Will we ever feel—for this generation and the ones that follow—that it's a good place to be young? To be old? To fall in love? To have a Fourth of July parade? Will it ever be the place we want to call home?

Robert Fishman, a Rutgers historian who is one of the few academics successfully to examine Edge City, thinks he knows the answer. "All new city forms appear in their early stages to be chaotic," he reports. He quotes Charles Dickens on London in 1848: "There were a hundred thousand shapes and substances of incompleteness, wildly mingled out of their places, upside down, burrowing in the earth, aspiring in the earth, moldering in the water, and unintelligible as in any dream."

That is also the best one-sentence description of Edge City extant.

30   Edge City's problem is history. It has none. If Edge City were a forest, then at maturity it might turn out to be quite splendid, in triple canopy. But who is to know if we are seeing only the first, scraggly growth? I once heard an academic with a French accent ask Fishman, seriously, what the *ideal* of an Edge City was. What a wonderfully French question! Who *knows* what these things look like when they grow up? These critters are likely only in their nymphal, if not larval, forms. We've probably never *seen* an adult one.

If Edge City still gives some people the creeps, it is partially because it confounds expectations. Traditional-downtown urbanites recoil because a place blown out to automobile scale is not what they think of as "city." They find the swirl of functions intimidating, confusing, maddening. Why are these tall office buildings so far apart? Why are they juxtaposed, apparently higgledy-piggledy, among the malls and strip shopping centers and fast-food joints and self-service gas stations? Both literally and metaphorically, these urbanites always get lost.

At the same time, Edge City often does not meet the expectations of traditional suburbanites, either. Few who bought into the idea of quarter-acre tranquillity ever expected to take a winding turn and suddenly be confronted with a 150-foot colossus looming over the trees, red aircraft-warning beacons flashing, its towering glass reflecting not the moon, but the sodium vapor of the parking lot's lights.

The question is whether this disorienting expectation gap is permanent or simply a phase, a function of how fast we've transformed our world. I discussed this with scholars who had examined the history of Venice. Venice today is venerated by American urban planners as a shrine to livability. What was Venice like when it was new?

"People forget that Venice was built by hook or by crook," replied Dennis Romano, a social historian of the early Renaissance. "Venice was just as mercantilist as Tysons. It was full of land speculators and developers. The merchants' primary concern was the flow of goods, of traffic. Those who now romanticize Venice collapse a thousand years of history. Venice is a monument to a dynamic process, not to great urban planning. It's hard for us to imagine, but the architectural harmony of the Piazza San Marco was an accident. It was built over centuries by people who were constantly worried about whether they had enough money."

35   In his plan for the urban future that he christened Broadacre City, that most relentlessly American of urban visionaries, Frank Lloyd Wright, anticipated with stunning accuracy many of the features of Edge City.

"Nonsense is talked by our big skyscraperites in the blind alley they have set up, defending urban congestion by obscuring the simple facts of the issue," he trumpeted in the 1950s in *The Living City*. "Their skyscraper-by-skyscraper is…the gravestone of …centralization."

Wright viewed as interchangeable the concepts of individualism, freedom, and democracy. He saw them as fundamentally in opposition to the despised, exploitative "monarchy" of the old downtowns. He yearned for a system in which all men fled the evils of big capital, big authorities, big cities—troglodytes of every stripe—for a connection with nature, the earth, the ground. He thought an acre per person was about right. He saw individuals newly freed coming back together in totally modern agglomerations, on new terms, stronger, growing together "in adequate space." He saw the automobile and aircraft as the glorious agents of that dispersion and reintegration, and he knew exactly what would happen when, inexorably, we blew Edge City out to their scale:

"After all is said and done, *he*—the citizen—is really the city. The city is going where he goes. He is learning to go where he enjoys all the city ever gave him, plus freedom, security, and beauty of his birthright, the good ground."

How *about* that. We've done it! Just as he said. But are we in our new Edge Cities ever going to reap the benefits of what he knew we'd sow?

40   "Try to live…deep *in* nature," he exhorted us. "Be native as trees to the wood, as grass to the floor of the valley. Only then can the democratic spirit of man, individual, rise out of the confusion of communal life in the city to a creative civilization of the ground."

Edge City has quite clearly released us from the shackles of the nineteenth-century city—out into that valley and wood, just as Wright foresaw. It is common for a first-generation Edge City to arise ten miles from an old downtown, and a next-generation one twenty miles beyond that, only to attract workers from distances forty-five minutes beyond that. At this rate, it is easy to see how a field of Edge Cities can easily cover more than ten thousand square miles. This is why the San Francisco area now statistically is measured as halfway across California, pulling commuters out of Stockton, in the Central Valley, into its Edge Cities east of Silicon Valley.

Whether that spatial liberation leads to Wright's "creative civilization of the ground," however, came to be my main concern, for it is central to the battles being fought in America today over such amorphous essentials as "growth" and "quality of life."

The forces of change whose emblem is the bulldozer, and the forces of preservation whose totem is the tree, are everywhere at war in this country. The raging debate over what we have lost and what we have gained, as we flee the old urban patterns of the nineteenth century for the new ones of the twenty-first, is constant. Are we satisfying our deepest yearnings for the good life with Edge City? Or are we poisoning everything across which we sprawl?

Getting to the bottom of those questions leads directly to issues of national character, of what we value. They come down to who we are, how we got that way, and where we're headed. It is why, when the reeling feeling caused by Edge City finally subsides, I think it is possible to examine the place as the expression of some fundamental values. Nowhere in the American national character, as it turns out, is there as deep a divide as that between our reverence for "unspoiled" nature and our enduring devotion to "progress."

45   In *The Machine in the Garden,* the cultural historian Leo Marx writes about our complicated attitudes toward utilitarian versus pastoral landscapes. For Americans, he observes,

> …regenerative power is located in the natural terrain: access to undefiled, bountiful, sublime Nature is what accounts for the virtue and special good fortune of Americans. It enables them to design a community in the image of a garden, an ideal fusion of nature with art. The landscape thus becomes the symbolic repository of value of all kinds—economic, political, aesthetic, religious…
>
> A strong urge to believe in the rural myth along with an awareness of industrialization as counterforce to the myth—since 1844, this motif appears everywhere in American writing…It is a complex distinctively American form.

One springtime, over lunch near his MIT office, Marx observed that Edge City represents "an escape from the negative aspects of civilization. Too much restraint, oppression, hierarchy—you justify building out there in order to start again and have another Garden. You want the best of both worlds. This would be Thomas Jefferson's Virginia; he very explicitly wanted a land that is midway between too much and too little civilization."

In fact, says Marx, the whole thing goes back to the very dawn of our civilization. Captain Arthur Barlowe, captain of a bark dispatched by Sir Walter Raleigh, described Virginia in 1584 in what became a cardinal image of America: an immense garden of incredible abundance. Virginia is a land of plenty; the soil is "the most plentifull, sweete, fruitfull, and wholsome of all the worlde"; the virgin forest is not at all like the "barren and fruitles" woods of Europe. We "found shole water," Barlowe wrote, "wher we smelt so sweet and so strong a smel, as if we had bene in the midst of some delicate garden abounding with all kinde of odoriferous flowers…"

What Barlowe was describing, of course, was Eden. That image inflamed the popular imagination as the first English settlement succeeded in America, in Jamestown, Virginia, 1607. It drove Shakespeare when, three years later, he wrote *The Tempest.*

What is so striking about these reports depicting Virginia as Paradise Regained—tapping a deep and persistent human desire to return to a natural idyll—is how sharply they conflict with the views of the second set of Englishmen to show up in America to stay. Those were the Pilgrims of the Massachusetts Bay. When the *Mayflower* hove to off Cape Cod in November 1620, what William Bradford saw shocked him. He described it as a "hidious and desolate wilderness, full of wild beasts and willd men." Between the Pilgrims and their new home, he saw only "deangerous shoulds and roring breakers."

50   This wasn't heaven. Quite the opposite.

"Which way soever they turnd their eys (save upward to the heavens) they could have litle solace or content...The whole countrie, full of woods and thickets, represented a wild and savage heiw."

His people, said Bradford, had "no freinds to wellcome them, nor inns to entertaine or refresh their weatherbeaten bodys, no houses or much less townes to repaire too, to seeke for succoure."

There was, in short, no civilization. Bradford found this void horrifying, hellish.

Here, then, is established the enduring divide in the way Americans have related to their land ever since. The hideous wilderness appears at one end of the spectrum, and the Garden at the other. These are such antithetical ways for man to understand his relation to his environment that Leo Marx calls them "ecological images. Each is a kind of root metaphor, a quite distinct notion of America's destiny." These vastly different systems of value, noted Ralph Waldo Emerson, would "determine all their institutions."

55   It comes to this. One vision of the American natural landscape was that it had inherent value and should be treasured for what it already was and had always been. The other saw in the land nothing but satanic wastes; there could be placed on it no value until it was bent to man's will—until civilization was forced into bloom.

The history of America is an endless repetition of this battle. We are fighting it to this day, nowhere more so than in our current frontier, Edge City. In the unsettled, unsettling environment of Edge City, great wealth may be acquired, but without a sense that the place has community, or even a center, much less a soul. And the resolution of these issues goes far beyond architecture and landscape. It goes to the philosophical ground on which we are building our Information Age society. It's possible that Edge City is the most purposeful attempt Americans have made since the days of the Founding Fathers to try to create something like a new Eden.

Edge City may be the result of Americans striving once again for a new, restorative synthesis. Perhaps Edge City represents Americans taking the functions of the city (the machine) and bringing them out to the physical edge of the landscape (the frontier). There, we try once again to merge the two in a new-found union of nature and art (the garden), albeit one in which the treeline is punctuated incongruously by office towers.

If that is true, Edge City represents Americans once again trying to create a new and better world—lighting out for the Territory, in the words of Huckleberry Finn. If that new world happens to be an unknown and uncharted frontier, well, that's where we've headed every chance we've had—for four hundred years. Frank Lloyd Wright genuinely believed that Americans continued to be the sons and daughters of the pioneers. He called us "the sons of the sons of American Democracy." Wright saw us as heading out of our old cities, freed from old verities, creating a new spiritual integrity in community. The enduring, exhilarating, and frightening themes to be examined in Edge Cities are if, whether, and how we are pulling that Utopian vision off.

This goes to the ultimate significance of Edge City. The battles we fight today over our futures do not have echoes only back to 1956, when Dwight D. Eisenhower changed America forever with the creation of the interstate highway program. Nor does it go back only to the New Deal of the 1930s, during which Franklin Delano Roosevelt shaped America into a society of home-owners. It goes to the core of what makes America America, right back to the beginning, with the Pilgrims in 1620 and the Virginia Cavaliers of 1607.

60   It addresses profound questions, the answers to which will reverberate forever. It addresses the search for Utopia at the center of the American Dream. It reflects our perpetually unfinished American business of reinventing ourselves, redefining ourselves, restoring ourselves, announcing that our centuries-old perpetual revolution—our search for the future inside ourselves—still beats strong.

It suggests that the world of the immigrants and pioneers is not dead in America; it has just moved out to Edge City, where gambles are being lost and won for high stakes. It adds another level of history to places already filled with ghosts. That is why one day Edge City, too, may be seen as historic. It is the creation of a new world, being shaped by the free in a constantly reinvented land.

Rereading Actively

1. With a partner, identify the several meanings that Garreau attributes to the word "edge" in the context of "Edge City," and talk about his definition of an Edge City. In your journal, define Edge City in your own words and list some of the examples of Edge Cities that Garreau mentions.

2. In your journal, write a brief summary of Garreau's view of the Edge City phenomenon that he describes, and explain how this view positions him in relation to what he says is the common opinion.

3. In a small group, review the article, noting Garreau's discussion of the "expectation gap" (¶ 33), and of the relationship between utilitarian and pastoral landscapes and the phenomenon of Edge Cities. In your group, formulate your own understanding of the relationships among these terms, and then, on your own, use a journal entry to explain these relationships as your group has explored them.

4. Garreau seems to say that edge cities add value to sites "where little save villages or farmland lay only thirty years before" (¶ 5). In your journal, write an interpretation of this statement that analyzes Garreau's apparent assumptions about the value of "villages" and "farmland."

5. Evaluate with a partner whether Garreau presents a persuasive case that edge cities are a promising sign of a positive form of future communities.

Exploring Your Responses

6. Garreau suggests that edge cities are the culmination of a generation of value decisions about the best ways to live, work, and play. In a small group or with a partner, discuss what values you infer in the appearance of edge cities: looking at edge cities, what statement would you say they make about what Americans value in terms of living, working, and playing?

7. Are the value decisions that you see expressed in edge cities compatible with your own vision of the "best ways to live, work, and play" (¶ 21)? Write a one- or two-page informal response in your journal.

8. Think about areas near where you live that may resemble or in fact be what Garreau calls edge cities. Revisit one of these areas, and then make a list of its

features that are identical to those that Garreau describes. Do you notice elements that he doesn't mention?

9. If you were asked to do it, how would you respond critically to Garreau's generally effusive, positive view of the growth of edge cities? That is, what negative aspects can you point to that weigh against Garreau's position?

How Suburban Design Is Failing Teenagers
William L. Hamilton

William L. Hamilton is a writer for the New York Times *and editor at large for* Martha Stewart Living *magazine. Covering the house, home, and style beat, Hamilton has written about topics ranging from an emerging collectors' market for toys from the 1940s and 1950s to furniture design. And whether the subject is "pornography chic" in fashion advertising and entertainment or devices for the high-tech kitchen, Hamilton's work links the artifact in question to the cultural pattern of which it is a part. The story included here was written in the wake of the 1999 shootings at Columbine High School. Looking at the style of life built into suburban design, Hamilton probes the possible effects of isolation on suburban youth. Tracing the causes and implications of the neglect of adolescents in suburban developments, the article is structured by a series of references to authorities on the subjects of community design and architecture, and at least one reference to a mother of teenage children.*

As quickly as the word "alienation" can be attached to the idea of youth, the image of isolation can be attached to a picture of the suburbs. Is there an unexplored relationship between them? It is a question parents and urban planners alike are raising in the aftermath of the Columbine High School shootings in Littleton, CO.

At a time when the renegade sprawl of suburbs themselves is being intensely scrutinized, the troubling vision of a nation repioneered in vast tracts of disconnected communities has produced uneasy discussion about the psychological disorientation they might house.

Created as safe havens from the sociological ills of cities, suburbs now stand accused of creating their own environmental diseases: lack of character and the grounding principles of identity, lack of diversity or the tolerance it engenders, lack of attachment to shared, civic ideals. Increasingly, the newest, largest suburbs are being criticized as landscapes scorched by unthoughtful, repetitious building, where, it has been suggested, the isolations of larger lots and a car-based culture may lead to disassociation from the reality of contact with other people.

Designers of the newest American suburbs say they have largely ignored or avoided one volatile segment of the population—teenagers. In recent conversations, three dozen urban planners, architects, environmental psychologists and sociologists, and experts on adolescent development agreed that specific community planning and places for teenagers to make their own are missing.

5   "They're basically an unseen population until they pierce their noses," said William Morrish, a professor of architecture and the director of the Design Center for American Urban Landscape at the University of Minnesota. "They have access to computers and weaponry. The sense of alienation that might come from isolation or

neglect will have a much larger impact than it might have before. And there are no questions coming from the design community about what we can be doing about this. We don't invite them in."

Virtually every other special interest has been addressed by enlightened suburban designers—the elderly, the disabled, families with young children. But, said Andres Duany, a planner who is a leading proponent of the "new urbanism," a model of suburban design based on principles of traditional towns, "it's the teenagers I always bring up as a question mark." Mr. Duany said that he had only once or twice included teenagers in the public process of planning a suburban development.

"It's a good point," he said, as though it were an unlikely idea. "I should talk to the kids."

Though teenagers tend to resist advice and choose their own turf as a territorial issue of establishing self-identity, most experts interviewed say that design could constructively anticipate and accommodate anxieties of adolescence. They agreed that teenagers need a place to congregate in and to call their own; it is a critical aspect of relieving the awkward loneliness of adolescence. Between home and school—spheres compromised by the presence of parents or the pressure of performance—places for teenagers in the suburbs are as uncommon as sidewalks.

"It's a paradoxical situation," said Ray Suarez, host of "Talk of the Nation" on National Public Radio and author of "The Old Neighborhood" (The Free Press, 1999), a study of suburban migration. "Parents move there for their children; their children are dying to get out."

10   Like much of the Western United States, Denver is experiencing vertiginous suburban growth. From 1990 to 1996, the metropolitan area expanded by two-thirds, to its current size of 535 square miles.

"Typical of the Denver metro area are the new suburbs, where 'downtown' is a four-way intersection with three shopping centers and a condo development," said Charles Blosten, community services director for Littleton's city planning division. Highlands Ranch, Denver's largest suburban development, has its own ZIP code, "nothing but rooftops and miles and miles of nothing," he said of the numbing vista of houses. "It's got to affect people."

The idea that place has an impact on adolescent development and socialization is accepted by most experts on the suburbs but is only now beginning to be studied. "A culture of impersonality has developed in the suburbs by the way they're laid out," said Jonathan Barnett, a professor of regional planning at the University of Pennsylvania and author of "The Fractured Metropolis" (HarperCollins, 1996). In the newer suburbs, "the standard of houses is high, but the standard of community isn't," he continued, adding, "It's most people's impression of modern life."

And the people it stands to impress the most are children. "They are the most vulnerable people growing up there," said Dr. Jose Szapocznik, a professor of psychiatry and behavioral sciences and director of the Center for Family Studies at the University of Miami. "As a child you're disabled by not being able to walk anywhere. Nothing is nearby."

Mr. Morrish said he thought that public transportation to metropolitan downtowns was crucial for highschool students. He said that the ability to access "the system"—the world adults create—was a vital form of empowerment.

Figure 9.6 Highlands Ranch
A development south of Denver, has its own ZIP code. Does it nurture community?

15   "What to do after school, how to get to the city, to see other people and how to negotiate this without parents," he said, posing the issues. "Teenagers have to have better access to the public realm and public activity." He recalled a conversation with a group of high school students who met with the Design Center, which invites teenagers to group meetings when it is commissioned to study neighborhoods.

"One girl said, 'All I've got is the Pizza Hut,'" Mr. Morrish said. "'You go there a lot or you go to somebody's house—we're tired of both.'"

Between home and school, in a landscape drawn by cars and the adults who drive them, is there even a particular place that teenagers can call their own? Peter Lang, a professor of architecture at the New Jersey Institute of Technology and an editor of "Suburban Discipline" (Princeton Architectural Press, 1997), a collection of essays, said: "In most suburbs, there's not even a decent park, because everyone has a backyard. But older kids never play in the backyard. They'll find even the crummiest piece of park."

Typically, the students at Columbine High School went to Southwest Plaza, a two-level mall that has video arcades, food courts and stores, supervised by security guards and closed by 9 P.M. "Like any suburban community, there's not a lot of places to go and hang out," Mr. Blosten said of Littleton. "I tell you this because that's where my daughter goes—the mall."

Mr. Lang said he thought that places like malls were not adequate gathering spaces for teenagers, calling them, like many public suburban venues, commercially and environmentally "controlled space." He added, "They are not places for free expression or hanging out."

20   Disagreeing that suburbs create greater alienation is Dr. Laurence Steinberg, a professor of psychology at Temple University and director of the MacArthur

Foundation Research Network on Adolescent Development and Juvenile Justice. But he said that he thought recent tragedies like the incident in Littleton do "wake people up to the notion that there is parental disengagement in affluent suburbs." He added: "We did a study on latchkey kids. The kids most likely to be left unattended for long periods were middle class, in sprawling professional suburbs. Isolated for long periods of time, there's no counterbalancing force to fantasy."

The desire for more and cheaper land that has pushed suburbs to rural exurbia may result in teenagers who are alone for large parts of the day. Mr. Morrish pointed out that in communities like Modesto, in the San Joaquin Valley in central California, people commute to jobs in the San Francisco area, where they enroll their children in schools.

"Some people in California are taking their kids with them," he said, "making the kids commute."

The planners who have been most vocally and visibly at work on restructuring the suburban model have been "new urbanists" like Mr. Duany. Their solutions to the wheeling nebulae of tract development are based on tighter concentrations of houses, businesses and public spaces connected by townlike elements—porches, sidewalks and parks—that have largely disappeared from the new residential landscape.

If teenagers find their place there, in new towns like Columbia and Kentlands in Maryland or Celebration, the Disney-built town in Florida, it is not because of any bravery on the planners' part. They often foster nostalgic views of families with young children. But like conventional suburbs, they overlook the inevitability of teenagers in their design.

25   Peter Katz, who with Vincent Scully wrote "The New Urbanism: Toward an Architecture of Community" (McGraw-Hill, 1993), spoke of the importance to teenagers of a place that existed only for them, neither hidden and ignored nor exposed and supervised—in effect, a secret place in full view.

On a visit, Mr. Katz discovered that for Celebration's teenagers, it was a narrow bridge, "with low railings, that goes from downtown to the health club." He continued: "They find each other. They sit on the railing. It's on the route to daily life—not a back alley, but not the town square." Mr. Katz suggested that such a structure could become a conscious part of a community design for teenagers.

For Diane Dorney, a mother with two teenage children who lives in Kentlands, MD, a 10-year-old "new urban" suburb of some 1,800 people, the hallmarks of town life work well for both parents and children. Ms. Dorney and her husband, Mark, moved their family from a typical townhouse development.

"We wanted to raise our kids in a place that provided more than just a house," she said. "It's a diverse community, of age and income," with older people, young couples, families. Ms. Dorney said that she thought the gaze of the town created a sense of extended family and moral weight that were its most important success.

"Someone sneaking down the street to have a cigarette—they don't get away with it," she said. "I don't think teenagers should be left on their own until they're caught at the small things." She continued, "When they go into the big things, they know how big they are." She added: "And we have another way of knowing these kids, other than the bad things. They're your neighbors, too. You're always seeing them. You give them another chance."

Rereading Actively

1. Review the structure of the article with a partner or in a small group, identifying the places where Hamilton discusses the following ideas: the "psychological disorientation" produced by sprawl, the neglect of teenagers in community design, and teen-friendly design alternatives.

2. With a partner or in a small group, discuss what Hamilton reports about the cause–effect relationship between suburban design and teenage alienation. Summarize your discussion in a brief journal entry.

3. Identify the sources of information (the authorities) Hamilton uses as he builds this story about suburban design. Among these authorities, whose words do you lend the most credence to? Why?

4. In a small group or with a partner, study the image of Highlands Ranch. Discuss the following questions:

   - What features in this image are striking to you?
   - What is your impression of Highlands Ranch, based on this image?
   - Based on what you see in this image, discuss the plausibility of the claim that "[a] culture of impersonality has developed in the suburbs by the way they're laid out," (¶ 12), as one of the experts quoted in the article states.
   - Reflect on your discussion in your journal, describing what you noticed in the image and what conclusions you came to in your discussion.

5. According to the article, what are the characteristics that make up the ideal place for teenagers to hang out?

Exploring Your Responses

6. Hamilton offers us glimpses of the ideal place for teenagers to be together. Apart from home and apart from school, it was "a secret place in full view" (¶ 25). Do you (or did you) have a place to go with your friends that has this essence? If so, describe this place in your journal. If not, describe the places where you and your friends would congregate to spend time together.

7. Afforded the opportunity to do so, would you choose to live in Highlands Ranch or a community like it? Why or why not? Explain your answer in a journal entry.

8. What changes would you make to the spatial design of your neighborhood that would make it a more teen-friendly environment?

CASE-IN-POINT ASSIGNMENTS

As Dolores Hayden points out, "place" is a word with several meanings. In part, it refers to a geographical or physical location. But we also understand it to refer to a social position—we know our "place" in a group, or in society. The readings here examine different sites where social and geographical places are being contested—that is, where an issue of geographical or physical location is also an issue of social positions or places. In one sense or another, each of the authors here presents information, questions, or arguments about border disputes where Americans are negotiating their future relationships to one another. Underlying these cases are abiding questions of community: what can it mean that we may live together? Freedom and security conflict with one another in these cases. Opportunity and tradition also clash. Patterns of community we inherit from the past weigh on our actions as we seek, sometimes in struggle, to invent the future.

Making Connections

1. Compare the positions Rodriguez and Kaplan take on the border relationship between the U.S. and Mexico, explaining how their understanding of this relationship affects their views of the future of the U.S. Suggest how your position compares with theirs.

2. Considering McLemore's account of the controversy over Sandra Cisneros's purple house as a similar case, review Greg Hanscom's report on the effort of Indian tribes to recover land they believe should rightfully be under their control. Take a position on the issues raised by these cases, weighing the history that lies behind the present facts along with the viewpoints of the contesting parties.

3. "Good fences make good neighbors," the poet Robert Frost declared. Do they? Compare Kaplan's depiction of a "rusted iron curtain" with Hamilton's discussion of the benefits and social costs that seem to be inherent in suburban sprawl development. Is the value of security worth the costs of isolation in these cases?

4. What form will the American frontier take in the 21st century? Explore the possible futures for America that are suggested by the case readings—for example, Garreau's description of edge cities, Rodriguez's comments about "el norte," or the "rusted iron curtain" described by Kaplan.

5. With Diane Barthel's discussion of historic preservation and attempts to revive "Main Street" in mind (Chapter 3), think about the future form communities may take. Consider the issues of suburban design discussed by William Hamilton and the edge cities that Garreau celebrates. What do people seem to be missing (or finding) in these new forms of communities? What role does consumer culture seem to play in the quest for community?

Collaborative Exchanges

1. In a small group, discuss your reaction to Greg Hanscom's report on Indian land claims, examining the evidence on both sides of this issue. Develop a collaborative position on this issue. Be prepared to present your position to the class.

2. In a small group, discuss your reaction to David McLemore's report on Sandra Cisneros's purple house, examining the evidence on both sides of this issue. Develop a collaborative position on this issue. Be prepared to present your position to the class.

3. With two or three classmates, brainstorm the images of borders that you find in the case readings. Explore how these images of borders symbolize the space between different groups of people. With this as a context, pick a border that affects the campus community, analyzing it in light of the idea of a border that you synthesized from the case-in-point readings. Be prepared to present your interpretation of this border to the class and to explain how your group perceives it in relation to the reading you have done.

Net Approaches

1. Point your browser to <www.census.gov> and at the U.S. Bureau of Ceusus homepage choose to "search" a "place" that you identify by zip code—have the zip code ready before you begin the search. Be creative in choosing your place; pick one that sits on a border of one sort or another, perhaps one mentioned in the readings. Using the census survey tables (the Tiger map is cool but really complicated), generate a profile of the neighborhood that reveals the following characteristics: persons, families, households, racial makeup, Hispanic population, occupations, household income, and urbanization. Review the tables and describe the demographics of the neighborhood. Then, scroll through the place search and select three other variables—poverty, age, details of racial and ethnic makeup, languages spoken in homes, and places of work are all possibilities. Explain why you chose the additional variables and what the results tell you.

2. Visit a national news site and enter the following string in a site search: *Indian and Native American and lands*. (You may decide to use the AJR Newslink <ajr.newslink.org> to help you find an online news site.) Make note of the focus of discussions. Then, run the same search in a single, western newspaper. Describe any differences in perspective that you notice.

3. Point your browser to <www.liszt.com> and search for listservs that deal with Latino immigration by searching for the terms "Latino" and "immigration" separately. Select a list or a newsgroup, subscribe (following the posted instructions), and browse through archived postings. Generate a report that describes the group or list and explains the issues and perspectives you found there. Follow the instructions for unsubscribing from the list or group when you have finished the project.

4. The issue of sprawl is implicated in many of the readings in this chapter. Go to <www.hotbot.com> and enter the following search: *urban sprawl*. Scroll through the results and identify the pages of a group that opposes sprawl, a group that is skeptical about the seriousness of sprawl, and an individual who is concerned with sprawl. Be prepared to share with the class descriptions of the page authors and their positions.

WRITING PROJECTS

OUR PLACES, OUR SELVES

Project 1

Likely Readings

Background Readings
- Berry

Case-in-Point Readings
- Garreau
- Hamilton

Task and Purpose

Wendell Berry focuses on the need to rethink community relationships, including the relationships among people and between people and the land. As he describes the emergence of edge cities, Garreau points us past what is visible—the office parks, the acres of parking lots, the beltways ringing our cities—to the shaping hand of the American frontier spirit that guides new trends. Similarly, in his discussion of suburban design and teenage isolation, Hamilton talks about the motives and values that have led people to create this form of neighborhood. Using the evidence presented in these readings along with your own observations and experience, evaluate the phenomena of edge cities and suburban communities. Do they bode well for the future of "community"?

Project 2

Likely Readings

Background Readings
- Tuan
- Jackson
- Hayden

Case-in-Point Readings
- McLemore
- Hamilton

Task and Purpose

Take a walk through your neighborhood, and write a narrative of your experiences and observations. You will want to focus your narrative on some aspect of your response, on a theme of one sort or another, so that you can organize your impressions, showing the significance of the things you observe and describe. Look back at the reading as sources for questions or themes with which you can frame your work. There are several directions in which to take this project, but perhaps the encompassing question is how the relationships among people who interact with each other and share this neighborhood are expressed by the buildings and streets and the "transition zones" where public and private spheres meet. You might look, for example, at how housing and yard landscaping seem to express certain values, or what kind of space is devoted to public gathering, such as park space, a town hall, or a library. You might pay attention to automobiles, noticing what concessions have been made to cars in the built landscape. With these examples, you can think about what ties a neighborhood together as a community, if anything, and what forces seem to work against the establishment of networks of interdependence.

Project 3

Likely Readings

Background Readings
• Berry
• Tuan

Case-in-Point Readings
• Hanscom
• Kaplan
• McLemore
• Rodriguez

Task and Purpose

In the context of the questions of private property and community values explored in the background readings, consider the disputes that are detailed in one of the case-in-point readings listed above. Remember that we are thinking about how place functions within a consumer culture. Analyze how private interests ought to be balanced against a public interest in a common good. For example, how much control should the historical district in San Antonio be allowed in governing the choices of homeowners? How should that question of control be decided? What are the arguments on both sides of this issue? What position do you take? Another example might be to focus on the question of Indian land claims. How should the interests of the tribes involved be measured against the interests of the white farmers who earn a living by farming the disputed land?

Project 4

Likely Readings

Background Readings
• Hayden
• Tuan
• Jackson

Case-in-Point Readings
• Kaplan
• Rodriguez
• McLemore

Task and Purpose

One way to see more clearly the meaning of our daily experience is through the lens of history. But history need not be conceived as ancient or distant events, involving people in far-off places. Indeed, discovering the historical traces in events in our day-to-day lives can illuminate them, showing the effects of large social and economic events on our neighborhoods, our families, and us. This project calls on you to begin a family history. The background readings suggested here introduce themes that can be helpful starting places. The case-in-point readings stand as sources of themes or as models for this project. Richard Rodriguez traces his immediate family's history, relating autobiographical details to larger historical trends. McLemore's account shows how the history of a place can be controversial and relevant to how we live there today. Kaplan's densely detailed descriptions show how a place can come alive in words. Your task in your family history is to link the details of your family's experience to the history of the place you live. How did your family get here, when did they come, and in the future does it appear that your family will remain in this place? Remember that we are thinking about how place interacts with family history in the context of consumer culture. You will need to think about how making exchanges based on commodity value has affected the place and the history you are writing about.

Project 5

Likely Readings

Background Readings	*Case-in-Point Readings*
• Tuan	• McLemore
• Jackson	• Hanscom
• Hayden	• Garreau
• Berry	• Rodriguez
	• Kaplan
	• Hamilton

Task and Purpose

Pull together common themes in the background readings here regarding the possibilities and problems of community. Using ideas from the readings, synthesize a definition of "community" and identify some of the elements that help to build a sense of community and of belonging to a place. What assets seem to foster a sense of community across racial, ethnic, and economic lines? What liabilities seem to stand in the way of realizing this goal? Generate a prediction or a series of predictions for the future: Are we moving progressively toward improved communities? Will our ideas about "community" become more and more separated from the places we live?

Points of Exchange

INFORMATION AND CENSORSHIP IN CONSUMER SOCIETY

John Fiske. "Radical Shopping in Los Angeles: Race, Media and the Sphere of Consumption"

Andrew J. Hacker. "Dividing American Society"

Joshua Wolf Shenk. "America's Altered States"

Ira Shor. "Is Education a Great Equalizer?"

Farai Chideya. "Race Right Now"

What cannot be said in a consumer culture? News divisions are profit centers in corporations. High ratings for electronic media, or circulation numbers for print media, attract increased advertising dollars. In the "information age" in consumer society with twenty-four-hour news cycles, access to information would not seem to be a problem. Or would it? Veteran journalists like Gary Web assert that newspaper publishers are influenced in their coverage by corporate interests, and that publishers freely admit this. The truth is published—but not at all costs.

In his introduction to *Censored 1999: The News that Didn't Make News* (ed. Peter Phillips. New York: Seven Stories Press, 1999), Web offers a prime example. The *Cincinnati Enquirer* fired Mike Gallagher and paid the Chiquita Corp. $10 million after it was discovered that Gallagher had stolen some voice mail from Chiquita personnel in order to uncover allegedly shady business practices in Central America. Action was taken in this case not because the facts were disputed (Gallagher's allegations, though challenged by Chiquita, have never been independently evaluated), but because the pursuit of the story violated written and unwritten rules in the culture. The twenty-five unreported news stories in *Censored 1999* document case after case of corporations from Coca-Cola to Monsanto to the prison industry exerting direct and indirect pressure on what the public learns.

Closer to home, many consumers feel that local television news is inconsequential at best, pandering to viewers' prurient interests. But so what? How much information does the public need in a healthy democracy? While conspiracy theorists and scandalmongers seem to be ever more present (especially on the Internet), is the quality of information in our society today really much different than in the past? Does the United States' position as a global superpower bring with it even more need for an informed populace, or is the average citizen removed enough from influencing global affairs that reliable information hardly matters? Is the truth out there?

There are several ways to explore the issues that this point raises. Start by reading the pieces listed above, focusing on how each writer talks about the quality of information available in the United States on the topics of social inequalities, violence, race, "outsiders," drugs, and education. Then, try one of the following projects:

- Isolate the most interesting claim about misinformation that is raised in the readings, and then find between six and ten Web sites—personal pages, organization pages, Web 'zines—that offer additional information on the topic. Use the readings to write a paper that evaluates the quality of information on the Web.

- Working with *Censorship 1999* or the Project Censored Web page <www.sonoma.edu/ProjectCensored>, pick a "censored" story. In an analytical paper, argue a position on why the story was censored. You might decide that consumers don't need to know whether Coca-Cola really recycles or whether genetically programmed potatoes might cause diseases; you might decide that they need to know but don't care or need to know but are denied crucial information because of corporate interests.

- Spend a week tracking a single news outlet—consider newspapers, TV news, Internet news services, listservs, newsletters, and so on—for representations of one of the topics raised in the readings. Then, using the readings as a reference point, evaluate the coverage of the topic and argue for whether or not the concerns of the writers represented in the text are valid.

FREEDOM, CONTROL, AND RESPONSIBILITY

Stan Davis and Christopher Meyer. "BLUR"

Malcolm Gladwell. "The Science of Shopping"

Barbara Ehrenreich. "The Yuppie Strategy"

Deirdre McCloskey. "Bourgeois Blues"

Stuart and Elizabeth Ewen. "Shadows on the Wall."

Jacob Sullum. "Victims of Everything"

Sallie Tisdale. "Silence, Please"

Mark Edmundson. "On the Uses of a Liberal Education"

Wendell Berry. "Conservation and Local Economy"

A market-oriented culture offers previously unimaginable freedoms. In *Consumer Culture and Postmodernism* (London: Sage, 1996), sociologist Mike Featherstone asserts that consumers can consciously pick a lifestyle; that is, they can select a life project and then purchase goods, services, and images to realize it. Of course, there are problems with the assumption that creating a life for oneself amounts to a series of purchases; indeed, a tendency throughout this book is to portray each of us as "consumers," as if this were the sum total of our being, as if we had no meaningful existence apart from the economic exchanges in which we partake.

Still, we recognize that as members of a consumer culture, we have an unusual ability to create ourselves. We buy and sell information, purchase personal styles through fashion, pay for educational and social enrichment. Viewing personal and cultural development in these economic terms, the argument holds that as long as we keep buying, advances in productivity and technology will keep providing new possibilities. At one level, individuals have never been so free to create and re-create themselves. On the other hand, as "consumers," we must make our choices within the roles that the market defines or risk having no choices at all. Ultimately, according to Featherstone, we don't choose between fashioning our own identities or accepting cultural constraints on who we can be: we do both. So what are our obligations in taking up roles like the good citizen, the helpful neighbor, the caring family or group member, or the respectful user of the environment? What spheres of freedom do we enjoy that are not defined by consumer culture?

As you read the pieces listed above, look for images and descriptions of individual freedoms and responsibilities, and think about areas of our experience where the role of consumer and the roles of citizen or neighbor or the like don't match up. Then, pick one of the following topics to pursue.

- Focus on a single consumption habit such as fashion, entertainment, education, information, food, technology, and so on. Go to the Internet and find sites that offer products and services related to this habit. Use the library to find additional discussions of your topic. Write a paper arguing whether consumers have meaningful choices in the area you are focusing on—that is, whether consumers can pursue their interests in new ways or whether we are really controlled by the strategies of advertisers and the producers of consumer goods.

- Some might argue that the freedom of choice supposedly provided by consumer society is really a false freedom: as long as every act and decision we make is interpreted in terms of our spending habits, we remain players inside a system of exchange that is driven by the profit motive. These people argue that though we tend to give much attention to consumer exchanges, the important events and activities in our lives and in society take place alongside, or outside, consumer culture. Write a paper in which you identify ways of acting that are not reducible to acts of consumption, showing how our lives add up to more than the sum of the purchases we make.

REPRESENTATIONS OF GENDER

Malcolm Gladwell. "The Science of Shopping"

bell hooks. "Re-thinking the Nature of Work"

Daniel Harris. "Out of the Closet, and into Never-Never Land"

Jib Fowles. "The Surface of the Advertisement, Composed and Consumed"

Susan Douglas. "Where the Girls Are"

Jill Birnie Henke, Diane Zimmerman Umble, and Nancy J. Smith. "Construction of the Female Self: Feminist Readings of the Disney Heroine"

Erik Hedegaard. "The Undergraduate"

Gloria Steinem. "Why Young Women Are More Conservative"

All of these writers assume that gender refers to the cultural situation that men and women find themselves in at any point in time. What it means to be masculine or feminine changes as historical conditions change. In a consumer culture, gender issues like sexuality, family roles, and power relations are at once fluid and rigid. As shoppers, women are as free to choose what they want as men are. Yet while marketers invite women to shop at Sears, for example, they are invited to the "softer side." Men are still expected to buy the hard stuff. The consumer world treats all of us as equals—as long as our credit is good—but at the same time tries to squeeze us into gender roles that limit, focus, and direct our desires.

The readings listed here consider how women and men are represented at work, in the mainstream press and advertising, and in social life. Men and women find themselves playing the roles of providers of services and consumers; they conform to cultural ideals, and they live as individuals with the freedom to make choices. With these representations in mind, try one of the following projects.

- With a partner, brainstorm recent representations of gender in niche magazines, advertising, entertainment, or politics. Select a specific situation—say, an issue of *Cosmopolitan, GQ,* a Fubu ad, a sitcom, or an interview with a member of the U.S. women's soccer team—and freewrite about how you respond to the image of gender that surfaces. Then, search the Internet and do some library research to find reviews and analyses of the situation you are working with. What have other people had to say about this representation of gender? Develop a report that first explains the important elements of the image—body type, character traits, social status, relative autonomy, and so on—and then summarizes some possible interpretations of the image. In your conclusion, suggest why this particular image has been created.

- Following the same approach described above, turn your focus to idealized gender images from the past. Examining sources such as popular magazines for men or women, find a series of images from advertisements in these magazines in which you see striking gender ideals being portrayed. To frame your investigation, try going back two or three generations, viewing the magazine issues your parents' generation would have, your grandparents' generation, and so on.

- Develop a comparison of the consuming roles of men and women. Here, Paco Underhill, the marketing consultant/anthropologist from from Malcolm

Gladwell's article (Chapter 3), should be your guide. Start by selecting a market in which both men and women are active, such as fashion, entertainment, technology, education, and so on. Once you've identified a market, observe a store, a theater, or a classroom where the product/service is delivered; analyze the strategies used to market the product/service; and interview some consumers. Drawing on your observations and analysis, write a paper that evaluates the role of gender in this market and draws some general conclusions about the relative autonomy and power of men and women as consumers.

CELEBRITY

Louis Uchitelle. "Keeping Up with the Gateses?"

Anita Gates. "America Has a Class System. See 'Frasier'"

Mary Kuntz. "Is Nothing Sacred?"

Darrell Dawsey. "Hard to Earn: On Work and Wealth"

Jamie Wolf. "The Blockbuster Script Factory"

Darcy Frye. "The Last Shot"

Our consumer culture places a high value on celebrity status. Because we are encouraged by advertising to look for goods and services that make us look, feel, or perform better, we are fascinated by those people who appear to look, feel, or perform the best. According to Stewart Ewen (*All Consuming Images.* New York: Basic Books, 1988), consumers find a kind of complete wish fulfillment: Celebrities are "someone" in a cultural situation where most of us are just another consumer. We come close to worshiping the mass-produced image of the celebrity. These superlative figures bring us together to communal events, challenge us, entertain us, and give us pleasure. But they can also separate us from who we are and can be. The tragic, accidental deaths of Princess Diana and John F. Kennedy, Jr., led millions of people across the world to mourn the passing of an important friend—but a friend they had never met. For millions of young men and women, Michael Jordan has been a more compelling example of success than family members, teachers, or employers. Jordan may tell young people frankly that they have almost no chance to imitate him, but Gatorade encourages us to "wanna be like Mike." A constant media barrage encourages us to live in the imaginary company of stars we will never meet and who will never know we even exist.

The readings listed above describe alternately the creative power and the unreality of celebrity status in individuals and products. Work through these pieces, noting how consumers construct and relate to stars.

- Brainstorm celebrities and celebrated products that draw your attention. Focusing on a single celebrity, freewrite in your journal about what draws you to this person or product and what that appeal has caused you to do and believe as a consumer. Then, search an index of popular magazines and journals for information on this celebrity, keeping in your journal a record of what you discover and how each discovery affects your perception of the celebrity. Review your journal and write a paper recounting your exploration of this celebrity. Aim for a conclusion that reveals how reflecting on a celebrity affected the appeal of that celebrity.

- Use the Internet to explore the social currency of a celebrity. First, pick a star; then, locate any official sites—fan clubs, pages operated by the celebrity or her or his people—and also find the pages of products that the celebrity endorses or appears in, from shoes to movies. Using a search engine or a link search, try to find the pages of six or eight regular people who make extended positive or negative references to the celebrity. Write a synthesis of your findings, offering an interpretation of the Internet identity and social function of the star.

THE WEALTH GAP

Louis Uchitelle. "Keeping Up with the Gateses?"

Judith Williamson. "Consuming Passions"

bell hooks. "Re-thinking the Nature of Work"

Robert Suro. "Children of the Future"

Susan Sheehan. "Ain't No Middle Class"

Linda Chavez. "An Emerging Middle Class"

Robert Kaplan. "The Rusted Iron Curtain"

Richard Rodriguez. "Pocho Pioneer"

Greg Hanscom. "Tribes Reclaim Stolen Lands"

The three richest people in the world have more money than the combined wealth of the poorest nations, a 1999 *Time* report says. Bill Gates, Warren Buffet, and Paul Allen own combined assets of $156 billion—almost $20 billion more in personal wealth than the combined GNP of the 43 least developed countries in the world, whose population totals 600 million people, according to *Time*'s figures ("Numbers," July 26, 1999). Similarly, while more citizens of the United States own stocks than ever before, it remains true that most citizens have not directly benefited from the enormous increase in value of the stock market, and indeed, only a small minority of the U.S. population controls a vast majority of the nation's wealth.

People draw different conclusions from facts like these. Those who express confidence in the productive power of the consumer economy point to rising standards of living enjoyed by many classes. Let the operation of global markets continue to produce more prosperous living conditions, these people argue. Others, viewing the inequitable distribution of wealth, call for interventions—for example, adjusting tax laws to reverse the two-decade-long trend in the United States of cutting tax rates for the wealthiest families. For example, every year the United Nations Development Program (UNDP) produces a report on economic conditions around the world. The 1999 report, "Globalization with a Human Face," points out that while free markets are very efficient, they cannot be relied on for equitable distribution of wealth <http://www.hndp.org/hdro/99.htm>.

Short of governmental intervention, many people urge that we examine our personal values. They point out, for example, that from the standpoint of function, one or two pairs of shoes is all anyone really needs, so why not take the money we might spend on more shoes and donate it to a charity? With these perspectives in mind, review the readings listed above and pick one of the following projects.

- Gather information and produce a report that summarizes what you find in a variety of sources on the topic of the wealth gap. For example, go online to <www.lexis-nexis.com> Lexis-Nexis Academic Universe and type the phrase "wealth gap" in the keyword box, searching major newspapers for stories on this topic. Skim through the articles you find, gathering information that outlines the problem. From your research, produce a report that explains the important terms used in these articles (e.g., "minimum wage," "the poverty line," "consumer price index") and the trends that are described. (One very detailed source for data relevant to the United States is *The State of Working America 1998–1999,* by Lawrence Mishel, Jared Bernstein, and John Schmitt [Ithaca: Cornell University Press, 1999]. Other sources, such as the United Nations Development Program report, can be consulted for information on the global distribution of wealth and comparisons of living standards in industrialized and less-developed nations.)

- Focus on children in poverty. Since approximately 40 percent of "poor people" in the United States are in fact children under the age of eighteen, citizens concerned about the health and welfare of the future of our nation might take time to ponder the implications of this figure. To find initial information, tap sources like the Children's Defense Fund <www.childrensdefense.org>, the Child Welfare League of America <www.cwla.org>, and the National Anti-Poverty Organization <www.napo-onap.ca>. Then, run a search on the Internet and in a periodical index that links "poverty" and "children" and a relevant issue that interests you—nutrition, violence, income, success, and so on. Write a paper that provides basic information about children and poverty, that suggests or explains some of the effects of poverty on children's growth, learning, and development, and that talks about the consequences for our society of having so many children grow up in impoverished circumstances.

- Focus on the optimistic interpretations of economic data offered by some analysts. Consulting sources such as the CATO Institute <www.cato.org> or the American Enterprise Institute <www.aei.org>, or a work such as *Myths of the Rich and Poor: Why We're Better Off than We Think,* by W. Michael Cox and Richard Alm (New York: Basic Books, 1999), explain the arguments these thinkers present in support of their view that the economic expansion our nation has enjoyed for nearly two decades has had beneficial effects across society.

SUSTAINABLE LIVING

Mark Sagoff. "Do We Consume Too Much?"

Sarah Boxer. "I Shop, Ergo I Am: The Mall as Society's Mirror"

Barbara Ehrenreich. "The Yuppie Strategy"

Michael Mandel, Mark Landler, et al. "The Entertainment Economy"

Rebecca Jones. "Kids as Education Customers"

Wendell Berry. "Conservation and Local Economy"

In *How Much Is Enough?* (New York: W.W. Norton, 1992), Alan Thein Durning notes that "Economists use the word consume to mean 'utilize economic goods,' but the *Shorter Oxford Dictionary's* definition is more appropriate to ecologists: 'To make away with or destroy; to waste or squander; to use up.'" As a researcher at the Worldwatch Institute, Durning focuses this book on the global environmental threat posed by consumer lifestyles. He marshals an array of evidence that points to social and ecological disequilibrium that results from excess consumption. Durning argues that the global environment simply cannot sustain for the whole population the consumption-based lifestyle now enjoyed by a small minority. The effects of consumer culture on the natural environment are comparable, Durning argues, to a force of nature itself: in 1990, he points out, "mines scouring the crust of the earth to supply the consumer class moved more soil and rock than did all the world's rivers combined."

These writers all ponder whether a consumer society is sustainable, and they come to a variety of conclusions. As you read, notice the benefits and costs of a consumer's approach to life and reflect on what it takes to keep consumers consuming.

- Investigate the voluntary simplicity movement, visiting Web sites like <www.awakeningearth.org> or <www.simpleliving.com> and reviewing literature in the mainstream and alternative press that describes this phenomenon. Track down practitioners of voluntary simplicity in your area and ask them about how they make this lifestyle work.

- Combine information from marketing research with your own direct observation to create a document that details the daily consumption of a typical college student on your campus. By all commonly accepted definitions, we live in a high-consumption society, absorbing far more of the world's resources per capita than other countries around the world. But what does that high-intake lifestyle really look like in terms of day-to-day living? Your goal in this project is to create a document (a brochure or a video, for example) that objectifies this concept.

- The argument over the sustainability of consumer society often turns on the issue of whether improvements in technology and economic productivity can mitigate the environmental damage caused by high-consumption lifestyles, and whether the real issue is world population growth rather than the rate of consumption of world resources. Start by looking on the Web and in a general academic index for perspectives on population growth and the sustainable use of natural resources. Write a report that synthesizes your discoveries and offers recommendations about how seriously your classmates should take population growth.

SHOPPING AND THE INTERNET

Malcolm Gladwell. "The Science of Shopping"

Judith Williamson. "Consuming Passions"

John Fiske. "Radical Shopping in Los Angeles: Race, Media and the Sphere of Consumption"

Stuart and Elizabeth Ewen. "Shadows on the Wall"

Marc Spiegler. "Marketing Street Culture: Bringing Hip-Hop Style to the Mainstream"

John Brinckerhoff Jackson. "The Accessible Landscape"

In a *Business Week* article, "Forget the Mall. Kids Shop the Net" (July 26, 1999), Roger O. Crockett points out that by the year 2002, kids from ages five to eighteen are predicted to spend $1.3 billion a year shopping online. In a *Time* cover story (July 20, 1998), "Click till You Drop," Michael Krantz compares the Internet revolution in shopping to the mushroom of shopping malls in the 1970s and 1980s. Krantz writes: "The malls themselves became essential parts of a new suburban design, where castles of consumption shaped town layouts in the same way the Colosseum shaped Rome." By the end of the 1990s, Krantz goes on, the Internet was proving to have similarly profound effects—not only on how people shop, but on how they relate to one another in "a new culture of convenience and speed."

- Consult information about e-mall designers from sources like the ones Michael Krantz cites (the Gartner Group <www.gartner.com>, Anderson Consulting <www.ac.com>) or those cited by Roger O. Crockett (NFO Interactive <www.nfor.com>, Concrete Media <www.macromedia.com>). Then, visit an online store like Amazon.com or the online Disney Store. (You might also stop by a magazine like Bolt.com to see how sales and lifestyle blend on the net.) Develop a report that explains how designers court Internet shoppers and how designers' strategies are realized in an online store or publication.

- Write a narrative essay in which you record your personal response to shopping transactions in "real" and virtual stores. Brainstorm your favorite retail experiences. Find a virtual store (or "real" one if you're a webhead) that sells the same merchandise. Then, go through the act of buying something at each site. (You don't really have to buy anything.) While the experience is fresh, write up each experience and then develop a substantial conclusion that compares and interprets the two experiences.

- Find the pair of stores described in the previous exercise. But instead of narrating your shopping experience, analyze both environments in an effort to explain how marketing strategies compare. (It might be especially helpful to keep some of Malcolm Gladwell's ideas from "The Science of Shopping" in mind as you undertake this description of your shopping experiences.) Write an evaluative essay in which you argue about which environment is better, that is, more effective or more human or less manipulative—you pick the criterion.

SPRAWL

Joel Garreau. "Edge City: Life on the New Frontier"

William L. Hamilton. "How Suburban Design Is Failing Teen-agers"

Dolores Hayden. "Urban Landscape History: The Sense of Place and the Politics of Space"

Robert Suro. "Children of the Future."

Mark Sagoff. "Do We Consume too Much?"

David Guterson, "Enclosed. Encyclopedic. Endured. One week at the Mall of America"

Stan Davis and Christopher Meyer. "BLUR"

Michael Pollan in "Land of the Free Market" (*New York Times Magazine*, July 11, 1999) argues that the debates about sprawl have elevated "'livability' to a national issue." In doing this, sprawl injects two ideas into the national political debate that the right, according to Pollan, thought had faded from the scene. One is the idea that "the personal is political"; the other is "the habit of questioning the wisdom and sovereignty of the free market." Sprawl perhaps epitomizes how encroaching urban/developed culture can hollow out but also energize human life and community.

- Explore a metropolitan area, using the U.S. Bureau of Census homepage to see how sprawl looks in a specific locale. Point your browser to <www.census.gov>, and at the Bureau of Census homepage choose to "search" a "place" that you will identify by place name or zip code—a zip code map from a print version of the white pages still seems to be a great way to find zip codes. Using the census survey tables, generate a profile of activity in your target area: consider looking at households, household incomes, occupations, places of work, means of transportation to work, travel time to work, industry, housing units, sewage disposal, median rent, and vacancy status. Then, look for newspaper accounts and interviews with residents that highlight issues of sprawl: traffic, cost of city services, deteriorating city centres, loss of farmland, and so on. Write a synthesis that pieces together how sprawl is affecting life in this locale.

- Investigate the national debate on sprawl, identifying the different positions people take on this issue (including the perspective of those who argue that sprawl isn't really a problem at all). General searches on the Web and in a popular literature index will turn up a wide range of positions. After reviewing the arguments, formulate your own position, recommending what—if anything— should be done about sprawl.

- Use the Internet to visit the virtual presence of a city that is known for sprawl— the readings identify several likely candidates, but you can pick one that is closer to home. Once you have a sense for how the city wants Web surfers to see it, look for newspaper reports on sprawl in this city. Write an evaluative comparison of the city's tale and the one that shows up in the media.

WELL-BEING, ECONOMIC PROSPERITY, AND SOCIAL HEALTH

Mark Sagoff. "Do We Consume Too Much?"

David R. Guterson. "Enclosed. Encyclopedic. Endured. One Week at the Mall of America"

Barbara Ehrenreich. "The Yuppie Strategy"

Diane Barthel. "Consuming History"

Deirdre McCloskey. "Bourgeois Blues"

Wendell Berry. "Conservation and Local Economy"

William L. Hamilton. "How Suburban Design Is Failing Teen-agers."

It can be argued that the "American dream" has two aspects, one comprising the freedom and social responsibility entailed in democracy, the other comprising the economic opportunity to amass fortunes. Still, research suggests that the relationship between material wealth and personal happiness is tenuous at best, and that we engage in socially and psychologically destructive behavior when we sublimate our longing for human connection in the consumption of goods and entertainments. A Merck Family Fund survey, reported by Jim Motavalli in "Enough!" (*E*, March–April 1996), states that "Americans would be happier with a lifestyle based on personal relationships rather than consumption." Further, he notes that "consumption has increased 45% since 1970, but the Index of Social Health reports that quality of life has dropped 51%."

In their book, *The Social Health of the Nation: How America Is Really Doing* (New York: Oxford, 1999), Marc Miringoff, Marque-Luisa Miringoff, and Sandra Opdycke outline the troubled relationship between economic prosperity and social health in the United States. The authors examine indicators such as infant mortality, drug abuse, and food stamp coverage, as well as the number of children who live in poverty, reported cases of child abuse, teen suicide rates, health-insurance coverage, and the gap between the rich and the poor. They conclude that while the United States has enjoyed nearly two decades of economic expansion, the nation's social health as measured by these indicators has steadily deteriorated: infant mortality and drug abuse rates have decreased, for example, but the number of children living in poverty, teen suicide rates, and reported cases of child abuse have gone up.

Think about the phrase "well-being" to define the good life. Are we "better off" than our parents or grandparents, and what does being better off mean? What sources of well-being are available to us in our consumer society? Consult the readings above, examining how each presents a perspective on the meaning(s) of well-being in our society. How do the views presented by the authors compare with your own? What useful insights, helpful terms or distinctions, if any, do you find in their writing that assist you in understanding the question of what it means to live "well" in America? Several different kinds of projects could be pursued to explore this question.

- Turn to the work of Miringoff et al., focusing on one of the indicators they identify for further research. For example, with the overarching idea of the health of society as the context, research the issue of teen suicide or of children in poverty, looking especially for explanations of these things that you can relate to the values that are forwarded by a consumer society.

- Take what you have thought about and learned from the readings you've consulted here, and interview people of different generations about the subject of economic prosperity and social well-being, focusing perhaps on the topic of "necessity." Do people in our society today routinely confront "necessity" as they make a life for themselves? (For example, one of our grandfathers immigrated to the United States as a young boy in 1908 and learned the necessary lessons of frugality and "making do" during the Great Depression. This man saved things—like the wafer-thin remains of soap bars—that many of us would casually throw away. Tested by necessity, his views of the relative merit of individual economic prosperity and social well-being might very well differ from ours today.) Use what you discover to develop a report on changes in the relationship between well-being and necessity.

- Identify what might be called "counter-traditions" in U.S. thought—that is, avenues for action, examples of figures or ideas that explicitly confront the materialism that seems so much to dominate our society. Counter-traditions range from the sublime (e.g., much of Christian as well as other religious thinking) to the more mundane (e.g., staying fit, eating organic, recycling). (Each of these avenues has a healthy Web presence.) Think about it this way: If we aren't spending time making more money, picking the right stocks, "moving on up," then what is worth thinking about and acting on? What can we learn from the counter-traditions you identify about alternative values and lifestyles in American culture? And are any of these alternatives really free from materialism? Write a reflective essay in which you explain the alternative offered by the counter-traditions you've looked at, and reflect on where this alternative might lead a self-conscious consumer, maybe you, yourself.

- Can market forces and careful planning be harnessed to engineer healthy communities? In "Consuming History," Diane Barthel refers to developers who have tried to do this in places like the Seabury Shopping Center in Cape Cod, or in the town of Seaside, Florida, using building codes to recreate a small-town atmosphere. Review the readings listed with this assignment, focusing on what they reveal about qualities like "connectedness," or "neighborliness" in a consumer culture. Use the Internet and a local library to find five recent analyses of Celebration, Florida, a model community developed by the Disney Corporation. Evaluate the success of Celebration, Florida. Does it seem to have succeeded in recreating small-town connectedness and neighborliness? Was it reasonable thing to try?

Credits

Figure 3.1 ©1999 Mall of America

Figure 4.1 Courtesy OUT Magazine. Photograph: Bob Frame/La MoinePhotoGroup, LLC

Figure 4.2 Photofest

Figure 4.3 Universal Pictures/Fotos International/Archive Photos

Figure 5.1 Advertisement on page 214 used with permission from Logitech.

Figure 5.2 Courtesy Bestform Foundations, Inc.

Figure 5.3 From Adbusters Magazine. http://www.adbusters.org

Figure 5.4 Partnership for a Drug-Free America

Figure 5.5 Partnership for a Drug-Free America

Figure 5.6 Partnership for a Drug-Free America

Figure 5.7 Partnership for a Drug-Free America

Figure 5.8 Partnership for a Drug-Free America

Figure 9.1 California State Library. California Historical Society

Figure 9.2 National Japanese-American Historical Society

Figure 9.3 Southern California Library for Social Studies and Research

Figure 9.4 Bently Historical Library, University of Michigan

Index

Note: Page numbers followed by *f* indicate figures.